THE INSTITUTION OF PROPERTY

A Study of the Development, Substance and Arrangement of the System of Property in Modern Anglo-American Law

BY

C. REINOLD NOYES

THE LAWBOOK EXCHANGE, LTD.
Clark, New Jersey

ISBN 978-1-58477-737-3

Lawbook Exchange edition 2007, 2018

The quality of this reprint is equivalent to the quality of the original work.

THE LAWBOOK EXCHANGE, LTD.
33 Terminal Avenue
Clark, New Jersey 07066-1321

Please see our website for a selection of our other publications and fine facsimile reprints of classic works of legal history:
www.lawbookexchange.com

Library of Congress Cataloging-in-Publication Data

Noyes, C. Reinold (Charles Reinold), b. 1884.
The institution of property : a study of the development, substance, and arrangement of the system of property in modern Anglo-American law / C. Reinold Noyes.
p. cm.
Originally published: New York : Longmans, Green and Co., 1936.
Includes bibliographical references and index.
ISBN-13: 978-1-58477-737-3 (cloth : alk. paper)
ISBN-10: 1-58477-737-0 (cloth : alk. paper)
1. Property. 2. Property--History. 3. Property (Roman law) 4. Property--United States. I. Title.
K720.N69 2007
346.04--dc22 2006036097

Printed in the United States of America on acid-free paper

THE INSTITUTION OF PROPERTY

A Study of the Development, Substance and Arrangement of the System of Property in Modern Anglo-American Law

BY

C. REINOLD NOYES

NEW YORK · TORONTO

LONGMANS, GREEN AND CO.

LONDON: HUMPHREY MILFORD

1936

NOYES
THE INSTITUTION OF PROPERTY

FIRST EDITION

PRINTED IN THE UNITED STATES OF AMERICA

To the memory of

WILLIAM GRAHAM SUMNER

A PIONEER AMONG SCHOLARS
AND A GREAT TEACHER

FOREWORD

As this study has gradually developed from small beginnings and over a long period of years, it has grown to a scope which, if I had foreseen it, would doubtless have seemed to make of it too ambitious a project for me to undertake. Because the creeping nature of its expansion has led me into fields in which I had no previous training I am sure that in many respects I must have failed to observe some of the finer points of scholarship which specialists in each of these fields would naturally expect. I hope, therefore, that each reader will judge the work by his impression of those parts in which he finds himself also in my condition.

For the convenience of the non-specialist reader I have relegated to foot-notes the supporting authorities for my own conclusions. But in these notes I have, for the most part, quoted fully from, rather than merely referred to, these authorities, since the range of subject matter is so large that few will be familiar with the theses of *all* these authorities or even have their works readily available. Additional supporting material for my two major conclusions is supplied *in extenso* in the first and third appendices. Case citations for the fifth chapter, which are not likely to be extensively used, are placed in the second appendix. A complete list of authorities used, with editions, will be found under the caption "List of References" just preceding the index. This does not pretend to be a bibliography of the various fields covered in the study, nor does it include many works which I myself have used if there has been no occasion to make reference to them in the text.

In numerous cases, for the sake of clarity, I have found it necessary to assign a special sense to a common word. The definition has, I think, always been made clear by discussion in the text. Where it has seemed doubtful to me that the reader would continue to bear in mind this special sense I have reminded him by placing the word in quotation marks at all subsequent appearances. Double quotation marks indicate a word the special meaning of which I have imputed to others. Single quotation marks indicate a word for which I myself have adopted a special meaning.

The work of research has been conducted largely in the libraries of the Johns Hopkins University, Columbia University, and Dartmouth College, and to a small extent in the library of the Bar Association of the City of New York and the Minnesota State Law Library in St. Paul. To these institutions I wish to express my appreciation of the facilities and assistance so generously extended to me. In the course of preparation I have been greatly aided by the suggestions and criticisms of a number of friends. Among these I wish to make acknowledgement particularly to the following: Knight Dunlap, Professor of Experimental Psychology, and P. E. Dumont, Professor of Sanskrit and Indology, at the Johns Hopkins University; Walter W. Cook, Professor of Law, School of Law, Northwestern University; Hessel E. Yntema, Professor of Law, Law School, University of Michigan; Wesley C. Mitchell, Professor of Economics, Department of Economics, Robert L. Hale, Professor of Law and A. Arthur Schiller Professor of Law, Law School, Columbia University; Ashbel G. Gulliver, Professor of Law and Assistant Dean, and Wesley A. Sturges, Lines Professor of Law, School of Law, Yale University; and Vserolvd Basanoff, a former fellow of the Rockefeller Foundation and now lecturing on Roman Law at the University of Paris. It is hardly necessary to add that this acknowledgement does not imply any responsibility upon the part of these friends for any of my views or conclusions, nor even necessarily that they are in agreement with me. It is a pleasure also to acknowledge here the help I have received, in the etymological sections, from Anthony F. Paura, A.M.; in the historical and juristic sections, from Mary F. Finkelstein, Research Assistant to Professor Schiller; and in the case and text-book citations, from William Messing, of the School of Law (all of Columbia University), who have verified all references and aided in putting the manuscript in final form for publication.

CONTENTS

INTRODUCTION

Chapter I

THE ORGANIZATION OF EARLY ROMAN SOCIETY

Chapter II

THE DEVELOPMENT OF THE ROMAN SYSTEM OF PROPERTY

Chapter III

THE FOUNDATIONS OF THE ENGLISH, OR FEUDAL, SYSTEM OF PROPERTY

CHAPTER IV

THE MODERN JURISTIC ANALYSIS OF PROPERTY – LEGAL THEORY

Chapter V

PROPERTY IN MODERN AMERICAN LAW – LEGAL PRACTICE

Chapter VI

THE SUBSTANCE AND STRUCTURE OF MODERN PROPERTY

APPENDIX II

APPENDIX III

THE NATURE OF CREDITORS' RIGHTS IN PRACTICE

THE INSTITUTION OF PROPERTY

THE INSTITUTION OF PROPERTY

INTRODUCTION

A. *The Field of Institutional Economics*

It is not merely a coincidence that the particular method of approach to the subject matter of the science of economics which has been given the name of "institutional economics," should have for the first time become self-conscious in the twentieth century. Nor is it fortuitous that this new approach should have especially concerned itself with the particular institution called property—including therein contract. The chief popular battle ground among the social philosophies of this period is in the field of economics; more particularly in that part of the field which concerns the institutions composing the economic organization of society: and most particularly in that special section of the latter which is called property. But the scientific attack upon these questions is only in its beginnings. Those who are making haste to diagnose the particular ills of society for which its institutional constitution is accused of responsibility and to advise major operations thereon, are doing so in spite of the almost complete absence of exact knowledge on the subject. Institutional economics may be understood as the beginnings of an effort to supply this deficiency and, for this purpose, to extend the purview of the science beyond the classical limits, or, perhaps, to review the same area in another and different aspect.

There is another and even more practical mandate for the undertaking. In the eighteenth century, when the claim of the science of economics was first staked out, economic organization in general and property in particular were relatively simple, direct and obvious arrangements—so much so that they were hardly envisaged as a part of the subject matter except in the somewhat conventionalized aspect of distribution. But recently they have developed a degree of complexity, of indirectness, and of obscurity which has permitted them to get out of control, even of the most astute managers, and beyond the comprehension even of the most acute observers. And this very lack of control and understanding is the basis of a common intuition that in the workings of the financial structure as an element in the economic organization—particularly in the institution of credit, which is a part of it—may be found the source of many of our more recent types of economic malaise. In other words, the more orthodox school of economic medicine—that one which is content to avoid major surgical operations and the introduction of new and artificial organs if it can make the present ones work better—is rapidly becoming equally interested in developing this new institutional field.

1. *The New Point of View*

To a considerable extent institutional economics deals with the same subject matter but in a different aspect. For this reason it requires a new point of view. And this point of view is especially one which must enable us to see the unseen, to visualize the social abstractions which lie between the concrete persons and the concrete objects with which the science has hitherto largely concerned itself. In this view it is the arrangements, the practices and the rules of society which become the most influential realities. The relations depose the relata from their pre-eminence as facts. In thus accustoming ourselves to dealing with such abstractions as the greater realities we are neither becoming doctrinaire nor are we pioneering. For the abstractions of property—of the financial structure—have come to be the realities of business and of its handmaiden accounting, as they have long been of the law. The business world thinks in terms of "rights" almost more than it does in terms of men and far more than it does in terms of objects. The chips in the economic game today are not so much the physical goods and actual services that are almost exclusively considered in economic text-books, as they are that elaboration of legal relations which we call property.[1]

It is probably true that transactions of which one side involves the exchange of possession of a physical good or the receipt of an actual service, do not constitute one quarter of the total volume of transactions in the United States today. All the rest, and the other side of all these, consist of exchanges of various types of property rights—including credit money—which are more or less remote from and do not affect the physical locus of a good nor involve its handling. And, except to a small extent, neither do they involve services of any kind—even of the most abstract nature. Not only is this true in

[1] Ihering, *Geist des römisches Rechts*, II, p. 435, says, "The commerce of exchanges, looked at from the legal point of view, is not a circulation of objects; it is a transfer of rights. Isolated from the law which relates to it, the object is deprived of all value. Neither utility nor economic use determines the value of things; that is the result essentially of the circumstances that the use of the object is legally assured and depends on the manner in which it is protected by law. The law is an essential factor in the notion of value; in a revolution all values suffer; they recover when confidence in the certainty of law returns. Legally the transfer of an object signifies the transfer of the right over that object; legally commerce in objects is no other than the establishment of rights, their transfer, their extinction."

respect of transactions, but it is true also of the process of production in other aspects as well. Insurance, banking—both commercial and investment—security and commodity exchanges, etc., are vital elements in the modern scheme. But their product is not principally those ephemeral, intangible economic goods which we call services. On the contrary what they produce are certain very lasting, if equally intangible, things—namely property interests of various subtle and intricate kinds which are of fundamental importance and come near to being the key to the working of modern business. Finally it is most conspicuously true in the arrangement of the economic organization. Personal position in the scheme is no longer a matter of possession of material objects. It is almost wholly a matter of an elaborate system of relations running to the person and *placing* him.

All business deals in terms of property. Of course it is not a case of enter property, exit wealth. Nevertheless an economics which focuses its entire attention on the concrete is necessarily failing to envisage the true—or whole—character of our economic life. The very terms which we choose to designate the special character of the régime under which the economically civilized peoples of the world are now operating, are terms which demonstrate this point. We call it "capitalism" or the "money economy." Even we are beginning to speak of the "profit economy." But how is it possible descriptively to designate the peculiarity of an institutional system in terms whose only scientific content is the physical and mechanical notions of classical, and even of current, economics? The peculiarity that it is thus attempted to name lies not in the accumulation of capital, in the economic sense of physical goods. Russia has, or soon will have, that idiosyncrasy. Nor does it lie in the substitution of payments in money for barter or for payment in services. The Phoenicians had accomplished that. Finally its peculiarity is surely not the profit incentive, because that is as old and as ubiquitous as is free exchange. Professor Wesley C. Mitchell has felt these "malapropisms" and has discarded such terminology in favor of the phrase, the "business economy." The name is perhaps vague, but its connotations are complete and directly applicable. It at least adumbrates the core fact of the peculiarity—the fact that in these recent centuries, for the first time in the history of mankind, and in this limited domain, out of all the habitable area of the globe, there exists a complete and almost independent organization exclusively devoted to the economic sphere of man's activities. It is to the structure and functioning of this separate business organization particularly that institutional economics directs its attention. The framework of this organization is property.

2. *The Relation to Other Schools*

There are perhaps two half-unconscious resistances to this method of attack – in addition to the usual one of inertia. The first is due to the fact that many economists have been inclined to feel that their science must come to be quantitative, as physics, for instance, is quantitative. The newer dictum that science is measurement merely annoys the biologist. But it converts the economist, because he is less sure of his ground. And so he pursues his new ideal by devoting himself to the statistical method. But the statistical economist, if he will question his assumptions, will become an ally of the institutional movement. He will perceive that, in the physical sciences, it has always been necessary for qualitative to precede quantitative analysis. One must first recognize the peculiar characteristics of what he is to measure and be able to classify his data in fairly homogeneous and well-differentiated categories. If, now, the statistician comes to see that the data of economic life are not wholly reducible to the accustomed economic categories of physical objects and of hours of work, or their values, and that, in fact, the most salient and vital of them are of a different order altogether, he will become convinced that it is a necessary preliminary to an adequate metric to analyse first the nature and variety of the non-conformable data; to determine in what respects they reflect their physical counterparts – the goods and services of economics – and in what respects they do not; to classify them into some sort of periodic system; to determine their valences or relations in combination with each other; and to devise for them a standardized and recognized nomenclature. Another consideration should clinch this conviction. Economics is, curiously enough, the one science where, in certain of its aspects, the data already exist in terms of measurement. The story of economic life, in its aspect of value, is written in the books of account. But these accounts and the statistical summaries of them are the record of institutional behaviour. They do not deal for the most part with the economic categories of physical objects or hours of work. They do not fit the old qualitative analysis. Rather they deal primarily with property and its transactions. With this tempting supply of ready-made measurements at hand, the statistician, once he appreciates that the things so measured are not the substances of his accustomed economic categories, should be among the leaders in pressing forward through the preliminary work of institutional analysis without which it seems that he cannot have an adequate qualitative technique as a basis for his quantitative constructions.

The other resistance is found more especially within the classical and neo-classical schools. The objective of these schools has been felt to be the searching out and exposition of those fundamentals which lie beneath the superficial variations of different economies—the universals which apply to all and are the inescapable conditions of economic activity. But I think it may fairly be said that an economics which is interested in the particular economies in vogue at different times and places only as they serve to demonstrate or illustrate the general principles that are common to all economies will never be a realistic science. It will remain speculative and theoretical, as it so largely is at the present time.

What would the biological sciences have been today if the anatomy and physiology of apes, of arthropods, and of amoebae had merely been explored to the extent necessary to determine the general principles of structure, circulation, respiration, etc.? Comparative anatomy and physiology have been valuable adjuncts in these particular fields of study. But one has never heard of a biologist endeavouring to construct an abstract animal composed of the common or general attributes and functions of all animal life. The very idea is ludicrous. Yet a somewhat analogous scheme seems to have been the goal of these schools of economics.

Nature exists in diversity, not in general principles. Economics is a branch of the science of human nature and of certain of its relations to the rest of nature. Comparative economics is a useful adjunct thereto. But the field of the science of economics *par excellence* is and must be the study of individual economies, their ontogeny, their anatomy and physiology, and their pathology.

3. *The Three Parts of Economics*

One takes his intellectual life in his hands today when he broaches the subject of the biological analogy in the field of the social sciences. Nevertheless, with a limited application, some such analogy is essential to a presentation of the fundamental place of institutional economics in the scheme. The whole subject of economics itself must be conceived and represented in some graphic form which will display its various aspects and its various departments. Since there is at present no such conventional representation in use, it is necessary to develop an analogy in order to illustrate. And, for such purpose the biological analogy is far more appropriate than the mechanical. In the study of the human body we conveniently order the subject matter into three general parts. The first deals with the component cells as individual and viable organisms with a life cycle, urges, habits and needs. This part includes cytology, histology, pathology, etc. The second deals with the collectivity in two aspects; one aspect consists of the various parts of the structure and their inter-relations, which are imagined and depicted in the form of a single instantaneous photograph as if they constituted a static fact (anatomy); the other consists of the functioning of this structure as a whole and in its several parts, which is analysed and depicted in the form of a conceptual moving picture as if it were a dynamic process (physiology). It must be recognized that both these representations are inadequate and conventionalized. Finally, the third part puts aside the factor called life and examines the whole subject in its physical (including mechanical) and chemical aspects; as a system of levers, pumps and fluids; as a system of energy, heat, and perhaps electricity; and, at the foundation of it all as a matter of physiological chemistry.

Some such division is also necessary in the field of economics. There is, in the first place, the part which is concerned with the individual human being, the member of a society, with his life cycle, his urges, his habits and his needs. He it is who is the motive power of the economy. It operates only when and as he operates. The social equivalents of the sciences of the cell are the sciences of individual behaviour. But it is this same individual who, by some usually indirect collaboration, composes and conforms the social organization with its institutional ways and habits and its relations. Once organized this collectivity becomes a negative constraint, if not a positive stimulus, to the individual. He is now a part of a whole and to a certain extent not only is his freedom of action limited, but there seems to be created some impetus and inertia under which the group acts as its component individuals would not act separately. The single man is caught up in the current of the crowd. Thus while individuals collectively grow institutions, the institution adds thereafter something more than the sum of the individual sources of behaviour. At least it does so in directing and determining behaviour, if not in initiating it. For that reason there appears a collective regularity which is different from the statistical regularity of a group of discrete units. Such social organizations have two aspects, just as the multicellular organism has—aspects which correspond to the anatomical and the physiological. There is first what we may call *structure*—the differentiated system, or design, into which the component members are fitted by a complex web of inter-relations. This is the static aspect. A diagram of this order usually adorns the office walls of every chief executive of an American business. The second aspect we may call *functioning*—the behaviour habits of the collectivity, the channels, movements, and activities, which may or may not be formulated into rules but which tend nevertheless to become conventionalized. This is the dynamic aspect. These two branches constitute the second, or institutional, part of economics.

Finally, in the third place, there is the quasi-mechanical part. And it is this, I think, which has been the almost exclusive concern of classical economics. For the first part of the subject it has merely assumed a lay figure—the *homo economicus*—to fulfill the need of a foil for the attributed and very simple set of wants, efforts and satisfactions which it has required as putative motive power for the mechanism—a mere catch-all concept like that of "force" in physics. For the second part it has been content with a simple functional analysis—of the order of air, fire, water, earth—which originated in a landlord-farmer agricultural economy, and therefore contained three elements, land, labour and capital; and to which has been added, in order to offer some concession to the realities of the last century, the fourth function of enterprise. But the part of the subject to which classical economics has largely devoted its attention and that in which its successes lie, is the mechanical. It has produced a mechanics of production—dealing with the processes by which the various chemical (or alchemical) compounds are produced from this air, fire, water and earth; a mechanics of exchange—dealing with the processes by which the resulting compounds interact upon each other; and finally an over-simplified rationale of distribution—the beginnings of a scientific approach to the subject of economic metabolism.

To point out in this way the narrow limits of the field already cultivated by the major school of economic thought is not, however, to depreciate the importance of the work done or of the results accomplished. It is rather to emphasize the relative immensity of that which remains outside, comparatively unexplored, and still to be systematized. And it is also to suggest a certain defect in the method, a defect which seems to arise from this very preoccupation with the seemingly mechanical (or inorganic) aspects of social phenomena. It is by reason of this point of view, perhaps, that economics seems to have been developed on the basis of the familiar illusion of the existence, and possibility of apprehension, of an absolute or norm. As a matter of fact, even in the seemingly mechanical phenomena of production, exchange and distribution, human beings are the sole agencies and they are driven by urges, wishes, foresights, estimates. They think that they want things; they estimate values; they are guided by currently accepted economic doctrine and practices as to what to do, to pay, to expect. Thus the facts of price represent merely what two or more men think a thing is worth, or think they must buy or sell for. The results of these human responses are largely fortuitous and are only formulable statistically as probabilities. The purely mechanical elements of economics are very limited and are practically confined to the inherent tautologies of the institutional system.[2] The rest are psychological or social in character and therefore of a nature more analogous to the biological than to the mechanical. By that very classification the absence of a background of norm or absolute is demonstrated.

B. *The Approach to this Study*

1. *Analysis of the Socio-economic Complex*

The aim of institutional economics is not, however, to correct the mechanical bent of the classical school. It is, rather, to devote itself to the exploration of its own preserve, the analysis of the organization and behaviour of the socio-economic complex. Although abandoning the foregoing analogy, let us use the framework we have thus laid down as a basis for a closer examination of this particular preserve. We have said that economics is a branch of the science of human nature and of certain of its relations to the rest of nature. Thus, in analysing the preserve, we may think of individual man as the economic agent and motive power; of social organizations and institutions as the organic apparatus, evolved by him and composed of him, through which the motive power, supplied by him, is applied; and of nature, or natural resources, as the *milieu* in which these activities take place and the stuff upon which they are exercised.

Those economic arrangements which concern principally the relations between man and nature, its materials, forces and resistances, are covered in the economic concept of technique, or the "state of the arts"; those which concern principally the relations between men themselves—the economic agents and motive power—are embraced in the indefinite concept of an "economy." We are provided, in law, with a fairly exact descriptive analysis of this second group of institutions and, in accounting, with a beautiful mathematic thereof. But as to the first group, in spite of the voluminous data available, we have almost no systematic studies. Both classes of arrangement are of human origin and both limit the freedom of the human animal as well as express it. We think of the state of the arts as a stage in a continuous progress, projected along a vague but conceivable scale upon which differentials can be measured. But the group of institutions which are defined by law and measured by accounting, while the facts with reference to them are of similar order and while they are subject to the same conceptual trick, are generally thought

[2] For instance the fact that aggregate wealth cannot be increased by increasing credit and debt, or that loans to governments, if the proceeds are consumed, represent a total loss to the community.

of in a different way. They are not usually regarded as a process of piecemeal invention and gradual improvement in availability and control, but rather as a creation; either a natural foreordained system to be retained intact[8] or, on the other hand, a temporary constitution subject to replacement as a whole at will. And this latter is a curious piece of self-deception. It is based on the false assumption of the pliability of man in contrast to the realistic assumption of the refractoriness of nature.

The study of man as the economic agent and motive power should be the foundation of any realistic approach to the subject of "economies." But, unfortunately, the basis for an individual economics does not, as yet, exist. Our knowledge of individual human motivation, of the way man acts alone or in the mass as a result of his internal stimuli, is of the slightest. Psycho-physiology is only in its beginnings as an objective science and the terms for the urges, such as hunger, sex, vanity, acquisitiveness, etc., are but words to hide our ignorance. We know that man makes the economic machine go, but we do not know what makes man go. This fundamental branch of economics—its energics—is, and will doubtless remain for a long time, a vague and metaphysical matter. Perhaps economic psychology can never reach the standing of a true science and will submit only to statistical treatment; like the microcosm in the physical field, from the erratic and indeterminable individual acts of which, only statistical averages can be derived. So we may come to measure the end-reactions of human motives and, since it is impossible to avoid imputing a motivation, we will ascribe the results to forces as to which we have no qualitative analysis or mensuration, and therefore no accurate nomenclature.

When we come to consider the apparatus of organization and customs into which man builds himself for wholly or partly economic ends—the special field of institutional economics, as a branch of social science—we find that it can only partly be separated from the study of the individual. For, in the first place, this apparatus is actually laid down by a process like growth; it is not designed or volitional. As with the parts of an organism it is the function of these institutions which may be said to formulate them. Thus they are, in the beginning, but the crystallized effect of the mass of individual motivations. The study of established institutions, therefore, does not explain their *raison d'être*. To understand that, it would be necessary to understand the original and individual motivations. Nevertheless the fact that they are crystallized does differentiate

[8] As Professor J. M. Clark puts it (*The Economics of Overhead Costs*, p. 2), "Our economics . . . is often tempted to regard these customs and conventions as laws of nature."

them from the original and individual. Once grown they become refractory and are not renewed in each period or altered to suit each current modification of impulse, but are themselves durable, continuing and only to be changed gradually. Thus, once established, they gain a certain independence and in turn give rise to a reaction upon the motive power (individual) in the shape of a tendency or necessity for the individual to conform and thus produce a coherent mass action. In other words the effect of this crystallization is to produce a certain degree of mechanical determinism in social behaviour because man has become a no longer wholly free agent, though he is by no means as inert and disciplined as the cells of an organism or the particles of a mechanism seem to be. He is carried along by the nature and process of the organization. And the ends achieved may come to have little reference to the current individual wishes of the human beings so organized.[4] Thus is produced a standardization in the functioning of organizations which greatly restricts the range of the motives and urges which inspire an individual.

In the second place there arises the question of the degree of conformity with which the individual and the mass of individuals will react to this dynamic scheme of things; how far will the collective behaviour depart from the standard because of variance in the current motivation of the individuals who energize these processes; and how far will this current motivation modify or determine anew the habits and customs which exist at any time and place? By reason of the first consideration, especially, it is necessary to recognize that the mores[5] may be regarded as either of two things. They may be considered to be the norm or rule of social conduct, rather a statement of intent than of fact—an influence, an idea, a guide, a plan. Or they may be considered to be the behaviour itself, which is the result of the process of individual motivation impinging upon and being deflected and restrained by these norms or rules. In the latter sense the mores and their institutions are both more and less than their rules. They are less, because they depart from the theoretical line of action. They are more because they express all social impetus and inertia which tends to follow the particular line of least resistance for future action which has been laid down by past action.

By reason of this partially standardizing influence on social behaviour, the study of organizations and institutions, economic, polit-

[4] For instance the standard work day has been eight hours. Human motivation might prefer six hours at three-quarters as much real return, and with more leisure. But custom rules. It can be modified by rebuilding the institution, but in the meantime it ignores and overrides individual human motivation.

[5] Professor Commons uses the term "working rules" for mores and their systems, institutions, and the term "going concerns" for social organizations. I see no advantage in this novel terminology.

ical, etc., at present offers much greater possibilities of inclusion among the sciences than does that of individual behaviour. In so far as it limits and compels human behaviour, the institution or organization does so by reason of the nature of its constitution and the channels of its functioning. If its relations and its identities are fully analysed and diagrammed, then at least we have a full knowledge of the constitution of society; and if the sequences of cause and effect which should follow from this constitution are studied in the same way, we have presumptions as to its functioning. Since, to a certain extent, the institution or organization, once established and in operation, is not greatly subject to the influence of individual motivation, but rather carries on as an independent and somewhat controlling force or movement, its necessary effects can be far better understood by thus separating the analysis of its constitution from that of the behaviour itself. We learn the habits of a chemical substance the better by separating it *in vitro* from all interfering factors, though we recognize that in nature it is never free from them.

By this means, though bearing in mind that institutions and organizations vary in different times and places and are continually undergoing modification, we are nevertheless able to deduce that, in a given case, as is and at a moment, the application of certain types and qualities of motive power should work in a certain way and produce certain necessary results, due to the design of the apparatus itself. Finally, by comparison of these hypothetical results with the results actually observed we can then determine the extent, always considerable, of the influence of this design in guiding and regulating the motive power and, in some respects, controlling and determining the results. Followed out along these lines such data as are reducible to measurement may be made the basis of a fairly exact science.

In any problem of institutional economics, therefore, the human motivations (individual), the natural forces and the resistances (technical) must be "given." Then, to the extent that the design and operation of the particular apparatus are understood, the results are mathematically calculable. Even the scatter of non-conformity is subject to some degree of statistical observation, and a certain regularity exists in the development and modification of the institutions and organizations which is reducible to a formula. But if the conditions are not given, since they are the product of unknown motivations and resistances, the results can only be forecast by guess. It is almost a fair presumption that every night the world's books are balanced. The motion of every minute part of the economic machine has been recorded each day and its changed position and the number of r.p.m. it has performed, noted. But this record does not tell us whether the fuel was coal, or oil, or wood; whether the power was applied by push or pull, and what was the degree of resistance and the loss by friction. It tells us exactly what has resulted. The how can be partially understood by understanding the mechanics of the machine. But the why cannot be understood at all. Changes in the volume of output may be due to functional efficiency or deficiency, or to changed resistance or to changed power. We do not know. This penultimate why, which would also explain the original development and the subsequent variations of social institutions, is the subject of individual economics—a branch of psychology, the keystone of all social sciences. For this we will have to wait until the new objective psychology has more nearly replaced its speculative predecessor. We are obliged, in the meantime, to deal with human nature, of necessity. But we can treat of it only crudely and where its motive forces are simple, obvious and generally recognized. Thus must we recognize that we are only beginning to build a behaviouristic economics when we study institutions and organizations by themselves, either in diagram or in action as going concerns.

In addition to which, when all is said, it remains true that institutional economics is confronted with the same general and extreme difficulty which faces the organization of a science in any department of human behaviour. This difficulty arises from the advancing irregularity which is found as we proceed from the comparatively simple and orderly activity of the inorganic world, through the biological scale to man, the last word in relative spontaneity, complexity and multiplicity. It is for this reason of course that the physical sciences enjoy the distinction of being the exact sciences and that doubt has been cast on the possibility that human behaviour can ever be brought, to any large degree, within the reach of scientific method.

2. *The Reality of the Abstractions*

As we have already pointed out institutional economics requires a new point of view. To one studying society objectively it appears that the realities of human life are in fact not so much the physical surroundings of men—realities which are perceptible to the senses—but rather the "dream world" in which they live. "We dwell in a world of conceptual thought. . ."[6] This "dream world" consists of the bonds of habit, individual and social—the institutions—by which men live. The social apparatus is itself invisible and its operation is even abstruse. The individual is hardly conscious of it. He

[6] Briffault, *The Mothers,* I, p. 1.

takes it for granted. But he does not understand it. Nevertheless it is so real that, though it is not seen, it is accepted, perhaps unthinkingly. Or it may be concreted in its physical representations; buildings, officials, regalia, ceremonies. Man is largely in its power, but he fails to recognize that fact. Popular social dynamics is anthropomorphic or demonistic. Some man, or men – evil spirits, profiteers and malefactors of great wealth, or leaders – are always held responsible for trends and movements, for actions and reactions, which are in fact for the most part the inevitable results of the way things are organized. Given the usually tritely simple motive forces applied at certain points and the apparatus willy-nilly produces certain results.

The so-called "dream world" of the unadapted (neurotic) is merely a different "dream world," an individual one which does not fit that of others. But the stuff of which both are made is conceptual – a purely internal process. The one works and is confirmed by experience only because the rest of society is living according to it. The other does not work and is not confirmed, unless perchance in the case of the vision of the so-called genius it proves to be truer to the physical surroundings or to the inner needs of men. But the general conventional "dream world" of a time and place is the social reality.

One is led, by studying its development, to conceive this social reality as a web of intangible bonds – a cobweb of invisible filaments – which surround and engage the individual and which thereby *organize* society. These bonds are relations; man and nature are the relata. Thus it is less the sensible relata which count in social life than it is the invisible inter-relations – our relations among ourselves and to external nature. And the process of coming to grips with the actual world we live in is the process of objectivizing these relations. Since it is this conventional "dream world" which concerns institutional economics, we must be forgiven if we discard the crude and primitive intellectual process of concreting; if we refuse to identify this world with its mere symbolisms or its anthropomorphisms; and if we insist on the superior behaviouristic reality of the conceptual abstractions with which the physical facts are invested.

3. *Structure and Function*

The presentation of this system of relations, which in the social sciences corresponds to anatomy in the biological, is necessarily conventionalized. It is a picture of society in its static aspect. But a static aspect is inherently a convention; for in fact, in all fields, the only phenomena are activities and therefore of a dynamic nature. For this reason statements of static relations are no more than presuppositions of the groove or channel through which activities will occur.

By a peculiar twist in the growth of language an incidental corollary of the physical concepts, represented by the words "static" and "dynamic," has developed itself into a usage of these terms in economics which may preclude their use here in the more standard sense. In economics "static" has been used to refer to the condition of absence of change in process — a condition which has unfortunately been described as equilibrium; by which is meant the condition in which inflows and outflows, or counterflows, are equalized; or in which the forces, on the analogy of pressure and suction, are equal, so that the volume, energy and direction of movement remain stable. This is a far cry from the "static" aspect of physical phenomena. In physics "statics" has to do with bodies and forces at rest — with the equilibrium of immobility. Thus a force conceived to be at rest is potential. When it becomes kinetic it is dynamic. In this sense nothing in economic life is static, for the life itself is an activity and therefore dynamic. The body economic is always in motion. On the other hand, in economics the usage of the term "dynamic" is the antithesis of its usage of "static." It is the term for the condition of changing processes. Economics has to some extent differentiated between the varieties of change; those which are irregular or mere disequilibrium; those which are pulsating (i.e., those periodic changes, ranging from seasonal to cyclical and even secular, which are called waves); and those which seem to be progressive or retrogressive in an evolutionary aspect (trends). The last sense complies with Adam Smith's differentiation of the "progressive" from the "stationary" (static) or "declining" (retrogressive) state. But the peculiar usage of "static" and "dynamic" seems to have sprung from Mill. It is unfortunate, like much of the rest of economic terminology which continues to be composed of words in common use, used, not merely in a special or refined sense as is necessary in any science,[7] but in a wholly different sense. The result is that the technical language of economics has none of the advantages which should accrue from its freedom from coined words

[7] The law is faced with the same difficulty. But there the difficulty seems unavoidable because the law is primarily an art, not a science. Maitland says, (Pollock and Maitland, *The History of English Law*, II, p. 31), "Few, if any, of the terms in our legal vocabulary have always been technical terms. The license that the man of science can allow himself of coining new words is one which by the nature of the case is denied to lawyers. They have to take their terms out of the popular speech; gradually the words so taken are defined; sometimes a word continues to have both a technical meaning for lawyers and a different and vaguer meaning for laymen; sometimes the word that lawyers have adopted is abandoned by the laity."

because its common words are used in coined, and therefore deceptive, senses.

If we desire to avoid confusion, we should substitute for the economic term "static," the word "stable" or "unchanging," and for "dynamic," the word "unstable" or "changing." The first pair again represent a conceptual artifice. The most stable condition we find in nature – external or human – is nevertheless tidal. There is an ebb and flow even in growth. And after growth is completed the grown man continues to be tidal; he sleeps and he wakes; he is active and he rests; his energy and activity are constantly rising and then declining. Moreover this conceptual artifice of stability is open to even more serious objections than the artificial idea of a static aspect. If it is a useful hypothesis it should be exactly defined. Not only does the condition not exist, but I suspect the idea leads to illusions with regard to the inter-actions of actual unco-ordinated conditions in the natural continuous state of flux.

However, it is futile to quarrel over words and it would only be confusing if we were here to use the term "static" and "dynamic" in an application analogous to their use in physics. Moreover the whole analogy is defective. The form of activity which has more resemblance to economic life is biological, the activity of an organism, not that of mechanical (or abstract) forces which can inhabit bodies and which can exist apart from motion. What we need is a term for the pattern of relations between the economic relata while they exist in a theoretical state of rest, or better at an infinitely brief moment. These relations are those of arrangement, connection, stress, strain, potential. As the antithesis for this we need a term for the condition of activity of the relata, activities which can be analysed into sequences. With the understanding that any terms borrowed from another field will always trail a modicum of connotation which is inexact, we shall use for the first the term "structural," and for the second, "functional." Structure is something which never *is*. This notion is a convenient intellectual artifice, or diagram, of relations, spatial, energic, etc., that may be conceived to occur *en passant*. But the pattern of the functioning cannot be analysed or described except on the framework of such a diagram. The sole purpose of the analysis of structure is to determine its interrelations and thus to find a basis for determining the probabilities and the improbabilities as to chains of sequence in functioning. If two parts are directly related (connected) it is probably impossible to affect one without the other. If they are indirectly related the degree of mediacy probably results in a corresponding degree of *non sequitur*. Thus the relations determine the channels or sequences of activity.

4. *The Special Field*

In thus narrowing down step by step the front of our attack we have attempted to show its relation to the whole. The special subject of this study is the structure *only* of that particular social organization and institution which is called property. The financial structure of the modern economic world, both in respect of the constitution of the individual elements composing it and of their knitting together into a complex whole, is but another name for the institution of property. The one is the institution in its economic aspect; the other, in its legal aspect. But the totality of the present system of property is embraced in the current concept of the financial structure. For property today has no other than an economic function. And, since this is the case, it is essential that the whole institution, in its legal as well as in its business and accounting aspects, should be envisaged in the economic viewpoint. If we are really to understand the financial structure we must grasp the nature of the modern institution of property, how it developed and what are its relations of identity or of sequence with the different forms of the past. We must see the structure in detail and as a whole, and analyse the connections which bind its diverse parts together.

Therefore, for the purpose of its application to economics or any other social science, the necessary prelude to any systematic and realistic analysis of the structure and functioning of the institution of property, at least in its non-mechanical aspect, is an analysis of property in the law. For law defines and represents all that portion of this and every other element in the complex of mores or social habits, denominated institutions, which is not wholly voluntary or merely customary. It was a matter for surprise to the writer to discover that there is no such analysis in the literature either of law or of any of the social sciences. This work is an attempt to supply the deficiency. It is limited in its scope to the purpose in hand; that is, to laying the necessary groundwork for subsequent studies of the economics of the property system (financial economics). It confines itself to the structural aspect of the institution, both because it is preliminary and, as well, because, in a study of the functional aspect, the legal cannot, even to this extent, be separated from the extra-legal, or economic, aspect; and it confines its objective to elucidating the particular case of the institution which is at this time operative in the United States. It suffers from the difficulties which are inherent in a new angle of approach to any subject, and doubtless reflects the disadvantages—as well, I hope, as the advantages—which result when one who is not a specialist in a particular field attempts to elucidate that field for the benefit of others also strange to it.

In such an undertaking we must perforce classify, define and name. Here, as generally, many difficulties are avoided by eliminating the intriguing search for the absolute. Our classifications will be but convenient groupings, not fixed concepts. Each class is roughly defined in terms of differences from, and of resemblances to, other classes. Thus the same fact may be viewed in different aspects and classified in as many different ways. Each class in turn is but an arbitrarily selected range in a gradually differentiating series. We recommend, particularly to any legal-minded readers, the consideration that, in the spectrum, one can contrast red and blue at certain points, but one cannot say when red ceases and blue begins, for they blend into each other, one character subsiding by degrees as the other emerges by degrees.

In this particular field of social science we are treading dangerous ground. Perhaps no other is quite so charged with emotional entanglements. Nevertheless it is my firm conviction that so long as the literature of economics is even in part inspired by, or pervaded with, the wishes of the observer, and expresses what he *thinks should be* rather than what he *finds to be*, it will remain a war of words—not a science. It is true that an understanding of what *is* in any field is largely of interest for the purpose of learning how to apply it as a means to the ends we desire. But it is also of considerable interest purely as a satisfaction to the craving for understanding for its own sake. And the determination of what we want is another and difficult problem in itself. Moreover, experience shows that whenever the reconnaissance in any field of knowledge becomes imbued with questions of purposive objectives, of practical results, it is betrayed by its changed point of view. It ceases to be science, for it loses, through some subtle psychological mechanism, its intellectual and emotional integrity. Social reform has its place. But it should not parade under the aegis of science.[8] It may be built upon scientific results. But science itself must be disinterested, if it is to constitute a sound foundation. Nevertheless, when that is said, one must admit in all humility that it is probably impossible to free oneself entirely from assumptions, prejudices, and a code of values.[9]

[8] As Professor Wesley C. Mitchell says in another connection, ". . . it is confusing to mix considerations of welfare with considerations of process." *Business Cycles*, p. 105, Note 1.

[9] As exemplified by Thorstein Veblen, for instance. He so implicitly accepted the *bourgeois* code that one is hardly conscious that the subtle ironic humor in his view of the leisure class arises entirely from the fact that he was viewing their satisfactions by comparison with and in the light of *bourgeois* satisfactions, and that his *reductio ad absurdum* is based on a purely subjective assumption.

C. *The Dualisms of Law*

1. *Substance and Form*

Property is not an idea nor an instinct. It is an elaborate social institution which presents a continuous sequence of development from the first record of the customs and organization of early society. If we were able to accept the extreme legalistic view that it is created by law and exists only in the contemplation of the law, an analysis of the institution for economic purposes would be a relatively simple matter. For then we would only need to adopt such definitions as are provided ready to hand in legal doctrine and practice. However, the most cursory examination of the history of legal systems must convince us that such a view is untenable. The law finds the institution of property in existence, as well at the earliest as at all later stages of growth, and, far from creating its varieties, is occupied only in defining, maintaining and validating them.[10]

Thus at the outset it is well to distinguish between the legal form and the real substance of the institution of property—a substance far more substantive than substantive law—the institutional reality which occupies the space within the outline which the law has somewhat hazily carved out for it. The substance consists of a certain system of relations among men which are devised, developed and practised in social economic life. These relations exist as independent phenomena. They are social habits, capable of being viewed in many different aspects and therefore seemingly a complex of several different orders of activity. But the legal clothes in which this institution is wrapped, and the so-called rights, according to which these relations are analysed and classified when from time to time they need to be validated or protected, are but conventionalized abstractions from the facts themselves. To be sure such forms, while they are not of the essence of the substance itself, nevertheless to a considerable extent delimit it and exercise a great degree of control over its development. For the law is more conscious than the social habit. And men can, for the most part, act only as they think.[11] The original or variant act that does not conform to precedent is rare. Nevertheless it does occur. And, if it survives and grows by imita-

[10] "Car en droit se sont les nécessités sociales qui font surgir les institutions." R. Saleilles, *De la personnalité juridique*, p. 45.

[11] Maine, *Ancient Law*, p. 226. "Nothing in law springs entirely from a sense of convenience. There are always certain ideas existing antecedently on which the sense of convenience works, and of which it can do no more than form some new combination."

tion, it compels, eventually, some modification in form.[12] Nor is form entirely extraneous to substance. It is, rather, an attempt—or the tradition of an attempt—to represent the substance. Thus neither substance nor form is independent of the other.

In all history and today we see the ideas, urges and activities of men struggling within these bonds of legal form.[13] If we disregard the form and look only through it to the substance we fail of understanding. For then we fail to appreciate the ways in which the substance is functionally constrained and even structurally modified by the form. On the other hand, if we look exclusively at the form we are misled as to the true structure and functioning of the reality beneath the form. But if we think of form as the costume of reality; if we recognize that it is partly an expression of that reality and partly a tradition derived from its own history; that it is constructed from the materials available at the time upon general patterns acquired from the past; conforming in some varying degree to utility and in some respects to abstract notions of an intellectual aesthetic; we will then have, perhaps, the most helpful point of view in coming to grips with the nature of such social phenomena.[14]

In this survey, for our special purpose, of the institution of property in various times and places we are looking primarily for the cognate relationships, for the spontaneous modes of action which inform the various manifestations. In doing this we may at times

12 "Mit der wirthschaftlichen Entwicklung aber hält die des Rechts gleichen Schritt, letzteres lässt sich als das Flussbett wirthschaftlichen Strömung bezeichnen, d. h. es ist zu jeder gegebenen Periode so weit und breit, als das Verkehrsbedürfniss es erheischt." Ihering, *Geist,* II, p. 431.

13 Bonfante, *Histoire du droit romain,* French Trans., I, p. 11, "Dans le monde spirituel, comme dans le monde organique, les formes antiques s'adaptent à de nouvelles fins qui conservent toujours la trace de l'ancienne finalité à laquelle elles ont servi . . . le juriste dans les phénomènes juridiques, sait distinguer, d'un côté, la structure, la forme, de l'autre, la fonction, la signification, la finalité . . . d'un mot, d'une institution."

14 Justice Holmes, considering the two aspects of the law itself—the substantive and the procedural—seems to regard the former as fitting the institutional facts rather closely. He says (*The Common Law,* p. 1), "The substance of the law at any given time pretty nearly corresponds, so far as it goes, with what is then understood to be convenient; but its form and machinery, and the degree to which it is able to work out desired results, depend very much upon its past." If we were to accept this somewhat euphemistic qualification it would perhaps be necessary to change our simile and to treat substantive law as the *underwear* of the social institutions, while for doctrine and procedure would be reserved the character of ruffs and bustles, fardingales, furbelows and crinolines. I think this procedural concept of form is what Ihering has in mind when he refers (*Geist,* III, p. 328) to "die aüssere Erscheinungsform des Rechts," and that he is distinguishing between the procedural and the substantive when he says (*Geist* III, p. 312), "Oder haben auch sie sich dem Wechsel der Dinge und Ansichten gefügt, und ist es vielleicht nur die Gleichheit des Namens, die uns die Änderung der Sache selber übersehen lässt, nur dieselbe Schale, aber mit anderem Kern?"

need to ignore the legal principles constructed after the fact and the actual genealogical relationships of legal forms among themselves. For in all ages and localities the individual systems of law have only plastered with their conventions and concepts the somewhat uniform structure of the current manner of thinking and of living. Thus these vestments and trappings of property are but disguises of a little varying body. Fashions in clothes vary widely according both to time and place. But fashions in bodies are conservative.

2. *Instances and their Generalizations — Law*

In addition to this deceptive dualism of legal form and institutional substance we find another disconcerting impediment which lies in the very nature of law itself. In the beginning, at least hypothetically, there are no laws, or rules, but only individual judgments "breathed for the first time by a higher power into the judge's mind at the moment of adjudication."[15] But human nature demands regularity and certainty and this demand requires that these primitive judgments be consistent and thus be permitted to crystallize into certain rules — into "this body of dogma or systematized prediction which we call the law."[16] From this, in turn, arises the application of such relatively simple legal principles to particular cases. Sir Henry Maine establishes a fundamental antithesis between these antique judgments (*themistes*) or Bentham's and Austin's "commands,"[17] on the one hand, and laws, on the other; between adjudged cases, and precedents, rules, principles and distinctions; between individual and always unique instances and those "uniformities, successions and similitudes," to which, by analogy, the term law is now applied in so many other fields.[18] This is another dualism of law — the individ-

[15] Maine, *Ancient Law*, p. 7.

[16] Holmes, *Collected Legal Papers*, p. 169. Tarde, *The Laws of Imitation*, Trans., p. 310, says, "If his [the chief's] method of settling them [differences between members] is continuous and self-consistent, if he possesses a system of jurisprudence, as our jurists would say, he comes to prevent their occurrence. And from that time on law exists in his little society; the memory of his past decisions implies the prevision of his future judgments."

[17] But Vinogradoff, *Outlines of Historical Jurisprudence*, I, p. 367, points out that these are not equivalents. "The notion of θέμις cannot be rendered by our term 'command': it implies a pronouncement as to right, and a direction as to conduct." It is a *iuris-dictio*.

It is not necessary for us to subscribe to Maine's somewhat imaginary explanation of the origin of the legal process in order to use his suggested antithesis as an analogy for the modern dualism — that between the case and the principle. Our own analysis of the earliest available data finds already in existence a body of rules, "mores," to which the *lex* seems at first to be opposed as a sort of legislative or statutory exception. See Chaper II. But that may mark but a phase in a transition, and the Roman *fas* (the "spoken") may have originally corresponded to the Greek θέμις.

[18] Maine, *Ancient Law*, p. 8.

ual instance supposedly judged on its merits as if *sui generis*,[19] *versus* the process of induction of general principles from many such instances, which eventually leads to inverse deductions by which future judgments are determined from such germane principles. Thus development proceeds from diversity toward uniformity; life, diverse, changing, growing; the mind attempting obstinately, but in vain, to reduce it wholly to order. In summary one may say that the law itself is always a matter of cases, not of principles. Principles can only be built up out of cases with some guidance from current usage, opinion and ideals. Therefore they are but secondary aids to enable courts and citizens to find their way with some consistency through the maze of cases. No more do principles evolve the law than did the Linnean or Jussieuan systems evolve the vegetable world.[20]

Professor Corbin, in the preface to his edition of *Anson on Contract*, says: "In the long history of the law can be observed the birth and death of legal principles. They move first with the uncertain steps of childhood, then enjoy a season of confident maturity, and finally pass tottering to the grave. It is during their middle period only that they can be used with confidence as the major premise of a deduction." And only at this stage, when the principle is fairly consistent with all the customary facts, does the law have that degree of certainty which is necessary to enable those subject to it to know in advance the precise limits of their rights and duties. At an earlier stage there are diverse decisions upon similar sets of facts and at a later stage there are uniform decisions upon sets of facts already becoming again diverse. Thus generalizations become too strait as the facts continue to change, and must in turn give place to new ones. This is the common characteristic of all processes of growth. Viewed in the aggregate, it is not so much a rise and decline as it is a continuous outgrowing of the abstract arrangements on the part of the actual data.[21]

The practical convenience of the public, as well as of the practitioners, compels this elaboration of rules, or laws, from single cases. And, with increasing complexity of laws themselves, the same consid-

[19] See Note 15, p. 20.

[20] In his *Personnalité juridique* (p. 45 ff.) Saleilles gives an excellent demonstration of the common development of legal theories or reasons as rationalizations after the fact.

[21] To be sure these facts themselves are but sets of circumstances capable of being viewed in many different aspects. And the individual judgment upon the case, even if it were wholly independent of legal principles, would be determined by many other criteria of no greater inherency.

Justice Holmes, *Common Law*, p. 36, takes the same view. He says, "The truth is, that the law is always approaching, and never reaching, consistency. It is forever adopting new principles from life at one end, and it always retains old ones from history at the other, which have not yet been absorbed or sloughed off. It will become entirely consistent only when it ceases to grow."

eration leads to recurrent efforts to systematize (codify) the body of laws. The demand for codification is a demand of the people to be released from the mystery and uncertainty of unwritten or even of case law. Finally this leads to the development of a rationale of all law, which is known as jurisprudence.[22] These successive efforts to systematize are the hygiene of the law in so far as they make possible a general knowledge and certainty which is preventive, not merely remedial.

3. *Generalizations of Law — Jurisprudence*

The rationale of law, jurisprudence, is referred to by many of its expounders as the science of law. There is certainly a science of the evolution of law, as carried on by Maine and his followers, including the subject which Justice Holmes calls "the history of legal doctrine."[23] But these subjects are in fact the genetics of the social arrangements with which law deals and of the ideas, forms and procedures in which it clothes them and through which it deals with them. They are distinctly of a different order and method from jurisprudence as it is practised. To the writer this jurisprudence appears to be not so much a science as a philosophy; at its most scientific an effort to discover a system in all law; and, at its most philosophic, to find that system upon which law should endeavour, or is endeavouring, to model itself. Jurisprudence is of the order either of classical or of welfare economics.

On some such principle Jeremy Bentham divides jurisprudence into two parts; the "expository," which ascertains what the law is, and the "censorial," which ascertains what it ought to be.[24] The latter, a philosophic criticism, is clearly not science.[25] Nevertheless

[22] Justice Holmes says (*Papers*) that the object of the study of law is "the prediction of the incidence of the public force through the instrumentality of the courts" (p. 167), and "every new effort of legal thought is to make these prophecies more precise, and to generalize them into a thoroughly connected system" (p. 168).

[23] Holmes, *Papers*, p. 212. This may be regarded, either as "an exercise in the morphology and transformation of human ideas," or as the study of "a great anthropological document" (loc. cit.).

[24] *Works*, I, p. 148.

[25] It should be said that even the partial realization of the ideal of Justice Holmes, namely the application of scientific method to the determination of the criteria upon which law should be patterned — an ideal which has not yet begun to bear fruit, but which we may hope is prophetic — might well give to this branch of jurisprudence a scientific rather than its present speculative or philosophic character. ". . . historic continuity with the past is not a duty, it is only a necessity . . . An ideal system of law should draw its postulates and its legislative justification from science." *Papers*, p. 139.

Bentham's "censorial" branch of jurisprudence is referred to in the current dis-it has pervaded and inspired a great part of the literature on the subject for more than a thousand years. Holland says, "There floated always before the eyes of the later Roman jurists a vision of a *ius naturale;* a universal code, from which all particular systems are derived, or to which they all tend, at least, to approximate. . ."[26] And Maine derives modern international law through the Grotian school from this same philosophic source, of which he finds the beginnings in the *ius gentium.*[27] The relation of this belief in a system of absolute legal values to the science of the evolution of law, has been stated with nicety by the scientific Maine in a frequently quoted passage. Even Bentham and Austin, he says, "sometimes write as if they thought that, although obscured by false theory, false logic, and false statement, there is somewhere behind all the delusions which they expose a framework of permanent legal conceptions which is discoverable by a trained eye, looking through a dry light and to which a rational Code may always be fitted." But the fact that certain legal notions belonging to the "osseous structure" of legal systems may nevertheless be found decaying and dwindling "suggests very forcibly that even jurisprudence [legal systems] itself cannot escape from the great law of Evolution."[28]

The "expository" part of the subject which Holland conceives to be obviously alone entitled to bear the name science, he defines as a "formal, or analytical, as opposed to a material" science, dealing with legal relations, not *a priori* as they might or should have been, but *a posteriori* and abstracted from actual systems.[29] And this sci-

cussions as the "normative" branch of a science of law. But this "normative" seems to describe, in fact, not so much a science as what Professor Yntema calls a "subjective and authoritarian intuitionalism." As such it identifies itself with the philosophical jurisprudence of the past rather than with Justice Holmes' scientific criteria and critique of the future. Perhaps this future application of scientific criteria and critique will not be apparent until it is disclosed, after the fact, as a by-product of the current more scientific approach to the field of "expository" jurisprudence. If so – as is quite usual – the "expository" will turn out to be the "pure" science of law and the "censorial" to be merely the "applied" science – the application of the results of the "pure" science. See, on this subject, H. E. Yntema, "The Rational Basis of Legal Science," 31 *Columbia Law Review* (1931) p. 925.

26 *The Elements of Jurisprudence,* p. 6.

27 *Ancient Law,* p. 96.

28 Maine, *Dissertations on Early Law and Custom,* pp. 360, 361.

29 This definition of the "expository" branch is certainly unsatisfactory. It is the definition of a technique – a method – not of a science. Therefore it is too narrow and exclusive. So, too, mathematics and logic (the prototypes of the formal or analytical) which are sometimes called sciences, are but techniques – elaborations which are by definition necessarily true. Science is the result of applying such techniques to the data of experience. The science of law is a social science. It is therefore new, like other social sciences, and subject as yet only to those vague beginnings of a formal and analytical technique which are involved in what we call the descriptive approach. See Yntema, loc. cit., pp. 927-929.

ence must be progressive. "Its generalisations must keep pace with the movement of systems of actual law."[80] We shall have occasion to use the analytical methods which this branch of jurisprudence has developed. But, in so doing, it is necessary for us to remember that the generalizations of jurisprudence—and even those contained in laws themselves—do not "keep pace with the movement" of the actual judgments upon which they are based any more successfully than the legal forms maintain a strict conformity with the social practices they are endeavouring to define and regulate. This double dualism, which we have already suggested, is a treacherous source of error, against which we must be on our guard. The statement of the legal idea is one thing, its application another, and the social reality behind it still a third. Each influences the others. We cannot safely ignore any of the three if we are to secure a definite and accurate analysis of the structure of property for purposes of economic science.

D. The Line of Attack

By way of preparation for an examination of modern property we shall make a rapid survey of its ancient forms, of its developments in the two great systems from which our own is derived, and, finally, of its representation in this philosophic summation of legalistic theory called jurisprudence, as well as in the practice of modern law. The purpose is not to present a study in this compass of such a vast and ever-changing subject matter, but wholly to prepare the reader's mind to see the things of today as they are, by reading forward from the simple to the complex instead of using the deceptive but common methods, either of philosophizing the complex as is, without reference to its origins, or, on the other hand, of reading back from the complex to the simple. Since this is the limited purpose, it is necessary to be highly selective, both as to periods and authorities. The following brief sketches are each confined roughly to one time and one place and are largely viewed through the eyes of one authority or school.

The practical utility of this method may be suggested in another way. As we have seen, the social reality of property is one thing; its legal conventions another. Each has developed somewhat separately from the other, but today they are so woven together as to be distinguishable with difficulty. By tracing the colours of the warp and of the woof, each from their earlier conditions, we shall be the better able to distinguish these constituents in the pattern of the present—to determine what is actual and what is conventional. And,

[80] Op. cit., p. 9.

for the very reason that they seem to us outlandish, it is easier for the modern student of the legal history of property to see through these external forms and to view objectively the exemplifications of the institution itself when he begins with ancient Rome and medieval England, than it is for him to escape his preconceptions, *ab initio*, and perceive at once the realities of today. Therefore we shall begin with a survey of these two early systems, in the belief that by so doing we may better train our eyes to see the inner nature of the modes of our own times.

CHAPTER I

THE ORGANIZATION OF EARLY ROMAN SOCIETY

A. *The Prepossessions*

1. *Survey*

SEARCHING for reasons for all the tacit presuppositions with reference to the institution of property which lie behind our modern law, we are led to examine the Roman law. But there, in turn, we find in the period of the development of the classic law through the late Republic and early Empire, an even larger substructure of such inherited prepossessions. In order to bring these latter to light – to make them evident as well as explicable – it is necessary for us to extend our perspective and to postulate a long history of institutions and of manners of thought, so traditional that they seemed to the Romans a part of the nature of things, and so taken for granted that they were hardly discussed or even realized. There were legends, it is true, of lawgivers – of a Creation – as in other instances; but in the realm of the history of institutions, as in other fields of scientific investigation, modern criticism is engaged in breaking down such traditions of creation and is substituting those of evolution. "History, like nature, does not make leaps," says Ihering.[1] And Briffault puts it even more specifically. "Traditional heredity, like natural heredity, is strictly determined by what went before and no phase ever passes without leaving its imprint on all subsequent phases."[2] On the other hand, "evolution is not a road, but a network of anastomosed roads."[3] As the development of the individual is a product of environment as well as of heredity, so the history of institutions is the result of borrowing, of imitation, as well as of growth.

To reconstruct such a preceding setting, from which historic Roman concepts of property could have arisen, we must depend almost wholly upon hypothesis constructed from the various hints

[1] *Geist,* I, p. 209.
[2] Op. cit., I, p. 80.
[3] Tarde, *Les transformations du droit,* Pref., p. III.

available, and projected, in part, from the later facts.[4] Such hypothesis has little or no value as an account of prehistoric Roman or Indo-European society, for it is quite impossible to identify the various successive stages of development of any particular institution with a definite period or habitat. We are not attempting a picture of things as they were in, let us say, the Regal period of early Rome or even at the time of arrival in Italy. On the contrary we are undertaking to elaborate, from the available results of a thorough process of historical higher criticism, the diagram of a development which took place over an indefinite period of time. Such an hypothesis has value in elucidating the thing that was when it began to stand forth in the dawn of Roman history. Before that, for our purposes we posit merely an "Urzeit."

In order to prepare our minds, accustomed to complexity, for the simplicity of this *Urzeit*, and thus enable ourselves to arrive at some notion of the true nature of the early institutions which gave rise to modern property, we must effect a synthesis and then submit the product to a new and partial analysis. It is a natural prepossession in modern times to differentiate the several aspects of social activities and even to assume a separate set of institutions for each. Among these we have the religious, the domestic, the economic, and the political. In early societies these functions seem to have been indistinguishably blended and any one activity partook of some or all these characters. At first one organization seems to have served all purposes. We shall not expect to find, therefore, an institution which we can denominate as property.

In the second place psychological investigations among savages of today indicate that we should not assume by any means so definite a distinction between men and other objects as exists among modern civilized peoples.[5] On the whole the somewhat speculative evidence indicates an earlier state in which far less objectivity existed than even that limited degree to which we have attained, and in which there was some considerable extent of diffusion of personality. These suggested cautions, by way of a preliminary restoration of the point of view to a relative homogeneity, will enable us to commence, in the next section, a new analysis along other lines.

[4] This method is inescapable. R. Schröder, used to say in the 5th (and earlier) edition of his *Lehrbuch der deutschen Rechtsgeschichte*, p. 60, "Eine vollständige Übersicht über das Privatrecht der germanischen Urzeit lässt sich bei der Lückenhaftigkeit der gleichzeitigen Quellen nur durch mehr oder weniger gewagte Rückschlüsse aus den Verhältnissen der folgenden Periode gewinnen."

[5] Says Schrader, *Prehistoric Antiquities of the Aryan Peoples*, Trans. p. 314, "Primitive man feels that he is an animal with the animals, and the language of the Vedas still groups man and the animals together under the word *paçávas : paçú*, 'cattle.'" He thinks this is typical of the primitive Indo-European.

It is also necessary to be on our guard against certain common failings among the authorities whom we shall cite. It is, at best, subject to great psychological difficulties to see correctly the thing that was, eye to eye with prehistoric man. Nevertheless it is essential to disabuse the mind of the trick of reading into the past the refinements and conventions of the present. This is a trick which Maine finds very embarrassing and only due to "the error of ascribing to the mental condition of an unformed society a faculty which pre-eminently belongs to an advanced stage of intellectual development, the faculty of distinguishing in speculation ideas which are blended in practice."[6] Particularly because the study of Roman law has remained a live subject to this day, and because much of the original terminology is still in use, the citations from legal authorities will seem to presuppose the existence in ancient times of the corresponding modern institutions.[7] In fact this delusion seems often to be in the minds of the writers themselves. Therefore such descriptions should be translated into terms which do not carry these connotations. Perhaps the reader can perform this feat for himself. In addition to this, and particularly where the subject concerns race, religion, marriage, the family, human rights, and private property, especially that in land, one must be on constant guard against the sentimental viewpoints and the prejudices of the investigators themselves which seem to distort, both pro and con, the presentation of the evidence. Only rarely does one find a seemingly dispassionate statement of the bare facts of the picture—a picture that has been reconstructed out of the limited evidence available to us by the enormous, but often highly emotional, diligence of scholars in many lines.

As we have before remarked, in contrast to a narrative or a descriptive account, what we require for our purposes deals with the *Urzeit* as a whole and with the broad institutional outlines only. As Clark puts it, it is an examination of "the prehistoric antiquity of certain primary constituents of the Roman state . . . upon which a great part of the Personal and Property Law . . . of historical Rome may be shewn to depend."[8] Fortunately, "by no other Indo-European nation have so many institutions dating from primitive times been maintained as by the Romans. . ."[9] "The Roman law is the

[6] *Ancient Law*, p. 306.

[7] So Ihering, *Geist*, III, p. 312, ". . . aber über die Rechte des alten Vermögensrechts scheint der Wechsel der Dinge keine Macht gehabt zu haben; . . . Hat die Zeit keine Gewalt über sie, sind sie für die Ewigkeit gemacht—unvergänglich und unveränderlich, weil absolut wahr? Oder haben auch sie sich dem Wechsel der Dinge und Ansichten gefügt, und ist es vielleicht nur die Gleichheit des Namens, die uns die Aenderung der Sache selber übersehen lässt, nur dieselbe Schale, aber mit anderem Kern?"

[8] *History of Roman Private Law*, Pt. III, *Regal Period*, p. 3.

[9] Ihering, *The Evolution of the Aryan*, Trans., p. XIII.

most complete heritage of antique civilization," and its history, "that is to say the history of the rules which have presided over the social life, under the guardianship of the state, among the people who recapitulated and dominated the whole of antique civilization, is the most organic of all juridical histories." In fact it was "the formation and interpretation of law in which [this people] concentrated, in an almost exclusive manner, its being."[10] Our subject is the development of these institutions and customs, not the history of the people.[11] Moreover, since the greater part of the early private law of Rome traces its descent to the practices of the patricians, most of the institutions we study will be limited to those in vogue among that order.

Nor is it our purpose to add another summary of the scholarly but contradictory views held upon the subject of the Indo-European social organization, which seems, in many respects, to be common to Italic, Celtic and Teutonic peoples. Many of the details are disputed. However, there remain some broad generalizations which seem well supported by evidence and by fairly general agreement. For our purpose these are sufficiently explanatory. Schrader holds that "we have a right to speak of a common European culture,"[12] and that the devolution of this inheritance may be traced through language, since the institutional heredity is likely to be joined with the linguistic rather than with the physical strains.[13] It is generally agreed, largely upon the basis of the etymological relations and content of the Indo-European languages, that the original home of the mother people or group of peoples lay somewhere in Western Asia. At some period all—or the predecessors of the European branches only—moved west to a "second home" in and near the lower valley of the Danube. The beginnings of the Italic peoples, as a separate branch, may be established from the time of their separation from the rest as they spread westward from this "second home." Up to the time of this separation a certain degree of homogeneity is assumed,

[10] Bonfante, op. cit., I, pp. 3 and 4.

[11] Therefore, as Bonfante puts it, op. cit., I, p. 8, we shall not follow the chronological or even the synchronous (periodic) method, but that for which he suggests the names ideological or etiological.

[12] Op. cit., p. 131. While we are following, for convenience, the general view of our sources that these strains were carried and these movements performed by human beings in their physical aspect, the whole thesis is equally valid if the strains and the movements are conceived only to have taken place in the medium of human cultures. Nothing is gained for our purpose by discussing this moot question. But the reader is requested to bear in mind the dual possibility. "Le problème des langues est différent de celui des races; le peuple, au sens historique, considéré comme un ensemble d'éléments doués d'une conscience commune, d'institutions communes et d'une langue commune, n'est pas le peuple dans le sens anthropologique constitué par des caractères somatiques communs." Bonfante, op. cit., I, p. 26.

[13] Op. cit., p. 110.

for at least the entire European group, both in language and in customs. After that comes divergence, due to different conditions, contact with other civilizations, and mere physical separation. But we have reason to see that while conditions were diverse and changeable nevertheless customs were very durable. The thread of the common heritage of custom, as that of language, can be detected continuing and recurring, however modified as to all but its core, through changing conditions. The Italic peoples, after their arrival upon the peninsula, came, almost as quickly as had the Greeks, into contact with peoples of superior culture. Nevertheless, as Schrader says, "All these foreign populations [Etrurians, Ligurians, Iapyges, and Iberi] . . . in the course of centuries, yielded in tongue and customs to the nucleus of Indo-Europeans in ancient Italy."[14] Italy was exposed, as well, to the influence of Greek colonies for several centuries before the beginning of the Roman record[15] and was dominated for a time by the, probably Lydian, Etruscan race. But, except for the absorption from Greek, or from Etruscan, or from Carthaginian and thence from Phoenician sources, of a certain law merchant, which came much later, the alteration of the fundamental habits of the stubborn and vigorous Roman strain does not seem at first to have been marked.[16]

Our prehistoric perspective is constantly deepening; the span of the lifetime of mankind constantly elongating; and presumptive incidents in the *Urzeit* which were formerly placed ten or twenty centuries before our era are now pushed back many times that distance into the past. Current opinion places the separation of the Italic peoples from the "second home" in the third millennium B.C., and their appearance in the Italian peninsula as a gradual process extending over the second millennium B.C. The settlement of Latium by the Latins may not have occurred until the eighth century B.C.[17] But evidence seems to be accumulating that it began as early as the middle of the second millennium B.C. Girard holds that "the Kingship phase is the most remote one to which the political history of Rome can be

[14] Op. cit., p. 112.

[15] Op. cit., p. 242.

[16] Bonfante, op. cit., I, p. 33, speaks of the Italian peninsula as "*ab antiquo*, le champ de tous les peuples"—a sort of ancient "melting pot"—and suggests (p. 34) the analogy between the consolidation of England under the Normans, after a series of invasions and hegemonies, and the Roman closing of the doors of the frontiers of Italy after a similar "suite continue d'invasions et . . . mélange de dominateurs et de races dominées." But he holds that, "Le vrai peuple de la péninsule italienne . . . est le peuple ombrien," and guesses that the Sabines and Latins were an offshoot therefrom (p. 41), driven into southern Italy by the development of the Etruscan domination. In spite of an overlay of Etruscan civilization, the influence was not very profound. The Sabellian race had guarded its own institutions (pp. 55-56).

[17] Tenney Frank, *An Economic History of Rome*, pp. 2-3.

carried back,"[18] and this he estimates to have ended about 500 B.C.[19]

At least we have three phases—a common Indo-European *Urzeit;* a phase of differentiation during which the new habitat was invaded; and, finally, an Italian phase during which the settlement of Latium was effected. The close of this prehistoric and the beginning of the historic, or at least legendary, time is called the Regal period. Then the outline of Rome begins to appear.

Considering that some 1500 years is supposed to have intervened between the so-called "departure" of the Italic peoples from the "second home" and their appearance in the valley of the Po, it is not necessary to assume that what took place was a migration (trek). Quite likely what occurred was merely an irregular and intermittent growth of population with a coincident spreading out to the west and south. As the distance between these geographical branches of the mother people increased, their cultures become differentiated.[20] One can perhaps best conceive the situation as involving great but thinly populated areas occupied by mobile and largely pastoral tribes, settled and at peace during certain periods and restless and disturbed at others. Exhaustion of pasturage and unfavourable climatic cycles, on the one hand, and radical improvements in technique and resulting growth of population, on the other, might well have given rise to movements and the search for and conquest of happier hunting grounds. During quiet times the economic aspect and organization would be to the fore. Perhaps even the beginnings of inter-community trade would appear. And when times were troubled the military organization would suppress the economic, and "economic civilization" would receive a set-back. But this is purely speculative. It is inserted in order to offset the common notion which seems to picture such movements as if they were compressed into a few years and were processes with a systematic course.

Here was a long period of gestation. True the embryos were already divided by a vague cleavage of outline; but the inheritance was common and, until certain of these branches emerged upon the southern peninsulas, the environment was much the same. There is, therefore, no apparent reason for denying the obvious relationship between the different manifestations of social organization among the

[18] *Manuel élémentaire de droit romain,* p. 11.

[19] Op. cit., p. 24.

[20] Ihering's picture of a long migration on the model of the later "Barbarian Invasions" seems to the writer fanciful. See his *Aryan.* The *ver sacrum* may have accounted for the settlement of Rome itself (see Bonfante, op. cit., I, p. 41) and for many previous short movements of colonization. But Bonfante conceives the general movements to have been a combination of conquest, colonization and slow infiltration (p. 26).

Indo-European cultures in Europe. The systems everywhere seem fundamentally to resemble each other in their broad outlines. It is not necessary for us to generalize *a priori* principles of human nature which *would* naturally lead to such systems of organization. For elsewhere apparently the same human nature has frequently produced different systems. All we need to do is to judge by the results.

We have to see that early Indo-European societies were subjected to a duplex organization on two radically different principles by two radically different sets of conditions.[21] When they were settled, one system of organization was uppermost; when they were wandering and fighting, another. The two subsisted alongside of one another, were intimately knit together in origin and structure, and continuously influenced and modified each other. The relative emphasis seesawed according as the people were spread out upon the land as dwellers—pastors and perhaps tillers—or were moving as a horde from place to place. If we start from such an assumption of a dual arrangement much seems to be clarified that is otherwise completely puzzling, and we detect many resemblances between the eventual systems appearing in the north and in the south during historic times.

It is also necessary to assume, in order to account for the resemblances between the northern and southern orders in their more settled and peaceful states, that the first of these, the fundamental organization by which they lived, had been established and hardened into inveterate custom before these peoples began to separate by expansion to the west and south and during the period when they were developing their common root tongue in propinquity to each other. The persistent uniformity with which this system seems to reassert itself when, after possible turbulent and migratory periods, it has presumably been reduced to a mere skeleton, argues that it is the age-old and traditional customary organization of settlement.

Many of the authorities seem to take it for granted, because the evidence of the general existence of monandry and at least official monogyny among the Aryans is strong, that it follows that the social unit which was the basis of this fundamental organization was what we call a "family"—that is, man, wife and progeny.[22] Conceding the apparent fact of monogamy it does not follow, however, that the group, which functioned domestically, politically, economically and religiously as the social unit, was such a family. All that the evidence for monogamy proves is that, in "official" marriage, a man

[21] See Ihering, *Geist*, I, pp. 181-2.

[22] Vinogradoff, *Jurisprudence*, I, p. 238, says, "In the Aryan household there is emphatically no idea of strict monogamy." I am inclined to think early imputations of this order were highly idealistic.

had one wife, a woman one husband, and that they had offspring. The organic social grouping need not have followed these lines and there seems to me to be sufficient indication that it did not.

The difficulties of matching the social grouping with biological relationship have proved insuperable. Here we find lineal relationships: there collateral: at other points none at all. Everywhere we find indications that the actual social grouping followed the line of paternity more nominally than it did really—that the biological pattern of organization came to be honoured, though it was breached as much or more than it was observed. It appears that the simple idea eventually showed itself as paternity—but that the simple fact was always the strong man. Our thesis will be that the forces which organized this integer of early Aryan society were *propinquity* and *power*, not *paternity* (or maternity).

In essence such a social grouping differs not only from the war organization but from the marital organization. One conceives it as the outgrowth of a putative Aryan and pastoral patriarchate.[23] It is in essence a grouping of men and animals upon the land. In appraising it for what it actually was many difficulties seem to be overcome if we do not impose upon it our own hard and fast notions of the necessity of biological domestic relationship, of property or of political organization. It was what Ihering has called a "state in little."[24] It was, too, an "economy in little." Finally it was, in some respects, a "sect in little." It functioned, jointly and integrally, as a producing organization, as a self-governing organization and as a church. Any larger group was built of these fundamental integers. Any larger group was a compound. This unit, as I conceive it, was bound together for the most part by two factors, propinquity and the power of the head—a power qualified by immemorial custom. Doubtless the arrangement of the modern family—man and wife and children—existed within it, singly or multiply; perhaps this element originated it. Doubtless, too, other biological relationships such as fraternity entered into it and related it to other units. Certainly it was per-

[23] Vinogradoff, *Jurisprudence*, I, p. 224, considers that "the Aryans had certainly reached the patriarchal stage before their dispersion"; nay more that "the central fact of Aryan culture is a patriarchal state of society." It should be noted that we use the term patriarchal to designate that form of social group, arranged in a hierarchy of generations (a truncated pyramid) and governed by a patriarch—one among the elders. This point needs to be made because anthropologists seem to be using the term to designate any father, as opposed to mother, government, even that of a modern family, and sometimes to indicate merely patrilineal descent (paternal right). Bonfante holds that the fact is established that the Aryan system was agnatic and that where we find evidence of early cognatic relationship it was non-Aryan, a survival of the matriarchate (op. cit., I, p. 30).

[24] Bonfante, op. cit., I, p. 30, calls them "agglomérations politiques minuscules."

vaded with the tradition – perhaps largely supposititious – of such a binder and of such a system of external valences. But the idea does not account for the facts, the facts of a miscellaneous congeries of men and animals upon the land – a polity – an economic enterprise.[25]

As to the military order we have to think of something in the nature of a horde or host, rather than an army; the men organized for military purposes under a leader, the women and children and cattle accompanying them on their slow trek. There is no need of supposing such movements and conquests to have been greatly different from those which were observed during historic times, except that they may have been much slower and for shorter distances. The term for these moving groups seems in the Roman case to have been *tribus*, and for their headman or chief, eventually, and perhaps originally, *rex*. The men were evidently organized in tens and hundreds, which is taken to account for the constant recurrence of the decimal system in the more artificially organized features of the later Roman political constitution, and also in the more legendary early system of land distribution among colonists. This same decimal system appears constantly in the north, as well, but there it occurs particularly in the terms for, and the arrangements of, the early political organization upon the land.

2. *Propinquity – The Group*

It is certain that the Roman institution of property is an outgrowth of the early social unit which we are about to describe. In fact Ihering holds this unit to be the original source of all private law.[26] At any rate, the beginnings of the law find it already in existence and, as we shall see, the law does not at first intrude within it. It is, therefore, only possible to deduce the nature of the primitive institution from the legal terms and provisions applied to it in historic times. Behind these terms and provisions lie the *prepossessions*, the assumptions, which the Romans took for granted and which determined the budding legal structure. Of these several prepossessions those in which we are particularly interested are:

25 Bonfante has summarized the development of doctrine as to primitive social organization. See op. cit., I, p. 73 ff. The nineteenth century doctrine was that "le lien de l'agglomération primitive est . . . le lien du sang. L'organisation politique naît postérieurement dans la cité et dans l'Etat, sous l'influence du territoire, c'est-à-dire de la cohabitation stable d'individus de diverses origines à la même place." Now, on the contrary, it is held that "ni la famille primitive, ni la *gens*, ni la tribu n'ont une nature différente de l'Etat; ce sont des agglomérations nées pour l'ordre et la défense et uniformes dans leur composition."

26 Ihering, *Entwicklungsgeschichte des römischen Rechts*, p. 49. He says, "Zum Ausgangs- und Mittelpunkt meiner ganzen Untersuchung nehme ich das römische Haus. Alles Privatrecht geht vom Hause aus. . ."

1. The content of the idea of the early social unit and of its relations.

2. The content of the idea "belong to," and the field to which it was applied.

3. The genesis and nature of that certain aspect of such relations which we term legal and, in particular among the latter, the legal institution of property which arose from and was defined by such legal relations.

The structure of this social unit in Rome was already fixed in the Regal period.[27] It bears the ear-marks of descent from a patriarchal régime and this, as we have seen, is assumed as the original Aryan form.[28] Schrader expresses the view generally held, that the Aryan form has, in respect of its composition, persisted especially in the joint household of the Hindus, the Irish sept and above all the Southern Slav house community. The latter contains up to 60 or 70 members, all being blood relations, on the male side, up to the second or third degree. But in that case there is no patriarch. Rather it is an elected house-administrator who lives in the true *house*—the "place of the fire." On the other hand, it is in the Roman *familia* particularly, according to this view, that the original form has persisted most exactly in respect of its governance; that of the patriarch, or house head. And it is possible to account for the alteration away from the patriarchal model, in respect of composition, which eventually took place among the Romans, Greeks and Teutons, by the change from the pastoral or nomad state, when the group was bound together by the indispensability of the herd, to the agricultural state where, as among the latter peoples, the sons eventually divided on the death of the father or even left the group as soon as they were married. It is probable that the migrations themselves also tended to break down the patriarchal community and to submerge its organization beneath that of the military host. This might account for the fact that the large house communities continued among the Slavic peoples who remained longest in or near the "second home"; for the remnants of the form among the Greeks and Romans and certain Celtic peoples whose movements were, among the western branches, presumably earliest and briefest; and finally, for the almost complete disappearance of patriarchal forms and the apparent substitution of the small modern family and the military organization among the

[27] "To this pre-Tarquinian period will generally be admitted to belong the peculiar family organisation with the extreme power of the male head, the old religious marriage, possibly the original rules of succession. . ." Clark, *Regal*, p. 455.

[28] Girard, op. cit. p. 148, says, "Mais, quels qu'aient été ses antécédents, la famille romaine nous apparaît dès la fondation de la ville comme une famille rigoureusement constituée selon le type patriarcal. . ." And Bonfante, op. cit., I, p. 30, "Aux Aryens appartient le système de la parenté paternelle, base de la famille dite patriarcale. . ."

other Celtic and the Teutonic peoples whose migrations were still continuing when they appear in history. It is sometimes assumed that with the original patriarchal form went primogeniture, traces and restorations of which survive among many of the Indo-European peoples.

The seemingly artificial organization of this patriarchal prototype indicates a slow development over an enormously long period; and the persistence and reappearance in historic times of its characteristics over an area reaching from Hindustan to Ireland (and even Iceland) demonstrates its enduring character. It appears to be a necessary hypothesis to account especially for the Roman social organization which we will undertake to appraise and analyse.

While there is some risk in giving much weight to the very uncertain etymologies, nevertheless the derivation of the ancient terms themselves remains the most available and effective means of coming at the viewpoint of prehistoric times. Presumably the development of meaning and application – the semantics – demonstrates the contemporary connotation. It is, for example, a striking fact that the words which pervade the Indo-European languages to describe this fundamental social unit, which in one form or another is common to all the Aryan peoples, have none of them any significance of *kinship*. The Latin term is *familia*. Its probable source is a root developing the idea of settlement. And, in turn, it is the source of our "family." But it did not mean "family," except in later times. It signified at first more especially this social unit; whence it came to designate a special part of the patrimony, a body of property, or even, later, a body of slaves, as property. I think its original meaning may be given as "dwelling," "habitation," and thence, in general, "household."[29] Two other Latin terms which are intimately related to this early household and with which we will be much concerned as we proceed – since the facts of property are largely built thereon – are cognates of the Greek and Sanskrit words which seem to have denominated the corresponding units among the ancient Greeks and Hindus. These are *domus* and *vicus*. The first is supposed to be derived from a root signifying "to build"; the second from another

[29] This is the sense which Walde, *Lateinisches etymologisches Wörterbuch*, gives it. He says, "Das Gesinde; die ganze Hausgenossenschaft (Freie und Sklaven); Familie." And Ihering, *Entw.-Gesch.*, p. 50, says, "*Familia* ist sprachlich die Wohnstätte, also das Haus, aber nicht das Haus im natürlichen Sinne (*domus, aedes*), sondern im wirtschaftlichen und juristischen Sinn: die Grundlage der gesamten wirtschaftlichen und privatrechtlichen Existenz, das Haus mit allem, was darin ist und dazu gehört: Weib, Kinder, Sklaven, Ackerland, kurz das Hauswesen und zwar wie wir unten sehen werden, das Hauswesen des Bauern." Clark, who of English writers on Roman law seems to have given the closest attention to etymology, agrees that "*familia* is the household, i.e., the house inclusive of the persons dwelling therein." *Regal*, p. 53. See also Ihering, *Geist*, II, p. 161, Note 214.

root signifying "to settle." *Domus* meant a house, and *vicus* a group of houses. Thus the early contemporary concept of this social unit may be said to have been that of a settlement, partly in its personal and partly in its material aspect.[80]

Why this peculiar sequence of meanings, beginning with the sense of building and ending with the broad—and, in our derivative, with the narrow—sense of kinship? Much of the history of the development of property is bound up in that progression and we shall do well to keep it constantly in mind. At this point it is sufficient to point out that *familia* did not mean "family." Philologists have not succeeded in uncovering a group of cognates represented in the Indo-European languages, which clearly signify "family"—in the sense father, mother, children.[81] If such a unit had been obvious in its physical segregation or its functional effect there would have been a term for it. Moreover, there appears to have been no term for the husband-wife relation—our "matrimony."[82] The obvious inference is that society in early times was otherwise organized.

I submit that the reason we find it so difficult to determine the exact sense of the words which have been used at various times and places to cover the fairly general resurgence of this hypothetically original Aryan unit, is that we attempt to read into them a degree of specialization which did not exist and that we unthinkingly assume that already certain institutions had arisen to define this unit in spite of the fact that we know, when we stop to think of it, that they themselves were later outgrowths of the operations of the unit itself. "One of the chief difficulties," says Hearn,[83] "in the study of history is the tendency to judge early men and early institutions by the standard and the lights of our own day. This tendency is indefinitely strengthened if we use the same name for both the ancient and the modern institution. There is, for example, little hope that we shall understand the nature of the archaic family if we permit ourselves to call it by that name. It is not only that the word family, or Familia, is hopelessly ambiguous, but also that the archaic Household is essentially different from the family, as we understand the term."

[80] For a discussion of the very interesting and important etymologies of these terms, see Appendix I A.

[81] Schrader, op. cit., p. 396, "It seems, therefore, almost impossible to establish a primeval term for the concept 'family.'"

[82] Vinogradoff, *Jurisprudence*, I, p. 224, ". . . there is no common name for marriage."

[83] *The Aryan Household*, p. 63. Bonfante supports the same view. He says, op. cit., I, p. 83, "Ce qu'on appelle *familia*, organisme bien distinct de la société domestique à laquelle il a fini par donner son nom, est le plus restreint des groupes politiques, c'est-à-dire des sociétés d'ordre et de défense formées à l'époque primitive." Even Cornil, whose views are in the main more conventional, says, *Ancien droit romain*, p. 31, that the term *familia* is used to cover many varieties of concentric groups, of all of which the axis is the *paterfamilias*.

For the sake of maintaining a reminder of this distinction, and in order to separate the prehistoric polity from the discrete institutions of marriage and of the modern family, which did not correspond with it, we shall apply to it the term *house community*.[84] Where we refer to its later place in the Roman law of property, the term *familia* is appropriate as suggesting many associated ideas. And, as an adjective, the convenient "familial" will do for both.

If the primitive Indo-European house community was not a family, what was it? We think of organization in terms of such fixed and distinct notions as those of the state, the municipality, the corporation, of sects and churches, of families, broad and narrow. If all these concepts are merged in one we seem to have something resembling the early Roman, or Aryan, house community. It was a village – farm – church – household – composed of *propinqui*. It was a "state in little" functioning in all fields.[85] It was also a "church in little," and it was as well the economic unit, organized and managed for commercial and industrial as well as agricultural purposes. To Ihering it seems particularly a unit of governance. Therein the individual "appears to us as a member of an association, which is to his life as much a support as it is a restraint."[86] Hearn holds that the core idea was ancestor worship.[87] Schrader, who doubts the great antiquity of ancestor worship, would, I presume, transpose this archaic core into a cult of fire.[88] At any rate, authorities, I think, agree in giving the house community a nature and binder blended of worship, governance, business and, in part, of kinship.

It is extremely difficult to estimate the degree to which kinship constituted the house community. We have denominated the cement of this original social unit, as *propinquity*. And this gives the key. *Propinquus* meant indiscriminately "neighbour" and "relative." Does that signify that originally all neighbours were relatives and all relatives neighbours? Certainly that was not true of the Roman

84 By "marriage" we mean the official *husband-wife* relation, or union; by "family" we mean the *husband-wife-children* relation or union.

85 Ihering, from whom this term is borrowed, uses it only of the gens.

86 *Entw.-gesch.* p. 50.

87 "The theory upon which it rested was the paramount and continuous obligation of ancestral worship. The practical object at which it aimed was the regular and proper performance of the *sacra* . . . The machinery by which the *sacra* were maintained was the corporate character of the Household, and the perpetual succession of the House Father." *Aryan*, p. 63. And, "The tie between the members was neither blood nor contract, but community of domestic worship" (p. 65).

88 See op. cit., Chapter XIII. He says, "The sanctity, however, of fire in general, and of the fire of the hearth in particular, is an idea which must be regarded as common to all Indo-Europeans . . ." (p. 130). He does admit, p. 424, that "the belief in and worship of the *dei parentes*, the *divi Manes*, the *Lares*, &c., are so engrained in the life of the Roman that, as regards Rome, we have no reason to doubt that these ideas are primitive." Nevertheless they do concern themselves particularly with "the place of the fire" – the hearth.

familia when it begins to be exhibited to us. But it may have been true of the *free* members. In fact this may have been the criterion of freedom – membership in a fellowship of traditional consanguinity – a partly supposititious reminiscence of the primitive patriarchal group and a practical recognition of the general reason for propinquity, the common descent by the fission of the patriarchal family.[39] Such a presumed, or actual, development would explain the secondary use of *familia* to indicate "kin" as well as the whole supposititious structure of the gens and its cognate Indo-European forms. Perhaps, so far as the free were concerned, *familiae* grew by fission among the male descendants of a common patriarch.

Certainly the agnatic principle, so-called, was universal[40] at the time of the "dispersion" of the Indo-Europeans. The cognatic relationships only came to be recognized later as settlement and civilization advanced, or under the influence of other cultures.[41] But within the larger or smaller circle of agnatic kinship we are left to wonder whether the terms describe generations or social economic functions.[42] Surely they do not describe exact lineal or collateral relationships.[43] Fathers were not given the name of father as to

[39] The connection of *liberi* (children) with *liber* (free) is tempting evidence for this thesis. Ihering, *Entw.-gesch.* p. 53, so holds, believing that *liberi* originally had the double sense of "free persons" and of "the children." Perhaps there was such a connection pre-ethnically, but Walde, *Latin,* prefers to relate *liber* (free) to an IE. **(e)leudh-,* though he cites Schrader approvingly in his establishment of certain cognates with the sense of *Volk. Liberi* (children), on the other hand, he prefers to derive in the sense of "growing," from IE. **leudh-.* And at this pre-Latin stage he relates the two. "Davon auch nhd. *Leute,* ab. *ljudŭ* (Volk) usw. (s. *liber*) als 'Generation,' und auf Grund der schon Idg. **Bed.** 'Volk' auch *liber, ἐλεύθερος* (frei) als 'Volksgenosse.'" Thus, much further back, the thesis seems established.

[40] Schrader, op. cit., pp. 375-380.

[41] For the Romans this is accepted by all authorities. For the Teutons, Schröder says, op. cit., p. 6, "Der Aufbau der Sippschaft war rein agnatisch, die Blutsfreunde von mütterlicher Seite wurden nicht als Verwandte, sondern nur als Freunde angesehen. . ." And, in general, Schrader finds (loc. cit.) that the Indo-European terms for relation through the wife's family are terms for, or derived from, friendship. Marriage severed the woman's previous family ties. "The wife vanished, so to speak, into the house of her husband." The term *affinitas* used later for the relation to the wife's family meant originally only "neighbourhood." Walde gives its sense from *ad fines* as *in agris vicini.* Thus it was but a later term for propinquity.

[42] Westermarck, *History of Human Marriage,* said, in the earlier (single volume) editions of his work, "There can scarcely be any doubt that the terms for relationship are in their origin, terms of address" (p. 89). They are applied according to "sex and age, as also to the external, or social, relationship in which the speaker stands to the person whom he addresses" (p. 90). The larger the body of kinsfolk who keep close together, the more comprehensive the terms (p. 94). These statements are substantially confirmed in the 5th (3 vol.) edition of 1921; see I, pp. 251-252. See also L. H. Morgan's "Classificatory System" as described in his *Systems of Consanguinity and Affinity of the Human Family.* Bonfante, op. cit., I, p. 83, regards the Roman terms as titles, "the same as those which relate to any political community."

[43] Schrader, op. cit., p. 373, says the terms, other than for the immediate family, were "in a state of continual flux."

their offspring alone but also as to many others. Brothers were not necessarily sons of a common parent. *Parens*, like its French derivative, covered any "relatives" as well as "parents." *Avus* originally signified "forefather in general" and *nepos* meant "descendant in general."[44] The daughter-in-law was the "female son."[45] Also these terms seem to describe a general relation, or define a status – outside the house community as much as in it. The outline of the social unit does not correspond with any certain degree or variety of kinship.[46] One sees its internal and external relations pervaded with a terminology that has, in historic times, become converted into the expression of varying precise varieties of true consanguinity. But its usage in the *Urzeit* covers a loose and vague notion of 'belonging' together – of kinship of some kind, fellowship, and neighbourhood in general – not that of an organized genealogical tree.

We may take it for granted that these early house communities were not uniform in size or composition. Yet it seems to be often assumed that the pattern was regular and systematic, although this is not only contrary to the evidence but is not in accord with conditions existing in any state of society with which we are directly familiar. Certainly there were always great men and little men, great "houses" and little "houses," great house communities and little house communities. Nevertheless, while recognizing that types do not exist, we may conceive one as a convenient diagram. And, for that purpose, we shall select a great house, though it be not typical. For such complex and larger units are more indicative and of more interest, since from them first developed the practices and principles which we find in later law. It is the growth of these more successful aggregating nuclei that we must watch.

Such a house community, by the time of early Rome, consisted of a master, perhaps his official wife and children, perhaps still some of his brothers, their wives and children, perhaps more distant relatives such as his widowed mother, his father's brothers and their families (agnates). These, by that time, were of the blood. In addition there might be adopted or arrogated members. At some stage the class of clients appeared, perhaps not usually in-dwelling.[47]

[44] See Schrader, op. cit., p. 379. At some time the matrilineal relation was incorporated. *Avunculus* (little forefather, or grandfather) came in Rome to stand for the mother's brother, and *nepos* (descendant) for either the brother's or the sister's son.

[45] Schrader, op. cit., p. 375.

[46] In Rome, says Schrader, op. cit., p. 394, it was *not uncommon* for blood relatives to dwell together.

[47] "Further, the Household, if no separation had taken place, extended not only to lineal but to collateral relatives. It included servants and dependents. It included children by adoption." Hearn, *Aryan*, p. 65. Bonfante, op. cit., I, p. 30, describes it as consisting of "toutes les personnes liées par un lien de descendance paternelle,

Also we find a sort of membership existing for the *hospites* – the guest-friends. Certainly from the beginning there were slaves.[48] And with slavery came freedmen, who still continued a quasi-membership. At any rate so important and effective did this social organization become in many cases that it proved a magnetic core around which other persons were gathered, or clustered, whose relation was economic and political and only in form one of mock-kinship.

In addition to human beings there were within the group the domestic animals, which we shall discuss later, and doubtless certain objects (chattels) such as armour, weapons, vessels and garments, together with small stores of product (hoards). Always there was some dwelling, some shelter, which eventually became a fixed habitation, a settlement, and appeared as the later inclusion in the *familia* of land and buildings. Together this complex formed the house community.

Of the members of this compound house community "the house itself (eventually) occupied the most prominent place." It was the asylum; the inviolable "place of the peace." It was holy. Gods lived there. The hearth, its center, was the "place of the fire." Divine law, *fas*, as well as human, *ius*, defended it.[49] It was the physical representation, the locus of the household – the *home*.

"All civilization begins with the establishment of a fixed residence in a determined place."[50] The Aryans are presumed to have been nomads without such fixed dwellings. They lived in wagons. But with the development of agriculture came fixed residence and wagons were displaced by dug-outs, huts, block houses.[51] Even "when the

les étrangers agrégés à la famille, qui sont égalés aux descendants dans le droit, ou ceux qui sont accueillis et protégés (les clients), ou ceux qui en sont proprement les instruments (les esclaves). . ."

[48] Girard, op. cit., p. 103, thinks slavery existed at the origin of Rome as a *cité.* Ihering, *Geist,* II, 172 ff., believes slaves were at first largely prisoners of war, existed in small numbers and, for this reason and because community of work and life raised their station, were helpers rather than servants. He holds, *Aryan,* pp. 394-6, that, "The mother-nation [Aryan] knew but one way of dealing with their vanquished enemies – they made them slaves." He is uncertain whether, during the migration, such a prisoner was *praeda* (public booty) or *spolia* (private booty) and cites the old etymology of *servus* (the saved). Walde, *Latin,* states that this etymology, given in the Institutes, is incorrect. "Ist nicht 'der in Gewahrsam genommene,' sondern der 'Hüter, Wächter' (des Viehs) ;" though from *servo* (to keep safe). In this view there is no etymological indication of the source of slavery.

[49] Adapted from Ihering, *Geist,* II, pp. 157-158.

[50] Ihering, *Entw.-gesch.,* p. 50.

[51] Schrader, op. cit., p. 338, says, ". . . there can be no doubt that the use of wagons as dwellings is a trait from the life of the primeval period which the northern tribes preserved." It was continued by the Germans even when settled for the time being. "In general, however, in winter the domestic animals either shared the human habitation . . . or wintered in the open. . ." (p. 347). Settlements "tended to become more and more permanent, the more the Indo-Europeans devoted themselves to agriculture" (p. 340). Of these the typical hut was of wood, basket-work and

Greeks and Italians immigrated into the two classical peninsulas, they knew no other form of dwelling than the hut made of straw, twigs, and loam."[52] There are no indications that the Romans knew the use of stone or brick even during the Regal period. "The Temple of Vesta was originally a hut, with walls of wicker-work and roof of straw."[53] It is not necessary, however, to assume that the residence of a prehistoric Roman house community was a single hut. The identification of the residence with a curtilage, rather than with a single building, which we shall examine later; the description of the Indian, Slavic and Teutonic house communities; and the use in Latin of *vicus*—a cognate of the Greek, Sanskrit and even the Umbrian words for the house community—to designate a little group of buildings, all conspire to suggest that the "house" was often rather a yard enclosing a group of huts, or even a straggling village.[54]

It may have struck readers unfamiliar with this subject, as peculiar that we should thus compose the house community of persons and objects indiscriminately, as if it were an undifferentiated homogeneous whole. Yet so the evidence is construed by most students of the subject.[55] If there was differentiation it was not along the lines we would expect. Of that more later. If, as well, it has seemed a work of supererogation to examine in such detail the structure and functioning of this early house community in connection with the

loam, and usually circular in form (p. 342). "It is conceivable that the round hut was the dwelling of the ordinary man, while more spacious blockhouses were built for the kings and chief men . . ." (p. 346). But he quotes Geiger, commenting on a passage from the Vendidâd—". . . in the case of a man who has died [away] from home two alternatives are mentioned as possible: either to take the corpse to the dwelling or the dwelling to the corpse" (p. 345) to indicate that even when placed on the ground the huts were readily movable. Ihering, *Aryan*, p. 106, states that the Teutons included houses among movable goods, since they were of wood and capable of being taken apart and moved.

[52] Quoted by Schrader, op. cit., p. 343, from W. Helbig, *Die Italiker in der Poebene*. But Bonfante, op. cit., I, p. 37, holds that these relics were Ligurian and not Aryan.

[53] Quoted by Ihering, *Aryan*, p. 105, from Helbig, op. cit.

[54] Bonfante assumes a connection between *familia* and *vicus* analogous to the one between *gens* and *pagus*. See op. cit., I, p. 85 and elsewhere. This is supported by the etymology of the terms. *Vicus* is elsewhere synonymous with house or household. Evidently in early Rome these households were often straggling villages. *Pagus*, on the other hand, may be related to *paciscor*, and so be the area of the "peace," and therefore probably of the gens, the earliest informal aggregate of households.

[55] Citing only Ihering, for example. He speaks of the term "*familia* (dem Hausstand desselben, Personen und Sachen gleichmässig umfassend)," *Geist*, I, p. 240; either as a figure of speech as we say "of both persons and things, house, household, farm;" *Entw.-gesch.*, p. 85; or more especially as something more unified than we can readily comprehend. . . "es behält auch, . . . einen besonders ausgezeichneten Charakter für sie bei, der sich dem Vermögen, welches das Haus in sich birgt, mittheilt." "In dieser räumlichen Gemeinschaft der Personen und Sachen, in dieser Bestimmung der Sachen für die unmittelbare persönliche Existenz und das Familienleben liegt für die Sache selbst ein sittliches Moment." *Geist*, II, p. 157.

objective which we set ourselves in the Introduction, may I recall to the reader that the subject of economics, as its name implies, began as the management of just such a house community. Here we find not only the beginnings of property but the beginnings of economics as well.[56]

3. *Power—The Person*

The governance of the early Roman house community was the despotism of a single master. As representing the authoritative view and that held universally, I believe, by students of Roman law, we can do no better than to present in full the description given by Girard, which we shall then proceed to qualify in certain details. He says,[57] "In respect to private life, the earliest Romans lived, as did many pastoral communities and some agricultural communities, under the patriarchal régime. At the head of each household, there was a patriarch, a *paterfamilias*, whose absolute authority, limited only by custom and opinion, extended equally over everything connected with the household, both human beings and things. He also alone represented the household to the outside world, whether in respect of the rare commercial transactions necessary at this period, when each family was, as a rule, sufficient unto itself, or in respect of the disputes provoked by the conduct of its members towards third parties, or by that of third parties towards them. He was in his household, it has been said, in specific terms borrowed from the categories of more recent times, at the same time, the proprietor, the judge, and the priest. He was sole proprietor, not only of the products of the labour of his slaves, his wife, and his children, but strictly of everything, including his wife and his children, whom he could sell as he could his cattle and his slaves.[58] He was the priest who took charge of the maintenance of the worship of the domestic hearth, of the sacrifices to ancestors. He was the judge, if not in civil matters,—in respect to which there were no separate rights, and, consequently, no possible legal proceedings between the persons composing the

[56] The Greek word *οἰκονομία* had probably as its original sense "mistress, or manageress, of the household" and the abstract or functional sense was derived. One cannot be certain whether, before its formation, that sense of *νόμος* had been reached whereby it became the word for "law," through the sense of tradition (custom, that which is handed out or down), just as "tradition," in turn—derived from *traditio* (delivery)—meant originally "to give over to"; or whether it still contained the original sense of *νέμειν* and thus meant "a dealing (or dealer) out to the household." The development is similar to the French *ménage, aménager, aménagement* from the Old French *mesnage* (house). But to assume that the Greek term meant merely "the domestic economy" is to misread the facts. For the economics of the house community was almost the whole of the economics of that day.

[57] Op. cit., pp. 13-14.

[58] He could not sell the wife *in manu* into slavery. See Cornil, op. cit., p. 36.

household,—yet at any rate in penal matters, where he could inflict all penalties even up to death, not only upon his slaves but upon his wife and children; though usage required him in the last two cases to take the advice of a council, composed of near kinsmen, but did not oblige him to follow it. In short, he possessed an absolute authority, identically the same over everything which entered within the sphere of his action: —over his dead chattels, over his living chattels, such as domestic animals and slaves, over his wife, and over his children—to whom must be added, in an enumeration which at all pretends to be complete, as being under his power which was inseparable from his protection, his guests (*hospites*)—the members of foreign cities [*cités*], temporarily at Rome, who could have no security except by placing themselves under the authority of a citizen, and who placed themselves under his at Rome, as he would place himself under theirs if he went to their city [*cité*]—and his clients (*clientes*), fugitives come to place themselves under his ægis, or slaves freed by him, who in those days would have as little security as the others, unless they remained under the *potestas* of a citizen." This "power, in accordance with the most perfect form of the patriarchal régime, lasted for life at Rome."

Let us attempt to reduce this picture to terms of its archaic prototype. That was an original political, economic, domestic group almost absolutely independent of all others. It was ruled according to age-old custom administered by its chief, whose power was supreme only because there was practically *no external power*. Its internal relations were among persons, for persons represented almost the whole household. It was a polity. While we perceive that the institution of property developed out of this unit and its mastery—out of propinquity and power—it is to overlook the political nature of the internal relations to apply thereto the term property. Before the existence of law—as we conceive it; before the opportunity, and perhaps the power, of alienation existed; while the relations remained almost wholly those between persons with regard to themselves; we have the precursor of property, not property itself. The position of head was that of priest, judge and chief, not that of owner.

We may conceive this house community as an independent and separate polity, at first only connected with others, on the one hand, through the "kinship" of related and similar communities maintaining a shadow of this intra-familial relation and, on the other, through the common army organization.[59] Thus the predecessor of the Roman household is a world closed to all interference from without; the head

[59] This explains the sense of the old term *caput*—the head-ship—which came later to stand for the status of the head as a link between these integers and their federation in the state.

alone dominates it, without control of anyone,[60] simply because there is no super-familial polity.[61] When, later, the state and its administration of justice does begin to appear it concerns itself for a long time solely with matters outside the sphere of the house community, because the house community was already an ancient and well-established institution at that time. Its affairs and administration continued to be its own concern.[62] Eventually the later super-familial power came to deal with individuals instead of with house communities as its integral units, and then the independence of the house community came to an end.[63]

There is much reason to assume that the power of the head was less despotic than it has been made to appear. In the first place early written law consisted largely at first of modifications of ancient custom; which modifications, because of the nature of the early super-familial organization, were often by way of assertion or confirmation of the powers new and old of the heads of the house communities. Thus we may suppose that early law, as well as early literature, theorized and idealized the position of the *paterfamilias*. We have no knowledge of what limitations there may have been upon the power of the *paterfamilias* by reason of the internal rules or customs of such groups. Autonomy consisted largely in non-interference from outside. And the exclusive representation of the *familia* by the *pater* in all these external dealings may have been fostered if not inaugurated by the later exclusive oligarchy of the *patres*. Moreover, it is difficult

[60] Ihering, *Entw.-gesch.*, p. 92.

[61] There was, of course, "aussi la *gens*, le village, le clan, groupements de familles," as Bonfante, op. cit., I, p. 30, puts it. But "le maître de maison . . . et le maître du village ont des dénominations communes," which, as we shall suggest later, is one of the grounds for supposing that the outline of the house community was very irregular, not that it was the base of a hierarchical organization.

[62] Ihering, *Geist*, II, pp. 196-199, describes the change. When the external law began to develop, at first "Eine Klage zwischen den Hausgenossen, sei es des Herrn gegen die Seinen, sei es der letztern gegen ihn oder der letztern untereinander ist ein juristisches Unding. Est ist Sache des Hausherrn, alle diese Streitigkeiten zu schlichten, er ist der Richter des römischen Hauses (*domesticus magistratus*)" – because he was such before the existence of other judges. After the state arose the authority of the *Hausherr* "ist zugleich ein Amt, das ihm vom Staat anvertraut." Eventually the internal isolation is invaded and "Unser heutiges und schon das spätere römische Recht hat jene unbeschränkte hausherrliche Gewalt aufgegeben oder, was dasselbe sagen will, das Recht ist in das Innere der Familie eingedrungen."

[63] "L'Etat, dans sa forme la plus parfaite, comme celle à laquelle il atteint dans la société civilisée, sur la base de la cité ou de la nation, tend à s'affirmer non comme le plus vaste dans la série des groupes politiques, mais comme *l'unique*; il vise par conséquent à désagréger, à absorber les groupes subordonnés, à en altérer la physionomie et la nature, en transformant les organismes politiques, autrefois souverains, en organes qui lui appartiennent, en institutions destinées à d'autres finalités ethico-sociales, il tend enfin à concévoir, comme terme de sa souveraineté, de son action, non les groupes immédiatement subordonnés, mais l'individu." Bonfante, op. cit., I, p. 86.

to connect a completely successful arbitrary power with the Indo-European sources. One of the sins first dealt with by the *Pontifices* was *parricidium.* It is disputed whether this meant originally killing or only striking, and whether it referred to all relatives or only to the father.[64] But in any case it shows the early necessity of upholding the discipline of the *magistratus domesticus* in serious affairs, which seem therefore, at times, to have got beyond his control. "Filial affection is not one of the characteristics of the Aryans."[65] "When father and mother became old and weak, useless for work or war, when power and property passed to the son, it was in accordance with the hard and cruel mode of thought common to primitive man, that these old people should be viewed as somewhat superfluous portions of the general household." "The custom of putting a violent end to the aged and infirm survived from the primeval period into historic times not infrequently amongst the Indo-European peoples. . ."[66] This too suggests a source of struggle and a reason for moderation and the assertion of power beyond that attained. Moreover, the fact, as Bonfante points out[67] that, in historic times, the son could become senator or consul shows clearly that the relation was one of "subordination but not of servile subjection."

There is little question, however, that the authority of the chief was great.[68] Certainly it was greatly modified by custom, doubtless considerably restrained by resistance, and, in all events, of the character of that of a ruler over his subjects, rather than that of an owner over his possessions. The great variance in the outcome of the operation of these two influences, propinquity and power – grouping and government – among the different Indo-European peoples shows their somewhat complementary nature. Moreover, it shows that the element of power in Rome is not the sole source of the institution of property, because where it was deficient elsewhere property developed as well, though along somewhat different lines.[69]

[64] See Clark, *Regal*, p. 590. He construes this as a demonstration that the *patres* needed to combine to back up their own authority.

[65] Ihering, *Aryan*, p. 34.

[66] Schrader, op. cit., p. 379.

[67] Op. cit., I, p. 182.

[68] Schröder, op. cit., p. 71, speaks of the "extraordinary severity with which the authority of the 'Haus-herr' (* poti) must have been established in the Indo-Germanic period."

[69] Ihering would seem to hold that power was the indispensable element. In *Der Zweck im Recht*, I, p. 204, he says, "Der Hausherr, welcher die Familie gründet, muss das Regiment im Hause haben, wenn das Haus bestehen soll, und die Natur selber hat im diese seine Stellung in ihren wesentlichen Grundzügen vorgezeichnet. . ." This is Ihering's thesis. There is another side to it. Laveleye, *Primitive Property*, Trans., p. 183, describing the Southern Slav house community, says, "The chief represents the community in its transactions with any third

The oldest Latin term for the chief of the house community is *herus* (or *erus*) which may be translated as "lord and master." This term was still in use so late as the *lex Aquilia.*[70] Its etymology and therefore its early connotation is entirely uncertain. The latest term was *dominus*, which we shall consider later. But the principal title, especially with reference to the relations to the persons of the house community and to the state, was, at least later and in the law, *paterfamilias.*[71] Nothing could be more absurd than to translate this compound into the modern cognate and derivative "father of the family." We have already shown that the *familia* was not a "family." In the same way the word *pater*, in this connection, indicates that this later term for father did not in early times have so much the connotation of paternity as it did that of manager, governor, or chief.[72]

At any rate the title *paterfamilias* was the title given to the position or office known as the *patrimonium.*[73] In early times it was the headship of the house community. It did not necessarily involve fatherhood. In a patriarchal family there may have been many fathers, but there was only one head. The composition of the group was such that the head was certainly not the father of a considerable portion. He was only such in name to any collateral or adopted

party, and in its relations with the state. He settles all disputes which arise within the family circle, and is the guardian of all infants." In most respects he is a replica of the *paterfamilias*, but he is *elected*. Perhaps for that reason he is "far less despotic than in the Russian family," or in the Roman.

[70] According to Girard, op. cit., p. 40, the *lex Aquilia* dates from somewhere between the beginning of the 3rd century B.C. and the middle of the 2nd. Ihering takes for granted the almost irresistible relation to the German *Herr*. *Geist*, II, p. 162, Note 216. Walde, *Latin*, does not dignify this by mention. He states that *erus* is more correct than *herus*, gives the cognate *anhuš* (master) in Avestan, suggests that its relation to Gaulish *Esu-* is uncertain, and calls attention to Brugmann's "very peculiar" suggestion that it is developed as * *es-es* (acc. * *em-em*) from pronoun stem * *e* (the "he"). *Hera* (mistress) makes this even more peculiar. Clark, *Regal*, p. 107, believes that the connection with *heres* (heir) is still "generally though not universally admitted."

[71] Vinogradoff, *Jurisprudence*, I, p. 232, calls attention to the fact that "in the Roman term, *paterfamilias*, the ancient genitive in *as* indicates that the word has been preserved in an archaic form, probably current about 1500 B.C."

[72] Clark, *Regal*, p. 52, believes that "In the old Roman word *paterfamilias*, the first part, so widely spread among the Aryan nations, would seem . . . to be accepted by the best authorities as meaning the *nourisher*, *protector* or *maintainer*, rather than the *owner* or *lord*." This, I presume, on the ground of an old etymology from the IE. **pā-* (to feed), confused with **pō(i)-* (to guard – cattle). But Hearn, *Aryan*, p. 85, says, "The word father was, in its original sense, a title of dignity. It denotes not a physical relation, but an office." Bonfante, op. cit., I, p. 79, Note 7, derives it from the root of *potestas* and says it means "lord" or "sovereign," and is synonymous with *princeps*. This is tempting. In Appendix I A this important etymology is fully discussed.

[73] Upon the analogy of *matrimonium* (the state of being *materfamilias*), we may presume, I believe, that at first *patrimonium* referred to the hereditary office as head of the house community, not, as later, to the house community itself – or a part of it – as a body of property.

members under his power or tutelage.[74] He was *patronus* to his clients, freedmen and *hospites*, and the master, not the father, of his slaves, land, draught animals and other elements of the *familia*. The relationship—and the organization of the house community—was largely an artificial, not a natural, one.

Doubtless the character and extent of the patriarchal pattern was irregular. It varied with the head. The position was a convention. The individual head and his strength was the fact. And according to the degree of this strength varied the degree of subordination and the extent of the group. When the younger males, their wives and children, remained with the new head after the death of the chief; when the position and importance of the head brought an aggregation of slaves and of voluntary subjects; when, later, large quantities of land were acquired; the group tended to grow great and complex. To this extent the power of the head—or rather his ability and his success in dealing with the outer world—constituted the adhesive which expanded the group, if not exclusively the cement which bound it together.

4. *The Classificatory Genitive*

In the foregoing we have endeavored to present a preliminary view of the content of the idea of the prehistoric Roman social unit and of its internal relations. In so doing we have given reasons for excluding from that idea the concept of property and of substituting that of a polity. To be sure, with the advent of external law, the legal institution of property developed from this source. But the relation cannot properly be called or thought of as a property relation at this stage. This idea of a polity seems to the writer the first of the prepossessions of Roman law. It naturally introduces the second. If the concept of property was not at that time developed and clarified, what was the content of the idea "belong to" which permeates the organization; to what field was it applied; and how did it give rise to that special sense of the phrase which came specifically to denote the idea of property?

Perhaps we can best illustrate the probable original view and the course of development of the idea of "belonging" by means of two pertinent illustrations, the usage of the genitive case in this connection and the Roman system of proper names. The term "genitive" is derived from the Greek γενική through the Latin *genetivus*. In Greek it "probably meant 'the case of genus or class.'" "In rendering γενική by *genetivus*, the Roman grammarians falsely interpreted

[74] ". . . a widow is sometimes described as having been, in contemplation of law, the daughter of her own son." Hearn, *Aryan*, p. 89.

the case as that of source or origin, misled, doubtless, by the frequent use of the Greek genitive in that function."[75] One genitive termination in the Indo-European mother tongue served also as ablative. It continued to do so in Greek. It did not in Latin. This may account for the "genitive of source or origin" in Greek, which purpose is only served by the ablative in early Latin. The two other Indo-European genitive suffixes convey the sense of "the sphere into which something was brought or to which it belonged."[76] According to Bennett, Brugmann and others hold that the original genitive was the *casus indefinitus* of an adjective.[77] Delbruck derives all the adnominal types from the *Genitiv des getheilten Ganzen*, which, for our purpose, comes to the same, though a narrower, point.[78] Thus the original significance seems to have been one of identification of reference or classification, not one of possession in any narrow or legal sense, as the common name "possessive case" might lead one to suppose. In fact when we come to analyse the early Latin usage, which Bennett cites, of even the individual type of genitive among many which he defines as possessive, we find that it consists of relations of the person (in the genitive) to his blood relatives, to his mental and moral qualities and to parts of his body, as well as figurative uses of the same, far more often than it does of relations to material objects as to which it could positively be regarded as implying legal possession.

In early Latin literature (prior to the first century B.C.) it would be more appropriate to give the title "possessive case" to the dative than to the genitive. Not only does the sympathetic dative of reference (usually as predicate and perhaps always with a verbal idea) cover the same field of the person's body, mind, personal relationships or possessions (including attributes), but its use, principally with *mihi* and *tibi*, is "decidedly more frequent than the possessive pronoun or genitive."[79] In addition we have specifically the dative of possession which, "in Early Latin," "is a very common idiom," especially with

[75] Bennett, *Syntax of Early Latin*, II, pp. 1-2.

[76] Bennett, op. cit., II, p. 9.

[77] Op. cit., II, p. 11.

[78] Delbruck, *Grundriss*, III, p. 333. He says "Der Genitiv (bei Verben) unterscheidet sich von dem Akkusativ dadurch, dass bei dem Gen. der Verbalbegriff nicht auf den vollen Umfang des Substantivbegriffs zu beziehen ist" (III, p. 308). He holds that the adnominal developed from this and that therefore the partitive is the "ältesten Kern" (III, p. 333).

[79] See Bennett, op. cit., II, p. 144. Landgraf, quoted by Bennett, p. 145, holds that, "Die Gesetzessprache und der amtliche Stil überhaupt bezeichnet mit dem Dativ das Recht- und Pflichtverhältniss, in welches eine Person zu einer anderen oder einer Sache gestellt wird."

Roughly the dative appears twice as often as the genitive or possessive pronoun. Three quarters of the instances of this dative are with pronouns, and two thirds of these are with *mihi* and *tibi*. Only the last was inherited from the parent tongue. But "the Sympathetic Dative was already [in early Latin] invading the field of the other pronouns and of the nouns."

tibi and *mihi*.[80] Further we may perhaps draw an inference from a contrast of the genitive of quality with the ablative of quality (instrumental) which would be characteristic of the genitive in general. In the genitive the association has the sense of permanency; in the ablative it is transitory. And while the ablative is beginning to be permanent, the genitive always remains so.[81] On the basis of such evidence as I have examined it would be better to describe the genitive in early Latin, either in general or in particular, not as the possessive, but rather as the associative case, in a permanent and static (non-verbal) sense.[82] It is the adjective, or type, case, though it may be used as a predicate as well as adnominally.

The parts, or members, of the early house community – whether persons or objects – were associated together by reason of the fact or presumption of propinquity – in its double sense. They 'belonged' to, or in, the group; they 'belonged' together; they 'belonged' *there*.[83] And, except for the head, they 'belonged' there exclusively. They had no other – no external – relations. By way of identification of the locus of this dual propinquity – place and kinship – it was natural to use the name of the *paterfamilias* as the class name for the group of persons and objects. For "every person who was in the Hand of the same Father was a member of the Household. . ."[84] The whole and all the parts were *of* Titus – they were identified and named by the genitive of his name. But this genitive was probably not applied in its later specialized possessive sense. If that had been the idea the dative might have been more suitable. Nor was it used in the sense of descent (source or origin). For that, in Latin, the ablative would have been natural. It was rather used as a means of denomination in an associative or classificatory sense. The elements were regarded not as possessions but as members. The nature of the relationship was practically uniform. Gradually, as the beginnings of the law developed the idea of property out of the power of the master, this genitive of class began to become in legal phraseology a true genitive of possession, pointing always to the one *in whose name* the community stood.[85] The 'belonging,' from being general, became specific – centred upon the power and the name. And, while this 'belonging' was being concentrated at one end, its

[80] Bennett, op. cit., II, p. 159.

[81] See Bennett, op. cit., II, p. 318.

[82] Perhaps the term "denominative" is even better, in connoting that it assigns or attributes the nominative (the subject) without the sense of action.

[83] In English one is a member *of* an organization. But he 'belongs' to it, or to-gether with the other members of it.

[84] Hearn, *Aryan*, p. 66.

[85] Pound, *An Introduction to the Philosophy of Law*, p. 228. "Later the head of the household ceases to be thought of as symbolizing the household and the property was regarded legally as his individual property."

originally indiscriminate application to all persons and objects over which the head had mastery was being diversified by the very resistance which its conversion to the connotations of property set up against it. Thus came the differentiation of the internal relations. Property—the possessory sense of 'belonging'—began to be applied in its pure form only to slaves, animals, inanimate objects and land, and less and less to those out of whose membership was appearing the embryo of the later purely domestic and political relationships.[86]

With the beginning of this process new terms for the latter relationships began to appear, as we shall see. The nature of the original homogeneity of the internal relations of the house community, as well as the gradual differentiation which took place, may be best depicted by tracing the beginnings of the development of each principal relation separately. While perhaps special names came to be attached to them only after each had matured, nevertheless these names themselves shed much light on the process, and on the original fact. But from the beginning to the end the classificatory genitive held the foremost position and retained its general application, though its content of sense changed or diversified. Frequently it stood by itself as sufficient; or to it was attached a technical term to describe by what rule the object, or, in the beginning, the person, was so classed. It is the form of the earliest claim. And, surprisingly it remains a technical term for *dominium* in the latest treatise. To say that a thing is *of* a man is to say enough. That was the general term. Others were the particular.[87]

This same classificatory genitive is at the root of the Roman sys-

[86] This change took centuries. In Rome the relation of the *pater* to the *filius familias* never ceased to be tinged with the possessive idea. In fact, until very recently, wives and children in Europe generally have been subject to the remnants of the property relationship. And slavery only disappeared from Europe in the nineteenth century.

It is worth noting that so eminent an authority as Fustel de Coulanges is sufficiently impressed with the Roman concept of the *familia* as the object of property—as in fact the patrimony itself—that he would confine the use of the term to that portion which at the parting of the ways continued to be the object of property, strictly speaking. He says, *L'Alleu et le domaine rural*, p. 42, "Le terme *familia*, dans l'ancienne langue latine, signifiait un objet possédé, un corps de biens, un ensemble de meubles ou d'immeubles, où l'ésclave avait naturellement sa place."

This interpretation, quite generally held by legal scholars, is a curious commentary upon and confirmation of the view we have presented. The naïve suppose the Roman *familia* to have been composed of persons—father, mother, children—in a family; these scholars suppose it to have been composed of non-human objects of property. The fact was that it was composed of both, held almost indiscriminately in a uniform relation.

[87] The genitive (possessive) pronoun was used in the same way and alternatively. Cornil, op. cit., p. 32, speaks of the "puissance complète, que longtemps il a désignée indistinctement par l'emploi du possessif."

tem of personal proper names. Without dealing with this subject elaborately we may say that the basis of this system lay in the designation, "of the house of," and that the sign was either an adjectival suffix or the closely allied genitive. Schulze concludes that the *praenomina* were the original individual and single names;[88] that they declined in importance and in number as, with the development of the *nomen*, they came to be used only in the household and among friends;[89] and that eventually they were largely replaced as a means of designation – at least among the *parvenus* – by the later developed *cognomen*.[90] He concludes that the *nomen* (*Gentilnamen*) had its genesis solely in the original *praenomen*[91] – presumably of the founders of the houses of the early period which became the *gentes* of the later – and developed as a pure adjective,[92] on the analogy of "Peter Peterson," because – presumably with the crystallization of the Roman *familia* and its *persona* – it became more important to relate a person to his gens than to distinguish him as an individual.[93] In the early days of the Republic one name – *nomen* or *cognomen* – was usually enough to designate an individual,[94] which speaks for the concentration of all external relations on one member of the house, or even the gens.[95] The wife took the *nomen* of her husband (in the feminine). So did the slave; but there it was followed by the master's *praenomen* in the genitive.[96] In addition, the slave frequently received, as his own individual name, a name compounded of the genitive of his master's *praenomen* with *puer* (as *-por*).[97] Finally the freedman followed a similar system, though in a different order – perhaps as Schulze suggests, for the sake of distinction from the slave.[98] I conceive this system of nomenclature to have been originally of one and the same order with the classificatory genitive, and that its obvious freedom from the import of property

[88] Schulze, *Zur Geschichte lateinischer Eigennamen*, p. 514, says, ". . . einmal das *praenomen* . . . ein Ding eigenen Rechtes und im Besitze der vollen Selbstständigkeit gewesen sein muss."

[89] Op. cit., pp. 515 and 487.

[90] Op. cit., p. 495.

[91] Op. cit., p. 517. "Aber nachdem uns einmal die Genesis der Familiennamen aus alten Individualnamen klar geworden ist. . ."

[92] Op. cit., p. 514. "Damals wird das Gentilicium noch ein reines Adjectivum gewesen sein. . ."

[93] Op. cit., p. 515.

[94] Op. cit., p. 487.

[95] Which as we shall suggest and as he evidently holds, may often have been, in earliest Rome, one and the same.

[96] Op. cit., p. 512. Originally perhaps just the *nomen*. "Von Haus aus genügte die Bezeichnung nach der Gens."

[97] Loc. cit., ". . . die aus dem Genitiv des Vornamens erwachsenen Sklavennamen. . ."

[98] Op. cit., p. 513.

lends weight to my suggestion that the original Roman usage of the genitive of the name of the head of the house, in general, denoted identification, pure and simple, and not possession.

Obviously the hypothetical process we have described must have taken place in the *Urzeit* or, at least, have been completed in the early course of the development of super-familial law. The evidence adduced as to the character of the genitive in early Roman literature, since the remains date almost wholly from a later time, bears on the question only indirectly. And the wholly speculative analysis of the previous development of the genitive is even less positive. Nevertheless I think the point of view which is obtained by these indirect means gives us an insight into the true nature of the precursor of the property relation, and aids us in explaining a problem which has long divided students of Roman law. To Girard it appears that "the notion of familial co-proprietorship, which has left profound traces in the language and in the institutions of Rome . . . has never *au fond* completely disappeared from Roman law," though it was "restrained and masked by the power of the head of the family to the point of being confounded with individual proprietorship."[99] On the contrary Clark says, "The position of a quasi-trustee or even of a mere joint-owner is sometimes attributed by modern writers to the original *paterfamilias* in regard to what is termed the 'property of the family.' I do not find sufficient evidence to support this view, in times of which we have any record, and consider it still less probable for earlier."[100] The problem is resolved and the later evidence referred to is explained if we entirely eliminate the idea of property at this early stage and substitute that of membership in and rule over a polity. There remained the tradition and the partial survival of the 'belonging' by each part to the whole—the polity. And there was developing out of the monocracy a 'belonging' by the whole to the single head, which was destroying the old idea, and causing internal resistance to the change, or sundering the unit. But the change lay not in the manner of the ruling. It lay in the conversion of political and domestic governance into ownership. That was not merely a change of name or of viewpoint. What it involved we shall see more clearly as we proceed.[101]

While, however, this analysis presents that part of the whole prepossession—described as the "classificatory genitive"—which bears particularly upon the nature of the pre-property relation, it is in

[99] Girard, op. cit., p. 282.

[100] Clark, *Regal*, p. 62.

[101] "C'est seulement après une longue évolution que la répresentation de la famille par le chef de maison arrive à être conçue comme une véritable droit qui lui est propre et qu'elle s'émancipe de toutes les limites et de tous les liens des phases précédentes de la collectivité." Bonfante, op. cit., I, p. 196.

another aspect that it will recur in our future considerations. For, as we have noted, this genitive, in some of its applications, came in time to be the very "rune" or hall-mark of property. But when, in this use, it lost its original significance and became converted in this respect, it nevertheless retained other connotations from its origin which we shall see as a cause of that peculiar blind-spot of Roman law which has been inherited by at least the theories of later times. We refer to the curious presumption of physical placement, of a walled-round preserve and of the single possible proprietary classification of the object, which lay at the root of the Roman idea of property and, as a subtle, tacit and perhaps unconscious presumption, prevented, or rendered unnecessary, the definition or analysis of its central idea—*dominium.*[102]

B. *The Internal Relations of the House Community*

Let us bear in mind this somewhat hypothetical early Roman house community, with its single head and representative, and the resulting prepossessions, as we proceed to trace the development of the two systems of relations which differentiated from its original homogeneity. It is probable from the internal evidence that, at many periods in the course of its development, this unit tended to be highly integrated and relatively isolated; even definitely circumscribed and separate. Such conditions left their mark in custom. They had taught the house community to be *selbstständig.* Thus it is a useful means of analysis sharply to divide its internal from its external relations. We will proceed to examine these two types of relation with the understanding that they were, in the pre-legal period we are considering, at one and the same time, domestic, political, economic and even religious, and that they were primarily relations concerning groups, not individuals. Under the first heading we will consider, in a more detailed analysis, the gradual differentiation of the internal relations of the various constituents of this independent early Roman house community, without attempting to assign the changes to any certain period.

1. "*Manus*"

As we have already noted, the earliest term for the head of the house community was probably *herus.* It is agreed that the corresponding early term for his general relation to all his subject persons and objects was *manus*, and that the special relations—and the terms for them—which we shall presently describe, were originally differ-

[102] See Bonfante, op. cit., I, pp. 206-213.

entiated from this primitive *manus*, which in the end remained in its pure form only to cover the relations to the wife.[103] Ihering[104] says, ". . . in this word, unless appearances deceive us, survives the original expression to signify the whole of the power of the head of the house over his *familia*, persons and things." All the later forms "are only the developments of a single primitive idea." "*Manus* and *familia* are correlative. *Familia* designates the domain of the power . . . *manus* the symbol and instrument of the power, the power itself. . ." It is evident that this term is of great significance for our purpose. Upon the theory that in the content of *manus* – its cognates and its derivatives – we may uncover much of importance with regard to that inchoate social institution out of which the later specialized institution of property developed, we shall proceed to a careful examination.[105]

It was customary in Roman times, and has been since, to assume that the word *manus* was merely the word *hand*. If we accept this view, it is natural to relate the term closely to all other compounds in use in Roman law in which the stem *man-* appears. The "hand" is thus found to be pervasive. And, if we do not – if we attach to

[103] See Maine, *Ancient Law*, p. 307; Muirhead, *Historical Introduction to the Private Law of Rome*, p. 37; Hunter, *Roman Law*, p. 223; Girard, op. cit., p. 14, who only goes so far as to say, "À l'origine, les distinctions (*manus, potestas, dominium*) durent être plus effacées, n'exister qu'en fait tant que vivait le *pater-familias* dont, selon la forme la plus achevée du régime patriarcal, le pouvoir est à Rome viager." The distinction arose at the death of the head. Terry, *Some Leading Principles of Anglo-American Law*, p. 356, says, "The rights which the head of the family had in or over the whole of it must have been nearly if not exactly the same." Ihering, *Entw.-gesch.*, p. 90, says, "*Familia* bezeichnet also in der ältesten Zeit die dem Hausherrn in völlig gleicher Weise, d.h. in Form der *manus* unterworfene Welt, sein Herrschaftsgebiet." Later it was divided into *manus, potestas, dominica potestas* and *dominium*. "Aber in ältester Zeit wurde die Gewalt über sie unter einen und denselben rechtlichen Gesichtspunkt, den der *manus*, gebrachte" (p. 91). "Im älteren Recht ist *manus* der technische Ausdruck für die Macht des Hausherrn schlechthin, er erstreckt sich auf sämtliche Bestandteile der Familie" (p. 95). "Die rechtliche Stellung des *paterfamilias* zu allen Bestandteilen der *familia* war ganz dieselbe, er hatte die gleiche Gewalt wie über die Sklaven und Sachen, so auch über Weib und Kind, wie im Innern der *familia*, so auch noch aussen hin" (p. 91). He holds that all legal qualifications of power were later introductions into the "ursprüngliche Anlage" (p. 95). For early development of distinctions see *Geist*, II, p. 164, where he refers to the three branches, "das Eigenthum, die väterliche und die eheherrliche Gewalt."

[104] *Geist*, II, pp. 162-3.

[105] Ihering takes this view. Speaking of *manus* he says, "Diese ungeheure Gewalt des Hausherrn ist übrigens nichts spezifisch Römisches [though the Romans supposed that it was]; das Römische steckt nur darin, das sie sich in Rom länger als anderwärts in ihrer ursprünglichen Gestalt und Kraft behauptet hat. Sie ist vielmehr nur ein Ausfluss uranfänglicher patriarchalischer Anschauungsweise, wie sie sich auch in anderen Rechten wiederholt, insbesondere auch in altgermanischen und zwar hier in einer mit der altrömischen Hausherrschaft so unverkennbar identischen Gestalt, dass man darin einen Rest der ursprünglichen Rechtsgemeinschaft der indogermanischen Völker erblicken muss." *Geist*, II, p. 163.

the term a different meaning, of which "hand" is perhaps merely the symbol and a specialized and derivative sense or, perhaps, a phonetically identical and therefore confused though unrelated word – then it is equally logical to relate all the other terms to *manus*. These other terms are *manceps*, whence *mancipium*, *mancipatio*, *mancipare* (or *mancupare*) and *e-man-cipare* (to liberate "children" from power); the important classifications *res mancipi* and *res nec mancipi*; *manumissio*; *mando* and *mandatum*: and finally the more questionable *manus iniectio*, *manus conserere* and *asserere*, and *manubiae*.[106] As to the simple term *manus*, it seems to me quite impossible to give that the immediate sense of "hand." The phrase for the entry of the wife into *manus* is "*convenire in manum*" (literally "to come together into *manus*"). When that phrase was originated it is obvious that *manus* did not mean merely "hand." "To come together into the hand"

[106] The group based on *mancipium* will be discussed in the next section. As to *manumissio* (the freeing of a slave) Ihering suggests that, "Dieser letzte Akt liefert uns zugleich einen Beleg für die obige Behauptung, dass die Hand nicht bloss ein Mittel zur Begründung der rechtlichen Herrschaft, sondern auch ein Symbol für sie hergegeben hat; in welchen Masse dies auch rücksichtlich des Namens (*manus*) der Fall war, ist bereits an anderer Stelle [II, 163] bemerkt worden." *Geist*, II, p. 577. It seems to me quite mistaken to assume that *manumissio* meant merely "letting go from (or with) the hand" (unhanding). Moreover the staff, *vindicta*, wielded by the *adsertor libertatis*, entered into this ceremony, quite as much as did the hand of the master. See Buckland, *A Text-Book of Roman Law from Augustus to Justinian*, p. 73. The obvious sense is "sending from *manus*." The earliest mandate of which we have record is that of a mancipation of the *familia* to a *familiae emptor*. Walde, *Latin*, derives *mando* from *manus* and root * *dō-* (*dare*). But he suggests that the fact that *mando* is of the 1st Conj. makes *mani* or *manum* more plausible. While he translates this "In die Hand geben," it is more appropriate to attach the sense "give *manus*." Pliny (Men. 783) gives *mandare* = *manum dare*. Buck, *A Grammar of Oscan and Umbrian*, s.v., translates Oscan *manafum* as *mandavi* and *aamanaffed* as *mandavit* or *locavit*. Apparently the Samnites had the same custom, inherited from a time before the separation of the two peoples; but here the sense of "give" is absent, and another verb stem is attached, in the form * *fefed*. This may arise like *facio* (Oscan *fakiiad* = *faciat*) from * *dhē-* (like *abdo*, *credo*, etc.) meaning, as in τίθημι, "put." It suggests also the same origin for *man-do*. This, in fact, is Muller's, *Altitalisches Wörterbuch*, construction. See Appendix I B. The case of *manus iniectio* will be discussed later. *Manus conserere* and *asserere* were symbolized by and meant "to join hands," or, perhaps, "to claim *manus* jointly, or singly." Nevertheless Ihering suggests that even these may be part of "des ältesten Manussystems." *Geist*, II, p. 163. And the closeness of the root * *ser-* (in *conserere* and *asserere*) to the "geschlechtliche Verbindung" (cited by Walde) supports this possibility. *Manubiae* ("the price of booty" and thence by transfer, the "booty" itself) is, according to Walde, a compound of *manus* and *habere*. It refers to the early practice of regarding *praeda* as collective – to be distinguished from *spolia*, individual – booty, and of selling it; the proceeds (earlier) being divided, or (later) going to the commander. Ihering associates this term with *manus* and conceives this system as the original source of property; *Geist*, I, p. 114, Note 21A. Also see his *Aryan* on *praeda* and *spolia*. It appears evident to me that the stem as used herein means *manus* and not "hand," and I would regard it as the only Roman instance where the term had, or retained, the sense of price, as happened so often in the case of its Germanic cognate. See Appendix I B.

is absurd. As we shall suggest, the term usually indicated a mutual relation and the whole concept of *manus*, even in later law, is that of something which is entered into, or something which can be taken or given (i.e. transferred).

The hand was the symbol of much among Indo-European peoples. It indicated friendship as well as power, protection and exchange. But, as we shall see, the spear, or the staff, seems almost symbolically synonymous with it. Perhaps as we proceed this seemingly diverse symbolism will coalesce into a consistent single idea. Ihering[107] has described the importance of the symbolism of the hand among the Romans. In Roman law he believes that the grasping of the "thing" has "as well the meaning of a seriously intended act to the end of physically controlling the person or object as that of a symbolic act to the end of asserting the claimed legal mastery."[108] But I think the view of Girard is more consistent with early psychology. He suggests[109] that all this symbolism, and the verbal formalism accompanying it, had in it the element of conjuration. Men had not arrived "at the idea that the human will could by itself alone dispose of a right of property, create an obligation, or produce an effect at law." For that reason they sought "instruments . . . recognized as apt for that purpose." And Pound[110] suggests that, "in primitive thinking forms have an intrinsic efficacy," the idea of which belongs "to the same order of thought as faith in forms of incantation." For these interpretations the spear, etc., might serve as a symbolic synonym of the hand.

At any rate the word itself and a part of the symbolism of the institution may indicate that the whole sense of the term was "hand," with the connotation of power, protection and control. As opposed to this the usage of the word in this connection, and the stem which appears in the compounds, frequently support the notion that the idea conveyed was quite distinct. In support of the first view we have the common impression that early Latin expressed its abstract ideas in concrete terms. Nevertheless nothing is more certain than that many of the concrete terms of later times, and especially those like *manus* which were feminine, were at first abstract and became "concreted." This question is discussed more fully in Appendix I B.

To approach the subject of prehistoric *manus* we must first relate it to an intimately connected *process*, which, with the development of law out of custom, came to be the central legal process and endured

[107] Geist, II, pp. 568 ff. And he says, II, p. 424, "Das Handgreifliche, Aüsserliche, Sinnliche, in die Augen Fallende ist der Grundzug aller Begriffe des ältern Rechts: überall das Überwiegen der Erscheinungsform über den Gedanken."

[108] *Geist*, II, p. 570.

[109] Op. cit., p. 29.

[110] *Philosophy*, p. 247.

throughout Roman law as the type of *actio in rem.* This process is the *vindicatio.* While the process, and its name, has reached forward almost into our own time, long after *manus* had given place to *dominium,* there is no reason to suppose it did not also reach back into the *Urzeit,* paralleling the early history of the institution which it supported. In the formalities of the eventual legal process it would appear that the *vindex* was engaged in acting out, in the form of a stilted ceremonial, the originally quite spontaneous behaviour of the house head who beat off with a spear or staff any one who laid hands on a person or object that belonged to his house community.[111] Perhaps the act might originally be performed by any kinsman, or neighbour. At any rate it is evidently the most primitive form of self-help as to another – force justified by right. In early law, and evidently previously in custom, *vindicatio* "supposes that a fragment of the family is come into strange hands"; it represents "the contest over *manus,* in the sense of ancient law; it has the 'de jure' existence of *manus* as its presumption and its 'de facto' recovery as goal."[112] At this stage, according to Ihering, if the *paterfamilias* has *manus* he has *vindicatio;* if not, not.[113] He holds this as the basis of the distinction, which we will discuss later, between *familia* and *pecunia* and the corresponding *res mancipi* and *res nec mancipi.*[114] If this is correct then, originally – before the advent of property in land and before agriculture produced work cattle, when the *res mancipi* could have consisted only of persons – *manus* must have been exclusively a relationship as to persons. And *vindicatio* must have confined itself to the assertion of the right over, and the protection of, persons.

If the *vindex* in the *Urzeit* concerned himself exclusively with persons we are furnished with a further connection between *vindicatio* and *manus* in another legal process which was also taken over by the law from the previous form of self-help. In the early legal process called *manus iniectio,* where the debtor or offender was, or was to be put, under arrest by the plaintiff, a third party, the *vindex,* could intervene. But he did so not in order legally to defend the captive. Instead this vindication immediately and automatically freed the captive. The similarity of the terminology and of the behaviour

111 ". . . the vindex takes the spear (the *vindicta*) in his hand." Ihering, *Entw.-gesch.,* p. 100. But, *Aryan,* pp. 327 and 331, he disagrees with Gaius, who construes the staff as representing the spear and thus the sign of lawful possession, and holds that the staff and spear had different meanings.

112 Ihering, *Entw.-gesch.,* p. 96-97. "For both parts of the family, persons and objects, there was originally the same law. It can be viewed in three aspects: 1. The legal situation of the head of the family within – *manus;* 2. The legal situation without – *vindicatio, actio noxalis, actio de pauperie;* 3. Acquisition of *manus – mancipatio*" (p. 91).

113 Ihering, *Entw.-gesch.,* p. 100.

114 *Entw.-gesch.,* p. 49.

indicates that *manus iniectio* was not originally arrest, in the sense in which it is later used in general—translated as "to throw hands" on a person. Rather, I think, it meant "to throw into *manus*," and is to be identified primarily with the *domum ductio*. And this is supported by the earliest available records of the phrase.[115] Such an interpretation fits the general thesis that all pre-legal and early legal processes against a debtor or tortfeasor had as their object the acquisition of his person. The injured party took the offender, if he could, and submitted him to his own domestic judgment and authority. Or he acquired him by noxal surrender. And it also explains the entry of the *vindex* who, it would seem, interfered because *manus* was his.[116] The use of the staff, the *manum repellens*, indicates the same beating off of someone who had laid hands on a person who belonged to the house community of the *vindex* which we have already noted in the *vindicatio*. The dispute, therefore, seems to have been one over *manus*. *Manus iniectio* asserted a new *manus*. The *vindex* asserted the superior force of the old.[117]

The clearest light on the original nature of *manus* and the proof that it was "an emanation from the patriarchal beginnings" is its "incontestible identity" with the old Germanic *mund*.[118] Here we have an admittedly unsolved etymological puzzle which is fully discussed in Appendix I B. *Mund* stands for this institution as well as for "hand" (early) in the Germanic languages, just as *manus* stands for both in Latin. Yet, in the German, good authorities dispute the identity of the two words, which they have never done, so far as I know, as to the Latin. We shall proceed on the theory, which is supported by considerable evidence, that in both groups of languages, Italic and Germanic, either there were originally two words, one for the institution and another for "hand," which, on account of their similarity and the symbolism, were eventually confused and became one; or, that the sense of "hand" is entirely a derivative sense acquired through its use in the symbolism of the institution.

For a description of the Germanic institution, *mund*, we can do no better than to quote from Schröder's careful, selected *résumé* of the authoritative opinion on the subject.[119] "In contrast to the Aryan

[115] In the 1st of the XII Tables the phrase appears "*manum endo iacito*" (let him throw into *manus*), and in the inscription of Luceria it is "*manum iniectio estod*" (let there be a throwing into *manus*). Again in the *lex Coloniae Genitivae Juliae* it appears as [*Cui quis ita ma*]*num iniicere iussus erit*." It is true that in the 3d Table the reading is "*Post deinde manus iniectio esto*."

[116] See Note 162, page 70, showing how *manus* superseded all other rights and claims.

[117] For a discussion of the meaning and etymology of the word *vindex* and its possible relation to *manus*, see Appendix I C.

[118] Ihering, *Geist*, II, p. 164.

[119] Schröder, op. cit., p. 63.

period the Germans differentiated between the property law mastery over slaves and things and the family law protective authority, the *munt* . . . over the free house community.[120] . . For the thing-owner they lacked a substantive designation." Doubtless this was for the excellent reason that they also lacked "things"—except cattle.[121] "They had expressions for the masters of slaves only, such as *frauja*, *hêriro*, *hêrro*. The *munt*-holder was called *muntwalt*, *muntporo*, *foramundo;* also *gêrhabe* from the spear representing the symbol of his authority; his *Schutzbefohlener* (person 'commended' to his protection) was called *mundling*." [122]

The symbolism, as well as the terminology, was cognate with the Roman. "As the symbol of mastery over land the gauntlet later served the West Germans. All legal business was accomplished *mit Hand und Mund* in that the necessary symbolic handling received the intended legal meaning through the accompanying expression of formal words. While with the Saxons all declarations took place '*mit Finger und Zunge*,' that is, accompanied by a particular movement of the fingers of the right hand, among the other West Germans the action *persisted* of the surrender or casting of a weapon, usually the spear. This form of spear-reaching remained among the Lombards longest; among others the spear was everywhere later replaced by a staff (*festuca*, *fustis*) or a strong stalk of reed or straw tied in knots (*festuca nodata*, *stipula*); so staff reaching and stalk throwing (*festucatio*, *stipulatio*, *werpitio*) appear along with the old *Gairethinx* (spear reaching).[123] Among the North Germans the *Staben* (*stafa*) oc-

[120] This confirmation of the original unity for which we have contended is worthy of note. It is presumably supported by the failure of such discrimination to appear in the very earliest Roman law.

[121] For which see p. 82.

[122] He relates (loc. cit.) the term *muntwalt* to the Medieval Latin *mundoaldus; muntporo* to the later *momper*. In Medieval Latin *munt*, or *mund* became *mundium* and the term for the head of the house was *mundualdd*. In his glossary, Thorpe, *Ancient Laws and Institutes of England*, gives *mund* and *mundium* (M.Lat.): *mund-byrd*, *mundiburdium*, (M.Lat.) and *munimen* as the abstract noun, and *mund-bora* as the agent (protector, patron). He says "these words are also commonly used to signify the price of violation of the *mund*, or *mund-bryce* [literally breach]." They were also commonly used to designate the purchase price of the bride, so much so that Walde, in his *Vergleichendes Wörterbuch der indogermanischen Sprachen*, translated the O.Ice. *mundr* as "the price of the bride and the tutelage over her acquired by the purchase." This, in Germany, is more properly analysed by Schröder, op. cit., p. 330. "The purchase price of the bride is called *Wittum* (OHG. *widem*), Lombard *meta* or *Muntgeld* (*mundium*), Frisian *Muntschatz* (*mundsket*)." Thus we see the ramification, as against the old assumed single nature (bride-price), of *mund*.

[123] One of the terms used for this process has led to further identification with the hand as symbol. As the writer thinks this view mistaken it seems worthy of comment. Schröder said, in the 4th ed. of his *Lehrbuch*, p. 60, Note 5, "Statt des Handschuhes (wanto) diente auch der noch nicht enträtselte andelang oder wandelang, den man mit frz. gantelet (Fechtbinde, Kleinerer Handschuh) in

curred partly by way of a casting, partly by one party extending the spear or staff toward the other who touched it with his spear or hand, a *manu firmatio* (*Handfeste*) as in the confirming act of later time. Very often in the north they also contented themselves with the simple handshake (*handsal*)." I have quoted Schröder *in extenso* not only to show the close resemblance of the northern symbolism to that which we have noted and will note in Rome, but also to show that there existed an equally general and valid symbolism of the spear — one which we have recognized in the case of the *vindex* — which goes to show that the institution of *manus-mund* was not identified with the one more than it was with the other.

Among the Germans the paternal *mund* over the son was maintained until he separated himself from the house community of his father, by founding one of his own or by seeking his fortune among strangers. Transfer from one family to another was accomplished by adoption, with the ceremonial of spear-reaching.[124] The daughter was separated from the paternal *mund* when the father gave her to a man in marriage.[125] "Marriage by capture" was recognized with strangers and tolerated with natives along with "marriage by purchase," but the latter was the only contractual marriage. The bridegroom paid the "price" and the father, or representative of the *Sippe*, with the spear, or other symbol of *Muntrecht*, turned over the bride. Schröder thinks this did not have the significance of the sale of a "thing," but of giving the bride in adoption.[126] In this we concur, for we shall hold that all ceremonial "sales" of "things" were only imitations of adoption and were "substitutions of the content" of this form, not themselves original.

Ehemündigkeit for men was reached at the end of the twentieth year. *Mundigkeit* (majority) is obviously derived from *mund*. We know that the term *selb-* or *self-mundig* was used, as in Rome, of the sons of free citizens, deceased, when they arrived at majority, and Würth translates *selb-mundualdˆ* as *sui iuris*. At the death of the father (husband) the widow and children entered the *Gesamtvormundschaft* of the *Sippe*.[127] Later this was transformed into a

Verbindung gebracht hat." The fact that this statement was partly and then wholly deleted from later editions indicates that Schröder has discarded the interpretation. DuCange, in his *Glossarium Mediae et Infimae Latinitatis*, gives the term as *andelangus*, *andelago*, *anlagus*, *vandilago*, used of "per festucam et per Andelangum tradere, donare." So he says, "Itaque Andelago est ex Hand et lagen, legen vel langen, quod hodie vocamus Handschlag."

If *wandelang* may be taken as the most complete form of the word it seems to be *wand* (Goth. *wandus*, a rod or staff) + *langen* (to reach) and thus a term for "staff-reaching" (*festucatio*), as above.

124 Schröder, op. cit., p. 72.

125 Op. cit., p. 74.

126 Op. cit., p. 75.

127 Op. cit., p. 77.

tutelage of the nearest relative on the male side, of which the eldest son was first in the series, or, as regards the widow, under certain circumstances a return to the *mund* of her own blood relatives.[128]

So far this system was very close to that of Roman law, though it embraced the whole of the house community, as *manus* may or may not have done. But it is the *Gesamt-* or *Obervormundschaft*, similar to the practices found in Rome under another name,[129] that we wish to emphasize, not only as an indication of the expansive nature of *mund* but also for its light on the character of the beginnings of law. "Along with that of the father the *Sippe* exercised a certain *Obervormundschaft* which was in part supplementary, but in part extended protection to the *Hauskind* against the encroachments of the father."[130] As this community authority became organized in the hands of leaders it extended its perquisites until eventually there appeared *die königliche Obervormundschaft* which we shall recognize in the early English law.[131] The breadth of the extension of *mund* is particularly emphasized by Green who interprets *mund* to mean the protection conferred within any group and the peace consequent upon it. The "'mundbryce' . . . was the violent breaking in on this peace and the sum paid as atonement. . ." "Every man of the folk lay in the folk's 'hand,' and, wrong-doer as he might be, it was only when the 'hand' was opened and its protection withdrawn, that the folk could suffer him to be maimed or slain."[132] Thus, in Germany, the arena of *mund* extended far beyond even the confines of the integral house community.

Because of its survival in Rome (in the pure form) solely as an element in marriage many have been led to identify *manus* entirely with that relation, or to assume that it had its origin therein. The foregoing description indicates enough of the extent of the cognate *mund* to suggest that marriage and *manus* were never coterminous. But let us examine the relation of *manus* to marriage in Rome. In historic Rome, women were always under power (or protection) of some kind—*manus, potestas,* or *tutela.*[133] The first—*manus*—was, in the earliest recorded law, applied only in connection with the relation of the wife to the husband. But, at the same time, marriage might take place by three methods, with all of which were associated

[128] Op. cit., p. 353.

[129] These cognates are the rights and duties of the *gentiles* with reference to inheritance and to land (early).

[130] Schröder, op. cit., p. 351.

[131] Is it possible that this also existed in Rome in the Regal period? See Justinian, *Digest,* 1. 2. 2. 1, ". . . *omniaque manu a regibus gubernabantur.*"

[132] Green, *The Conquest of England,* p. 21, Note 2, and p. 22.

[133] Hearn, *Aryan,* p. 96.

manus. These were *confarreatio*, *coemptio* and *usus*.[134] The association of *manus* with both formal marriages and with *usus* is, to my mind, conclusive evidence that all three were methods of bringing wives within the patrician house community and that, if none but *confarreatio* were used by the patrician *cives* for their own marriages, then the other two were nevertheless methods of bringing women indirectly within their *manus*—or under their *potestas*—either as wives of clients or freedmen.

All these three forms transferred *manus* just as did the "sale" of *mund* among the Germans.[135] Under the later marriage *sine manu* the woman, not passing into the *manus* of her husband, remained in the *potestas* of her father."[136] Since, by that time, legal property had commenced to develop and *manus* had begun to savour of the later "courtesy right," marriage without *manus* can then only be accurately defined as marriage without property in the wife or a right to the wife's property. Thus, eventually we find marriage as something separate from *manus*, though in the early times it was inseparable. And yet even then the use of three other terms to describe marriage, or the entry into it, indicates that *manus* was something

[134] The first was exclusively patrician and the second plebeian. See Ihering, *Entw.-gesch.*, p. 59. Schrader, op. cit., p. 381, says that "the original custom, of which the symbolical process of *coemptio* has preserved a reminiscence, yielded in the very earliest times among the Romans [patrician] to the purely religious *confarreatio*, which contained no notion of purchase." It is worth while to call attention to the fact that the form of *confarreatio* resembles certain of the marriage ceremonies found elsewhere among the Indo-Europeans, and is therefore, perhaps, to be construed as a special practice of endogamous marriage among the members of a noble caste who could dispense with bride purchase. See Vinogradoff, *Jurisprudence*, I, p. 251. The rule was at first endogamous within the limit of the gens but exogamous among the agnates to the sixth degree. After the Punic war this limit was reduced to the fourth degree. The form of *coemptio* also somewhat resembles that part of the ceremony of "bride sale" which among the Germanic peoples took place in the father's house. However, the function, or symbolism, of the "copper and the balances" in the latter, common to many early Roman transfers, is doubtless an acquired one—perhaps of Greek or Carthaginian origin. And it is curious that the transaction should be called *co-emptio* (literally "co-taking") instead of merely *emptio* (later "buying"), if it came from the same source as the Germanic "bride sale," or if the German transaction was really a sale. It is true that both may have consisted in an exchange of gifts (*co-emptio*)—of the *mund*, the price of the bride, for the *dos*, the dowry. Schrader, op. cit., p. 382, finds that the terms for dowry developed out of words which originally designated purchase money. We may conceive these two forms of marriage as fundamentally associated with the several parts of the at first triplicate Indo-European ceremonial; the transfer of *manus* in the father's house (*traditio*) with *coemptio*; the ceremonial carrying home (*deductio in domum*) and the installation in the husband's house with *confarreatio* proper. Perhaps, too, *usus* might be associated with Indo-European bride capture.

[135] Ihering, *Geist*, II, p. 164, Note 223, quotes Grimm, *Deutsche Rechtsalterthümer*, I, p. 447, to the effect that, marriage founded on the *mundium* of the husband had all the effects of the Roman *conventio in manum.*

[136] Clark. *Regal*, p. 83.

other than marriage or the marriage relation itself.[187] It appears in this connection as a familial relation which, in the realm of certain racial customs, was at first, but later need not be, established by all marriage.

If, then, *manus* came in Rome to relate to something savouring of property in (or the property of) the wife; and if, in the case of the German form of marriage and perhaps in the case of the *coemptio* among Romans, the acquisition of *manus-mund* bore the ear-marks which have come to be identified with a purchase; and if we are right in holding *manus-mund* to be the focal point in the beginnings of our Indo-European property system; does that all indicate that our early forbears held their women as *property* and that the whole ambit of *manus-mund* and the whole institution of property are but developments of the relation of the woman to the man? We do not know. Most of the legal scholars, with their fixed notion of *manus* seem to think so. So I read Girard. He sees in the freeing of marriage from *manus* the first break in this old patriarchal edifice.[188]

There is much evidence for the legal view. Let us quote from Schrader. He says, "Indo-European marriage was based on the purchase of the bride" (p. 381). It "equally warranted the master of the household originally in exercising the same right of sale and death over the wife herself as over the children" (p. 390),[189] though there was a distinction between the free wife and slaves or concubines (p. 392). Everything "indicates that the power acquired by the man over the wife . . . was in the primitive period no empty legal form, but a hard and cruel reality against which our modern sentiment rises in revolt" (p. 387). The wife was merely a servant and known as the "childbearing woman" (p. 386). There was no term for a married pair and the name for husband was "lord and master," the same term as for the head of the house community (p. 385). "The same conception of the husband's absolute right of property in the wife accounts for the Scandinavian's offering the marriage bed to his guest. . ." And he interprets this and the other customs, which we shall instance, in agreement with the view of the other authorities cited, to indicate that "the wife belongs to the man, body and soul, and what she produces is his property, as much as the calf of his cow, or the crop of his fields. The husband therefore regards the child of his wife and another man as his own, provided only it was begotten with his will" (p. 388). Adultery, he holds,

[187] Girard, op. cit., p. 162, distinguishes marriage from *manus* but in a note he gives a reason for assuming that originally they were one.

[188] Op. cit., p. 163.

[189] Hearn, *Aryan*, p. 98, cites the case of Periander, Tyrant of Corinth, who murdered his wife. Her father could not interfere because she was in her husband's power and therefore he had the right to kill her.

was an infringement of a right of property. Rules against adultery by the wife, with freedom to the husband, were common to the European branches of the Aryan stock. The supposition of so early a development of the principle of exclusiveness as to the use of the wife by another without the husband's consent, while the custom of permitting it as hospitality or in his interest persisted much later, is consistent with the idea of property, but not with the principle of paternity. But it does not prove the fact of property, for it remains the law today; and even as early as the sixth century it seems to have been as likely that adultery was classed with the personal injuries as with the offenses against property. In the case of the laws of Aethelbirht, about A.D. 600 (England),[140] out of the 90 provisions therein 17 have to do with such sexual injuries to a man's household, 40 with personal injuries and most of the rest with killing, theft and robbery. Therein, however, is the curious provision, "If a freeman lie with a freeman's wife, let him pay for it with his *wer-gild*, and provide another wife with his own money, and bring her to the other."[141] By that time, of course, the principle of paternity was recognized. But this rule has the look of property—a sort of *restitutio in integrum.*

On the other hand, as to the Germanic custom at least, Westermarck believes that[142] ". . . marriage by purchase did not imply the purchase of a piece of property [sic]: the ancient Teutons bought the *mund*, or protectorship over the woman and the other rights which marriage conferred on the husband." And Maitland[143] supports this view. "The 'bride-sale' of which Tacitus tells us was no sale of a chattel. It was different from the sale of a slave girl; it was a sale of the *mund*, the protectorship over the woman. An honourable position as her husband's consort and yoke-fellow was assured to her by solemn contract. . . He became her 'elder'—her *senior*, her *seigneur*, we may say,—and her lord." In early English law the price of the bride is "for the expense of upfostering her."[144] We must also note that marriage among the Roman patricians always constituted the appointment to an office. The wife was the official mate; later, at least, the *materfamilias.*[145] And marriage was by no means the only sex relation.[146] There were concubines in early Rome, and female slaves. So that the wife's position was something of a different nature. The wife of the Roman citizen, Ihering believes, "lived rather on an equality with, and as a companion to, man," and

140 Thorpe, op. cit., I, pp. 2-25.
141 Op. cit., I, p. 11.
142 Op. cit., II, p. 412.
143 Pollock and Maitland, op. cit., II, p. 364-365.
144 Vinogradoff, *Jurisprudence*, I, p. 253.
145 Ihering, *Entw.-gesch.*, p. 70.
146 Ihering, *Entw.-gesch.*, pp. 52-53.

as "mistress of his house." In certain respects the exclusively paternal right of the patriarchal state developed in Rome into a joint parental right.[147] The unique position which Roman wives of the upper class eventually attained suggests that, even in the early days, their status was more subject to legal than to real disabilities, and that it was a convention of the past which early Rome preserved in its patrician institution.[148] Or, it suggests that *manus* had in it from the beginning far less of the notion of property than has been supposed.

Even if *manus-mund* came not to be confined to the marriage relation and even if the marriage relation was not originally of the nature of property, did *manus-mund* have its origin in marriage? Or was it only an incident thereto and its principal significance along other lines? We have assumed, on the authority of the students of Roman law and of Indo-European languages, the existence among the Aryans of the patriarchal type of social organization. Such an assumption is directly contradicted by the apostles of the matriarchate.[149] But this issue does not concern us here, since even this school will agree that the early Aryan group was a large one and that, in any large group, marriage is not the binder.[150] Marriage, there, is but an incident which may exist within the group in numerous cases. Propinquity is the binder, a propinquity which comes later, at least, to be presumed to be due to consanguinity on the male side – to common descent. If *manus* originally covered the entire ground of the relation of the chief to the components of the Roman house community, just as *mund* seems to have done among the Germans, then it is more likely that we will discover its nature in this general binder than in the straiter relations of marriage. It is necessary therefore to inquire what was the nature of the original theory of propinquity. Was it consanguinity and thus related to marriage? Was it refined still further by the recognition of true paternity and thus confined to agnatic consanguinity? Or was it rather of the nature of mere recognition of membership in a group, a group maintained solely by the adherence of the males and so necessarily following what came to be termed the agnatic principle?[151] Among the early Germans there survived the rule which is described by

147 Ihering, *Aryan*, p. 40.

148 Bonfante, op. cit., I, p. 182, speaks of the position of Roman women as one so elevated that its contrast to that of the Greeks was a favourite theme with the ancients.

149 See, however, Briffault, op. cit., I, pp. 420-430.

150 See Briffault, ibid., I, pp. 199 ff.

151 J. J. Atkinson in his *Primal Law*, p. 289 says, "We must remember that, in so early a group, personal descent as such was in no way recognised. Mere local contiguity alone constituted the sense of relationship. . ." And Lubbock, *Origin of Civilization*, p. 160, says, "Relationship is, at first, regarded as a matter not of blood, but of tribal organization."

Schröder as follows:[152] "The paternal authority rested on the 'munt' of the married man, over the mother, which included children born by his wife to a third party in breach of marriage." And a child born outside marriage, or in marriage without *munt*, did not stand in the *munt* of the father, but under the *muntwalt* (whoever he might be) of the mother. This is not a question of paternity, nor of agnatic consanguinity. It is that the child belongs where the *mund* of the mother belongs. Among the Indians, Greeks and Teutons the custom prevailed, in case of a failure to secure the much desired male heir,[153] that the husband might "obtain progeny from his wife by means of a substitute, who was originally perhaps the husband's brother."[154] Even in Rome, as elsewhere, the child of the female slave, who was a *res mancipi*, followed the status of the mother. There is abundance of other evidence to the same effect.

Why such rules and evasions if paternity, paternal descent or paternal right, were the determining factors? Girard[155] supposes that paternity could not be recognized at all until "the relations between the sexes acquired a certain character of exclusiveness which they have not always had," and that the original paternal right appeared through "the assimilation of the right of the husband over the child of the wife to that of the master over the child of the slave."[156] Starcke[157] also takes the view that paternity was in early times a matter of ignorance or of no interest to the house head. "Whether they [the children] were of his begetting was a point to which he gave no weight, as everything which the woman belonging to him produced became his property." And Maine points out[158] that "paternity . . . is a matter of inference, as opposed to maternity, which is a matter of observation." In the view of these authorities, then, the steps to the establishment of paternity as the basis of group organization, of descent and of consanguinity, must have been, first, monogamy (on the female side) or, as they put it, "property in the wife," and, second, complete exclusiveness as to her possession. The first step may have taken place before the origin of *manus-mund*. But, according to the evidence cited, the second came only later and gradually. Therefore

[152] Op. cit., p. 350.

[153] Marriage was "a means to an end. That end was the birth of a son. It was the son alone who could continue the Household," Hearn, *Aryan*, p. 69. Schrader, op. cit., p. 388, also says that the main object of ancient wedlock was the obtaining of male progeny.

[154] Schrader, op. cit., p. 388.

[155] Op. cit., p. 148.

[156] Elsewhere he imputes this idea to the ancients themselves. ". . . l'idée ancienne selon laquelle le droit du père sur l'enfant vient de son droit sur la mère. . ." Op. cit., p. 161.

[157] C. N. Starcke, *Die primitive Familie in ihrer Entstehung und Entwicklung*, cited by and quoted from Schrader, op. cit., p. 370.

[158] *E. L. and C.*, p. 202.

the true agnatic principle (paternity) could not have been the binder of the original group and the foundation of *manus-mund*. Instead the order of precedence seems to have been reversed. If we substitute for his term "property" the content we are reading into it – namely the idea of 'belonging' to a ruled group (membership) – then Vinogradoff's summary of these principles is illuminating. He says[159] that the fatherhood principle "centers on *property* [membership], for the law of marital union depends less on the law of relationship, . . . than on the law of property [membership] and authority. . . In all cases the principle obtains that the children belong to the male [group] to whom the wife belongs." In relation to fatherhood procreation is subsidiary to property [membership] "in a way we have almost ceased to understand, save in the case of a stepchild." He assumes the Aryan "taking up of the child by the father [head] directly after birth" to have been "a special acknowledgement, a 'seisin,' of the child," establishing the legal relationship. So too Dargun.[160] But this is usually construed in its cruder aspect of a decision that the child should live – i.e. not be exposed.

In attempting to interpret these facts, selected from a great quantity of similar evidence, in order to come at the early significance of *manus-mund*, we are obliged either to accept the general legal viewpoint that our notion of property is an original and pre-legal category, the beginnings of which are, in this view I think, identified with primitive marriage, and that *manus-mund* is this early property – an interpretation seemingly inconsistent with the breadth and kind of the relations later included thereunder – or we must offer an acceptable alternative. In any event, Schrader's "linguistic paleontology" and the legalistic views of Girard and others constitute an interesting indication of the prehistoric (or early) content of one of the relationships in the group out of whose internal relations developed the institution of property, and help to eliminate any squeamishness we may have about accepting, as the origin of property, human relations. But, after all, do they define for us the content of *manus-mund?* The field of that appears to have been wider than marriage. It extended beyond the man and the woman; on one side to minors and perhaps slaves, to unmarried sisters and widowed mothers; and upon the other to the head's agnates, perhaps to the whole sib, or even tribe, in their relation to him as well as to his. Neither did it follow the lines of paternity, nor even those of agnatic consanguinity. Rather it was coterminous with the presumably patriarchal group. Anyone who was born into; or captured, or bought, and brought into; or adopted into the group, came under the

[159] *Jurisprudence*, I, pp. 197-8.
[160] *Mutterrecht und Raubehe*, p. 49.

mund, principally of the particular house head, but also of any wider circle united by propinquity.

When we face the question as to the cause of this propinquity; as to the influence which formed this group, as to what existed prior to our putative patriarchate out of which it developed—we will not venture even to hazard a conjecture. This is the battle field of anthropology and the outcome is, as yet, uncertain. We shall look no further but will content ourselves with an hypothesis traced back along these two lines to the point of juncture of the Indo-European languages and social traditions.[161] Prior to the separation of the Italic and the Germanic peoples the social organization appears to have consisted of units, large or small, containing several adult males, of which one, perhaps the eldest, was chief. These units, if they grew and prospered, tended to divide by fission—the separation of a part headed by one of the junior adult males. Thereafter the new and old retained a remnant of the intra-familial relationship in the form of an inter-familial relationship which gradually dissipated itself as the degree of propinquity decreased. In these groups all, male and female, were subject to the power of the chief, though in Rome the adult males retained a degree of independence and of power as the *populus*. In connection with this group there arose a gradually expanding social thesis or groundwork of customs which the term *manus-mund* seems to have described.

Manus-mund was not property. It extended beyond the relationships that gave rise to property. And when, later, certain otherwise competent means of transfer of property began to appear *manus-mund* at first superseded them. It was something greater. Thus the *vindex* in *manus iniectio* freed the delinquent against the claimant on account of debt or delict. His claim was stronger.[162] And *manus* could not be transferred by *traditio*. True, when we use the term property, we are referring to the legal institution, not to the mere control of persons or of objects. But the distinction is important. The source of most of the early forms of the legal institution is the

[161] Certain statements in the work of one of the most recent exponents of the matriarchal theory (Briffault, op. cit.) somewhat confirm the opposition we have endeavoured to establish between the house community and the family. He says, I, p. 192, "The group produced as the manifestation of the masculine instincts, is the very reverse of the family. It is the herd." And, I, p. 193, ". . . the herd is the masculine group; the family, the feminine, or maternal group. . ." "The masculine herd is patrilocal, the animal family matrilocal." While he asserts that "it may also be confidently concluded that the human group did not develop out of the animal herd," I, p. 195, he also concludes that the patriarchal grouping eventually developed. And I do not find his hypothesis as to the transition to that state at all convincing.

[162] "The particular character of the ancient *vindicatio* is not that it is an *in rem actio*. The point is the way it is." Nothing can stop it. "Whether the defendant is possessor by *bona fidei* or by *mala fidei*, whether he has paid for the thing . . . makes no difference. . ." Ihering, *Entw.-gesch.*, p. 99.

forms in prior use in dealing with persons with reference to this group. But if the 'belonging' together in a group under the power of a head – if even the possession of a woman as slave or wife – gave rise to the forms of property, that does not indicate so much that the early husband or chief regarded his wife or group in the light of our modern concept of property, as it does that he at first regarded certain of these objects which he began to acquire later, outside the field of persons, much as he had regarded his wife or his group.

Manus-mund was not "the hand." The spear was as often the symbol as was the hand. This point goes deeper than a dispute over words. The evidence shows that the part of the ceremonial, or symbolism, connected with the hand meant much more than a literal "taking by, or in, the hand" and something quite different than "taking by force."

Manus-mund was not marriage as a ceremony or "title." That, in Rome, was *confarreatio*, or *coemptio*, or *usus*. Nor was it marriage as a woman's status. That was *matrimonium* and gave the title of *materfamilias*. Nor was it the relation between the man and woman in marriage. That seems to have had no early name either in Latin or in other Indo-European languages. Among the Germans *mund* never seems to have confined itself to marriage. And among the Romans we presume it did not in early times. On the basis of the evidence I am inclined to think *manus-mund* was originally not more particularly associated with marriage than with any other entry into, and membership in, the group. Its particular significance therewith was similar to our modern adoption by the wife of the husband's name. It did not govern the position of the wife. Marriage, being only a special case of change of *manus*, and being in fact a separate institution, could, and apparently did, vary and change while the term remained constantly applicable.

Manus-mund was not exclusively familial. Thus the Germanic evidence suggests that it followed in some degree the extent of the *frith*, or *pax*; in fact that it was that which gave rise to this compact of peace. While we do not find the term in use in Rome to cover the wider relation of the gens, nevertheless the fact of the *Gesamtvormundschaft* and the *pax* consequent upon it, existed there as well.

Apparently it was at first exclusively concerned with personal relations. We have seen that Schröder finds it in earliest historical Germany dealing only with the *free persons* of the family. And in the case of Rome, if we delete such of the *res mancipi* as did not exist at the pre-agricultural stage – land and work cattle – we have left nothing but persons, though here slaves are included (see page 59).

Evidently it involved propinquity. It concerned itself with a neighbourhood or a group of neighbours (if moving). This grouping followed the male line because it was the males who held together and who controlled the groups, while the females were passed from one group to another. It was the males, too, who separated and established sub-groups, becoming semi-, and eventually perhaps wholly, independent, depending upon the degree of physical propinquity maintained. While the system of propinquity was not at first recognized as – nor was it of necessity – one of consanguinity, nevertheless by the mere rule of fission according to males it appeared to conform to the agnatic principle. As paternity became recognized and certified, this propinquity and this agnatic principle came to be converted into a system of true blood-, rather than merely local, relationship. And, then, so far as the female side was concerned, a new and secondary system, based on *affinitas* – a very similar idea – had to be created to contain it.

Manus-mund involved power and protection. For that was the political element which converted the group from a crowd into an organization. And it involved peace – the very basis of its integration and the original cause of its exclusiveness. One was in the *manus-mund* of the group, or one was *hostis*. Enemy and stranger were synonymous.[163]

Introduction into the group occurred by birth, by force or by the peaceful ceremony of initiation. All persons born therein were automatically in the *manus-mund*. Introduction by force took place in the case of the captive bride, or the stranger (*hostis*) who was enslaved, and in the case of the delinquent (debtor or tortfeasor) belonging in the *manus-mund* of some other group, if he were not vindicated (also perhaps by noxal surrender). It took place by initiation in the case of bride purchase, adoption, arrogation and hospitality (*hospites*) and later by self-surrender (*clientes* and *gehörige*) and the purchase of *filii*. In this initiation appears the origin of formal exchange.[164] This relation to early exchange, through bride purchase in Germany and, perhaps, through purchase of captives in Rome, may have given rise to the sense of "purchase price of the bride" and of *manubiae* which we have noted.

In coming at the true content of the thing that was we must rid our minds of the inclination to attach a specific meaning to the term *manus-mund*. Early terms are all-inclusive. But if we are to at-

[163] Briffault, op. cit., I, p. 157, says the "attitude of uncultured human beings towards any individual who is not a member of their own restricted social group is one of profound distrust and generally of active hostility."

[164] Church and state, in later Rome – the *pontifex* and ten witnesses representing gens, or curia – established the marriage by *confarreatio*. They were not mere functionaries. See Ihering, *Entw.-gesch.*, p. 65. Similar ceremonies accompanied *adoptio, arrogatio* and, in modified form, all other changes of *manus*, such as *nexum*, *mancipatio* and one form of *testamentum*.

tempt to focus the concept let us say that the term stood for *membership in the house community* – this early "state in little" – and all the different functional relations which that position implied. It seems to have been the central fact of '*belonging*' to the patriarchal group.

It represented the principle of exclusiveness – of exclusion.[165] *Manus-mund* was the antithesis of *hostis*. Peace and relative safety within was the centripetal force. It was secured by the "wall around," a wall difficult to climb and only to be scaled by elaborate ceremonies. Other walls in concentric circles embraced the multiple groups and widened the circle of the peace pact. Outside was *war*.[166]

It represented the relation existing therein – participation in a highly practical political structure, which we must still hesitate to call domestic, and in religious connections as of a private sect.

It represented the power of the head and the subjection of the others thereto. But this was not inherent. Its degree was variable. Power was imposed, not automatic. And protection was, practically, the obverse of the power; its success depending upon the success of the power and the resulting degree of organization and effectiveness. The headship was a management (*mesnage*) not, primarily, a perquisite.[167]

Finally it represented the "name" and all that stood for. In it was the early magic of the "word." Perhaps it involved the tradition of an original common chief – later called a common ancestor – the idea of *Mannus* (Germanic) or of *Manu* (Indian).[168] Perhaps it

165 We may, perhaps, connect this original practical exclusiveness with that of the (later) patrician and *Adel*. Ihering, *Entw.-gesch.*, holds that the Roman aristocracy was maintained by *connubium* on the same principle as the German *Ebenbürtigkeit* – the idea of founding or maintaining a house (p. 61). He says, p. 63, "– Absperrung nach aussen hin war die unerlässliche Bedingung des festen korporativen Zusammenhaltes im Innern." And concludes that the refusal of *connubium* to *plebs* was the natural result of the constitution of the ancient familial state. Rather, I should say, it was in part a sign of success, and of conservation and retentiveness of ancient and originally necessary customs. In part, presumably, it was the more practical pride of purity of blood.

166 Tarde, *Transformations*, p. 96, "L'intensité de sentiment qui serrait le faisceau des parents ou des voisins aux anciens âges s'alimentait surtout de leur isolement dans une milieu hostile."

167 The sense of perquisite, to which the power gave rise, should be regarded as a by-product. It was not functional. I note that Clark, *Regal*, p. 126, refers to "the *primitive* character of *tutela*, as established in the interest of the *tutor*." This does not seem to me at all apparent. In our view of the early state of society it is clear that this protection to the female and minor was a matter of life and death to them.

168 Pound, *Philosophy*, p. 25, speaks of a "convention, which, in a society framed on the model of an organized kindred, required that the citizens have a common heroic ancestor . . ." Bonfante, op. cit., I, p. 78, says, "Les members de la *gens* croient, il est vrai, qu'ils descendent d'un seul auteur commun dont ils font dériver leur nom, mais cet auteur commun est toujours légendaire et remonte à un temps

is derived from the word *man* which was the original Aryan "name" – the Adam. At any rate, when the bride, or the adopted individual, or arrogated group, were initiated into the community they, in effect, changed their names just as we, in such cases, adopt new surnames and with the same significance. That was partly a means of identification and partly a sign of a certain brotherly (or sisterly) union – a conjuration.

2. "*Mancipium*" – *A Method of Acquisition becomes a Relation*

The most direct offshoot from the original idea of *manus* appears to have been *mancipium* (from *manceps*). The term is interpreted by the authors of Justinian's *Institutes* to mean "taking by the strong arm" (or hand).[169] On the other hand Ihering translates the term as "acquisition of *manus*."[170] Muirhead says that the older interpretation "has been accepted in many quarters much too readily," and asserts that "the fundamental mistake lies in supposing that the notion embodied in the word is *manu capere* instead of *manum capere*."[171] According to Walde, the term *manceps* is the source form.[172] To this form it would appear more natural to assign the sense "acquirer of *manus*," than that of "acquirer by the hand."[173] Another hint to the same effect is furnished by the fact that Plautus used the term for a *surety*, thereby allying it to the original institution of *manus* along the lines we have suggested in connection with the *vindex*.[174] Moreover, it is difficult to reconcile with the idea of force, or capture, the ceremony *per aes et libram* which constituted the essential element of the transfer when it first appears in the record.

immémorial (*cuius memoria non exstat*) ; il est le héros éponyme, le chef antique de la *gens*. . ."

169 ". . . quod ab hostibus manu capiuntur," Justinian, *Institutes*, I, 3, 3. This literal translation of the classic period has been accepted by many. So Clark, *Regal*, p. 548, says, "*Mancipium* must have meant originally a physical taking *with* the hand. That it ever meant the acquisition *of manus*, in the metaphorical sense of control I do not believe." In support of which he cites Goudy's Note 23 in Muirhead's *Roman Law*, p. 60. This objection of Goudy's that, at that stage, the forerunner of *mancipatio* could not have been abstract seems to me quite trivial in view of the almost wholly abstract *vindex*. But others have been equally convinced that *in manu* should be translated as "in the hand of" ; witness this favourite phrase used in describing the familial power.

170 *Entw.-gesch.*, p. 111.

171 Op. cit., p. 56. "In every case, without exception, in which the process of *mancipium* was resorted to there was acquisition of *manus* in the old meaning of the word. . ." P. 58, Note 27. The etymology *manu-captos* (see Ernout and Meillet, *Dictionnaire étymologique de la langue latine*) may also be doubted.

172 He cites Varro's translation as "*qui manu capit*," and gives the ground form as **manu-capos*. But see Appendix I B.

173 See Appendix I B.

174 If the *vindex* was the "family-speaker" then perhaps the *manceps* as the "*manus*-taker" was synonymous, and *man* = *vin*. See Appendix I B.

The term, according to Ihering, appears for the first time in the XII Tables and continues until the third century of the Republic to cover the idea of the act of acquiring by formal purchase, with the copper and balances, a certain class of things – the *res mancipi*. Varro and Cicero knew no other sense.[175] But in the juristic writings of the Empire the term *mancipatio*, which we discuss below, has been substituted as describing, in general, this process of selling and buying *res mancipi* (construed as *mancipii*) and, in particular, the act of selling free persons in power into that specialized status for which *mancipium* had by that time come to be reserved. This status, in historic times, was that of domestics who had been sold by their *pater* into the household of another. Bonfante[176] includes in this status *filiifamilias* "surrendered in expiation of a delict committed by them" (*noxae dediti*). Girard believes[177] that, in ancient times, it was very close to slavery and in later times to be distinguished with difficulty from debtor slavery (*servitus*).[178] But the person *in mancipio*, as well as the debtor slave (*nexus*, perhaps originally the same), the condemned (*addictus*), and the surrendered (*deditus*) remained free and a citizen though, if he were a *paterfamilias*, some of his rights, such as the *potestas* as head of his *familia* were in abeyance (a degree of *caput deminutio*).[179] When emancipated the person was *ingenuus* not *libertinus*, and he remained subject to rights of patronage. Thus these relations were more personal than that of slavery. As Poste says, the condition "was relative; a man could only be *in mancipio* in relation to a given domestic lord: whereas the status of slavery was absolute; a man might be a slave without an owner. . ."[180] In fact one is tempted to see in this very lasting distinction between the status of slavery – the status of those who had perhaps in reality been "taken by the strong arm"; strangers of another blood captured in war, together with their offspring – the bondage of the debtor and of the domestic, and the patronage over *clientes* and *hospites*, the basis for that ubiquitous medieval discrimination which ranged along a scale from absolute chattel slavery, at one extreme, to the position of the "freeman" who had put himself, or had been born, under the protection of the lord as "his man," at the other.

In the beginning *mancipium* seems to have been the process, growing out of the introduction of peaceful ways and commercial prac-

[175] Muirhead, op. cit., p. 57, thinks that the word was used in three different senses, the power of the *manceps* ("synonymous with *manus*"), the thing over which the power extended, and the process of acquisition.

[176] Op. cit., I, p. 179.

[177] Op. cit., p. 143.

[178] The condition *servire* and *servum esse* were quite different. See Note 302, p. 115.

[179] Muirhead, op. cit., p. 144, disputes this. But the view seems generally held.

[180] Gaius, *Institutes*, p. 76.

tices, for effecting a transfer of membership from one house community into another. It established a new and artificial, though similar, relationship. And though, in the course of time, this process—as *mancipatio*—came to extend to such transfers when applied to any person or object that was construed to be part of the *familia*, the survival of *mancipium* to distinguish the position of *free members only*, when so mancipated, leads us to suspect that the process itself was at first applied principally to the transfer of "children," especially daughters, from one *familia* to another.

3. *"Potestas"—The Relation of the Head to his Persons*

If *manus* is the oldest term for, and described originally, the fact of membership in a house community—the element of propinquity—we must suppose that *potestas* constituted the first specialized name for the element of "power" which constituted the government of this early patriarchal system of human grouping. As *patria potestas* it defined the power of the head of the house over his own and his adopted children and, at certain periods, over his wife as well, since she was technically his daughter. And the term *potestas*, alone, seems to have stood, as well, for the power of the head over all other persons of the household, free or slave.[181]

It is tempting to assume from the possible etymological relation of *liber* (free) and *liberi* (the children) that even in prehistoric times the household was divided into the free and the servile "in power." [182] So far as their absolute status in the later aggregate of the community at large is concerned, this was no doubt true. But within the household the position of both relative to the head seems to have been much the same.[183] His power was despotic as well over the son as

[181] In later—I believe post-classic—times the term *potestas dominicale* was used to distinguish the power over slaves from that over the free members of the house community.

[182] See Note 39, page 40. Bonfante, op. cit., I, p. 180, suggests that "la dénomination de *liberi*, par opposition aux *servi*, ne devait probablement pas se restreindre [à cette époque ancienne], comme elle le fit dans la suite, aux seuls *filiifamilias*."

[183] Girard, op. cit., p. 151, says, "Mais, en tout cas, par rapport au père, le fils joue un rôle symétrique à celui de l'esclave. . ." And Ihering, *Geist*, says, "Für das ältere Recht lässt sich meines Wissens nur eine einzige wirklich nennenswerthe Differenz zwischen der herrschaftlichen und väterlichen Gewalt nachweisen. Hinsichtlich der Veraüsserung der Sklaven ist der Hausherr unbeschränkt, hinsichtlich der des Sohnes nicht; wenn er denselben drei Mal veraüssert hat, so soll derselbe einer Bestimmung der XII Tafeln zufolge für immer frei sein. . ." II, p. 184. Each sale ended at the close of a lustre (five years). And he also believes, II, p. 166, that "das Gewaltverhältniss über die Sklaven, die herrschaftliche Gewalt, hat den ursprünglichen Charakter und Gehalt der hausherrlichen Gewalt am reinsten bewahrt." Clark, *Regal*, p. 54, inclines to the view that both slaves and children were originally chattels. He says, "In the writings of the later legal authorities, the *patria potestas* presents itself to us as undergoing successive *limitations*, by custom or statute, which

over the slave. "At first, the father is despot or owner; he has all the essential rights of ownership, the right to use the son's services, the right to part with them [i.e. mancipation], the right to destroy [i.e. power of life and death]. . ."[184]

We see here the original oneness of the mastery—which can neither be called ownership nor merely authority—and the assimilation of the power over the free to that over the slave. Nevertheless, though the "condition of the slave . . . bears the character of absolute submission to his master,"[185] it seems, rather, that at this early stage the condition of the slave was assimilated to the condition of the free members, than that either were actually in the position of owned objects.[186] We note that the authorities liken the position of the free "in power" to that of slaves. But they do not liken that of either to cattle, the only important element of the group of those times which has continued to be the object of property. Shall we say that in the political constitution of Aryan society at this stage—an organization confined almost wholly to these small autonomous house communities—the evidence indicates a nearly uniform power of the head over the whole, with some more considerable distinction between human beings and cattle, than, among human beings, between slave and free?

On the other hand it is clear that the use of the term *pater* (father) in connection with the Roman house community, did not indicate either that this group was more nearly a "family" than we have admitted, or that the relation of the *pater* to it was more paternal than the authorities quoted have conceived. The original term for this type of "fatherhood" in Rome was *patrimonium*, which in historic times came to have exactly the sense of our "patrimony." And the only term for the relation of this "father" to his children was *potestas*. Not only was *potestas* at first exercised indiscriminately over the children and the slaves, but the term itself is the immediate cognate of the Greek term δεσπότης (head of the house community)—whence our "despot"—and of the Sanskrit term *viç—patiḥ* (head of the village community). **Poti-s* is presumed to be the original Indo-European term for "lord and master," used of such group chiefs, and the only

e converso go far to show that the original . . . unlimited rights of the Roman *paterfamilias* were at one time those of *ownership* over both goods and persons."

184 Hunter, op. cit., p. 192. Schrader, op. cit., p. 389, believes that among the prehistoric Indians, Teutons and Romans, children were exposed unless the father "took them up."

185 Ihering, *Aryan*, p. 394.

186 Vinogradoff, *Jurisprudence*, I, p. 259, says, ". . . the primitive slave had a better standing, not on account of sentiment, but for practical reasons." And, p. 258, ". . . according to the general Aryan conception the servants are a part of the household. Even the slave is not regarded as an outside subject; he is a member, though an inferior member, of the family."

original term for "husband." So completely does this connect with the general system, and reverse the usual connection of *pater*, that it becomes difficult to understand the use of the latter term in this connection in Rome—either in the simple form or as *paterfamilias*. Nevertheless, as we note in Appendix I A, modern philology refuses any longer to admit the near relation of the two, classing *pater* with the biological terms derived from the infantile *pa-pa*, and *potestas* with the political terms given above.

While the term *pater*, in this connection, and its attribute *potestas*, do not connote "fatherhood," neither does the latter connote force. *Potestas* was used with reference to human beings alone. It means "an office or delegated authority, and is rarely used to express independent or physical power."[187] The sense of power is secondary, and the general Latin terms for potentiality (*potis*, *possum*, etc.) are all derived from the same original Indo-European **poti-s*, the title for the head of the house community, the "self" of the lord and master.[188] We start with the fact of the head. We end with the abstract idea of power. But we can impute no greater content to the word than that derived from the source. The idea comes from the fact, not the reverse. Thus if *manus* was the word for propinquity—the idea of kin or 'belonging'—and arose from the "name," so *potestas* was the word for power—the idea of control and protection—and arose from the term for the chief.

4. "*Dominium*"—*The Property Relation*

Eventually and very slowly there was differentiated still a third relation, which, under the title *dominium*, is the direct ancestor of the later concept of ownership and the source of the specialized modern property relation. Muirhead[189] finds that "it is impossible to say when the word *dominium* came into use," and assumes that it was after the time of the XII Tables, for then "it is mine" was enough. Gaius, in the Middle Empire, hardly ever uses it. But he does speak often of the *dominus*. By the time of Justinian, and his most recent sources, *dominium* is not uncommon, though by no means standard. The classificatory genitive is even then the "last word."

But *dominus* (whence *dominium*) is an old word. It is only its appearance in law that is delayed. While we have accepted the authorities to the effect that *herus* was the original general term for

[187] Hearn, *Aryan*, p. 86. So too Ihering, *Entw.-gesch.*, pp. 58 and 93, speaks of the relation of *potestas* as one of government of the order of the *imperium* of a magistrate. And Ernout and Meillet, op. cit., s. v., define it as "pouvoir politique."

[188] For a discussion of the etymology of *potestas* see Appendix I A.

[189] Op. cit., p. 120. Ihering, *Entw.-gesch.*, p. 52, considers the use of the term *dominus* in the antique epoch as doubtful.

the head of the house, it is a question whether, in fact, this term did not merely precede and cover the same limited ground as *dominus*. In Plautus it is the term of address used by slaves to their master. The phonetically similar German word * *hēriro*, (*Herr*) which Ihering assumes to be a cognate, was, according to Schröder, used only of the master of slaves. But whatever the early specific usage of *dominus* it meant literally the "master of a house."[190] The developing use of *dominium* seems to follow the new line of cleavage between the free members of the household on one hand and the slaves, cattle and all else on the other — a cleavage which gradually displaced the older one between human beings and cattle. It indicates the beginning of a revolution in the status of the free members — their liberation from a condition closely resembling slavery. Perhaps, too, it indicates a deterioration in that of the slave into something resembling the cattle — "chattel slavery," under which human beings came to be dealt with more as if they were objects (*pecunia*, cattle), whereas formerly objects (in the *familia*) had been dealt with more as if they were human beings. The eventual exact coverage of the word *dominium* in late Roman law, if it can be said to have arrived at exactitude, covers the relation of the master of the house only to the slaves and to non-human objects, animate and inanimate. It covers that part of the whole field still described by the classificatory genitive which pertains to those things which come later to be called *corporeal*.

One of the purposes in thus tracing from their common source the development of the later elements in the system of management of a Roman household is to point out that the nidus of the Roman system

[190] It is thus identical in sense with the Saxon *husband* — literally "house-dweller." Its etymology has been carelessly traced to the verb *domare* (to tame). So Maine construes it. "There must have been a time when a wild animal tamed, which was a rarity, was of more value than a hundred acres of land, which was superabundant," *E. L. and C.*, p. 338. On the contrary both the words *domare* and *dominus* derive from the early word *domus*, whence the late Latin *doma*. And these in turn are cognates of the Greek δόμος, from δέμω (to build). That which is "tamed," is and always has been, that which is "domesticated" or "brought to the house"—"made part of the household." Walde, *Latin*, says *dominus* meant *Herr*, not as the *tamer*, direct from *domare*, but "the one who is in the house"— essentially "belonging to the house." He also confirms the secondary character of *domare*. E. Littré, *Dictionnaire de la langue française*, says, "On tire *dominus*, de *domus*, maison ; mais le suffixe *-ĭnus*, avec *i* bref, n'a pas, dans la latinité, le sens possessif." Another confirmation of the original classificatory genitive ! This pair of terms, *potestas* and *dominium*, is then cognate etymologically and semantically with the Greek δεσπότης and the assumed IE. **dems-potis* (the head of the house). Ernout and Meillet, op. cit., s. v., say of *dominus* that "le rapport avec *domus* etait senti des Latins. S'oppose a *servus* (comme *erus*) *vilicus*, *ancilla*, *familia* ;" and that it designated by extension all kinds of masters including tyrants (despots). Thus this later term for master (after *paterfamilias*) did not follow the oriental Indo-European pattern but was distinctively western — like *tribūnus* from *tribus*, Goth. *þiudans* (literally the chief of the *þiuda*), and *kindins* (ἡγεμών — literally chief of the "kind" or gens).

of mastery was the original group or, eventually, its fixed place of abode. The terms *familia*, *manus*, *mancipium*, *potestas* and *dominium*, though they arose at different stages and from different sources, all seem to have had their roots in the house community of the preethnic stage, in the position of its lord and master, or in the terms, perhaps developed from it, to cover its home.

5. *Wardship and Patronage – The Semi-dependents*

Lest we seem to have over-emphasized the subjection of these early house communities to their heads it is well, in support of the presentation, to mention the institution of tutelage and the several classes of persons who were attached to the house community, or who attached themselves, purely for the sake of the protection afforded. Even in Rome such memberships (*manus*) though they went by other names had especially the connotation of *mund*.[191] Again we have to think of these communities as walled round preserves – within, peace; without, war. Those within, women and children, if left without a *pater*, needed to be taken under the tutelage of another house head. Also the stranger – the man from without – was an enemy (*hostis*).[192] If he desired to trade or dwell with the community he needed to become a *hospes* – that is he put himself under the patronage of some house head, by means of the institution of "hospitality."[193] Thus it was the necessities of living in a society in which these house communities were practically the only organized centres of peace, which compelled the adherence of those who for various reasons were incapable of fending for themselves. And the growth in power and prestige of the more successful units encouraged this aggregation of hangers-on to an extent which crystal-

[191] A section of the *manus-mund* system had received a special terminology in Rome as *tutela* (from *tueor*, to protect), but there are traces of its relation to the *manus* system, as, for instance, in the earliest will. In the north, as *Vormundschaft*, it became the major and most enduring element. It is interesting to note that in Rome *manus* gave rise to the later *potestas* (power) while in the north the cognate *mund* retained or developed the significance of "protection" for which the Romans needed a new term *tutela*. Patronage was, of course, an institution independent of tutelage. Nevertheless it seems to have been constructed, in many respects, on that as a model – as if it were adopted or arrogated tutelage.

[192] The Latin *hostis* and OHG, *gast* are the same word. ". . . this equation shows . . . that the fundamental meaning of both words is 'stranger,' and that in a hostile sense." Schrader, op. cit., p. 142, Note.

[193] The term itself is, according to Walde, *Latin*, built from **hosti-potis* (*Gastherr* or guest lord) and thus originally signified the house head who extended such protection, or the protection he gave. Schrader, op. cit., p. 351, thinks "the necessities of trade . . . awoke the conception of guest-friendship in the breast of man." The exchange of presents was the "memory and a symbol of the exchange of wares" and changed the term for enemy into one for guest.

lized the various relationships and made of them the basis, as we shall see, for the later organization of medieval society.

In the course of time there developed from several other sources, but for similar reasons, the class of the half-free.[194] We may conceive a military horde composed of many of these house communities invading and conquering a territory, and subjugating the indigenous population. Thereafter with the development of a super-familial political organization by the conquerors, in which they exclusively shared—literally a fellowship—it became necessary for the subject peoples to attach themselves to one or another house in order to participate thus indirectly in the economic and political advantages established by the association.[195] This may have occurred where the people already on the land were "too numerous to be enslaved."[196] But it also occurred when those who had been slaves were liberated.[197] The relation thus established was called patronage—the house head the *patronus*, the subordinate the *cliens*. Like the son, the client was submerged in the autonomous house community. He had no legal (super-familial) rights against whoever stood to him as patron. In fact he had no legal position whatever. The patron was his representative in all external relations.[198] And the tie thus formed continued to the heirs of the patron and to the descendants of the client.[199] It is true that the condition of half-freedom seemed to

[194] See Schröder, op. cit., p. 52, who speaks of the insertion among the West Germans, between the free and the unfree, of the class of the *Hörigen*, or "half-free." See also Tacitus, *Germania*, Ch. 25. Among the Greeks (helots, *perioeci*) and the Slavs there existed a similar status. See Ihering, *Aryan*, p. 395. The clients in the Gortyn inscription are ϝοικεῖς. See Vinogradoff, *Jurisprudence*, I, p. 260.

[195] Clark, *Regal*, p. 266, says, "Whatever be the main source of *clientela*, Mommsen winds up with the conclusion that in the old patrician community every domiciled freeman, not a patrician, must have been under patrician Patronage." Bonfante, op. cit., I, pp. 80-81, recalls that *clientela* was older than the beginnings of Rome, that the ancients considered it an institution not peculiar to the Roman people, and that comparative ethnology now shows it to be a world-wide method of aggregating or reinforcing the primitive group by means of prisoners of war, persons expelled from other groups and poor strangers. He says, I. p. 112, "Il est certain que, à l'origine, les vaincus étaient partagés entre les *gentes* et que les étrangers cherchaient spontanément la protection d'un puissant patron. . ."

[196] Ihering, *Aryan*, p. 395. In fact Bonfante ascribes to the *plebs* somewhat the status of clients of the *civitas*.

[197] Ihering, *Geist*, I, p. 243, ". . . es kann in meinen Augen nicht zweifelhaft sein, dass alle Nichtbürger, also ursprünglich auch die Freigelassenen in diesem Verhältnis standen."

[198] Ihering, *Geist*, I, p. 237, Note 133. "Daher *patronus* noch in späterer Zeit = Fürsprecher."

[199] See Ihering, *Geist*, I, pp. 236-8. He says, there, "Die Abhängigkeit, welche das Verhältnis begründet, prägt sich deutlich in den beiden Ausdrücken *patronus* und *cliens* (Höriger) aus. Der erste Ausdruck stellt das Verhältnis als eine Nachbildung der väterlichen Gewalt dar, und mit dieser Bezeichnung hat die Sprache das Wesen desselben treffend ausgedrückt." So far so good. But his connection between *cliens*

constitute, both among the Germans and the Romans, a semi-membership in the larger agnatic circle. The client was protected by the *gens.*[200] But in other respects the relation is extra-legal and we cannot learn much of it from the literature of the law, but only from the allusions to it from other sources. However we know that it appeared as a going concern at the dawn of history and later "largely modified the course of events. . ."[201] Tradition has it that the *gens Fabia* contained some four or five thousand clients as against only 306 *gentiles.* So it is evident that the mass of the *familia* was greatly enlarged thereby, at least among the powerful houses and in early historic times.[202]

6. "*Pecunia*" and "*Peculium*" — *The Status of the Cattle*

In the earliest evidence we find many indications that the primitive and most enduring line, drawn within the house community, was that between the human beings and the cattle. Of this the most notable relic in early law is the favourite dichotomy *familia pecuniaque,* which already at the time of the XII Tables is a merely traditional phrase having lost its original meaning.[203] Ihering, Girard and Bonfante all assume as probable the identity of the *familia* with *res mancipi* and that of *pecunia* with *res nec mancipi.*[204] We have then, if our relation of *mancipium* to *manus* holds good, an identification of the original *familia,* at the pre-agricultural stage (pastoral), with the *persons only* of the house community, including, perhaps already,

and *Höriger,* while formerly held and suggestive, is probably incorrect. He assumes, on the one appearance as *cluens* in Plautus, that it is derived from *clueo* (hear). "Im deutschen haben wir das Hören in demselben Sinn, z. B. Gehorsam, gehorchen, angehörig, Höriger." And in his *Aryan,* p. 395, he says that both the "Latin and German languages describe it as obedience (*cliens* from κλύειν = *hören* (to hear) = '*hörig*' (audible); both derive the idea of obedience from the same word (*ob-audire* = *obedientia, hören* = Germ. *e-hor-sam.*" As to the German it is correct and significant, for thus we have a parallel development of personal submission into property. But Walde, *Latin,* dismisses this probable slip of the pen (?) in Plautus and suggests, after L. Meyer, that *cliens* — as "depending on someone, seeking support and protection from him" — is connected with *clino* (to lean). Bonfante suggests the source *colere* (op. cit., I, p. 80) presumably like the name Esquiline (see Ernout and Meillet).

200 See Ihering, loc. cit.

201 Hearn, *Aryan,* p. 111. Cornil, op. cit., p. 18, speaks of the relation as one "de dépendance personelle régi par d'anciennes coutumes antérieures à la fondation de Rome."

202 It is the view of some (see, for instance, Tenney Frank, op. cit.), that during the Regal period, as a result of the Etruscan occupation and overlordship and the remarkable agricultural prosperity, a semi-feudal system existed around the *villae* as centers. This was built upon clientage, with the plebs as clients. Whether the holdings of the clients, and their condition, were free or servile is uncertain.

203 See Girard, op. cit., p. 272, who goes so far as to hold that by that time the "two words were employed indifferently for each other."

204 See Ihering, *Aryan,* p. 18; *Entw.-gesch.,* p. 84; and Girard, op. cit., pp. 271-272.

slaves. It is then reasonable to assume that the rules and customs developed for dealing with the *familia* were adapted to the control and government of a human group. Thence too we find an easy transfer to the sense of the relatives of the household, and that of the slaves of the household, which the word always retains. The other *res mancipi* are later additions; the work animals being included at the entry into the agricultural stage;[205] and the land and rustic servitudes when landed property arrives on the scene.[206] Why these latter things should have been attached to the *familia* under the rules of *manus*, as if they were human, we shall consider later. At any rate this thesis gives us a sharp original outline of the *familia* as a human group of a strictly political or domestic form of organization.

But from the beginning of the pastoral stage there subsisted alongside this human group its one important accessory, the flocks. *Pecunia* is constructed from *pecus* and it is assumed that it originally designated these flocks.[207] The flocks consisted for the most part of the smaller animals, sheep, goats, and swine, which directly furnished food and clothing. With the *res nec mancipi* was also included, as time went on, the slowly growing stock of inanimate objects (other than land) which went to make up the equipment and stores of the group. But the cattle constituted the principal non-human wealth, as witness the later use of the term *pecunia* also for money.[208]

It will become apparent, as we trace the development of the legal institution of property, that its persistent dichotomies—*immobilia* and *mobilia*; *alod* and *feud*; land and chattels; the heritable (hereditament) and the non-heritable; real and personal property; formal property and informal property—had in certain respects their common source in this early traditional division, though not altogether through the channel of Roman law.[209] Originally the shepherd

[205] *Boves, muli, equi, asini*, or, as Ulpian puts it, 19. 1, "*quadrupedes, quae dorso collove domantur. . .*"

[206] Girard, op. cit., p. 72, considers that the distinction between the *familia* and the *pecunia* became obscured from the time when *fundi* and *servitutes rustici* were included among the *res mancipi*.

[207] "Idg. **peku-* is at first the domestic animal whose wool makes him useful, especially the sheep." Walde, *Latin*. Schrader, op. cit., p. 260, connects the words to the root **paç-*, which meant "fasten," "capture." "The domesticated animals were then perhaps originally 'the fastened,' as opposed to those which ran wild" (*cf.* Curtius). *Pecus* (*pecoris*) was the collective term (*troupeau, bétail*); *pecus* (*pecŭdis*) was the individual term (head of cattle); and the two were still distinguished in the Republican epoch (Ernout and Meillet).

[208] Schrader, op. cit., p. 349, says ". . . as early as the primeval period [that is before the "dispersion"] . . . the cow was the special standard of value amongst the Indo-Europeans. . ."

[209] Practically all legal historians note the universality of this dichotomy, which Bonfante describes as one between "things having social importance" and "things abandoned to free individual disposition" with little interference by the state. This however is the result of the distinction, not its cause. He speaks of the classifications

groups consisted almost exclusively of men and their flocks. The connection of the first to the head was a personal governmental relation; that of the second was what we should now call proprietary, though somewhat of the nature of a joint ownership.

We have first to suggest that the *patrimonium*, in its pure original meaning, was the headship of this originally wholly human group, a headship which passed by various types of automatic and customary selective succession. This conclusion is supported by the fact that *patrimonium* and *familia* come to be synonymous when both have arrived at the objective stage of designating a body of heritable property, the *res mancipi*.[210] Neither term is applied to the *pecunia* (the *res nec mancipi*). The *patrimonium* was still that which was ancestral, which passed by perpetual succession; the governance of a group of persons, a political *job*. And it pertained to the autonomous and independent group to which all 'belonged.' Finally it was an absolute and original, if in part also a communal and not wholly individual, right. Walde says that *proprius* (whence *proprietas*), meaning "belonging exclusively to someone," "wholly belonging," is very probably derived from **pro-p(a)trios*, which signifies "ancestral, received from the ancestors as inherited possession." [211] Thus the word "property" (*proprietas*) is, perhaps, originally identified with the *patrimonium*, the *familia*. Such an absolute right as *dominium*, the successor of *patrimonium* in the field of property, we must then ally with the equally absolute "divine right of kings," the direct successor of *patrimonium* in the field of governance. In fact we must see in *patrimonium* originally more of the latter, the succession to an office, than of the former, the inheriting of an estate.

If in Rome we find this sense of headship over a patriarchal house community—the *patrimonium*—confined at first to the original *patres*, or patrician class, only, so among the northern peoples we find a similar connection between the words *Adel* (nobility) and *odil* (patrimony),[212] as if such a tradition of an ancient political hereditament, confined to a caste, were common to both races. In the Dark Ages the latter term, in the derived form *alod* or *alodium*, had become the sign of a right (of property?) *held of* no one—an absolute and original heritage.[213] The two sets of terms, the Roman and

"visibles et invisibles du droit attique, les biens réels et personnels du droit germanique, les biens immeubles et meubles du droit médiéval et moderne. . ." Op. cit., I, pp. 211-212.

210 See Clark, *History of Roman Private Law*, Pt. II, *Jurisprudence*, II, pp. 544 ff. Gaius, 2. 102, uses the terms *familia* and *patrimonium* as synonymous.

211 *Latin*, s. v, *proprius*. But see Appendix I D.

212 Grimm, *Deutsche Rechtsalterthümer*, I, p. 265, says, under *adal*, ". . . ich habe . . . vermuthet, dass *uodal* . . . dazu im ablautsverhältnis stehe."

213 For discussion of these etymologies see Appendix I D. The Latinized term (viz. *ex alodis*) was not at first applied exclusively to land, but signified rather "by

the German, seem to fit together in detail and argue that both were descended from the earlier rule of succession of the patriarchal headship. And *alod* appears to have had much the same connotation as *familia*.

Thus we find an original distinction between the governance of the household—in Rome the *familia*, or *patrimonium*—to which was later added the homestead and its appurtenant beasts of burden, and, on the other hand, the control of the herds—in Rome the *pecunia*—to which was later added all other inanimate objects. The "title" to the two was different. The first gave rise to formal property; the second to informal. The change of 'belonging' of the first involved an elaborate ceremony savouring at first of adoption and later of what seems to us a publicly attested purchase and sale, applied to persons and objects alike. Perhaps at first alienation of the succession to the former was impossible. The latter could be alienated *inter vivos* by the simple act of delivery (*traditio*), and was at least the first element to be subject to legacy, or testament in the modern sense. It was also the first subject of ready exchange. While the former remained qualified by the rights of those subject—rights expressed in rigid custom—the latter represented more particularly the developing wholly individual property of the head. And yet even this *pecunia* of the master was not exactly the immediate source of truly individual property because, as we shall suggest, even as to the herd there were, in the pastoral stage, common rights.

It is in the *peculium* that we find the immediately perfect form of individual, or private, property, though on the other hand a property in no wise absolute, but rather *derivative and dependent*.[214] As its name indicates it was originally used to designate the small herd (or single head) of cattle, separated from the capital herd and consigned to the care and use of an individual or sub-group.[215] It consisted, of course, wholly of *res nec mancipi*. Therefore it corresponded always and exactly to, and was, in a sense, a subordinate part of, the *pecunia* of the master; something entirely outside the *familia*, or patrimony. It is supposed that the practice originated with the clients and was

inheritance." Later it became the special term for an absolute title to land (allodial) which is distinguished in the Lex Salica as capable of descending only through the male line although all other "property" descended through both sexes (see Title LIX, Lex Salica). Here is another hint that this term was of old allied with the traditional principles of the government of the house community, to which the land was eventually attached.

214 Walde, *Latin*, says *prīuus* (standing for itself, single; own; deprived of something) is from *prīvo* (to take, *berauben*, a thing); is related to Umbrian *prever* (*singulis*), Oscan *preiuatud* (*privato, reo*); and apparently rests on **prei̯*— (to like, to save or spare). Festus says "*privos privasque antiqui dicebant pro singulis.*"

215 Ihering, *Geist*, I, p. 242, "Der Name [*peculium*] weist auf die Beziehung dieses Vermögens zur Landwirtschaft hin; wörtlich übersetzt bedeutet er 'kleines Vieh,' d.h. einen von der Hauptherde gesonderten Viehstand."

later applied as well to the *filii* and the slaves.[216] But this I think is unwarranted. Maine says that the ancient law of Rome never contemplated the possibility that *filii* "under power" should claim a separate ownership of property.[217] But he refers there only to a super-familial property for, as he says himself, at that stage, "law had not yet penetrated into the precincts of the Family."[218] The fact was that the early house community was autonomous and therefore above the law. Whatever rights existed therein, whatever arrangements were made with clients, freedman, *filii* or slaves, were, in that sense, extra-legal. Later, it is true, the law did penetrate these precincts and confirm some of these rights. And it is by that light that we perceive the *de facto* practices which probably existed previously. Certainly their lack of early recognition in law is no evidence that they were not among the most ancient of customs, existing, perhaps, long before the custom of patronage. When this dependent but private and individual property came to be recognized in law it was because in the eyes of the law the house community had been resolved into *disjecta membra*. But there are reasons to assign to it great antiquity in the epoch before there was law. Eventually *peculium* became the general legal term for the private property of one "in power" or one not fully free. It long remained a mere life estate, not alienable, not fully segregated and reverting to the common or chief stock of the head at death.[219]

Obviously the name *peculium* (from cattle) dates back to the time of the "*paysan romain primitif*," as Girard puts it.[220] And the practice we find widely spread and persistent among the Indo-Europeans, under a terminology which divides itself into two classes. Either there arises from the term for cattle a general term for derivative and dependent property, or there arises from the sense of a share of the chief (or chief's) herd the term for cattle which, curiously enough, does not long retain the connotation of dependence. We have not the space for an exhaustive treatment of this interesting point. But, by way of example, we will cite certain typical cases. Of the first class we have the Roman *peculium* and, not impossibly, *pecunia* as well. The OHG. *fihu* (cattle) and Gothic *faihu* (*pecunia*) are cognates of *pecus* (cattle). Thence developed the various me-

[216] Ihering, *Geist*, I, pp. 240 and 242.

[217] *Ancient Law*, p. 136.

[218] *Ancient Law*, p. 141.

[219] The 5th of the XII Tables (as reconstructed by Mommsen) reads, "Ex ea familia qui liberatus erit, eius bona in eam familiam revertuntor." The *peculium profecticium*, or *ex re patris*, was subject to reversion to the father and was inalienable; the *adventicium* was subject to a life estate in the father with the reversion in the son, and only the *castrense* (military) and the *quasi-castrense* were held in absolute ownership by the son. See Poste, *Gaius*, p. 43.

[220] Op. cit., p. 272.

dieval terms, *fief*, *feodum*, "feud," "feudal," with their specific connotation of derivative and dependent property.[221] It is possible that this word retained, at the beginnings of feudalism, its traditional sense of a share divided from the chief, or common, fund or herd, and in this way was appropriated in the west of Europe to cover the method of the land-loan,[222] by which the individual was "enfeoffed," which pervaded the whole cast of the feudal system, and which furnished a contrast to the term *alod*. It is also possible, on the other hand, that, as a term for cattle, it came to describe the system by which the domanial lord stocked his tenants' farms (see below), and was from that usage transferred to apply to land.

Starting, on the other hand, from the idea of the chief or common herd, we find in two cases, among others, the term *caput* (head) giving rise to the terms for cattle, chattels and eventually capital. We have the Umbrian *pequo castruo*, which one must suspect is related to the idea of chief herd,[223] and the Oscan *eítiuvam* (*pecuniam*) which seems to be cognate with Oscan *aeteis* (*partis*).[224] While any construction on the basis of these faint traces is highly speculative it is also very suggestive to consider the possibility that the Sabellian *pecunia* began as a share (of the herd) and is probably cognate with the Latin *usus*, while the Umbrian *pequo castruo* may be related to the Celtic process to be next described. The French name for the early Gallic and also Irish institution which came to be called *chatel* or *cheptel* (from *caput*) with all the variant forms, is most certainly the source of the words "cattle," "chattel" and, through a reversion to *capitalis*, of our "capital." The semantic chain is clear. "In the ancient Irish laws [Brehon], we constantly see the chiefs making grants of cattle *en cheptel* to men of their tribe, and various forms of vassalage spring therefrom."[225] In both these latter cases the idea of "dependent and derivative property," which seems to spring naturally from the derivation of the terms, has disappeared. This leads to the reasonable inference that these "uses" (or shares) de-

221 That the institution of the *peculium* was native in Germany is indicated by the term *suntarscaz* (*peculium*) which appears in Old High German (*MHG. sunderschaz*). Schade, *Altdeutsches Wörterbuch*, holds *scaz* to be a borrowed word from Slav. *skotŭ* (*Vieh, Zuchtvieh, Heerdenvieh*) ; Russ. *skotŭ* (*Tier, Vieh*). Graff, *Althochdeutscher Sprachschatz*, gives for *suntar* and its allied forms much the same series as we have already noted with *priuus*. It has the sense of sundered, single, private. Thus the idea is "that which is sundered from the main herd."

222 The nature of this *feodum* is well shown by the fact that the German word for *fief* was *Lehn*. *Lehn* originated as *leave* but always had the sense of "loan," and the word "loan" is derived from it. Thus Pollock and Maitland, op. cit., I, p. 498, speak of the fief as the " 'land-loan' of the old Frankish world."

223 See Appendix I D.

224 See Appendix I D.

225 Laveleye, op. cit., p. 234. See also D'Arbois de Jubainville, *Études sur le droit celtique*, I, pp. 118 ff.

veloped, by a sort of prescription, an absolute title among some peoples while they remained dependent among others, according to the force and authority with which the original right continued to be asserted. Even in Rome it seems plausible to hold that this type of prescription occurred, that, upon the analogy of *mancipium*, it eventually took the name of *usucapio*, and that it came to intrude even upon the field of the *res mancipi*, though originating as a share of the common herd.[226] Such a share (*οἶτος*) called *usus*, might, if held for a long period, create a right, by *usage* or custom, to its *use* and thus by the predecessor of usucapion become eventually a prescriptive title, if the prior claim were not defended, to the thing itself. The distinction between the *usus* (*corpus*) and the *fructus* is a relic of the dependent stage. Such a process is at least typical of the development of property throughout later times.

By way of setting up an hypothesis which might account for the rise of this apparently original, wide-spread and persistent dichotomy in the classifications of property and in the character of title, let us outline a potential source. Given the form of a large nomad patriarchal group, of which the head is only one among many in his generation, a tendency might grow toward distinguishing between the descendants of the chief and the descendants of his collateral fellow members. Certainly such a distinction would arise wherever subject peoples were absorbed into the group. Thus in time there might occur a cleavage of strains between one, a noble (*adelig* or patrician), strain — in whom by custom remained the hereditary headship and therefore a peculiarly absolute relation to the whole, a divine right to rule — and all others whose relation was dependent.[227]

To such a group was certainly attached but one important possession — the herds[228] — held in common under the direction of the chief. As the group grew and divided by fission, or as, in settled times, it spread out over a large area, this capital herd might be broken up temporarily for better use or for better pasturage. The title would remain in the whole or in the head — if it could be maintained. Thus little herds, *peculia*, might be assigned, as a sort of loan or life estate, to individual branches, a division not absolute but temporary, and dependent as well as derivative. At the same time the capital herd would remain the *pecunia* of the chief.

[226] So *usus* (*usucapio*) may have become a means of acquisition of *manus* over wives (*usus*), of property in land and its accessories, *via* and *iter*, the while it continued in its original form and gave rise to the *servitutes*.

[227] Such a thesis might explain the necessity among the Germans of electing the king and even the *Gaufürst* from among a select few in whom the hereditary capacity rested. See Schröder, op. cit., p. 29.

[228] See Tacitus, *Germania*, Chapters 5 and 18, attesting to this fact in early Germany.

In some such fashion a distinction might arise. On the one hand would exist the patrimony (*odil*), which, from designating the office, might come, through the avenue of the power of that office, to designate the group of persons (*familia*).[229] This office would attach to a privileged class in absolute right as a hereditary perquisite. On the other hand the cattle would stand on a different footing. The capital herd belonging to the whole or, more particularly, to the chief as *pecunia*, would be partly divided and these shares (*usus*, *eítiuvam*, *fihu*, *peculium*) would be held by a tentative and relative right, until and unless, by prescription, they became the *pecunia* (*faihu*) of the individual, and eventually independent, chiefs of off-shoot groups.

Thus may have developed a distinction between two kinds of government—of control—that over the human group itself and that over its cattle; a distinction which continued and was reproduced on a smaller scale in the less patriarchal Roman family as the antithesis in character between the *familia* and the *pecunia*. And, resurgent from the same source, this distinction may have reappeared again in the Dark Ages in northern Europe to create that persistent antithesis between *allodial* and *feudal*, between that which was held in absolute right and that which was dependent and derivative. Certainly it is more than a coincidence that the etymological source of "feudal" and of *pecunia* and *peculium* is the same, and that the term *familia* as applied to the patrimony very evidently had in its early use in Rome much the same significance as had *alod* and *odil* in the north. The dichotomies of *familia* and *pecunia*, of *alod* and *feud*, of real and personal property (chattels), are in respect of heritability and the common etymological source of their second members convincingly similar.[230]

In Rome, when, in the early agricultural economy, the accessions to the house community of land and its accessories and the addition of work animals has taken place, we have on the one hand the *familia*, at its apex, as the plant, and the *pecunia* as the inventory.[231] "The *familia* is fixed, stable, continuous; the *pecunia* is passing, changing, floating."[232] Eventually the distinction was lost and the terms had

229 Just as did *patrimonium* later. See Clark, *Jurisprudence*, II, p. 544, Note. Gaius, 2. 102, explains *familiam* as *suum patrimonium*.

230 Ihering calls attention to this in *Geist*, II, p. 157, Note 205. "Auch im englischen Recht ist das Hausthier der etymologische und historische Ausgangspunkt einer besondern Sphäre des Vermögens geworden (*chattels real* und *personal* von *catalla, chattels.* Hausthiere, fahrende Habe) im Gegensatz des Grundeigenthums (*freehold*)."

231 The stock of work cattle, implements, seed and other stores necessary for production, together with the labourers, were *plant* and were called *instrumentum fundi*. See Vinogradoff, *Jurisprudence*, I, p. 276.

232 Ihering, *Entw.-gesch.*, p. 51.

been replaced by *bona*, an introduction of the Praetor,[233] by the end of the Republic.[234] But it reappeared in the Middle Ages, partly, as we shall see, rising from the persisting intra-familial and extra-legal institutions of *peculium* and *precarium*, and, at least so far as nomenclature was concerned, from the Germanic institutions of the *alod* and the *feud*.

From the foregoing discussion it may appear to the reader that we have admitted that the relation which we now call property existed first as to the *pecunia*, and its tributary *peculium*, rather than as to the *familia* (of persons). If one identifies property with its modern field of exercise – rights over non-human material objects – I do not gainsay it. But, on the contrary, the legal institution of property in Rome – the legal forms and processes – developed almost wholly *via* the power of the head to rule and the arrangements for holding and dealing with the other portion – originally wholly human – of the house community. If we wish to trace the development of the institution we must look to the principal, not to the accessory, portion of the group, to the *res mancipi* not to the *res nec mancipi*.[235] Of course the chattels (*pecunia*) of the head of the house did develop different forms from those applied to his real property (*familia*). But the really important result of this accessory portion, the *peculium* – that which remained dependent and derivative and retained the character of a loan (owed), *held of* rather than owned – plays an insignificant rôle in Roman law. It is only later that it gives rise to the major principles of a new system of property.

7. *The Projection of the "Familia" upon the Land*

The great diversity of views among students of the subject as to the beginnings of property in land among the Indo-Europeans – which is no doubt due in part to a variety of social ideals for which historical justification is sought – makes it quite impossible to present any authoritative statement as to the way in which land came to compose a part of the Roman *familia*. Three schemes are put forward and they are treated as if sharply distinguished. I am impressed with the fact that they merge into each other and that the difference between them is one of theory and of statement more than it is of fact. For all assume something like our modern ideas of landed

233 Ihering, *Entw.-gesch.*, p. 82, assumes this to have been a later reading where it appears in the XII Tables.

234 See Ihering, *Entw.-gesch.*, pp. 81-83.

235 This characteristic of the development is so marked that a legal scholar like Bonfante is inclined to refuse the denomination "property" to the *res nec mancipi* in early times; ". . . d'après les textes de Cicéron, il semblerait . . . que les *res nec mancipi* n'etaient pas encore de vrais objets de propriété." Op. cit., I, p. 215.

property, and all proceed from the conception of a hard and fast hierarchical organization of early society; so many persons to a family, so many families to a gens or sib, so many of these to a tribe. This organization we are not prepared to admit. Rather we have assumed a fluctuating, merging and dividing grouping of people, of which the only durable principle was propinquity, to which was loosely applied a highly variable nomenclature; a grouping in which the most stable element was the tradition of the patriarchal house community and its relationships.

The three schemes may be illustrated by typical examples; the late Southern Slav co-proprietorship of large tracts by an extensive communal house community; the early Germanic household proprietorship of the curtilage and co-proprietorship by the *Sippe* of the arable and waste; the late Roman familial proprietorship of the whole. It is agreed that the pastoral or migrant group has no sense of, or plan for, proprietorship of land except perhaps as to the enclosure for man and beast, the curtilage or *hortus*. As agriculture develops the cultivation may be prosecuted "individually" or "collectively." No one holds, I believe, that the cultivator was in any case a lone individual (even in Germany).[286] What is meant by "individual" is in reality "household." And what, we may ask, was the household? Nor has any one defined exactly what they mean by collective cultivation; that is, how large and of what nature was the group jointly working the land. The Serbian house community was large, composed of 25 to 50 persons. Perhaps the German household was very small, composed of one couple and their children. Is the one communal and the other individual? The Serbian house community was weakly governed (i.e. it was only mildly patriarchal); the Roman house community was strongly governed. So too with ownership. Most of the evidence used to prove a stage of communal property in land simply proves that the first step in territorial claims was effected by large familial circles, representing several house communities acting jointly, and does not indicate a true communal property among the individuals within these smaller and integral political subdivisions. The difference, we see, depends not so much upon a principle as it does upon the degree to which the idea of territorial right had narrowed itself; upon the nature and size, rather than upon the name, of the unit conforming to this territorial ambit; and upon the degree of concentration in a single head of the authority within

[286] *Seebohm, The Evolution of the English Farm,* p. 25, describing the agriculture of neolithic man, says, ". . . but in a year or two it would be necessary to dig up a fresh piece of land"; and, p. 29, the working "must surely have been cooperative, for no man could cope with such problems single-handed." This suggests, as the common background of experience; first, rights in the product of a shifting cultivation rather than in the locus of that cultivation; and, second, original collective working.

this unit. The first two concern the boundary at which the idea of immediate propinquity may have become delimited. The last concerns the element of power.[237]

It will perhaps be generally agreed that in the roving pastoral state, before agriculture is developed, there was no semblance of property in land of any kind. Such a condition Schröder describes among the Germans of the *Urzeit*.[238] "The individual had in general no private property in land, and even the folk did not consider itself as permanently connected with it. To them the land was only the stage upon which their legal and practical relations found the necessary locus. But their law was folk-law and the governmental structure attached itself throughout to that of the folk" (i.e. not a land-law or a territorially districted government).

It may be presumed that the first step in the direction of landed property was the beginning of the idea of the territoriality of a group; an idea which we still retain in the political field; the idea of "England for the English." And this conforms to our presentation of early social organization, down even to the house community, as *par excellence* a political grouping with a political point of view. The size of the group in which this idea of territoriality might begin to awaken, the number or size of the house communities which composed it, would probably depend largely upon the size and density of the minimum group necessary to prevent encroachment by outsiders when it was entering the state of settled agriculture. Within whatever boundaries and groups the idea thus became established there would remain an enduring tradition that the land—their common country (*patria*, *Vaterland*) belonged to all together, was in fact an undissociable attribute of the whole aggregate to which they themselves belonged. As, in the course of time, existing or later subdivisions of persons effected corresponding subdivisions of territory, much the same attitude would attach to the immediate and smaller neighbourhoods in their relation to the smaller political units occupying them.

As to the beginnings of landholding among the Romans we have only the eventual institution, the early terminology and a group of fanciful legends to go by. Apparently the original Indo-European dwelling upon the ground was the hut we have described, which, as residence became continuous, was converted into an immovable

[237] Tarde, *Transformations*, pp. 74-6, says, ". . . on doit regarder la propriété collective des temps primitifs comme l'équivalent pur et simple de notre propriété individuelle" . . . "Le groupe familial . . . est la seule unité sociale, indécomposable et indivisible, comme l'individu à présent." He says that such early community of interest was far from "un banquet public. C'est un grand diner particulier dans une salle hermétiquement fermée."

[238] Op. cit., p. 19.

building. Such a hut or group of huts was placed "within an enclosure surrounded by a strong hedge or palisade. . ."[239] This enclosure is the *hortus* or garden. It is evident from the general appearance of cognates of this word that it was common to all Indo-Europeans and therefore probably the customary dwelling before the "dispersion," and that it represented the means for the earliest beginnings of cultivation of the soil.[240] Schrader[241] states that "subsequently the expression *Hufe*, in German, comprised all rights which the individual members of the community possessed in regard to the soil" (citing Brunner, *Deutsche Rechtsgeschichte*, I, p. 62) and that "in Greece all permanent occupation, and therefore all personal property, in land goes back to the garden (κῆπος)." In the legend of the early distribution of land to Roman citizens the term *hortus* appears in connection with *heredium*. It has been assumed that these represented two different holdings granted to each citizen. Thus Clark,[242] interpreting Festus and other Roman commentators, refers to "*hortus* and *heredium*, both terms apparently applying to land: *hortus*, the smaller, answering to the later villa (country house); *heredium*, the larger, answering to the later *hortus* (a small landed estate; cf. Festus)." Schrader concurs. He says, "In the terminology of the XII Tables, *heredium* (inheritance) means merely the garden (not the arable land) which belongs to a farmhouse (*hortus*)." Both cite Mommsen,[243] who viewed the *hortus* (curtilage) as the first private ownership of land in Rome, and regarded the *heredium* as of the nature of a corporeal hereditament. The *heredium* is stated to have been two jugera (about 1⅗ acres) and Clark identifies it with the later expression *sors* (lot).[244] Bonfante, with many others, rejects the possibility that any *familia* such as we have described could support itself on such a holding. He considers it more likely that this was the curtilage of the working population, or perhaps of the plebs, similar to the original English copyhold. He assumes the patrician holding to have been from 7 to 20 or 25 arpents (p. 215) for the

[239] Laveleye, op. cit., p. 183, describing the later Southern Slav dwelling which, I think, we may take as typical.

[240] Schrader, op. cit., p. 291, gives the equation, Lat. *hortus*, *cohors*, Osc. *húrtúm*, Gr. χόρτος (grass, fodder, farmyard), Old Ir. *gort* (*seges*), *lub-gort* (vegetable garden), Lith. *žar̃dis* (horseyard), Goth. *gards*, Germ. *garten*. The Greek κῆπος (Dor. κᾶπος) refers to this enclosure. It is cognate with OHG. *huoba* (hut) and Germ. *Hufe*. Thus we see a family of words variably referring to the enclosure, to the building within, and to the grain grown or stored therein.

[241] Op. cit., p. 291.

[242] *Regal*, p. 213.

[243] *Römisches Staatsrecht*, III, pp. 23-25.

[244] *Regal*, p. 221. He also suggests, p. 543, Note 254, that the Germanic land measure *hide* (originally AS. *hīgid*) is apparently connected with words meaning household, thus establishing a similar relation in Germany.

"ancient economy based itself more especially on the *ager publicus* than upon the *ager privatus*." Vinogradoff suggests[245] that "such a holding could only serve as a centre of grazing rights for a household chiefly dependent on pastoral pursuits."

As a means of interpreting these bits of evidence we may present as a parallel the better known facts of early Germany. "In Cæsar's time amongst the Teutons private property in land was unknown; the soil was rather the property of the various communities, into which the *civitas* was divided. The magistrates annually assigned the use of certain land to the individual sib communities. The landmarks, and with them the dwellings, were changed every year. The cultivation of the soil, within the *gentes ac cognationes*, was done in common." By Tacitus' time the transition to "private enjoyment by the various House-Fathers has already been effected."[246] There at first we find the whole use of land—even for residence—in a state of flux and, less than two centuries later, a permanent division, at least of arable, among the house communities. It should be noted that, as long as land (arable?) was redistributed periodically it was apportioned by lot (*sors*).

Authorities generally try to find, in these facts, evidence, which they apply to Rome, of a development of property in land first in the tribe, second in the gens or sib, and third in the house community, at which stage it is assumed to have become private property.[247] It

[245] *Jurisprudence*, I, p. 327.

[246] Schrader, op. cit., p. 290.

[247] Ihering, *Aryan*, p. 393, says that, in the second home, "land and soil were not private but public property. This is undeniably proved by the fact that both Teutons and Slavs, not only when first occurring in history, but also for a considerable time afterwards, were quite unacquainted with the private possession of pasture land, woodland, and arable land." And, p. xiii, he says, they "kept the Aryan system of communal property, even of arable land; the Romans did not . . ." Ely, *Property and Contract in their relations to the Distribution of Wealth*, I, p. 274, taking the economic point of view, agrees that property in *immobilia* (land) was of later development than that in *mobilia*. He says, "In primitive periods abundance of immobilia, including land, and migration rendered the exclusive appropriation of immobilia difficult. Yet another reason is that mobilia . . . represented at first more labour, more toil and effort than the immobilia. The mobilia stood for an incorporation of labour power. The immobilia in primitive society were the product of nature. . . In the course of development this particular difference . . . is diminished . . . more and more work is intermingled with the nature factor. . ." But on the whole this conventional view of the origins of property seems to overlook the primordial foundations of property in aggregation and mastery over man and beast rather than in work and enjoyment of inanimate objects or products. Mommsen, op. cit., III, p. 24, held that the soil was originally the common property of the tribe. Girard, op. cit., p. 13, "Il est infiniment plus douteux qu'ils connaissent déjà la propriété individuelle du sol." And he speaks, p. 282, of their knowing its collective proprietorship by all the people or by one of its subdivisions. As to the last, p. 12, he concedes that the gens may have held land, though it is doubtful if it had any political function. Ihering, Geist, I, pp. 198 ff. takes strongly this last view. He holds that the system of private property in land was not borrowed from the

appears to me that the process was exactly the reverse. Political occupation of a territory is one thing. Economic use is another. Property seems to have grown only out of the latter and it was probably by analogy that the idea of property was later applied to the unused but jointly occupied territory of the larger political units. On the other hand it is quite evident that the viewpoint, as to the circumscribed area thus acquired by the integral group for economic utilization, was of a political order. It was the territory of the *familia*. Let us conceive a moving body of people, or tribe, gradually having become stabilized in an area, which thereafter they come to regard as their country. Gradually each individual household, having settled in a certain spot, would build a fenced or hedged enclosure around their farmyard, *hortus*, for a dwelling, storehouse and barnyard. This then became the locus of, and an adjunct to, that household. It was put to permanent use by this group and so identified itself with them as a permanent site.[248] All the land which

plebs, and that originally in Rome it was neither non-existent nor unlimited. Rather he thinks that the *ager publicus* corresponded to an *ager gentilicus* and that the earlier idea was taken over in the later form. As such, I, p. 202, "Die Sachen der Gens gehörten sämtlichen Gentilen zusammen." It differed from individual property in that it was "kein exklusives, sondern ein ihm mit seinen Genossen ungeteilt-gemeinsames, und sodann, dass es kein veraüsserliches, sondern ein untrennbar mit der Eigenschaft als Verbindungsmitgleid verknüpftes war. . ." So too, I, p. 203, the later *res publicae* to the "sämtlicher Staatsangehörigen." Finally let us note that Schröder considers the earliest acquisitions of land to have been tribal and the final status communal within the house community. He says, op. cit., p. 66, "Solange es noch kein Privateigentum an Grund und Boden gab, konnten derartige Übertragungen nur bei Landabtretungen von Staats wegen vorkommen. . ." Later, "Sie galten als Familienangelegenheit, da Haus und Hof in Gesamteigentum der Hausgenossenschaft standen und nur mit gesamter Hand veraüssert werden konnten." Clark takes the more legendary view. He says, *Regal*, p. 225, "As to *exclusive individual* property, it seems to me, that such property must be recognized in the Roman *paterfamilias*, certainly as regards moveables, from the beginning, and as regards land, from a very early period, only preceded, in fact, by an invasive conquest, and the temporary community above referred to."

As to the application of these generalizations to Rome, the common argument (see Cornil, op. cit., p. 71, for instance) that the early appearance of the rustic servitudes and their equal standing with *dominium* as property rights, proves the prior existence of a *régime* of collective cultivation, or even of collective property, at which time these necessary accommodations were arranged, seems to me fatally weak. For had there been at any stage such an imposition of encumbrances upon land, either by collective or by superior authority (i.e. the *patres gentis* jointly, or, if there was such, the *pater gentis*), some relic or survival of this eminent domain would certainly have persisted. But, on the contrary, the only evidence we have as to the means of originating servitudes indicates that they were wholly voluntary arrangements, arrived at by transactions, two of which were presumably the results of bargains. These means were *mancipatio, in iure cessio* and, at least at later stages, *usus*. Even the last assumes a period of uncontested enjoyment of the right, as ground of title, which argues its voluntary nature.

248 Schrader, op. cit., p. 291, says, "Private property in land amongst the Teutons and Slavs started with the farmyard, which we may picture to ourselves even in primitive times as surrounded by a fence of twisted thorns and reeds."

remained outside would be pasturage – range – the territory of some larger political unit, but obviously no more economically used than had been the areas over which they had wandered in the past. Such land would not be prized. The *cité* was only a citadel or fortress in their midst; a walled round refuge, perhaps unoccupied except in the time of danger, perhaps containing their domiciles.[249] Gradually agriculture would be extended by neighbourhoods of various sizes and degrees of subdivision. As this took place, by expansion of the original enclosure, *hortus*, or by enclosure of other contiguous arable – for it must have been protected from the herds – it would widen the area put to economic use and establish the tendency to stabilize and make permanent this accession. So much would be transferred from political territory to economic land utilization. This general process of the development of agriculture would tend toward the relative isolation of the *familiae* living upon the land. "Isolation is the necessary consequence. . ." says Vinogradoff.[250] Thus the individuation of these holdings would parallel and correspond to the individuation of the communities. If the normal house community was called a "gens" or "sib" and their territory a *pagus* the result would appear later to have been communal. Where the unit was called a *familia*, it would appear later to have been individual, or rather familial.[251] Yet, as a matter of fact, the distinction is without a difference. In the first case the real patriarchate was the "gens" or "sib," in the second it was the *familia*. Neither was communal nor individual in the modern sense. Such expansions would in the course of time become permanent like the *heredia*. In cases where large groups had expanded jointly, their at first undivided interests in the whole, exercised as shifting severalties, would be gradually translated, as they themselves divided, into permanent divided shares, though these might well retain the name of *lots* (*sortes*, or the Greek *κλῆροι*). Eventually, with the development of the identification of such land with individual house communities by reason of regular economic use and the resulting change of point of view in regard to it, the

[249] Girard, op. cit., p. 12, speaks of the settlement being "autour d'un refuge fortifié (*Roma quadrata*)" and apparently considers the *heredia* to have been within this refuge (see p. 284). Ihering, *Aryan*, p. 88, thinks the town not originally a place of habitation for the townspeople, but a "fortified bulwark for the whole populace." And Schrader, op. cit., p. 140, says, ". . . as H. Zimmer has conclusively shown . . . the *púr-as* [Gr. *πόλις*] are nothing more than 'strongholds situated on high ground and strengthened by earthworks and ditches, whither in time of danger (of war or floods – the only occasions on which these places were occupied) the inhabitants betook themselves with their goods and chattels.' "

[250] *Jurisprudence*, I, p. 197.

[251] "La propriété familiale, toutefois, n'est pas encore la propriété individuelle, parce que le chef de maison n'en dispose pas absolument et les familles primitives sont de larges groupes, qui embrassent toute une vaste parenté." Bonfante, op. cit., I, p. 196.

occupied but unused area, the *ager publicus* or common, might come to be viewed by analogy in an economic as well as in its original political aspect, and thus be conceived as the joint property of all the house communities forming the federated state. At that stage of sophistication in property over land it is possible to see the beginning of the positive distinction between the land which had already for generations been lived upon or used, which had become a part of the *familia* and subject to a claim of right so immemorial that it could present no contrast to the earlier right of the house community to itself or of the head to it – the classificatory genitive – and, on the other hand, that lesser claim to the subsequent occupation of this *ager publicus* as a squatter which gives rise to the later term *possessio*, a claim more of the nature of the *usus* or *peculium*.[252]

Such a process of learning by gradual experience as we have described, may have been cut short by the Romans who, after their passage south to Latium, came, in the course of several centuries, in contact with more advanced peoples. But to assume that there was a systematic distribution of land when Latium was first occupied is, it seems to me, to accept in spirit if not in detail, the naïve and hardly credible legends of early Rome.[253] Landed property developed out of the ever-widening small circles of utilization within, but of a different order than, the large circle of political occupation. And yet, at first, the point of view as to the former was probably very similar to the still existing point of view as to the latter, for the *nidi* of these small circles were, after all, the house communities, still the most fundamental and enduring political units, and not yet, at all, bodies of property. The limited needs for economic utilization had determined the boundaries; but territorial occupation (i.e. political) was the basis of the title and continued to be so.[254]

Coincident with this dual development of political connection with the land – one of which was to become the institution of landed property – and as the avenue of transition, there gradually took place a transfer, or projection, of the personal organization over upon the land. Settlement effected fixation. And the structure which had

[252] It is this later expansion of economic utilization upon the basis of a different title which, I think, leads Bonfante to reject that ground for the measure of the land originally acquired by territorial title. "Comme le territoire appartient à l'Etat, ainsi la propriété quiritaire appartient à son titulaire, jusqu'à la limite politique de sa conservation et de sa défense, mais non jusqu'à la limite économique de son utilisation." Op. cit., I, p. 208.

[253] Unless we construe the settlement, as Bonfante does, as a Sabellian (Alban) colony, founded on the principle of the *ver sacrum* – with 300 families. See op. cit., I, pp. 41 and 55.

[254] ". . . dans le droit romain la propriété a toujours conservé son caractère souverain." Bonfante, op. cit., I, p. 210. "Le fonds est le territoire, le siège de la famille : l'*ager* du quirite et *paterfamilias* est le parfait parallele de l'*ager romanus*" (p. 208).

been mobile — a matter of *Volksrecht* — became immobile — a matter of *Landesrecht.* As a result of this fixation the whole political organization began to be converted into one of land districts, such as we have today, rather than of groups of persons.[255] So too the immediate and earliest domain of the "state in little." That came to be regarded as "the necessary home of the family" and as inalienable as the house community itself.[256] The persons came to be identified by the land, rather than the reverse. In the course of time those members of the *familiae* who were not free or who were only half-free became *attached* to the land — became almost a part of it. That which belonged *in,* or *to,* the *familia* — the patrimony — belonged *on* certain specific land. The *familia* began to become a *fundus* or *villa.* The land, the site, became the crux of the matter.[257]

Because of this origin of the relation to the land in the political sphere and the entry of the land, as an intimate element, into the personal circle of the *familia* — as its arena, in fact — the earliest and central portion at least, which was the seat of the *familia,* became a *member* of the household. It entered into the sphere of *manus* as a *res mancipi,* subject to vindication; that is, to the "declaration of 'belonging.'"[258] It was a part of the *familia.* It was the territory upon which the hereditary rule, the *patrimonium,* was projected. Its control, and the rules by which it was dealt with, followed the political system applied to the persons, not the economic system applied to the cattle — the *pecunia.* It even entered into the religious scheme, and there came to be gods of the *termini.*

And yet, while this title to the land of the "state in little" seemed as absolute as did the right of the group to itself or that of the customary succession to the headship, nevertheless it will not do to exclude entirely the familiar viewpoint derived from the handling of the herd. The line was not so sharply drawn as that. Obviously

[255] This view, to my notion, is part and parcel of the thesis that the early organization of Roman government was arranged by districts rather than by groups of persons, and that the terms tribe, curia, gens, appearing in that connection, whatever may have been their original sense, had then come to mean such districts — like our wards and precincts. Thus there came to be four urban *tribus* and sixteen rural. And this consideration makes even more sharp the distinction between a political subdivision projected upon the land (the basis of the communal notion) and property in land.

Mommsen considered the tribe a district or quarter. But Bonfante considers it a group of *gentes* until the Servian reform, when it becomes a "circonscription territoriale." Op. cit., I, p. 115.

[256] Laveleye, op. cit., p. 164.

[257] "Le corps permanent de cette personne immortelle," according to Tarde, *Transformations,* p. 76.

[258] So too were the later *fundi,* and the rustic servitudes, way (*iter, actus,* and *via*), and water right (*aqueductus*). See Bonfante, op. cit., I, p. 195. Only these became "les vrais objets dont la propriété pouvait être protégée par la *rei vindicatio.* . ." Op. cit., I, p. 213.

the tentative division of the principal herd, for life or at will – the principle of dependent and derivative property which we have already described – would appear as a *peculium*, or loan, when it occurred within a unit having a chief, such as the Roman or Teutonic house community, but it would seem to be rather a non-permanent division of an undivided community property when it occurred among the independent parts of such larger groups as the gens, which had no chief, or where the chief had died. I think the latter explains, as a sort of transfusion, the apparent early idea of communal property as to land in Rome and as to the whole *familia* in the case of an orphaned house community.[259]

The general terminology goes to confirm the foregoing thesis. Property in land is associated with settlement. Always one finds the same necessity of *sitting on* or being *set* on the land. The *settler* sits; old English *seisin*, which was the ceremony or title of possession of land, was derived from "seize," which in turn originally meant to "set," the factitive of "sit"; even the settler without legal title, the "squatter," was conceived as thus tentatively possessing the land in a half-sitting posture. Allied with the last seem to be *possessio* and *besitz*. The former is probably from *pos-* or *post-sedeo* and the latter certainly eventually from *bei-sitzen*.[260] Perhaps both have the sense of sitting or setting (dwelling) *near* rather than *upon*.[261] For a landed estate there seems to have been no original Latin term. Such a holding was apparently an indistinguishable element or basis of the

259 While Bonfante's view is that "la propriété primitive est une propriété gentilice . . ." I am not sure that he has in mind a super-group or anything other than the house community we have described. At any rate he thinks the resemblance to the Germanic system "une pure chimère." "L'opposition entre la propriété germanique et la propriété romaine peut se résumer dans les deux axiomes suivants: (a) la propriété individuelle germanique est la possession consolidé et élevee peu à peu au rang de propriété; la propriété individuelle romaine est la souveraineté territoriale mutilée et peu à peu réduite à la simple propriété; (b) la propriété individuelle germanique a pour type et pour point de départ la propriété mobilière; quant à la propriété romaine, on peut bien dire qu'elle a pour type et pour point de départ la propriété de la terre, du fonds." Op. cit., I, pp. 210-211.

260 Ernout and Meillet do not accept this etymology but hold the, to me, doubtful thesis that it is derived from *potis* and preserves the primary sense of that word which was "exercising the power over." But note the contrast between *assiduus* and *possessor*.

261 According to the Neibuhr-Savigny theory of the origin of *possessio*, in law, the term was first used in connection with the possessory interdicts originally devised in order to guard the interests of those using the *ager publicus*, the public domain. Obviously these users were practically "squatters" and perhaps not living on the land. Perhaps the same holds true of the *besitzer*. Ihering, I think, takes a wholly legalistic view when he depreciates the absolute sense in which the terms allied with "settle" have been used in popular speech. He says, *Geist*, II, p. 572, Note 776, "Die relativ niedere Natur der faktischen Herrschaft des Besitzes gegenüber der rechtlichen des Eigenthums drückt die Sprache dadurch aus, dass sie jenes Verhältniss als blossen Zustand des Seins auf und in der Sache (Sitzen: Besitzen, *sedere; possidere*) erfasst. . ."

heredium (patrimony), or of the *familia,* or it was a share in that of the gens—a *sors. Fundus,* the later term, means "*Grund und Boden.*" It is the ground, the soil, itself.[262] Later the term *villa* appears. Contracted from *vicula,* did it at first mean a little *vicus* (village or group of houses) or merely a little house (ὄικος)? At any rate the villa has its roots in antiquity and in the centre of this early system of land holding, and we shall presently see its branches becoming the manorial domain of medieval times.

8. *Succession—The Hereditary Headship*

It is in the field of succession and the development of its property forms—intestate succession and the testamentary creation of heirs, guardians and legatees—that we find the greatest difficulty in following the general legal authorities. For, so imbued are their minds with the practices, forms and terms of the developed institution that, even when they examine what preceded it, they seem only able to envisage those details which appear to present traces of the same order of things and they overlook the obvious evidence of a quite different order.[263]

Upon the basis of the foregoing hypothesis as to the organization of pre-legal Roman society we shall attempt to outline a putative system of early succession and its development into the later property system, using as evidence the judgments of fact of our authorities but not always their interpretation of these facts. And in this way, I believe, we will arrive at a point of view which will clarify much that is otherwise obscure.

Assuming the prehistoric social unit of a character and form of organization such as we have now described, what would occur when the chief died? Obviously everything would remain as before. The persons would be there on the same land with the same accessories. All would 'belong' together in the same way. Life would go on uninterruptedly. Under conditions which had created and maintained the circle of this community as an oasis of peace and refuge in

[262] Ihering attempts to make out a case for construing *praedium*—a probably later term for any piece of land rural or urban—to indicate that these original rural residential and agricultural landholdings were considered booty. He says, "the Latin tongue does not designate land by its salient quality (*immobilia*) but envisages it as the object of booty (*praeda*). . ." *Geist,* I, pp. 111 and 115. He relates *praedium* to *praeda* and assumes it derives from *prae-hendere.* But it is more probable that that term came into use later when real estate was offered as the basis of security (like our requirement of real property for bail bonds), and derived from *praes,* for which Walde gives the older form *praevides,* from the joining of *prae* with *vas.* See Walde, *Latin,* and Ihering, *Geist,* I, p. 112, Note 15. It seems to me that *praeda* itself conveyed at first rather the similar idea of "hostages" than the later one of "booty."

[263] In this respect we must except Bonfante whose views seem to us wholly realistic. See, especially, op. cit., I, pp. 186 ff.

a hostile world, there would be no tendency to disperse. Fission might have taken place on other occasions, under favourable circumstances, through the secession of some strong subordinate. But on this occasion the loss of their leader would only bring the orphaned community closer together.[264] The only change, the only lack, would be a chief. Thus the essential thing would be to provide in advance against this very contingency. It is evident that such provision had been developed and had gradually acquired the weight of an age-old custom, the custom of some sort of perpetual succession – a rule under which, upon the death of one, another chief automatically and immediately took his place. The existence of such an immemorial rule is testified to not only by the fact that this principle is wide-spread and enduring in the sphere of government but also because of its near universality in the sphere which later became metamorphosed into property. In the former it has remained as it was, the continuity of an office with a succession of incumbents. "Le roi est mort; vive le roi." In the latter it has been disguised – or devised again in a new form – as the concept of the continuing "legal personality."

In the earliest Roman record we find this continuity expressed in the term *suus heres*, which is usually interpreted as the "successor to his own" or perhaps "presumptive lord of his own."[265] A more con-

[264] Vinogradoff, *Jurisprudence*, I, p. 261, says, "In ancient life the principal fact governing the relations was the continuity of a family organization, and there was no compelling reason for dissolving it in connection with the death of a particular member, even if the member in question happened to be the ruler or manager of the concern."

[265] Viewing this feature as it had developed in later times helps to demonstrate its eventual significance. But I think it is clear that the concept of an interest in a body of property should not be projected back into the times when this office was wholly one of governance over persons. Poste, op. cit., p. 188, translates *suus* as self-successor, which is obviously twisting the idea of *suus* (possessive pronoun) to fit the later philosophic theory. No such theory accounts for its early use in the XII Tables. It is opposed to *extraneus*.

Girard, op. cit., p. 895, presents the matter in this way, except that he does not rid it of the idea of property. "Ils sont considérés comme succédant moins à des biens nouveaux qu'ils ne continuent une propriété préexistante, comme étant plutôt les héritiers d'eux-mêmes (*heredes sui*) que d'un tiers (*heredes ejus*)." And he holds this a mark of its antiquity because it recognizes the fact that it is a mere prolongation of the pre-existing state of the aggregate. "Ils continuent d'y vivre après la disparition de l'un d'entre eux qui d'après le régime patriarcal était leur chef. . ."

Girard, op. cit., p. 904, also emphasizes, in this idea of *suus*, the previous interest, the presumption which existed in the *heres* during the life of the *pater*. "Le *suus heres* n'acquiert pas proprement l'hérédité à la mort du père, il ne fait que continuer avec des pouvoirs plus étendus une propriété qu'il avait du vivant de celui-ci sur le patrimoine commun." And he speaks of the "vocation successorale . . . à la copropriété existant entre eux et le chef de famille."

Ihering, *Geist*, II, p. 436, having shown that early Roman law – and hardly even the late – is unable to envisage the acquisition of a single right but only the occupation of an object, undertakes to explain the reason for the exception in this case of

sistent and grammatical interpretation would be "his own successor" indicating a successor from among "his own," the "his" referring to the predecessor. Upon the analogy of the development from the term *mancipium* of the later term *mancipatio* we may, I think, presume that the original term for the heirship was *heredium* which we have already seen applied to the territory of the *familia* — the area to be governed. Certainly the later term *hereditas* meant originally, and always strictly, the "heirship" rather than the heritage, though just as in the case of the title to the position of headship to which it was presumptive — the *patrimonium* — it came in time to mean loosely that which was inherited — the *universitas rerum* or *bonorum.*[266]

universal succession *in loco defuncti.* He says, III, p. 204, ". . . der Erbe werde lediglich berechtigt, denn er überkomme nicht unmittelbar die einzelnen Rechte und Verbindlichkeiten, sondern das ideale Objekt der *hereditas,* den ökonomischen Niederschlag der Persönlichkeit des Erblassers." This explains the origin of the "legal personality" concept, which was the Roman legal philosophers' way of accounting for the facts. But the origin of the practice cannot be explained in terms of individual property. The *heres* did not acquire a group of objects. He acquired an office as head of a *familia* which continued all its assets and liabilities. The form was corporate, not personal.

Hearn, *Aryan,* p. 83, seems to me to come nearer to the early substance, though even he seems to overlook the extent to which originally the "property" consisted of persons. He says the *heres* "did not take the property for his own use : he merely acquired the defined and well-understood position of manager of the common property. He succeeded to an office, and not to an estate."

Bonfante's view, op. cit., I, p. 193, seems to me by far preferable. He interprets *suus* as meaning belonging to the family of the deceased and calls attention to the fact that the XII Tables reserves the word *heres* for *suus heres,* using the term *habeto* for others. The *suus heres* succeeded *ipso iure* not *suo iure.*

The same practice eventually resulted from the common source in Germany. As Schröder puts it, op. cit., p. 356, "Das gesetzliche Erbrecht hat seinen Ausgang von der Vermögensgemeinschaft der Hausgenossen genommen, deren Träger und alleiniger Vertreter nach aussen der Hausvater war. Der Erbe erwarb nicht ein neues Vermögen, das bis dahin dem Erblasser gehört hatte, sondern die bisher von diesem ausgeübte Verfügung und Vertretung ging auf den Erben über."

[266] *Hēres* was formerly assumed to be connected with *hĕrus,* in spite of the difference in quantity. Clark, *Regal,* p. 107, thinks this connection is still "generally though not universally admitted." And Bonfante, op. cit., I, p. 189, adopts this version. But the present accepted etymology would seem to be the one given by Walde, which allies it with the Greek cognates χῆρος (bereaved) and χᾶρος (empty space), to the root **ĝhē(i)*- (forsake, be empty). Schrader, op. cit., p. 290, coincides. He says there is no primeval term for inheritance or inherit. "The words used by the individual languages to express this idea frequently start from the sense of 'orphan,' 'orphaned.'" The other case he cites is Germ. *Erbe,* Goth. *arbi* (inheritance) ; Ir. *orbe* ('hereditas') which belong with the Latin *orbus,* Gr. ὀρφανός. It is, of course, not necessary to assume, as Walde does, that what was meant was, by analogy, a body of orphaned property. As well as the heir, the heritage — the *familia* — was at first composed wholly of persons. If the etymology is correct this is merely another confirmation of our general thesis. But to my mind the semantics are here almost incredible if the term originated as one for *suus heres.* It is difficult to see how early times could have denominated the heir apparent as "the bereaved," or have appointed the mourners while the *pater* was living and lusty. Nevertheless Vinogradoff notes, *Jurisprudence,* I, p. 228, that "in Scandinavian the same word, *erfa,* is used both for taking up an inheritance and for offering funeral prayers and rites, and

Bonfante[267] describes the "specifically Roman" feature as the indirect transmission of the patrimony as a result of the title of the heir.

Both Ihering and Schrader agree that, before the "dispersion," the process of the "son" displacing his "father" as head took place when the latter began to be incapacitated, or sooner. "Dominion belongs to him who has the power to uphold it."[268] Obviously the concept of *hereditas* did not exist at that stage, which explains the absence of a common term for it. The transaction was *inter vivos*, and probably under duress. The delay of succession until the "father's" death was then a later and, to him, advantageous step. But, whether during life or at death, the substitution was a matter of grim necessity. In the pastoral and even in the early agricultural stage there had to be an arrangement for the protection of the dependents and the continuity of the economic enterprise, as well as an assurance that the *sacra* would be performed. Only when the "family," as a group of persons and, later, as a farmstead, was finally superseded, in this connection, by a body of quick and saleable assets, could it be apportioned and dispersed or the unit discontinued. At first the *heres* acquired primarily liabilities rather than assets. He must protect and support the dependents and maintain the going concern. And this result of its origin as a political office is most clearly shown by, and particularly marks, the distinction between the *hereditas* and the modern inheritance of a body of property.[269] Even the later

erf means both 'succession' and 'funeral.'" Curtius, *Grundzüge der griechischen Etymologie*, p. 246 (Root 189, χερ), and Leist, *Zur Geschichte der romanischen Societas*, p. 22, assumed the word was *hĕrĕd-* and from the Gr. χείρ, Old Lat. *hīr*, or *īr* (hand, palm). This older etymology connected it to *herus* and thence to the idea of "grasp" or "take," whence also χείρ and *hīr*. It is also well to note that Schröder, op. cit., p. 223, Note 24, cites Sievers to the effect that "the fundamental meaning of the word *erbe* (OHG. *arbi*), later technically for land ownership, is 'cattle,'" which suggests *fihu* as the source of the German institution rather than *odil*. We treat these very doubtful constructions more fully in Appendix I A.

267 Op. cit., I, p. 138. "Le nom de l'héritier ne sert pas à désigner comme chez nous la personne à qui est attribué l'héritage en tout ou en partie, mais la personne qui doit recevoir l'institution d'héritier" (p. 188).

268 Ihering, *Aryan*, p. 33, says, "With the marriage of the eldest son the father's possessions and the household government pass into the son's hands. Brothers and sisters, even parents, henceforth have to respect him as the head of the house." He believes that the idea of "senior" is first-born, or oldest living. Schrader, op. cit., p. 379, says that when the parents became old and weak, the power and the property passed to the son. Thereafter the parents were superfluous and the custom of putting them to death appears frequently as a survival in historic times.

269 Bonfante, op. cit., I, p. 84, says, ". . . la structure du droit héréditaire romain qui, dans les origines nous présentait la désignation non d'un acquéreur du patrimoine, mais d'un successeur dans la souveraineté nommé par le *paterfamilias* pour le temps après sa mort." "L'essence objective . . . comprenait certainement, outre le patrimoine, les *sacra*, les sépulcres, le patronat sur les affranchis, les dettes du defunt" (p. 134).

Roman *heres* could not abdicate the inheritance after *aditum* (entry) and, if he was *heres necessarius*,[270] he could not abdicate it at all. His own *persona*, if he had one, merged with that of his predecessor and he acquired, with the rest, the liability for all debts, which evidently, at times, exceeded the assets. A successor was then at all times a necessity; and in earlier times this necessity was so pressing that it overrode all difficulties. Lack of a male heir warranted divorce, the marriage of a sole female heir by next of kin (compelling him to divorce his own wife) and, in the case of impotence, even the bringing in of the next of kin as breeder.[271]

What we have now assumed is the prehistoric existence of a customary rule of succession to a political office upon the death of the previous incumbent. It is begging the question to describe this rule by the later negative term "intestate succession," for such a term presupposes the prior introduction of the testament.[272] While it is impossible to set up, out of the welter of different views and contradictory judgments, an authoritative picture of the early practice of succession in Rome in historic times, I take it that some explanation and hypothesis of a gradual evolution must be inserted between this common Aryan institution of the continuing community with its succession of heads and the eventual Roman institution of devolution where the owner dealt with his property pretty much as he liked. For, during the transition, and in spite of the change to an absolute power of testation, we have to recognize a persistent influence which enabled this aggregate somehow to remain intact and to add to itself great accretions, so that we find it surviving in the great landed estates at the end of the Empire. The question divides itself into two parts. To what extent did the patrimony maintain itself intact through the customary rule—or perhaps the appointment by the *paterfamilias*—of a *single* successor—a *suus heres*? And to what extent did the *paterfamilias* have, or exercise, or acquire the right to alienate, by distributive will or legacy, part or all of that which was under his control away from this patrimony and from its automatic or selected single line of descent? These are two different questions, though they are frequently confused.

It is difficult even to found any definite judgment as to an early rule of succession in Rome. The authorities agree that there is no trace of primogeniture and most of them assume that some sort of

[270] Or, at first, even *suus heres*.

[271] See Hearn, *Aryan*, pp. 102-103.

[272] Schröder, op. cit., p. 78, refers in this way to Germany. "Jedenfalls gab es nur ein gesetzliches Erbrecht, letztwillige Verfügun waren unbekannt." So Laveleye, op. cit., p. 178, considers that testamentary disposition was completely unknown originally and that the group descended by custom.

equal sharing by all existed in the earliest as well as in later times.[278] If these shares remained undivided, this thesis requires an extraordinary application of *consortium* or *societas* to explain the holding together of the *familia*. And if they did not it is difficult to account

[278] Clark, for instance, *Regal*, pp. 107-108, finds no evidence of one principal taker or of primogeniture or of exclusion of females. Yet neither is there any mention of the children taking equally. Dionysius says the wife shared with the children. And Girard, op. cit., p. 948, Note 2, thinks the *familia* was always divided among those who were *sui iuris* except when held together as *herctum non citum*, *consortium*, or *societas bonorum*. ". . . à la mort du père chacun de ses fils a fondé un foyer séparé. . ." But Ernout and Meillet, op. cit., state that *heres* was at first only masculine ("l'enfant mâle seul pouvant hériter à l'origine").

The old term *herctum* (inheritance) and the phrases *herctum ciere* (to divide an inheritance) and *herctum non citum* (an undivided inheritance), together with the old action (or process) *familiae erciscundae*, which seems to be associated with them, all appear at first sight to be evidences that the processes of dividing the inheritance are very old. These data are the usual basis for the construction. But as to their weight see Bonfante, op. cit., I, p. 204. Though they were all applied, and adapted, to division at some period, probably by the time of the XII Tables, I think an examination of the terms indicates that they did not originate in that connection but rather had to do with the installation of a single successor. Certainly they are so ancient that, when they first appear, the terms have become garbled almost beyond recognition, and have apparently lost their original sense.

Bruns, *Fontes Iuris Romani Antiqui, Scriptores*, p. 8, quotes Festus, p. 82, "Erctum citumque (Scaliger, del. que) fit inter consortes, ut in libris legum Romanorum legitur. Erctum a 'coercendo' dictum . . . Citum . . . a 'ciendo.'" And Gellius, 1.9.12: "Anticum consortium quod iure atque verbo Romano appellabatur 'ercto non cito.'" If, as Festus suggests, *erctum* is pp. of *arceo* (*erceo*) it meant "enclosed," or perhaps "settled." But Walde finds both *herctum* and *hercisco* from *heres* and *cieo*; the former a contraction from **hero(m) *citom* and the latter of **hero(m) *cisco*. Thus the phrase *herctum ciere* or *non citum* would be a repetition of the original idea, by that time lost in the old word. Now *cieo*, or *cito*, means "to set in motion" and thence "to call or cite." It has nothing to do with dividing. If this derivation is correct the phrase meant the "citing of the *heres*" and had perhaps to do with the installation (*aditus*) of the successor, or even the settlement of the succession. I venture the suggestion that the compound in the case of *herctum* may either be *heres*, or *heredium*, or *hereditatem*, (or even, according to the new passages of Gaius, *erum*; especially since he construes *erctum* as equivalent to *dominium* rather than *hereditas*) and *citum*. Bonfante, op. cit., I, p. 193, thinks "probablement, dans le temps ancien, l'acceptation de l'hérédité ou *aditio* était toujours accomplie dans cette forme solennelle qu'aux temps historiques on appele *cretio*." Lévy-Bruhl, "La fonction du très ancien testament romain," 45 *Nouveau revue historique de droit français et étranger* (1921) pp. 634, 655, thinks the two separate. "La *cretio* n'est pas seulement un mode d'adition d'hérédité, elle est aussi et peut-être surtout un procédé de substitution." Bonfante, op. cit., I, p. 91, calls attention to the fact that the rules of the kingship were analogous, and that the king "lui-même . . . nomme (*creat*) son successeur." Now if *citum* may be construed to refer either to this *cretio* or this *creatio*, *herctum* would signify literally "the decided or nominated" *heres* or *erus*, or "the settled or appointed" *hereditas* or *heredium*. *Herctum* would then be a "settled succession," and *herctum citum* an inheritance for which the *heres* had been settled or appointed. Certainly it cannot be merely "heritage," for, as Karlowa, *Romische Rechtsgeschichte*, II, p. 914, points out, the form shows it to be verbal, so that it can only designate an act, just as *furtum* is originally not a "theft" but "stealing." The process, eventually legal, of bringing this settlement about would be the *familiae erciscundae*, "of the settling of the family succession" – of the closing of an

for the notable continuity. Muirhead[274] calls attention to the evidence that many *heredia* remained in the same families for generations and even centuries, which would seem to be impossible if the *familiae* were divided.[275] Therefore what we have to account for in Rome is extraordinary aggregation, not the reverse. It is also worthy of note that in the XII Tables *suus heres* always appears in the singular. And "the single agnate, as successor, seems rather contemplated, as the ordinary occurrence, by Gaius, in his notice of the *cessio legitimae hereditatis*."[276]

The custom of primogeniture, while it crops up repeatedly in later times, as if it were an ancient habit, is not so general that we can safely take it for granted in this case. Bonfante declares that both private and public law in Rome were ignorant of it.[277] In later Germany we find it mixed with *mainete* (succession of youngest son) and with election, in the larger political units.[278] In the Southern Slav house community the rule is election. On the other hand, the contingency which required most of the early public acts with reference to succession seems to many authorities to have been the failure or minority of the customary or selected *suus heres*. These acts were *adoptio*, perhaps *arrogatio*,[279] and perhaps the earliest three forms

estate. The occasion when this would become a joint concern of the free members of the house community may have been the instance when there was no *suus heres*, or when the heir had declined, or when for any other reason this process had not been gone through with – when, in other words, the *heres* had not been determined – *non citum*. *Herctum non citum* would therefore stand at first, not for "a *familia* not divided," but for one "not inherited," to which there was no head, and which therefore must operate as a *consortium* or *societas*, or disintegrate and disappear. And this last – a distribution – might be accomplished eventually by the same action which had originally been required for the official determination of the *heres* in disputed cases. Its later importance rested on the intrinsic difficulty, introduced by multiple *heredes*, of dividing the *persona*, so that it became the first means, along with the praedial servitudes, of attaching a liability to a fund (*fundus*, or undivided interest) rather than to a person. See Lévy-Bruhl, ibid., p. 634 and Audibert, "Nouvelle étude sur la formule des actions *familiae erciscundae* et *communi dividundo*," 28 *Nouvelle revue historique de droit français et étranger* (1904), pp. 273, 401, 649.

[274] Op. cit., p. 42.

[275] Nevertheless, Ihering, *Geist*, II, p. 150, finds that unlimited divisibility "was never, so far as we know, restrained by the laws of Rome." Divisibility of what?

[276] Clark, *Regal*, p. 119, referring to the XII Tables.

[277] Nevertheless, Vinogradoff, *Jurisprudence*, I, p. 285, says, "If *authority* is the most important element [and it certainly was in Rome] . . . then seniority and primogeniture are clearly indicated in the case of the inheritance. This is the case in all *patriarchal* arrangements." And, "there can be no doubt that the Romans started from the same principle as the other branches of the Aryan family in regard to succession: *heredes successoresque sui cuique liberi, et nullum testamentum*" (p. 289).

[278] Succession is only possible to one who has not left the home. "Wer von der Hausgenossenschaft abgeschichtet war, galt gegenüber den in der Gemeinschaft Verbliebenen als abgefunden." Schröder, op. cit., p. 357. This, says Vinogradoff, *Jurisprudence*, I, p. 285, "is an exceedingly widespread custom."

[279] *Arrogatio* "in its primary and direct signification, is the transfer of an adult and independent citizen, of course with his own consent, into the *patria potestas* of

of testament, *in comitiis calatis*, *in procinctu* and *per aes et libram.* It is assumed by many to be probable that these represented expedients to care for the exceptional cases – the emergencies – where no son, of age, was available. If any member of the *familia*, male or female, would serve, why this necessity? On the other hand, unlike Germany, where sons could separate themselves from the paternal household at majority and always did so when married, the Roman sons, the only members of the family capable of founding new houses, were, unless they were previously emancipated, incapacitated from so doing until, at the death of the *pater*, they became *sui iuris.*[280] Thereupon, if the practice was not to reserve the *familia* to a single *heres*, division would be in order, some one assuming the tutelage of the mother, unmarried sisters and minors.[281] And this would be the only means and occasion for fission in Rome.

Recognizing that there were probably wide variations in practice according to the variations in the availability of sons past majority, I am inclined to believe that the original standard Roman practice was the continuance of the patriarchal family under the headship of a single *suus heres* appointed by the father. And this largely on the ground of the Aryan heritage, the Roman emphasis on *potestas* and the indivisibility of the *persona*. This is the view of Bonfante and, while it is incapable of proof positive, it seems by far more reasonable and consistent with the data than any other.[282] In this view it was, on the one hand, the splitting of the *familia*, which had been a body

another." Clark, *Regal*, p. 373. With him went all that had been in his power. The presumed purpose was thus to secure an heir. It should be noted that, as Bonfante points out, op. cit., I, p. 133, the two universal successions *inter vivos, adrogatio* and *conventio in manum* are expressly stated by Gaius not to be mentioned in the XII Tables because they were primitive customs of the Roman *familia*. So, too, evidently, is the original *testamentum*. The XII Tables deal only with the new exceptions not with the rule as to that; legacies, *tutela* and the *actio familiae erciscundae*.

280 ". . . parental control was not ended by maturity of the son, but lasted, unless artificially determined, till the death of the father." Buckland, *Text-Book*, p. 101. "A la mort du *paterfamilias*, toujours dans la période historique, la famille se divise en autant de familles qu'il y a de *filiifamilias* immédiats du *paterfamilias*." Bonfante, op. cit., I, p. 83. But he holds (I, p. 187) that at the time of the XII Tables the gentile organization was still intact and that after the death of the *paterfamilias* "tout le group devait rester uni sous le nouveau chef désigné par le défunt."

281 If then, all women and minors in the household came under the tutelage of one of the sons, their interest remained undivided and the *familia*, to this extent, a unit under one management. Ihering, *Entw.-gesch.*, p. 57, holds that the tutelage of women past majority was not personal, and only over *familia* not *pecunia*, thus tending to the conservation of the familial fortune. This also, in his opinion, accounted for the ancient testamentary incapacity of the wife.

282 Bonfante admits the difficulty that, while appointment is "largement répandu et reconnu sans obstacles dans un grand nombre de peuples, sur toute la face de la terre," it "semble presque étranger au peuple aryen." Op. cit., I, p. 31. It is only the probability of a single heir which I ground on the Aryan heritage.

of persons on the land, needing to hold together and be protected and ruled by one *heres*, into a group of *heredes* to a body of property, still called the *familia*, which they could divide; and, on the other, the abandonment of the practice of inliving by the other sons after the death of their father; which represented the breaking down of the old patriarchal system.[283] Certainly such a putative revolution had already begun to take place by the time of the XII Tables and the term *familia* had lost its ancient meaning.[284] When, later, *heres* became *heredes* the old régime was gone.

It is evident that the earliest custom transfers the custody or guardianship of the orphaned house community, with no *suus heres*, to the gens.[285] At some later time, prior to the XII Tables, the nearest agnate is interposed. From our knowledge of medieval wardship it is not a wild presumption to hold that, as the acquisition of land and the accumulation of *pecunia* began to make this *Obervormundschaft* a perquisite, the house head would attempt to avoid the contingency. In default of an *heres*, or during the minority of his *heres*, he would wish to protect his *familia* from coming into the hands of a wastrel or being absorbed into that of another. And this, it seems to me, is the best way of accounting for the third of the early *testamenta*. None of these *testamenta* were wills. Perhaps they can be construed as anticipations of the customary action of the gens, made at the instigation of the *testator* while he was still alive.[286] He himself, with the approval of the *gentiles* as a whole or under their guaranty, chose and appointed the heir or the guardian (*tutor*) over his *familia* in the two earliest, and, before representative witnesses, the *familiae*

[283] The religious requirement would be satisfied by division among male heirs each maintaining the *sacra*. Propinquity might hold the *familia* together, but the very existence of the *gentes* shows that the custom of fission of younger houses was ancient and general. These could only begin in Rome at the death of the father. Certainly the strong would keep their range of power as wide and as enduring as possible and the development of property in land seems to have been an influence in keeping the units undivided.

[284] Pound, *Philosophy*, p. 226, refers to the fact that "in Hindu law partition is thought of as partition of the household primarily and as partition of property only incidentally." This seems to me to represent also the earlier Roman point of view.

[285] Girard, op. cit., p. 854, construes this to have been a complete power of disposition. "Antérieurement c'était le peuple qui *legebat*, qui *legem dicebat*," as to his *res*, his patrimony (*familia pecuniaque*) the tutelage of his children and the "*sort des biens*" (*tutela pucuniaque suae rei*).

[286] Girard, see Note 285, objects to the view that the term *testamentum* merely signified that it was a declaration before witnesses. Undoubtedly the early term *testis* has in it more the sense of "guarantors" than of our mere functionless witness. But it certainly does not put the authority for the act upon the witnesses (even the *comitia*). By way of the Oscan *trstus* (*testes*) the Italic primitive form **tristo* is established which, according to Solmsen (cited by Walde, *Latin*) is **tri-sto* (to stand third between two in a quarrel or in a deal). *Dritte* and *tiers*, as our "third party," have much more this functional sense than does our phrase.

emptor, as agent and custodian (executor and trustee), in the latest.[287] In this way the early testament may be regarded as a means of avoiding the ancient custom of *manus-mund*, (in Rome, *tutela*) at the time

[287] So far as I know, we have no certain knowledge as to whether the appointment in the two earliest was of an *heres* or only of a guardian. But the fact, to which Bonfante, op. cit., I, p. 188, calls attention, that even in later law no testament was valid which did not appoint an heir, would indicate that, from the beginning, this was the prime purpose and the guardianship was an interim appointment during the minority of the heir only. While the status of the purchaser of the *familia* in mancipatory testament is disputed, it seems to me that Gaius' account of the words he used, "*famili(a) pecuni(a)que tu(a) endo mandatela(m) custodela(m)que mea(m)*," is conclusive. That also jibes with our relation of *mandatum* to *manus*. Buckland, *Text-Book*, p. 283, says, ". . . what is said to be bought or acquired is not the property but the guardianship of it." Gaius, 2. 103, does say that "*heredis locum obtinebat*." But he does not say that he *was* the *heres*. Girard, op. cit., p. 856, says, "Dans la première phase, la *mancipatio familiae* n'était pas un véritable testament ; *l'emptor familiae* était seulement *loco heredis, heredis locum obtinebat*." Appleton, *Le testament romain*, p. 125, has shown that this mancipation was probably transformed into the testament *per aes et libram* in the sixth century (of Rome). There is, however, a seductive resemblance between the original process and that described in the Lex Salica, Title XLVI, which suggests that this was the ancient and general Aryan mode of assuring the desired succession *via* a trustee or executor. In fact it is tempting to assume that the origin of the word *testamentum* in *testis* is the same as the origin of the word *trust*, whence *trustee*. See Note 286, above.

If so, the so-called *testamentum per aes et libram* was not at that time a *testamentum* at all, since it appointed no heir. This conclusion seems to accord with Bonfante's view. See op. cit., I, p. 494. He says the later *testamentum per mancipationem* "a été établi par la jurisprudence, convertissant en un testament l'alienation fiduciare de son patrimoine (*mancipatio familiae*) que faisait, en faveur d'un ami, à la probité duquel il s'en remettait pour l'exécution de ses dernières volontes, celui qui était surpris par une fin imminente, sans avoir eu le temps de faire son testament dans les formes publiques et légales et aux jours fixés. . ."

In this view it remains possible to consider that the *suus heres* was automatic, not appointive ; to admit that the power of true testament (including legacy) was limited to the minor accessories, the *pecunia tutelave* ; but to hold that this *tutela* embraced not only those running to the testator but also the appointment of that one who would be *tutor* to his after his death ; and finally to reconcile this incapacity to divert the *familia* from the customary line with the fact that in section four of the Table it may be assumed *e converso*, that there is in the testator power to defeat the right of the agnate or the gens, not by creating an *heres* (which would be breaking away from the customary line), but only by creating a substitute guardianship in an *emptor* by mancipatory testament, or in some specified person by other will. But the strongest point against the existence of the power of appointment of an *heres* at the time of the XII Tables is that, if a *suus heres* could be appointed, the word *intestato* is redundant in section four. It would be enough to say "if there is no *suus heres*." In other words *suus heres* does not seem to be limited to an appointive heir. Vinogradoff, *Jurisprudence*, I, pp. 291-292 thinks the appointment of an heir was unusual, was reserved for cases of *exheredatio* and that explains the later requirement of *exheredatio*. But Bonfante, op. cit., I, p. 496, explains this as a later requirement "par réaction au droit absolu de tester du *paterfamilias*, qui, après avoir perdu sa signification primitive, pouvait être utilisé au prejudice de la famille. . ." It is possible to harmonize these two views by following Levy-Bruhl, op. cit., p. 634. He distinguishes three groups, the *heredes sui* and the *agnati* – conceived in the Greek sense of *domus* – and finally the *gentiles*. ". . . le testateur ne peut choisir son héritier que parmi ses *sui heredes*, ou, à défaut, parmi des agnats. . ." (p. 645). He could not go outside the *domus*.

when it had begun to be disadvantageous or abused, and of providing for the maintenance and protection of the *familia* as a separate unit."[288] Perhaps from the beginning the heir was appointive, as he certainly was later; perhaps not.[289] At any rate he was probably single. If he was always appointive then testamentary preceded intestate succession and the latter occurred merely in default of the former. If he was at first determined by a rule, then customary succession preceded both, and the field occupied by the later rules of intestacy was merely that of the prior rule of custom – though largely invoked only in default of both a *suus heres* and a testament. The evidence of the record up to and including the XII Tables does not seem to prove either.

Our second question bears on the power of the "father" to leave some of that which was under his control, away from this appointed or customary line of descent. Such a question concerns the beginnings of testamentary division – the substitution of *heredes* for *heres* – which we have already discussed; and it concerns legacies. The latter term is derived from *lex*, which shows the route through which the practice arose. But I judge that few will hold that *legassit*, in the XII Tables, already meant anything more definite than "he had

[288] Ihering, *Geist*, I, p. 207, thinks the effort to introduce the testament in place of *Intestaterbrecht* was due to a natural reaction of family affection to the artificial legal-constituted family. "Bei den vorrömischen Völkern hemmte die Familie die testamentarische Freiheit, bei den Römern treibt sie durch ihre teilweise verschobene Stellung hervor. . ." But Bonfante, op. cit., I, p. 188, points out that testament and *adrogatio* are the only acts of which one can establish the existence in the Regal period.

[289] Hearn, *Aryan*, p. 105, thinks the origin of testament was the appointment of an heir, failing a natural one. And Clark holds, too, that he was appointive. He says, *Regal*, p. 445, in the case of the testament *in procinctu*, "In such a moment there would be little time to do more than name a *heres*; and probably in the *testamentum comitiis calatis* a selection among the persons, who would naturally have taken on intestacy, was all that was competent to the earliest testators." This point fits as well the theory that it was a *tutor* not an *heres* who was so appointed. Girard, op. cit., pp. 850-852, takes the position that testament was not only from the beginning the naming of an heir (not tutor or trustee), and not merely in default of a natural one, nor merely a division of some goods (legacy), but that it was a full-fledged modern system at the time of the XII Tables. He does recognize a previous custom, however, "le testament étant une dérogation à la loi générale des successions comme l'adrogation est une dérogation à la loi générale de la famille . . ." (p. 852). This *loi générale* was surely at the time but an ancient and unwritten custom. But see Muirhead, op. cit., p. 154, giving what seems to me the soundest reasoning for placing the development of the power of appointing an heir in the later interpretation of the XII Tables. Cuq, also, *Les institutions juridiques des Romains*, I, pp. 124-125, says that the liberty of appointing an heir "n'existait pas encore, à notre avis, au temps des Douze Tables." The text "ne fait pas la moindre allusion à l'institution d'héretier." And it would have been inconsistent with "la conservation de certains biens de famille," though hardly inconsistent with the conservation of the family itself.

publicly declared." Such at first is the sense of the word *lex*.[290] And this instance seems but the usual occasion of a "private law." In general we may cite the view of Clark as fairly representative. He thinks that the alienation of the *familia* (by legacy?) away from the *heres* was not allowed in the Regal period (though perhaps alienation *inter vivos* was),[291] but that "other property (the *pecunia* or *res nec mancipi*) might be left away from the *heres* by *legatum* even at the beginning."[292] In general there seems to me to be no evidence prior to the XII Tables that permanent alienation of any part of the *familia* away from the customary line of devolution was possible.[293] "Ancient society, and in this expression Rome is to be included at some time prior to the XII Tables, admits slowly the power of free alienation."[294] And, at the time of the XII Tables, it was just beginning. The beginning seems to have been made with the *pecunia* and the *tutelae*. The patrimony itself—the *familia*—still automatically followed the line of political succession to a single officer.[295] When the

[290] Yet Clark, *Regal*, p. 448, seems to assume that the legacy, not the appointment of a *tutor* or an *heres*, was a new power confirmed at the time of the XII Tables. Of course the word *legatum* and the verb *legare* eventually referred to legacies. But that its sense was originally not so circumscribed is evidenced by the term *legatus* with the sense of public appointment. Cuq, op. cit., I, p. 124, assumes that the word used would have been *testare* if more than a legacy was intended. On the other hand Bonfante says, op. cit., I, p. 192, that the testament was never a law; "il se réfère à une époque où le concept d'une puissance législative du peuple et d'une loi au sense propre . . . n'était pas encore né."

[291] *Regal*, p. 544-545.

[292] *Regal*, p. 223. Ihering, *Entw.-gesch.*, pp. 88-90, cites cases of the free disposition of *pecunia* and the inalienability of *familia*. Laveleye, op. cit., p. 178, took the view that testation was late and then, at first, the testator could will only what he had acquired but not what had come by descent. "The same distinction," he says, "appears both in the old and the new customary laws of France, between the *héritage* and the *acquêts ainsi que les meubles*." And Schröder, curiously dividing from the *Erbrecht* all succession to the family headship, says of the Germans, op. cit., p. 77, "Das Erbrecht beschränkte sich, solange es kein Sondereigentum an Grund und Boden gab, auf die fahrende Habe. Innerhalb der Hausgenossenschaft bestand Gütergemeinschaft, so dass der Tod eines Mitgleides nur ein unentziehbares Anwachsungsrecht zugunsten der übrigen, aber kein eigentliches Erbrecht begründete." It is this indivisibility which we have construed, not on grounds of property but of continuing political unity, in Rome. He also, p. 357, refers to the Lex Salica, "die ein eigentliches Erbrecht nur bei der Fahrnis (*alodis*) kannte," though he admits that "der Grundbesitz ging zwar auf die Söhne über."

[293] The instances given by Ihering, *Geist*, II, p. 437, are all temporary and the residual title remains at home. So mancipation of those in power (5 years); creation of the servitudes (retaining *dominium*); the creation of *obligatio*, retaining right of *vindex*; the creation of *tutela*.

[294] Hunter, op. cit., p. 258.

[295] Bonfante, op. cit., I, p. 133, holds that the phrase relates "à la liberté, accordée alors pour la prémière fois, d'ajouter des libéralités dans l'acte solennel par lequel on désigne son héritier et à la faculté, nouvelle peut-être, elle aussi, de conférer l'office de tuteur à d'autres qu'à l'heritier." He says, p. 184, that "peut-être, avant les Douze Tables, l'héritier lui-même était nécessairement le tuteur," and that

newer liberties as to the former intruded also into the sphere of the latter, they joined with the simultaneous conversion of the *suus heres* into *sui heredes* to destroy the patriarchal system and convert the *familia* into owners and owned. Certainly when we first see the ancient rule of succession to an office appearing in the law it is already in process of disappearing into the new system for the inheritance of wealth, wherein the distinction between the patrimony, the real property—*familia*—now coming to be confined to land and slaves, and the personal property—*pecunia*—is lost. If this thesis is correct then the origin of the modern system was the legacy, not the testament.

C. *The External Relations of the House Community*

These house communities, the early character of which we have attempted to depict, while apparently they were the fundamental and persisting autonomous political units of prehistoric times, had no permanent delimitation. Constantly dividing by fission, there remained relations of attenuated propinquity with neighbouring units, and in times of stress or movement, the military organization doubtless encroached upon their independence and ended their comparative isolation. Thus there must always have been relations, religious, political and economic, between such loosely grouped aggregates of house communities, called *gentes* or tribes. The most important formalities concerned with these relations or dealings between particular house communities—or their respective heads, as representatives—seem to have given rise to the earliest forms which appear in the law. If we consider the law as beginning with the effective constitution of a permanent and established super-familial organization, which begins to convert traditional customs into express rules with some machinery for their enforcement, then we must agree that these earlier transactions between individual groups preceded law. While we are concerning ourselves at this point with the pre-legal organization of Roman society, and will therefore attempt to present these formal transactions as they may have existed at that stage, it is necessary to recognize that practically all we know of them is derived from their appearance and survival in later law.

The most important of these forms are *mancipatio*, the transfer of *manus*; *nexum*, the personal bond; *stipulatio*, the formal promise; and *mutuum*, the informal loan. Out of the first arises the formal

"la disposition célèbre *uti legassit* . . . sanctionne probablement une nouveauté, c'est-à-dire que pour la première fois la tutelle se détache de l'hérédité et le *paterfamilias* peut désigner dans son testament une personne distincte de l'héritier pour la charge de tuteur" (p. 185).

conveyance, or deed; out of the others the contract of later times. The older authorities, seeking the source of contract, took different views. Savigny found the origin of *stipulatio* in *mutuum*; Maine and Ortolan held that it began with *nexum*; and Hunter, for example, held all three original. We shall see, in the more recent view, warrant for believing that *nexum* arose from, or was one with, *mancipatio*, that *stipulatio* was original and that *mutuum* was not a form at all, but merely a commercial practice not recognized in the law until much later.[296]

1. *"Mancipatio"* – *The Transfer of "Manus"*

We have already identified *mancipatio*, under its supposed earlier name *mancipium*, with the *manus*-system, and have conceived it as representing the transfer of all those elements of the original patriarchal group which were conceived as coming within the classification of *membership*. It signified the "taking under familial power." When the group had come to be regarded as an inseparable unit upon the land – the *familia* – then land and the permanent agricultural essentials became naturally, as we have seen, identified with the previously altogether human elements and were incorporated as part of the *familia*. All such were *res mancipi*. The herds and flocks and their institutional offspring were merely accessories, separable and transitory. These were the *pecunia* and were *res nec mancipi*.

Ihering conceives the deed of *mancipatio*, the transfer of *manus* before witnesses, to have been of Roman origin, according to much the same view we have adopted. He suggests, however, that the actual ceremony which accompanied it, the use of the copper and the balances (*aes et libram*) and the presence of the *libripens* (scale-holder) was of Babylonian origin, introduced to Rome by the Carthaginians, much as the practices of the law merchant were later introduced into England from the Continent.[297] This plausible suggestion raises the question whether it was only in respect of this

[296] *Nexum* and *stipulatio* were both of great antiquity, but the latter did not become of importance in law until after *nexum* had been abolished. *Mutuum* arrives still later, during the late Republic. But, on account of the general reluctance of primitive law to recognize the contract, this is not indicative of the respective ages of the economic processes involved. Muirhead, op. cit., p. 205, believes the *stipulatio* was legalized later than the time of the XII Tables, and states that with the rise of the *ius gentium*, advance of money as a loan put the borrower under obligation without stipulation (p. 258). Hunter also believes *mutuum* was "a substitute, not for the *nexum*, but for the *stipulatio*." Op. cit., p. 530.

[297] *Aryan*, p. 204, Note 1. Clark, *Regal*, p. 570, assumes that *mancipium* was adopted as a legal process at the time of the Servian reform. And Cornil, op. cit., p. 28, supposes that its extension from the original and only antique use in transferring slaves and cattle, was the work of the pontiffs.

feature of the ceremony that *mancipatio* was allied to other transfers *per aes et libram*, such as *nexum*, *coemptio*, *adoptio*, *emancipatio*, and the *testamentum* of that form – whether, in other words, the ceremony became merely a method of "signing and sealing" all important conveyances. I think not. *Coemptio* and the testament transferred *manus* or *mandatum* respectively, which seems to identify them with the *manus*-system; *emancipatio* was a release from *manus*; and *adoptio* transferred the successor to *manus*, *potestas*. The more recent view of *nexum*, which we shall present, seems also related in other ways.[298] In this view, then, *mancipatio* is the prototype of all formal conveyance in Roman law and the pure survival of the most primitive ceremony which effected that parlous business of making a change in the *propinquity* of a member of the earliest group.[299] It was the only means sufficient to overcome the prestige of the classificatory genitive, which seemed to have had its basis in the very nature of things. Yet in the end it became, as Gaius says,[300] "an imaginary sale," functioning rather as the "signing and sealing" of certain important legal acts. And *traditio*, the mere physical transfer, which had been derived from the practices concerned with the less important *pecunia*, became the focal point of the system of conveyance.

2. *"Nexum" – The Personal Bond*

It was evident in our description of the operation of the presumed pre-legal process of *manus iniectio* that the ordinary recourse, in the case of debt or delict, was for the creditor – or injured party – to take possession of the person of the debtor – or wrong-doer – or to have him delivered in person by noxal surrender. Thereupon, if in the first instance a *vindex* had not interposed, the debtor became subject to the creditor who could punish him as he chose, or retain him *in servitio*. It is evident from this and many other sources that no distinction was made between a delict and the failure to repay a debt when due. The latter was viewed as an injury of the same order as theft.[301]

[298] See Muirhead, op. cit., p. 66.

[299] *Adrogatio*, the merging of one *familia* in another, is said by Bonfante, op. cit., I, p. 180, to have had its "counterpart in the annexation of a state." See Cornil, op. cit., pp. 39-41, as a demonstration of the great difficulty of altering these natural ties.

[300] I. 119.

[301] In this connection it is interesting to note that in the various early translations of the Bible, the phrase in the Lord's Prayer reads sometimes, "Forgive us our debts," and sometimes "Forgive us our trespasses." The two were hardly discriminated. Ihering notes, *Aryan*, p. 54, Note 4, that Skt. *ṛṇa* means both "guilty," or "thief," and "debt," or "loan."

Pound, *Philosophy*, p. 244, says that, in early Indian law "the debtor is looked

When, with the beginning of legal processes, it became necessary to secure the sanction of the *sacramentum* before applying *manus iniectio*, a system appears to have been developed, which by prejudging the case—or publicly acknowledging the debt—provided the sanction for *manus iniectio* in advance without further legal action.[802] Thus the old practice was legitimized by mutual agreement beforehand. This arrangement was called *nexum*, and the person so prejudged was, in the case of debt at least, called the *nexus* or *nectus*.[803]

There is a close relation between this old practice of proceeding for debt, just as for delict, against the body of the debtor[804]—which here reappears merely under a new name[805]—and the sale of the person or of a dependent by *mancipium*, which gave rise to the special status of that name. And *nexum* was effected by the same means—"an imaginary sale," *per aes et libram*. Perhaps it was another name or another aspect of the same act. This is the warrant for the previously mentioned identification of early debtor slavery with *mancipium*.[806] The *necti* seem like bond-servants,[807] and it is even a question whether the creditor did not immediately assume some sort of power over the debtor.[808] In the legendary final case mentioned by Livy, it would appear that the *nectus* was in the *familia* of the creditor before ever the debt was in default. Moreover in that case it is the

on as one who wrongfully withholds from the creditor the latter's property and hence as some sort of thief." This is decidedly Bonfante's view of the Roman origins. See op. cit., I, pp. 220 ff.

802 See Girard, op. cit., p. 31. Muirhead, op. cit., p. 87, says, ". . . a borrower gave his creditor the right to apprehend him on his failure to fulfill his obligation of repayment and, without any process of law, carry him home and detain him, and employ his services as *de facto* (though not *de iure*) a slave." He was *servitus* not *servus*.

803 This is one of the words so frequent in Latin legal phraseology which connotes the idea "to bind." It is derived from *necto* (to bind) of which the etymology is uncertain; see Walde, *Latin*. Perhaps, in the case of delict, he was distinguished as *addictus*.

804 Sohm, *The Institutes*, Trans. p. 287, says "The aim of execution in the old times was not, as it is nowadays, primarily to satisfy the creditor, but rather to punish the debtor. . ."

805 Clark, *Regal*, p. 570, refers to the "personal *nexus*, a remarkable species of bond, which appears to have been developed in practice at some time posterior to the Servian adoption of *mancipium*, and prior to the legislation of the XII Tables."

806 Bonfante refers to *nexum* and *mancipium* as perhaps the same thing (op. cit., I, p. 134) or at least as signifying the same act (op. cit., I, p. 221).

807 Varro, *De Lingua Latina*, 7. 105, says, "Liber, qui suas operas in servitutem pro pecunia quam debebat, dum solveret, nexus vocatur. . ." This indicates that he performed work as a *servitus*—the term for debtor slavery.

808 See Brinz, "Der Begriff *obligatio*," 1 *Zeitschrift für das privat- und öffentliche Recht* (1874), pp. 11, 22. Bonfante, op. cit., I, p. 222, assumes that, as in *mancipatio fiduciae causa*, "la personne ainsi vendue était d'ordinaire laissée, elle aussi, dans un état de liberté de fait précaire," but since "juridiquement elle était asservie au créancier, celui-ci conservait la faculté de s'en emparer à n'importe quel moment."

son of the debtor who is *nectus,* as if he were a hostage (or *praeda,* pledge) given at the time the debt was incurred.[809] Certainly, at that time, *nectus* was the general name for debtors in *pecunia credita;* they could be kept in fetters;[810] and the term for their liability was *corpus obnoxium* – literally "guilty of, and corporeally punishable for, *pecunia credita.*"[811]

While the feature of *nexum,* as a tentative condemnation serving as the prerequisite for a money loan, or as the acknowledgement of a delictual debt, is perhaps the principal one, it is worthy of note that among the older authorities dealing with this much discussed subject there were some who found for it a different origin – in an incompleted exchange – and who made it in turn the source of certain other forms of legal security connected with contract. The idea that it was a bilateral transaction, a mancipation, but conditional – that, in fact, it was a personal *mancipatio fiduciae causa* or exactly similar to it – seems to be repugnant to the legal mind.[812] Nevertheless that view seems tenable. In general it is that of Maine.[813] Thus *nexum* occurred when any two persons committed themselves to a transaction *per aes et libram* – that is, in the form of a purchase and sale (*mancipium*). It ceased and the two *nexi* (or the one *nectus*) were released if the exchange were completed at once. If not the one who had not completed his part in the exchange remained *nexus,* or bound.[814] Therefore *nexum* is conceived to have been the obligatory (juridical) element of any formal exchange which continued until the exchange was completed, or until matters were restored to

809 Livy actually says "*se dedisset*" (had given himself). Muirhead, op. cit., p. 146, assumes that the father was deceased.

810 Livy, 6. 36. 12, speaks of the patricians' houses having become like private prisons.

811 See Livy, 8. 28. 8.

812 This was the interpretation of Neibuhr. So Sohm, op. cit., p. 59, construes it. But Cuq, op. cit., I, p. 117, Note 7, cites opinions to the effect that loan and pledge were two separate transactions. I think we may visualize *nexum* as a mancipation of a person or object, upon a conditional *nuncupatio.* All *mancipatio* had this element in it, since title was never acquired by the bare form. The material completion of exchange was necessary (Sohm, loc. cit.). And Cuq, op. cit., p. 116, Note 6, shows that the word was used as if *nexum* were the juridical, or obligatory, feature of all mancipation. Certainly the two terms are much confused. But the semantic identity of *nexum* and *obligatio* seems to me to warrant this view. Muirhead, op. cit., App. Note C, seems to hold that *fiducia* (as security) was the *nectus* (person) or *res nexa* (hypothecated object) to be delivered when demanded under an obligation to restore when the whole transaction was placed *in statu quo ante*; just as the *nexum aes* was the debt – perhaps a loan, perhaps the unpaid purchase price of a sale, and perhaps a debt incurred in any other way.

813 *Ancient Law,* pp. 305 ff.

814 Not bound, be it noted, to complete the transaction, but bound to surrender what he had received if he did not complete the transaction. So, in an incompleted mancipation the buyer could not compel delivery but only the return of his money. This, in turn, makes an incompleted exchange even closer to a loan; see infra.

their previous condition. And Maine says, "if it be true that, both in the popular and in the professional view, a *Contract* was long regarded as an *incomplete Conveyance*,"[315] it is consistent to hold that this source is "the Nexum, in which a Contract and a Conveyance are blended."[316]

The reconciliation of these two seemingly opposed views – the one that this earliest known contract covered only the advance condemnation, or that together with the money loan or debt, and, the other, that it arose from an incompleted exchange, a conveyance by one party requiring a later conveyance by the other and in the meantime submitting this latter to personal bondage – while it may present technical legal difficulties in accounting for the history of the divergence, is merely a matter of eliminating preconceived ideas. Originally a sale and a loan were identical in appearance. Money or other object was bartered on one side for some object or person on the other. Whether the party of the first part delivered as purchase price or as loan, and whether the party of the second part delivered as sale or as pledge, did not appear evident. The two were indistinguishable except as, according to the expressed intention of the parties (*nuncupatio*), it was made evident that the sale was a permanent exchange, while the loan was a temporary one. We may take it, I think, that originally loans were always also exchanges, exchanges of a pledge for the object loaned; the pledge either of an object, or of the (or of a) person of the borrower,[317] or of a surety who became

[315] *Ancient Law*, p. 311.

[316] *Ancient Law*, p. 327. It should be noted that Maine assumed that *nexum* originally covered the conveyance and that *mancipatio* was a special term used later, when the former had gone over to contract. The current view would, I think, reverse this process. But this seems a mere dispute over terms. Referring to this as the general source of at least all Roman contract, Justice Holmes says, *Papers*, p. 217, "Sohm, following a thought first suggested, I believe, by Savigny and made familiar by Maine in his *Ancient Law*, sees the beginning of contract in an interrupted sale."

[317] Sohm, op. cit., p. 64, Note 16, says, "German law confirms the view that all the oldest contracts originated in some kind of pledge (obligatio), whether of one's person or of portions of one's property." The English word "borrow" confirms this view. It is derived from words for pledge or security, whence also "burg," as fortress.

While it is not safe to argue too far upon the ground of comparative law and while I have confined myself in the text to a statement of the generally accepted – the new and the old – views on this subject, I venture to suggest that the end of the *nexum* controversy will consist in the confirmation of Niebuhr's theory by identifying *nexum* with the Germanic *wed*. This would construe it as not so much a personal bond as a development of the idea of hostage, a sale of the person subject to defeasance. On this subject see Wigmore, "The Pledge-Idea: A Study in Comparative Legal Ideas," 10 *Harvard Law Review* (1897), pp. 321, 389; 11, p. 18. "Since the *wed*, in its original form, was the transfer with a right, but no duty, on the transferor's part, to redeem, it might seem a not inaccurate description to call it a sale with right to repurchase (*Verkauf auf Wiederkauf*, *vente à réméré*)" (10, p. 389). Thus it was a conditional sale; not the purchase of an article on credit,

thereby himself personally pledged.[818] In fact the same held true of a sale on credit.[819] In no other way was the "haver" originally induced to part willingly with his possessions, either as a loan or as a sale on credit. Thus this interpretation does not require Maine's anachronistic supposition of the prior arrival of the idea of legal liability. The liability (*ligo* = bind), or *obligatio* (*ligo*) or *nexum* (*necto* = bind) was physical, or potentially so. These two forms of debt, a loan and a sale on credit, equally constituted *pecunia credita.* So did the price of composition for a delict until it was paid. What would be more natural than that, in the beginnings of law, the method of contracting and securing debt voluntarily incurred should, in the earlier stages of economic activity, graft itself upon the seedling of the peaceful method of composing for delict, particularly since the default on debt was itself construed as a delict? Later distinctions must not blind us to the original identity. The delictual nature, the contractual nature, the aspect of prejudgment, and the aspect of personal bond all seem to be phases or characteristics inextricably woven together in a *mélange* of pristine crudities.[820]

nor the purchase of a person with money, but the purchase of an article or money with the person. It was effected with or without possession of the pledge and at first without a clear title. The pledgor's right had to be foreclosed. Really the condition was precedent. The natural overcame the artificial *manus*. And the pledge – or hostage – was redeemable at any time.

In early Germanic law Wigmore, 10, p. 334, says "complete transfer of a property-right involved three distinct elements,– the sale or *traditio*, the *gewere* or *investitura*, and the *Verzicht, uplaten, werpitio, dewerpitio, Auflassung* or *resignatio*." The first two merged as delivery; the third was abandonment. A sale included both; a life estate and a pledge did not include abandonment. This division must remind us of the difficulties to be overcome in the case of altering a 'belonging' which were referred to on page 114, Note 299. Also it is worthy of note that *werpitio*, which we discussed in connection with *manus*, is the equivalent of abandonment. Wigmore remains on safer ground; relating *wed* to *pignus*, not to *nexum*. He suggests, 11, p. 23, that *pignus* was "the generic term for the subject, like *wed* in Germanic usage;" says, p. 31, that "the Sale-for-Repurchase form is represented in Roman law by *fiducia*," which effected a conditional transfer by mancipation or (?) *in iure cessio*; and calls attention to the fact (p. 32, Note 1) that the sale of the pledge in either case required *denuntiatio*. I suspect that the original Roman term was *praeda*.

818 As to sureties see next section on *stipulatio*.

819 Bonfante thinks that there were no early sales on credit. See op. cit., I, p. 221. But this is an extreme view.

820 On the other hand, it would be quite consistent with the surviving traces, and far more consistent with the significance of early Celtic and Teutonic practices, to construe the whole of early Roman contract in exactly the opposite way. If we suppose (with Frank, for instance) the immediately prehistoric organization of Roman society to have had something more of the nature of the semi-feudal character of pre-Roman Gaul – conglomerates of households under a chief – then it might appear that the original fact was the personal bond, the labour service owed, a sort of property over the person owned by the lord. And *pecunia credita* may have been originally "cattle (not money) entrusted." If now the Mediterranean influence should have introduced to early Roman society the beginnings of a money economy – the copper and the scales – then we might read into the earliest apparent contract

This leads us directly to the second point, the development from *nexum* of other contracts of a not dissimilar character, covering the transfer out of possession of objects, with the obligation of return. We have already seen that in the later classic law the term *res nexa* was frequently used as a general term for objects pledged. The relation to *mancipatio fiduciae causa* seems to have been close. Hunter says, "It is also a fact that certain contracts – such as *depositum* [custody] and *pignus* [pledge] – were derived from the ancient *nexum*.[321] On the whole it seems to me we can agree with Sohm[322] that "nexum and [perhaps] mancipatio fiduciae causa were the original sources of real contracts."[323]

3. "*Stipulatio*" – *The Original Formal Promise*

The formal verbal promise, which took its place somewhat later in the developing Roman law of contract, was *stipulatio*. It appears to be a compound.[324] The name seems to come from one source, new or old, and the content from another. Perhaps it was first called *sponsio*.[325] At any rate the ancient ceremonials (the *sponsiones*)

a commutation of labour service, perhaps combined with a commutation of the chief's claim over the cattle.

On this construction the personal bond becomes the principal not the accessory of the contract – and the *pecunia credita* becomes its commuted form. If the latter is not paid, then by the simplest and most primitive thinking the original status, of bondage or of vassalage, is restored.

321 Op. cit., p. 538.

322 Op. cit., p. 374.

323 It will not do to leave the subject of *nexum* without at least a brief reference to the intensive study which has been given to this institution and the resulting perennial controversy. In general Niebuhr proposed the interpretation of a self-sale (*mancipium*) under a suspensive condition – substantially a pledge – and a resolutive condition – the *solutio* upon payment. Huschke, on the other hand, outlined the interpretation of the prejudgment. On this basis *nexum* bore the same relation to *iudicatum* that *mancipatio* bore to *in iure cessio*. Mitteis proposed, and then rejected his suggestion, that there were two *nexa* – the loan and the bondage – but then reverted to a similar construction to that of Niebuhr. Becker, finally, revised Huschke's version along lines substantially those now given by Girard and others. I am told there are still more recent modifications with which, however, I am not at this writing familiar. One makes a moving picture, not a portrait, of the current thesis as to *nexum*. For much of the foregoing analysis the writer is indebted to the most complete summary of this subject, in English, known to him. See F. de Zulueta, "The Recent Controversy about Nexum," 29 *Law Quarterly Review* (1913), p. 137.

324 The name was derived by Paul from *stipulum* (firm). But this seems too abstract to be consistent with early Roman terminology. Ihering, *Geist*, II, p. 558, Note 747, connects it with *stips* (gift, money) which he says comes from Sanskrit root **sthâ*, from which also "staff." And the Latin *stipula* means straw. This has led to identification with the various symbolic acts of staff reaching or straw throwing which we have seen described by Schröder, op. cit., p. 65. This is a tempting connection; particularly in view of the probable religious source of the form and the well known antiquity of Roman religious practices.

325 See Leist, *Graeco-italische Rechtsgeschichte*, pp. 465-470.

which it apparently adopted, were of religious origin,[326] connected at first with sacrificial libations (σπονδή), treaties of peace, betrothals,[327] etc., and brought to Rome, perhaps from Greece, perhaps from other Aryan sources.[328] It is assumed that the religious significance was retained, though the promise no longer continued the old form of the oath — the ancient self-curse.[329] It is this which leads Sohm to say that[330] *stipulatio* resembled *nexum* in so far as the underlying idea in both was "originally a kind of self-pledge"; but it differed from *nexum* in that the pledge implied in *stipulatio* "could only be enforced by the gods."

This introduces, and creates a convenient place for a brief mention of, the subject of third person guaranties, which seem to have formed so important and original an element in early law. Without attempting to unravel the complex and disputed technical relationship, it is safe to say that just as *stipulatio* eventually became almost wholly a means of contracting sureties, so it is quite possible that it commenced to be used in law for that purpose. Certainly *adstipulatio* and *adpromissio* — the latter both by *sponsores* (*sponsio*) and by *fideipromissores* — were of great antiquity.[331] We have seen that the probable original meaning of the term *testis* (witness) was "to stand third." That was no empty form. The witness assumed a liability. Almost he *praestat* — that is, according to Walde, he "stood responsible" for him ("*bürge fur etwas*").[332] *Vadimonium*, which was "one of the formal contracts of the XII Tables"[333] was the earliest legal contract of surety. And *praes*, as we have suggested, seems to have been an outgrowth of it, and to have had the connotation of "hostage." In Bonfante's view the legal origin of obligation — the bond — was in connection with the guarantor not the debtor. He says[334] that, in

[326] Ihering, *Geist*, I, p. 311, contrasts *sponsio*, from the religious system, with *nexum*, from the profane system, in his presentation of the traces of both in the later law.

[327] Originally, in exogamous marriage, a formal treaty between two polities, two house communities. It is this use which leads Hunter, op. cit., p. 525, to say, "Hence, in betrothal, an extremely ancient institution, we find the opposition between contract and conveyance, between promise and property. This distinction, if Sulpicius is right, corresponded with that between *stipulatio* and *mancipatio*."

[328] See Muirhead, op. cit., p. 206 and Goudy's Note 8.

[329] At first "if one had called on the gods to witness his promise or sworn to fulfill it, he was liable to pontifical discipline. The presence of an impious oath breaker was a social danger." Pound, *Philosophy*, p. 245. The gods were supposed to wreak their vengeance for such impieties on the community, not on the individual.

[330] Op. cit., p. 64.

[331] See Buckland, *Text-Book*, pp. 443 ff.

[332] *Praes* (the security, or a surety — the one who *praestat*) is a contraction (Walde, *Latin*) of *prae-vides* from *prae-vas*. *Vas* is allied with Goth. *wadi* (pledge), AS. *wedd* (promise, pledge), whence *vadimonium*.

[333] Muirhead, op. cit., p. 252, Note 23.

[334] Op. cit., I, pp. 224-225.

the beginning, personal guaranties (*praes, vas* and *vindex*) represented a state of obligation analogous to *nexum*, and that originally the guarantor only was bound. Thus the debt and the obligation were separate. Eventually the obligation became conjoined with the debt by the curious means that the debtor in effect became his own *vas, praes* or *vindex*.

Thus *stipulatio* is intimately associated, not only with the introduction into Roman law of the unilateral promise, which has had so great an influence on the Roman law of contract and on the juridical ideas built upon it, but it is also intimately associated with the system of third party guaranty which is one of the principal primeval elements from which the law of contract evolved.

4. "*Mutuum*" – *The Informal Loan of Money*

The last of the original sources of contract to appear in the purview of the law was *mutuum*. Bonfante considers it, according to his thesis already described, the first form of obligation which was truly contractual, though this too retained a penal character.[335] Muirhead says[336] that the loan of money, and of other things returnable generically, was at first effected by *nexum*. When this was abolished for the purpose, the loan was effected by stipulation. Only with the rise of the *ius gentium* did the loan itself become actionable on its own merits, and "the *res* – in this case the giving and receiving of *mutui causa* – completed the contract." Thus it is the first of the contracts which are called, from this word *res*, *real* contracts. Such real contracts are "contracted *re*."[337] By which term are distinguished those obligations which are contracted, not by a form (viz. *nexum* or *stipulatio*), but from a fact, or act, or thing. "This fact, or *res*, consisted in the delivery by one person to another of some property, with the intention of imposing duties on the receiver."[338] And this giving constituted a transfer of property (*traditio*) so that the title passed, as in the case of *nexum*, to the borrower. Upon this basis, the editors of Justinian's Institutes derive their, as usual, incorrect etymology of the term: "Whence it is called *mutuum*, because I so give it to you that from being *meum* it becomes *tuum*."[339] The fact was that the loan was originally called *mutui datio*, or the giving of *mutua*.[340] It was the giving which constituted the loan. *Mutuum* was a description of the character of thing loaned. So Poste describes the

335 Op. cit., I, p. 221.
336 Op. cit., p. 258.
337 Gaius, 3. 90.
338 Hunter, op. cit., p. 471.
339 Justinian, *Inst.* 3. 14. pr.
340 "Re contrahitur obligatio velut mutui datione," Gaius, 3. 90.

term *mutuum* as identified by, and derived from, the special nature of the things lent.[341] This view is confirmed by the accepted etymology of *mutuum* from *muto*,[342] which meant "to exchange," and hence "to interchange." Thus the giving of something interchangeable, to be repaid in kind, not specifically, was the *mutui datio* or *mutuum*.

While, of these three early sources of contract none but the first can with certainty be considered part of primitive law, they are considered here since they represent the origins of transactions which remained open, or continuing; and because they provide in the ceremony, the promise, and the act, the foundation of all later evolvements of the Roman law of contract. Two of the three were confined, when not delictual, to bilateral transactions (including loans) which were, and have continued to be, the only sources of contract which are treated by the layman as property. The wide difference between them seems to lie in the fact that whereas in *nexum* the exchange was at first complete, but tentative—leading to a further exchange or a reversal of the first—in *mutuum* we have the earliest important recognition, in the more sophisticated law, of the creation of a liability—of what we would call a property right—out of the mere lack of balance of the two sides of a transaction. The third form, *stipulatio*, could be applied to any one-sided agreement, which is not now—nor was it then—considered (except in law) to establish a property relation until and unless, as between the principals, such lack of balance can be shown.[343]

D. *Summary*

We have now outlined, as the source of most of the elements in the Roman system of property, a partly hypothetical earlier form of social organization, of the order of a patriarchal house community. We conceive this to have represented the permanent, fundamental groundwork of the time—the "state in little"—constituting almost the whole of the religious, political and juridical organization and the

[341] "Such members of a genus as are naturally capable of mutual substitution (quae vice mutua funguntur) received from modern civilians the barbarous name of res fungibiles. . . The classical name was . . . Quantitas, Dig. 44. 2. 7. pr." Poste, op. cit., p. 323.

[342] Walde, *Latin*, gives the word *mutuus* the sense "*im Austausch stehend*, interchangeable, mutual." It is interesting to note that Schrader, op. cit., p. 348, thinks *mûnus* "(return-)gift," is related to *mûtare* (:**moi-ta*), just as he holds that **vesno* (IE.), his source of *venditio*, was "the object given in exchange for something." Exchange was barter and was indiscriminately give and take. While Walde does not confirm this he does relate *mūnus* to root **mei-*(exchange), and, giving no root for *muto*, does allude to *mūnus*. If this is correct it is another confirmation that the loan came originally out of the incompleted exchange.

[343] This point is discussed in detail in later chapters.

original economic unit for such production and trade as existed. It was, as well, the forerunner of later domestic institutions; but, as such, it must be sharply distinguished from what we have come to call the "family" (father, mother, children), for it consisted of a group united in the main by other relationships than those of consanguinity, and the larger and more successful it became, the more heterogeneous was its composition. The chief of this group was, in Rome, called *pater*, or *paterfamilias*, which as a title of office, seems to be allied more closely with the Hindu *viç-patiḥ* and the Greek δεσπότης than with the sense of "father" which it may originally have had, and which it came later to have.

The two major influences cementing, organizing and characterizing this social unit were *propinquity* and the *power* of the head. While the first seems as much effect as cause, it must be emphasized that the fact of being born, bought, or brought by force into such a group created quickly a sense of accustomedness, of familiarity, of "at-home-ness," as contrasted with the strangeness, hostility and danger of all outside, and that this polarization was centripetal. Moreover the fact of propinquity fostered consanguinity – if that can be considered a unifying influence. The legally minded, seeking the property concept, and the socially minded, seeking signs of communism therein, seem to be imputing sophisticated notions to early society. The indications are rather that they conceived of themselves as '*belonging*' *together*, eventually in a certain place, and that all non-human objects which surrounded them also 'belonged' there in much the same sense. This sense we have considered to have been expressed in the "classificatory genitive," which for so long identified 'belonging to' by a purely physical localization and rendered slow and difficult the entry of the idea of a right to a thing separated from its actual physical presence. As to the influence of the power of the head, we must admit that its development was the source of most of the later idea of ownership – *dominium*. If, too, we assume, as many do, that the origin of the primeval patriarchal group lay in the power of a man over his woman and, thereby, over her children, we emphasize the element of power – the bringing and holding together – rather than that of propinquity – the clinging together – as the source of this form of organization. But at the same time we also demonstrate the reciprocity of the original relation, the importance of the Germanic element of *mund* (protection) as the obverse of that power which was the more conspicuous feature in the Roman *manus*.

From the practical facts of this situation there developed certain habits, or inertias, which eventually grew into, and were accounted for by, corresponding ideas. The first of these we may call inseparability. Only by the most elaborate and perhaps occult ceremonials could members of one group be moved (except by force) to another. This has been especially indicated in tracing out the *manus*-system, of which the externalized forms were largely concerned with such transfers. Only as the power of the head became more despotic, as the accumulation of non-human elements became important, and as development of commercial relations with other groups made exchanges possible and advantageous and the unit less completely self-sufficient, did the question of alienability come to be a pressing one. The resistance to this invasion has given rise to the supposition that there existed a sense of co-proprietorship. No such doctrine is necessary to account for the indivisibility of England, for instance, or the tariff and immigration wall around the United States. And these modern examples express, I believe, the attitude to such matters on the part of the infant "state in little."

The second of these inertias was that of continuity, represented in the later concept of perpetual succession. This principle had no ideal or mystical source. It was a mere matter of observation. The group clung together, when moving; they remained together when the development of agriculture settled them upon the land. Individual persons and animals came and went, generation after generation; the leader died and was replaced. Nevertheless through these changes the group remained intact. It was a continuing entity. This continuity expressed itself in *manus* – the grafting upon or sprouting from the stem, of the individual – the relation of subjection to power and of enjoyment of protection which membership involved. And it expressed itself in the *patrimonium* and *heredium* (eventually *hereditas*) of the succession of actual and presumptive leaders. Only the leadership passed automatically. Membership did not pass. It occurred, or it was arranged.

The third characteristic fact was the independence or autonomy of this early unit. And this had two aspects. These people may have accounted for their origin and location by legends as to ancestral creators and organizers, and as to migrations, conquests and arbitrary distributions of land. But the cause of origin was that the group had always existed – or had split from some other which had – at least for a time so long that "the memory of man runneth not to the contrary." And we have already suggested the gradual development of the, at first, dimly apprehended idea of location. Its early status was the political idea of *territory*. This independence as to origin of the right to be, and the reason for being, together where they were, is the apparent source of the notion of absolute, rather than derivative, right – a notion which has always pervaded the concept of *dominium*, *domaine* and "allodial" – terms which, later or elsewhere, referred to the successors of this continuing heritable unit and expressed the idea of *Selbstständigkeit*. And this notion is due to the nature of the political beginnings.

Another expression of independence arose from the fact that this social grouping was the first, and at first the only, form of government. To say that it was self-governing is a pleonasm. When, in Rome at least, a super-familial government and law first began to appear, since it was wholly supplementary, it did not intrude within these units, of which and by which it was constituted. Not only was this system developed by the heads of the groups composing the pre-existing sub-structure, but it was largely a replica of that which had already existed within the *familia*. It was the application of the same principles in a wider field. And, as a result, it respected for centuries, though in a constantly lessening degree, the prior, though lesser jurisdictions and familial governments from which, by a sort of federation, it had arisen.

Ihering, the background of whose point of view seems to be Hegelian, would establish as the principle back of this system of organization, the idea of physical force.[344] "Where has there been a right, which did not proceed from individual force, and of which the origin is not lost in the obscure background of physical power? . . . The human sweat and blood which sticks to the beginnings of law, is concealed in the nimbus of its divine origin." "The Roman world was founded with the sword, and the sword or the spear is the oldest symbol of Roman law. It was not the gods who gave to the Romans their first endowment, as the God of Israel bestowed the 'Promised Land' upon the Jews; purchase and craft were not employed, as once by Dido for the founding of Carthage; – the Romans had no derivative property in the legal sense, derived from God or other men; theirs was original; among them the owner is his own *auctor*; he has taken it as he found it."[345] "It is the right of booty, in which the Roman concept of property first shows itself . . . in the oldest law, the transfer of property through agreement had no force and validity in itself, but only as it conformed to the idea of booty."[346]

These statements, founded upon the literal acceptation of early terminology and symbolism, are representative of the ideas which also seem to have been held by the jurisconsults in the classic period of Roman law. The portrayal we have made is based upon wholly different interpretations and has arrived at very different principles and forces to account for the result which we discover in early

[344] Not *potestas* (power) which was rather the idea of authority.

[345] *Geist*, I, pp. 107 and 109.

[346] *Geist*, I, p. 117.

Roman history. We have found the sources of property in the relations existing within the early groups and between friendly congeries of such groups, not in those with the hostile, strange, outside world. To us the source has seemed the beginnings of government, or religious, economic and even of domestic life. Property, in our view, seems the outgrowth of peace – of security – rather than of war. Doubtless physical force, at home and abroad, played a large part in the life of early society. But the force which bound together these early units and developed them into aggregating nuclei, was not primarily aggressive force: it was rather the restraining force of law and order, the energies of which were devoted, not to maintaining the predatory condition of a state of nature – "red in tooth and claw" – but, on the contrary, to maintaining refuges against the predatory – to the reclamation of these oases in the primordial waste of lawlessness. In human, as in non-human, nature the evolution of civilization has been domestication; that is, the wresting and protection of a conservatory of tame life from the surrounding wilderness of wild life. And it was the attraction and opportunity offered by these domestic asylums which brought to them most of their acquisitions.

While, in certain respects, we have appeared to hedge the issue, presenting the political aspects in economic terms and the economic aspects in political terms, our purpose has been to spike in advance, so far as possible, all preconceived ideas, and to demonstrate the original condition as something of a different – not merely undifferentiated – order, not entirely characteristic of either. But we may definitely assert that what existed prior to the development of superfamilial law was not property.[847]

The point of view of the early Romans in reference to this social unit seems to have corresponded to ours of a governance more nearly than to ours of modern property over non-human objects. The house community was a "state in little." It had its territory – the early view of landed property. It had its members, divided between free and servile (those of the blood and those not of the blood). It

[847] This seems to have been partly envisaged by Clark. He says, *Regal*, p. 225, ". . . of the names for *owner* and *property* – the former seems generally to indicate either the headship of a household or acts of physical acquisition [he is referring to his view of the *manus*-system] : the latter either the most important groups of living creatures subject to such head, or proximity to his person, perhaps as being acquired by him." Bonfante calls it "la propriété-souveraineté." Op. cit., I, p. 213.

Bonfante, op. cit., I, p. 132, holds that "les trois points capitaux," that is, "la propriété privée, le testament, la distinction des droits réels et des obligations" are three "*idola theatri*" in that their content was so different and represented so wholly an organization and an *ensemble* of primitive ideas that the modern content which has been substituted within their framework "aurait été souvent incompréhensible à une intelligence romaine."

had its flocks and other chattels which may have been regarded as different from the rest—not because they were non-human, but because they were readily separable non-members. The house and land and the work cattle were also non-human, but they were an inseparable part of the house community. The whole was divided into ruler and ruled, the master and the rest. The *familia pecuniaque* as well as the *tutelae*[348] were "of Titus," who held the office as his patrimony. The classificatory genitive did not originally imply possession. No one owned anything. All members 'belonged' *in* the group and only in that sense *to* the group. The idea was of a politico-economic organism, not of a proprietary fund. Just as in our corporation, the going concern, the body of managers and employees is the essential element, the body of property incidental; so in the early Roman household. What was valued was not the very limited possessions, but rather *place*—the place of the member and particularly the place of headship.

Therefore it seems quite impossible to impute, at this stage, a sense of, or a system of, property—even one confined to material objects; land, animals, products. This would presuppose a differentiation for which there is no evidence whatever and against which there is abundant evidence. The system was homogeneous except in respect of the *pecunia*—a difference which we have already explained.

And if there was no system of property, neither was there one of employment. It is difficult for us to conceive a society in which there was no such thing as employment—that is, service rendered for pay. Yet such was ancient Roman, or perhaps pre-Roman society. The economic function of employment was then performed by this system of government. It consisted in a relation of mastery over human beings in the condition of slavery, of *mancipium* (probably similar to the medieval bond-servant—the worker bound over to a master), of debtor slavery—a condition half way between the two—and of the nearly assimilated labour of the free. One had *potestas* over his workers; he did not hire them.[349] But, as Ihering well says, there is no reason to suppose that the condition of the unfree was what the modern concept of slavery would imply. That has been a result, as he points out, of a racial difference; of a plenitude of slaves; of a breaking off of the personal relations and the co-working of master and servants. Doubtless, however much the original

348 Were the "tutelary gods" conceived as having a proprietary relation?

349 Ihering, *Geist*, II, p. 432, says, ". . . was waren die wirthschaftlichen Factoren des ältern Verkehrs? . . . Sachen und als Sachen behandelte Menschen. Die freie menschliche Kraft, das Talent, die Fertigkeit u.s.w., waren noch nicht als solche, d.h. unabhändig von den Producten, in denen sich verwirklichen und ökonomisch—mittelst des Kaufs—verwerthen, auf den Markt getreten."

relation savoured of property, it was rather that the category of pre-property was thus elevated than that the status of persons was thus degraded.

"Nothing shows that the idea of property has historically preceded that of domestic power and is its prototype. The similarity of the two is not to be ascribed to the fact that one is copied from the other, but that both have branched off from a common idea." [350] This common idea was the primarily political organization of early society, an organization which also performed the limited economic functions of the time, co-operatively and communally but under a dictatorship, and which contained in it the germ of the later domestic organization.

Out of this prehistoric social system which perhaps existed among the Roman people when they first entered Italy and which, during the transition, was doubtless submitted to many other influences and was blended with many foreign strains, there developed in the course of a millennium the institution of property found in the classic Roman law. Concurrently, from the same source were specialized that system of organization which we call political—the control and ordering of groups larger than, and constituted of, these early units—and that which we call domestic—a control of constantly attenuating authority and importance over households constantly diminishing in size.

In varying degrees in different times and among the different branches of the Indo-European stock the pattern of this early house community was retained with more or less of traces of its original pastoral patriarchal form. And, conversely, in varying degrees, more or less of its functions had become stranded, so to speak, during the process of successive fissions, in a hierarchy of gens or sib, perhaps tribe, and even *civitas*,—a stranding which resulted in a degree of co-ordination, gradually largely displaced by subordination. Eventually only the residue of the original functioning remained in the integral unit.

Not only did this fundamental group, eventually based on the land, give rise to the political hierarchy, and thus reduce its own political functioning to the so-called domestic ambit, but, as the precursor of property, the assimilation of government and property therein remained so intimate that in the Dark Ages the latter could readily revert to its former condition and become government again. And when this occurred there was displayed in more vivid light the contrast that had previously existed, the contrast between the two different principles of government within the house community—

[350] Ihering, *Geist*, II, p. 165.

that of the persons and that of the cattle—the one patrimonial in origin, the other pecunial.

In its Roman forms the precursor of property as an institution is found not so much in these pecunial relations, established among persons as to material objects, as it is among those established among persons as to themselves. The origin of Roman property lies in the antecedent personal relations within the framework and applied to the internal and external arrangements of the early house community. So far as this and other Indo-European peoples are concerned there are striking indications that these features were largely embraced in what we have called the *manus*-system. From these relations as to persons arose the principal early features of succession, conveyance, contract, *dominium*, and its subordinates *possessio* and the servitudes. From the lesser relations as to objects may have come the corresponding minor and later practices of legacy, *traditio*, the informal contract *mutuum*, and the *peculium*.

To some extent to argue that the precursor of property was not property is merely a dispute over words. Control existed, to be sure, over both *familia* and *pecunia*, and something of the nature of use or enjoyment at least over the latter. But if we take the four principal criteria by which it is usual to define the modern institution and to separate it from other forms of control and enjoyment which are excluded from its field, we see good ground for rejecting the application of the term. If property is the separation of *meum* from *tuum*, then, as to individuals, within the early social unit, we see only the dim beginnings of such an idea—principally as to the chief, faintly as to the rest. If property is an institution of what we call legal character—that is, one which consists of a similar separation but between *familiae*—then, obviously it could not have existed prior to the development of super-familial government and its law.[351] If

[351] In his *Philosophy*, pp. 225-226, Pound describes this process, though always from the legal viewpoint, and in terms of property. He says, "Recognition of individual interests of substance, or in other words individual property, has developed out of recognition of group interests. . . The statement which used to be found in the books that all property originally was owned in common means nothing more than this: When interests of substance are first secured they are interests of groups of kindred because in tribally organized society groups of kindred are the legal units." Super-familial control secures them in the occupation of their possessions. "In this sense the first property is group property rather than individual property. . . Two ideas gradually operated to break up these group interests and bring about recognition of individual interests. One of these is the partition of households. The other is the idea of what in the Hindu law is called self-acquired property." The first process is that which we have described as the substitution of *heredes* for *heres*. The second development was, in Rome, included in the *pecunia* and in certain of the *peculia*. And, in early French law, it was that which we have seen Laveleye citing (Note 292, p. 111) as "acquêts ainsi que les meubles."

property is concerned only with non-human objects then, as to early times, we can find its field only in the slightly discriminated relations as to the flocks. Such a criterion suggests that there was no need for a true institution of property until the modification of the relation to the land and the accumulation of non-human and man-made products had proceeded to a point where a system was necessary in order to deal with them. And, finally, if we adopt the very frequent, though mistaken, criterion which associates it with the attribute of alienability we must see that property over the principal elements of the early social unit hardly existed at all. However, the point we have sought to make has served its purpose if it has convinced the reader of the original homogeneity of relations, practices and viewpoints in the all-embracing functioning of a single type of organization.

CHAPTER II

THE DEVELOPMENT OF THE ROMAN SYSTEM OF PROPERTY

A. *The Evolving Super-familial Structure*

1. *Source and Character of Organization*

In the previous chapter the early organization of Roman, or pre-Roman, society has been presented as a system of irregular unit groups of which the most conspicuous character was political (i.e. governmental), though in the course of time, with the partial supersession of this political functioning by a new and external political power and the gradual dwindling of the field of influence, this grouping contracted into what we now call the domestic organization. The system of control originally exercised therein, indiscriminately over persons and objects, though it also developed into, and at first gave form to, the differentiating super-familial (political) and intra-familial (domestic) controls of later times, was preserved most nearly intact in the later system of property—the control over objects. And this presumably because, in that field alone, no human interests intervened in behalf of the objects to alter the original relation. Because of this finally single survival of form many have been led to denominate the whole original type of control as property. We have preferred to call it 'pre-property' in order to distinguish it from the remnant of it which gradually appeared under a new sanction, in a limited field, and designed for a single function. This distinction particularly emphasizes the fact that pre-property functioned politically and domestically as well as it did economically.

In outlining the arrival on the scene of a new sanction we must avoid the impression that this was an event which occurred. As a matter of fact, like all growths, it is impossible to say when it began or ended.[1] There is evidence that at all times the early house communities had inter-familial relations, and some super-familial sanctions. At times action was joint. In times of peace the neighbourhood—

[1] As Bonfante puts it, op. cit., I, p. 87, "Le processus organique d'intégration de l'antique commune de Rome se clôt avec la féderation des collines tibérines et la formation de l'*Urbs*."

confounded with, or the same as, the kindred [2] – in the indefinite concentric circles of gens and even tribe, may have to some extent limited and supported the autonomy of the integral units.[3] And, in time of war, the hosts, or hordes, "in some rude military order," may have effaced, to a considerable degree and for the time being, the familial organization. But with concentration, development of agriculture and consequent settlement, the relative emphasis began to change. Propinquity began to extend its scope in a permanent and systematic union. Then it becomes what Thucydides called συνοίκησις, "that process of *coalition*, which is held to be a law of national formation, at least in the West, by most modern research and theory." [4] It is at this stage that we discern the beginnings of a continuous and territorial super-familial government. Thus our purpose is to contrast with the beginning, the end of this process of imperceptible development of pre-existing institutions. By comparison with the original independent and perhaps isolated house community we find ourselves now at a stage where the mounting tide of federation has created a form – the *civitas* – which marks the beginning of a new integration and the gradual breaking down of the at first autonomous familial units which compose it.

It has been frequently assumed that the evidences of hierarchical form, which are recorded in early historical Roman and German political organization, reflect a pre-existing *systematic* structure of the same pattern; a union of families in gens, *Sippe* or sib; of *gentes* and *Sippen* in tribes; of tribes in nations.[5] But, while there is little doubt

[2] Tarde, *Imitation*, p. 315, ". . . relations of neighborhood combine with those of kindred in the creation of legal ties."

[3] Propinquity of place seems to have led to the assumption of propinquity of blood, at least among the free, probably because, as paternity came to be recognized, the notion of agnatic relationship grew out of, and was found to conform in general to, the fact of neighbourhood.

[4] Clark, *Regal*, p. 333.

[5] Fustel de Coulanges, *Ancient City*, Trans., p. 153, seems to assume that the gens was the unit dwelling together, and that largely on the ground of a religious community. This too I judge is Schröder's view of the prehistoric Germans. He says, op. cit., p. 70, "Die Sippe zerfiel in den engeren Kreis der Hausgenossen (Eltern, Kinder, Geschwister) und den weiteren Kreis der Magschaft." Schrader, too, op. cit., p. 398, assumes an "ancient political significance of the *gens*," which he says, "was lost in that of the state." And Pound, *Philosophy*, p. 74, seems to hold the same view. He says, "The system of organized kindreds gradually breaks down. Kin-organization is replaced by political organization as the primary agency of social control."

Originally, before the settlement of Rome, Ihering sees as "das Gentilitätsprinzip die Identität des Staats und der Familie: den Staat mit familienartiger Organisation, die Familie mit politischen Funktionen," *Geist*, I, p. 308. In the previous chapter we have suggested our reasons for doubting the antithesis between political and familial – between state and kin – which is the prepossession of these writers. We have Bonfante's support. He says, op. cit., I, p. 75, "ni la famille primitive, ni la *gens*,

that such a systematic arrangement had already begun and gave rise to certain of the configurations of the political framework when these peoples became settled and organized into communes and states, I think the evidence of the terminology itself indicates that as an element of political organization it was a comparatively late growth, and that the early condition of all the Indo-Europeans, before settlement, extended beyond the single or multiple house community only to the vaguest and most irregular groupings. Many of the terms for groups of various supposed orders in all the various languages refer indiscriminately to groups of buildings or to groups of persons and, by the time they appear in the literature, also to land districts. The terms are often terms of residence rather than of relationship. And while most of them appear wide-spread, in the form of a number of cognates, the usage or the thing designated is apt to be different in the different languages. Also the system of nomenclature of groups has the earmarks of a spreading out by fission; in which process the descriptive titles had as much tendency to stick to the expanding whole – as the designation of a continuing group of actual persons – as it did to remain as the definition of a certain type of group with a fixed place in the structure – a continuing system of relations through which persons passed. A discussion of this terminology appears in Appendix I A.

When permanent settlement took place, it would appear that besides the integral isolated house community there were frequently and quite generally multiples of such integers, constituting villages. But apparently at least some, even, of such villages were simply large integral house communities. In these, or in still wider neighbourhoods, there existed also a vague grouping of "kindreds" in which there was reputed consanguinity through the male side. Such extended relationships were probably a relic of the "fraternity" of several house communities separated by fission from a single source, and might persist for generations. Naturally the groups so joined

ni la tribu n'ont une nature différente de l'Etat; ce sont des agglomérations nées pour l'ordre et la defense et uniformes dans leur composition."

In spite of the weight of these authorities to the contrary, it seems to me the evidence of language demonstrates that, aside from the military groupings, there was practically no organized political or judicial relation of kindred beyond the confines of the individual house communities, until the time of permanent settlement in the eventual homes. And this point is well presented by Ihering himself. He says, *Geist*, I, p. 317, "Für den Begriff sowohl wie für die meisten Institute des Rechts hat jede indogermanische Sprache eine andere, dieselben von einer verschiedenen Seite erfassende Bezeichnung. Was also auch die indogermanische Völkerfamilie an gemeinsam Rechtseinrichtungen ursprünglich besass, die Tätigkeit der Sprache in der Bezeichnung derselben, d.h. das Erwachen des Bewusstseins über dieselben, fällt in die Zeit nach der Trennung." Bonfante, op. cit., I, p. 30, says, "Le groupe le plus ample, la tribu, avec, à sa tete, un roi ne se trouve que très irregulièrement. . ."

would then vary greatly in numbers and in concentration as well as in the simplicity or multiplicity of their organization.[6]

As we have noted, Schulze presumes that the gentile names—the *nomina* of historical Rome—were formed from the *praenomina* of the founders of the early Roman houses. Thus it is entirely possible that the patriarchal house communities or *familiae* of the period, at or before the time of settlement of Rome whenever the practice of nomenclature developed, were the source of the later *gentes*, and that prior to that time only such larger circles of "kindred" as the tribes were recognized, at least by a common name. But, since the term "gens" is cognate with the Greek *γένος* and has the same sense, it seems probable that for several generations, or at least as long as they remained contiguous, house communities of a common stem had from the beginning recognized such a relationship. These two somewhat contradictory viewpoints may be reconciled if we suppose that such kinship was not a system of organization but rather an habitual recognition of the propinquity of groups of house communities whenever and for as long as such propinquity existed in fact—in other words that it depended not so much on consanguinity as upon neighbourhood and that it meant "of the same 'house,' or stock" (as was assumed) and not a well defined element in organization or grouping. In this view we eliminate the idea of a hard and fast pattern.[7]

Such an informal reminiscence of a preceding closer familial union would account for the dimmed reflection of some of the internal arrangements of the house community which we see reaching over the larger circles.[8] In particular we need to mention three respects in which it is usual to assume that this expanded familial relationship entered in important ways into the constitution of the eventual super-familial government. Schrader speaks of the "agnatic exclusiveness of the Indo-European family, as regards those outside it."[9] And

[6] If, as Bonfante concludes, op. cit., I, p. 85, "la *gens* et les agglomérations similaires prennent les extensions les plus variées, oscillant, comme nous l'avons remarqué, entre une nombreuse maison et une communauté de village," I conceive it to be more consistent with a correct representation of the facts to ignore the name and to represent the house community as one fact and its loose federations or communes as another. Even this does not envisage the possibility that, in certain cases, the latter form may have come under the domination of one strong *pater* and thus have become a compound, or multiple, house community. Doubtless there were such variations. We should therefore conceive the probable structure as irregular and the terminology as even more so.

[7] It is more in accord with this view that Schröder says in another place, op. cit., p. 67, that "the general German designation for the *family connection in its entirety* was *Sippe*" (Goth. *sibja*). In other words the *Magschaft*, not an organization.

[8] Bonfante, op. cit., I, p. 73, "Jusqu'à une période avancée de l'époque historique, au-dessous de la *civitas* survivent deux couches de vigoureuses organisations [the *familia* and the gens] constituant les noyaux politiques qui la précèdent."

[9] Op. cit., p. 393.

elsewhere he says, "Primitive man only regards those who belong to the same tribe as himself as enjoying common rights with himself. . ."[10] It is this principle which constitutes the caste system under which the early Roman Government formed itself as an association of the heads of patrician house communities.[11] And the equality within these gentile fraternities doubtless contributed the element of co-ordination rather than that of subordination which characterized the later Republic.[12]

We have already touched upon the *Obervormundschaft* which existed within the wider circles of "kinship" among the Indo-Europeans and have seen the relic of this duty (or right) reappearing in the Roman law of property with reference to the guardianship established among the agnates or *gentiles* over the *familia* left without a head.

Upon the evidence of communal land holding, by units perhaps larger than single house communities, which is found in early Germanic custom and later among Germanic and Slavic peoples, it has seemed necessary to some authorities hypothetically to construct the gens as a proprietary unit in prehistoric Italy and to assume the degeneration of this system of organization before the constitution of the *civitas*, in order to account for the almost complete absence of any traces of such gentile land holding in later Rome.[13] All this is

[10] Op. cit., p. 350.

[11] Ihering, *Geist*, I, p. 226, defines it. "Gentilität und volle Rechtsfähigkeit, Nicht-Gentilität und volle Rechtlosigkeit ist ursprünglich gleichbedeutend. . ." And, *Geist*, I, p. 230, he points out the contrast with modern conditions. "Recht und Freiheit sind heutzutage gleich der Luft und dem Wasser eine *res communis omnium*, an der jeder Mensch, der Einheimische wie der Fremde, partizipiert, und deren Wert wir, weil wir sie überall vorfinden, nur zu leicht übersehen, und die uns daher nicht mehr wie einst, wo man sie nur in der Heimat fand, an letztere fesseln."

[12] Ihering, *Geist*, I, p. 190, ". . . das einzelne Mitgleid steht nicht unter der Gens, sondern neben den Gentilen." And, *Geist*, I, p. 259, ". . . die Verfassung der *gens* ist durch und durch republikanisch organisiert. . .'

[13] Ihering, *Geist*, I, p. 197, "Die römische Gentilverfassung war nicht vereinbar mit der vermögensrechtlichen Freiheit der späteren Zeit, letztere kann sich erst auf den Trümmern jener gebildet haben. Sollte die Gens stetig und fest sein, so musste sie ein festes materielles Fundament unter sich haben, es musste eine gewisse gesicherte Verbindung zwischen ihr und dem in ihr befundlichen Vermögen hergestellt sein." And elsewhere he suggests that the *ager publicus* is modelled upon an earlier *ager gentilicus*. But, I, p. 204, he admits that "Welcher Art die Beschränkungen waren, denen die Dispositions-befugniss des Eigentümers im Interesse der Gens unterlag, lässt sich für die Veräusserung einzelner Sachen nicht näher bestimmen."

Bonfante, op. cit., I, pp. 205-213, arrives at the conclusion that the "*propriété primitive est une propriété gentilice*." And he excuses the absence of evidence of this in later times and the extraordinary anomaly that *dominium ex iure Quiritium* (which he says himself, "se conserve dans une forme stéréotypée pour désigner les institutions fondamentales, qui ont une saveur plus archaïque," I, p. 167) always retains "tout le caractère, tout l'esprit d'une vraie souveraineté territoriale, fermée en elle-même et indépendante," by imagining the following process. "Comme l'Etat-cité a opéré peu à peu la désagrégation des *gentes* et les a réduites à l'état de la famille classique, il a accompli la même oeuvre de désagrégation dans le territoire genti-

unnecessary if we distinguish between the notion of political territory and that of landed property. For then we may assign any pre-existing super-familial (gentilican) domain to the former category exclusively and see it as absorbed in the purely territorial notion of the state as fast as the *foedus* of *gentes* or *pagi* gave rise to the state. And we may reserve for the pre-existing familial domain – perhaps preceding, perhaps a section of the gentilican territory – the source of the proprietary category with its peculiar continuing autonomous and absolute character. This is even less necessary if the circle of *propinqui* is regarded, according to the view we have suggested, as an informal and only lately organized relationship based largely upon contiguity, which appears in the constitution of Rome principally as a classification of membership by districts, through which groups of house communities came to speak and act as units.[14]

It is apparent that, in times of movement and of war, circles still wider than those of neighbourhood or "kindreds" had always functioned as units. Such larger groupings seem to have been knit together primarily for military (and migratory) purposes – aggression or protection.[15] The skeleton of this war organization was apparently retained in times of settled peace. It was this larger grouping which constituted the tribe and the folk or people (perhaps *populus*).[16]

lice. . . Mais, ceci posé, la propriété nouvelle, classique, concentrée dans la *paterfamilias*, n'étant pas une concession ou une sous-concession de la *gens*, mais une division du territoire gentilice entre plusieurs souverains, favorisée par l'Etat, a conservé les caractères mêmes de la propriété gentilice." This seems to me a twisting of the facts from their direct to an indirect induction in order to fit a theory. I assume, on the contrary, that the final, original, and absolute "propriété-souveraineté" was always and remained in the house community, and that the gens, if it was not a term for such a community, was only a loose federation of such communities.

[14] We have already spoken of the projection of the structure of society upon the land at the time of final settlement. It is, I believe, not too unorthodox to hold that the terms curia and tribe, and perhaps even gens, when they appear in early Roman history, refer rather to districts – in conformity to our views of propinquity and of political territory – which by the nature of the slowly dividing house communities and by the rule of marriage within the gens would also conform roughly to the arrangement by consanguinity. Certainly at first, land was plentiful. There was plenty of room to spread out, agriculturally speaking. In general this seems to be the theory of Girard and before him of Mommsen. See Girard, op. cit., pp. 283-284. See Mommsen, op. cit., III, pp. 161 ff.

[15] Bonfante, op. cit., I, p. 30, says, "Au-dessus [the small groupings of house communities], on ne voit aucun lien qui embrasse tout un peuple, sauf des coopérations militaires sous forme de fédérations internationales, le plus souvent très relâchées et passagères."

[16] Schrader, op. cit., p. 403, "In those wandering times people and army were one. . ." Schröder, op. cit., p. 19, also says that among the Germans *Volk* and *Heer* were synonymous concepts. Ihering, *Geist*, I, 248, says ". . . das Volk ist Heer. . ." Also, p. 249, he refers to Kuhn's etymology for *populus* from *pulus* (young) like *puer* and *pubes*, and says it meant "those past majority capable of bearing arms." Thus, p. 251, "*Populus Romanus Quiritium* ist also die junge römische Mannschaft der Lanzenträger. . ." But this etymology is very doubtful. See Appendix I A.

Here too we find at least a supposititious descent from a common hero, or ruler. Clark has outlined the apparent traces of the military order in the political structure of early Rome and has shown its connection with the system of "hundreds" which is seen in the later German and Anglo-Saxon organization upon the land.[17] War taught "the value of an ordering," says Ihering.[18] And he holds that "the military organization established the fundamental form of the state, and the religious and political interests conformed to the arrangement thus constituted." [19]

This interpretation undertakes to construe the fact that the earliest Roman government of which we have any record was regal. Such authorities hold that the original Indo-European *rex*, or *rí*, was not a king but a military leader in time of war, who appears to have carried into times of peace the function of a judge. But "as the military arrangement of a warlike people is the most important and oldest and the starting point for the political, so the office of army leader, who arranges and maintains this external and artificial ordering is more indispensable and older than that of magistrate. . ." [20] Ihering points out that, since military interests were inconsistent with what he supposes to have been the hereditary honors of the patriarchal system and its special method of transmission of office, the earliest kingships were probably incompatible with, and, in Rome at least, did not at first follow, the patriarchal pattern.[21] As Ihering puts it, "The oldest state stands with its feet in the family, and with its head and limbs in the defense organization." [22] Eventually we see, however, that the king in early Rome was less of an army chief than he was a chief magistrate and high priest; which functions were at

[17] See *Regal*, pp. 195-206 and 214-218.

[18] *Geist*, I, p. 263.

[19] *Geist*, I, p. 248. ". . . das Volk ist Heer, das ganze Heer hat seinen Gottesdienst und seine politischen Funktionen, ebenso aber auch jede Heeresabteilung."

[20] Ihering, *Geist*, I, p. 252. "Der erste *rex* war ein Feldherr . . ." (p. 253). And, p. 252, "*Rex*, der Richtende (*reg-ula, reg-ere*), heisst der König, nicht weil er richtet im juristischen, sondern im militärischen Sinn." Clark's view is the same. He says, *Regal*, p. 479, "Among really original constituents of a state the first person exercising anything like general command appears, at least in our Western nations to be the War-chief: any civil organisation is of a vague and incoherent character. The molecules are beginning to crystallise into the elements of a permanent law abiding society. . . The immediate antecessor of the final and true King is, I believe, the Judge." Schrader, op. cit., p. 403, adopts the view that the *rex*, or *rí*, was originally a military leader and cites as proof the fact that the Slavs who remained peaceably in the "second home" were also longest in ignorance of regal power. Bonfante, op. cit., I, p. 30, confines the spread of "un terme commun pour signifier le roi" to Sanskrit, Latin and Celtic (whence Gothic), which goes to support this view.

[21] *Geist*, I, p. 182.

[22] *Geist*, I, p. 178. And, p. 247, he says, "Die Ordnung des Heeres, die Wehrverfassung verbindet sich mit der Ordnung der Familie, dem Geschlechterstaat, zu einer militärisch-politischen Einheit, der altrömischen Verfassung."

first, perhaps, hardly separable.[23] In certain respects in the time of the Regal period, the *rex* appears, therefore, to have come to occupy a relation to the folk as a whole similar to that which the *paterfamilias* occupied to the house community,[24] although his authority reached only to the *patrifamilias*, and not within the autonomous groups they ruled, except perhaps in so far as the latter contained grown sons of military age. While we must admit the evidence of dual structure, I am inclined to follow Bonfante who, while conceding that "the regal system seems the primitive phase of any people," sees that possibly passed by the time of the Regal period, so-called, of Rome. There he finds evidence that the system was originally that of an oligarchy rather than a monarchy – corresponding to the later consulships – that the system of succession was not hereditary, but rather that of designation by the predecessors; that the chief functions of the king, or kings, were pre-eminently religious, incidentally civil (judicial and administrative) and hardly at all military; and, finally, that the organization of the state was not dissimilar to that of the later Republic.[25]

In the earliest organization of the Roman state we see, at any rate, two elements combining, the patriarchal, or "hierarchical," and the military.[26] The former is represented primarily by the *senatus* – the heads of the constituent autonomous house communities who themselves form the association, acting by districts within the dimmer reflection of past patriarchal relations denominated the *gentes*[27] – and perhaps by the *rex*. The latter is represented by the *comices* and the *populus*, though these too come in time to be affected by the patriarchal influence.

"We run the risk of unconsciously carrying over our modern

[23] Ihering, *Geist*, I, p. 253. "Die Religion erscheint bei den Römern als unzertrennliche Begleiterin jeder wichtigen Institution. . . Sowie der Hausvater für die Seinigen den Hausgottesdienst versieht, so der König für das Volk." Clark, *Regal*, p. 242, ". . . Sovereignty itself is, in my view of the Roman Royalty, a gradual development through the judicial function, but principally under religious influences." And Bonfante says, op. cit., I, p. 238, "La cité, dans ses origines, présente vraiment une forme semi-théocratique."

[24] Clark, *Regal*, p. 458, says, "The king standing in the same relation to the community as the 'paterfamilias' to the family . . . is a stock matter of comparison with authors ancient and modern." Bonfante, op. cit., I, p. 165, says, "La famille, autour de laquelle se concentre le droit privé, est un organisme identique à la *civitas*."

[25] Op. cit., pp. 89 ff.

[26] Clark, *Regal*, p. 244, says, ". . . while the fundamental unit of the Roman Polity is the Family, and the first directly constituent parts of it are either combinations, real or assumed, of the Family, or combinations of those combinations – we also find, in its earliest history, unmistakable traces of occupation by a Host, in rude military order."

[27] Ihering, *Geist*, I, p. 205, says, "Nach den Gentes sind die Rechte und Lasten des Staats verteilt, mit dem einzelen Bürger steht der Staat in keiner unmittelbaren politischen Beziehung."

view of the state to a time and to conditions to which they in no way apply. To the name sticks the idea!"[28] The earliest functions of such super-familial government were extremely limited. If at first its prime activity was war, it came also to serve certain religious and judicial purposes. Of administration there is little. Its officials and official bodies were principally the repositories and the means of expounding the traditional customs of the whole group, both religious and ethical. The greater the antiquity of the contiguity of the elements of the whole, the more sacred and revered – though, too, the more attenuated – was their common heritage of memories and ideas. Super-familial authority was solely the weight of this old tradition which the officials expounded. The state was in essence a mere confederation of autonomous house communities, or of groups of such, which continued to conduct their internal affairs as before.[29] Therefore the association was highly exclusive. It was primarily the chiefs of these smaller units who constituted the association itself. In a secondary way the men of military age participated.[30] All others were excluded. It was a close corporation of the *patres* – the heads of patrician house communities.[31]

As we have already noted, the form which this super-familial organization at first took was that of a compound, a super-patriarchate modified by the military organization.[32] But the classical view of the Roman *regnum* seems to have been an imputation based on the later meaning of the term rather than upon reality.[33] Girard minimizes the shift to a Republic. He says,[34] that the change "proceeded from

[28] Ihering, *Geist*, I, p. 177.

[29] Ihering calls the *Gesamtstaat* a *Staatenbund*. *Geist*, I, p. 205.

[30] Vinogradoff, *Jurisprudence*, I, pp. 352-353, holds that "the principle of the assembly is not that of political representation, but of military organization. The general assembly of the people is identical with the army or host." And Clark, *Regal*, p. 357, has the same view. ". . . the early popular assembly is solely a gathering of warriors under a tribal military chief." But Cornil, op. cit., p. 34, thinks that, in all *res publicae*, the personalities of the *filii* were independent of the *paterfamilias*.

[31] Beneath these organized households were the plebeians. Whether this system of caste corresponds to the Germanic distinction between *Adelheit* and *Freiheit*; whether the two were derived from a common past; and whether either or both arose originally from a differentiation between conquerors and conquered – invaders and indigenous population – from hereditary leadership, from a sifting out of the rich and powerful, or from some other source, I am not prepared to guess. At any rate "les institutions fondamentales du droit romain sont essentiellement les institutions des dominateurs, les *patres*." Bonfante, op. cit., I, p. 227.

[32] Ihering makes much of the hierarchy. "Die Architektonik des ältesten Staats beruht wesentlich auf Nachbildung des kleineren Kreises im grösseren, auf imitation und Symmetrie." *Geist*, I, p. 260.

[33] One distinction between an early *rex* and a medieval king is suggested by Schröder, op. cit., p. 31, when, speaking of early Germany, he says, "Der gesamte Grund und Boden galt als Volksland, nicht als Königsland. . ." But Bonfante thinks the Roman *rex* could dispose of the public land. Op. cit., I, p. 94.

[34] Op. cit., p. 22.

a general movement which took place about the same time in nearly all the neighbouring states, and which tended to substitute an annual change of officials for the chiefs for life which had existed until then." "To the consuls (as they were later called) went the political power of the *rex*." In effect this change of form, which Ihering thinks came from Carthage,[85] converted the organization from a patriarchal pyramid to an oligarchical truncated pyramid. The formal remains of the apex merely served as the instrumentality for the joint will of the *patres* or *gentiles* to a greater extent than it had, at least, during the latter part of the kingship. Authority rose wholly from the heads of households.[86] We may unthinkingly conceive the Roman Republic, as well as the Greek Democracy, to resemble what we mean by those terms today. They did not. The Roman *patres* were equal, it is true; but the *patres* were but the apices of the constituent house communities which formed the basis of the whole, the *cives* or *populus* had limited powers and functions, and the population may have outnumbered the *cives* some five or ten to one.[87] In Greece too the "actual democracy was however restricted to a comparatively small number of privileged citizens selected on the basis of descent."[88]

2. "*Actio*"—*The Appearance of Law*

The earliest administration of justice, if it can be called such, seems to have been revenge, taken by an individual who conceived himself to be wronged and secured with the aid of his *propinqui*, who were bound to help him.[89] In the terminology of the jurists this was "self-help." The obverse of it was the corresponding liability of the *propinqui* of the supposed wrongdoer to defend him. Obviously the result was always a feud between two more or less extensive circles of kinsmen or neighbours. This latter liability may be identified with the institution of *manus-mund*, which we have already described. Within the circle of the house community the head

[85] See *Aryan*, pp. 221-224.

[86] As Ihering puts it, *Geist*, I, p. 210, the state is not "ausser und über ihnen," but is themselves. ". . . Staat und Volk ist gleichbedeutend." "*Res publica* . . . bezeichnet daher ursprünglich nichts weiter als was allen gemeinsam ist. . ." Bonfante, op. cit., I, p. 243, rests at least the Republic on a *foedus*. "C'est l'accord international entre les *gentes*, représentées par leur chefs, qui établit ou change les bases de l'Etat." Thus it was like the other primitive municipal organizations—at least the Italian—the *municipia foederata* or communes, all of which retained their autonomy.

[87] Clark, *Regal*, p. 401 and Note 1, refers to it as "an aristocratic democracy." "Aristocratic in so far as those family associations, which had reached the fuller development of the paternal system, held themselves superior to those which had not, even before the distinct separation of a certain ring of families: democratic, in the evident equality of these families as between themselves."

[88] Vinogradoff, *Jurisprudence*, II, p. 265.

[89] Ihering, *Geist*, I, p. 126, says, "Der Geist des ältern Rechts ist der Geist der Rache, der Genugtuung für jegliches widerfahrene Unrecht."

maintained peace among the inmates, and he and his fighting men protected the group against all attack from without.[40] If one of the members of this group – human or animal – committed a wrong outside the circle, he was protected or recovered, and the responsibility for his act assumed, by the predecessor of the procedure of vindication which we have already described. But if the wrong was admitted by his chief, then the wrongdoer was repudiated and delivered to the injured party in noxal surrender.[41] Thus it was the *magistratus domesticus* of the defendant who, so to speak, adjudged the case when he determined whether to protect or surrender the supposed culprit.[42] If the latter was surrendered, vengeance was taken upon him alone. If not, the party of the plaintiff made war upon the party of the defendant. At certain times and places this same system seems to have extended itself to larger groups composed of several kindred house communities. But there the decision rested on the verdict of the *patres* jointly.

What was, perhaps, the earliest appearance of law – defined as a super-familial institution – seems to have resulted from the application of this same negative procedure to the larger circle of federated house communities. There too the decision confined itself to the question whether vengeance by an outsider was to be permitted or prevented, whether the normal protection of the supposed culprit – a member – was to be withdrawn or maintained.[43] It was not so much the determination of right as it was the repudiation of wrong. But as to disputes within this larger circle the beginnings seem to

[40] Speaking of the early Anglo-Saxon custom, and with an individual in mind (though such individual could only be the representative head of a house community), Green, op. cit., p. 21, says, "Older than 'the peace of the folk' . . . was the 'frith,' or peace of the freeman himself – the right that each man had to secure for himself safe life and sound limb. He lay, as the phrase ran then, 'in his own hand.' "

[41] Bonfante, op. cit., I, p. 233. "Pour les délits des personnes en puissance, libres ou esclaves, le chef peut toujours se libérer, conformément à l'usage général et perpétué, même par l'Etat romain dans les rapports internationaux, en livrant le coupable (*noxae deditio*)."

[42] This point is made most explicitly by Cornil, op. cit., p. 37. He says "le chef de famille du délinquant choisira entre les deux attitudes suivants," (1) 'noxae deditio' (2) "il prendra fait et cause pour la *subiecta persona* coupable."

[43] Green, op. cit., p. 22, says, "Every man of the folk lay in 'the folk's hand ;' and wrong-doer as he might be, it was only when the 'hand' was opened and its protection withdrawn, that the folk could suffer him to be maimed or slain. The earliest conception, therefore, of public justice was a solemn waiver on the part of the community of its right and duty of protection. . . Till such a waiver was given the wrong-doer remained in the folk's 'mund'. . ." Without appeal to the folk and their waiver of protection, vengeance (punishment) constituted "a breach of the peace or frith to which his 'mund' entitled him" – a *mund-bryce*.

It appears to have been a survival of this practice that we detect in the *deditio* (presumably analogous to *noxae deditio*) of an individual who had broken a treaty of the folk as a whole, which was regarded as a collective obligation of all members and therefore incident upon each member. See Ihering, *Geist*, I, p. 215.

have been different. If this larger group is conceived to have been federated by a pact (*foedus*), then this *pactum* seems to have had as a corollary the keeping of the peace (*pax*); or if it is conceived to have been unified by a single ruler, then this peace may have been imposed; or, finally, if there was no unification or federation but merely the fact of propinquity, the peace may have been the result of public opinion which was opposed to the inconvenience of internal warfare. Whatever the basis, the result of the more extensive groupings of house communities was to extend the arena of the familial peace, or *frith*, over the whole sib or folk – commune or *civitas* – and eventually to produce a condition like the "King's Peace" of early England.[44] Obviously such a peace did not deal with the matter of putting a stop to the commission of wrongs. It was not police. And its only effect in that direction may have been the moral effect of withdrawing support from wrongdoers. But in the time when the rule was "tit for tat," it served to distinguish the "tit" from the "tat," and indirectly to endorse the former – vengeance – while it condemned the latter – the wrong – in such a way that, of the two acts, which might be identical in appearance, the one was declared to be white, just, and self-help, while the other was declared to be black, unjust and a tort. Yet otherwise the acts were indistinguishable, since vengeance was *talio* – an eye for an eye, a tooth for a tooth. And only if vengeance had undergone this preliminary whitewashing was it possible to distinguish it, as restoration of balance, from the original disturbance of balance.[45]

It is evidently because of this limited and "timid taking hold of the administration of justice upon the part of the state,"[46] that Girard overlooks it and states that "the origin of civil procedure lies in the practice of doing justice for oneself, of assuring to oneself, with one's own force and according to one's own mind, satisfaction of the right

[44] It is apparently this process which Pound has in mind when he says, *Philosophy*, p. 35, "In the beginnings of law men had no more ambitious conception than a peaceable ordering of society at any cost." Ihering, *Geist*, I, p. 224, treats this peace as a contract. He says, ". . . das ganze Völkerrecht löst sich in Verträge auf." And, p. 209, "Der Zustand der Verträglichkeit, in dem der einzelne mit dem einzelnen lebt, ist die Folge eines ausdrücklichen oder stillschweigenden Vertrages, der Friede, *pax*, die des *pactum*, des *pacisci*." But one is inclined to attach the original sense of these words to the fixing of territorial boundaries between groups, as in *pagus* and *pango*, or *pago* (see Ernout and Meillet), and to consider the peace as the indirect outgrowth of this particular pact. The Anglo-Saxon *frith* seems to be allied semantically to freedom and to friendship and to have in it no sense of agreement. But it was allied intimately to this process for it was also used as the term for the third of the composition which went to the king. See d'Arbois, *Droit Celtique*, I, p. 154.

[45] See, for the rationale of this distinction, Girard, op. cit., pp. 421-422.

[46] Bonfante, op. cit., I, p. 169. Elsewhere, I, p. 246, he says of the state that "il intervient timidement, par voie indirecte, presque en s'excusant, sous un prétexte religieux, de se charger de la défense juridique, et ce n'est pas l'intérèt de la justice qui l'anime, mais celui de la paix."

which one conceives he has and reparation of the injury which one judges himself to have received." [47] We may better say that self-help preceded law and persisted throughout its early stages—in fact that early law at first incorporated the methods of private vengeance in its procedure. "The proceedings," says Hunter,[48] "are essentially a private act of force legalized and restrained by law." Through all the changes in the character and mode of sanction with which this fundamental act was clothed and the change in the form of reparation, which we will later discuss, the act itself—execution upon the wrongdoer by the wronged—persisted until well into the classic period of Roman law.[49] In the earliest Roman actions, where a defendant is involved, the summons (*vocatio*), and the execution (either *manus iniectio* or, perhaps earlier, *pignoris capio*) were all effected by the plaintiff. *Manus iniectio* (arrest) was certainly one of the prior means of self-help, and probably *pignoris capio* (distraint) was far more general in pre-legal than in legal times. The submission to the tribunal was at first voluntary, to avoid organized resistance and to secure the distinction of the act of self-help as punishment rather than itself a delict.[50] As such the submission came to appear as an arbitration, under a binding agreement to abide by the result, which Moyle has called "the contractual decision of disputes." [51] And eventually such submission became compulsory; that is, no execution could be made without it.[52] But the execution itself remained for long in the hands of the plaintiff, the precise manner becoming more and more definitely prescribed and circumscribed.[53] It continued to be "doing justice for oneself," though only a sanctioned justice.[54]

Early law did not distinguish along modern lines between public

[47] Op. cit., p. 1025.

[48] Op. cit., p. 1035.

[49] Bonfante, op. cit., I, p. 168. "Mille ans s'écoulèrent . . . avant que le procès ne vint entièrement entre les mains de l'autorité publique et du magistrat. . ."

[50] Vinogradoff, *Jurisprudence*, I, p. 351, "Procedure begins to develop at a time when the element of public compulsion is absent or insignificant;" and Ihering, *Geist*, I, p. 123, says that he knows of no provision of ancient law which imposed on the plaintiff the co-operation of authority.

[51] *Imperatoris Iustiniani Institutionum Libri Quattuor*, I, p. 618.

[52] Girard, op. cit., p. 1026, Note 2, "Le droit de se faire justice était resté intact durant toute la République où son exercice n'était puni ni de peines publiques, ni de peines privées." Here he refers only to extra-legal *vis privata*. At the end of the Republic, it was by the law *de vi publica et privata* "non seulement permis, mais commandé de demander justice aux tribunaux" (p. 1026).

[53] Vinogradoff, *Jurisprudence*, I, p. 357. ". . . if he is willing to conform to certain rules established by authority, his self-help will be sanctioned: if not, he will himself be guilty of a misdemeanor." And Girard, op. cit., p. 30, "Celui qui croit avoir un droit, ne demande pas justice. Il se fait, en suivant d'ailleurs des formes rigoureusement arrêtées par l'usage, en s'exposant à commettre un délit s'il agit sans droit ou en dehors des formes."

[54] Bonfante, op. cit., I, p. 169, says, "Mais . . . si la contestation n'a pas lieu, ou que le défendeur avoue, ou qu'il ne comparaisse pas . . . le rôle du pouvoir public

and private law,[55] nor between crime, tort and breach of contract. It is true that in Rome the first judicial matters, about which the men banded together in the super-familial organization seem to have concerned themselves, were injuries to their joint interests, such as treason,[56] acts which might evoke the wrath of the gods upon the community and, already in early Roman days, murder.[57] But in the main all lesser injuries to individuals were undiscriminated and were left to the individual to redress. Moreover, such injuries were not distinguished according to whether they were injuries to the person of the chief (now called personal injuries) or injuries inflicted on him indirectly through some controlled person (now called injuries to domestic rights) or through some controlled object (now called injuries to property rights). The absence of distinction between the last two was obviously due to the fact that pre-property was a power over both controlled persons and controlled objects indiscriminately. The absence of all distinction within the house community was due to the fact that it was regarded as a whole, a subsidiary autonomous unit.[58] And this resulted as well in the continuing exclusive jurisdiction of the head over disputes between members of one house community. The household was judicially as well as administratively autonomous as to internal affairs.[59] Law dealt only with the relations between these basic political units. It was *as if* international.[60]

est fini ; le demandeur obtient la reconnaissance du bien-fondé de ses raisons *in iure* et la coaction est abandonnée au citoyen et à ses clients et amis, lesquels désormais, en se faisant justice ou en prêtant main-forte ne commettent pas de violence illégale (*vis iniusta*) ou bien il renonce à l'objet du procès, qui se termine toujours, *in iure*, par une espèce de traité de paix (*pactum*)."

[55] Or perhaps it is better to say that public law dealt only with the peculiar business of the *foedera* – the collective affairs. The distinction of *ius privatum* and *ius publicum* was a distinction of spheres. In the latter field we note "le parallélisme du droit privé et du droit public." Bonfante, op. cit., I, p. 165.

[56] *Perduellio* (*perduellis* is the enemy) and *parricidium*, which according to Clark's interpretation of its etymology (q.v.) must first have meant "striking or killing of father or parent," then that of any near relation, then of any free citizen and finally treason (*parricidium patriae*).

[57] "Der Übergang von der Volksjustiz zur organisierten Strafrechtspflege erfolgte weit früher als der der Privatrache zu dem System der Privatstrafen." Ihering, *Geist*, I, p. 212. And Girard, op. cit., p. 1026, says, "L'Etat romain se fait justice à lui-même, à toutes les époques. . ." Nevertheless, as Ihering points out, *Geist*, I, p. 219, ". . . nicht das Privatrecht ist nach publizistischen, sondern der Staat nach privatrechtlichen Prinzipien konstruiert."

[58] Ihering, Geist, I, p. 219, says, ". . . das Gefühl der individuellen Selbständigkeit ist das absolute erste. . ." And elsewhere he refers to the idea of autonomy as "the basis of ancient private law." Geist, II, p. 147. I am not certain that in making these statements he is visualizng an independence and autonomy strictly limited to the heads of households. But that is as far as the principles reached.

[59] Clark, *Regal*, p. 619, says, "There could be neither offence nor contested claim [at law] between members of a family, as to property which is, in the eye of the law, exclusively owned by the head."

[60] Bonfante, op. cit., I, p. 169, says, "En case de controverse entre les particuliers, c'est-à-dire entre l'un et l'autre *paterfamilias*."

It would appear that the character of the early tribunal depended upon the organization of the group within which a *manus-mund* and its peace existed. If this group had a single head – that is, if it was a house community or a folk – then the single leader, the *pater* or the *rex*,[61] would usually constitute the tribunal. If the group was merely a multiple of such units then the several heads, the *patres* or elders, constituted the tribunal.[62] All such functionaries had, however, many other duties. They were perhaps the military and certainly the religious officials, as well as the judicial. So, in the course of time, specialization began to appear. Then, in Rome, the judicial seemed to cling at first to the religious function.[63] And this apparently not so much by reason of a special priestly concern for the ethic, as by reason of concern for the *sacra* and thus the business of preserving the households intact.[64] Apparently changes of *manus* required the approval of the *pontifices*, and all legal processes were at first directed toward a change of *manus*.[65] The *pontifices* were also, at one period, the exclusive depositories and interpreters of the law – or at least the rules of procedure – which they kept secret; and they were usually the judges.[66] The actual *rôle* of all judges, up to and including the early *iudex*, was that of a jury not that of a court.[67]

Speaking of ancient law, Maine says,[68] ". . . the primitive Codes . . . all seem to begin with Judicature, and to distribute substantive law into 'heads of dispute'" (i.e. between members of different groups). And elsewhere he coins this striking and oft-quoted aphorism, to which we shall need to revert later since it seems to explain so many of the present differences between the legal philosophy and the factual social structure which it is intended to represent;

61 It should be noted that the process of repudiation could not have covered the whole ground of disputes *within* a group. Mere peace-making was there a considerable part of the function of judge or arbitrator. As Vinogradoff says, *Jurisprudence*, I, p. 346, "Hesiod, for instance, in the sixth century B.C. describes the function of kings sitting in judgment as the action of 'middlemen' who conciliate contending parties by persuasive words, and induce them to make peace and not resort to hostilities."

62 Clark, *Regal*, p. 394, suggests that "possibly this plurality [of judges] may be the older form of nascent Sovereignty or pre-Sovereignty," and the Council of Elders was "certainly a primeval institution at Rome" (p. 259).

63 Ihering, *Geist*, I, p. 299, says, "Der älteste römische Prozess war das Werk der *Pontifices*, oder genauer, er war nichts als der Prozess am geistlichen Schiedsgericht." And Clark, Regal, p. 422, says, "the function of Judges – which can at least at Rome, be shewn to be a development, both in civil and criminal cases, of the Priesthood."

64 Ihering, *Geist*, I, p. 269, says, ". . . die Wächter dieser Ordnung [the 'sacra'], die pontifices, tragen dafür Sorge, dass bei Erbfällen und Arrogationen die Verhältnisse der Privatsakra geregelt werden. Letztere ruhen wie eine Erbschaftssteuer auf jeder Erbschaft (*nulla hereditas sine sacris*)."

65 See Ihering, *Aryan*, p. 359.

66 See Bonfante, op. cit., I, p. 247.

67 See Girard, op. cit., p. 1037.

68 *E. L. and C.*, p. 382.

". . . substantive law has at first the look of being gradually secreted in the interstices of procedure. . ."[69] This is confirmed, in the Roman case, by Hunter.[70] "The order of development of juridical ideas among the Romans stand thus—ACTION, OBLIGATION, JUS." Thus the action (*actio*) is the first appearance of law, under our restricted definition. Derived from the pastoral *agere*, it describes originally this voluntary submission—the driving or conducting of the defendant by the plaintiff before the tribunal—in order to secure approval of his proposed execution of justice (vengeance). Thus the earliest known Roman actions, the *legis actiones*, are for the most part reproductions of pre-existing complete procedures for "doing oneself justice," and therefore combine in themselves several, or different, elements from the modern action. They are legalized procedures; processes rather than pure actions.

We have already discussed the process of *manus iniectio*, and its defence by vindication. Evidently it was of great antiquity, and the action was the legal replica of the original procedure. *Pignoris capio* was the ancient and almost universal procedure of "distraint." But the more immediate source of the later action seems to have been the *sacramentum*, of which the formalism was a curious mimicry of the settlement of disputes by force, reminding one of the English "trial by combat."[71] The essence of this action, according to the view coming to be generally accepted, was the countering oaths of the parties, made at first before the *rex* and later before his religious successors, the *pontifices*.[72] And the issue was the question which one

[69] *E. L. and C.*, p. 389. Pollock and Maitland, op. cit., I, p. 230, find this same precedence in early English law. They speak of "that characteristic mark of ancient jurisprudence, the prominent place given to what we sometimes speak of as 'adjective law,' the apparent subordination of rights to remedies . . . and naturally, for our common law is the law of courts which gradually acquired their jurisdiction by the development and interpretation of procedural formulas."

To a layman this "characteristic mark," derived from its origins, seems to persist as a survival and handicap in later law as well. Ihering, *Geist*, III, p. 368, says, that the standpoint of the Roman jurists "war der unmittelbar praktische der Klage"; whereas "das Fundament unserer heutigen wissenschaftlichen Systematik bildet nicht die Klage, sondern das Recht."

[70] Op. cit., p. 125.

[71] Bonfante, op. cit., I, p. 170, speaks of them as "probably representing primitive institutions." With reference to the last he says, op. cit., I, p. 172, ". . . dans cette procédure, la série des symboles rappellent l'époque où l'État n'intervenait pas, où c'était la lutte entre les parties qui décidait."

[72] Girard, op. cit., 1047, "Il consistait probablement à l'origine en un serment, prêté par chaque partie de son bon droit, qui amenait le roi, à la fois à la tête des affaires civiles et religieuses, à vérifier qui avait raison pour savoir qui devait l'amende de son parjure." The later *praedes sacramenti*, the *cautiones* or deposits, made by each party, were at first these "amendes." The older view (viz. Maine, *Ancient Law*, p. 363) that these deposits constituted a wager, simply took the wrong one of the two final senses of an originally single notion. Wager and gage (guaranty, *cautio*) are at first one. Clark has conceded the correction. He says, *Regal*, p. 451, "The loser's

had perjured himself. Clark[73] thinks this is the starting point of all early true actions. ". . . the *form* of procedure originally common to all actions involves the preliminary creation of a religious liability by making of oath. . ." Girard says "its precise office is to transform into debts upon which *manus iniectio* might be based, certain debts which did not themselves support it."[74] Presumably these debts might have arisen, as we shall suggest later, as well from delict as from contract. And I am inclined to think, judging by the description of the ceremonial which Gaius gives us,[75] that at first all such disputes consisted, in accordance with our previous thesis, of a vindication and a counter-vindication (imitations of that of the original *vindex*), of disputes between two chiefs of house communities as to where this natural or even the artificial *manus* belonged over a wrongdoer, a debtor, or any other person or object indiscriminately.

The point of first appearance of the institution of property in the law is merely a matter of definition. The point at which the developing legal procedure may be said to begin to take cognizance of disputes concerning property, depends on what we consider to be property. The range of injuries running from bodily hurts, through involuntary loss of possession of a person or object, to failure to restore when due such person or object voluntarily surrendered, is treated as a homogeneous whole. We can follow our modern categories and beg the question; or we can say that property appeared when first, in any of these cases, any kind of interest of one person in some other person or object was legally recognized. If so, property appeared in law as to such interests indiscriminately, more especially as to those over persons, but incidentally also those over objects; and there was hardly a distinction between property and obligation, or between the two classes of obligation. Over the person of the transgressor, be he debtor or tortfeasor, the action of the creditor was similar to a vindication, perhaps opposed by an actual vindication—which was similar to a counter-vindication—of one from the transgressor's own house.

Perhaps coincidentally with its appearance in connection with the form of the action, the institution of property begins to appear as well in connection with other forms, so similar to the action as to be hardly distinguishable, except in the light of later times. These are the transfers—the "transactions"—permanent or tentative, conditional or unconditional, of persons and objects from one system of relations in the social fabric—one *manus*—to another. If the system for

forfeited deposit is not a gain of the winner, but a fine paid in atonement of his false oath by the loser."

[73] *Regal*, p. 451.

[74] Op. cit., p. 31.

[75] Gaius, 4. 16. 17.

the decision of disputes seems to us contractual, the system of contract and conveyance seems to the same degree judicial. When these acts become legal acts – that is, when they begin to be incorporated as parts of the now developing legal institution of property – through some form of public validation on the part of the super-familial organization, then the form is much the same as that used in the settlement of the dispute. It is, in the same sense, an adjudication. It is a pre-judgment, an authorization of a changed *manus*, differing only in being voluntary. "The chief matters of the Roman law were decided under public guaranty. . ."[76] "The fourth fundamental principle in the constitution of the Roman house is publicity for all the legal acts concerning the whole *familia* or any member, that is the conclusion in the presence of witnesses."[77] But this witnessing, this publicity was more than a guaranty. It was a judicial authorization of much the same character as the action; ". . . its proper public is originally the assembly of the people in arms or in its civil capacity." Gradually this public is symbolized by a "skeleton *comitia*."[78]

Vinogradoff says[79] that "neither succession, nor property, nor possession, nor contract started from direct legislation or from direct conflict. Succession has its roots in the necessary arrangements of the household on the death of its manager, property began with occupation, possession is reducible to *de facto* detention, the origins of contract go back to the customs of barter." It is true that the static customs which were to become elements in the legal institution of property had already developed out of the internal relations of the household, and that the corresponding dynamic customs had already developed out of its external relations, such as the predecessors of conveyance and of contract, and vengeance for wrongs done to it. But these anterior customs were not the legal institution, nor equally its early source. The first set of customs was left by the infant law almost undisturbed; and only the second was taken over and became the avenue through which developed the legal institution of property. The sanction of the first – of property, of possession – remained for a long time non-legal. Nor for that matter does it seem to have rested overtly even upon custom. Rather it was regarded as a matter of fact. On the other hand the sanction of dynamic customs – of conveyance or contract and even of succession, as well as

[76] Ihering, *Geist*, I, p. 220. He considers that *testamentum in comitiis calatis* and *in procinctu*, and *arrogatio*, are effected immediately, while *mancipatio*, *nexum*, *coemptio* and *confarreatio* are effected mediately, that is through a small representation of the *comitia*.

[77] Ihering, *Entw.-gesch.*, p. 108.

[78] Vinogradoff, *Jurisprudence*, II, p. 237.

[79] *Jurisprudence*, I, p. 368.

of vengeance for delict or breach of contract—grew quickly to be legal.[80] And that which was added to these dynamic customs by the law was at first one almost uniform judicial authorization applied alike to actions and to transactions. It is proper to state, therefore, that property appeared in law as events—as actions or transactions—not as rights or states. Only gradually do we see signs of the projection of the incident into the condition existing before or after; of the sanction of the event spreading its aegis over the state; of the concept converting itself from that of a remedial fact or right to that of an antecedent fact or right. So the institution of property seems, like substantive law, to have consisted at first of its procedural incidents exclusively.

3. *"Ius"—The Super-familial Power and Its Sanction*

The field which we are now entering is among the most difficult and disputed of all those connected with early law, since it concerns especially the point of view of ancient men—the central core of the conceptual structure they were in process of developing as their guide to the ordering of social life. But since it is also peculiarly the foundation of much of the later organization of theory and practice, its elucidation, so far as possible, is necessary to our further studies.

We have already examined the course which the early developing state took as to the form and the nature of its entry into the judicial (legal) field. Vinogradoff has identified the two as inseparable. He says,[81] "In this sense law requires the State as a condition of its existence." But no political body "can exist apart from the Law, in the sense of a set of rules directing the relations and conduct of their members." "In short, law and the State are to that extent interdependent that it would be idle to derive one from the other. From this point of view the State may be defined as a juridically organized nation or a nation organized for action under legal rules." But such a definition produces a dilemma for us. If law begins with the state, when does the state begin? We have held that the preceding house community and the transitional gentilican communes, or federations of house communities, were also essentially political organizations. Therefore they too must have had law. The line to be drawn is necessarily arbitrary and merely convenient rather than significant. For there was no point at which pre-property was converted into the legal institution of property. It was an evolution, not a creation. Therefore we choose to fix this point and change the terminology

[80] See Appendix I E.
[81] *Jurisprudence*, I, p. 85.

at the moment when the lasting super-familial organization — the *civitas*, the *cité*[82] — which was to convert pre-property into property — began to appear. At that point, it seems, a new sanction came into being — a sanction which was to displace in this regard the earlier *mores* with their *fas* and *fides* — the sanction of *ius*.[83]

This was not at first a practical sanction. The practical sanction of this early law — in the legal sense of "means or methods of enforcement," or of promise of reward or threat of punishment — was very different from that of today. ". . . the origins of law in these communities depend on the *recognition of the community*."[84] The sanction was the withdrawal of this recognition — *outlawry* or ostracism. In a society constituted on the principle of its still autonomous component parts — the principle of *manus-mund* — one either enjoyed the protection of one's fellows, or of one's superiors, and participated directly, or through a representative, in the benefits of membership, or one was a lost soul consigned to outer darkness. The practical sanction of the super-familial authority was repudiation, exclusion, withdrawal of protection, the "opening of the hand."[85]

The true sanction — in the sense of the criterion according to which the decision of disputes was made — was the consensus of a more or less select body of opinion as to the accepted moral code — the prior and so-called customary law. As a determination of right and

[82] It is in line with Bonfante's satisfying thesis of the origins of Rome as a *civitas* to conceive that — since in general, "La cité n'a pas probablement une origine aryenne," because "aux agglomérations politiques sur des bases plus vastes [than communes] l'esprit aryen semble opposer une résistance indomptable," perhaps the consequence "de l'impossibilité à souffrir le joug (op. cit., I, p. 30) — the initial push which converted this particular one, among the many loose federations of Italic communes, into something more centralized, more viable, more dominating, than the rest, was the influence of the Etruscan overlordship during the Regal period. If so the point at which the change took place from an inter-familial to a super-familial government might be placed in this period which Frank conceives to have lasted about a century, about or prior to 600 B.C. (see op. cit.). Homo, *Primitive Italy and the Beginnings of Roman Imperialism*, pp. 99 ff., places it during the sixth and the last half of the seventh centuries, B.C.

[83] See Bonfante, op. cit., I, p. 245, for the relation of the sanction *fas* — of familial matters — and that of *fides* — of commercial matters — to the *mores*, and their continuance in those fields, or recognition later in the super-familial field.

[84] Vinogradoff, *Jurisprudence*, I, p. 359.

[85] Ihering, *Geist*, I, p. 122, says that injustice provoked in the breast of the community the same reaction as in that of one wronged — the idea of right — and that the preponderance of physical force threw itself regularly on the side of him who had the right. In pre-legal times it would appear from the evidence that the intervention of friends and relatives was based on fellowship in the *mund*, and was usually regardless of right or wrong. And in the beginnings of Roman law it is clear that there is no use of organized or official force for the revenge or punishment of wrongs to individuals. Even wrongs to the collective interest are dealt with by repudiation (outlawry) and the vengeance or punishment is left to any individual who wills. ". . . schlug tot, wer da Lust hatte." Ihering, *Geist*, I, p. 212.

wrong, with the connotation of the weight of tradition, of the authority of the deciding tribunal, and of the support of the body politic in the background, this sanction in Rome was *ius*. But *ius* differed from and was greater than its predecessors. While the modern views as to the significance of this word are almost as numerous as the writings on the subject, and while the etymologies which might shed light on the subject are almost equally numerous and quite uncertain, we may venture a general thesis which has considerable support. The etymology is discussed in Appendix I E.

We attach much significance to the early words of Roman law because, as Ihering says,[86] nowhere is the general primitive belief in the word, as something mystical and of supernatural power, stronger than in ancient Rome. On the other hand we must not expect as content a precise idea. All these early terms have large, vague and ramifying coverage, in which the best we can expect is to discover the core or characteristic idea implicit throughout, or the historical source from which the use was extended to related facts and processes.

The core and original idea of *ius* would seem to be "the truth" with the connotation of the oath – and thence the general notion of "the right," as norm or good. From this there develops the notion of the sanction of the determined right. And this in turn confers its own weight upon those to whom is conceded the authority to determine the right – the *iuris-dictio*. Thus the word comes later to stand for this specific authority,[87] or even for the place in which it is exercised. Since this early, principally judicial, authority is one of the two sources of all later governing, *ius* comes to share with the magistral *imperium* the general field of super-familial power. But, since its source is in the co-ordinating and autonomous features of the early constitution, rather than in the subordination, it continues to remain on the side of the constituent citizens as against *imperium*, which comes more and more to identify itself with the increasingly separate

[86] *Geist*, II, p. 441.

[87] Clark, *Regal*, p. 392, says, "The priestly judge . . . has behind him the general feeling of some elementary association of human beings, which causes the rule on which he bases his decision to be practically obeyed." And, p. 393, he takes "cognizance of Crimes as Sins requiring atonement in the interest of the community. . ." But "in all cases this primeval administration of Justice seems to occur in connexion with an *assembly* of the body [of citizens or army], before which we find some influential person or persons declaring what is right or fitting [*ius*] for the case." Thus the *ius Quiritium* (which gave rise to the *ius civile*) perhaps originally meant the authority of the host, doubtless signifying not so much the force of a military organization (not Ihering's probably erroneous etymology as "the spear-men"), but rather the fellowship within which there was a peace (Walde's etymology as from a "place name"). Bonfante, op. cit., I, p. 69, says ". . . le nom de *Quirites* servait à désigner les citoyens des *colles* [Sabine, as opposed to the Roman or Etruscan *montes*, centered on the Palatine] ou de la plus grande colline, appelée ensuite Quirinal."

entity, the state. *Ius*, at the beginning of the classic period, still stands for the collective or the individual authority of the group of citizens.[88] *Imperium* has come to be the authority of the super-entity, conceived as beyond and above the individual members. Taking "the right" as the central idea of *ius*, and that of jurisdiction or authority as the secondary thought, we find the usage of the word spreading until it includes that vague thing we signify by "the law," as well as its more specific accessories such as court and judgment.[89] In spite of authorities to the contrary I do not think it ever had, through the time of the classic Western Roman law, the sense of "a right," which it is frequently given in translation. To the Roman individual his *ius* was an absolute or a delegated power over others, no more than authorized self-help.[90] It does, however, at times convey—as well as the sense of authority and implicit responsibility of those upon whom it is conferred—the sense of the subjection and support that are derived from it by those who are submitted to it. The English word which comes nearest to translating its entire developed content is "rule," with its double sense of principle, or precept, and of mastery.

The words derived from *ius* shed considerable light on its original meaning. Ihering says,[91] "The distinction between the right or the injustice, the contestable or incontestable," is *ius* (or *iustus*) versus *iniustus*. It would appear from the term for oath, *ius-iurandum*, (strictly, "swearing"), that *iurare* (to swear) meant literally "to declare, or asseverate, the truth, or right," and that *per contra*, *iniuria* meant "a wrong declaration," or a "declaration of the wrong"[92]; whence it came to mean the harm done by such false

[88] Ihering, *Geist*, I, p. 219, says, "Die Normen, welche die Gesamtheit sich gesetzt hat oder stillschweigend anerkennt, und über deren Befolgung sie wacht, verhalten sich zu ihr in derselben Weise, d.h. sie erscheinen nicht als subjektiv beziehungslose Rechtssätze, sondern als ihre Rechte, Befugnisse."

[89] As examples of other all-inclusive legal terms we may cite *assize* (*assisa*) and *lis*. To the former Beames, in his translation of Glanville, p. 36, gives the following principal meanings: 1. Writ; 2. Jury; 3. Statute; 4. Court, place or time where writs of assize were taken; 5. a certain number; 6. it imported a tax or tribute; 7. it was used for a fine. Yet the word came from *assidere* (to sit beside) and came into this use through *assessor*, a judicial assistant. For the various meanings of *lis*, see Note 188, page 179.

[90] When, in early English Law Latin, we first meet a word which we have to translate as "a right" it is the word *rectus*. It is worthy of remark that the verbal sense which *rectus* should be given, as a past participle, leads one to suppose that, as "straightened" or "ruled," it derives secondarily from the judicial process which we connect below with the verb *regere* in its early stages.

[91] *Geist*, I, p. 123.

[92] In the early *sacramentum* the plaintiff challenged the defendant with the phrase, "*Quando tu injuria vindicavisti* or *provocasti*." Finally the judge "déclare de qui le *sacramentum* est *justum* et de qui le *sacramentum* est *injustum*." Girard, op. cit., p. 1049. The *ius* was abstract truth or right; *iuria* would have been a rightful assertion or claim; and *iustum* was the judicially confirmed rightness of this assertion or claim.

claim and then the prior harm resulting from the state of facts, forsworn by the *periurium*.[93]

The word *lex* has the sense of "*public declaration* rather than *binding law*."[94] On the basis of its most probable etymology[95] and of its early usage, it seems plausible that it at first expressed the *collected* verdict, or the verdict of those *collected* in the *comitia*, and thus came to mean any disposition arranged and announced in that manner.[96] The verb *lēgo*, derived from it, was used to cover the appointment of an ambassador,—whence *legatus*—and, as we have seen, was associated with the appointment of a guardian (perhaps also the heir) of a *familia*, as well as with specific dispositions of *pecunia*—whence the later term *legatum* (legacy).[97] The latter, in fact, may have been the original of the *privi-legium*, or *Sonderrecht*, and analogous to the early English sense of "specialty."[98]

The point which requires emphasis is the absence in the early stages of the idea of a legislative function. That was a gradual growth. In the beginning one sees a pronouncement, or verdict, an authoritative version or application of a traditional custom to a specific case, or a decision on a piece of business,—or even a special exception to, or qualification of, custom—proposed in general by the *rex*, affirmed or rejected by the *comices*, and confirmed by the *auctoritas patrum*.[99] The citizens made disposition of all their important affairs, collectively or individually, by the same means—a *lex*. To some extent there seems a contractual element, such as Ihering finds (see Note 105) in these pronouncements. The form, *sponsio*, like our vote (*votum*) and the early assimilation of the *foedera*, or treaties,

[93] See Appendix I E for Ihering's different interpretation of this accepted derivation. Pound, *Philosophy*, p. 151, construes the word to have meant particularly "insult."

[94] Clark, *Regal*, p. 375.

[95] See Appendix I E.

[96] It has the sense, perhaps, that made *legio* from *lego* (to collect).

[97] Clark, *Regal*, p. 450, says the "word *lex* . . . undoubtedly existed before the Twelve Tables, for *legare* in that code is evidently to make a *lex*, for the guardianship of a man's property generally, or the disposition of a particular part of it."

[98] See Salmond, *Essays in Jurisprudence and Legal History*, pp. 93-94.

[99] See Girard, op. cit., p. 17. It is as if this function had in general been limited to a consent or veto of exceptions to the customary rule—as if the chief could proceed without special authority so long as he remained within the *statu quo* or the customary rule. The formula of submittal of the *lex rogata* was, "*Velitis, iubeatis, Quirites? Rogo vos, Quirites.*" That of the affirmative response was "*Uti rogas*"; and that of the negative "*antiqua* (or *antiquo*) *probo*." In other words the king seems to have asked, originally, for authority to make an exception. Consent was "As you ask"; denial was "I approve the old (or former)"—perhaps even the "*ante quo* (or *qua*)," like our "*statu quo ante*." One sees a possible similar origin for the antithesis between *iubeo* (*iussus*) and *veto*; the one being to "hold right" (ordain) the other being "to *antiquare*" (reject, abrogate), perhaps related to *vetus*, itself in opposition to *novus* of which the verb was *novo* (innovate). See Appendix I E. Bonfante construes the sense of *iubeo* to be "consent" not "order" (op. cit., I, p. 100).

lends colour to this view. Some say that legislation "was thought of originally as declared and published custom. Later it was thought of as resting on the authority of the [new] state:"[100] early law "is really a codification of matter previously familiar," that is, custom:[101] or, "at first enactments are no more than declaratory. But it was an easy step from publication of established custom to publication of changes as if they were established custom and thus to conscious and avowed changes and intentional new rules through legislation."[102] But I am inclined to follow Bonfante and see the original legislation – that is, *leges* dealing with more than an individual piece of business – only in exceptions and qualifications to customs which were themselves so old and so well known that they were tacitly accepted and did not need to be promulgated; to deny at first "a true legislative activity" to the ancient *comitia curiata;* and to ascribe the initiation of even this limited legislation to the king and the senate as "the organ of all change" – legislation (public declarations) to which the *comices* committed themselves by their approval.[103] The XII Tables themselves, the first Roman codification, seem to have been publications of an accumulation of such modifications, more than they were enactments of new or fundamental rules, and to have resulted especially from a demand by the people (particularly the *plebs*) to know the rules that were governing judicial procedure.[104]

Of these two terms *ius* was the substance and the sanction of law; *lex* came to be its form and expression. From the beginning *ius* was the idea, the abstract criterion and sanction; *lex* was the specific, gradually becoming the general, rule of application.[105] In the Greek there

[100] Pound, *Philosophy,* p. 28.

[101] Clark, *Regal,* p. 390. Schröder, op. cit., p. 19, has much the same to say of the early German unwritten law. "Geschriebenes Recht gab es nicht, alles Recht war Gewohnheitsrecht, das teils in Urteilssprüchen von Fall zu Fall teils in abstrakten Urteilen oder Weistümern und in Rechtssprichwörtern zum Ausdruck kam."

[102] Pound, *Philosophy,* p. 21.

[103] See Bonfante, op. cit., I, p. 244.

[104] But see Girard, op. cit., pp. 27-28. Bonfante, op. cit., pp. 133-134 and 168, compares the XII Tables to the Magna Charta and points out that they did not codify all the customs which were in vigor, nor even sanction the fundamental institutions (which are presupposed), and that they were neither complete nor organic. They were largely "*dérogations particulières,*" that is, exceptions or qualifications of the old rules (*brèches à une système*), and regulations of procedure.

[105] While his view is coloured by a concept of the *peace* as a contract and by an etymology for *ius* which imputes to it a sense of which I see no traces in Roman usage, it seems worth while to cite a summary of Ihering's interpretation, as a possible corrective to the one we have presented. He says, *Geist,* I, p. 216, "Wille des Staats ist Wille sämtlicher Bürger, das Gesetz ein Vertrag, wodurch sich letztere gegenseitig zu einer gewissen Handlungsweise verpflichten, Recht im objektiven Sinn ist die daraus entstehende Verpflichtung aller." "Das Gesetz also ist nichts als eine auf das ganze Volk angewandte Obligationsform." In support of this he cites the fact that the form of the question and answer in *stipulatio* is the same as the question submitted to the populace, in connection with a *lex,* and its voting answer. And

is a similar distinction. *Τὸ δίκαιον*, the near equivalent of *ius*, has rather the connotation of abstract justice than of authority. The Greek sanction is ideal; the Roman practical.[106] But *θεσμός*, the declaration of customary law, and *νόμος*, the written law, correspond to *lex* at its two stages of development. They are the express, or expressed rules of the right.[107] To the end the Roman distinction endured. *Lex* became legislation. *Ius* became that great body of legal lore, mainly the work of the jurisconsults, which corresponded to our law and precedents. But the latter always retained the idea of something beyond – of a goal or norm – which fulfilled the original idea of "the right."[108] Through the avenue of the authority it conferred it came to be extended, in later times, to cover an idea which corresponds in some respects to our notion of "a right." It is worthy of remark that the French and German languages also suffer from the same inconvenience of having one word for these three ideas.[109] *Recht* and *droit*, like our "right" and "rule," come from (or from the source of) the Latin *regere*, meaning "to direct or govern," and are derived from a root meaning "to fit," or, perhaps, "to make straight."[110] The double sense of *regere* still survives in our word

Papinian called such voting "*communio reipublicae sponsio*." He holds, p. 217, that *lex* is "gleichbedeutend mit Auflage." ". . . das Gesetz soll keine *lex privi*, d.i. *privilegium* einführen." "Der Sprachgebrauch, der diesen Ausdruck gleichmässig von Gesetzen wie von Privatvereinbarungen gebraucht, zeigt, dass beide ursprünglich in der Vorstellung der Römer auf einer Linie standen." "Eine *lex publica* ist ein Vertrag aller und umgekehrt eine Privatvereinbarung ein Gesetz für die beiden Kontrahenten." And, p. 218, "Diese Wirkung des Gesetzes, dass jeder gebunden wird, drückt der Ausdruck *jus* aus. *Lex* bezeichnet den Grund des Rechts, den Akt des Auferlegens, *jus* die Folge, den dauernden Zustand des Gebundenseins. Die *lex publica* begründet das *jus* im objektiven Sinn, die Rechtssätze; die *lex privata*, der Vertrag, das *jus* im subjektiven Sinn, die Berechtigung. Wie Gesetz und Vertrag, die später so weit auseinander gehen, ursprünglich identisch gewesen sind, so auch Recht im objektiven und subjectiven Sinn. *Jus* ist das Band, das Bindende, die Rechtsnorm, und zwar *jus* im objektiven Sinn das, welches bindet, allen eine Pflicht auferlegt, beziehungsweise ein Anrecht gewährt, *jus* im subjektiven Sinn, was bloss einen einzelnen bindet und dadurch einem andern das Recht gewährt."

106 Δίκαιον and δίκη, since, like the Skt. *diçā*, they arise from IE. **deik-* (to show) and thus correspond to the process covered in the Latin *iudex*, are in reality semantic equivalents of the Roman *fas*, not of the Roman *ius*. *Fas* – with *fāri*, *fātum*, *fateor*, *fāma* – is from the IE. * *bhā-* (to say). Thus *fas* was divine because it was the traditional or antique "spoken" law (like δίκαιον) whereas *ius* was human because it was the modern or current authority, the sworn or voted right.

107 See Vinogradoff, *Jurisprudence*, II, pp. 19 and 74.

108 As Pound, *Philosophy*, p. 31, puts it, "The Latin equivalent of τὸ δίκαιον (the right or the just) became their [the jurisconsults'] word for law. They said *ius* when Cicero said *lex*."

109 Ihering, *Geist*, I, p. 222, makes a play on this *double entendre* which also well interprets the Roman *ius*, when he says, "Das Konkrete was hier wie so oft in der Geschichte des römischen Rechts die Brücke zum abstrakten; aus dem Schutz der Rechte entwickelte sich der Schurtz des Rechts."

110 See Appendix I E. Schröder, op. cit., p. 18, says, "Das Wort 'Recht' (got. *raihts*, an. *réttr*) bedeutete ursprünglich das gerade gemachte ('gerichtete'), also das subjective Recht, erst erheblich später, davon abgeleitet, die 'Richtung,' das objektive

"ruler," which may mean either a governor or an instrument for making a line straight. That this diagrammatic psychic trick is fundamental is also shown by our words "crooked," as evil or wrong, and "straight" as honest or *square*. It is supposed that "law" is derived from a root signifying "to lie," perhaps in the sense of something established.[111] So, since "statute"—or "established"—means literally that which is set up,[112] it is not entirely beside the mark to see in the phrase, "lay down the law," an etymological contradiction. While the modern world has selected a new, and a larger, vocabulary, principally from Latin sources, to cover the various meanings of *ius*, we have paid the original word the compliment of letting it supply us with "justice," with "judges" and "juries" and their "jurisdictions," and even with "injuries" and "perjuries."

4. *"Res"—The Subject of Dispute*

The extent to which the coming of law created the institution of property, as if it were an overlay, gradually deposited by the expansive super-familial organization upon existing practices, which converted them into something new—at least in seeming—is prettily demonstrated by the history of the terms which it has developed in various languages to represent the very substance of property, the *thing* itself. Certainly some of these terms, and perhaps all, have passed through a process the recognition of which illuminates the whole of legal history. The most certain example of this process is the French word *chose* which, from medieval times, while it has retained, as well, its earlier sense of a legal case or cause (as in *chose jugée*), has come to signify in law all objects of the right of property, and more particularly material objects. It is derived from the Latin *causa* which, in general, meant "cause" or "reason," but, in law, signified particularly a "case" or a "pleading" and perhaps, originally and more technically, the grounds or documents of pleading or of title.[113] Thus the word which, from more specialized beginnings,

Recht, die Rechtsnorm [in this connection *gerichtete* = set right and *Richtung* = direction]. Die gelaüfigste Bezeichnung für die letztere war bei den Nordgermanen *lagh* and *laeg*, bei den Westgermanen 'Ehe' (ahd. *êwa*, as. *êo*, *êu*, ags. *â*, *ae*, *aew*, afrs. *â*, *ê*), d.h. Billigkeit (lat. *aequum*)," (i.e. fairness, justness).

111 οἱ κείμενοι νόμοι.

112 The corresponding German *Gesetz* and *Satzung* may have come from the sense of a "settled" society. So Ihering assumes, *Entw.-gesch.*, p. 50, as already quoted, in connecting *Sitte* (custom), *Satzung* (statute) and *Gesetz* (law or statute) with *sitzen* and *setzen*, and *Gewohnheit* (custom) with *wohnen*, all in the sense of dwelling, or settling "*an einem bestimmten Ort.*" But it is equally possible that they were "established" or "set up" entirely independently of this process. The French *loi* is *lex*.

113 For the etymology, see Appendix I E.

came to mean a case at law, has since become the substantial or insubstantial object of property.

The German *Sache* has reached an even broader scope. Technically it means the objects of property, usually in a material sense. But in its compounds it stands for all legal matters (viz. *Sachenwalter*) and even for property in general (viz. *Sachenrechte*). Yet its well known origin has no relation to objects. It is a cognate of *sake*, that term which has puzzled the students of Anglo-Saxon law. Perhaps, on the analogy of "sake" and "forsake," we may attribute to it a very early sense of "claim, or blame." Certainly it had a contentious connotation.[114] As, in the course of time disputes came to be brought before a tribunal, the words *Sache* and *sake* were used to refer to such disputes, or combats—the predecessors of law suits,[115] and thence came to mean a case, or cause, at law. From this point their congener, *soke*, diverged along the line of the court or its jurisdiction or authority, and *Sache* followed almost the same course as *chose*.

Again with the word "thing" (German *Ding*), the earliest sense seems to have been "the council of the folk."[116] Thence or also, it meant "the public handling before the folk," or a matter so handled. And the verb *thingian* meant "to deal before the folk," and thence "to compose a dispute" or "to contract" (i.e. agree publicly). Thus through the channel of "the law suit" both the English and German words have come to mean, in law, property or its object. *Ding* shares this field with *Sache*, but has become so real that it expresses the very fact of materiality (*Dinglichkeit*). "Thing" means nothing definite in common speech, but in law it means, as we shall see, property or its object, with a decidedly material sense in its use in theory.

Upon the basis of these and other analogies and in spite of the generally accepted doctrine as to its sense and etymology, we have to suggest that the word *res* had a similar origin and development of meaning; one which cannot, however, be positively proved since it was wholly prehistoric. By classic times it had come to cover much of the field of "affair," "cause" (legal) and "thing," in English. Its early legal usage can only, I think, be arrived at by inference. Of the various eventual senses the one by which we denominate "reality"—that of physical objects—has been chosen by authorities to be the original idea and the search for a derivation has been made on the theory that the word meant "riches." Our thesis is, on the contrary, that *res* represented originally a litigious concept, connected in some

114 For the etymology, see Appendix I E.

115 Schröder, op. cit., p. 91, says that the only early legal process in Germany was a combat between the parties before the judge. Hence *widersacho*, the counterclaimant, (OHG. *widersacho*, AS. *andsaca*, Old Franconian *gasakjo*).

116 Schröder, op. cit., p. 21, The "gemeingermanische Bezeichnung der Volksversammlung war Ding (lang. *thinx*, an. *þing*)." For the etymology, see Appendix I E.

indeterminable way with the family of words represented by *rex* and *regere* in Latin, old Irish *rí*, and by *Reich* and also *Richter* in German, and that its growth from the seed of the process of settlement of disputes to the later wide range of meanings was along the same channels as that of the other words cited above. The grounds for this thesis are fully laid out in Appendix I E. Here we may note merely a few points relating to it. We catch an early hint, by way of confirmation, in the word *reus* which meant not "owner" but a participant – later the defendant – in a lawsuit. It is also clear that the *rex* was, either at the beginning or at an early stage, particularly a judge; that the process of governing, except for military leadership, continued, even into historical times, to consist very largely of the judicial or magisterial function; and that the idea of direction, of straightening or arranging, which pervades this family of words, while it may have risen at first from military leadership, indicates a common judicial period for both eventual groups, those which came to pertain to political *regulation* as well as those which remained at the stage of judicial *richtend*.[117]

We have now come to the conclusion that the use of *res* and *ius* in early Roman law corresponds generally to the similar pair of terms, *sake* and *soke*, in early Anglo-Saxon law. The first of each pair meant something like the claim, or the case itself, and the second of each pair meant particularly the authority to decide the case, the jurisdiction of the superior. Such vague and purely dynamic concepts have more the sense of the doing – almost verbal – than of some abstract notion.

From the time we can trace them with some certainty the development of sense of *Sache*, *chose*, *thing* and *res* flow from different or uncertain sources into a common channel. *Sache*, as dispute, and *chose*, (perhaps) as the ground of dispute, joined *thing* (*Ding*), the tribunal, and all became a lawsuit. On the basis of *reus* we may

[117] We refer to the citations already made to Ihering's views, see supra, p. 137, Note 20 as to the original military function of the *rex*. The idea of arranging, "not the civil organization, but the battle array" fits the root *ar* (from which this family is supposed to have arisen) and many of its derivatives. *Aryan*, p. 324. But he concedes the judicial as a major, though later, function. So Schröder, op. cit., p. 32, says "Mehrfach begegnet die Bezeichnung der Fürsten als 'Richter' (*iudices*)." Clark holds that the judicial was the original function. He says, *Regal*, p. 456, that *rex* inclines etymologically "rather to the idea of Judge than to that of Priest," and passes over the possible military origin. Believing himself to be on common ground with Mommsen, he states, p. 457, "My own theory is that when the office of *rex* first arose at Rome, before the full development of the Sovereignty, [pre-Regal], the functions specially intended by the name were judicial or magisterial. . ."

It is quite in line with this thesis and with the process of development we have described, that the phrase *res publicae*, should have developed from the matters or judgments of the public assembly into the affairs of the body politic in general (*res publica*), its form of organization (republic) and its property (*res publicae*).

assume *res* to have appeared at this stage from some uncertain source. Thence all become more particularly the matter, or subject, of a lawsuit, as such the dawning concept of the property interest, and eventually the object of property. At the last they have all been *concreted.*[118] Nevertheless, we should notice the fact that these terms, while they have pervaded their respective languages, from litigious sources, in many other ways, have hardly influenced the popular terminology for the objects of property.

If we attempt to impose upon the word *res* in its early, or even classical, legal use, its own eventual popular sense, or that to which *thing*, *sache* and *chose* have arrived in legal literature—that is, if we follow the general practice of students of Roman law—we will fail, I think, almost entirely to understand the contemporary viewpoint as to the institution of property. For it is true that the whole of Roman property law centres upon the word *res*, and can only be seen as it was if one has clearly in mind the meaning, the connotations, the conceptual *milieu*, and therefore the history of this word. The legal institution of property developed out of procedure. This procedure consisted of litigation and the closely similar processes of transfer. *Res* was the subject of such procedure—the matter in hand. While it developed many specialized uses,[119] some of which were objective, we shall do well to remember that its general use was to cover the subject or basis of any action or transaction. This viewpoint will enable us to see the extent to which the idea of the right of property—the central concept of the legal institution—grew out of the right of action; was in fact the right of action and to some extent still is in legal theory. In early law, property was the legal means of securing it. Only later did it come to be conceived as something which existed independently of the action or transaction and which the law merely confirmed.

5. *"Poena"—The Original Objective of Action*

We have assumed that the original method of doing oneself justice was to seek or take vengeance. The idea of vengeance which one may detect within the emotional rind, is the idea of equalization. Its purpose and satisfaction was a reverse liquidation of that which had

[118] In the same way our word "property," which purists agree means only a right or relation, has come, in popular usage, to mean the object, not the relation of property—the object owned. This is a very common form of psychological ellipsis resulting gradually in a substitution. It seems to be a common cause of the semantic process which Breal calls "concretion," and of which we shall cite a number of other examples as we proceed. See Bréal, *Semantics*, Ch. 13.

[119] For an analysis of some of these specialized meanings, see Note 186, page 178; also see Note 89 on *assize*, p. 152, and Note 188 on *lis*, p. 179.

upset the original reciprocal equality (*aequitas*), and thus a restoration of the normal equilibrium. It may have been expressed at first as *talio*.[120] But at some early stage the word *poena* became the general term and somewhat changed the objective.[121] Perhaps borrowed from the Greek, or perhaps the cognate of ποινή, it never seems to have had the sense of vengeance, as did the latter at first, but to have progressively run the gamut of "expiation," "punishment," "penalty," "compensation," "fine."[122]

As Maine has said,[123] early "Courts of Justice existed less for the purpose of doing right universally than for the purpose of supplying an alternative to the violent redress of wrong."[124] True; yet at first it was this very "violent redress of wrong" which was legitimized into a formal self-help. Moyle[125] finds it necessary in order "to bridge over the gulf between the primitive system of private vengeance, and the earliest Roman civil process," to proceed both by "tracing this gradual incorporation of self-redress with a regular procedure" and by recognizing the beginnings of three more advanced ideas, "the introduction and development of the idea of composition for injury; the plan of guaranteeing a man's rights by collective action through witnesses [i.e. formal conveyances and contracts]; and the contractual decision of disputes" (i.e. the assimilation of judgments to the foregoing).

The first step away from vengeance or private punishment was the substitution of a money composition. At first the wrongdoer and his party had either to "buy off the feud or fight it out."[126] And

[120] From *talis* (i.e. of the same kind). This practice continued at least until the time of the XII Tables, for Gaius, commenting thereon explains that it is called *talio*, '*propter membrum quidem ruptum talio erat*;" Gaius, 3. 223.

[121] Perhaps this took place at the point, which Ihering seems to think he detects, when *Privatrache* gave way to *Privatstrafen*; see *Geist*, I, p. 212. And at the same point – perhaps the appearance of the prestly concomitant to the judicial function – entered the idea of sin and expiation which regarded "das Verbrechen als Vergehen gegen die Gottheit, die Strafe als Sühnemittel" (p. 275).

[122] Thus it has given rise to *punio* (*poenio*) (avenge, punish), *poenitio* (freq. of *poenio*) (tr. displease, intr. feel displeasure, repent) and *poenitentia* (penitence). Ultimately from *poena* are our words "pain," "pine," "penance," "penitent," "repent," "penal," "penalty," "punish," etc. And these, I think, give a fair notion of the early content. Ihering, *Geist*, I, p. 277, says "*Poena*, worin man wie im griechischen ποινή zunächst das Sühnegeld erblicken will, weist etymologisch auf die Idee der Reinheit hin, ebenso *castigatio* (*castum agere*) : der *incastus*, *incestus*, der Schmutzige, wird dadurch gereinigt, und *luere*, büssen namentlich auch in Verbindung *poenas luere*, ist *lavere*, *lavare*, waschen." Ernout and Meillet suggest that its first use, when borrowed from the Greek, was popular and designated "le châtiment infligé à un serviteur."

[123] *Lectures on the Early History of Institutions*, p. 288.

[124] Holdsworth, *A History of English Law*, III, p. 278, says, "The first business of the law, and more especially of the law of crime and tort, is to suppress self-help."

[125] Op. cit., I, p. 616.

[126] Pound, *Philosophy*, p. 148.

the individual wronged "did not waive his private vengeance in return for a ransom unless he chose to do so, fixing the amount to his own liking."[127] The composition was a ransom, a buying of peace. "As the social interest in peace and order—the general security in its lowest terms—comes to be secured more effectively by regulation and ultimate putting down of the feud as a remedy, payment of composition becomes a duty rather than a privilege. . ."[128] It becomes either a compulsory compromise or "the public imposes on the wronged the necessity of contenting himself with a ransom fixed by itself, a legal composition, a '*créance d'amende.*'"[129] The result is "the detailed tariff of compositions that is the staple of ancient 'codes'."[130] And thus *poena* becomes a sum of money.[131] "The next step is to measure the composition, not in terms of the vengeance to be bought off, but in terms of the injury. A final step is to put it in terms of reparation."[132] Nevertheless there lingered even to the time of the XII Tables certain relics of *talio*; until much later times certain processes of self-redress; and even throughout classic Roman law, *poena* retained vestiges of penalty rather than pure compensation or reparation. Accompanying this evolution was another. In the course of time "the state, to protect order and peace, enlarged little by little its sphere of action and altered the conception of the ends of penal law."[133] Penal public law, from being concerned only with *political* crimes, came to treat as crimes also acts which had been hitherto only delicts.

Legal historians are apt to see the modern categories of actions

127 Girard, op. cit., p. 29. Poste, op. cit., p. 412, for instance, cites the declaration of Rotharis, giving "the relatives of the slain their election between the primitive vengeance for blood (feud or vendetta) and a composition or pecuniary fine (wergeld or poena) to be recovered by action before the public tribunals." Moyle, op. cit., I, p. 616, conceiving its origin to be at this point, says, "There can be little doubt that the term 'poena' originally meant not so much penalty as composition for injury . . . sums in consideration of which the injured person consented to forego his customary right of self-redress. . ."

128 Pound, op. cit., p. 148. And, p. 151, "In juristic terms, the central idea of the beginnings of liability is duty to make composition for or otherwise avert wrath arising from the affronted dignity of some personality desirous of vengeance, whether an injured individual, a god or a politically organized society. Greek law and Roman law give the name of insult to legally cognizable injury to personality." Perhaps we can seize the idea so well put, without accepting the interpretation of *injuria* as *insult*. See page 152, supra.

129 Girard, op. cit., p. 29. He describes the evolution of delicts, p. 421, as passing through "la phase de vengeance privée, celle des compositions volontaires, celles des compositions légales et celle de la répression par l'Etat."

130 Pound, *Philosophy*, p. 150.

131 Ihering, *Geist*, I, p. 127, says, "Denn das ist das höchste Ziel der Gerechtigkeit, wie in der einem Wagschale das Verdienst, so in der andern die Schuld rechtig abzuwägen, das Gleichgewicht herzustellen zwischen dem Verdienst und der Schuld auf der einem und dem Lohn und der Strafe auf der andern Seite."

132 Pound, *Philosophy*, p. 149.

133 Bonfante, op. cit., I, p. 167.

(and the derived rights) already distinguished, or distinguishable, in the early stages of the law. But to a layman the evidence indicates rather that they were as yet undifferentiated, though of course the lines of the later distinctions were already being laid. The most prominent features of the law and probably the almost exclusive subjects of legal actions were wrongs, or injuries.[184] But there seems to have been little distinction in the nature of these wrongs. In the beginning the failure to return what one had borrowed, or to pay for what one had bought, seemed hardly distinguishable from theft. Injuries suffered by reason of failure to carry out promises (negative acts) and injuries suffered to persons or objects by positive acts were closely allied. All were wrongs. And the remedy for wrongs was vengeance. It is difficult to distinguish the treatment of the debtor from that of the wrongdoer.[185] Moreover, as soon as composition appears, we have debtors for this judgment.[186] It would seem in general that in early times the distinction of method was rather according to whether the transgressor (debtor or wrongdoer) was of another gentile household or of a poor, weak or *ungehörig* household, than that it discriminated debt from delict.

There are also some signs that the loan of person or object did not at first, as we say, transfer property. Pound, writing of early Indian law, says "the legal idea [in debt] so far as there is one, is not of obligation but of a property right in the creditor."[187] We may venture the thought that it is consistent with our view of the major operation which was required to effect a change of *manus*, that ordinary loans or "uses" were not, until the beginnings of mature law, conceived to alter the classificatory genitive of 'belonging.' Certainly, once the debtor had consented to the prejudgment of his debt (*nexum*) he was within the *manus* of his creditor and the means of dealing with him were indistinguishable from that of any other subject of *vindicatio*. Nevertheless a *natural* vindication instantly released him.

[184] Muirhead, op. cit., p. 136, says, "In the XII Tables . . . delicts are much more prominent than contracts,—wrongs entitling the sufferer to demand the imposition of penalties upon the wrong-doer, that in most cases covered both reparation and penalty."

[185] For instance, even in later times according to most authorities, the defaulting debtor, after *manus iniectio* could be killed or sold into slavery. Ihering thinks this was a substitution by the Romans for the old Indo-European public exposure. See *Aryan*, p. 57. The creditors, if there were several, had the joint right of killing and dividing (?) the corpse (?). See Girard, op. cit., p. 1044. If the *vindex* interfered in *manus iniectio*, and the debt (or tort) was proved, the claim against him was for double the amount otherwise assessed, showing the idea of injury or wrong rather than of repayment or compensation. See Girard, op. cit., p. 1043.

[186] *Manus iniectio iudicati.*

[187] *Philosophy*, p. 244. In this connection it is well to point out that several of the earliest contracts, *commodatum*, *depositum*, *pignus*, did not transfer property. Also the "uses," to which we shall advert later, left *dominium* unchanged.

As the scope of the judicial function expands – or perhaps coincidently from the beginning – it comes to include other types of dispute as to the *manus* of persons and even of objects. In these cases, the objective of the action is not to avenge an injury but rather to secure the vindication or restoration of the subject of the dispute itself. This *thing* the plaintiff asserted was his, or ought to be given him; he sought to pursue (*persequor*) it. Thus in the public mind the matter or subject of dispute – the grounds of action or the dispute itself – comes to be identified with the objective, the thing sought, and, in this way, the word *res* begins to be used as both subject and object. Eventually we have, then, two types of objectives; one *poena* – vengeance or its equivalent in money – and the other *res* – the thing itself. And, since by that time, it had been found more convenient to apply, at least to voluntary surrenders of possession, the same principle of money equivalent, in place of restoration, there arises in early law a similar distinction as to the latter – one between *res* and *quanti res erit*, its money equivalent. So *res*, or *res persequenda*, the subject of dispute itself or its equivalent in money, comes to be distinguished, as an alternative objective, from *poena*, the element of vengeance or punishment, by that time a compulsory composition of compensation or reparation, also in money.

We have now perceived that, so far as the institution of property was the child of a super-familial law, its first appearances resulted from the antique power of the chief (or agnate) over the members of his house community (*vindicatio*); or from the customary claim of the wronged to the person, or body, of the wrongdoer (*manus iniectio* and *noxae deditio*), or in default of that to vengeance (*talio*, *poena*) or the price of forbearance (*poena*). The subjects of legal disputes were largely persons; the occasions were either losses of possession, involuntary or voluntary, of persons or of objects (including money) or they were injuries; the objective was either the subject (*res*) or satisfaction (*poena*). These seem to be the original incidents of property in the earliest Roman law of actions; a system of property consisting, for the most part, of direct relations between superior and subordinate persons, between the layers of which, as a sort of wedge, the beginnings of the money economy is driving a partial substitute.[188]

B. *The Classic Scheme*

The most difficult part of the task of presenting the essential facts in the development of our own law of property faces us when we attempt to analyse the complex finished structure of Roman law as

[188] Bonfante, op. cit., II, p. 81, thinks money began to come into use about 350 B.C.

it appeared at the end of its classic period in the Western Empire. The final codification, under Justinian, into a consistent *corpus juris* does not truly represent the law of the Romans. It is a sophisticated summation applied in a new *milieu*, subjected to amending influences, and only compiled after the "decline and fall." Nevertheless it contains much of the "source material" for the previous period. Moreover it is particularly this latter which represents the heritage which Rome bequeathed to the world, analogous to that which Greece left us in the philosophy of her apogee. As a philosophy it has been the gospel of the so-called civilians for more than a thousand years and the source, in principle, of much of modern law. There are today, as Pound says, "two great systems of law, the Roman or Civil Law and the English or Common Law."[139] The characteristics of civil law have persisted and spread over half the civilized world among "those peoples who," as Maine puts it, "built the debris of the Roman Law into their walls."[140] And, while the other half professes the common law, one would be blind not to perceive that this English system is itself somewhat a hybrid, infused since the days of Bracton with ideas from the more sophisticated system, borrowing from Canon Law, and beginning with Bentham, Austin and the moderns to try to fit its disorderly growth into the orderly arrangement of a Roman or pseudo-Roman jurisprudence. So much of the study of this classic Roman law by the almost continuous series of scholars, from the glossators through to the moderns, is distorted by the medieval and modern rationalizing and the structures of legal theory that have since been erected upon the original foundation, that one cannot always trust the picture they present. Theirs is a modern *restoration* from the "debris," not the original,—though, in part, the old plans still survive. Therefore we shall deliberately shut our eyes to all these subsequent developments from Roman law and shall endeavour to see it as it was in the heyday of Rome itself by considering it only in the light of its ancestors and not in that of its descendants.[141]

It would be impossible to discuss in any detail in this brief space the mature Roman law of the classic period. In many respects, as we have said, it is the foundation of our modern law of property and in this, as in the latter case, we must assume a general knowledge of the subject on the reader's part. What we shall undertake is a tracing, through this period, of the course of those particular enduring and fundamental concepts that we have already examined. This will enable us to see the way in which these old inherited prejudices have

[139] *Readings on the History and System of the Common Law*, p. 26.

[140] *Ancient Law*, p. 45.

[141] And this is made the more exact by the fact that Roman law developed consistently from its original basis by modification only. See Bonfante, op. cit., and particularly I, p. 497.

unconsciously become the basis of the later theory of the law of property and have confused and often misrepresented the fact of modern property and its law. In other words we wish to convert the disguise of our modern institution, which arises from this source, from a state of opacity to one of transparency, so that we may see through the surviving old forms and old theories to the new facts.

The three original relations of citizenship in Rome were *connubium*, *commercium* and *actio*, terms which described the three graded privileges of the Roman caste system. These relations have persisted as the internal, the external and the procedural and have given rise, with modifications from another source, to the arrangement of the Institutes of Gaius and thence to those of Justinian. But with the growth of the subject matter the titles have changed and have become the "Law Concerning Persons," the "Law Concerning Things" and the "Law Concerning Actions." The internal structure and functioning of the house communities have now in some respects come within the purview of the law. Status is now crystallized in law as it doubtless always was in domestic custom. And status now includes not only the position of the individual with respect to the *familia* but has come to include that of free men in respect of citizenship, a growing problem in the increasingly conglomerate Roman population. Domestic mastery over men — even slaves — has now been partially differentiated from mastery over land, animals and inanimate objects. The former has assumed the position of status with a lingering and still strong tinge of property. The latter has become concerned exclusively with material objects (and, in some respects, with slaves) and the purview of the law with regard to it is still largely confined to its external relations.

1. *The Two Fields of Power*

Yet this rough statement is neither quite accurate nor completely illuminating. The organization of the classic law goes deeper than that. In the previous pages we have outlined the development of the external relations of the *familiae* and have identified therewith the gradual growth of a jurisdiction, or *ius*, in regard to these inter-familial relations, which comes to be known, in our terminology, as law.

As this inter-familial *ius* (*ius privatum*) developed from its beginnings in the voluntary, but supposedly binding, submission to arbitration, it became a more and more powerful sanction as to what was right. Whereas previously the only sanction was the mores — *fas* and *fides* — and the conscience and the power of the individual house head, the collective sense of *ius* came later to descend upon this individual from above: whereas, at first, his authority was no stronger than his own power, the super-familial power came later to lend strength to him. He became subject to it, but also privileged under it. Thus *ius* came to mean, not only "the right," but law and rule, when viewed from above, and sanction and subordination when viewed from beneath. Nevertheless in this aspect it retained the sense of an authority conferred rather than that of a result assured, because the process of relieving the plaintiff of the necessity of himself asserting his authorized power, within or without the household, was itself a product of the classic period and was never completed in Rome.

At some point the term *ius* and its content was transferred, as a whole, from the inter-familial field, wherein it seems to have been developed, to the intra-familial field, which was now commencing to become subordinate.[142] There it was confined for the most part to human beings and rarely extended to material objects, just as in its larger sphere it concerned primarily the relations between men and men, and only secondarily those between men and objects. The transfer had been at least partially effected prior to the XII Tables, for its affirmation appears therein. When the process was finished the assimilation was complete. The *paterfamilias* was conceived to exercise the same kind of *ius* over the *familia*—at least, over its human elements—that had already begun to be delegated to him as a result of awards in specific disputes with persons outside the *familia*. When this authority recognized (or granted) the power to name the guardian (and perhaps the heir) of his *familia* and the disposition, *causa mortis*, of his *pecunia*, the term *legare* was used, which is the same term used of appointments by the *comitia*. The XII Tables directed of what he so "publicly declared," "let it be settled right, or law" (*ius esto*). And, for the letter of a will, the expression of this *ius*, the Romans used the term *tabulas* just as they did of their early written law.[143] It is highly probable that this process confirmed the

[142] It is possible that the term was already used of, and had been developed in connection with, the sanction of the *iudex domesticus*. We have no means of knowing, since there is no remnant of a written intra-familial code. But the antithesis of *fas* and *ius* and the later entry of *fides* into the law, perhaps from the source of the gens, suggest that it was not. Also the antithesis between the *iudex* and the *vindex* suggests that it was not. Nevertheless, since the super-familial organization was, as we have seen, developed at first in part on the familial model, it was natural to apply the term, used with reference to the former, to the latter as well.

[143] Muirhead, op. cit., p. 22, shows that the power of the house head, which was originally that of *manus*, became latterly that of *ius*. Thus as the form of jurisdiction, or power, called *ius*, entered the sphere of the smaller political unit it displaced the antique relation of *manus*, except as to the wife. As to her it asserted the new *ius*, as *in manu*; as to those purchased by mancipation it did likewise, as *in mancipio*; as to those born *in potestate*, the same. *Ius* became the inclusive term for the jurisdiction, or rule, of the master over the people of the household.

concentration of the newer idea of property upon the *patrifamilias*, or at least that the stripping off of the customary restrictions upon their dealing with the subject matter was simultaneous. For, as the heads of all the constituent small political units established among themselves a public and superior *ius* to which, at first, only they themselves were related, they, as an oligarchical group, became capable of usurping a certain freedom of action which had perhaps not been theirs before. The group power of the heads of households began to supersede the group power of the households themselves.[144]

Thus we find in later law that the word *ius* has come to cover the whole ambit, respectively, of domestic and of the limited original private or inter-familial law. Nevertheless these are conceived to be two separate fields of power, originally absolutely distinct and even then to a considerable degree independent.[145] The component sources of the chief's authority (domestic law) are still *manus*, *mancipium*, and *potestas*, now jointly called *ius*. The component sources of the collective or delegated authority (private law) are the *Quiritii* (*ius civile*) and the Praetor (*ius honorarium*), or, as we should say, Quiritary and Praetorian law.[146] The exercise of the first by the *patrifamilias*, as the *ius* within the *familiae*, is merely sanctioned and supported by new authority. The exercise of the second by them individually, and outside the *familiae*, continues, as it has been from the beginning, to be a new sanction—a substitute for unauthorized force—and the specific delegation, in particular instances, of the encroaching super-familial power itself. The pattern of the law follows the division of its sources, and the old authority of the chief within the autonomous "state in little" remains dimly different from the new authority of the individual but confederated chiefs outside the confines each of his own constituent subdivision.

2. *The Arrangement of the Institutes*

Let us proceed to relate these categories of the fields of power to the arrangement of the two leading, extant, contemporary text-books of Roman Law. The Institutes of Gaius and thereafter those of Justinian follow almost the same arrangement, shown in the following outline.

144 It is perhaps a relic of this earlier view which survives in the classic expression for the integral house community. The *familia iure proprio* is therein opposed to the later agnatic circle, or *familia iure communi*. See Ulpian, *Dig.* 50. 16. 195. 2.

145 In the XII Tables, we see this law of the household already emerging from its independence. The fourth and fifth tables are concerned with the *potestas*, and the limits upon it, and with succession.

146 Thus *ex iure Quiritium* means successively "on the authority of the *Quiritii* (Roman citizens)," "under the Quiritary jurisdiction," and finally, "according to the Quiritary (civil) law."

Gaius	*Subject*	*Justinian*
Book I	Law Concerning Persons	Book I
Book II	Law Concerning Things	Book II
	Ownership, Possession and Servitudes	
	Testamentary Succession	
Book III	Intestate and Involuntary Succession	Book III
	Obligations from Contract	
	Obligations from Delict	Book IV
Book IV	Law Concerning Actions	

This arrangement—and particularly the division of the subject of succession between Books II and III as well as the inclusion in Book III of all obligations, in the one case, and obligations from contract, in the other, with intestate succession—is not explained in the text and has never, so far as I know, been satisfactorily explained by interpreters. It has proved so baffling that many authorities have come to assume that the subdivision into books is merely a convenient break in the narrative, like chapters in a novel. But in no other respect are these carefully reasoned and nearly identical text-books so casual. Moreover these divisions are not at all of the same length, in number of titles, or sections, or lines. Hence it would appear probable that this arrangement and division of books is grounded in some fundamental principle or viewpoint of Roman law which was so implicit in legal thinking as to have become unconscious or at least to require no explanation. Perhaps, even, it may have become the conventional arrangement for certain purposes long before the time of Gaius.[147]

The key to this scheme seems to be the categories of the two original fields of power, the jurisdiction within the *familia* and that without. The first two books deal with the intra-familial field; the last two with the inter-familial.

In Book I is discussed the familial authority to which the various orders of men, women and children are submitted, and it is set out to whom this power appertains and how it may be attained, or modified.

[147] It is not the conventional arrangement of those earlier works of which portions of the text or descriptions have come down to us. Roby, *An Introduction to the Study of Justinian's Digest*, p. 181, supposes Gaius' to have been the "first institutional treatise in the history of Roman law." But Girard concludes, op. cit., p. 8, that Gaius "l'avait lui-même certainement trouvé chez un jurisconsulte plus ancien." See also his Note 1, p. 7. Bonfante, op. cit., I, p. 442, says that it is certainly not of Gaius' devising. And Buckland, *Text-Book*, p. 29, says, "He [Gaius] has been credited with the invention of the division of the law into *Ius personarum, rerum, actionum*, but it is more probable that it was already traditional." At the opening of his chapter on the Law of Persons, Buckland describes the two chief theories as to the basis of this arrangement.

In Book II is described the power of the head of a family as to certain *things*. The first is that with reference to corporeal *things*. But, this is not conceived to be a *ius*. It is still of the undifferentiated and undefined order of the classificatory genitive. To this is added a small section to cover those cases where the familial *ius* is acquired with reference to certain *things* of another household *in situ*. This we shall examine and explain later. Finally comes the whole subject of voluntary (appointive) succession, which had perhaps subsisted as to the office of the *patrimonium* from pre-legal times but which had now come to be sanctioned wholly by law[148] under the exercise of the power conferred by the transfer of the *ius* into the familial field and thus the especial area of maximum interference within the domain of the hitherto autonomous *familia*. With this we leave the subject of the intra-familial field.

Book III begins with intestate succession and touches on succession to the estate of a bankrupt, inter-familial succession *inter vivos*, and surrenders. These are the involuntary successions – in part the relics of former customs but now prescribed under the powers conferred in specific cases by the state.[149] While the first is the survival of the original consuetudinary and intra-familial form it has now become wholly statutory. And it never was subject to the familial *ius*. It was fixed by the gens, or by rigid custom.

From this we pass to the other branch of the power exercised or authorized by the state. For the *iuris vinculum* – the name which Justinian[150] gives to the obligation – has always been, as we have seen, a chain imposed, not under the familial authority, but under that of the state as between heads, or in rare cases other members, of different households.[151]

Finally, in Book IV under actions, we pass to the very essence of the jurisdiction of the state – the thing itself. On this basis the puz-

148 It also prescribes who can take, i.e. who has the *ius successionis*, and who can refuse to take. In general those who are *of* another familial jurisdiction cannot take, those *of their own* or of the *familia* can; but only those who are *of their own* can refuse. In the light of this scheme of jurisdictions this would seem logical.

149 They are much changed by the time of Justinian.

150 So-called for convenience; actually the editors of the Institutes prepared under the presidence of Tribonian at the Emperor Justinian's direction.

151 Upon the basis of these inherent and persistent, if unconscious, categories it would doubtless be possible to explain many of the early oddities, corrected by later law, in the law of succession. For instance, there is the curious fact that when the heir first accepted the *hereditas* and then rejected it by *in iure cessio*, the corporeal *res* are merely divested (for they must by their nature be *of* someone); the debts remain attached to the heir (for having assumed them he is subject to the *ius* of another and cannot surrender liabilities); but the credits are extinguished. (For, after succession, they are surrendered and being specially conferred *iura*, and thus wholly personal, they are not transferred but are released and disappear.)

zling separation between Books II and III is adequately explained,[152] and we find a general division into two halves. The first half deals with the exercise of the recognized, but now restricted, pre-existing authority of the heads of the constituent "states in little." The second half deals with specific authorities conferred upon them from the reservoir of the new public *ius*.

C. *Intra-familial Field—Domestic Power over Human Beings within the "Familia"*

1. *The Law Concerning Persons*

Almost the whole of the Law Concerning Persons represents a major invasion by the super-familial power into the affairs of the formerly autonomous household. This interpretation is quite contrary to that formerly given to the dichotomy between the Law of Persons and the Law of Things by modern authorities on jurisprudence. The older view is stated by Sohm:[153] The Law of Persons, "as a department of private law . . . is identical with the law of the *subject* of private [i.e. proprietary] rights, in other words, it is concerned with proprietary capacity, the capacity of holding property." And Holland[154] says, "'Ius quod ad personas pertinet' aptly enough expressed the law as to those variations in rights which arise from varieties in the Persons" and "'Ius quod ad res pertinet' very ambiguously indicates the department of law which treats of such modifications of rights as result from varieties in the objects or in the acts with which they are concerned." On the other hand Maine, though he, curiously enough, considers the distinction between the Law of Persons and of Things "entirely artificial" because it has no meaning in the infancy of the law,[155] nevertheless diagnoses its meaning and origin more nearly on the basis we have suggested. "All the forms of Status taken notice of in the Law of Persons were derived from, and to some extent are still coloured by, the powers and privileges anciently residing in the Family."[156] Hunter interprets

[152] This leaves unexplained Justinian's separation of the two classes of obligations, and his inclusion of those from delict in Book IV with the subject of actions. To me this seems a last refinement of the idea presently to be suggested as to the source of delictual obligations. These were at first obligations imposed during and by means of actions—not previously existing like those from contracts. It is almost as if we were to discuss the subject of judgment debts in the section on procedure. While this would not be regular, neither would it be so far amiss.

[153] Op. cit., p. 159.

[154] Op. cit., pp. 136 and 137.

[155] *Ancient Law*, pp. 251-252.

[156] *Ancient Law*, p. 164.

this particular division even more along our line:[157] "The law of persons contains an account of the different species of authority to which a person in Rome might be subjected." And Moyle, in the introduction to his translation of the Institutes of Justinian, blames Austin[158] and his *a priori* division of law into that of Persons and that of Things for the quite general misunderstanding of what the Romans meant by the dichotomy. For what they meant he stands on the authority of Savigny's metaphysical concept, which, he thinks, also accords with scientific observation. Savigny divided the exercise of the will into three concentric circles; the first, self; the second, self expanded in the family—the legal relations of which are comprised in family law (the Law Concerning Persons); and third, the external world apart from the family. The rights which arise from the relations to this third circle on the part of the individual will, belong to property law, (the Law Concerning Things) in its two departments, the Law of Things and the Law of Obligations.[159] Savigny's identification of the Law Concerning Persons with the original family law—if by "family" is intended the early political unit of a house community—accords with both of our foregoing presentations. But it does not adequately recognize the elements of the Law Concerning Things which remained so largely subject to this familial *ius* (i.e. Book II). Nor does it recognize either the original oneness of the power over persons and objects, nor the original duality of the sources of power arising from the fact of confederation of autonomous units.

2. *The Inherence and Incidence of the Power*

Before we examine the Law Concerning Persons we must discuss the question of what the jurisconsults meant by the word *persona*. The word itself—*per-sona*, or "sounding through"—refers to the mask worn by actors in early Roman drama; whence it came to mean a character, or part. While in later times it evidently had come to be used popularly and loosely to mean any individual, the indications are that its original and accurate sense was that of the public character or part played by him (and only by him) who represented, or *personified* the *familia*.[160] Such a one was a *personage* and his *person* stood for the *corpus* as its *caput*, or head. These senses are all of

157 Op. cit., p. 129.

158 See Holland, supra, expressing the Austinian view.

159 See Moyle, op. cit., I, pp. 69-70.

160 Thus Terry, op. cit., p. 356, "The further we go back toward the primitive institutions . . . the more clear traces we come upon of a time when the *pater familias*, the actual head of a family or the man *sui iuris* who might be head of a family, was the only person recognized as having a separate legal personality. . ."

Roman origin. The *corpus* was indiscriminately a body of men (a *familia*, or a corporation) or a body of objects or "things" (a fund, the principal of a fund), for the original *corpus*, the *familia*, was a blend of the two and was now coming to constitute as to the latter, and in some respects as to the former, what we should call a body of property.[161] Out of this scheme of thought *caput* came to mean the status of headship.[162] The important connotation is this. Strictly speaking there was probably but one *persona* to each *familia* or *corpus*. This *persona* persisted and clothed unchanged the successive heads. Even it could remain in suspense during an interregnum (*hereditas iacens*). But, with divided succession, the problem of the "split personality" arose and was never adequately solved. As, in time, other types of *corpus* (corporations) were developed, a *persona* was conceived to attach to each. Thus arose the question whether one man could sustain two or more *personae*. And in the end, as we shall see later, a *corpus* existed, the *persona* of which was worn by no man but was conceived as immanent in the body of "things" which composed it.[163]

It is difficult without examining for oneself every instance of the use of the word *persona* in Roman legal literature to prove this interpretation. For the modern authorities are so imbued with their notion of a legal person, as now conceived, that they read their idea into the text and largely ignore many of the distinctions of Roman legal usage. Thus Poste, in his translation of Gaius, constantly inserts the word *person* when it does not appear in the text. Abdy and Walker, on the other hand, conclude from their examination of both Gaius and Ulpian, that the slave had no independent *persona* until after manumission, and consider it probable from the evidence of the *dispensator* that no member of a *familia* had an independent *persona*.[164] And Buckland[165] says, ". . . slaves and young persons,

[161] *Corpus* is perhaps originally the stem as opposed to the *fructus*, or fruit. Hence it becomes, on the one hand, principal as opposed to yield and, on the other, the trunk from which the genealogical tree branches – the continuing substance of the *familia*; ever changing, ever renewing itself; that which is continually giving off but is never depleted. The Latin *stirps*, (a stem) has exactly the same history. Gaius, 3. 16., speaks of the various direct lines of descent in the family, as *stirpes*. That represents an old and allied concept.

[162] Girard, op. cit., p. 90, speaks of "la personnalité, designée, surtout dans la langue récente, par le mot *persona*, dans une langue plus ancienne et plus technique par le terme *caput*. . ."

[163] *Corpus* is "at other times, a collection of goods devoted to a definite permanent purpose (FOUNDATION, universitas bonorum) to which personality and legal capacity of its own is attributed by the State for the sphere of Property Law." Salkowski, *Institutes and History of Roman Private Law*, p. 327.

In fact, "ordinarily [that is, in late law] the term *corpus* is used to denote a corporation. . ." Sherman, *Roman Law in the Modern World*, II, p. 122.

[164] *The Commentaries of Gaius and Rules of Ulpian*, p. 242, Note 2.

[165] *Elementary Principles of the Roman Private Law*, p. 16.

incapable of taking part in legal proceedings, are regarded as having only an imperfect *persona*." Slaves and young persons, in Rome, included all under power, regardless of age or sex. It is true that Gaius uses the term *persona* in connection with slaves and "children" in power. But he does not speak of them as persons. Rather it is *in persona servorum*,[166] or *in ceteris vero liberorum personis*,[167] as if he meant "*via* a representative." Doubtless by the time of the Empire correct legal usage was more honoured in the breach than in the observance and popular usage was loose, after the manner of our word "property." It seems to be instances of such popular usage that leads Clark to conclude, after a careful study, that the *personae* of the *ius personarum* are individual men who may be slaves or free, *sui iuris* or not; men for whose sake law was established, not status or characters.[168] It is possible that this humanistic spirit had invaded Roman law by the time of the Institutes and that what we detect here and there, which tempts to the view I have presented, is but the relics of an archaic system of thought. But I am inclined to follow Girard.[169] He says that personality in Rome did not belong to every one. It was a privilege. And this conforms to Bonfante's interpretation of the change which took place in the classic period by which the term *paterfamilias*, accompanying the conversion of the *familia* from a subsidiary state to a body of property, became a *nomen iuris* for the person with legal capacity rather than the person as a representative.[170] At any rate the old notion required, to have personality – and the later notion required, at least to have complete personality – three elements of which the whole constituted the *caput*. The first was to be free not slave; the second, to be a citizen, not a Latin or *peregrinus*; the third to be the head of a household and not in power. Thus *caput* was the status of the *persona*, and *persona* at first was the *part* of headship – that of the independent.

The Law Concerning Persons defines dependents and independents. But it deals with the subject almost wholly from the standpoint of the independents – the *personae*, limited as above.[171] It is a description of the various forms of subjection of an individual to the power of a selected few – an oligarchy.[172] These selected few were

[166] Gaius, I. 123.

[167] Gaius, I. 134.

[168] *Jurisprudence*, II, p. 457.

[169] Op. cit., p. 101.

[170] Op. cit., I, p. 481.

[171] Bonfante, op. cit., I, pp. 482-483, says, "La doctrine du sujet juridique dans le système romain coïncide avec le droit de famille, . . . Dans son organisation essentielle, la famille romaine subsiste." "On ne nie pas, . . . l'autorité intrinsèque du *paterfamilias*."

[172] The various types of subjection, now in general grouped under the word *ius*, have for the most part been described in the previous chapter. There was,

confined, in varying degrees at various stages, to the three successive concentric circles, the original patrician patriarchs, the heads of both patrician and plebeian families, and finally all *cives* who were full-fledged Roman citizens. As a group it included, and throughout much of its history was restricted to, the heads of the wealthy land-owning families.[173] Thus the Law Concerning Persons is a series of sieves, graduated as to mesh, through which one must have passed to arrive in this oligarchic company. The series is well presented in Hadley's analysis.[174]

1. *Libertas*
   a. Is he free or unfree?
   b. If free, is he born free (*liber*) or freed (*libertinus*)
2. *Civitas.*
   a. If free, is he a *peregrinus dediticius*, a released prisoner of war of limited status?
   b. Or a *peregrinus* (*Latinus*) with the privileges of *commercium* and *actio.*
   c. Or a *civis* (Roman) with these privileges together with *connubium*, the right to found a Roman family.
3. *Familia.* If a *civis*, a Roman citizen, is he[175]
   a. *Alieni iuris*
      1. *In potestate—domini*
         —parenti
      2. *In tutela*, or *in curatione*
   b. *Sui iuris*

Only those who pass into this final, or thirty-second degree, enter the pearly gates and are entitled to all the privileges and, at least theoretically and in the cognizance of the law, are *sui iuris* and subject to none but self-imposed duties (i.e. via *commercium*). And the

in addition to wardship (*tutela*), guardianship (*curatio*) which was exercised over incompetents on analogy to wardship over minors. Both of these classes would, except for such special subjection, be *sui iuris.*

[173] This constitutes the key to the organization of Roman society and to the Roman law. The organization of equality, perfected under the Republic, persisted in practice, somewhat impoverished, through the period of the Empire. And the law continued, as usual, to describe it as it had been. Fustel de Coulanges, *Les origines du Système féodal*, p. 92, says, "Rome avait alors une constitution démocratique, et pourtant l'aristocratie y régnait. C'est que, si elle était démocratique par les lois, elle était aristocratique par le groupement des intérêts, par la condition de la plus grande partie du sol, surtout par la pratique du précaire. La République romaine était, en fait, l'association de quelques centaines de famille très riches et très puissantes. . ." Actually the constitution was oligarchic, not democratic.

[174] See Hadley, *Introduction to Roman Law*, p. 104.

[175] Gaius refers only to this "3. *Familia,*" as *status hominis*, 1. 162.

law has little to say of those who are *sui iuris* (i.e. not subject to anyone).[176] Subjection, on the other hand, is dealt with fully. It was of two or possibly three sorts, as we have seen. The Institutes of Justinian divide men who are in power into two classes, those who are in the power of the parent (i.e. *filii*) and those who are in the power of the master (i.e. slaves and perhaps *mancipii*).[177] Those who are not in power are also divided into two classes, those either in wardship or guardianship and those *neutro iure*.[178] There is one other relation not fitted to this scheme but of great importance both in the history of Rome and in the history of the Middle Ages. This is the relation of the client to his patron and other relations built up on this analogy which we have already briefly touched upon. The special privileges and powers of the patron and the special duties and fealty of the client seem to be the origin, in part, of the relation between the feudal lord and vassal. As such we shall deal with them later.

D. *Intra-familial Field—Property Power over Objects within the "Familia"*

1. *The Law Concerning Things*

The Law Concerning Things[179] was, in respect of its origin, peculiarly a development of the external rather than of the internal relations of the *familia*. It therefore concerns itself largely with transfers between households (i.e. means of external acquisition) of material objects or of non-free persons, together with that curious double survival of the vengeance upon, and sometime acquisition of,

176 Ulpian, 4. 1, says "Sui iuris sunt familiarum suarum principes. . ." That is, "Those who are heads of their own families are *sui iuris*." And Gaius, 1. 48, says, "Nam quaedam personae sui iuris sunt, quaedam alieno iuri subiectae sunt." Which may be translated somewhat freely, "for some are persons under their own rule, while some are subject to the rule of another."

It is interesting to note the survival or revival of the classificatory genitive in this newer term. Literally a man *sui iuris* is "of his own jurisdiction." So to speak, he "*belongs* under the classification of himself." The sense is exactly that which we have heretofore given and in this case, of course, the supposed possessive sense is necessarily excluded.

177 ". . . aliae in potestate parentum, aliae in potestate dominorum sunt," Justinian, *Inst.* 1. 8. pr.

178 "Nam ex his personis, quae in potestate non sunt, quaedam vel in tutela sunt vel in curatione, quaedam neutro iure tenentur," Justinian, *Inst.* 1. 13. pr. This suggests another class of those who were neither *sui iuris*, nor yet *in potestate*, perhaps non-citizens, perhaps *clientes* and *amici*.

179 "*Ius quod ad res pertinet.*" We are using the term "things" as a convenient translation here of the word *res*, because, as we have already pointed out and will later demonstrate by further evidence, the word "thing" has had in our law much the same history and broad significance. Henceforth, when we use the word 'thing' (with single quotation marks) we do not mean material object.

free persons of other *familiae*, which went by the name of *obligatio*. But this section of the law, as well, had by this time incorporated certain interferences with the internal familial relations. There is a minor reference to *dominium*, which is only slightly touched on and is restricted rather than defined.[180] For, in accordance with the development described in the previous chapter, there now remains under this title but the remnants of the pre-property power. All that which dealt with free persons within the *familia* has been removed into the Law Concerning Persons. There is also a major intrusion covering the laws of familial succession and devise, the beginnings of which had already appeared at the time of the XII Tables.[181] Both these subjects, *dominium* and succession, were in the beginning wholly internal relations of the *familia*. The first seemed hardly to require treatment in the law. Its character and incidence had not changed with the appearance of the super-familial *ius* and with the reduction in its scope. And it was still held within the jealously exclusive and autonomous jurisdiction of the *familia*, by the classificatory genitive. The only aspect in which it entered the purview of the law was that concerned with changes of classification.[182] But testamentary succession to property, while it followed decidedly the same forms and was only an enlargement of the old intra-familial authority of the head, nevertheless had evolved under super-familial authority, still required its support, and had come to be regulated by it. So it receives full treatment. These two elements, then, of the Law Concerning Things, formerly the exclusive affairs of the autonomous states in little, represent not only invasions by the newer political régime into the field of the older, but also the special elements of the older power which, in the process of differentiating the domestic from the property power, are ranged principally within the field of property. The rest of this section consists of the elements of the institution of property external to the *familia*, developed from prelegal custom by a combination of the privileges of *commercium* and *actio*, or by the latter alone. These are intestate and involuntary

[180] Most of the space given to this subject is devoted to methods of acquisition of the rights and to the different qualities of title. There is no definition of *dominium* as such.

[181] Here we see the climax of the process already discussed whereby succession to an office – appointive or hereditary – had been converted into the devolution of property; whereby the chief of the household was enabled to use his new found accession of sanction from the super-familial federation to break the ancient rule of custom as to single succession, and to assure, *via* this independent authority continuing after his death, the carrying out of his living will against all and sundry, within and without the *familia*, who might otherwise, when he was gone, have defeated his purpose.

[182] For our purpose Praetorian property (*in bonis habere*) is unimportant. In this analysis *possessio* may be considered to be *de facto* property.

succession to *universitates rerum* and obligations from delict and from contract.

It should be noted that, in respect of its effect on modern law, the Law Concerning Things is the whole and only ancient source of the civilian law of property, for it covered completely all the then existing relations among persons, or between persons with relation to objects, which are now embraced in property. Those matters pertaining to the qualifications of an individual for holding property, which, according to the views of Austin, Sohm, Holland and others already referred to, one would expect to find in the Law Concerning Persons, are, as a matter of fact, quite consistently with our thesis, included in the Law Concerning Things.[183]

Thus the word *res* has already come to centre about itself the now fairly well defined and restricted legal idea of property.[184] It becomes, therefore, a matter of great importance in the analysis of the nature of the institution of property, to interpret the content and relations of this word. And this is even more essential as a part of our general study, by reason of the fact that much the same development of thought has repeated itself, as we have already suggested, in the legal use of the word "thing," with which we shall be much concerned in subsequent chapters. But this fact also adds to our difficulties. So much have expert translators and historians been influenced by their preconceived ideas – either from later jurisprudence, as to what the meaning of *res* ought to be, or from subsequent civilian law, and from the legal usage of our word "thing" (as if it were synonymous) as to what it was in classic Rome – that at every step one must be wary.[185]

[183] In Gaius one finds them discussed in Books II and III in connection with *de Rebus Singulis, de Rerum Universitatibus,* and *de Obligationibus.*

Clark, *Jurisprudence,* II, p. 542, says, ". . . most people, I think, who look at the Roman Institutes themselves, apart from modern theory, will allow that the framers of the distinction under consideration [*Persona, Res*] meant by their second division what may be correctly described as Property Law." And Hunter, op. cit., p. 129, says, "It is a mistake to regard the object of the jurists [in the Law Concerning Persons] to be an enumeration of the cases of legal incapacity. As a matter of fact, Gaius deals with incapacity under the several heads of Property, Testament, Contract, etc., connecting, very properly, the instances of incapacity with the particular rights that the classes of persons were incapable of enjoying."

[184] Not property in the Austinian sense (i.e. *dominium*) but in its broad modern scope.

[185] This imputation of meaning has gone so far that in the common legal phrase, "rights *in rem,*" *rem* is made to stand for "the world," somewhat figuratively of course.

With regard to the general effort to find in, or to attribute to, classic Roman law the foundation of a later scheme of jurisprudence, by means of the misinterpreted words *res* and *ius,* it seems apt to cite the remark of Fustel de Coulanges, made in another connection. He says, *Alleu,* p. 171, "Il y a une grande imprudence à batir tout un système sur un mot dont on n'a pas étudié le sens."

We have already suggested our thesis as to the origin and development of meaning of the word. By the classic period it had come—exactly as our word "thing" has come—to represent a convenient substitute for thought, that is, any indefinite object or category of loose thinking.[186] Its use in law was almost as broad and its content was frequently equally vague.[187] Nevertheless, if we put aside the looser colloquial uses, it seems possible to establish a reasonably definite group of technical meanings which can be related to a common origin from which they diverge. And in this way we discover the connotation and significance of each use. The common ground meaning is "matters for litigation." As there is, in an earlier time, no notion of legal rights, but only of persons and material objects (the visible and tangible) these seem themselves to be the very "matters," or subjects of the litigation. Since, as we have already pointed out, the subject or its equivalent is often as well the object sought,

[186] By way of confirmation we may cite Freund's analysis of its uses.

In general

A. A thing, subject, being

B. A matter, affair, event, fact, circumstance, occurrence, deed, condition, case

In particular

A. An actual thing, the thing itself, reality, truth, fact

B. Effects, substance, property, possessions

2. Whatever may be the subject (object) of rights

C. Benefit, profit, advantage

D. Cause, reason, ground, account

E. An affair, matter of business, business

F. A case in law, a lawsuit, cause, suit, (more general than *causa*)

G. An affair, especially military

H. Acts, events, as the subject of narration

. . . .

K. The common-weal, state

L. Political changes, revolution

[187] For instance Gaius in the section in which he appears to discuss the statute process *sacramentum* when *in personam* (4. 15, 16, 17) uses the phrase "*si de re*" (if about a subject of dispute). And when he speaks of those *in rem*, he describes the necessity of bringing the *ipsum rem* (material object or person) over which there was a dispute as to title, or some part of it, into court. To one of the claimants the court awarded the thing in the interim and him he bound to give a pledge to his adversary "*litis et vindiciarum, id est rei* [the corpus of the thing, or its value] *et fructum.*" As to the statute process *condictio* he states (4. 19) that the *lex Silia* made it apply to a *certa pecunia* and the *lex Calpurnia* to all certain things ("*de omni certa re*") (i.e. definite articles). In the statute process *manus iniectio*, the pronouncement began *ob eam rem*, (on account of that judgment). And in describing the *pignoris capio* he says "*de quibusdam rebus moribus*," (in some cases by custom).

Thus in a few short paragraphs he uses the word *res* to mean a case, a subject of dispute, a material object or person, a judgment, an article, the principal value of a thing.

The *praescriptio* of a *formula* began "*ea res agatur*," (let this be the issue to be determined). And this I think is an example of the original sense, though *lis* was perhaps the closer technical equivalent for our "issue" (legal).

the term *res* comes also to be used for the objective of the litigation.[188] In the course of time legal theory begins to discriminate the various characters among these "matters." As it does so it continues the use of the term for the whole original ambit, qualifying the specific divisions in some degree with adjectives or adjectival pronouns. Since the objects persist, and since the legal relations which are being established with regard to them also persist, the word comes gradually to be attached in a somewhat vague way to that dimly perceived something – the position or the relation to an object, or person – which is, even in the interval between actions or transactions, the potential basis of an action.[189] Eventually the word comes to be a blend of all these uses surviving from the various stages of the development. The safest generalization that we can make is that it was, in general, "the subject of a legal process," and thus came to refer to the various specific subjects or classes of subject.[190]

As the subjects of legal process, *res* were generally classified in Roman law somewhat as follows. Let us take that of Gaius.

188 This process of concreting is well illustrated in the case of *lis*. Its meanings are given by Freund:

1. In general. A dispute
2. In particular
   - A. A charge, an accusation
   - B. A lawsuit, action or process at law
     - 1. The cause
   - C. The matter in dispute (i.e. *litem aestimare*, "to fix the amount of the fine").

In general it may be said to be nearest to our "issue." Thus it proceeds from the "dispute" to the "amount of the fine," just as *res* proceeds from the "subject of the dispute" to the "value equivalent of the subject, or even of the object sought."

189 It is perhaps in this sense that *suae rei* appears in the XII Tables. But it should be noted that in all the various readings of this text *res* appears in the singular. *Res*, there, is not "thing" or "things." It is something more of the nature of a position, or status, or a collective whole. It is more the *res* of *res publica* than the *res* of *res publicae*. It is more like the *universitas* than like the *rerum* of the later *universitas rerum*. And this *universitas* included both persons and objects – "*pecunia tutelave suae rei*." It is translated by Bonfante in this connection, as *familia*. But perhaps it means no more than his *res privata* – that is his private affairs or jurisdiction – as contrasted with *res publica* – the affairs and jurisdiction of the public bodies.

190 The authorities usually translate the word *res* as "thing" with its legal connotation of the object of a right of property – or, worse still, of the material object of such – and then find it necessary to quarrel with the classic Roman analysis of *res*. If it is not so translated, the organization of the law seems quite reasonable. Those who attempt to make it even more specific, seem to the writer to go even further wrong. Kocourek, for instance, says, *Jural Relations*, p. 317, ". . . the term *res* was limited by the Roman lawyers to the concept of property. . ." If we go so far as to admit that the Roman lawyers had arrived at the *concept* of property, nevertheless the only grounds for this assertion is the dichotomy, *persona – res*. For the application of the word was almost unlimited. Buckland elaborates the same idea, even more unjustifiably. He says, *Principles*, p. 59, ". . . a Res was an element in wealth, an asset, something which would appear on the credit side in a man's statement of affairs. Essentially it appears to be an economic conception." This very well describes the word *bona*. But it is wholly inapplicable to *res*.

1. *Res extra nostrum patrimonium* (*extra commercium*) (Matters outside our legal capacity)
   - A. *Res divini iuris.* Matters subject to divine law
     - a. *Res sacrae.* Dedicated to the gods
     - b. *Res religiosae.* Dedicated to *dii manes*
     - c. *Res sanctae.* Under special protection of the gods.

     } "*Nullius in bonis est.*" (Among the goods of no one)
   - B. *Res humani iuris.* Matters subject to human law
     - a. *Res nullius* / *Res hereditariae* } "*Nullius in bonis est.*" (Among the goods of no one)
     - b. *Res publicae* } "*Universitatis esse creduntur.*" (Believed to pertain to the community)
2. *Res in nostro patrimonio* (Matters within our legal capacity)
   - B. *Res humani iuris* (And subject to human law)
     - a. *Res privatae* (Matters of private persons)

Justinian's editors ring slight changes in this order. The *res* subject to divine law become, in that more sceptical age, *res nullius*, but the sub-classes are the same. *Res publicae* are subdivided, in a way that has been adopted by modern law, into *res communes*, which are holdings for general use, or common to all, of objects which thereby become unappropriable; *res publicae*, holdings of objects which remain appropriable but are being held out for common use; *res universitatis*, holdings of municipalities rather than individuals; and *res nullius*, again, which may be defined as non-holdings,—i.e. the status of objects merely unappropriated.[191] In effect Gaius' classification was a way of saying "you cannot submit to private legal process *matters* (*res*) concerning religious or public bodies, for the former are in the jurisdiction of divine law (*fas?*) only, and both are *extra commercium*." It is a statement of jurisdiction, not a division of objects; and the genitive is the genitive of class not of possession. Reference to material objects and to proprietors is by way of illustration only. To this point of view Gaius, at least, is consistent

[191] Poste, op. cit., p. 127, among others, is impressed that this is not in fact a division of the objects of property (material objects) but merely a division of proprietors. Nevertheless, he translates it as if it were the former, for he is convinced that the word *res* means material objects. This comment serves as an example of the misunderstanding of the Roman thought which seems to the writer almost universal among the modern commentators. Actually this is, first, a statement of jurisdiction; second, one of legal competence; and only incidentally one of proprietors. One cannot have sub-classes of *nullus*. By imputing to the words meanings which they gained at later times a fairly logical structure is rendered absurd.

throughout.[192] If this is not conceded it is necessary to assume that, without any mention of the fact, this entire analysis deals only with *res corporales* and excludes *res incorporales*. A *reductio ad absurdum!*

It is this latter distinction between *res corporales* and *res incorporales* which is the real basis of Gaius' analysis of the law of property – the Law Concerning Things. *Res corporales* are defined as all material objects *in nostro patrimonio*, that is, *in commercio*.[193]

Res incorporales are all other subjects of legal process. "Incorporeal *res* are those which cannot be touched, which are of a nature such that they consist only of authority [over persons],[194] such as an inheritance, a usufruct, or an obligation by whatever mode contracted.[195] Nor does it pertain to the matter [*ad rem*] that an inheritance includes *res corporales*, and that fruits too . . . are corporeal [the *fructus* of *ususfructus*], and that what is owed us under some obligation is often corporeal, as land, a slave, a sum of money. For *ipsum ius successionis et ipsum ius utendi fruendi et ipsum ius obligationis incorporale est*."[196] This phrase is one of the justifications for translating *ius* into our word "a right" (legal). Yet, if that be correct, it seems that here the *res* itself has become a *ius*, and therefore also "a right."

Later legal theory quarrels with this Roman distinction between *res corporales* and *incorporales*, largely, I believe, because of imputing to the words *ius* and *res* their later civilian meanings roughly corresponding to our ideas of "a right" and "an object," rather than those of "an authority over persons" and "the subject of a legal process" which we are attributing to them. Thus Hunter finds it invalid, since all *rights* are incorporeal, those of ownership as well as the others, and because the *right* cannot be the *thing* (i.e. material object), for rights cannot be objects of themselves. But he says,[197]

192 To quote from Gaius literally: "Those which are of human law are either public or private. Those which are public seem to be *in bonis* to no one; they are believed to be *ipsius universitatis*, [i.e. of the community itself]. Those which are private are of individual men," 2. 10 and 11. There is no question that Gaius visualized most of these matters as concrete physical objects or subject persons, but it is equally obvious that he was not thinking of them as the objects of property, but as the subjects of actions and other legal processes.

193 Gaius defines them thus: "Corporeal things are those which can be touched." 2. 13.

194 ". . . qualia sunt ea quae iure consistunt . . ." Gaius, 2. 14. Sometimes translated as, "Of such kind that they exist only at law." This entire phrase was translated by Poste, through his 3d ed., into the one word "rights."

195 Justinian continues this definition more generically, "In this class are *iura praediorum* [praedial servitudes], both urban and rustic, which are usually called *servitutes*." Justinian, *Inst.*, 2. 2. 3.

196 Gaius, 2. 14.

197 Op. cit., pp. 287-288. Girard, op. cit., p. 273, also says, "Cela revient à opposer les droits à leurs objets. . ."

"The jurists were led into this error by the accident that ownership in their law was transferred by delivery of the thing, whereas lesser rights than ownership were transferred in a different manner. . .[198] The association of ideas was strengthened, as Mr. Poste points out, by the fact that in actions for ownership, the plaintiff claimed a *res*, and in actions for usufruct or servitude, he claimed a *jus*."[199] While we cannot agree that these procedural explanations are statements of cause – rather they are statements of effect – they are of interest to us because they are quite generally and inconsistently used the other way round to explain the derivation of the distinction between the two classes of Roman actions, – the phrases *in rem* and *in personam*, which, with a new content, have since assumed such structural importance in legal theory.

We must at once admit that, in the distinction between *res corporales* and *res incorporales* the Roman legal theory, whatever it meant by *ius* and *res*, had clearly begun the perennial error, which still persists, of confounding ownership with its object. If it had not done so, the distinction between the two classes would not have been based on the criterion of corporeality.[200] If, in attempting to fit these categories to the modern notions of "rights" and "objects," we translate *ius* as "a right," and *res* as "object," then clearly there should be a *ius* associated with the *res corporales* exactly as well as with the *res incorporales*. Or, if we translate *res* into the medieval sense of "thing," and conceive of *res corporalis* as a possessory interest and *res incorporalis* as a non-possessory interest, there is then no room for *ius*

[198] Gaius, 2. 28, says, "Res incorporales traditionem non recipere manifestum est." Servitudes, both praedial and personal, were wholly inalienable. So were *hereditates*. Both were created by mancipation or surrender and both were extinguished by surrender. Obligations were only alienable by novation (i.e. substitution of a new debt running to the alienee).

[199] See Note 191, p. 180. Poste himself says, "Gaius was probably not entirely responsible for this confusion of thought, which, perhaps was too deeply inwoven in the formulae of Roman jurisprudence to be easily eliminated by an institutional writer." Op. cit., p. 125.

As to whether both authors, and others of the same view, have not misunderstood the meaning of the words *ius* and *res* and the nature of this division of the latter, the reader is left to judge from the evidence.

[200] Ihering, *Geist*, II, p. 438, commenting on this, says, "Während alle übrigen Rechte zur letzteren Classe [*res incorporales*] gestellt werden, figurirt hier das Eigenthum als *res corporalis*." He speaks of "die Verkehrtheit dieser Identificirung des Eigenthums mit seinem Gegenstande. . . Das Eigenthum ist ebensowohl eine *res incorporalis* wie die übrigen dinglichen Rechte, und bei der Übertragung desselben geht juristisch nicht die *res corporalis*, sondern das Recht, die *res incorporalis*, über." But he admits that the error has an historical basis: it is the exact expression of the conception of ancient law which confounds in ownership the thing and the right. Girard comes to a similar conclusion, op. cit., p. 273. ". . . il semble que parmi les droits on omet le plus important de tous, le droit de propriété; mais on ne l'omet pas en réalité; on le met dans la première catégorie [*res corporales*] en le confondant avec les choses sur lesquelles il porte."

at all, even in the latter case. But, having admitted the one blind spot, which we correct by identifying *res corporales* with "ownership" and *res incorporales* with all other varieties of property, we must note that all systems of law since that time have also placed "ownership" in a class by itself.

Very probably Roman law at the time of Gaius had not developed a theory of "right" or interest and its object, in spite of the fact that later theory began by grounding its divisions upon these distinctions and has attributed its own origin to the classic period. Very probably we should translate *res corporales* as "tangible subjects of legal process" and *res incorporales* as "intangible subjects of legal process." In this light we may imagine Gaius as explaining to the students of law to whom he was writing: "All these matters may seem corporeal to you. But some are not; because in certain cases the issue is not immediate to the material object, but only mediate to it through an authority *via* the owner and conferred by him, or over the owner and conferred by the state." Thus the *res* (subject of dispute) is corporeal if the claimant says it is his own; it is incorporeal if he admits it is "of another," but claims that he is for some reason entitled to it or to use it. This is but the beginning of an analysis of property. It is an erroneous basis. But it explains the classic Roman system, and that is what Gaius was undertaking to do. He was not founding a school of jurisprudence; he was teaching students the existing law.

Obviously this elision of the notion of "ownership" and the immediate juxtaposition of the object to the "owner" was a result of the general prepossession which we have called the classificatory genitive. According to this crude point of view every subject person or material object must be placed in some group. Where it is, it 'belongs.' There it is inside the wall and has no external relations. It is merely classified as *of* so and so—the *persona* of this group. While it is there, claims to it are not direct but reach it only indirectly since they consist of authorities over the *persona*, *of* whom it is: an authority of a similar order to the "authorities" embraced in the Law of Persons.

In other cases as well, as we have suggested above, the popular tendency was to identify the *res* with the material object or subject person sought. Hence the effort of the jurists to prove the incorporeality of these other *res* as subjects or issues of lawsuits. But the profession bowed in part to the popular usage and to the necessity of recognizing, even when the claim was based on other rights than ownership, that it was usually directed toward a material object. So the word *res* was used of this indirect objective as well. There was the *res persequenda*, which had come to be more often a *tanta res* (the money equivalent—not only of an object, but as compensatory damages in general) than it was an *ipsa res* (the object itself). Thus, in a somewhat different sense, *ipsa res* was corporeal and *tanta res* incorporeal. For the former was a specific object in contrast to the latter which was, during proceedings, as yet indeterminate. And this distinction tended to attach itself to the other. So that a legatee might recover even a specific sum of money as if it were his, if the coins had been physically segregated. Then he had a corporeal *res*. But if not, and his claim must be satisfied out of as yet indeterminate pieces of money, then he must sue as if he held an obligation. Then his *res* was incorporeal. So, too, the holder of a servitude, since its *praedium* was specific, was accorded certain rights of action as if the land were his, in spite of the fact that his *res* was incorporeal.

2. *Present and Prospective Property Power*

After this preliminary statement as to *res corporales* we are not surprised to find that there was practically but one property relation conceived as capable of existing with direct reference to material objects, and that this one relation was hardly described or defined. Perhaps we may venture to call this single possible corporeal relation to objects *dominium*, though Gaius rarely uses the term and it was never exactly defined in Roman law. It was only in later legal thought that this relation was fully elaborated and sophisticated. At any rate one could only have *dominium*, of one kind or the other (or *possessio*) with regard to *res corporales*, and only they, in turn, could be held in *dominium*. The physical concept of object made it impossible that a corporeal *res* (identified with the material object) could 'belong' in two co-ordinate classes at the same time, because the classification was as yet little more than a physical location. It still based itself on propinquity. And the original political notion of the *familia* made it equally impossible that a person or an object could have membership (citizenship) in two groups or be the subject of two collateral authorities at the same time. For these reasons there could not be two property relations of different kinds in the same object at the same time. Thus Ulpian[201] reconciles the idea of condominion by quoting Celsus to the effect that two cannot own one whole, nor can one own one part and one another, but each owns an undivided interest in the whole (i.e. the division is in the *persona* not in the object). And Paulus insists[202] that *dominium* is complete,

[201] *Dig.*, 13. 6. 5. 15.
[202] *Dig.*, 50. 16. 25. pr.

even if usufruct exists, for that is not part (or joint) *dominium* and since no part belongs to another then the whole is entirely "mine."[203]

It was this eminently physical and political view of property, still surviving from early times, which retained as its last stronghold the field of the classificatory genitive, the long unexplored relationship of dominion or "ownership," and prevented the full digestion or analysis of the newer genitive of possession, the idea of property in its strict sense. This *idée fixe* explains much. It explains the emphasis on *traditio*. It explains the claim to the body of the debtor. But it is in *dominium* that it sticks longest. Ihering presents clearly this particular form of blindness in early justice. He says[204] that in the transfer of property the right and the thing are confounded. The thing alienated changes place outwardly and, by being interested only in this external (objective) fact, it is easy to lose sight of the internal (subjective) fact, the transfer of the right. This is what the Roman law did. For its transfer was not the transfer of the right of property but the transfer of the "thing" itself. In the transfer of property the ancient law sees abandonment by the present proprietor of a "thing" of which a new proprietor takes possession. As in *in iure cessio* so in *traditio*. Succession is unknown in the ancient law — that is, they knew only entry into the "things" of another, not entry into the right of another. In other words, "in the ancient epoch, all rights, with the exception of the right of ownership, were practically inaccessible. To succeed to another in a thing was only possible for ownership; there only the thing and the right were blended."

The first of Gaius' illustrations of *res incorporales* is *hereditas* with which he associates the *ius successionis*. By his time *hereditas* had come partially to stand for the inheritance — that is, the body of property composing a decedent's estate — though it still appeared technically, at times, to retain its original sense of "heirship." It is in order to avoid this possible corporeal connotation that he associates with the term the newer phrase *ius successionis*. The substitution of this latter phrase for the original sense of *hereditas* supports our thesis. Heirship was at first an office. The authority to which the heir was presumptive had been, and to a lesser degree still was, that of the *iudex domesticus*. It was particularly and ex-

[203] The only exception was the case in which title was claimed under the two jurisdictions of the state, Quiritary and Praetorian, by two different men. Gaius calls this "divided ownership." 2. 40. It was in reality a case of conflict of laws. But by the time of Justinian usufruct, at least, and perhaps all servitudes (though none of the other incorporeal 'things') were conceived to be "a separation from *proprietas*," Justinian, *Inst.* 2. 4. 1.' Thus, in later times, it began to be possible for these particular two kinds of right to exist in the one object at the same time.

[204] *Geist*, II, p. 436.

clusively of the nature of an intra-familial *ius*. From this beginning as a prospective power over persons it had largely shifted to a prospective "ownership" of a body of property. Nevertheless the old terms and conceptual organization still persisted with a partial substitution of the content.[205] The *ius successionis* therefore was incorporeal, as well because it was, or had been, a presumptive office as because it was not as yet the actual occupation of the material objects of which the *hereditas* might now be thought to be composed.

The subject of succession, while it was one of the two great contributions of Roman law, bears upon our present study in only one important respect. Its always pertinent refinements have been the source of many of the modern rules as to testate and intestate succession. But it is the conceptual inventions—or artifices—in connection with it in which we are interested. As already pointed out the fact of succession was one of the earliest occasions for the rather crude analogies which appear to have been the first metaphysical notions of legal theory. The individual *paterfamilias* and *familia* required no theory. They were patent. But the succession in series of *patrifamilias* and the continuity of the *familia* in the face of its ever-changing content of individuals, excited thought. Out of the first came the concept of office; of a place to be filled, apart from the persons filling it. This office was the headship, the *caput*, and the body to which it was attached was the *corpus*. As *caput* was converted into a technical term for one special attribute, or aspect, of the office—the status—*persona* came into use for the general part played and became the source of the later concept of legal personality. Out of the second, the continuity of the *familia*, came both of the later notions of a collective whole, a supersensible reality. The group, the *familia*, at first composed almost wholly of persons, came later to consist as well of an important and valuable collection of objects. As the two component classes began then to differentiate and gave rise, on the one hand, to domestic organization and, on the other, to property organization, the term *familia* tended to stick to both. A body of persons related in a certain way constituted a *familia*. So did a body of objects (and slaves) within a certain preserve. Along both these lines the word *corpus* followed, so that, in later times, the term was used of any body of persons constituted in a certain way (our corporation) as well

[205] Bonfante, op. cit., I, p. 492, says that in the classic period, "L'hérédité a désormais, depuis longtemps, perdu son caractère de transmission de la souveraineté et bien que ses principes fondamentaux y soient peu propres, elle s'adapte peu à peu à des nouvelles fins essentiellement patrimoniales. Peut-être aucune institution ne nous permet de contempler avec une plus grande évidence l'adaptation progressive d'anciennes formes à de nouvelles fonctions."

as of any body of property constituted in a similar way (our foundation and our trust fund).

The conceptual trick by which this aggregate, or collectivity, was presented as something other than its constituent parts is shown by the term *universitas*, literally "turned into one." Apparently the term was first used of the *familia*, either as a body of persons or as a body of property. In turn the distinction appeared by which the latter was termed a *universitas rerum*, and the former—or perhaps by that time, only an artificial *familia*, or corporation—a *universitas personarum*. Finally the term *universitas rerum* became the term for a foundation, or body of property constituted upon the lines of a corporation, a *familia* detached from persons.

Thus appears in later legal theory the construct of a body of persons or of objects, existing as a sort of shell apart from the persons or objects which it comprises; and, of the same order, the construct of an office or place, also existing apart from the person who occupies it. Naturally these two metaphysical notions continued to be joined together. When the facts which had given rise to them became differentiated, in the course of time, into political and property, as well as domestic, organizations it is natural that the accompanying metaphysical notions continued to develop along parallel lines in the two principal fields. For this reason the notion of a corporate body, and the terms therefor, were applied indiscriminately in Rome to political and to property organizations.[206] On the other hand the notions of office became specialized. Nevertheless, from medieval times to our own day, the early metaphysical concept of office, the idea of *persona* or legal personality, now detached from any notion of office, came to be applied directly to, and to clothe, the *corpus*.

The literature on this subject is immense; the differences of opinion are manifold; and we have no need of going further in consideration of the various questions. But the main line of descent is clear. It was the "state in little" and its successor, the body of property, which gave rise to the collective notions of—and to many of the practices for dealing with—the municipality and the corporation, on the one hand, and, on the other, to that of the estate of a living person and of a decedent. Moreover, it was the head-

[206] Bonfante, op. cit., I, p. 481, says, "Le point de départ [of the theory of the juridical person] est constitué dans le droit romain, comme dans tout droit, par les organisations politiques; la *res publica* ou le *populus* est le modèle du sujet collectif du droit privé, et les premières institutions reconnues de ce genre furent les cités, autrefois, elles aussi, organisations politiques et souveraines. Mais ce concept s'étendit à d'autres organisations de simple caractère privé et commercial et perdit toute empreinte publique."

ship of this original state and the succession thereto, which gave rise to the notions of public office, to those of owner and of heir, and finally to the somewhat mystical concept of legal lore embraced in the *persona*, at least so far as it concerns the legal personality of an artificial person.

Thus the nature of the original collectivity and the relation of the person thereto have given rise to prepossessions which have persisted throughout the history of law, in spite of the changing character of the relations which have come to exist within the subsequent successors to this prototype. We shall try to trace, as we proceed, the alterations of substance, and shall, in the end, hope to cut through the traditional legal clothing, so much of which has been inherited from this source, in order to disclose the new collectivity and the new relation into which the old have gradually evolved.

3. *Detached Intra-familial Power*

It is quite evident that Gaius had not successfully classified the second of the incorporeal *res*, the usufruct, which is included as a sample of the group called servitudes (*servitutes*). The group was to him neither flesh, fish, nor fowl. So he skips over the subject ingloriously. Justinian, however, though including the group among the incorporeal *res*, nevertheless classifies and analyses them.[207] In the case of usufruct he describes it as a "*ius alienis rebus utendi fruendi*,"[208] and as a "separation from *proprietas*."[209] Some such vague notion, that the servitudes were allied with if not part of *dominium*, accounts for the fact that they are discussed by both authors immediately after *dominium*. Thus, while they are associated with *hereditas* and *obligatio* as incorporeal *res*, they are in all other respects treated as unlike these others.

[207] The Roman servitudes were the antique rural and the later urban easements appurtenant to land, as well as the *ususfructus* and the *usus*. The usufruct is described by Salkowski, op. cit., p. 453, as a combination of *usus* (bare use) with *fructus* (products or revenues) which gives the right of using and enjoying the objects of another whilst the *corpus* (substance) remains unimpaired. Both applied to slaves as well as to land.

[208] This phrase has formed the basis of a later sophistication used to describe the whole group of divided allegiances, securities as well as servitudes. They are called *iura in re aliena*. In Gaius – and probably in this case – *ius* invariably takes the genitive, not *in* with the ablative. Gaius speaks of "*ius utendi fruendi*"; "*ius . . . edicendi habent magistratus*"; "*ius aureorum anulorum*"; and Justinian of "*ius praediorum*"; and "*succedere in ius demortui.*" In fact, in the phrase quoted in the text, *utendi fruendi* is probably intended as the object of the *ius* and *alienis rebus* is the locus of the usufruct. Thus we find *ius in re aliena* to be another "barbarism," as Poste would call it.

[209] Justinian, *Inst.*, 2. 4. 1.

There seems to the writer to be a fundamental basis for explaining at one and the same time the incorporeality of the servitude, the use of the word *ius* in pleading and elsewhere in connection with it, together with the apparent inconsistency of including actions in regard to servitudes with actions *in rem* while those in regard to the obligatory *res incorporales* were *in personam*.[210] The servitudes seem to be a hotch-pot from two different principal sources, which have undergone a long process of legal philosophical welding into something like unity.[211] The praedial servitudes, particularly the ancient rural ones, are obviously necessary practical arrangements which, in the earliest development of individual use of land, would require to be added as attributes of the land itself.[212] As such the earliest were *res mancipi* (i.e. part of the plant) and were inseparable from the land. That they were only philosophized later is indicated by their persisting designation by individual names rather than as a class. As to the other group, we have already suggested the source of the word *usus* and that the term originally meant "share," thence "the accustomed having of this share" and thus, finally, the benefit therefrom – our "use." In other words it would appear that the practice was originally analogous to the *peculium*. This is somewhat confirmed by indications that both *usus* and *ususfructus*, when they appear in the late Republic, commenced as life-estates granted by legacy – a sort of *post mortem peculium* which did not permanently separate the object from its native *familia*, but merely created a similar temporary division within it. The arrangement was very likely used at first for the assignment of slaves.[213]

Probably much of the terminology as to the servitudes is late. But there is a curious savour of personal relations about it. In the case of praedial servitudes – the servitudes *par excellence* and perhaps the only ones properly so called –[214] the relation of the two *fundi* come to be described as that of master and servant, the one *dominans*,

[210] Poste explains the inclusion of servitudes with incorporeal things on purely procedural grounds. The *intentio* of a vindication to land or a slave began, "Si paret illum fundum (illum hominem) ex iure Quiritium Auli Agerii esse" ; but that to a servitude began, "Si paret ius eundi per illum fundum ex iure Quiritium Aulo Agerio competere," Poste, op. cit., p. 125.

[211] Bonfante, op. cit., I, p. 488, states that the term personal servitudes and the enlargement of the category which includes them is not the work of the jurisconsults but of the so-called compilators after the fall of the Western Empire.

[212] Girard, op. cit., p. 399, thinks that, perhaps, the most ancient praedial rustic servitudes were not at first distinguished from "*droits de propriété*."

[213] One of the supports for this thesis is the apparent absence of the idea of our economic "use" in early thought – at least in law. Ihering speaks, *Geist*, II, p. 435, of the rudeness of the economic conception "der nur das sichtbare und greifbare Object, die Sache selbst und die Früchte, nicht aber das übersinnliche Stück der Sache ; die zeitweise Möglichkeit ihres Gebrauchs als wirtschaftliches Gut und als rechtlich zu verfolgendes Object erschien."

[214] Girard, op. cit., p. 382.

the other *serviens*. This is intimately related to the term *servitus*,[215] which primarily described the condition of a person "in bondage" to another *familia*, used in the special and limited sense of debtor slavery. It is also consistent with the suggestion of personal relation that the term *ius* should have been used, as in *ius eundi*, *agendi*, etc. But this, in turn, is inconsistent with the idea of *dominans*, for in Roman law one does not find *ius*, the term for a peculiarly personal authority, used in conjunction with the idea of *dominium*. The *dominus* has *res* not *iura*. Which suggests that the expressions *dominans* and *serviens* started with the servitudes over persons and not those over land, and were only applied to the latter when the two classes coalesced.

In the case of *usus* and *ususfructus*, however, the analogy to a purely personal relation is far clearer. Here not only was there a *ius utendi*, etc., but the inherence was purely personal as well. Not only did these servitudes cease at death but also *per capitis deminutionem*, along with all other intra-familial *iura*.[216] Nevertheless, in both cases, since the *ius* granted is assumed to be intra-familial, servitudes have actions *in rem*; for all actions founded on the *ius* over the *familia* (in the Law of Persons) are equally actions *in rem*.

What we have to suggest is that the servitudes were incorporated into the early system of Roman law on the analogy of personal relations – perhaps particularly that of *mancipium*. They were regarded as tentative or separable and yet as continuing in one *persona* until surrendered. The transfer was of the *ius*, or authority only. Thereafter this special power was *of* the transferee, but the object remained *of* the transferor. The transferee assumed over the object, in whole or in part, a position *in loco parentis*, so to speak. The object was *in iure alieno*, as a son or other member of the *familia* might be. But, by the classificatory genitive, it continued to be a member or part of the original *familia*. The theory was not consistent, and naturally so, for these were the first dim gropings of legal theory in its process of converting the powers over persons, of which pre-property almost entirely consisted, into the protections as to specific interests in material objects of which the institution of property itself

[215] Moyle, op. cit., I., p. 204, says, "Properly speaking, the term servitus denotes the quasi-nonfree condition of an object over which rights are enjoyed by a person other than its owner. . ."

[216] In *capitis deminutio minima*, that form of reduction of status in which only the loss of the headship of a household was incurred, the intra-familial powers exercised outside the boundaries of the *familia* of the *capite minutus* – the personal servitudes – disappeared. They were of a patrimony (*familia*) but not of his. But the inter-familial powers exercised beyond these boundaries – the credits – persisted and passed to the new *paterfamilias* or to the creditors. Poste, op. cit., p. 101, calls this inexplicable. It seems to me the foregoing explanation makes the practice entirely logical.

has come to consist. In reality this particular brand of *iura*, though they were modeled upon them, were not authorities over persons; they were the first clear cases of protections against interference with a specific liberty as to an object—the *eundum*, *agendum*, etc.—the modern right of property.

E. *Inter-familial Field—Property Power Beyond the "Familia"*

The third of Gaius' examples of *res incorporales* is the *ius obligationis*. With this we enter a new field of *ius*. For, as we have already noted, the form of power over a person beyond the confines of the *familia*, which went by the name *obligatio*, was not the inherent authority of the head of the autonomous household, merely confirmed by the later super-familial power—*ex iure Quiritium*—but was, on the contrary, a fraction of the authority, or sanction, of the super-familial power itself, conferred in specific cases upon the head of one house over the head of another house.[217] In the classic law the obligation was conceived to arise—or the *ius* to be conferred—for two classes of reason: the one contracts, the other delicts. We have discussed the forms of pre-legal agreement and of early legal contract in the previous chapter and have surveyed in this one the early treatment of delict under the caption of *poena*. Here our chief concern is at first to analyse more completely the history and rationale of the major and enduring dichotomy of the institution of property which divides all that has gone before from this new class, the obligation. This is of vital importance to our study, for the practical Roman distinction has now become the basis for the theoretical division of the modern system of property rights into two classes, those *in rem* (against the world) and those *in personam* (against a person or persons). These terms are borrowed from the two general classes of Roman action to which we now turn our attention.

1. *Obligation—The Procedural Distinction*

The two general classes of Roman action conformed to the divisions of field upon which we are constructing our study. Actions *in rem* were actions supported by intra-familial authority (including that of *dominium*); actions *in personam* were supported by inter-familial authority. The jurisconsults themselves seem to have used these terms merely as names for the two types of action without, to

[217] As Bonfante says, op. cit., I, p. 219, ". . . pendant que les droits réels se rapprochent ["en parcourant à rebours le long chemin de l'histoire du droit romain jusqu'au droit primitif"] des droits de la famille et constituent la sphère interne de la puissance du *paterfamilias*, les obligations s'opposent aux uns et aux autres comme une sphère externe et prennent la position du moderne droit public international."

any considerable extent, grounding the distinction upon any fundamental basis other than the procedural form itself. In this manner Gaius describes the classes.[218] He says, "An action *in personam* is one by which we bring an action when someone is obligated to us either *ex contractu* or *ex delicto;* that is when we claim he ought to give, do or make good something. An action *in rem* is one in which we claim either a corporeal thing (*corporalem rem*) to be ours, or that the authority over something (*ius aliquod*) belongs to us, such as a use or usufruct," etc.[219] He then proceeds to give a formulary explanation. ". . . it is certainly not possible for us to demand our *rem* from another so [*ita*] 'if it appears he is bound to give.' For it is not possible that what is already ours should be given us, since what is so given is understood to be given to us in order to make it ours; but things which are already ours cannot be made more ours." [220] The formula from which he quotes is that of the vindication.[221]

These excerpts are inserted in full to demonstrate to the non-technical reader, among other points, that Gaius is a commentator expressing opinions as to what seems to him the character of the law which has grown up before his time. He is an interpreter, of the same sort as his successors. And he is attempting to explain why things are as they are from a limited and, it must be suspected, often inadequate knowledge of origins.

The explanation of this division of actions given by most modern authorities, on the other hand, is that it arises from and is based upon a fundamental difference in the nature of private rights, a difference which divides rights associated with obligation from all other rights.[222] Says Sohm,[223] "An action arising from an obligatory right is an actio in personam, an action arising from any other right is an actio in rem." [224] And he explains, as does Poste after him, that this is due to an antithesis in the *intentio*, based on a fundamental difference in the nature of private rights.[225] This same point of view is presented by

[218] Gaius, 4. 2-3.

[219] In Justinian this is somewhat differently stated. The action is *in rem* when "he sues one who is obligated to him *nullo iure*, but he created a controversy with him about something." *Inst.*, 4. 6. 1. And he says such actions are permitted in civil law only when one indicates his ownership, though the Praetor allows actions *in rem* to others at times. *Inst.*, 4. 6. 4.

[220] Gaius, 4. 4.

[221] Gaius, 4. 5, says, "Actions *in rem* we call *vindicationes* [i.e. determinations of familial jurisdiction]; actions *in personam*, in which it is claimed [*intenditur*] that one ought to give or do something, are called *condictiones*."

[222] "*Obligatio* was coextensive with actions in *personam*." Hunter, op. cit., p. 131.

[223] Op. cit., p. 264.

[224] This statement, while generally true, is subject to many exceptions. For instance holders of security, which in Roman law were classed with obligations not with servitudes, were given certain actions *in rem*.

[225] Sohm, op. cit., p. 263; Poste, op. cit., p. 446.

Hunter, who believes[226] that Gaius unconsciously organized the law "according to the character of the rights or duties. . ."[227] Having in mind our previous analysis and the thesis built upon it we are led to suspect, on the contrary, that it was the somewhat peculiar form of organization of early Roman society, with its two originally separate levels of authority, which created the distinction and the gradual differentiation in the actions. If this is so then we may also suspect that subsequent thinkers, influenced by the unique authority of Roman law, have unconsciously organized the system of rights and duties upon this rather accidental and local, or at least primitive, foundation.[228]

The question, then, goes to the root of the nature and history of our institution of property. All we can do at this point is to examine the suspect facts, attempt to see them as they were, and leave our suggested alternative possibility to its full development in the course of our study. In the first place let us try to learn the rationale of this separation of actions by tracing the growth of the distinction in form. We might assume from the terminology that the distinction resulted from the fact that certain actions were brought against a *res* – that is, a subject person or object – and that others were brought against a person who was not subject and therefore not as a *res*. But the usual legal view is different. That assumes the real distinction to be the nature of the question submitted for decision (i.e. whether the claim was grounded upon a right of "ownership," or analogous to that, or upon a right to some performance by a person). The earliest legal process to which our authorities give the designation *in rem* is the *sacramentum in rem*, described by Gaius.[229] In this action we have no difficulty in identifying the *vindicatio* with which we are already familiar and which always remained the type of action *in rem*.[230] It would appear that, as a legal process, vindication was a copy of the previous pre-legal practice of asserting and defending

[226] Op. cit., p. 125.

[227] But he bases this statement upon what may be a vicious circle. For he says "To understand the connection [arrangement] . . . we must look to the forms of action. Delict and contract were alike enforced by actions *in personam*; and in this respect they stand in contrast with the other topics dealt with by Gaius, where the proceeding was by an action *in rem*." Hunter, op. cit., p. 131. But if this distinction in the character of rights and duties is in turn based on the Roman distinction between actions *in rem* and *in personam*, in fact as well as in name, it is rather an effect than a cause. See Girard, op. cit., p. 1081.

[228] As Bonfante, op. cit., I, p. 219, points out, this supposedly precocious evolution in early Roman law of a distinction of mature law is suspect – "Bien loin d'être un fruit du progrès, la distinction des droit réels et des obligations est plus prononcée à mesure qu'on remonte dans le passé, tandis qu'elle s'atténue au cours de leur évolution . . . elle était moins profonde dans le droit classique que dans le droit archaïque."

[229] Gaius, 4. 16-17.

[230] But by no means the only action *in rem*; see Girard, op. cit., p. 1081, Note 1.

manus and that, as such, it had always had a certain inherent and recognized sanction over and above mere physical force.

It is generally supposed that there was also a *sacramentum in personam.* Where it should be described in Gaius' text there is a lacuna. Nevertheless he seems to establish an antithesis.[231] If, as Girard supposes, the *sacramentum in personam* was used to give ground for *manus iniectio* in cases where this did not arise "from certain sources of credits regarded as evident,"[232] it was, in spite of the technical inconsistency according to the view of modern law, no more than a test or ratification of the *manus iniectio* itself. It is then not far-fetched to consider the pre-legal *manus iniectio* as the prototype of personal actions, just as we have assumed the *vindicatio* to have been that of real actions. But this recognition deprives us of most of the basis for the distinction between the two types of process. For vindication was, as we have noted, a frequent element in *manus iniectio,* itself, and other forms of taking of *manus* gave grounds for vindication (viz. *mancipium*). Perhaps by supposing that *vindicatio* was a vindication (assertion, protection) of natural *manus,* and that *manus iniectio* was a forcible taking of artificial *manus,* we have hypothetically reduced the original difference to its simplest terms.[233]

If we ground the distinction in the class of actions upon the legal criterion, namely the nature of the question submitted, the difference arises only later. When, about the close of the third century B.C., the *formulae* were introduced in the place of the *legis actiones* we find a rapid change in the direction of establishing the differentiation. The form of these actions consisted of three or four parts. The content of the *intentio,* or statement of the claim, is the point where the differentiation appears.[234] It is true that there may have been

[231] Poste does not attempt fully to fill the blank (see op. cit., p. 456), merely recognizing the antithesis. Girard cites Valerius Probus to the effect that the phrase of the formula was "I say you ought to give me." Op. cit., p. 1048, Note 2. And Muirhead, op. cit., p. 178, gives both; the real, "I say that this is mine"; and the personal, "I say that the defendant is bound to pay me so much." The latter, being in the third person, suggests the *formulae,* not the *sacramentum.*

[232] Op. cit., p. 1045.

[233] Girard seems to conclude that the model of *in rem* is *vindicatio* without *contravindicatio* (i.e. uncontested) and of *in personam, manus iniectio* without *vindicatio* (i.e. uncontested). We cannot follow him in assuming that the terminology began at this stage. See Note 244, p. 196. He says, op. cit., p. 1048, Note 5, "L'action *in rem* est, d'après son nom, une action exercée contre la chose comme l'action *in personam* l'est contre la personne, une action où celui qui a mené devant le magistrat une chose, un animal, un esclave pour s'en dire propriétaire et a fait son affirmation (*vindicatio*) sans être arrêté par l'affirmation d'un autre personne qui se prétende le propriétaire (*contravindicatio*), emmène cette chose avec lui, comme celui qui a exercé la *manus iniectio* sur la personne de son débiteur sans être arrêté par la contradiction du *vindex,* l'emmène chez lui."

[234] The form was as follows: the *demonstratio,* beginning with *quod* (whereas), was a statement of the reason, a showing of fact. Gaius says, 4. 40, "Demonstratio . . . ut demonstretur res de qua agitur." Thus he calls the reason *res.* The *in-*

an antithesis between the forms of claim in the *sacramentum*. But because the *sacramentum*, and in fact all actions prior to the *formulae*, was based on assertions which were then converted into the determination of an oath, both Hunter and Muirhead agree that the form was *in personam*.[235] On the other hand certain other authorities conceive all those original actions to have been in form vindications.[236] This difference of opinion indicates that the true ground for the distinction had not yet arisen.

If we ground the distinction upon the presence or absence, in court, of a *res* as the subject of dispute, or of the person of a defendant, we meet other difficulties. It is true that there may have been vindications without counter-vindications under the *sacramentum*—in other words cases where the object in question was brought into court with no other claimant—while if the *sacramentum* was ever *in personam* it obviously required the presence of the defendant in court. But this is no true distinction since the *petitor* out of possession needed also to secure the presence in court of the defendant in possession, in a real action. Nevertheless it is noted that there were distinctions in this respect in the *formulae*. "Ordinarily the *intentio* did not name the defendant in real actions and did in personal actions."[237] "A real action named no party but the plaintiff in the 'intentio' . . . a personal action named the defendant as well as the plaintiff in the 'intentio'."[238]

According to the strict legal test the action *per formulam petitoriam* was the first action which was in a form which we can identify as *in rem*.[239] Gaius states that a *petitoria formula* is one in which the plaintiff alleges in the *intentio* that the thing is his.[240] However,

tentio, beginning with *si paret* (if it appears), was a statement of the claim or objective. Gaius says 4. 41, "Intentio est ea pars formulae, qua actor desiderium suum concludit." Here the objective itself is named but is not referred to as *res*. The *condemnatio* was a statement of the alternative verdicts suggested.

In certain cases—the mixed actions—there was an *adjudicatio* following the *demonstratio*.

235 See Muirhead, op. cit., p. 327. And Hunter says, op. cit., p. 983, "The recovery of property was accomplished by an action that in form was *in personam*."

236 See Muirhead, op. cit., p. 178. And Holdsworth, op. cit., III, p. 5, says, "As in Roman Law we see in the Legis Actio Sacramenti the most primitive form of real action. . ."

237 Girard, op. cit., 4th ed., p. 1012. In the 7th and in the last (8th) edition, p. 1081, a part of this statement is omitted, apparently in error, so that it is made to say the opposite, which is neither correct nor consistent with Girard's accompanying statements. See also Poste, op. cit., p. 447.

238 Moyle, op. cit., I, p. 629, "The intentio is either directed against the person of the defendant, and names him . . . or it merely specifies the object to which the plaintiff's claim relates. . . In the first case the action is in personam. . . In the second case it is in rem, and asserts either ownership or a ius in re aliena."

239 Muirhead, op. cit., p. 327.

240 Gaius, 4. 92. Technically *actio* was always in *personam* and *petitio*, derived from this, the first action to be real in form, was the exact name for an action *in rem*.

it was not the allegation which was new but the fact that it was the allegation itself which was submitted for decision. In this last stage (the *formulae*) "the fiction of a wager is dropped, and the right of the plaintiff is submitted directly for the judgment of the *judex*. It is at this point for the first time that we reach a true *actio in rem*."[241]

Thus we see one presumed gradual differentiation according as to whether only the subject of dispute (*res*) is brought into court; or both the subject (*res*) and the person (*persona*) against whom the complaint is directed; or, finally, only the latter. As a result of that another difference arises. Where the subject can be introduced without the *vocatio* of another person it is unnecessary to name a defendant in the *intentio*; but where the subject cannot be reached, either because it is withheld, or because it is of a non-physical nature, a person must be named and called. Only at the last does the issue itself become differentiated.

At whatever stage we conclude the essential difference in form to have developed it is clear, I think, that the terminology for the classification of actions could only have been a product of a late period in Roman law—a sophistication applied in retrospect, always remaining somewhat explanatory and neither controlling the law nor quite able to reduce the facts to fit the theoretical system.[242] And this for two reasons. In the first place the phrase *in rem* is inconsistent with the terminology in use in the actions themselves, even that of the *formulae*. There, for instance, the objective is called a *ius* in the case of the real actions on servitudes.[243] And *res persequendae* are constantly referred to in personal actions. In the second place the word *persona*, as we have seen, came from the drama and was probably not applied to the legal personality of the representative of the *familia* until long after the forms and phraseology of the *legis actiones*, and perhaps even of the *formulae*, were settled. The early term was *caput*.[244]

See Moyle, op. cit., I, p. 332, and *Dig.*, 44. 7. 28; 50. 16. 178. 2. Later it was called *vindicatio*.

[241] Hunter, op. cit., p. 983. Bonfante, op. cit., I, p. 498, says, ". . . dans la revendication de la procédure formulaire . . . on abolit le système des *vindicationes* et *contravindicationes* et celui qui possède est exonéré de la preuve; c'est pourquoi *possessor* devient synonyme de défendeur dans une action *in rem*."

[242] Such non-conformist cases are cited by Justinian as mixed actions. Justinian, *Inst.*, 4. 6. 20.

[243] Gaius, 4. 3.

[244] Girard, op. cit., p. 1081, says that the designation came into use under the *legis actiones*, because the action *in rem* had for direct object the thing and the action *in personam* had for direct object the person of the debtor. So far as I can learn there is no evidence that these terms were used at the time when the *legis actiones* constituted the only processes. Of course the use of the latter persisted until the early Empire. If by "person of the debtor" Girard means his physical person, then certainly the term must have been applied very late, for its early popular and its continuing legal significance was far from a physical notion.

From these considerations it appears that the differentiation of actions evolved not from some early theory which consciously organized the system of actions according to a scheme, but from some more practical and inherent necessity, the results of which were only recognized after the fact. Was this necessity a "fundamental difference in the nature of private rights," or was it rather the result of the somewhat fortuitous system upon which early Roman society happened to be organized? For the sake of future reference let us set up at this point as our hypothesis the latter explanation, basing it upon an interpretation of this distinction in the light of the conclusion we have already reached as to the nature of the Roman social organization.

The essential prehistoric social fact was *manus*. This was the basis of the subsequent intra-familial *ius*. It was the prepossession we have called the classificatory genitive. It was not conceived as a right. Rather it inhered in the very nature of things. It was not granted by the super-familial power and it could not be removed in early times by that power. It stood on its own feet. It was the binder of an autonomous "state in little." Its existence could be disputed but was a matter of fact, not of law. It could not be changed without the voluntary consent – the acquiescence or repudiation – of him who had *manus* (i.e. usually the *paterfamilias*, but also in certain cases the *patres* of still larger groups). This consent expressed itself as surrender – that of *traditio*, *mancipatio*, *in iure cessio*, *noxae deditio*, etc.

Vindication was the maintenance of *manus* and all that involved.[245] The *vindex* was the one whose duty or privilege it was to maintain it – the *mundebour*. *Manus* and its maintenance (vindication) applied equally and without distinction to all subject persons or objects. Nothing could stand against it.[246] It superseded all other claims because it was absolute. In fact it excluded all other claims not

[245] The field of meanings which this family of words covered confirms this interpretation. *Vindex* = he who maintains *manus*; *vindicatio* = the process of maintaining; *vindiciae* = the objects or persons over which it is maintained; *vindicare* = to maintain *manus*; *vindicta* = the implement with which it is maintained (the rod or spear).

	In general	Against injury	Against captivity (legal or otherwise)	For recovery (*rei-vindicatio*)
Vindex	Protector	Avenger, Punisher	Deliverer, Surety	Claimant
Vindicatio	Protecting	Avenging		Claiming
Vindiciae				That claimed
Vindicare	Protect	Avenge, Punish	Deliver, Liberate	To claim
Vindicta		Vengeance, Punishment (transf.)	Deliverance (transf.)	Symbol of claiming (*festuca*)

[246] See Note 162, page 70.

founded upon itself.[247] For this reason the only question concerning *manus* was the question where it lay. That question could be settled by a simple uncontested vindication (*manum adsertum*) which appears alike in actions and transactions.[248] Or it might need to be settled by a *vindicatio* and *contravindicatio* (*manum consertum*), the contested action.[249]

Actions *in rem* developed from this source and were assertions of the intra-familial *ius* over persons and objects, in whole or in part (servitudes), or of the Praetorian analogues to the same. They began by being tried before a tribunal and under an authority which pretended no power to interfere within a *familia* or to change whatever relation was found to exist within that subordinate but nevertheless independent jurisdiction. Adjudication was at first merely the confirmation of a state of fact.

Since, because of the notion of *manus* and the fact and idea of two co-ordinate and mutually limiting jurisdictions, the super-familial power could not or would not at first go behind the head of a *familia* and deal with his subject persons or objects without his consent, there remained but one recourse in all other questions; namely to proceed against the head himself. He was a free person. But he it was who had submitted himself in a sense to the joint authority of his fellows and himself in the constitution of the confederation of heads. And he it was who, as the representative of his *familia* toward the world outside, was the only legitimate point of attack. He assumed all responsibility to his fellow *cives* for the affairs of his *familia* and of himself. His patrimony remained safe, but his person was entirely exposed.[250] Even when the proceeding was against the head it was at first true that, though the *ius* conferred was a fragment of the super-familial power, it could only be attained by proper ceremonies and with the consent of him who was to be subjected to it. It was not granted arbitrarily. He must bind himself (*obligatio*) either by means of a publicly made agreement in the form of a self-surrender (*nexum*), of an oath with guarantors or pledge, or, under pressure of public opinion and perhaps fear of a feud and vengeance, by a voluntary agreement to abide by the result of an arbitration and to settle for any delict or breach of other contract which might be proved against him or his. And the last was probably the first.

[247] The *ius utendi*, etc., being a fraction of itself, stood against it.

[248] The vindication of *status hominis* in an action, or in a transaction. The latter is shown in adoption and in manumission by *in iure cessio*, for instance. We have already suggested that actions and transactions were not originally distinguished.

[249] Whether *manum adsertum* meant "assertion of manus" and *manum consertum* the "joint assertion of manus," or signified the symbolizing of the same – a single or joint laying on of hands – is a question. Poste supposes the latter meant "a grasping of the hand" of the adversary; see op. cit., p. 461.

[250] Ihering, *Geist*, II, p. 153.

The sanction (in the legal sense) in support of this obligation was solely *manus iniectio*; that is, execution upon the person, who had, by this time, been converted into a debtor whether the source had been contract or delict. But this sanction, though it derived from the consent of him who was to be submitted to it and had received the authentication of the super-familial power, nevertheless was as nothing in face of the natural *manus*. Although the subject was a *paterfamilias*, and had therefore a *persona* and was *sui iuris*, still even the weaker natural *Obervormundschaft* of a *propinquus* sufficed instantly to release him. Conversely, the failure to vindicate argued something in the nature of noxal surrender by his *propinqui*. But if the subject himself was not attained by *manus iniectio* it was only because his *vindex* had substituted himself for him. Therefore this was, in lesser degree, the same assumption of responsibility that took place within the smaller familial circle. Only, in this case, a new but equally independent *person* became the object of execution.[251]

Thus, though the *familia* could not be touched by the super-familial *ius*, the *paterfamilias* could be—though at first only with his own consent.[252] While the *familia* could not be separated from the *pater* by the super-familial *ius*, the *pater* could be separated from the *familia*. The result, in his case, however, was not acquisition of him in a property sense. Rather it was a taking for punishment. After a certain opportunity was given for ransom he could be killed or sold outside Rome into slavery. In either case he suffered death, natural or civil, and therefore his position became vacant. If he suffered death an heir succeeded to his debts; if he suffered *capitis deminutio* his position (*patrimonium*) was extinguished along with his personality (*persona*).[253] Then, according to Girard, his creditor or creditors acquired the orphaned, or abandoned, subject persons and objects composing his *familia*.[254] Whether even this addiction of the *familia* was at first possible, is doubtful. However with the introduction of the *venditio bonorum* by the Praetor it became so. The *emptor* or *curator* was in effect a "praetorian successor" who took by *addictio*, if his predecessor were living, and as fictive heir, if dead. Property did not pass directly to the creditors. Instead the buyer acquired subject to the debts, or his purchase price was the creditors'

[251] Later when the system was in process of breaking down he was admitted, in *manus iniectio pura*, to an inconsistent vindication of himself.

[252] An exception was *pignoris capio* (distraint). But, as Girard points out, op. cit., p. 1040, this common primitive legal process had been suppressed in Rome in prehistoric times. Its only survival was in public law and, from that source, in a few analogous cases of private law. This suppression strongly confirms the thesis as to the inviolability of familial precincts.

[253] Girard, op. cit., p. 212.

[254] Girard, op. cit., p. 212 and p. 110, Note 3.

dividend.[255] By this avenue execution upon the property came into use, first as a secondary result of, and later as a substitute for, execution upon the person.[256] But it occurred, when the *pater* refused to defend or to pay, only by way of the arbitrary substitution of a new *pater* who would.

We can take two views of this ultimate sanction (legal) of most early actions *in personam*. It can be regarded only as bodily execution, which it most certainly was.[257] In this view the ultimate right of the creditor was as real as any other right.[258] The debtor became a subject person, an object of a sort of *dominium*. He was taken under *manus*. And the purpose seems to have been punishment for a wrong done – punishment in default of payment of composition for delict or for breach of contract. But the matter can be looked at in another way as well. Ihering combines the two as alternatives. "The execution of the debt was the annihilation of the personality of the debtor; of his legal *persona* when there was only a single creditor (sold abroad as a slave); of his physical personality when they were many (*in partes secare*, according to the law of the XII Tables, that is to say dissection of the debtor)."[259] In this view execution was at least indirectly and alternatively upon the *persona*. It appeared as a right to depose the debtor from his office and later, at least, indirectly to succeed him. Perhaps, the latter view would be more emphasized by the sense of the word *persona* at the period in which the terms for the types of action were probably adopted. But doubtless both were in mind.

The real basis for the distinction in the actions seems to be due, then, to the peculiar constitution of Roman law, which was based on a weak confederation of autonomous units. In general there was

[255] Girard, op. cit., p. 113. See also Bonfante, op. cit., I, p. 519.

[256] Bonfante, op. cit., I, p. 518, says, "En principe, l'exécution de la sentence, même dans la période des formules, est toujours faite sur la personne. En pratique, cependant, l'exécution sur les biens a remplacé l'exécution sur la personne. A cet effet, l'institution fondamentale est la *venditio bonorum* introduite par le préteur Rutilius Rufus."

[257] It is this view which Ihering presents in one place, *Aryan*, p. 55. "The popular mind was loth to give up the idea that the body of the debtor belonged, even after death, to the creditor – the *actio in personam* in its full consequence. . ." And Girard, op. cit., p. 413, Note 2, says, "On a même pu se demander si très anciennement le droit de créance n'a pas été consideré comme portant sur la personne du débiteur de la même façon dont le droit de propriété porte sur la chose."

[258] Ihering, *Entw.-gesch.*, p. 123, says ". . . das *nexum* begründet die *manus* über einen freien Menschen ganz so wie das *mancipium* im späteren Sinne des Wortes, und die zuständige Klage im Fall ihrer Bestreitung ist daher die *vindicatio*, sie richtet sich nicht gegen den Schuldner als Subjekt (*in personam*), sondern als Objekt (*in rem*)." P. 102: "Allerdings will der Gläubiger sein Geld, aber der Schuldner hat es nicht, und damit schlägt – um in der Sprache der Juristen zu reden – sein obligatorischer Anspruch in einen dinglichen um, er erhält ein Recht an dën Korper des Schuldners. . . Der Mann gehört fortan dem Gläubiger. . ."

[259] *Geist*, II, p. 153.

but one classification of subject persons or objects. And this withdrew them from the purview of the law. There was a single general relation within these groups; and but a single claim to them — wholly defensive, and only to be brought by the head, his delegate or his successor. From without there was but one point of attack. The only offensive claim was against the head, the *persona* of the group, upon the ground of his or his subordinates' commitments or responsibilities, and enforcible, in the last analysis, only against his person in its dual aspect. Thus the term *in rem* seems to have visualized only subject persons and objects — *res corporales* — as its eventual objective; whereas the term *in personam* visualized only sovereign heads of the constituent units — persons *sui iuris* — as its eventual objective. But the character of the power defended or acquired, by the two means and over the two objectives, seems not, at first, to have been widely different. As to whether this dichotomy applies generally to all times and societies, we shall need to suspend judgment until we have examined the other systems of organization which come within the field of our study.

2. *Differentiation of the Two Forms of Obligation*

In suggesting this curious and somewhat accidental origin of the foregoing division of Roman actions we have necessarily presented the development as if it were a much more consistent and systematic affair than it probably was. It is necessary now to modify this presentation and to introduce still further inconsistencies in order to show the confused way in which another related classification arose, which distinguished the actions springing from the two kinds of obligation, those from delict and those from contract. In this way we may succeed in viewing the thing that was — and still is — freed from the usual blindness toward the accepted and conventional.

We may first re-examine briefly the source and nature of obligation, a concept which, as is normal in Roman law, is hardly distinguishable from the processes which supported it.[260] In the classic period we find two sorts of obligations, those arising from contract and those arising from delict (tort). To the layman this seems a strange mixture. In what respect were injuries and contracts assimilable? If a delict — an injury to a person or property — occasions an obligation, then it would seem that, in the case of contract, it would be the breach of contract which corresponded — which occasioned

[260] Buckland, *Text-Book*, p. 405, suggests that "there are not wanting signs of a view that they [*obligationes*] are not *res*, but a conception with a close affinity to the notion of *actio*." It has been our contention that all *res* had this same close affinity; were in fact originally and primarily the substance of actions and had in the earlier times existed, strictly speaking, only in that aspect.

obligation – and that this would be treated as a delict. But if, on the other hand, it is the entry into an agreement which gives rise to obligation then it is difficult to see in what manner a delict becomes the occasion for one. There is no such joint association in obligation indigenous in English law, though there the breach of contract did savour of delict.[261] Therefore, the lumping together of such diverse matters, while it has coloured all legal thinking since and to this day occasions many practical difficulties in American courts, seems so illogical that we are tempted again to look for an evolutionary rather than a rational explanation.

Such an explanation has already been outlined. It lies in what Moyle has called "the contractual decision of disputes." In the beginning, as we have seen, the remedy for delict was vengeance. Then the interposition of law resulted in the substitution of a monetary composition, at first voluntary upon both sides, by which the feud was bought off.[262] The effect of this composition was the same as, and the form not far different from, a contract. And this is natural for, as we have noted, early actions and transactions were closely allied. Contracts, conveyances and judgments upon them and upon delicts were all conceived to be ratified by similar methods, the formal procedure *in iure,* by which ceremony there was either transferred a sort of artificial intra-familial *ius* or there was sanctioned or imparted to one party a delegated and separated fraction of the super-familial *ius* over the other in respect of the particular transaction.[263] Therefore the result of any *incompleted* action or transaction alike was a debt. The parties were thereupon united by a bond – the later *obligatio* – originally probably a real and later a conceptual chain by which one held the other.

It is apparent that, at first, the obligation arising from delict was only conceived to come into existence after the action was brought before the arbitrators as a joint submission and the stamp of a contract had been placed upon it. This exact point may not have been reached

[261] Pound, *Philosophy*, p. 174, says "Roman law may have a contractual conception of obligation *ex delicto* – thinking of the delict as giving rise to a debt – and the common law a delictual conception of liability upon contract – thinking in terms of recovery of damages for the wrong of breaking a promise. . ."

[262] The means of the contractual decision of disputes are described by Moyle, op. cit., I, p. 618, as *confessio* or the "reference of the matter by common consent to arbitration; from this [the latter], beyond the shadow of a doubt, the whole Roman system of actions tried before a judge or judges took its origin." Girard, op. cit., pp. 421-425, shows clearly that the obligation *ex delicto* was the legal means of securing the legally imposed composition for the right of vengeance.

[263] Always the super-familial power because, as Girard says, op. cit., p. 420, ". . . la personne obligée par le délit, elle doit, même dans le droit le plus récent, appartenir à une autre *domus* que la victime. . ."

in the very beginning until judgment was given.[264] But at an early stage the obligation appears to have arisen already at the joining of issue. Then the matter became a *lis contestata* and was converted into a voluntary agreement to abide by the issue. This seems to be the only adequate explanation of the old exception to the rule that "actions on delict, even when partly rei persecutoriae, 'in heredem non dantur,'" (i.e. do not lie against the heirs).[265] In general the right of action for tort died with the person of the tortfeasor because, as Moyle[266] puts it, "the feuds and hostilities" of the deceased are no part of his *universitas iuris.* But if before his death he had incurred a potential obligation on account of the delict by joining issue upon the question, then the action did not die.[267] As time went on the originally voluntary, or quasi-voluntary, character of this obligation tended to disappear and the obligation began to be conceived as one imposed at the time of the delict.[268] Later distinctions (sophistications, however empirical) which imputed novations at each stage of procedure tended to confuse this rather obvious source of obligations *ex delicto.*

The only remaining distinctions between the two types of obligations, after this change took place, were the differences in results, which we are about to describe, and the differences in cause. The obligation *ex contractu* continued to be a voluntary subjection of one to the super-familial power delegated to the other by means of the legal confirmation of their agreement. A breach of such a contract was an interference with the power and authority of the inter-familial *ius.* But the obligation *ex delicto* was eventually conceived to be an involuntary subjection of one to the same delegated super-familial power, in the hands of another, which had come to be imposed automatically and at once by the authority of the *Quiritii,* when the one had interfered with the powers and protections accorded to the other in the intra-familial field.

264 The opening phrase of the *actio manus iniectio* reads "*quod tu mihi iudicatus (sive damnatus).*" Gaius, 4. 21, suggests that the *obligatio ex delicto* may, in its earliest stages, have come into being only at the point of condemnation (judgment) not even at that earlier point of *litis contestatio* (joining of issue).

265 Moyle, op. cit., I, p. 617.

266 Moyle, op. cit., I, p. 617.

267 Poste, op. cit., p. 452.

268 Poste presumed, op. cit., 3rd Ed., p. 434, that the obligation *ex delicto* existed from the first, as now, as a "liability to the legal sanction," prior to beginning of action. But all the evidence makes it seem to me clear that it did not. It is quite possible, however, that it was this extension of the idea of delictual obligation, this pre-judicial "liability to the legal sanction," the right of action before the joining of issue, which gave rise to the rule that the action died with the person. The adoption of the new theory as to the moment when the obligation sprang into being could not be made to change the facts of law and the rule arose to explain the discrepancy.

In the beginning, as we have noted, the objective of the delictual action was *poena.* As, in the course of time, the monetary award (*damnum*) came to include compensation for injury, or reparation, as well as the original element of vengeance now become punitive (penal), it became necessary to distinguish the reparatory from the penal element. The latter continued to be described as *poena;* the former was usually separated as *tanta res.*[269] This dual objective was frequently combined in one action. Thus delictual obligations were not only intimately associated, if not identical, with contractual obligations in their origin, but some of the actions based on them have in them an element of the action *in rem,* an assertion of a right of property, of which the cause, course and effect are quite similar to other actions *in rem* although, in later times, only the money equivalent of the object or subject person might be awarded.[270]

The case of obligations *ex contractu* presents an even less distinct character in its early stages. In respect of their relation to obligations *ex delicto* the possibility must be recognized that the original legal cognizance and confirmation of agreements (*obligatio*) may quite as well have commenced in connection with the composition of vengeance, and that other agreements came to fashion themselves upon this model.[271] It seems as likely that the origin of obligation on contract was delictual as that the origin of obligation on delict was contractual.[272] Moreover we have seen that there remained for a

[269] Or merely *res* (Justinian), the later expression for *quanti res erit.*

[270] *Actiones mixtae.* Or they gave rise to two actions and "l'action en dédommagement, c'est-à-dire l'action réipersécutoire, est nettement distincte de l'action pénale, et, par suite, bien qu'elles paraissent avoir toutes les deux pour objet l' *eadem res,* le fait d'avoir intenté l'une n'enlève pas le droit d'engager l'autre. . ." Bonfante, op. cit., I, p. 467.

[271] Bonfante, op. cit., I, pp. 219-220, says, "La finalité de l'obligation dans le droit le plus ancien n'est pas commerciale, mais pénale. . ." "Le délit émerge [in retracing the evolution of obligation] et envahit tout le système de l'obligation." ". . . dans l'ancien droit romain, *reus* signifie aussi bien le débiteur que le coupable, la langue allemande . . . a encore aujourd'hui le même terme (*Schuld*) pour désigner la dette et la faute . . . dans le droit du plus ancien peuple aryen, le même mot désigne la dette et la faute (*ṛṇa*) ; le voleur et l'emprunteur qui ne paie pas (le prêt est toujours la première forme d'obligation) sont mesurés à la même aune. . ." See also, op. cit., I, p. 221, for a summary of his view of the origins of obligation, having always for its object *poena* and its sources *noxae deditio, mancipium* or *nexum,* and of the parallelism between *noxa* and debt.

So far as the procedural results are concerned Pound seems to take this view. He says, *Philosophy,* p. 151, "In Roman law, the condiction, which is the type of actions *in personam,* and thus the starting point historically of rights *in personam* and of theories of obligation, was at first a recovery of a thing certain or a sum certain due upon a promise of this sort," (i.e. a promise of composition for delict, one causing a feud if not performed).

[272] Such an origin would help to account for one peculiarity. "*Obligatio* was so intensely personal that it seems that, at one time, it died with the party liable. This indeed was always so in delict, but in very early law it seems to have been not less true in contract." Buckland, *Text-Book,* p. 408.

long time evidence that the purpose of action and execution, based on contract, "was not . . . primarily to satisfy the creditor, but rather to punish the debtor. . ."[273] The having away from the owner of money or other objects, conditionally or unconditionally, and then defaulting in their restoration, specifically or in money equivalent, was not sharply distinguished, because the having had been voluntary on the part of the owner, from involuntary losses of possession. The result of the confusion appeared in many of the awards in actions upon contract persisting until later times.[274] The element of vengeance for injury subsisted along with that of equivalent for loss suffered. And, as has been made clear, execution upon the person retained always the punitive element of vengeance. Thus the reason for the similarity of result of breach of contract and of delict was partially due to their indistinguishable origin in wrongs.

The intimate relation of all obligations, but especially those from contract, to the field of corporeal *res*, presents an even more noticeable confusion, characteristic of the early law but persisting in some respects in the later as well. It is true that the gradual differentiation of actions along the lines discussed in the previous section had caused almost all claims founded upon contract to impinge, not upon the subject objects or persons sought, but rather upon their sovereign or owner. But this seems to have been a technical legal development upon the basis of a self-limitation as to jurisdiction, not carried out in complete consistency. At least the law continued to bow to the popular view that the objective even of personal actions was often the pursuit of such subject person or object.[275]

In the case of contract—and thence by analogy all debt—the early popular view looked past the person—the avenue of access—to the object. In the obligation, at its beginning, "the thing formed also the foundation, the base, as well as the end or objective of the claim. The thing was the foundation of the obligation; in the ideas of the ancient law all obligation rested on the fact that the debtor (*de-habet* = *debet*) had had some thing (*res*) of the creditor and that the creditor had given some thing (*cre-dedit* = *credidit*), so that either the delivery had been really effected (contract real) or that it had been legally promised (contract literal or verbal). The thing was also the object of the obligation; all obligation in the ancient law led to a *dare*, to the giving of a thing; in the expression *rem persequitur* the word *res* is originally employed in the literal sense as in the

273 Sohm, op. cit., p. 211.

274 See for instance Gaius 4. 9, and Girard, op. cit., p. 442.

275 Nevertheless, as we have already seen, no claim upon any artificial basis could, in the early days, stand against the true and natural *manus*. For example, the conclusive effect of vindication in *manus iniectio*.

expression *quanti ea res est. . .*"[276] Thus the action *in personam*, arising from contract, tended to model its objective upon the same lines as the action *in rem*, to seek specific restitution, though in the main it had to be satisfied, as did occasionally an action *in rem* as well, with a compensatory award.[277] Eventually, in Justinian's phrase, the distinction in objective is between those actions which are "*rei persequendae causa comparatae*" and those which are "*tantum poenae persequendae causa comparatae.*" This distinction was indiscriminately applied to actions *in rem* and to both kinds of action *in personam.* In this final stage, the actions *in rem* all pursued, and there was awarded only, the subject of dispute itself; in the actions *in personam* on contract all sought the subject of dispute only, but the award was usually of its equivalent in money, for specific performance was rare; in the actions *in personam* on delict both the subject and punishment might be sought, but the award was for the money value of both.[278]

Upon the basis of this analysis it is proper to say that actions on contract were closely related in origin both to penal actions on delict and to real actions; perhaps more closely to the latter than to the former; that the obligations of both varieties arose from a common origin and were the result of actions or transactions which took an almost identical form; and finally that these obligations at first envisaged as their eventual incidence almost the same character of power over the body, or *persona*, of the person at the head of a *familia*, as the domestic and property powers of that person himself represented

[276] Ihering, *Geist*, II, p. 440.

[277] "The *res intenditur* already at the time of the *formulae* might be the objective itself or a sum of money representing its value. This has led to much confusion. So Muirhead, op. cit., p. 184, speaks of the fact that disputed readings of Gaius (Gaius, 4. 48) lead to a difference of opinion whether condemnation in *legis actiones* "was in the 'ipsa res' and not in a pecuniary equivalent," or always in pecuniary equivalent. And Hunter, op. cit., pp. 41-42, when he states that under the original statute-process (*legis actio*) the Praetor gave title or damages is careful to cite the terms *addictio bona* and *damna*. For *bona* meant possessions, and *damna* might mean either *res*, in the foregoing sense, or *poena*.

[278] "We sue sometimes so that *rem tantum* is sought by us, sometimes *poenam tantum*, and sometimes both *rem et poenam*." Gaius, 4. 6. "*Rem tantum* is sought by us, for instance, in actions in which we sue on contract." Gaius, 4. 7. "*Poenam tantum* is sought by us, for instance, in action of theft and injuries and, in the opinion of some, in action of robbery, for we have the choice either of a *vindicatio* or a *condictio* of the *res* itself ['*ipsius res*']." Gaius, 4. 8. In other cases enumerated, "Both the *rem* and the *poenam* are sought. . ." Gaius, 4. 9. In the *Institutes* of Justinian the expression is different. Here all real actions are "*rei persequendae causa comparatae.*" Those which spring from contract seem to be the same. Of those which result from delict ("*ex maleficiis*") some "*tantum poenae persequendae causa comparatae sunt*," and some "*tam poenae quam rei persequendae et ob id mixtae sunt.*" Justinian, *Inst.*, 4. 6. 17-18. Thus the word *res* is used alone by Justinian to mean what Gaius earlier called *tanta res* and what originally was exactly described as "*quanti ea res erit, tantam pecuniam condemna.*" See original *formula*, Gaius, 4. 51. *Res* in the end means compensatory damages and *poena*, punitive damages.

over the subject persons and objects within his *familia*. Nevertheless always the *manus* of a *manus iniectio*, the artificial *manus*, seems to have been weaker than the *manus* of a *vindicatio*, the natural *manus*. Execution seems to have taken the same course whether the debt arose from contract or from delict. And, when this power over the person was acquired, its exercise seems to have been used as often for purposes of punishment as it was for the enjoyment of the benefits of property. It was a punitive more than an economic acquisition, nearer to the original noxal surrender than to *mancipium*.[279] The change in the nature of execution was only completed with the substitution of real for personal execution.[280] Then the final solution of the matter came to be in truth a monetary equivalent both of the *poena* and of the *res*. We may say that the early execution of a restorative award was penal and that the late execution of a penal award was restorative.

3. *Contract—The Voluntary Subjection to Inter-familial Power*

The normally slow growth of the law—if not of the fact—of contract in primitive communities brings us naturally, at the last, to this part of the subject. Gradually differentiated from wrongs in general, breaches of contract became segregated and classified by themselves according to the legal nature of the contract. For, to the extent that the obligation had been previously incurred by the

[279] Bonfante, op. cit., I, p. 228, says ". . . à l'époque des Douze Tables, la peine privée elle-même peut être afflictive, de sorte que la seule critère pour distinguer le délit public du délit privé est de voir si le sujet qui inflige la peine et en perçoit le montant est le magistrat ou bien le *paterfamilias*." But in the historic epoch "Le droit pénal public et le droit pénal privé se distinguent, . . . par le caractère de la peine, laquelle, dans les délits privés, n'est jamais afflictive, mais toujours pécuniare, et la peine pécuniare servit de transition au contrat et au nouveau type d'obligation."

[280] In the beginning, says Sohm, op. cit., pp. 287-288, "When the person of the debtor (whom execution placed in the position of a slave in regard to his creditor) passed into the power of the creditor, the same fate befell his whole estate and probably also his whole family, i.e., the aggregate of those who were subject to his potestas. Thus every personal execution necessarily—though only indirectly—involved an execution against the debtor's property, because it went, in all cases, against the debtor's entire person and estate, quite regardless of the actual amount due. . ."

"The praetor was the first to grant execution against the property of the debtor. . ." Thus the creditors had the option to proceed either by personal execution or by real execution. The *lex Julia* gave to the debtor the right to choose the latter by *cessio bonorum*. But he had the right to reserve a *beneficium competentiae*. It was not, Sohm says, until the later empire that specific execution came in and, through the revival of *pignoris capio*, the individual creditor could obtain satisfaction without seizing the whole estate of the debtor. Execution then became what it is now, solely "for the satisfaction of the person entitled," and limited to an approximate equivalent of the debt.

Bonfante, op. cit., I, p. 520, notes that execution on the estate only became a general right in the time of Caesar or Augustus. This was the *distractio bonorum*, eventually replaced, under Antoninus Pius by the *pignus ex causa iudicati captum*.

entry into a formal contract, such wrongs had a double sanction. They constituted the violation of a binding agreement as well, usually, as the securing of something for nothing. In the course of time, the idea of the latter became more sharply separated from delict, as the distinction between voluntary and involuntary loss of possession developed. Then, when the necessity of the formal agreement partially disappeared, the contracts *re*, including the innominate, were enabled to become implied contracts, and therefore obligations, by the mere fact (*re*) that something, not intended as a gift, had been secured for nothing. Some of the old forms were retained, however, or were revived, to care for those cases where the contracts were wholly executory.[281]

Partly because of its legal origin in wrongs and its resulting execution against the person of the debtor; partly because of the prepossession which limited property to the area of the classificatory genitive;[282] partly because the matter to be performed came to be more and more often the doing or not doing of an act (*faciendum* and *praestandum*) rather than the return of an object (*dandum*); partly because of the phraseology of the time-honoured *intentio* (*dare, facere, oportere*); and partly because of the almost universal condemnation of *res tanta*,[283] the Roman obligation *ex contractu* of the classic period was conceived in law to create a relation of a wholly different order from *dominium*. It was a power over a person *sui iuris*, not over a person *alieni iuris*, or an object.[284] Because what was asserted in an action was this intangible authority, the *res*, as the subject or basis of the action, was conceived to be among the incorporeal things. But because the contractual transaction itself had originally been an effort to create a new, if weaker, *manus*, and because in the action the claim was frequently based upon the past delivery of a tangible object and sought its restoration, the objective continued inconsistently to be called a *res persecutoria*, in spite of the fact that it was not usually *ipsa res* but *tanta res*.[285]

[281] So "l'obligation revêt définitivement, à cette époque, un caractère patrimoniel et assume une fonction commerciale." Bonfante, op. cit., I, p. 489.

[282] So that what I deliver to you on credit, after you have it in your possession, or what you buy with the money I lend you, is no longer *of* me.

[283] I.e. compensatory damages rather than specific performance.

[284] Whereas "le concept moderne de l'obligation signifie un rapport entre deux sujets. . ." Bonfante, op. cit., I, p. 219.

[285] In connection with obligations *ex contractu* the word *res* frequently seems to mean the object which ought to be given or the act which ought to be done – *res persequenda* – as well as that which had been done – *re*. Nevertheless there remains the connotation of legal action. It is strictly speaking only a *res* when viewed in its legal aspect. The word *bona* appears to have been the commercial word for elements of wealth and as such to have gradually intruded into law, particularly in its more highly developed meaning as assets or net assets. Thus Paulus in *Digest*, 50. 16. 39. 1, says, "That is regarded as *bona, quae deducto aere alieno supersunt*,"

In the end the legal philosophers, ignoring the remaining inconsistencies, crystallized this conceptual distinction between owning and being owed, effectively cut the last real survivals of the ancient bond between the creditor and the objects he had delivered to the debtor, and confirmed in its place the equally ancient bond upon the debtor—one reaching only as far as his person. Thus Paulus[286] says that "the essence of an obligation does not consist in its making any material object our property, or a servitude ours, but in its binding another person to grant something [*dandum*], to do something [*faciendum*] or to make good something [*praestandum*] in our favor." And the definition of Justinian is that "an obligation is a legal bond [*iuris vinculum*] by which we are bound by a necessity of performance of some matter [*alicuius solvendae rei*] according to the laws of our state."[287] Maine has stated that in "Roman legal phraseology . . . 'Obligation' signifies rights as well as duties. . ."[288] But in general one is impressed by the fact that the term is more often used to denote the subjection of the debtor than the power of the creditor. Originally the chain was the chain of bondage. It required little imagination to arrive at Justinian's figurative concept. For, from the beginning almost until his time, that had been the literal fact.

As we shall have occasion to examine the structure of later contract law it will be well, in passing, to present here the arrangement of the Roman contracts which Hunter gives and which is based on their analysis in the Institutes.[289] This arrangement is based solely on the manner in which the contract is effected and the obligation incurred. For those who had made an agreement, or pact, were conceived to be "drawn together," only by the bond, or *obligatio*, which the law might attach. Thus a pact made obligatory becomes a contract. But the *contractus* and the legally imposed *obligatio* are always carefully and consistently distinguished in Roman law.[290]

(i.e. which remains over after debiting money owed others). The legal connotation becomes still more obvious when, with the *formula incerti condictio*, the uncertain thing is first introduced; see Muirhead, op. cit., p. 325. For then the *res* is not only not material, but it is not even specific. Finally the word is often used to mean not so much what is to be secured by the action (the object) as that which gives rise to it (the reason), which may or may not be the same fact or object. Thus its use in *re contrahitur* and in *quid pro reo*, Gaius, 3. 127. So it may be said that in these contractual cases of *quid pro quo*, *res* is usually the *quid* but often the *quo*.

286 *Dig.*, 44. 7. 3. pr.

287 *Inst.*, 3. 13. 1.

288 *Ancient Law*, 314.

289 For instance, "id est sive re, sive verbis, sive litteris, sive consensu contractae fuerint obligationes," Gaius, 3. 119a.

290 According to Maine, *Ancient Law*, p. 313, "A Pact was the utmost product of the engagements of individuals agreeing among themselves, and it distinctly fell short of a Contract. Whether it ultimately became a Contract depended on the question whether the law annexed an Obligation to it."

Bonfante, op. cit., I, p. 489, says, "Le *contractus* ou *contractum* . . . n'est qu'une

Contracts

1. Real. Formless. Concluded by delivery. Unilateral or imperfectly bilateral
   - A. Named
     - a. *Mutuum* — Repayable in kind } "Ownership" passed
       - Payment in Error. Repayable in kind } "Ownership" passed
     - b. *Commodatum* — Returnable specifically
     - c. *Depositum* — Returnable specifically
       - Detention passed. Bailments
     - d. *Pignus*[291] — Returnable specifically
       - Pledge with right of sale. Possession passed
       - *Hypotheca*[292] — Returnable specifically
       - Pledge with right of sale, without possession
   - B. Unnamed (Innominate). Bilateral, for reciprocal performance and executed by one party.
2. Verbal. Formal. Concluded by a form of words at a meeting. Unilateral
   - A. *Stipulatio*
     - Suretyship
3. Literal. Formal. Concluded by writing in creditor's *codex*. Unilateral
   - A. *Expensilatio*[293]
4. Consensual. Formless. Concluded by letter, messenger or mere agreement. Bilateral, reciprocal and executory
   - a. *Emptio-venditio* (Purchase and Sale)[294]
   - b. *Locatio et conductio* (Letting and Hire)[295]
   - c. *Societas* (Partnership)
   - d. *Mandatum* (Agency)

ellipse de *contractus negotii* ou de *negotium contractum*. *Contrahere* . . . désigne . . . le fait de s'astreindre à une obligation quelconque . . . ; par contre, il ne signifie pas et ne peut signifier le consentement qui se dit *conventio* ou *pactio*. Mais le substantif *contractus*, dans lequel etait compris le mot *negotium* sousentendu, fut appliqué encore d'une manière plus spécifique et plus exclusive à la matière des obligations."

[291] The Romans did not treat pledge as among the *iura in re aliena*. Buckland, *Principles*, p. 63, believes the reason to have been that "the pledge possessor can take no economic advantage from the thing." We have already indicated a more natural explanation.

[292] Originated by a merely informal contract, without transfer of possession and protected, by certain actions *in rem*, in the right of sale. See Moyle, I, op. cit., p. 318.

[293] This prototype of the modern "account stated" was an entry in the creditor's ledger, presumably in the presence or with the knowledge of the debtor. The *codex accepti et expensi* was the book for recording debts arising from literal contracts and contained such entries as produced a legal result of their own force; Sohm, op. cit., p. 392. According to Hunter, op. cit., p. 526, it was used principally for the transfer of existing obligations. By the time of Justinian it had passed out of use; Justinian, *Inst.*, 3. 21.

We are not so much interested in the history and relation of these forms among themselves as we are in the various economic activities and the character of modern property to which they gave legal effect. The first question is, how far did these contracts inherently establish the relation of credit-debt—or, if it is different, that of creditor-debtor—between the parties? Ulpian defines credit as follows: "For when we agree to anything in reliance upon the honour of another, in order presently to receive back something by this contract, we are said to give credit."[296]

The *lex Cornelia*, according to Gaius,[297] defined *pecunia credita* in connection with limiting the liability of sureties. He says, "*Pecunia credita* includes not only that which we give as an instrument of credit, but everything which is an obligation when it is contracted, which it is certain will be due and which, without any condition, is provided for [debited] in the obligation. So money which we are contracted to pay on a certain day is included, in spite of the fact that it is to be demanded later, because it is certain that it will be due. By the term money in this law is meant everything. So if we are liable for wine or grain or land or a slave, this law is to be observed." This is an excellent definition of the modern "credit." The terms "creditor" and "debtor," however, were used in Roman law, we find, in a broader sense to cover the two parties to any obligation, except one which was *naturalis*.[298]

Applying the rule of the *lex Cornelia* to the foregoing contracts we find that the following contracts did not create the credit-debt relation: *commodatum*, or gratuitous loan for use; *depositum*, or gratuitous custody; *pignus*, or pledge. And this because they did not pass property, but merely detention or possession. The general *stipulatio* created a credit-debt only if its provisions were included in Gaius' definition. But the stipulation of suretyship, since it was

[294] "The contract is concluded, or complete, the moment the agreement of the will (consensus) upon object and price is declared, whereupon the risk and use of the article sold passes to the purchaser: it is regarded as already forming part of his substance, although until traditio [delivery] it is still in the ownership of the vendor." Salkowski, op. cit., p. 592.

[295] It is worthy of note that Roman law was already in its later days beginning to find it difficult to differentiate between the contracts of sale and of letting and hiring. "So nearly akin, indeed, is purchase and sale to letting and hiring, that in some cases it is a question to which class of the two a contract belongs." Justinian, *Inst.*, 3. 24. 3. And somewhat the same held true of the distinction between the latter and servitudes. *Emphyteusis* had been introduced as a form of servitude and it eventually became almost as difficult to distinguish the owner of land as it was, in later days, in England.

[296] "Nam cuicumque rei adsentiàmur alienam fidem secuti mox recepturi quid, ex hoc contractu, credere dicimur," Ulpian in *Dig.*, 12. 1. 1. 1.

[297] 3. 124.

[298] See *Dig.*, 50. 16. 11 (Gaius) and 12 (Ulpian), also *Dig.*, 50. 16. 10 (Ulpian).

a contingent liability, did not do so until the contingency occurred. The four consensual contracts created reciprocal credit-debt relations – the first two for definite sums or objects, the last two for indefinite sums or services. Only if one performance exceeded the other could the true credit-debt be said to be established. Thus *mutuum*, *expensilatio* and the innominate contracts were the only ones which certainly created credit-debt, either in money or in kind. The economically important contracts were *mutuum*, *stipulatio*, their accessory *pignus*, and the four consensual forms. The various forms of suretyship which had come and gone were legally of great importance, and perhaps *expensilatio*, when it was in vogue, covered much of the *pecunia credita* which later came to be classed as *mutuum*.

Two other minor additions and refinements of the Law of Obligations, to which we shall have occasion to refer incidentally, are the following:

Obligations *quasi ex delicto* are those, for the most part, arising from delicts for which the defendant ought to be held responsible, and is in law held responsible, though he did not commit them himself.

Obligations *quasi ex contractu* are those, for the most part, for which a liability is implicit in a relation and is imposed by law, though not created or undertaken by any direct act of the obligor. Poste thinks[299] that these relations are, in most cases, assimilable to agency or to partnership. It is far more illuminating to regard them as erstwhile purely internal familial relations, now projected outside the sphere of the family, and thus for the first time become reciprocal, i.e. subject to enforcement for the benefit of both parties.

F. *Summary*

1. *The Forms of Law*

Even if, in the foregoing, we have succeeded, to a considerable degree, in seeing through to the thing that was, it remains difficult to summarize the structure of the institution of property as it stood in Roman law at Gaius' time – the height of the Empire. We can be sure, however, that it was much less modern and civilized than it has been made to seem by those who have been deceived by the great technical progress that had been made and by reading into it the meanings and developments of later times. On the other hand, it is true that the emphasis we have given to the causes, rather than to the consequences, of the arrangements which had by this time

[299] Op. cit., pp. 386-387.

been evolved may readily have given to a reader, unfamiliar with the subject, an impression of a somewhat archaic system. That the classic Roman law certainly was not.[300]

This law was not specifically a law of property. Rather it was the whole private law of Rome. In its classic period it had come to deal with two kinds of power over persons according as they were within or without the family. The former was the Law of Persons; the latter the Law of Obligations. And it dealt with two kinds of power over material objects, again according to whether they were within or without the family. Of these the former was the various types or qualities of "ownership,"[301] and the latter the group of servitudes. Slaves were treated both as persons and as objects. But otherwise the division between persons and material objects had become nearly complete. Nevertheless, in form, the domestic relation had been applied over objects in the case of servitudes and, in real substance, the property relation had continued to a considerable degree to be applied over persons, both within the *familia* and without (in obligation). Thus the Roman view of property in classic times was still pervaded by the original distinction between that which was within and that which was without the *familia*, between the internal relations—familial law descended from the customs of the "state in little"—and the external relations of these still somewhat independent and autonomous units. Within there existed the original authority, under a new name (*ius*), and the old prepossession, the primordial classification by the genitive. As law developed—a new and external authority exercising its jurisdiction between the *familiae*—it had become possible for one person to superimpose this newer authority upon the person of another *familia* by means of obligation. But the classification of the objects within the latter's *familia* was not thereby changed. And, as domestic authority (or control) and *dominium*—the survivals of the as yet almost unexplored residuum of pre-property—became differentiated, it was possible in the servitudes for the *ius* to belong to one, though the corporeal *res* or *dominium*, belonged to another. Since both these relations were subjects of legal quarrels, and therefore *res*, in the strict legal sense, when one asserted such a segregated *ius*, his *res*, or reason, was incorporeal. And it was always incorporeal when he asserted the inter-familial authority over another person. But when

300 For in the classic law "les sages organes de l'évolution du droit romain . . . accommodèrent les vieilles institutions aux fins nouvelles, en atténuant au moyen de remèdes et de compromis, les contrastes les plus violentes entre les anciens dispositions et les idées nouvelles." Bonfante, op. cit., I, p. 481.

301 It is perhaps better to regard this power as various types or qualities of title to (i.e. grounds of acquiring) "ownership" and to consider the fact of "ownership" as one simple (i.e. irreducible) and unexplored concept.

he asserted the intra-familial power either over persons or material objects within his own *familia*, then, since no such segregation of the *ius* and the *dominium* had arisen, because both relations were retained in one hand, the duality did not appear and the *res* became, by ellipsis, the corporeal subject of dispute itself. Nevertheless *res* did not mean "wealth."

Even this statement exaggerates the accuracy of meaning. For it cannot be said that even in classic Roman law *res* had come to mean the object of property in the modern sense. True, it was beginning to stand, in part and as yet unconsciously, for the property (the right) itself. Technically it still meant any matter for legal process, with an occasional transfer to the sense of the objective. *Res* was still the *sake*, though in popular usage it had evidently acquired a considerable degree of *Dinglichkeit*. *Ius*, on the other hand, was the *soke*. It meant the power, or jurisdiction (authority), as well within the *familia* as without. Certainly *ius* did not mean "a right." No one can read the Law Concerning Persons and conclude that one who was not *sui iuris* had no rights. Yet he had no *iura*. And *ius*, in turn, was already beginning to take with it that differentiation of the original unity out of which was developing the political and domestic relationships; leaving *dominium* over *res* – in its popular sense – to be confined more and more to the economic relation. As *ius* became humanized, *res* became materialized. But both continued to refer to matters particularly in their legal aspect, as if, like meteors, they were only visible as they passed through this special atmosphere – the purview of the law.

Out of the original absolute independence of the groups which federated together to form the Roman state and the resulting limitations of the state's jurisdiction; and out of the contractual decision of disputes and the delictual character of contracts – or their breach – there developed the rigid line drawn between *dominium* and its satellites, on the one hand, and *obligatio*, on the other, a distinction which, ever since, has proved a trap for courts and a blind spot for jurisprudence.[802] The procedural foundation of this later theoretical distinction had been crystallized in classic Roman law. Witness the wholly technical and procedural explanation of the reason for the division of actions. Paraphrased the explanation was this. The *causa rei persequendae* was conceived to be the cause of almost all actions except for any penal aspect. If it was claimed that the *res* belonged

[802] Bonfante, op. cit., I, pp. 227-228, confirms this analysis exactly. He speaks of the fundamental principles of each institution of Roman private law remaining in harmony with their primitive function. Thus *manus* or *potestas* is a personal sovereignty; *dominium ex iure Quiritium* preserves the character of a territorial sovereignty; obligations are a reflection of the relations between different group chiefs; testament is the designation of the succeeding sovereign.

to the plaintiff, the actions must be brought against the object itself; for how could another person transfer what was not his! If it was conceded to belong to the defendant but the claim was that it was owed, then even the judgment would not effect a transfer. So in this case the action must be brought against the person of the defendant to compel him to effect a transfer, for only he was capable of so doing. We have seen how little this explanation of mature Roman law conforms to the probable reasons for the existence of the distinction.

As we have said, later law has accepted this second distinction as to actions and has even gone so far as to build upon it, at least in name, much of the structure of legal theory as to property rights. But in modern times it has only accepted the first distinction as to corporeality in so far as it has been obliged to do so by the persisting legal usage founded thereon. The reasons for this partiality will be considered later. Suffice it to say at this point that the civilians have retained the two primitive presumptions, derived from the classificatory genitive and from the right of the injured to the body of the injuror, and have largely discarded the adolescent forms of indirect property in objects, represented by the incorporeal things. And this in spite of the fact that the first two are relatively unimportant today, while the latter have become the major part of our property structure.

2. *The Organic Survival*

In this chapter our chief concern has been to disentangle, so far as might be, the theories and forms of the Roman law of property as they stood in classic Rome from those subsequent modifications which, because they have expressed themselves in the same terms and sought to found themselves upon the authority of Roman law, have led to the assumption that the ancient forms were practically identical with them. In directing ourselves at this particular objective it has been necessary to confine our attention to these theories and forms of law rather than to consider the legal and economic facts they clothed. It is obviously impossible within the compass of this study to treat the latter in any detail. But in one respect it is essential for the understanding of what we shall find in later times to look behind the structure of the law. During the late Republic and Empire Rome had become the most highly organized commercial economy of ancient times. One must be impressed with the fact that classic Roman law is concerned principally with this commercial rather than with the older agricultural economy—with that of the city rather than with that of the country—and that it represents the institutionalizing of this economic superstructure which had by that time been erected upon the simple foundations of the previous agricultural age. Nevertheless a study of the beginnings of the feudal period in Europe makes it most evident that the permanent mark of Roman organization upon subsequent economic and political life was more especially derived from the survival of the older organization upon the land. It is this which presents to us the continuity of the evolution of the institution of property. For it was this, and not the commercial superstructure, which survived the inundation of the Dark Ages and to a large extent determined the character of organization of medieval Europe. And here life and law diverge. For the organization upon the land, even in its developed state during the late Empire, was still quite largely extra-legal, customary, functional. The solution of continuity took place in the field of law and in that economic superstructure which it had come to be framed to fit. It was not until the revival of commerce in early medieval times that this law—which had originally sprung out of, but which in the meantime had become divorced from the early organization upon the land—began to reappear from its eastern refuge and the work of the glossators commenced the process leading to the "Reception."

It is this difference in the two periods we have already considered, matched by the two which follow, which compels us in our studies of early Rome and early Europe to emphasize the structure of the land organization, out of which law and its institutions have grown, while in those of classic Rome and modern Europe we emphasize the theory and structure of the law itself. True, in these latter periods, the law is considerably adapted and transformed because it has come to be transferred to apply to a different set of facts in the commercial field. Nevertheless we perceive in both cases that it continues to reflect, though in a purely ideal way, the somewhat inappropriate ways of thought, derived from the earlier and more fundamental arrangement of society in its territorial relations, at these stages become relatively unimportant.

In order now to pick up the threads of that which represents the continuous portion of this development we must survey briefly the stage at which the organization of the original social unit, the *familia*, had arrived toward the end of the Roman empire. We have already perceived that the word *familia* never at any stage meant what we mean by the word "family." In the beginning it covered all that pertained to the house community. Before there was much content within this unit, other than of human beings, it probably had the shade of meaning that our word "household" has. But always it was an organization of and for group government, or pre-property. Therefore, in the middle period it had come particularly to signify the patrimony as opposed to the *pecunia* and the *peculia*, which were the individual and somewhat separable holdings of the head and of the subordinate members. Perhaps it is a predisposition against regarding persons as property which has led scholars to assume that in this period it referred more to non-human objects (and to slaves) than it did to the human members. At any rate, in attributing to it the sense of an aggregate of so-called material possessions scholars seem to have erred in one direction as seriously as the naïve or the sociological views have erred, in the other, when they attribute to it no different meaning than that of a "family." The fact is that, throughout its ancient history, it was the term *par excellence* for the indivisible and basic unit of society, political, economic and domestic. It was the whole microcosm of men and objects upon the land, which, as a patrimony, persisted from generation to generation under the dominance of a perpetual succession of sons, or their analogues.

At the end of the era and at the brink of transition into the Middle Ages—a century or two after the time of Gaius—the *familia* is still to be recognized through the obscurities of a changing nomenclature and in an enlarged and complicated form, particularly where it has transplanted itself into the rich virgin soil of the western European provinces. It is now the *villa*, and the master of it is the *dominus*, rather than the *paterfamilias*. The binding relations among the biologically related members have somewhat broken down with the penetration of law within this charmed circle. No longer to the same extent are the brothers and sons of the eldest male subjected to and included in the unit. Nor are his wife and other children subjected to the same despotic pre-property power. But as to the rest the relations remain very similar and there have been large accessions from other sources. The period of the Empire has seen great concentrations of land and of stock, and therefore of men. Even in Gaul we find much evidence of this Roman institution, transplanted almost intact.

In the landholding in the provinces we see at first revived a theory something like that which had been applied to the prior *ager publicus*. In this period it is conceived that all conquered territory vests in the emperor. Those who hold it, hold it by *possessio*, not by *dominium*.[303] Gradually, however, and after accustoming the

303 "En Gaul, durant cette époque [the first two centuries of the empire], le propriétaire du sol était l'empereur, les hommes n'y étaient que possesseurs," Fustel, *Origines*, p. 66.

colonies to the concept of a very real eminent domain,[304] this possession seems to have ripened into dominion and the theory of alodial right displaced that of dependent possession. But the change went no further than the *dominus* of the *villa*. He it was to whom was now attributed complete dominion. All land came, therefore, to be in the *dominium* of some *dominus*, the chief of a *familia*, the successor of the patriarch.

The *villa*—the organization upon the land—had two aspects. The one was the land; the other was the persons upon the land. Within it there were relations that seemed to savour of the land only; relations of parts to other parts and to the whole; relations of dominance and of servience of the various *praedia*, within or to the *fundus*—or, if it was great, the *latifundium*. And there were also various relations of dominance and servience binding the persons thereon to the *dominus;* relations which, to some extent but not wholly, paralleled the first. Of these the law recognized certain, and others, equally important, were extra-legal.

The *villa* was also divided into two parts. That which contained and adjoined (figuratively speaking) the house of the master was called *villicus*.[305] There dwelt the family and most of the slaves. This land was reserved to the master and worked for him by the *familia*. The rest of the *fundus* was held by others, *of* the *dominus*, and by some sorts of right less than *dominium*. Of these the two principal legal forms seem to have been, on the one hand, usufruct—with its companion emphyteusis—which for the most part represented long term, or life, holdings, and, on the other, leases (*locatio et conductio*) for shorter or more definite terms. Finally, and extra-legally, there seems to have been prevalent a revival of the *possessio precarium*,[306] now applied to land in private ownership instead of, as in Republican days, to that held by possession out of the *ager publicus*. With all these subordinate holdings there went various sorts of rent, certain or uncertain, or of division of the profit. Thus, as Fustel says,[307] the economic activity was divided into two parts. With the *familia* working *en commun*, it was direct exploitation by the *maître*, who alone had the profits. With the little free farmers and even the *coloni*, it was the system of tenure with rent or division of profits.

[304] Bonfante, op. cit., I, p. 487, says, ". . . l'expropriation pour cause d'utilité publique non seulement était inconnue dans le droit romain classique, mais elle y était inconcevable."

[305] So Fustel construes the term. But both for classical and for Low Latin (see DuCange) this term was principally used to describe the *gubernator* or *dispensator*, later, in France, called the *major villae*.

[306] *Precario possidere* marks the absence of right and the impossibility of acquiring by prescription.

[307] *Alleu*, pp. 66 and 80.

To some extent the relations of the persons upon the land identified themselves with the foregoing land relations and to some extent they were independent. The free family was becoming freer. Probably usufruct was, to a considerable degree, a means of provision (analogous to *peculium*) for semi-independent free members. Other classes remained "in the household." The slaves (*servi*) retained their former status and became far more numerous. They worked the *villicus*. But many were freed—for a price or for services. Such either continued in the *villicus* or became *tributarii*,[808] renting on some basis distinguished from a lease. These *libertini* remained dependent however.[809] Then there were the free tillers of the soil, perhaps the indigenous population, perhaps small landholders forced to surrender their rights through debt. These were the *coloni*, the tillers of the soil.[810] According to Fustel they were, in the writings and the laws of the period, called *conductores*.[811] Finally we see the great resurgence of an extra-legal relation, that of patron and client. This extended from the intimates of the household (the *amici*) to the holders of land by *precarium*.[812] Under it the client or the *amicus* (then called *susceptus*) had given himself and his possessions to the patron so that his status was nearly assimilated to that of a member of the *familia*. Literally he gave himself into the *ius* (*in ius ditionemque eorum*), and thus became one of the *familiares* or *domestici*. But he was a free, not servile member, though he held his possessions thereafter by a right resembling the *peculium*.

All this conglomerate of men and goods upon the land were nearly

808 See Fustel, *Alleu*, p. 399.

809 ". . . les biens possédés par ces affranchis ne sont pas désignés par les termes *dominium*, *dominatio*, *proprietas*, *res juris sui*, qui sont ceux par lesquels s'exprimait le droit de propriété ; ils sont toujours appelés *peculium* ou *peculiare*." Fustel, *Alleu*, p. 396. He also says of their goods and land, "ils étaient donnés, vendus, légués avec lui. L'affranchi ne pouvait vendre. . ." Ibid., p. 397.

810 Girard, op. cit., p. 145, says, "Le colon (*colonus*) . . . est un fermier héréditaire, attaché à perpétuité, lui et toute sa descendance, au sol qu'il cultive moyennant une redevance en argent ou en fruits. Il n'est pas précisément esclave d'un autre homme ; mais il est esclave de la terre."

811 *Alleu*, p. 65.

812 Ihering, *Geist*, I, p. 240, says, "Ich . . . erblicke im *precarium* und *peculium* zwei Ausdrücke und Institute, die ursprünglich dem Klientelverhältnis angehörten." He construes Savigny and Mommsen in support of this view.

Of both *precarium* and *peculium* it was said by later jurists, "*magis facti sunt, quam iuris*." And to be sure, so was clientage. Perhaps by that time it was forgotten that they had been extra-legal because they were intra-familial and therefore of a different and independent jurisdiction.

"*Precarium* hiess alles, was der Patron dem Klienten auf dessen Bitten (*preces*, daher *precarium*) zum Gebrauch einraümte. . ." *Geist*, I, p. 241. It was usually land and perhaps a dwelling, the *habitatio* of later law.

Bonfante, op. cit., I, p. 114, describes it as "jouissance pleine et entière, mais revocable à volonté." He conceives it to have covered distributions of gentilican land by the chief of the gens to clients.

as much under the single dominion of the master as they had been at the time of the XII Tables. The right of *dominium* rested solely in him. The whole conglomerate passed as one (*universitas bonorum*) to his successor either by sale, by gift or by inheritance.[813] The structure endured generation after generation as the survival of the old *familia*, the fundamental rural unit in the social organism, integrated by a variety of species of legal or extra-legal bonds which were, or were assimilated to, property. The *villa* was the *familia* of imperial Rome.

[813] The men, the slaves, the freedmen, and even, among the free, the *coloni* passed with the land. The *suscepti* did not so pass. Their relation was personal and needed to be renewed to the successor or transferred to some other. As to the freedman, Fustel says, "c'était le maître qui vendait ou donnait ce lot de terre avec son affranchi." *Alleu*, p. 397. This was also true of the *coloni*, ibid., p. 404.

CHAPTER III

THE FOUNDATIONS OF THE ENGLISH, OR FEUDAL, SYSTEM OF PROPERTY

A. *The Organization of Feudal Society*

1. *The Feudal vs. the Roman Principle*

WHEN we come to deal with the other strain in our institutional inheritance we find that the development of property took place upon a very different basis. Whereas in Rome the peculiar cast given to the institution of property was due to its origin within that nearly self-sufficient social unit called the *familia*, the principal contribution of pure English character arose from the dependent relation between families, called the *feod*. The two social organizations were wholly different. The Roman consisted of independent groups, on a somewhat equal footing, and each represented by the person of the head of the *familia*. The early English consisted of a hierarchy, the units of which were, at least as they approached the foundation, more nearly the modern family. The result was that in Rome the property relation, so far as it came within the purview of the law (i.e. was presented as disputes over property) was concerned primarily with a collateral relationship between independent and equal units, while in England it was concerned very largely with a lineal relationship between dependent and ranked units.

We shall have so much occasion to construe the material examined hereafter upon these two principles that it will be well at this point to define the principles exactly. The civil law of Rome concerned itself, at first wholly and always largely, with the external property relations of the *familia*. Internally the *familia* was organized upon a hierarchical basis with a supreme head; with different ranks, or generations, of free members; with several classes of partially or wholly unfree members; and with other dependents. Title to the whole was conceived as resting in the head. Such internal property relations as existed were of a derivative and dependent nature, subject to the rule of the head and the rigid familial custom. For the most part, therefore, these internal property relations were sub-integral, and did not come within the jurisdiction of the law of the Roman state. This law, at least at first, dealt only with the property relations arising between such familial units, which were, relatively speaking, on a parity with each other. Thus we see already emerging two models upon which the structure of property may be arranged, the one the external familial and the other the internal familial. Roman law dealt with the first, for Roman family custom and rule jealously guarded the second. But early English law finds already installed a system, largely imposed there by fiat, which closely resembles these internal property relations of the Roman *familia*, though since it was stretched to apply on a nation-wide scale it had extruded into the purview of the law. Therefore the indigenous property concepts of England conform more closely to the *mores* of the Roman *familia* than they do to the organization of Roman law.

The Roman legal system of property, conforming to the external relations, we shall characterize as the allodial, or collateral, system. It is the holding in absolute and original right by independent and coequal units; the character of the interests being the same. The English legal system, conforming rather to the internal relations of Rome, we shall call the feudal, or lineal, system. It is the holding, except at the apex, in a dependent and perhaps derivative right by successive and ranked units, according to varying degrees of ascendancy; the character of the interests being mutually exclusive. But we must remind the reader that in both cases the institution to which we are applying the modern term property was still a conglomerate of relations consisting of those which today would be called political or domestic, as well as of those we would call economic, and that they applied to men on much the same basis as to land or other objects. In this respect the economic institution of property was in early Rome part and parcel of the domestic organization, while in England it was at first indistinguishable from the political organization.

2. *The Derivation of the Feudal Form*

From this point of view let us proceed to examine the detail of both the early and the maturing English law of property. It is impossible to describe its process of development and it is inaccurate to picture it as a perfected plan of organization, for no social institution ever arrives at this state. But, since what we are looking for is the beginnings of the present day structure, or analogies with modern facts, it is better to simplify the picture. While recognizing that new forms and relationships were constantly evolving and the old becoming extinct, we can achieve our purpose best by conventionalizing a plan toward which the institution tended at the beginning and at the end of its critical period, even if thereby we sacrifice historical accuracy. This period covers the development which took place from the Norman Conquest to the end of the thirteenth century, by which time the Norman feudal theories had become completely consolidated upon the foundation of Anglo-Saxon law and institutions, the process of conversion was well under way and the indigenous common law land system was already in its lusty infancy.

In order rightly to grasp the nature of the feudal institution which we discover in England almost full-fledged soon after the Conquest, we must briefly review the manner of its evolution from the organization upon the land as we found it at the close of the Roman Empire; an evolution which took place upon the Continent during the first three or four centuries after "the Fall."[1] Gaul, as a Roman colony, had received the dual organization of Rome. The economic organization upon the land, still with a tinge of political function,[2] was in the main the system of the *villa*, already described, itself an outgrowth of that originally autonomous social unit the house community or *familia*. The political organization proper was, on the other hand, the successor of that early oligarchy formed of the heads of the Roman *familiae*. With the barbarian invasions and the dissolution of the Empire the incompetent conquerors proved incapable of handling this elaborate political machinery and, in the course of time, it almost ceased to function and practically disappeared. But the Roman economic organization upon the land persisted.[3]

[1] In order to present the main outlines of this process of transition without unduly confusing the reader I am omitting all discussion of other viewpoints and of other influences upon the development of the feudal system on the Continent. The coherent thesis here presented is that of Fustel de Coulanges, whose views have for long received general acceptance. I am doubtful that they will ever be found to require serious amendment in one major respect. He practically destroyed the thesis quite generally held before his time that feudalism in France was largely Germanic in origin and was an organization imposed by the barbarian Frankish conquerors upon the Romanized Gallic peoples. On the other hand I am inclined to think that further researches are likely greatly to qualify the Roman character of pre-feudal Gaul. There is too much resemblance between the details of feudalism, on the one hand, and, on the other, the relics of the organization of pre-Roman Gaul – with its hierarchy of chiefs and its classes of retainers – the fairly complete picture of the closely related Celtic organization of ancient Ireland, and finally with the outcroppings of Celtic Britain which show through the Germanic community organization of Anglo-Saxon England, to leave much doubt that feudalism was in part indigenous to the Celtic north, as well as in some respects to the Germanic north-east. Perhaps, in the end, it will turn out to represent in large degree a generalization of a certain stage in the social organization of all peoples – at least of all Indo-European peoples.

[2] Fustel, *Alleu*, p. 438, speaks of the "internal government of the villa." And this was no mere phrase even under the Empire.

[3] Fustel, *Les institutions politiques de l'ancienne France*, ed. 1875, Part I, p. 461, says that the right of complete and absolute private property preserved its Roman character from the fourth to the seventh century. It passed without any "*atteinte,*" or interruption, the crisis of the Germanic invasion. He reiterates this in *L'Invasion*

During the period which we call the Dark Ages—a period of relative chaos, anarchy and political disorganization—the surviving political functions gradually accrued to this organization upon the land. Its units tended to agglomerate because of the absence of and the necessity for protection. The larger grew still larger by a constant absorption of the smaller. The political functions, justice, police, taxation and the military, were slowly absorbed or elaborated anew. Thus, in the course of several centuries, there developed by this means a new political structure, grown again from the soil. The economic organization upon the land, primarily of a proprietary character, had pyramided itself into a political hierarchy, the "feudal system." In the end we find an organization of which the function is predominantly political but which retains in general the proprietary design and relations of its origin, as well as, at its base and to some extent throughout, its original economic function.[4]

The work of more than a thousand years was destroyed. The complex political civilization erected by Rome upon the foundation of the ancient *familiae* had fallen in ruins. But the highly developed, though still patriarchal, successor of that viable grouping of the Romans themselves, which dated back to the time of the "dispersion"—the first barbarian invasions—survived, because it was projected upon the land itself, these later inroads of new hordes from the East and again built up a political structure. This time, however, it was far different in form. Instead of creating a wholly extraneous political system between the federated *familiae*, these *villae* simply expanded and became themselves the political system. The system was then within the *familiae*, so-to-speak. The Roman political organization was wholly super-familial. The feudal system was wholly intra-familial.

When we come to examine the individual factors—always recognizable though undergoing occasional changes of nomenclature as well as many modifications and fusions—which, continuous from the earliest times, became the constituents of the feudal system, we see that they were the artificial, rather than what we term the natural, relations and practices of the *familia*. The fundamental unit had now come to be called the *domaine* (*dominium* or *dominicum*) or "manor." The chief of it was the *dominus*, or *senior*.[5] His authority, as well as the arena of his authority, was also his *domaine*, *domi-*

Germanique, pp. 531-542. So far as the conquerors were concerned, "il n'y a pas le moindre indice que ce système rural ait été attaqué ni contesté." *Alleu*, p. 463.

[4] Fustel, *Alleu*, p. 464, says, "Ce régime dominal durera pendant tout le moyen âge et en se modifiant, plus loin encore." Feudality was simply erected on top of it.

[5] Fustel, *Alleu*, p. 458, says, "On voit par là que le propriétaire devient, dans les limites de son domaine, une sorte de chef d'État. Les hommes l'appellent *dominus*, terme qui signifie à la fois propriétaire et maître. Ils l'appellent aussi *senior*."

nium or *dominatio*. At first both this and the land itself were still sometimes referred to as *potestas*,[6] which demonstrates its nature. As to the internal regulation of the *domaine* the laws say nothing, just as they had originally said nothing of its source, the *familia*.[7] We may perceive, then, that the chief fact at the basis of continental society in the beginning of the period was this familiar unit – a group of persons settled upon a land district and under the domination of a single individual. It was still wholly autonomous in its economic functioning and largely so in its political, or domestic, functioning. But as an organization it was conceived to be of a different order from that of bodies politic – an order now already given the name of property. Along certain lines the rule of the *dominus* was absolute. The group and its territory 'belonged' to him. Along other lines the law and other political functionings invaded his precincts. In so far as they did not, the internal structure and relations of this group were extra-legal. And since it was these extra-legal internal relations – the informal or unrecognized proprietary and personal arrangements – which particularly gave rise to the feudal system, it is these, rather than the continuing features of the legal institution of Roman property, which we must examine.[8]

The structure of personal relations of the feudal system seems to have had its chief source in the Roman practice of patronage.[9] The terminology was varied.[10] But, in essence, the practice consisted in one man making himself dependent upon another by means of a subjection so complete that it required to be distinguished from slavery. Fustel concludes that "the original fact which gave birth to it is that the weak or poor man had need of the strong or rich man." Though the practice "is so repugnant to modern ideas that

[6] Fustel, *Alleu*, p. 445, says, ". . . le domaine était souvent appelé *potestas*. . ." See also Fustel, *Institutions*, ed. 1875, Part I, p. 464.

[7] See Fustel, *Origines*, p. 410.

[8] Since we are not attempting a history of the development of feudalism, but merely a brief view of the unbroken threads of development, it is most effective to follow the consistent and generally accepted view, for which Fustel is largely responsible. Though it may be one-sided to treat the Roman system as practically the only source, it seems unwise to confuse the reader with any reference to the complexities and perennial uncertainties engendered by the ancient Franco-German dispute as to which created the feudal system.

[9] Fustel, *Origines*, p. 83, finds the rules the same as those which had been the foundation of the rule of the patriciate – the chiefs of the patrician *gentes* – the bonds between patron and client.

[10] The terms for the "*ensemble d'usages*" were *patronage, clientèle, protection, defense, sauvement, recommandation, foi, mundebour, truste, vasselage*. See Fustel, *Origines*, p. 192. For the act of "celui qui se commende en puissance d'un autre," there were three precise terms, *mundeburdum, tradere, commendare;* for the authority of the superior, *potestas, mundeburdum, defensio;* for the subjection of the inferior, *servitium, obsequium;* he engaged *servir* but "comme *libri,* pas de la servitude." Fustel, *Origines*, pp. 267-9.

we have some difficulty in comprehending it, nevertheless it has been one of the most frequent practices which history notes and is apparently one which conforms most closely to human nature."[11] Thus, though the rules were Roman, the custom has been near universal. Since a particular foundation of the church as well as an individual could be the *dominus* of a district, so too it could be a patron of persons. In fact the early freedom from taxation of church lands and, during the invasions, the relative sanctity of church property made it advantageous to place oneself "under the *mainbour* or defense of a church."[12]

Thus it appears that "the men of the 7th century had . . . an idea which we no longer have; they conceived outside the entire administrative system, a way of governing men, directly, individually, without the mediation of agents or the action of general laws."[13] This governance was modelled upon property. It was one of the differentiated forms of pre-property; something like Roman *dominium*—the proprietary governance of slaves and objects; something like Roman *patria potestas*—the domestic governance of the wife and children, adopted or legitimate.

The most general source of the structure of land relations of the feudal system seems to have been the Roman practice of *precarium*, the precarious holding of the client obtained by a *prex*, or prayer.[14] The pre-feudal term was *beneficium* (benefice, or *bienfait* = benefaction, or good deed). It was neither conveyance nor contract, but rather an informal and extra-legal life use.[15] The term was used to

[11] Fustel, *Origines*, p. 195. He shows that it had not been a part of the political organization among the Germans or Gauls, but that it had come into use in these provinces prior to "the Fall." "Une sorte de vassalité existait déjà, mais en dehors de l'État" (p. 204). He also relates it, though not by way of origin, to the practice of property *en cheptel* found in early Ireland, to which we have already referred. This is also a term for an early French custom which suggests that the source of the medieval patronage was by no means solely Roman. Under the latter, in Ireland, "Le client, le futur vassal, a été le plus souvent un pauvre auquel le riche avait donné quelque petite part de sa richesse en bétail ou en argent, pour l'enchainer à soi par une sort de dette et faire de lui un sujet" (p. 199). We have already suggested a still more general and original source for this practice.

[12] Fustel, *Origines*, p. 252. "Le patronage d'église, qui avait été sous l'Empire un moyen d'echapper à l'impôt, devint dans les invasions un refuge contre la violence" (p. 256). This extended to proprietors themselves, who afterwards retained their proprietorship, so that "on y reconnaît deux propriétaires, l'homme qui vend la terre et le saint à qui il est dit qu'elle appartient" (p. 262).

[13] Fustel, *Origines*, p. 399.

[14] Fustel, *Origines*, p. 69, says, "Assurément le précaire n'a pas produit à lui seul le bénéfice merovingien, mais il est entré pour beaucoup dans sa formation."

[15] It was "un certain mode de concession." Fustel, *Origines*, p. 162. "Dans les conventions entre les hommes, *beneficium* était l'opposé d'un contrat" (p. 159). It was not *dominium*, a transfer. It was analogous to but contrasted with that (donation). One "*in beneficio habet*" (p. 160). Maine's thesis of the element of contract in the "express conditions which had been agreed upon when the infeudation

cover many practices, the most general – and perhaps the model – of which was *precarium.*[16] And "the only appreciable difference between the Roman *precarium* and the Merovingian *beneficium* is that the latter becomes ordinarily for life," with rarely "a change of will."[17] The consideration varied from full money rents to the most nominal services, according apparently to the circumstances and the whim of the benefactor.[18] It is evident that by means of this process there took place over several centuries a marked concentration, voluntary upon both sides, in the supposedly absolute or proprietary title to the land – the *dominium.* This proceeded *pari passu* with the conversion of *dominium* from a principally proprietary relation into one principally political. And it left the distribution and the use of the land much as it had been. Its practical economic consequences were not noteworthy.[19]

These two practices together tended to the development of an organization upon the land of which the form was proprietary though the substance became primarily political. "By patronage the man lost the property in his person; he belonged to another. . . By the act of benefice the land lost in the same way its independence; it became subject; it was obligated for rents and services, for duties of all kinds."[20] "The *recommandé* became the man of the patron; the benefice became the property of the proprietor."[21] Nevertheless the complexion was increasingly one of governance. There was land a plenty. The task was to arrange for its working. More and more the slaves of the household were given land by servile tenure, thus raising them approximately to the level of the *coloni,* those who

took place," *Ancient Law,* p. 353, seems not to hold. This was an intra-familial and therefore extra-legal arrangement beneath the level of contract.

16 It usually covered land, but often covered loans of money or other objects secured by the land of the borrower, transferred and re-received as a benefice. Fustel, *Origines,* pp. 162 ff, finds the usage of the term:

1. Excluded from donations; 2. covering, a sum of money with or without gage of land; 3. a piece of land, something like a lease *au fermage* or *louage viager;* 4. usufruct; 5. most frequently *precarium* of all kinds; 6. hardly ever in law.

If to the church the benefice is for "the salvation of his soul," or according to "the precepts of the religious law"; if to a layman for "the services which he had rendered" (p. 178).

17 Fustel, *Origines,* p. 179.

18 In general they were *fructus,* if from the demesne itself; *tributum* or *redditus* in money or grain, if from the free working tenures, and *suffragium, reliqua beneficia* (the feudal incidents) if from the tenures of greater dignity. See Fustel, *Alleu,* p. 445.

19 Fustel, *Alleu,* p. 464, says that the change in title was able to take place little by little without otherwise modifying in any way the intimate organization of the domains.

20 Fustel, *Origines,* p. 336.

21 Ibid., p. 333.

were personally free, but attached to the land.[22] The whole process was far from an oppression imposed from above.[23] It was rather an elevation of all ranks into new and eventually higher spheres, as the whole body moved up to fill the vacancy caused by the disappearance of government. It was a substitution of the landholders for the former officialdom in the sphere of government, and a substitution of lower ranks for the landholders in the agricultural economy.

The process by which the land organization, of which the chief function was economic, became converted into one of which the chief function was political, was at least initiated, as Fustel has pointed out, by the system of immunity. It was doubtless finished by the almost complete disappearance of the former government, a disappearance to which the grant of immunity contributed by undermining the structure. This immunity, commencing with the domains of the church and extending to those of the private proprietors, was a grant by the kings which freed the domains from the oppressions of the super-familial officialdom and converted them into independent jurisdictions and sovereignties, supposedly directly answerable to the king. "Perhaps the kings thought that immunity would fortify their authority, rendering it more direct and personal. What it especially and permanently fortified was the authority of the great proprietors."[24] "The immune proprietors became the trustees of the king and the men who lived on their land became their subjects."[25] For the immunity was granted only to the landed proprietors, not to those holding of them.[26] Thus "the proprietor, in the process of dispossessing the public officials, became the absolute master of his domain. . . He was the sole chief, the sole judge, the sole protector."[27] "The justice of the state ceased 'to have access' to the interior of the domain."[28] The successor of the *familia* became almost as independent a jurisdiction and almost as autonomous a "state in little" as its predecessor had been in the time before the organization of the early super-familial government.

In this new order, "the men were subordinated hierarchically, the one to the other, and bound together by the pact of allegiance or

[22] Fustel, *Alleu,* p. 462, speaking of the whole period from the fourth to the ninth century, says "La substitution de la tenure servile à l'ancienne servitude s'est continuée pendant ces cinq siècles. . ."

[23] For instance, Fustel, *Alleu,* p. 405, finds not a single line in all the texts of the fifth, sixth, seventh and eighth centuries, which gives the idea that the obligations of the *coloni* had been imposed by the strong on the weak.

[24] Fustel, *Origines,* p. 406.

[25] Ibid., p. 428.

[26] Ibid., p. 406.

[27] Ibid., p. 419.

[28] Ibid., p. 413.

personal subjection. The feudal régime already existed [in the seventh century] with its characteristic traits and its organization complete. But it did not exist alone."[29] "This patronage or this clientage had already become the social *lien*, the very same which, many centuries later, when the authority of the kings was obliterated, appeared as the feudal *lien*, to rule society."[30] For, when the super-familial government disappeared, this was the strongest remaining institution for the governance of men. However, it acquired title to its new function by abandonment. For, as to itself, "feudalism was not born of a political system; it had its origin in the customs of private life."[31] Neither was it at first of military character.[32] But "when the frame of civil society changed, the military system changed with it, adapting itself to the new social order."[33] Then the seignory of proprietors became a military and feudal seignory,[34] and the fief, held by military service, appeared.[35]

3. *Application of Feudalism to England*

There seems to be a tendency upon the part of the historians of English law to regard feudalism as the product of a self-conscious plan rather than as a continuation and development of pre-existing organization. In this vein Pollock refers to it as a "complex and artificial system."[36] The reason seems clear. While Pollock's appraisal of feudalism is not correct as to its original habitat upon the Continent, it is certainly correct as to the English form.

The situation which existed in England immediately prior to the Conquest was complex and unsystematic. To attempt to describe it in a few words one may say that it consisted of a partial overlay of economic and personal landholding upon the remains of the ancient rural community, itself a product of the old "tribal arrangements with its far-reaching family ties."[37] The newer form,

[29] Fustel, *Origines*, p. 429.

[30] Ibid., p. 247.

[31] Ibid., p. 63.

[32] Ibid., p. 429.

[33] Ibid., p. 430.

[34] Ibid., p. 430.

[35] Ibid., p. 11, he says, "Le fief ou le bénéfice militaire ne fut jamais une institution romaine." This particular feature of feudalism may have had its source in the German *comites*, or *gesinde*. But as to the rest, "La Republique romaine a été dominée par la pratique du précaire et de la cliéntèle, comme la monarchie du moyen âge a été dominée par la pratique du bénéfice et de la vassalité." *Origines*, p. 92.

[36] "English Law before the Norman Conquest," 14 *Law Quarterly Review* (1898), p. 291. Holdsworth, op. cit., Book III, Part I, Chap. I, seems to have the same idea when he imputes to contemporary ideas a supreme effect upon all the law of the Middle Ages.

[37] See Vinogradoff, *The Growth of the Manor*, pp. 212-235. It is impossible, in this limited space, to consider the varieties of strain – Celtic, Roman, Anglo-Saxon,

rising partly from the same conditions and along the same lines as the beginnings of feudalization upon the Continent and partly by imitation of the final manifestation of the latter,[38] came, after the Conquest, to be called the "manorial system."[39] The older form shows the earmarks of its antiquity in the "open-field system" of tribal custom.[40] But, as the needs of patronage and private protection compelled the cession of individual and group holdings, the primitive institution became more and more shattered. Some of its practices and some of its relations to the land were taken over into the manorial system. But its main outlines, the "hundred" and "vill," remained more as political subdivisions of the country than as economic landholdings,[41] although, in the latter respect, they lived on as a "hant" over the land. The *territory* was becoming *property*.

The superstructure of this transitional and confused organization upon the land was swept away by the Conquest.[42] The feudal system in its most highly developed form was substituted for it, as a whole, by the Norman dynasty.[43] But it was the lines that the economic manorial system had already begun to project upon the land, which political feudalism seized upon and at a stroke completed as the basis of its own projection.[44] The older tribal system practically

Danish and even Norman – which appear blended or confused in the land organization of England before the Conquest.

[38] Vinogradoff, *English Society in the Eleventh Century*, p. 232, says, ". . . one may certainly speak of old English land tenure as to a great extent feudalized even before the invasion of the Normans." Seebohm, op. cit., p. 99, thinks the change to the manorial system began to take place in the fifth and sixth centuries.

[39] Maitland, *Domesday Book and Beyond*, p. 108, says, "The term *manerium* seems to have come in with the Conqueror. . ." But, pp. 108-110, he indicates that the new manor and the old hall (*aula*) were practically the same. Vinogradoff, however, at times associates lordship with the older boundaries. Thus, *Manor*, p. 221, he speaks of "a lordship as a superstructure of the township," and, p. 223, he says, "Territorial lordship did not necessarily imply the existence of a demesne, that is of a special appropriation of one part of the soil to the use of the lord."

[40] See Vinogradoff, *Jurisprudence*, I, p. 340.

[41] One gathers from the studies of Vinogradoff, that the later villein tenure was related to the earlier, "vill" and its open field system, while the later indigenous notion of "common" was related to the earlier "hundred." Certainly the old English manor seems to have been "a standing combination between the township and the home farm or domain." *Manor*, p. 307.

[42] See Maitland, *Domesday*, p. 150.

[43] Haskins, *Norman Institutions*, p. 5, refers to Normandy at that time as "one of the most fully developed feudal societies in Europe." And Laveleye, op. cit., p. 249, says, "The feudal system, being at its full development at the time of the conquest of England by the Normans, was applied there in a more systematic and complete manner than anywhere else."

[44] Maitland, *Domesday*, p. 122, says, "In the first place, our record [Domesday Book] seems to assume that every holding either is a manor or forms part of a manor." Seebohm, op. cit., p. 122, says, "It remained for the Normans fully to carry out and crystallize this organization into the feudal system." And, p. 129, ". . . it was the work of the Conqueror not to upset this (the manorial) system but to see that it was firmly and systematically established in every corner of the realm."

disappeared at once, as a method of landholding. The conquerors had a free hand in England to work out in its entirety the idea of "dependent and derivative tenure," tenure in exchange for services, and thus give it "a dominance it could not obtain elsewhere."[45] Perhaps this "was possible only in a conquered country."[46] At any rate the very completeness of the application,[47] produced a surprising change in the institution. Moreover, this influence was reinforced by a peculiar native refractoriness, itself the vital element in the old Anglo-Saxon system, upon which feudalism had been imposed, which so to speak seeped up from the soil and in the following two or three centuries succeeded in disintegrating and digesting feudalism for its own economic purposes.[48] Almost at once, since all men were included in the system, tenure ceased to be a mark of class. When, in time, the economic relation to the land began to supersede the political, the choicest holdings gravitated to the ablest and most ambitious men who frequently came by this means to hold by lower tenures. Thus the lower tenures were assimilated to the higher and *vice versa*, and the "'feud' must lose half its meaning by becoming universal." This process "impaired . . . [the] intensive force of the system and had important effects in consolidating the population and in raising the lower estates.[49] In other words, "pure feudalism had but a short life in England."[50]

Holdsworth's view ascribes this levelling effect more particularly to the maintenance of direct relations between the Norman king and the people, especially through the king's courts and William's requirement of direct allegiance. He speaks of this "universality of tenure in our land law which was secured by . . . the existence of a central court strong enough both to repress the elements of feudalism which were hostile to the development of the state, and to make the feudal conception of land tenure the common law of the land."[51] Thus "the common law has levelled the status of the freeholder."[52] "The fact that this doctrine of tenure has been applied universally

[45] Pollock and Maitland, op. cit., I, p. 94.

[46] Pollock and Maitland, op. cit., I, p. 236.

[47] ". . . the assumption made by the Domesday commissioners that all land was held of some one," Holdsworth, op. cit., II, p. 183, and the phrase "*nulle terre sans seigneur*," are evidence of this completeness.

[48] Both the arbitrary completeness and the refractoriness are exemplified by the fact to which Holdsworth calls attention, op. cit., II, p. 200, that since the system of tenure was thus imposed from above it tended not to square with historical fact. Thus while the king's courts treated the "common" rights as having been granted by the lord, the manorial courts still adhered to the previous title (perhaps folkland) in the tenants.

[49] Pollock and Maitland, op. cit., I, p. 236.

[50] Digby, *An Introduction to the History of the Law of Real Property*, p. 41.

[51] Holdsworth, op. cit., III, p. 57.

[52] Holdsworth, op. cit., II, p. 303.

to the land law is a purely English phenomenon."[53] In other countries the term "feudal" was applied only to noble or military tenure. No direct relation existed between the sovereign and the people. There *feodum* tells something of the quality of tenure. In England it tells nothing of quality but only indicates heritability. By the end of the thirteenth century, with the beginning of the English Parliament and the continental assemblies of the time, the germ of this different development had already led to a difference in grouping of the social classes because of the existence in England "of a law which was more common than any law existing in any continental state of this period."[54]

In the view of Maitland, "in so far as feudalism is mere property law, England . . . [was] of all countries the most perfectly feudalized."[55] Feudalism, after it had developed, was never, even in part, "mere property law." Therefore it is more accurate to say that, since England was submitted to the most drastic political feudalization, it soonest traversed that stage of development and therefore produced the earliest and most complete conversion of feudal tenure into its successor, a "pure property system." The thirteenth century was the critical period in this transition.[56]

4. *The Union of Political and Proprietary Relations*

The system of feudalism in England was primarily what we should call a political organization. That is, it was primarily a system of control over men beyond the domestic circle. True its function was indiscriminately political and economic. But the control by men over material objects was incidental to the principal element in this unified control. On the other hand, because of their origin, the forms for achieving this unified control were to a large, though graded, degree what we should call proprietary. In order to counteract the bias of our preconceived notions we shall do well, therefore, in examining English feudalism, just as we did in the case of the Roman *familia*, to emphasize in its relations the elements of mastery, or authority, rather than those we now call ownership, or property. Maine describes a fief as "an organically complete brotherhood of associates whose proprietary and personal rights were inextricably blended together."[57] Maitland says that *dominium*, whence our

[53] Holdsworth, op. cit., II, p. 199.

[54] Holdsworth, op. cit., II, p. 302. See also page 247, infra, for the effect of this difference upon the two meanings of the words developed from *status*.

[55] Pollock and Maitland, op. cit., I, p. 235.

[56] For a discussion of other causes influencing this specialization of feudal law in England, see Holdsworth, op. cit., II, pp. 125-126 and 144.

[57] *Ancient Law*, p. 352.

"dominion," "has to stand now for *ownership* and now for *lordship*."[58] It "has to cover both proprietary rights and many kinds of political power; it stands for ownership, lordship, sovereignty, suzerainty."[59] Again it is more accurate to say that it stands for all these modern ideas which then were one. "The kingly power is a mode of *dominium*; the ownership of a chattel, the lordship, the tenancy, of lands, these also are modes of *dominium*."[60] And "in medieval English one spoke of the 'lord' of a beast or other chattel."[61] There was but one order of mastery and that applied in much the same way to men, to land, and even to movables.[62] The *dominium* of the Roman property system – that late arriving term for the specialized power over objects within the *familia* – had become the whole of the government of men and objects, with a territorial projection upon the land.

It is true that the present surviving effective element of feudalism is the Anglo-American land law. Nevertheless, in this transition period, the relation to the land was not only undeveloped; it was political rather than proprietary. "What is characteristic of 'the feudal period' is not the relation between letter and hirer, or lender and borrower of land, but the relationship between lord and vassal, or rather it is the union of these two relationships."[63] The political relation served also a proprietary purpose and *vice versa*.

Because this system was the result of a former private law (or extra-legal custom) usurping the field of public law, there was no separation of public and private law. "Feudalism, we may say, is a denial of this distinction."[64] There was no idea of the state, and no line was drawn between the king's public and his private capacities. "The king, it is true, is a highly privileged, as well as a very wealthy person; still his rights are but private rights amplified and intensified."[65] "It is characteristic of the time that rights of sover-

[58] Pollock and Maitland, op. cit., I, p. 230. And Gierke, *Political Theories of the Middle Age*, Trans., p. 88, says, ". . . in their concept of *dominium*, Rulership and Ownership were blent." In another work Maitland says, *Domesday*, pp. 342-343, "At the present day no two legal ideas seem more distinct from each other than that of governmental power and that of proprietary right." "But though this be so, we can not doubt that could we trace back these ideas to their origin, we should come to a time when they were hardly distinct from each other." That time, as he seems to have failed to grasp, immediately preceded the period he was studying. The two distinct ideas had, under pressure of events, reverted to type.

[59] Maitland, *Domesday*, p. 344.

[60] Pollock and Maitland, op. cit., I, p. 513.

[61] Pollock and Maitland, op. cit., 1st ed., II, p. 4, Note 2. The French phrase was "le seignur de la chose," loc. cit., Note 2.

[62] The lord "is not only lord of his men, but lord of the land. . ." Digby, op. cit., p. 44.

[63] Pollock and Maitland, op. cit., I, p. 67.

[64] Pollock and Maitland, op. cit., I, p. 230.

[65] Pollock and Maitland, op. cit., I, p. 231.

eignty shade off into rights of property; the same terms and formulas cover them both. . ." [66] Holdsworth says, "Political rights and privileges [under feudalism] were regarded as property; and the king's political rights and privileges—his prerogative— did not escape the influence of this idea." [67] So rigorously and simply was this single system of dominion applied that on the king's personal lands, the "ancient demesne," where he was himself lord of the manor, the "custom of the manor" assumed equal authority with the law of the land, since both alike were the exercise of the royal jurisdiction.[68]

Before we see signs of a return to specialized proprietary relations, the specialized political relation of today is already beginning to differentiate; and from this source. For it is in the direct functions which the king assumed that it first appeared. The higher administrative political structure and the special methods of financing it were already begun with the Domesday survey. Vinogradoff speaks of Domesday recasting "into a new mould of manorial hierarchy" the "ancient lines of the associations of shire, hundreds and townships." [69] But "the object of the survey, . . . was to provide a new basis of assessment for the levy of a direct tax imposed upon the land." [70] And this tax was not feudal. It was modern, though promulgated under the guise of the ancient Danegeld, and though assessed by means of the manorial machinery.[71] Thus Domesday has been called "the first English tax roll." [72] As politics builds itself a new structure it begins to leave the land to economics. The *state* is the first offshoot of *status*.

Nevertheless, with the exception of these faint beginnings of the state, the one hierarchical relationship covered practically all the aspects of the social organization, from the king down. It was the proprietary relation so far as there was any; it covered the economic relation of employer and employee; and on its purely political side it not only included the greater part of such public finance and police as existed at the time, but, until the introduction of the king's courts, was the whole and only basis of legal jurisdiction.[73] For freeholders the king's courts came gradually to usurp this administration of justice. But in theory the jurisdiction of each lord

[66] Pollock and Maitland, op. cit., I, p. 68.

[67] Op. cit., III, p. 462. See page 235, infra, for comment on this way of presenting the facts.

[68] Pollock and Maitland, op. cit., I, p. 384.

[69] *Manor*, p. 292.

[70] Holdsworth, op. cit., II, p. 156.

[71] Maitland, *Domesday*, p. 120, says, "A manor is a house against which geld is charged."

[72] Pollock and Maitland, op. cit., I, p. 70. "A rate book upon a large scale." Holdsworth, op. cit., II, p. 156.

[73] See Holdsworth, op. cit., II, p. 260.

extended over his landholdings and was his perquisite. Even in practice this jurisdiction of the manorial courts was long maintained over the non-free population. Jenks speaks of the "hundred court" lingering on "rather as a 'franchise,' or form of feudal property. . ." As such, he states, "it can be, and is, claimed at the present day."[74] Not only were these jurisdictions, unlike the private Roman *ius*, subject to farming out or granting for profit – and as such what we would call private property – but "the guardian's rights in the person, in the marriage, in the lands of the heir are regarded as property; they are saleable, assignable rights . . . indeed so thoroughly proprietary and pecuniary are these rights that they can be disposed of by will. . ."[75] Finally even administrative offices pertaining to the hierarchy were regarded as alienable, which leads Holdsworth to remark that "the proprietary element in feudalism was so strongly developed . . . that it was sometimes improperly extended to things which should never have been regarded as property at all."[76] This statement illustrates well the difficulty which the modern mind has in conceiving the original feudal oneness wherein all freeholdings in the organization, even including the kingship, together with their attributes, were implicitly alienable because heritable (i.e. birthrights).[77] The original single form of mastery – that of the house community – was subject to hereditary succession. The practice had survived into the Dark Ages only in connection with property. In feudalism property had become government. Again the original unity was restored. But merely because in our day the practice has again survived only in connection with property, and with the remnants of royal and noble power, one is not warranted in regarding the practice as proprietary.[78]

The one relationship had, however, two aspects. It was, we remember, the product both of the personal relationship of patronage and of the land relationship of benefice. At the outset "the lord is far more than a landlord. The tenant owes many other and different duties than a mere tenant. Lord and tenant are related rather as ruler and subject. The state is weak. The man wants

[74] Jenks, *A Short History of English Law*, p. 74.

[75] Pollock and Maitland, op. cit., I, p. 322.

[76] Holdsworth, op. cit., III, p. 76.

[77] The *feodum*, in all its details, was essentially a heritable though dependent right. See Pollock and Maitland, op. cit., I, p. 67.

[78] A few centuries later the full idea of office had developed to replace this early one. Gierke, op. cit., p. 62, speaking of the fourteenth century on the Continent, says, ". . . though it was conceded on all hands that the Ruler might have a vested right, and a right that was all his own, in his Lordship, still with equal unanimity men saw as the content of this right merely a call to the temporary assumption of an immortal *dignitas*. . ." But at an earlier stage he admits (p. 99) that jurisprudence "had accepted the *ius feudorum*, and was prepared to treat offices as objects of proprietary rights."

protection and the lord retainers."[79] The ceremony of homage well indicates the absence of differentiation of the two prime elements which existed in the relation of feudal tenure—the relation of man to man and that of land to land.[80] The phrase ran, "I become your man of the tenement that I hold of you. . ."[81] That is to say, "I am your subject, under your rule and jurisdiction, and in your service. I am resident on a certain tract of land which is owed to your domain, but over which I have certain rights and privileges."[82]

By the end of the thirteenth century "the land law was becoming more and more distinctly simply the law of property."[83] Externally, this was largely accomplished by the gradual stripping of its governmental and judicial elements from the feudal system of tenure, which left it to be regarded "from a commercial rather than a political point of view."[84] "In time the personal elements of the [feudal] relation dwindled away. The lord became merely a landlord and the vassal a tenant of land. . ."[85] In the process, what had originally been

[79] Holdsworth, op. cit., III, p. 55. Markby, *Elements of Law*, p. 176, says, "The one essential and distinguishing feature of the feudal relation was the obligation of mutual defense and protection. . . It was a bond of union as close as that of kinship, which it probably to some extent replaced." He finds all other features common to at least some other system of property. This one alone is peculiar to feudalism.

[80] Maitland speaks of tenure as a "complex of personal rights and of real rights." Pollock and Maitland, op. cit., I, p. 236.

[81] See Pollock and Maitland, op. cit., I, p. 297. Digby, op. cit., p. 38, says, "The personal relation of lord and man is closely connected with, and generally, though not always, merged in the relation of lord and tenant."

[82] As to the legal classification of these rights according to modern, or Romish, ideas, the authorities are poles apart. Maitland is inclined to attribute ownership to the tenant in demesne. Austin, *Lectures on Jurisprudence*, II, 866, says, "Consequently in English law, there is no property in land which comes up to the idea of absolute property." Digby says, "The tenant is conceived as having only an *estate* in the lands—an interest which though it may be capable of descending to heirs, *in infinitum,* was something short of absolute ownership" (op. cit., p. 43). Markby, with his Roman viewpoint, says, op. cit., p. 175, "In all cases of feudal tenure we find ourselves in presence of two persons—an owner of land, and one who has rights over the land derived from the owner." Elsewhere he speaks of the grantee as "being merely owner of a right over a thing which belongs to the grantor" (p. 175). Finally he goes so far as to state that "the feudal tenant enjoys all the rights of an owner, and yet has only a ius in re alienâ" (p. 177). For Digby only the easement and profit a prendre (incorporeal hereditaments) are *iura in re aliena* (pp. 306-307). One could continue such citations indefinitely showing the persistent effort to apply to the feudal conditions concepts of property which are inapplicable.

Vinogradoff, *Manor*, p. 308, seems to the writer to put the case exactly when he says of pre-feudal England, ". . . we have to recognise the lord [of the manor] as the exclusive owner;" and of the situation after the Conquest, *English Society*, p. 236, "There is no independent property in English feudal law, nothing like the *dominium* of Roman law, or even like the *aleu* of Southern France. . ."

[83] Holdsworth, op. cit., II, p. 347.

[84] Holdsworth, op. cit., II, p. 349.

[85] Terry, op. cit., p. 308.

a matter of public and political status, the whole position of the man in the community, came to be little more than the pure economic relation, an interest in the land.[86] Or one may perceive again the same process of differentiation that has already been noted in the development of the Roman system. Just as, there, the jurisdictional relation separated from the proprietary (or *vice versa*) and law divided into the law of *ius* and the law of *res*, so in England status separated from land, though by a curious twist of events the word itself stuck to the land relation.

B. *The Internal Relations of the "Feod"—Status and Tenure*

With this preparatory view of the general character of the feudal organization we are now prepared to examine in some detail the particular subject of "dependent and derivative tenure," as Maitland calls it, which is the feature that gave rise to the most individual and original characteristic of the Anglo-American law of property; a contribution of as much importance to the modern institution as the Roman law of succession, and one which supplies us with a better understanding of the intrinsic character of all modern property than does that survival of the primitive classificatory genitive to which we now give the title *dominium*, or "ownership."

1. *The Unit upon the Land*

In order to clarify the more intangible arrangements of the feudal system which we are about to examine, it is an essential preliminary to visualize its ground plan, the design and organization of the unit upon the land. In order at the same time to indicate the way by which the plan of operation developed naturally from that of the provincial Roman *villa* we may sketch briefly the course of this evolution.[87]

The description which Fustel gives of a Gallic *domaine romain*

[86] See Holdsworth, op. cit., II, p. 352. Digby, op. cit., p. 48, Note 5, says, "It is characteristic of the history of the growth of tenure that in Domesday (if the index is correct) we hear of different classes of tenants, but not of different species of tenure; of *liberi homines*, but not of *liberum tenementum*; of *milites*, but not of tenure *per militiam;* of *socmanni*, but not of *socagium;* of *villani*, but not of *villenagium*." Maitland, *Domesday*, p. 151, also remarks the absence of the abstract terms in the early documents. In other words, at first tenure depended on personal status; later the "estate" was the tenure.

[87] Fustel, *Alleu*, p. 1, says, "Il nous est impossible d'expliquer le régime rural du moyen âge sans présenter d'abord celui qui était en vigueur à la fin de l'empire romain. Il se peut que cela surprenne ceux qui aiment à se figurer le moyen âge comme naissant tout à coup et tout d'une pièce. Cela n'étonnera pas ceux qui sont arrivés par une observation plus complète et plus juste des faits à conceivoir la règle de la continuité historique."

of the sixth or seventh centuries agrees almost perfectly with that which Vinogradoff gives of the English manor of the eleventh. In Gaul, in spite of the invasions, the conditions remained Roman for both conquerors and conquered.[88] There too the free village of Germanic theory – analogous to "hundred" and "vill" – if the barbarians brought it with them, or if it had survived from the Celtic era, had yielded to the competitive and personal advantages of the Roman system, just as at an earlier stage the same practice must have yielded among the Gauls themselves. In Gaul "the domain was vast; the proprietor could not cultivate it himself. He arranged then to cultivate his land by means of his men." He could work it collectively, rent by the year, or distribute once for life or hereditarily. ". . . these were the three processes which prevailed in Gaul." "Sometimes he gave to a slave a small lot to cultivate himself; . . . more often to the freedmen; and still more often . . . to the 'coloni.' Thus collective working, without entirely disappearing, lost the land little by little, and individual tenure substituted itself unnoticeably for collective and impersonal cultivation."[89]

Through this process, which had already appeared in the Roman *villicus*, the area which the *dominus* worked with his own house servants tended to shrink, though the domain itself might, by the practice of "benefice" and the adherence of free men with their land, be greatly expanding. But "from the first the land was divided into two parts: that which the proprietor reserved for his personal exploitation or enjoyment,[90] and that which he conceded and distributed in tenures to his men."[91] The nomenclature is confused. But one may say that the land so reserved was called the *dominicum*, *terra dominica* or *terra indominica* (that is to say "the land reserved for the master") and that the principal house was the *mansus dominicatus*, or *domus dominica*, or *sala*.[92] But the term *mansus* or *manse* tended to follow the residence upon any permanent tenure,[93] so that we find *mansi serviles* of the *servi manentes*, or *mansuarii*.[94] The essential constitution of the *domaine* or *villa* was this division between a *dominicum*

[88] Fustel, *Alleu*, p. 199, ". . . le sol soit resté distribué après des invasions comme il l'était avant elles, c'est-à-dire avec le prédominance du domaine et la rareté du village libre."

[89] Fustel, *Alleu*, pp. 360-361.

[90] Fustel, *Alleu*, p. 425, says, ". . . la forêt était toujours comprise dans le *dominicum*."

[91] Ibid., p. 439. The division was not sharp, for the tenurial duties usually combined "les redevances de la tenure et un travail sur le dominicum." Ibid., p. 382.

[92] Ibid., p. 367, he says, "*Mansus*, sometimes *mansio*, properly designated the house only."

[93] Ibid., p. 372, he says, ". . . le mot manse, de *maneo*, être à demeure, porte avec lui l'idée de permanence."

[94] Ibid., p. 377.

and tenures. "The unit of property was the *villa;* the unit of tenure was the *manse.*"[95]

As we have noted, this unitary system was coming into vogue in England before the Conquest. There, as well as in France, the "most ancient forms of tributary subjection" seem to have been the "feasting progresses."[96] Next there came to be reserved some central place "which may be properly called a dominical house or mansion," though sometimes it was merely "a counting house or a storehouse."[97] Later there appears a "domanial farm round which dependent holdings are gathered"; the "home farm, *dominicum,*" and the "tributary manses," bearing out the "general distinction between demesne and tenant land."[98] It is this residence or mansion which seems to be the nucleus of the manorial system. ". . . the essence of the manor consisted in its economic organization."[99] And this was the centre of administration. "As a rule, the hall is necessary to constitute a manor, and it may be said, in a sense, to be the manor itself, inasmuch as the manor-house was a place of residence for the lord or his steward."[100] The arrangement is geographical, not personal. ". . . the history of a complex of property is derived, not from a person, but from a locality which appears as the chief seat of the honour, its capital manor. . ."[101]

"The structure of the ordinary manor is always the same. Under the headship of the lord we find two layers of population — the villains and the freeholders;[102] and the territory occupied divides itself ac-

[95] Ibid., p. 367.

[96] Vinogradoff, *Manor,* p. 223. The French term was *gîte.* Obviously this was not of Roman origin. It seems to have been an old Celtic tribal custom of feasting the chief.

[97] Ibid., p. 224. Vinogradoff, *English Society,* p. 354, says, ". . . the domanial centre was [often] a kind of adjunct, and served more as a counting house and the seat of a court than for purposes of husbandry."

[98] Ibid., p. 225. ". . . the word demesne ascending in its low Latin form of *dominicum* even to earlier Old English times. . ." Ibid., p. 226.

[99] Ibid., p. 301.

[100] Vinogradoff, *English Society,* p. 358. "To begin with [Domesday], the expression [manor, *mansio* or *manerium*] is clearly used in the sense of mansion, the residence of a more or less exalted personage" (p. 305). But it was also "currently used to designate estates organized under aristocratic administration" (p. 311), "of which the central house is the hall (*aula*)" (p. 305). "The hall may stand for the demesne as a whole, or for domanial authority" (p. 360). Even, "the hall or court, being the seat of the lord, may be called the head of the manor [caput manerii]" (p. 362).

Delisle, *La Classe Agricole,* p. 212, Note 71, as quoted by Godefroy, *Dictionnaire de l'ancienne langue française,* says, "In the language of the Middle Ages, in Normandy and particularly in England, *manoir* designated the whole of a feudal domain, comprising the habitation of the lord, the lands not fieffed which he exploited himself and the rights which he enjoyed over the lands fieffed to his vassals."

[101] Vinogradoff, *English Society,* p. 348.

[102] Vinogradoff, *Manor,* p. 351, says, "Roughly speaking, villains were peasants, as freemen were knights or rent-paying tenants."

cordingly into demesne land and 'tributary land' . . . of two different classes."[103] "The lord's part of the manor is naturally called *dominicum, demesne.* The term admits of two main acceptations; it may point to the estates, or part of the estates, assigned to the use of the tenant-in-chief [the lord], in opposition to those given over to military followers—thanes, knights, or sergeants. Or else it may point to the home-farm as distinguished from the holdings of the tenants, and it is in this sense that we find the expression in every page of Domesday Book."[104] Let us say that "demesne" was the feudal nucleus, as "manse" had been the manorial. It was a home farm or it was the home farm together with a system of dependent holdings. Therefore it was both productive and tributary or only the former. It was this economic organization upon the land—arrived in England, in the eleventh century, at the same stage which we have found existing on the Continent in the seventh—to which the political feudal system, which had in the meantime developed out of the latter, was now applied.

2. *The Lineal System—Derivative and Dependent*

The feudal system was imposed, primarily as a system of government, upon this mainly economic groundwork. The points of contact—the strategic positions of which it availed itself—were the manorial centres. It completed and, by subdivision, expanded the manorial system; but it did not at first penetrate it. The manorial lords and all above them were feudal. Within the larger circle of the manor—the demesne in its wider sense—all remained as it had been. The interior of the manor was not feudalized. Thus a political superstructure was transplanted and imposed upon an economic organization of the land similar to that from which it had itself developed several centuries earlier. Naturally we find two sets of ideas—one representing the fundamental and more indigenous strain and the other the superior imported strain, and both from the same original sources and conditions—at first distinguished and then during the subsequent two centuries becoming confused and blended.

Within the manor there were three concentric circles, the home farm, the land held by villein tenure, and that held by free but non-feudal tenure.[105] Moreover, by addition or subdivision, there

[103] Vinogradoff, *Villainage in England,* p. 223.

[104] Vinogradoff, *English Society,* p. 353. He thinks that the Old English expression corresponding to the Low Latin *dominium* or *dominicum* is *hired,* which is about the same as "household" today, though not as technical as the later *dominicum.* The immediate object of the home farm is to provide food and clothing for the lord and his household (p. 353).

[105] Vinogradoff, *Villainage,* p. 223, Note 1, points out that the theory of the king's courts did not follow the older distinctions between the home farm and all

came soon to be subordinate manors, primarily to provide for the lord's men, and which were held by strictly feudal, or aristocratic, tenure. Such subordinate manors might not even be contiguous. Within they were organized on the same pattern as the chief manors. But a distinction existed between these subordinate freeholdings and those free tenures which had existed within the old English manor, and which continued to exist therein. Finally, above these chief or subordinate manors, came the feudal hierarchy, reaching to the barons – or, according to the doctrine of his courts, to the king. And here relations were less those of land to land than of person to person. The English manorial system pertained to the soil. The Norman feudal system was governmental.

We have seen that in early France the distinction was made between the chief lord – the old Roman *dominus* who owned the whole domain but reserved only the *dominicum* for his own use – and his permanent tenants who held *manses*. It is evident that, in the course of time, the more important tenants had put their own lands to use in the same way as had the lord. They had acquired sub-tenants who held, thus indirectly, land owned by the chief lord. Apparently this latter practice became the principal factor in economic exploitation and was the generalizer of the manorial system. From the source of this term, *mansus* or *manse*, came the word "manor" and the word *mesne*, used to describe this intermediate landlord who was himself a tenant. He it was who, in perhaps a later sense of the expression, was described as the tenant *in capite*; that is, an immediate subordinate of the chief, or *dominus*. His tenants, however, were described as holding of a "mesne lord." It is possible, as well, that the spelling "demesne," for *domaine*, resulted from a confusion of the idea of *de mesne* – that is the land appertaining directly to the house (*mesne*) – with the Latin *dominicum*, whence *domaine*, and that this accounts for the dual use of the Latin term. For the etymology of these terms, see Appendix I F.

Either from Norman sources, because of this confusion, or from English sources, because the lord of the manor had been regarded as a true owner of the land, or from both, the term *dominus* was used in England immediately after the Conquest to describe the lord of any manor, chief or subordinate, and indeed all his hierarchical

else or between the whole, including villein and freeholdings, and the non-economic holdings (military, etc.) which were presumably subordinate manors. Rather it included in the demesne (*in dominico suo*) all villein holdings but no freeholdings, thus, in effect, throwing the economic freeholdings (socage, fee-farm, etc.) in with the non-economic. This would explain the rapid rise in dignity of these economic freeholdings during the subsequent two centuries. It is not consistent, however, with Bracton's definition of demesne at the end of the thirteenth century. He says, fol. 263, "Est autem dominicum quod habet ad mensam et proprie. . ." In other words the old household idea.

superiors, whose relation to him was personal rather than manorial. Thence the corresponding term *dominium* came to be applied to the authority of such a one, and *dominicum* or "demesne" to the dual or triple grades of its projection upon the land.

Most, perhaps all, such lords were also conceived feudally to be tenants as well. For William I, or perhaps his Barons, was the apex of the whole structure. "Every holder of land, except the king, holds it of (*de*) some lord. . ."[106] Thus the relation had two ends, an upper and a nether. Viewed in the upper aspect all were conceived to hold the land only *in servitio* when it was held through an intermediary lord. Only the manors, chief or subordinate, which they themselves occupied were held *in demesne*. And, viewed in their nether aspect, such tenures were at first *in capite* when they were held direct from the lord of the chief manor, and *via* a "mesne lord" when from the lord of a subordinate manor.

The term *feudum*, or *feodum*, was "imported into England by the French phraseology of the conquerors." It does not appear before the Conquest. Its most usual meaning is "the complex of estates held by a lord. . ."[107] It was applied only to the feudal superstructure and covered that whole group of holdings both *in servitio* and "in demesne" of which the lord was the apex. *In feodo* then had the sense at each level of that original *dominium* from which the structure had in the first place grown down. It corresponded to the lordly or domanial superiority.

In the course of the twelfth and thirteenth centuries the whole arrangement became greatly modified, primarily by the practice of sub-infeudation under which, as its name indicates, the feudal principle and tenure *in feodo* descended below the original aristocratic or military level to those tenures subordinate to the tenure in demesne (manorial), strictly so called. Thus, except as to those portions of the demesne, in its larger sense, which were held by tenure in villeinage, the term tenure in demesne (or *in feodo*) comes to be applied to all freeholdings, and to be, in effect, synonymous with "socage."[108] In this way the invasion of the precincts of the manor not only disintegrated the manorial system, but, as feudalism descended to these lower economic levels, it became itself unfeudalized and began to be converted into a system of property. The process was itself largely the result of the commutation of rents in kind and of services which we shall mention later.[109] As a result the feudal superstructure even-

[106] Maitland, *Domesday*, p. 151.

[107] Vinogradoff, *English Society*, p. 232.

[108] Pollock and Maitland, op. cit., I, p. 235, Note 3, say, "Perhaps the tenant in villeinage was not yet spoken of as holding *in feodo*."

[109] From the standpoint of an economist E. T. Powell, *The Evolution of the Money Market*, p. 6, gives a graphic picture of the process which was taking place

tually lost its relation to landholding – although its formal design continued as a relic of its origin in property. The English land system adopted the forms of feudalism and then superseded it, relegating its model to a purely political function.

The Anglicized feudalism of the period is described by the legal historians. The general theory of feudal land tenure put into effect by the Norman dynasty was pyramidal. It was coming to be contemplated that "every acre of land is immediately or mediately 'held of' the sovereign lord," the king.[110] All varieties of tenure existed between the king and his immediate tenants, so that the hierarchy was wholly irregular and there might be any number of graded tenures, from one to a dozen or more, between the king and the eventual occupying tenant. He who held immediately of the king was said to hold of the king in chief (*in capite*); he was one of the king's tenants in chief, or tenants *in capite*.[111] "The person who stands at the lower end of the [feudal] scale, the person who seems most like an owner of the land, and who has a general right of doing what he pleases with it, is said to hold the land in demesne [*in dominico* or *in dominico suo*]." The term was coming to be applied to any freehold, but of course to nothing sub-feudal. The lord was *dominus*; the tenant was *tenens*. The lord held, "not in demesne but in service (. . . *non tamen in dominico sed in servitio*) . . ."[112] "Every person who stands between the king and him who holds in demesne, every *mesne lord* or *mesne*, is both lord and tenant, lord as regards those who stand below him, tenant as regards those who stand above."[113] Holdsworth describes the process by which this structure had become modified. The tenant in chief "may either keep the land in his own hands, hold it in demesne, or he may grant it out to some one else. In the latter case he holds the land in service; and his tenant holds it in demesne or in service, according as he keeps it

during the latter part of the period we are describing. He says, "The rigidity of the feudal regime had been relaxed, and the flexibility of a money-economy had begun to manifest itself when Richard II succeeded to the throne in 1377. The money solvent had then been at work upon the crystalloid fabric of feudalism for nearly two centuries, if we reckon from the first traceable commutation of the feudal dues into money."

110 Pollock and Maitland, op. cit., I, p. 69.

111 Maitland says elsewhere, Pollock and Maitland, op. cit., I, p. 233, Note 3, "In the thirteenth century the term 'in capite' is merely equivalent to 'immediately,' 'sine medio'; thus even a burgage tenant may have 'tenants in capite,'" and "a tenant's 'capitalis dominus' is his immediate lord. . ." He says it only came later to be "equivalent to 'tenure in capite of the crown.'" Du Cange, op. cit., s.v., gives the sense as "subjected to no middle lord *ratione feudi*." See the discussion of *mesne*, Appendix I F, which I think clears this difficulty.

112 The second statement was still only true of the land held of the lord by free tenants.

113 Pollock and Maitland, op. cit., I, p. 233.

in his own hands or grants it out to another. There may be many steps between the tenant in demesne and the king."[114]

In order to grasp the essence of this relation to which was given the name "tenure" one must disabuse the mind of the modern idea of tenancy. The feudal tenant was literally the "holder" of the land, not a lessee. That which he held, the subject of the tenure, was the "tenement."[115] The lord was any one whom it was mediately or immediately "held of." The nature of the relation was still hardly proprietary in a modern sense. It was, as we have noted, a combination of relations with reference to the land and of personal relations. "Therefore 'tenet' and 'servit' are two sides of any tenure."[116] As to the personal element, "The lord owes defence and warranty [of title] to the tenant. The tenant owes services to his lord. He must swear fealty; and sometimes do homage."[117] This reciprocal relation applied as we have seen in different degree to everything.[118] The dominant or authoritative aspect was called *dominium*, which in Glanville's time must be rendered as "lordship," not ownership. And, since the subordinate became "the man (*homo*) of" a lord, the aspect of personal subjection was originally "homage."[119] But the personal was but an inseparable part of the whole. All the correlative obligations — even the personal ones — between the lord and tenant were in regard to, or *via*, the tenement. "We have further to conceive of the service due from the tenant to his lord as being a burden on the tenement."[120] So that in some ways these services were charges against the tenement rather than the tenant, or rather charges against its occupancy.[121] If a free tenant surrendered the tenement his liability for services ended. Those services which the immediate lord himself owed were incumbent on the tenement and

[114] Holdsworth, op. cit., II, p. 199.

[115] "Tenement" in English law means anything that can be holden provided it be of permanent nature. It includes much besides land. "Hereditament" covers only those tenements which will descend to the person feudally determined as heir. See Clark, *Jurisprudence*, II, p. 557.

[116] Vinogradoff, *English Society*, p. 239.

[117] Holdsworth, op. cit., II, p. 199. See also Digby, op. cit., p. 61.

[118] Vinogradoff, *Manor*, p. 294, speaks of "the element of mutual obligation inherent in the nexus of feudal tenure."

[119] Glanville, Book IX, treats dominion and homage as the two sides of the relation, each involving fidelity (fealty) to the other. "Mutua quidem debet esse dominii et homagii fidelitatis connexio." The *Regiam Majestatem*, L. 2. C. 67, seems to imply that warranty (i.e. the obligation of the lord) is not owed where homage is not paid in return. "But homage is due only for lands, free tenements, services, rents in certain, whether in money, or in other things. But in respect of dominion alone, homage ought not to be rendered to any one, except to the king."

[120] Pollock and Maitland, op. cit., I, p. 237.

[121] The mutual obligation "does not depend . . . on any contract between the parties, but is attached to the land." Markby, op. cit., p. 175.

must be divided between the lord and the tenant. They were *forinsec*. Those which this lord was himself to receive were adjusted by bargain between him and his tenant. They were called *intrinsec*. Thus the land was the locus for the performance of services. Of these the political, military, religious and managerial were the particular functions of the feudal organization and were prescribed in the relations of the aristocratic tenures. The relations within the old manorial organization, which continued on the lower rungs of the feudal ladder as it invaded the manor, were mainly economic in nature. The economic life of the time was almost wholly agricultural. But, before the substitution of the money economy, the function of the lord was one of employment more than it was one of ownership. The tenant was usually an employee, either directly or as the user of the land. The lord was both a landlord and an employer. "The whole of medieval society is held together by the services of tenants—the church is endowed, the kingdom is defended, the land is cultivated." [122]

3. *Tenures of Free Status*

At first there were five classes of tenure. The free tenures were military, by knight service; eleemosynary, by frankalmoin; seriential, by serjeanty; agricultural (or economic) by various tenures. The non-free tenure was villeinage. "Tenure by knight service was the typical tenure of the feudal system, and, as we have seen, the feudal system was far more than a system of land tenure." [123] This was in the beginning the general immediate administrative tenure, the tenure in demesne. But with the process of development of subinfeudation it became the residual, superior and noble tenure—the non-working status. To it especially were appended, in addition to or in place of economic services, the so-called feudal casualties. These were the levies made when the lordship descended (relief), or the tenancy descended (primer seisin), or at other times when the lord was himself subjected to levies (aids). There were also the lord's perquisites, later of much economic importance, connected with the wardship of the tenant's minor heirs and the control of marriage of the tenant's widow and his daughters, after his death. Such tenure was also subjected to the conditions generally applied to all free tenures, namely homage and fealty,[124] and escheat and forfeiture. Under the rule of escheat, the lord was in fact the final heir

[122] Holdsworth, op. cit., III, p. 46.
[123] Holdsworth, op. cit., III, p. 37.
[124] The former came to be omitted in the more economic tenures.

of the tenant so that when the latter's line became extinct the tenure was extinguished and the land returned to the immediate lord "in demesne." Upon this basis of the right of *ultimus heres* the tenement also escheated to the lord when the tenant defaulted in the services due or became a felon, for in these cases as well his rights ceased.[125] Frankalmoin was the early form of tenure under which gifts were made to the church, usually free of services other than religious. It was suppressed by the Statute of Mortmain, presumably because, once in the hands of the church, the "perpetual succession" of that institution eliminated all the profitable casualties and the possibility of escheat. Serjeanty was a special tenure attached to managerial offices of the household and of the domains of the lords.[126] It died out because, as has been noted, the confusion of offices with landholding made the former inconveniently hereditary.

It is evident that the foregoing classes of tenants found it increasingly advantageous not to work their land themselves, except perhaps the immediate precincts of the manor which were worked by the attached villein labour. And this produced the rapid introduction of an economic substratum by means of sub-infeudation. In addition to this new substratum there already existed at the time of the Conquest a numerous class of free tenants who were taken over on various different bases. For these reasons the early forms of free tenure, below the foregoing strictly feudal ranks, are very various. Holdsworth states that the oldest system was *feorm*, or the fee farm.[127] The *feorm* was originally the "amount of produce needed to maintain the lord's household for a certain fixed period," the *firma unius noctis*.[128] Gradually, as the lord found it more profitable to manage his own home farm through his own bailiffs, this system gave place to the system of definite labour service which was prevalent in the thirteenth century. Labour service in turn "was gradually replaced by a system of money rents. . . The lord cultivates his own land by

125 Escheat "forms as it were a basis for all his [the lord's] other rights. The superiority which he always has over the land may at any time become once more a full ownership [*sic*] of it." Pollock and Maitland, op. cit., I, p. 351.

126 As an example of these seviential tenures there is the one referred to by Digby, op. cit., p. 38, Note 5. Certain lands were held of the king *in capite* "by the serjeanty and service of holding the king's head between Dover and Whitsan whenever he crossed the sea between these ports and there should be occasion for it." Quoted from Hasted, *Kent*, IV, p. 39.

127 The Saxon word *feorm* originally meant "food," but by the process described above it came to mean "rent." See Holdsworth, op. cit., III, p. 198; also Pollock and Maitland, op. cit., I, p. 293. It was translated at this later stage into the Latin *firma* meaning "fixed" and implying a fixed rental.

128 Holdsworth, op. cit., III, p. 198. It was paid in kind, and "paid in kind" originally said what it meant, "paid in kine" (i.e. in money on the hoof, similar to the Roman *pecunia*). But apparently it was at first the "feasting progress" or *gîte*, to which reference has already been made.

paid labour, or lets it to a tenant who pays rent."[129] Thus in the end *fee farm* came to mean "to hold heritably and perpetually at a rent," and "farmer" came to mean "renter," in precisely the sense that we in America use the word "renter" today.[130] But parallel with this development another was going on which eventually absorbed it. This was socage, the substrate Anglo-Saxon free tenure which the Normans found and continued under their superimposed feudalism.[131] "Thus socage begins to swallow up the other tenures, and preparation is already made for the day when all, or practically all, tenants will hold by the once humble tenure of the *sokemanni.*"[132] By the end of the thirteenth century the process was nearly complete and "socage becomes the one great standing contrast to military tenure." Originally a peasant's tenure, it became the "great residuary tenure . . . it is non-military, non-seriential, non-elemosinary."[133] Holdsworth believes that socage absorbed the other forms because it was "least encumbered of all the tenures with obsolete and oppressive incidents"[134] – in other words because it was non-feudal and so more suitable to an increasingly economic age. But the essence of the formula remained intact even when the land was leased for a money rent. The lessee *holds* the land of the lessor.[135]

Under the early English feudal system all these tenures were primarily a matter of personal status. For the group as a whole the status was that of free men – freeholders. As landholding gradually developed into property the importance of status tended to disappear and the lower reaches of the system were converted from an organization of persons to an organization of property, from one of status to one of tenure. In Bracton's work (about the middle of the thirteenth century) *status* generally means personal condition.[136] But it

129 Holdsworth, op. cit., III, p. 199.

130 The term farmer was later applied more often to the lessee of a lesser estate than fee farm. "The lessee [for a term of years] is sometimes called the *termor*, sometimes, from the main object of the transaction, the *farmer* [i.e. rent payer]." Digby, op. cit., p. 242.

131 Vinogradoff says, *Manor*, p. 357, "Socage remains the typical free tenure, the holding in which the services are certain, whether they take the form of rent or of services in kind." And Digby, op. cit., p. 46, says, "It seems that the changes in the direction of feudalism wrought by the Conquest affected the small free proprietors far less than the lords of great districts."

132 Pollock and Maitland, op. cit., I, p. 356.

133 Pollock and Maitland, op. cit., I, p. 294.

134 Holdsworth, op. cit., III, p. 53.

135 Pollock and Maitland, op. cit., I, p. 235. It is not necessary for our purpose to discuss the special tenure of burgage which was eventually absorbed into socage. But it is of some interest to note that Digby considers its special character due to the fact that it was the last survival of the *alod* (absolute ownership). See Digby, op. cit., pp. 5-6.

136 "Bracton could still sharply oppose it [estate] to rights in land." Pollock and Maitland, op. cit., I, p. 408.

is already evident that tenure and status are becoming differentiated.[137] Soon thereafter the word "estate" (status) was set apart to signify a proprietary right in land or other tenement.[138] Even in Bracton a person already has a status in reference to objects; he may have several estates, according to different titles, in different pieces of land. So, because it is "characteristic of this age that a man's status—his general position in the legal scheme—is closely connected with his proprietary rights"[139] the word "estate" becomes a description of the successor of feudal tenure rather than one of personal status. The peculiarly English character of this metamorphosis of feudal landholding from politics to property is testified to by the fact that, in English, the word estate came to mean landed or other property, while, in French, its cognate continued up to the time of the Revolution to indicate the major class, or rank, to which a person belonged. In England tenure overruled status, while on the Continent status overruled tenure. Nevertheless in both (as in other feudalized countries as well) the political organization upon the land also retained the word in another form. It became the *state*.[140]

4. *Non-free Tenure and Status*

While the distinction between both the personal status and the tenure of the free and of the non-free was always difficult of practical application in England it was sufficiently clear cut in legal theory almost as soon as the distinction appeared at all in the law. Just as in Rome, the free man was in some respects a person, while the villein was only a member of the *familia*, or the *vill*. In this way freedom has always pertained to a unit under the law and unfreedom to a sub-unit; one who is completely subordinate to some person and therefore beyond the reach of the law. The free man could claim

[137] Digby, op. cit., p. 136, finds this even in Bracton. "What was formerly a distinction principally affecting the status of the holder [i.e. the distinction between holding by free or non-free services] comes now [in Bracton] to be regarded as the basis of two different classes of rights of property."

[138] The Year Books begin with the Latin word *status* meaning estate in land.

[139] Pollock and Maitland, op. cit., II, p. 79.

[140] This word "status" gives us perhaps the deepest insight into the character of feudal society. Originally it meant "standing," with especial reference to one's standing in the organization upon the land. Its first offshoot, in order of differentiation, was the French term *les états*, signifying the orders of society in respect of this standing. Thence the term *l'état* came to mean "the estates as a whole, the collective *organization upon the land*." This became our word for "the state." Meanwhile in England the first offshoot *via* the early French, the word "estate," which separated just at the time that standing with reference to the organization upon the land was beginning to be converted into property in land, came to mean this property alone, and later even the land itself. Having used both the early derivatives for these special purposes it is now necessary for us to use the original Latin word *status* to cover its original meaning, from which the others sprang.

the jurisdiction of the king's court. The villein could not. In theory the freeholder had a personal relation of subjection to the lord, but only through his holding land of him. He could leave the land and so be freed from the relation. The villein also had a personal relation of subjection, which at some times seems to be direct and at other times only, as in the first case, *via* the land. But he, on the other hand, was attached to the land and could not leave it in order to be freed from the personal relation. In other respects, in spite of this limited freedom, the freeholder resembled the adopted or dependent members of the *familia*, while the villein was somewhat like a slave.

In practice, however, the distinctions between personal freedom and unfreedom and tenurial freedom or unfreedom came to be entirely independent of each other. "The greater part of the land of England was cultivated by persons who held by unfree tenure."[141] But, in the course of time, it came about that "a man may be free and yet hold by villein tenure. He may be a villein and yet hold by a free tenure."[142] In the case of the personal status "there is no such thing as merely praedial serfage."[143] The serf was personally unfree. True, he was annexed to the soil, but he could be, though he seldom was, severed from his tenement and even sold as a chattel. But the character of his unfreedom was, in England, peculiar. It was a relative serfdom, hardly like the slave status, because as against others than his lord he had many of the rights of the free. So serfdom, as treated by Bracton, was "hardly [what we consider] a status; it is but a relation between two persons, serf and lord."[144]

In respect of the character of the tenure, it is best defined as being unfree in the case of "one who owes to his lord in respect of his tenement *uncertain* labour services, or who (by himself or his predecessors) has owed such services in the past, or who is subject to distinctively servile burdens. . ."[145] "This seems the point that is seized by law and that general opinion of which the law is the exponent: any considerable uncertainty as to the amount or the kind of agricultural services makes the tenure unfree. . . This doctrine has good sense in it."[146] In other words if the service was explicit the tenure was based on what we should call contract, so free. If it was not, then it was based on pure status, so unfree. But the extent to which status and contract were intermixed is shown by the assimilation of the rights of the unfree tenants on the ancient demesne of

[141] Holdsworth, op. cit., III, p. 198.
[142] Holdsworth, op. cit., II, p. 264.
[143] Pollock and Maitland, op. cit., I, p. 413.
[144] Pollock and Maitland, op. cit., I, p. 415.
[145] Pollock and Maitland, op. cit., I, p. 375.
[146] Pollock and Maitland, op. cit., I, p. 371.

the king to the rights even of the free holder of the high honour of a barony. The "custom of the manor" then seems to identify itself with the law of the realm and to affect both tenants alike. When such a tenement was enfeoffed it moved out of the ancient demesne and came to be "at the common law." Nevertheless the jurisdiction of the king's court reached both; in the first case subject to the "custom of the manor," and, in the second, subject to the common law. Thus we see the blending of seignorial with royal jurisdiction.

However "on the whole, outside the ancient demesne, the law maintains the dilemma, 'Freehold, or unprotected by law.'"[147] Obviously this was not a question of law or no law. It was merely a separation of the manorial from the royal jurisdiction. In effect, to extend the field of common law into the relations between the lord and his villeins would have seemed in that day like substituting law for factory rules between employer and employee in ours. When the royal jurisdiction was eventually so extended it was because, through commutation of labour services for rent, a new species of land tenure (i.e. property in land) came to displace the status (i.e. basis of employment) of the unfree labourer. At first the tenant in villeinage simply occupied the land by the custom of the manor, in the name of the lord, who held in demesne.[148] Transfer was effected by "surrender and admittance" rather than by feoffment. Later, records began to be kept, the so-called "roll of court"; and title was established by "copy of court roll"—whence the term "copyhold." Gradually and in the course of time, the uncertain labour services came to be compounded for money rent, without, however, changing the nature of the estate.[149]

Not only has this question of villeinage given modern scholars much difficulty, but it is evident that the connection between villein status and villein tenure and the application of the legal theory as between free and unfree was most puzzling to the courts of the period. On the whole we can agree with Holdsworth that the theory applied at the time "which threw together into the class of the personally unfree the majority of the humbler cultivators of the soil, had ignored the fact that many of those persons were personally free [merely dependent]; and facts revenged themselves upon such a theory."[150]

As the law of property in land developed out of a purely political organization on the land, in one of the later stages even the villein

[147] Pollock and Maitland, op. cit., I, p. 406.
[148] Pollock and Maitland, op. cit., I, p. 392.
[149] Pollock and Maitland, op. cit., I, p. 369.
[150] Holdsworth, op. cit., III, p. 493.

became a property owner and the copyhold estate appeared. The serf, who was originally unfree and attached to the soil—merely an agricultural labourer for the lord on his reserved demesne—was artificially merged with many another special status or tenure in the general legal class "villein." Unprotected by the king's courts; subject to and protected by the "custom of the manor" only; allowed to pay himself for his service to his lord by working a small holding held in uncertain tenure "in the name of his lord"; nevertheless, in the end, he escaped from the handicaps of status and became a full-fledged British landholder. After the middle of the fourteenth century, especially on account of the Black Death, commutation became an important influence in the process.[151] "With the completion of the transition from praedial services to money rents, tenure in villeinage may be said to have come to an end . . . the essence of villein tenure had consisted in the uncertainty of the tenant's services, and when the old agricultural services were commuted for a fixed money payment this uncertainty passed away."[152] This change also put an end to the principal contemporary employer-employee relation and thus "protection given by royal courts would no longer mean an interference with or an inquiry into the agricultural economy of the manor. . ."[153] Therefore the king's courts proceeded to take the copyholder under their wing and the last vestiges of status in respect of land disappeared. Thus just as the term *vassus*, or vassal, originally applied to an unfree servant,[154] came eventually to be the generic continental term for free feudal tenant, so the English tenancy in villeinage climbed the barrier of status and became a full-fledged and free estate in land.

5. *The Freehold Estates*

At the end of the period we are examining the servants of the military are becoming the masters of the economic organization. Economic civilization seems, for a long period, to have been submerged. Yet when one compares the institutions of the people—rather than those of their masters—of the provinces at the end of the Roman empire with those at the end of the intervening Dark

151 On the whole we may say that commutation of services for money rents was the process of introducing the money economy into feudal tenure. This was the second revolution. The first was, as heretofore described, that which inaugurated the manorial system, the change from *feorm* to service. Vinogradoff, *Villainage*, p. 307, says, "The same remark which applied to the passage from produce 'farms' to labour holds good as to passage from labour to money payments. There is no break between the arrangements."

152 Page, *End of Villainage in England*, p. 83.

153 Holdsworth, op. cit., III, p. 207.

154 Pollock and Maitland, op. cit., I, p. 68.

Ages, or with those of England at this later but equivalent period, one sees that, somehow or other and against great odds, the same characteristics, almost the same organization, have persisted, undergoing a mere change of terminology rather than one of substance. The head of the new and smaller unit, the husband of the modern family, has become the repository not only of the domestic power but of the new property organization; no longer absolute, it is true, because of its origin in the intra-familial mode – the *peculium*. There appears implicit in the facts the picture of the same acquisitive, coral-building human animal continuing the exercise of his peculiar faculties and only waiting for the restoration of relatively settled conditions and of *security*, doggedly to reassert his pre-eminence. The teeter right-might eventually shifts its angle. Those who have coined the antithetic phrase to defend their method – the method of work and wits and trading *versus* that of brawn and fighting – shake off their protectors when they are no longer needed. The age of chivalry and cavaliers – the romance of feudalism – passes into the age of morality and the *bourgeois* – the romance, if it can be called such, of business. Honour becomes honesty; virtue becomes caution, thrift, chastity, temperance; and courage becomes patience and perseverance.

In the end the feudal aristocracy yielded the working and administration of the land itself to the hitherto subordinate economic classes. They found it more profitable and pleasanter to draw their money rents and concern themselves with other matters. The manorial system, as a productive and administrative agricultural mechanism, gave place to another and itself retired as a *rentier* to the relatively functionless field of landholding. The change of management is reflected in a change of nomenclature and a change in the medium of exchange; but the form of the earlier structure continues in the later. We shall have to consider whether the lineal organization of landholding persisted merely as a survival because of a paucity of legal ideas, or whether, on the other hand, it was taken over by the economic organization in a modified form because it had proved to be an invention of great utility to the now full-fledged institution of property.

In the preceding two centuries the organization of society upon the basis of the land had been built up into a structure, increasingly complex in configuration and increasingly uniform in character. The process was that of sub-infeudation, which was unrestrained and which continually added more rungs to the ladder. This was a complicated and unsatisfactory method of transfer of possession (though perhaps the only way of evading restriction) so that the effort to accomplish alienation *inter vivos* by the more direct method of substitution and by the newer form of determinate estates was constantly battling against existing legal handicaps. In other words it was desired to transfer possession without the necessity of securing the lord's consent and sometimes without endorsement, so to speak. Finally in 1290, through the statute *Quia Emptores*, the effort was successful and the changes worked were revolutionary. Further sub-infeudation was prohibited; but all free tenants, except the tenants in chief of the crown, were permitted to alienate at will. When the tenement so alienated was in demesne – a definition which by this time included socage and all tenures *in feodo* (i.e. in fee or fee simple) – transfer was accomplished by substitution; that is, the purchaser took over the feudal obligations of the seller and wholly replaced him.[155]

The prohibition of sub-infeudation led to the gradual decay of mesne tenure.[156] For, whenever the rights of the mesne lord were from time to time forfeited or escheated[157] they could not be revived, so that the king came gradually to hold the only seignory. But this process of eliminating the feudal intermediaries[158] only added vigour to the already elaborated system of new estates issuing out of the tenures in demesne, a process which prospered because land was the principal form of wealth, the almost exclusive avenue for the investment of capital, and therefore, as the name indicates, the substance of nearly all estates. The gift of land was the disposition of the family fortune or its liquidation.

With this commercializing of feudal tenure came naturally a

[155] Bracton says, fol. 81, ". . . et incipit in persona feoffati, qui obligatur propter tenementum quod tenet, quod est feodum domini capitalis." This was before *Quia Emptores*.

[156] Holdsworth, op. cit., II, p. 348.

[157] Or, to judge from Glanville, III, 6, when the lord failed to appear for warranty of his tenant and the tenant thereafter did service direct to the king.

Digby, op. cit., p. 77, confirms the foregoing and elaborates the explanation. "If by any means, such as escheat for felony, or failure of heirs, or repudiation of his duties as lord, the tie was dissolved as between the tenant and his immediate lord, the intermediate seignory was as it were taken away, and the relation of lord and tenant arose between the tenant and the superior lord of whom the intermediate lord himself had held." For, as Bracton says, fol. 80 b, he had already been this lord's tenant as well, "*quamvis per medium . . . tenens suus.*" "In socage tenure, when no rent was payable and no value attached to the service, there was no motive for keeping up the empty ceremony of fealty, and thus in many cases the relation of lord and tenant became altogether obliterated. Finally, when all the valuable incidents attaching to knight-service were abolished, and the tenure itself converted into socage by the Statute of Charles . . . the relation between the freeholder and his lord fell into abeyance, and the freeholder became for all practical purposes owner of the soil." Digby op. cit., p. 235.

[158] The demilitarizing of the organization was hastened because services other than socage rents were tending to be eliminated, forcing the mesne lords to look to "other sources of profit – the incidents of tenure – aid, relief, escheat, wardship and marriage," Holdsworth, op. cit., II, p. 348; emphasis on which obnoxious burdens only served to increase the desire to escape from feudal tenure.

change of terminology. The thirteenth century is already beginning to use the names which we still use for the various estates in land. The word "estates" had already been applied to the various tenures, since the type of tenure indicated, or was supposed to indicate, something of the status of each tenant. So both the name and the concept were naturally carried forward into the newer form where different tenants held by various interests, all based upon the one tenure and, so to speak, divided into temporal parts (i.e. estate for life, reversion, remainder, etc.). Eventually, therefore, "as the difference between the types of free tenure tended to diminish in importance, the term [estate] came to be applied to the quantum of the tenant's interest rather than to the quality of the tenant's tenure."[159] Then the word *feodum* became "fee"; and, because the prevailing working tenure was socage (i.e. at a rent), the word "fee" came to have its other present sense of a periodic payment. The complete estate came then to be called the "fee simple absolute," by which was intended an estate given to a person and his heirs at law. One who holds in fee (*tenet in feodo*) "does not hold for life, he does not hold for a term of years, he does not hold as guardian of an heir, or as one to whom the land has been gaged as security for money; he holds heritably and for his own behoof."[160] Carved out from this complete estate were two others. The first, also in fee, was at first called "fee simple conditional"[161] but later came to be called "fee tail." It was a gift to a person and the heirs, or some class of the heirs, of his body only. This did not constitute a complete transfer. It did not grant out all the donor had to give. "The interest so created was called a fee tail because the descent of the fee was cut down (*talliatum*) to the heirs of the body of the donee."[162] Finally there was the estate for life, non-heritable and therefore not in fee, and obviously less than the nearly perpetual estate of the donor. Therefore "when there is a tenant for life there is always a tenant in fee of the same land."[163] "From the earliest period in our law the rule has been established that a gift to a man simply gives him only a life estate. Perhaps this shows that at an early period the life estate was the ordinary or normal estate."[164]

By creating a life estate from either of those in fee, or by creating one in fee tail from the maximum estate in fee simple, there remained a residue. Provision for this residue was by reversion and by re-

[159] Holdsworth, op. cit., II, pp. 351-352.

[160] Pollock and Maitland, op. cit., I, p. 235.

[161] At first all limited gifts were construed as conditional gifts. See Pollock and Maitland, op. cit., II, p. 17. Gages of land were made in fee conditional.

[162] Holdsworth, op. cit., II, p. 350.

[163] Pollock and Maitland, op. cit., II, p. 7.

[164] Holdsworth, op. cit., III, p. 120.

mainder. At the expiration of either of the lesser estates the land "reverted" to the donor, or his heirs at law. But the donor might qualify this reversion by directing that at such expiration it should "remain" out to some other person instead of so reverting. Thus were created the "reversion" and the "remainder." All these estates were the subject of gift. They were the devices of an age when wealth was land, to subject it to permanent control. Maitland[165] says of the donor, "he can make that land descend in this way or in that, make it 'remain,' that is, stay out, for this person or for that, make it 'revert' or come back to himself or his heirs upon the happening of this or that event." And he finds that in the thirteenth century the common law about *forma doni* is liberal, elastic, loose and vague. From Henry III on its main duty will be to establish certain barriers to this freedom.[166]

With the definition of the estate tail under Edward I and the differentiation of these future estates from the older feudal "escheat," matters were complicated. After the statute of *Quia Emptores* there was no reversion after a grant in fee simple but only after the grant of a lesser estate. For a grant in fee simple was a substitution. The alienee then held of the lord and the alienor was eliminated.[167] But there remained a possibility of escheat to the lord if the tenant in fee simple died without heirs, or if he committed felony. Therefore the right of the reversioner or remainderman to succeed at the expiration of a particular estate became differentiated from the tenurial right of escheat.[168] But, curiously enough, in the process of transition the older residual right did not attain to the dignity of an estate.[169] It was treated as a mere possibility of one, while a reversion was regarded as an estate because it was more intimately related to the new conception of quantum.[170] The remainderman also suffered discrimination, though a lesser one. He might be tenant in fee subject to a life tenancy to another. But the life tenant held of the donor not of

165 Pollock and Maitland, op. cit., II, p. 11.

166 Pollock and Maitland, op. cit., II, p. 27.

167 Holdsworth, op. cit., III, p. 165.

168 Holdsworth, op. cit., III, p. 67.

169 Digby, op. cit., p. 238, Note 2, makes it fairly clear that the system of estates, at least those created subject to rent charges, resulted largely from an effort to escape the prevention of sub-infeudation effected by *Quia Emptores*, so that the more favourable treatment of the reversion as an estate (escheat was not) was merely part and parcel of the general process of denuding the proprietorship of the mesne lords which, over five hundred years, succeeded in taking the land from them.

170 Holdsworth, op. cit., III, p. 133. It is true that the condition terminating the estate tail is a more probable one than that terminating the fee simple by extinction of the line; so in this respect escheat is more of a mere possibility than reversion. But the difference is one of degree only. And with escheat there was also the possibility of extinguishing the dependent estate for other reasons. Obviously the basis for the distinction was that no "honour" was a "status."

the remainderman, because the two estates were of independent origin. Thus the "remainderman can not use the writ of right [the principal proprietary action of the time] because neither he, nor any one through whom he claimed *by descent*, has been seised of the land."[171]

These three estates and the two future interests in them became the freehold estates.[172] By that time "freehold" had come gradually to imply, not the free status of the man as contrasted with the villein tenure of the tenant in villeinage, but rather the fact that the "tenant does not hold merely at the will of another, and that he does not hold for some definite space of time," "but heritably, or for life."[173] The category excluded the chattels real as well as the unfree holdings. Thus the system of freehold estates, or heritable interests, was subjoined to the system of free feudal tenures. At first the former rested upon several tenures; eventually only upon one, and that one the meanest, socage.

C. *The Nature of Coexisting Interests*

We are now prepared to grasp the essence of this system of organization of property and the novel and modern relation which it established. Maine describes it as a "long succession of partial ownerships, making up together one complete ownership, the feodum or fee."[174] Maitland, considering especially the system of tenures, distinguishes the peculiarity that "several different persons, in somewhat different senses, may be said to have and to hold the same piece of land," and goes on to say that "we have not adequately described his [the lord's] position by saying that he has a right to services from his tenant. Of him as well as of his tenant it may be said that he holds the land, not indeed in demesne but in service, that the land is his land and his fee, and even that he is seised, that is, possessed of the land."[175] Holdsworth, tracing the transplantation of this lineal system from the organization of tenures into that of estates, says, "There are a large number of different interests, recognized and protected by law, which may coexist in the same piece of land at the same time."[176] These three points of view, that of the scientist, the historian and the lawyer, practically coincide on the essential point. "It is obvious also that

[171] Pollock and Maitland, op. cit., II, p. 10, Note 2.

[172] Estates *pur auter vie*, and those of dower and of courtesy are nowadays also considered freehold. See Digby, op. cit., p. 310.

[173] Pollock and Maitland, op. cit., I, p. 357.

[174] *E. L. and C.*, p. 344. The term *feodum* was, as a matter of fact, applied to each holding and was inclusive – a summation – only from that point down.

[175] Pollock and Maitland, op. cit., I, p. 237.

[176] Op. cit., II, p. 351.

any system of land tenure necessitates the existence of two separate sets of interests in the land – the interest of the lord and the interest of the tenant; that the physical characteristics of land make it possible that it shall be enjoyed in succession; and that the large powers given to the landowner of carving estates out of his land, or of charging it in various ways, gives rise to many other simultaneous interests in the same piece of land. No such simultaneous interests were allowed to coexist in the case of a chattel. A chattel is not the subject of tenure, nor can it be carved out into estates."[177]

1. *Differences of Quality and of Quantity*

The estates were regarded as differing in quantity not, as was the case with the tenures, in quality. We see this idea coming to the fore in these citations from Holdsworth. And Maitland finds that at this point there appeared "the most salient trait of our English land law. Proprietary rights in land are, we may say, projected upon the plane of time. The category of quantity, of duration is applied to them."[178] Not only is this concept applied to an estate for life,[179] but also to the estates of future enjoyment. Thus, as Markby says, we have many slices carved out of the estate in perpetuity, and each slice conferred upon a different person. "English lawyers do not seem to consider this mode of dealing with ownership as any thing peculiar; but it nevertheless is peculiar to English law."[180] So invasive is this concept that it converts the term "freehold" from its original sense of status to a sense of duration.[181]

Thus a curious and seemingly invalid distinction is introduced into the theory of English law. Whereas it was possible, under the feudal system, for several tenures of different quality to coexist,[182] it is now considered possible for more than one estate to exist at a time only if they differ in quantity (i.e. time of enjoyment). With tenures the whole rights to the land might be assorted into several different bundles, so that a number of present tenures of different quality,

[177] Holdsworth, op. cit., III, p. 352.

[178] Pollock and Maitland, op. cit., II, p. 10.

[179] Modern statutes call the life tenant a limited or temporary owner. Pollock and Maitland, op. cit., II, p. 10.

[180] Op. cit., p. 167.

[181] Lord Mansfield, in Taylor v. Horde (1 Burr. 60, 108) says, ". . . the idea *modern* times annex to *freehold*, or *freeholder*, is taken merely from the *duration* of the estate." As Digby puts it, op. cit., p. 161, "When the rights over the land are given for a period the termination of which is not fixed or ascertained by a specified limit of time, the interest is a freehold interest."

[182] There could not be two seisins of the same quality (i.e. kind) at the same time. But there could be one in demesne and several in service, as well as several successive estates, to each or any, all at the same time.

summing up to unity, could run to several different men at once; with estates it is conceived that each estate is complete and exclusive as to enjoyment during its life, and that they may coexist in that respect only in succession to one another. And this theory is the more surprising in view of the fact that there seems to be no difference in the relations between coexisting estates as contrasted with those formerly established between coexisting tenures. In point of the "projection in the plane of time" the possibility of escheat was very real, greater than that of many reversions.[183] And, as to differences in quality, if there is any variation between the two periods it is that the assignment and protection of qualitatively different rights, concurrent in point of time, to the holders of various estates, is more energetically carried on after the change than it was before. The explanation seems to be that while the common law lawyers were familiar with coincident tenures and so accepted them as a matter of course, it did not occur to them to apply the same principle to estates, because estates seemed at first to be temporal divisions of a single tenure. In the second place, in establishing the system of estates, it was of course necessary as well to deny or disguise their resemblance to the hierarchy of tenures for the very reason that they were a means of escape from the prohibition upon sub-infeudation. Moreover the estates, as distinguished from the chattel interests in land, were designed primarily to succeed each other and their actual coexistence was a practical incident only discoverable by experience. These vested interests, projected into the future, were soon found to cast their shadow before them into the present.

2. *Several Coexisting Present Interests, "Real" and Possessory*

As we are now at the heart of the analogy between the modern Anglo-American and the medieval English property structure it will be worth while to examine in some detail the respects in which the feoffor, donor, and even the lessor,[184] maintained rights in land (i.e. were protected in a continuing relation to the material object itself). While it is clear that, whereas the benefits of the land were conceived to be divided among the tenures and, on the other hand, the possessory relation, which was enjoyed by one at a time, seemed to be the

[183] Maitland, in Pollock and Maitland, op. cit., I, p. 355, says, "However, in the thirteenth century the possibility, never very remote, that the land would escheat, was, when coupled with the power of distress, a quite sufficient manifestation of the idea that the land, though it was the tenant's, was also the lord's. The tenant's interest in it might at any time expire and leave the lord's interest subsisting."

[184] Littleton, *Tenures*, I, 6, 57, uses the term "feoffor" only of fee simple, "donor" only of fee tail, and "grantor" of anything less including (according to Coke) grants of estates for life, or *pur auter vie*.

only beneficial one among the estates, nevertheless to the extent that any concurrent rights were maintained, it should be said that the estates as well as the tenures coexisted qualitatively as well as quantitatively. The first and most important point is that the feoffor, the donor of any estate less than his own (i.e. the reversioner), and the lessor were all seised of the land. The remainderman, it is true, was not and, for that reason, his protection was scant.

We have already seen that, in the cases of tenures, the services owed the lord were not wholly, if at all, a personal liability upon the tenant. Rather they were "owed by" and "a burden on the tenement."[185] They were a real not a personal relation. At first there were three courses open to the lord who sought to recover from his tenant services in arrears:

1. Action in the king's court. This was proprietary and slow. Since it only established title and did not turn out (disseise) the tenant because he could not or would not render the services but only because he denied title to them, it was used only in cases of disavowal of tenure. By the time of Edward I, with the writ "*cessavit per biennium*," the lord could claim land to be restored in demesne if the tenant was in arrears for two years. Later on, in preference to distraint, there is an action, the Writ of Customs and Services, "an action of the realest kind."

2. Distress. This was the extra-judicial levy by the lord on certain of the tenant's movables, not for appropriation or for sale, but only as a gage. ". . . it is not a means whereby the distrainor can satisfy the debt [sic] that is due him," but a method of constraining the defaulting tenant.[186] It might be used before or after judgment in the lord's own court.[187]

3. Action in the lord's own court. This permitted, finally, the distraint of the land after that of chattels had failed, but again only as a gage. In fact the distrainor could not even retain the "profit" of the land, showing the "extreme reluctance of ancient law to deprive a tenant of his tenement. . ."[189]

If the tenant were distrained by some other lord to coerce him to pay rent to him, the lord disseised brought the "assize of novel disseisin" (recent dispossession) to recover his right by possessory action.[190] And if the terre tenant were distrained by the lord above

[185] Pollock and Maitland, op. cit., I, p. 237.

[186] Pollock and Maitland, op. cit., I, p. 353. The distrained chattels were regarded as being "*in custodia legis.*" Pollock and Maitland, op. cit., II, p. 576.

[187] The present meanings of the words "cheat" (from escheat) and the word "distress" (allied to distrain and district) may be interesting commentaries on the common viewpoint, at least, of the time as to the character of these legal processes.

[189] Pollock and Maitland, op. cit., I, p. 355, Note 1.

[190] Pollock and Maitland, op. cit., II, p. 128.

his own he had the Writ of Mesne against his own lord. By way of additional direct relation to the land it was "common practice for a feoffor or a lessor to stipulate that if the services due him were in arrear for a certain time, he might reenter on the land and hold it as of old: — he made his gift subject to the express condition that rent should be duly paid."[191] That is, a conditional tenure or estate was created which, upon default, expired. Sometimes there were stipulations giving the lord the right of pre-emption and sometimes restrictions on conveyance of other kinds.[192] In all these actions and arrangements the idea of qualitative division and the duplicate or conditional quality of the possessory right was evidenced.

It was not a far cry from this real and somewhat corporeal relation of the lord to the land, under which he had a right to part of the produce or its equivalent in part of the tenant's time, to the developing and popular concept of the rent charge, which while it had changed to an incorporeal thing, had also become itself a tenement (a holding) of which the donee, or the lord, was seised, and to which he had subjected the land, or which he had reserved from his feoffment or gift.[193] But this change did not change its real nature. It retained the power of distress, "a procedure that attacks the land. Into the land the rent-owner enters; he takes the chattels that are found there. . ." It retained the governing idea that the land was bound to pay the rent, and "it is by no means necessary to the existence of the rent that any person should be bound to pay it." "We may almost go the length of saying that the land pays it through his [the terre tenant's] hand." It was created in a manner "closely akin to seisin." "The assize of novel disseisin enables the rent-owner to

[191] Pollock and Maitland, op. cit., II, p. 25.

[192] Pollock and Maitland, op. cit., II, p. 26.

[193] Littleton's analysis of rents is summarized here, not only because it will explain the foregoing allusions, but because it sheds much light upon the manner in which rents came into being and the extent to which the estates and the incorporeal things it gave rise to were modelled upon, and were an evasion of the restrictions upon, subinfeudation. See op. cit., II, 12, Sect. 213.

Rent Service.

Where the tenant holds of his lord by certain rent, for which a distress is incident of common right.

a. Whether it be upon a gift in tail, for life or for years.

b. Or upon a feoffment made before the statute *Quia Emptores*.

Rent Charge.

a. When one grants a rent with a clause of distress (i.e. when one subjects to a rent his own estate or reserves one from a grant of his own estate).

b. Or when rent is granted upon equality of partition.

Rent Sec. By grant without clause of distress.

If one hold by fealty and rent, or by homage, fealty and rent and the lord grants the rent only, or grants the rest and reserves the rent.

coerce the tenant. . . It also protects him against the world at large in the enjoyment of his incorporeal thing. . . Every sort of action that can be brought for the recovery of land can be brought for the recovery of rent." Even a man could enter into and be ejected from a rent charge.[194]

Thus the relation of the lord or donor to the land, through services, commuted rents or the rent charge[195] remained alike real—though the last was becoming incorporeal. In all alike there was available Novel Disseisin. Even the owner of the rent in default was considered to have been "disseised of his free tenement"—so many shillingsworth of rent. And the resulting action was not the enforcement of an obligation but the recovery of a thing, as if it were part and parcel of the land. The element of obligation was subordinate and never gave rise to an action for debt. In Bracton's day the real action ran even against the termor.[196]

It is true that relations existed between man and man as well as between man and land, so that not all this complex system can be regarded as comparable to land law. And this in more respects than the exchange or protection and homage. The lord had given (*do*) his land to the tenant. And, though the tenant "held of" the lord, he held the land. What the lord had "given" he could not give again. What the tenant "held" he could give, though what he owed might impede this giving. So, at first, the increasing liberty of alienation did not work equally both ways. If the seignory were conveyed, an attornment by the tenant (novation of fealty) was essential. And the lord owed the personal obligation of "warranty" to the tenant. Nevertheless proprietary actions went on, as to the seignory, over the heads of the tenants and the two seisins were so independent of each other that ejectment of one tenant by another was not a disseisin of the lord. In certain respects the feudal superiority itself, with its accompanying rights to services, and the feudal inferiority, with its corresponding obligations, were regarded as things incorporeal, apart from the land though "issuing thereout."[197] Holdsworth considers that "the lord's duties were regarded as contractual in their nature—as a sort of chose in action which could not be assigned; whereas the tenant's duties were bound up with the land, and, so to speak, ran with it, so that they were assignable with the land."[198] In view of the unformed state of the theory of contract at that time and the fact that all other rights of property of one out of possession were at that time regarded as choses in action, I do not think this view of the

[194] Pollock and Maitland, op. cit., II, pp. 130-132.
[195] But not the rent sec, which is a rent without the power of distraint.
[196] See Pollock and Maitland, op. cit., II, pp. 125-127.
[197] Pollock and Maitland, op. cit., II, p. 125.
[198] Holdsworth, op. cit., III, p. 82.

relation, as a purely personal one, is as satisfactory as the one we have presented. It is the natural view of a legal scholar, thoroughly inured to the peculiarities of English law, who finds it difficult to conceive of two real interests coexisting in the same present. Nevertheless all these instances seem to indicate that such was the case.

3. *Several Coexisting Present Interests, Independently Alienable*

Alienation of tenancies by substitution and sub-infeudation seems to have had the same row to hoe that later retarded the similar process in the financial field – the alienability of choses in action. And Jenks and others think it was for the same reason. This view seems erroneous. As Digby points out [199] the restrictions upon alienation are at first "the relics of primitive custom antecedent to the growth of feudal ideas." The ancient inheritance of the family could not be alienated. The recent acquisitions of the tenant could. This primitive idea of the necessity of continuing property in the line of descent – the idea of perpetual succession – seems as indigenous in Saxon as in Roman tradition. There too, in early times, familial property could not be sold or devised. Digby is inclined to think that the feudal objections came later, and were "encroachments upon the freedom of the tenant devised by the selfishness and avarice of the lords." [200] But it would appear more consonant with the plan of organization to believe with Maitland that from the beginning "seignorial and family claims must be satisfied before there can be any alienation at all." [201] So far as the family claims were concerned, at first the consent of the expectant heir was required. Then, as the rule of primogeniture became general, that requirement was rendered absurd. So alienation was freed of this restriction. Nevertheless it could still only be effected *inter vivos* and not by will. ". . . the lord's consent to a gift by a tenant was thought desirable. . ." [202] But the law took the side of the tenants, the growing "estate" of property owners, and, in estimating the injury of alienation to the lord, minimized the loss of the precious feudal incidents as compared with the value of the services.[203] Digby believes the abuse which brought about *Quia Emptores* was the growing practice of sub-infeudation of part tenements which was held not to make the new holder a tenant of the feoffor's lord. He says, "It seems that at the beginning of the

[199] Op. cit., p. 100.
[200] Loc. cit.
[201] Pollock and Maitland, op. cit., II, p. 12.
[202] Holdsworth, op. cit., III, p. 76.
[203] Holdsworth, op. cit., III, pp. 79-80.

reign of Edward I the barons determined on attempting, where they could not prevent alienation altogether, at all events to diminish the loss sustained by the granting out of lands by their tenants to be held of themselves by subinfeudation."[204] In any case this statute, as we have already seen, put an end to alienation by sub-infeudation but freed that by substitution from all restrictions. Of course each could alienate, not the land, but only his own tenement or estate in it, which might be limited or conditional in many ways.[205] Nevertheless, after the restrictions were removed "the danger of the time was not that too little, but that too much, respect would be paid to the expressed wills of feoffors and feoffees, so that the newly acquired power of free alienation would involve a power of making land absolutely inalienable" (i.e. by entail).[206] It was not until the last half of the sixteenth century that a new restriction arose against this abuse by means of the rules against "remoteness of limitation."

Free alienation by the lords of their seignories, while always possible, was subject to somewhat greater and more persistent obstacles. The tenant was sometimes consulted and his services and fealty were always transferred by attornment, compulsory if necessary. There were also some "restraints upon alienation based on the feudal principle"; for instance to prevent the lord substituting for himself "a personal enemy of the tenant, or one incapable of fulfilling the duties of a lord."[207] As yet there were no involuntary alienations. Escheat, forfeiture and reversion simply caused the tenant's rights to disappear and the lord came to hold again in demesne. The only alienations were inheritance, marriage, gift. The last covered sale, exchange, gage and lease.[208]

4. *Limitations on the Right of User*

The real and present rights of coexisting interests which we have so far described were merely sustained with the incoming of the estates. It is in the matter of the preservation of the land, however, that we find an actual improvement in the protection of the concurrent rights of the holders of future interests as compared with that

[204] Digby, op. cit., p. 234.
[205] See Holdsworth, op. cit., III, p. 81.
[206] Pollock and Maitland, op. cit., II, p. 26.
[207] Holdsworth, op. cit., III, pp. 76-77.
[208] Pollock and Maitland, op. cit., II, p. 82. The apparent exception of the "fine" was not in fact involuntary. "A fine . . . is an action compromised in court, and by the leave of the court, upon certain terms approved by the court." Seisin was given by order of the court. Holdsworth, op. cit., III, pp. 236 and 241. Thus the "*finalis concordia*" of Glanville and Bracton is similar to *in iure cessio* of Rome. It was a means to a secure title.

accorded the qualitatively different tenures. At first the tenant had the "right to use and abuse the land, to cultivate it or leave it uncultivated, to keep all others off it. . ."[209] In fact he had an almost absolute Austinian right of user—"a general, indefinite right of using it as he pleases."[210] Even a life tenant was not liable and might lawfully waste unless debarred by bargain. Nevertheless actions for waste, while probably new, were brought.[211] In the course of time, "just as the law gave specific relief if the lord ejected his tenant, so the same relief was granted if the tenant used his land in a manner inconsistent with the nature of the interest granted."[212] "Thus the dowress, the guardian, and the lessee for life or years, could be prohibited from committing waste."[213] But waste must be due to the voluntary act of the tenant. Accident or *vis major*, as well as the defective condition of the premises, was a good defense. And the damage must not be too trivial. If the tenant simply permitted the premises to decay he was probably not liable for the "permissive waste." It was the "prevailing medieval view that liability was based on a positive act contrary to law which caused damage." By the end of the thirteenth century it was settled that the tenant for years must keep the premises in repair. And later both tenants for years and for life were held liable even for permissive waste.[214] Maitland speaks of the gradual development of the restriction on absolute ownership—that is the rights of the tenant for life—by repeated legislation requiring him to behave "*quasi bonus pater familias.*"[215] Thus the present rights of the possessor were gradually carved down and the coexistent interests became qualitative as well as quantitative.

Finally it should be noted that, in respect of the original character of coexistence, two estates, that of the reversioner and that of the freeholder subject to copyhold, retain at least the form of tenures to this day. While an estate rather than a tenure, the modern concept is, nevertheless, "that between the reversioner and the tenant of the particular estate a *tenure* exists—that the latter *holds of* the former."[216] And in the case of copyhold there are also two holders, "for the lord being the freeholder, his rights of ownership remain untouched, except so far as they are limited by the copyholder's rights which have supervened."[217]

[209] Pollock and Maitland, op. cit., I, p. 232.
[210] Pollock and Maitland, op. cit., I, p. 237.
[211] Pollock and Maitland, op. cit., II, p. 9.
[212] Holdsworth, op. cit., II, p. 249.
[213] Holdsworth, op. cit., II, p. 248.
[214] See Holdsworth, op. cit., III, p. 122.
[215] See Pollock and Maitland, op. cit., II, p. 9.
[216] Digby, op. cit., p. 260.
[217] Digby, op. cit., p. 292. And elsewhere Digby says, "A trace of the older meaning remains in the opposition of *freehold* to *copyhold* tenure" (p. 162).

5. *The Essence of the New Form of Property*

Thus in the course of time it developed that the junction of two or more property relations, in the same land, each so close to what is called ownership that the authorities give this title now to one and now to the other, did not as a practical matter inhibit land and the interests in it from moving in exchange as an article of commerce. In effect, when sub-infeudation was prevented, alienation by substitution, now made free, and the creation of the complex subordinate estates were greatly stimulated. Here, some six hundred years ago, at a stage which lawyers are apt to regard as primitive, we find fully developed a system of property in land, highly complex and yet so flexible and so liquid that even our modern specialties, the outgrowths of the chose in action, hampered as they are by antiquated theory, can hardly better it. In spite of the improvement of general law and order it is questionable if the effective protection now afforded these new forms is as good as the landholders enjoyed in the time of Henry II.

It should be clear to the reader by this time that the structure of landed property of medieval England, which we have seen gradually developing out of the political organization of feudalism, and which consisted of the various tenures and estates, fails to fit, if indeed it does not deny, the modern as well as the Roman concept of ownership. It is a bird of another feather. In some of the quotations we have cited the word is used—carelessly used—by modern scholars. But the word as well as the concept was unknown at the time.[218] Maitland remarks, "That the law of England knows no ownership of land, or will concede such ownership only to the king, is a dogma that has never entered the head of Glanville or of Bracton."[219] The reason is plain. If these writers were using the word *dominium* in a sense allied to "ownership," it was because they were mistakenly applying the classic Roman sense—revived by the Italian glossators—to the term *dominium* which had in the meantime come to signify rather the several orders of feudal mastery; something more like "seignory." At the time there was no word or concept for "ownership." It is

[218] Maitland states, Pollock and Maitland, op. cit., II, p. 153, Note, that the word "owner" begins to come into use in the fourteenth century, and "ownership" only in the late sixteenth century. Coke identifies absolute "ownership" with "property" and applies it to the tenant in fee. The Bankruptcy Act of 1623 helped to "give legal currency" to the word "owner." The word "possessor" is very ancient and runs through the Middle Ages. It was the predecessor of the word "owner." It is used in King James' Bible. But neither "property" nor "owner" appear there. The word "property" occurred throughout the Middle Ages in French and Latin forms, but it hardly appeared in the English form until the eighteenth century.

[219] Pollock and Maitland, op. cit., II, p. 2.

true that the thirteenth century used the word for lord and for lordship to apply indiscriminately to anyone having any sort of control over a thing. But it is the thought of later times which ascribes to what came to be called the "tenant-paravail," the terre tenant, something akin to ownership. And it is this afterthought which sees in the space of five centuries the transfer, at least in theory, of what is conceived to be "ownership," from the "tenant-paravail" to the "lord-paramount," from the terre tenant to the sovereign.[220]

The nature of this relation was not ownership.[221] It was, as we have said, lineal – "dependent and derivative" – a complex of concurrent but qualitatively differing seisins, culminating in one with which went occupancy.[222] Each was "held of" its predecessor up to the theoretical apex. It savoured more of loan than gift for, except in substitution, the givers were always "Indian givers."[223] Maitland says, ". . . the old land-loan was a temporary gift, the gift [feudal] was a permanent loan. . ."[224] And this aphorism has the rare distinction, for aphorisms, of being almost exactly true. Give (*do*) meant to transfer, or grant, seisin.[225] It was accomplished, as in Rome, by *traditio*, by "livery of seisin" (delivery of seisin). Seisin was not ownership (*dominium*). Nor was it possession in any corporeal sense. Several seisins, of different orders, could coexist in respect of the one piece of land. This is confirmed by all authorities, who nevertheless persist in the attempt to identify some certain seisin with their preconceived idea of ownership and to treat the variety as if they were only claims of greater or less validity to the one thing, seisin – their *idée fixe*. For example take Holdsworth. "Seisin, rela-

[220] If one ignores intermediate changes during the whole millennium from the seventh to the seventeenth centuries then one may discover that, at the end, such a transfer has taken place and that the *domaine* of Roman Gaul, which, as Fustel states, was tributary to no one and not even subject to eminent domain, has finally been converted into a qualified property subject to the eminent domain of the state.

[221] Pollock and Maitland, op. cit., II, p. 152, say, "Englishmen are accustomed to hear it said that our medieval law knew, and even that our modern law knows, no absolute ownership of land."

[222] Pollock and Wright, *An Essay on Possession in the Common Law*, p. 49, say, "It must be remembered that gradations of freehold tenure had already made men familiar with the conception of the lord being seised of rent and service while the tenant was seised of the land itself."

[223] An excellent insight into this crucial subject is presented by Vinogradoff, *Villainage*, p. 330. "That English law should regard these tenants under leases for life as freeholders, should, that is, throw them into one great class with tenants who have heritable rights . . . who are in fact if not in name the owners of the land, is very remarkable; hirers are mingled with owners, because according to the great generalization of English feudalism every owner is after all but a hirer."

[224] Pollock and Maitland, op. cit., II, p. 12.

[225] "Feoffment is a species of the genus gift." Pollock and Maitland, op. cit., II, p. 82, citing Britton, I, 221.

tively good or bad is Bracton's theme." ". . . his 'dominium' is really a seisin which no one can dispute."[226] "The best right to seisin is still the only form of ownership recognized by English law."[227] ". . . as the result of the doctrine of seisin in property law, the common law knew no such thing as absolute dominium: all it knew was a variety of rights to seisin, older or better, or younger or weaker, relatively good and relatively bad, but all alike entitling the person de facto seised to the rights of ownership."[228] "Seisin is prima facie ownership. The person seised has the rights of an owner: the person disseised . . . has none of the rights as an owner."[229] "A man [with possession] may have an estate in the land though he has no right to it."[230]

In fact the object of each coexisting seisin was coming to be regarded as itself a legal 'thing' – some sort of legal interest appertaining to a certain piece of land. And already the distinction was being made between those 'things' which were regarded as corporeal and those which were regarded as incorporeal. The estates were corporeal. And Holdsworth, following the lead which we have already seen applied to the same distinction in Roman law, lays it down that this doctrine of estates as corporeal things is due to a "defect in the analytic faculty." "An immature system of law has some difficulty in grasping the idea of a legal right apart from the thing over which that right exists."[231] He cannot reconcile his late Romanized cast of thought to the medieval English concept of the 'thing.' So imbued is his mind with the distinction between the thing as a material object (the civilian's notion of *res*) and the rights with reference to it (the civilian's notion of *ius*) that it is impossible for him to see that the early English idea, somewhat like the classic Roman, was that a 'thing' was never itself material but was always a relation of some character to, or in respect of, a material object. A corporeal 'thing' involved the present or prospective possessory right to the material object. An incorporeal 'thing' involved no possessory, or at best only a fractional possessory, right to the material object. Or, perhaps, it is better to say that it involved only a lesser material object or an immaterial benefit "issuing out" of the principal one. And,

[226] Holdsworth, op. cit., II, p. 263. Digby, op. cit., p. 109, says, "In the great majority of cases when litigation arose as to the right to land, it would be sufficient to decide which of the two litigants had the right of immediate actual possession."

[227] Holdsworth, op. cit., III, p. 93.

[228] Holdsworth, op. cit., III, p. 495.

[229] Holdsworth, op. cit., III, p. 95.

[230] Holdsworth, op. cit., II, p. 353. "A 'tortious fee simple' was valid against everyone but the person truly entitled." Pollock and Wright, op. cit., p. 5.

[231] Holdsworth, op. cit., II, pp. 350-351.

since it had to do with land, this concept of possession — a sort of privilege of various kinds of activity upon, or use of, the land as an arena — is in many respects more realistic than the modern concept of occupation which attempts to visualize the possessor as exclusively holding this arena in the hollow of his hand. At any rate these medieval categories are not an "immature system." The use of these terms is classic Roman, not English; somewhat sophisticated; certainly not naïve. We shall see whether, apart from the inappropriateness of the borrowed Roman phraseology this medieval idea, as compared with the legal concrete concept of the thing, does not continue better to represent the facts of today — jural as well as infra-jural.

D. *Subordinate Property in Land*

1. *The Incorporeal 'Things' — The Non-possessory Seisins*

In defining the incorporeal 'thing' Maitland says, "Any permanent right which is of a transferable nature, at all events if it has what we may call a territorial ambit, is thought of as a thing that is very like a piece of land. Just because it is a thing, it is transferable."[232] The relation is thought of not as "many ownerships of one thing," but as "many things each with its owner."[233] Thus, as we have said, it was the relation and not the land which was conceived as the 'thing.' Even the incorporeal 'things' were "tenements," since they pertained to land and were "held of" a lord. One was enfeoffed of them. And, as part of the feudal structure, they were thus included in the larger term "hereditament" and came, in time, to be known as the "incorporeal hereditaments." As hereditaments they descended to the feudal heir and were therefore real not personal property.[234] And even today they continue to be real rights.[235] All of which puzzles the modern lawyer with his confirmed notion of the *Dinglichkeit* of a thing. Digby says they "cannot be said to be rights over land, or indeed to have any subjects [objects] at all," although he concedes they "possess some characteristics common to rights over land,"[236] and are rights *in rem*. And we have noted that Maitland conceives they were "thought of as a thing that is very like a piece

[232] Pollock and Maitland, op. cit., II, p. 124.

[233] Pollock and Maitland, op. cit., II, p. 4.

[234] Today hereditaments include anything which can be inherited and may, therefore, be real, personal or mixed.

[235] Jenks, op. cit., p. 93, states that the development of incorporeal hereditaments as real rights was due to the fact that "real" or "proprietary" claims were, in the fourteenth century, becoming scientific and effectual.

[236] Op. cit., p. 303.

of land." The fact is that the earliest 'things' (i.e. bundles of property rights) "had a territorial ambit," or "issued out of" the land because the land was the basis of the organization of society, because the manor was "a highly complex and organized aggregate of corporeal and incorporeal things,"[237] all protected alike by the Assize of Novel Disseisin which "is regarded as a highly successful institution." While incorporeal 'things' "lie in grant," and corporeal "lie in livery,"[238] nevertheless the grant of incorporeal 'things' resembles livery of seisin and gives seisin. One had to maintain something resembling possession; to make use of the 'thing.' The donee of an advowson had to "present," etc. Rents were incorporeal hereditaments. So were the offices and dignities (the modern peerage). The favourite curiosity, which receives more attention than it deserves, is the "advowson," the right of presentation to a vacant benefice (perhaps a popular provision for younger sons). But the important surviving members of this group are the English correspondents of the Roman servitudes, principally easements and profits a prendre.

These incorporeal hereditaments are anomalies to the theorists. Modern jurisprudence has succeeded in fitting them in, so far as the servitudes among them are concerned. These are *iura in re aliena.* But the offices, etc., seem to be misfits. Their difficulties are well explained by the very explanations of the *raison d'être* of these curiosities which are given by modern scholars. The thirteenth century, says Maitland, "is fertile of 'incorporeal things.'"[239] "The yet feeble law of contract is supplemented by a generous liberality in the creation of incorporeal things. The man of the thirteenth century does not say, 'I agree that you may have so many trees out of my copse every year,' he says, 'I give and grant you so much wood.'"[240] And Holdsworth says,[241] "In a feudal state where property and office are confused [sic], under a primitive legal system which has a highly developed land law, but no theory of contract, the list of incorporeal things tends to expand, and to follow the most highly developed branch of the law." Thus it is the generally accepted system of property rights *in personam,* itself founded on the earliest presuppositions of Roman law and its primitive classificatory genitive, in the light of which the English system seems archaic. Perhaps, if it had not been for what Maitland speaks of, in another connection, as the early English "flirtation with Romanism," the peculiar English genius

237 Pollock and Maitland, op. cit., II, pp. 124 and 145.
238 Pollock and Maitland, op. cit., II, p. 93.
239 Pollock and Maitland, op. cit., II, p. 3.
240 Pollock and Maitland, op. cit., II, p. 146.
241 Holdsworth, op. cit., II, p. 355.

might have demonstrated as highly developed a law of incorporeal as it did of corporeal 'things.' As it was, the civilian theory of contract stunted it in its infancy. And the prepossession of the classificatory genitive came in with its hard and fast distinction between *meum* and *tuum*, to prevent the application of the same plan to other objects of property. Thus the idea was confined to this system of possessory rights in land. It was already too late to touch that. Today we can still see in these incorporeal 'things' the germ of the modern idea, just beginning to appear, that property in any object is a bundle of rights, separable into diverse assortments. Each may be, and then was, called a 'thing.' Each may be held separately. There may be no owner of the whole object.

2. *The Lesser Estates—The Non-seisinal Possessions*

At first "every proprietary right must have a seisin at its root," and the chain of title must be a transfer or inheritance of this seisin.[242] Since the tenure of land for a term of years was beneath the dignity of a seisin, the termor, or the tenant at will, did not have a true proprietary right but held, like the tenant in villeinage, in the name of the lessor or lord (*tenet nomine alieno*), and was excluded from the use of proprietary actions. The effect was "to exclude interests for a term of years from the category of real property"[243] because this category was reserved originally for those certain interests in land which were based on seisin and were therefore protected by the real, or strictly proprietary actions.[244] Later the classification was modified and the distinction between real and personal property came to be applied according as these interests were or were not heritable by the feudal heir.[245] But it was this "youthful flirtation with Roman-

[242] Pollock and Maitland, op. cit., II, p. 80.

[243] Holdsworth, op. cit., II, p. 205.

[244] Holdsworth says, op. cit., III, p. 29, "We do not meet the term 'real property' in the mediaeval common law; but the foundations of that conception were laid in the rules which determined the sphere of these real actions." And, III, p. 3, "In the developed common law a real action was an action in which the specific thing demanded could be recovered [not exactly the Roman action *in rem*]; and, as, in the great majority of cases, it was only certain interests in or incorporeal rights over land which were so recoverable," such interests and rights came to be defined as real property, or real estate. By the end of the thirteenth century real actions only lay (1) for land, (2) held by a free tenure, (3) under certain interests. See Holdsworth, op. cit., II, p. 261.

In this connection it is interesting to note that Holdsworth, op. cit., III, p. 359, says, "Everywhere we can trace the leading doctrines and fundamental distinctions of the common law to differences between the classes of actions and to epochs in the history of some one class of actions." Which appears to be a frank acknowledgement that Maine's aphorism, to the effect that substantive law seems to be secreted in the interstices of procedure, applies not only to primitive codes.

[245] Digby, op. cit., p. 243, says, "Thus [because they passed by will, not by primogeniture] leasehold interests came to be classed with personal property."

ism," as Maitland[246] calls the borrowing of the distinction in name—though not the distinction in character—between the real actions (*in rem*) and the personal actions (*in personam*), which resulted eventually in dividing English land law into two halves; that concerned with real property in land and that concerned with personal property in land. And it was in this way that there arose that special class of personal property (i.e. originally property protected only by personal action) called chattels real.[247]

Having erected this system of classification upon the foundation of the real (proprietary) actions, the development of English law proceeded to remove the foundation. The first step consisted in the introduction of the Roman concept of possession as a sort of secondary seisin—and eventually distinct from it—to be the special attribute of the lesser chattel interests in land as well as, later, of the non-possessory real interests.[248] The termor was beginning to get a real right by the end of the thirteenth century.[249] It came about through this new doctrine of possession and the accompanying possessory action, "*quare ejecit infra terminum.*"[250] And this in turn brought to him the dignity of an estate. Later the action of trespass began to be the more usual resort of both the copyholder and the termor. When, in time, the scope of this action came to include specific recovery and it became possible to recover by it more than damages, namely the restoration of the term itself, then it became the serious rival, as well, of Novel Disseisin and other real actions.[251] Finally, with the disappearance of the original proprietary actions, real property came to rest upon this foundation, which had in the

[246] Pollock and Maitland, op. cit., II, p. 115.

[247] Digby, op. cit., p. 243, says, "Since however they are rights over things immovable, they received the mongrel name of 'chattels real.'"

[248] At first (in the thirteenth century) seisin and possession were synonymous terms. Then, to comply with the Roman maxim that there could not be two possessions, it became necessary to treat the freehold and the reversion separately. The term seisin was still used of the freeholder so that, after Littleton, seisin is used of freehold and possession for anything less. Thus an occupying freeholder is both seised and possessed. But a freeholder letting for years is seised of the freehold but not possessed of the land. The lessee possesses that. In this way there was developed a "double set of rights, and (so long as the real actions were in practical use) also of remedies." Pollock and Wright, op. cit., p. 49. So Coke *On Littleton,* I, 1, 10, says, ". . . *seisin* is properly applied to freehold, and *possessed* or *possession* properly to goods and chattels; although sometime the one is used instead of the other."

[249] See Holdsworth, op. cit., II, p. 354.

[250] Digby, op. cit., p. 176, finds in Bracton a passage "very remarkable, as noting the precise point at which terms of years came to be recognised as estates in land." It is as follows: ". . . Ad feoffatum vero pertinet proprietas feodi et liberum tenementum, firmarius vero nihil sibi vindicare poterit nisi usumfructum, scilicet quod libere uti posset et sine impedimento feoffati percipere fructum" (fol. 27). Which leads Digby and Markby, op. cit., p. 169, to consider a term of years as a *ius in re aliena.*

[251] Holdsworth, op. cit., III, p. 27.

meantime been first built under the rights which, in the beginning, had not been even proprietary.

To the class of chattels real, containing these lesser estates, were also annexed the remains of the feudal casualties and, at various times, certain of the conditional (creditors') estates and even that created by the alienation of a life estate, the estate *pur auter vie.*[252] The surviving members of this group of legal anomalies are historical accidents, of interest to antiquarians only, and shed no light on the nature or substance of property. But the class is of interest because it explains the resulting status as personal property of the modern leasehold in American law—an evidence of the peculiar persistence of legal inconsistencies.

E. *Property Not in Land*

1. *Involuntary Loss of Possession*

We now leave the subject of the land law, which Jenks says[253] resembles rather a chaos than a system—the most jumbled part of what English lawyers themselves have called "that ungodly jumble"—and turn to the relatively unimportant (for our purpose) subject of movables. The term "chattel" was not coterminous with that of "movables" for, as we have seen, it extended to all personal property—property supported only by personal actions—and thus included the lesser rights in land. Nevertheless the etymology of the word shows that its principal original meaning was "cattle" (i.e. the chief form of early movable property). It is interesting in this connection to note that chattels were non-feudal (i. e. non-heritable) property. Whereas we have found that feudal property was a more or less direct descendant of those forms of intra-familial property in Rome which was represented by the term *peculium*—also derived from cattle—it was heritable on the model of the *familia*. On the other hand, chattels—semantically cognate in name—but not descendants at law, were, like the Roman *pecunia*, the first property to be subject to devise as soon as any system was available to carry out the will of the testator after his death. Thus real property in England, the descendant of the earlier derivative and dependent property of Rome, apes, in respect of succession, the system of *dominium*, the absolute property of Rome; whereas personal property in England, originally existing in a form which was doubtless derivative and dependent, had

[252] Holdsworth, op. cit., III, p. 123, says the thirteenth century regarded this as a chattel like a term of years, though it is now a freehold, like its parent.

[253] Op. cit., p. 241.

long ceased to be so and so could copy the early freedom of devise which was first attained in Rome by its congener, the *pecunia.*

"Owing to the apparently arbitrary decision of the old Common Law Courts not to allow a 'real' or proprietary action for the recovery of chattels, there has never been very much of what may be called 'objective' law of chattels corporeal in England."[254] "Indeed we may be left doubting whether there was any right in movable goods that deserved the name of ownership."[255] ". . . so far as chattels corporeal, or 'goods' were concerned, they did not build up this law as a code relating to proprietary interests. They approached it through the Law of Tort. . ."[256] Since, "the law gave no real action for the recovery of chattels, but only these personal actions of trespass and detinue,"[257] the criterion as to the right over a movable chattel came to be that of physical possession.[258] Already in the thirteenth century "Bracton's words show that . . . there was no real action for movables."[259] The remedy for the involuntary loss of a chattel was by personal action for tort (as above) and for its equivalent rather than its recovery.[260] Thus "the owner of goods has a real right; but it can only be enforced in a personal action for damages. He can get no specific restitution at common law."[261] On the other hand, "the person in possession of a thing which has gone out of its original owner's control without his consent has a title which is defeasible because another title may be asserted which is older and therefore better; and he runs some risk of being charged with theft. Subject to that he is a possessor, and as regards third persons is treated as though he were an owner."[262]

[254] Jenks, op. cit., p. 271.

[255] Pollock and Maitland, op. cit., II, p. 153.

[256] Jenks, op. cit., p. 124.

[257] Holdsworth, op. cit., III, p. 328.

[258] But we have seen how the possessory remedies came to supplant those of seisin. It is this process which leads Pollock and Wright to say, op. cit., p. 5, "The Common Law never had any adequate process in the case of land, or any process at all in the case of goods, for the vindication of ownership pure and simple. So feeble and precarious was property without possession, or rather without possessory remedies, in the eyes of mediaeval lawyers, that Possession largely usurped not only the substance but the name of Property; and when distinction became necessary in modern times, the clumsy term 'special property' was employed to denote the rights of a possessor not being owner."

[259] Holdsworth, op. cit., III, p. 322, and Bracton, fol. 102 b.

[260] Jenks, op. cit., p. 60, says, ". . . as Bracton informs us, it was the business of every plaintiff who sought to recover a chattel by action, to put a price upon it; and then, even if the defendant no longer held the chattel, he might be made liable for its value." And Jenks gives this as the reason – though "excessive respect for possession" of chattels had something to do with it – for the French rules, "*en fait de meubles, possession vaut titre*" and "*meuble n'a suyte.*"

[261] Holdsworth, op. cit., III, p. 328.

[262] Holdsworth, op. cit., II, p. 79.

2. *Voluntary Loss of Possession—Bailment*

"The general term used to express any voluntary parting with possession of a chattel is the term 'bailment'."[263] Maitland, speaking of the rights of the bailor says, "We may call him owner or say that the thing belongs to him, but our old-fashioned law treats him very much as if he had no 'real' right and no more than the benefit of a contract. Hence the dependent tenure of a chattel is impossible."[264] Nevertheless in the development of the indigenous institution of bailment there gradually appeared another instance of a dual property—the rights of the bailor and the bailee, which, if not dependent either on the other, were certainly coexisting and which, for this reason, deserve some attention. Holdsworth describes the early stage of this property interest as follows: with movables in early times "ownership as such, possession as such, is not protected; what is remedied is an involuntary loss of possession. The practical result is, to use modern terms, that an owner who has involuntarily lost possession can take proceedings to recover his property, and to recover a penalty for the theft, against anyone into whose possession the thing has been traced. But if he has voluntarily parted with possession—if, for instance, he has bailed his property to another—it is the bailee, and the bailee alone, who can act if the property is lost. In such a case the owner's remedy is against the bailee. 'Hand muss Hand wahren'—where I have reposed my trust, there I must seek it—was the rule of the old law; for 'mobilia non habent sequelam.' The person in possession with the consent of the owner is treated as though he were the owner as regards third persons."[265] But, "early in the thirteenth century, the bailor's rights of property are distinctly recognized, and the bailee's rights are based on his liability over."[266] The bailee was still given these rights of action, but it was coming to be on the grounds of his responsibility to the bailor. Terry[267] supposes that the peculiar form of permissive possession appertaining to the bailee, which "temporarily and provisionally changed the owner-

[263] Holdsworth, op. cit., III, p. 336. Actually bailments included in early times arrangements some of which would now be construed as agencies and some as loans. They included money entrusted to be "bestowed" in some business and money entrusted as a deposit—not a *depositum* but a loan. These came to be differentiated from bailments, but in the sixteenth and seventeenth centuries they were still usually called bailments.

[264] Pollock and Maitland, op. cit., II, p. 182.

[265] Holdsworth, op. cit., II, p. 79.

[266] Holdsworth, op. cit., III, p. 345. But Terry, op. cit., p. 324, says, "Afterwards, when an action was also allowed to the bailor and the ancient law had been well forgotten, the theory was inverted, and it was said that the bailee was allowed to have an action against the wrong-doer because he was answerable over to the bailor; which is the principle that we now find laid down in the books."

[267] Op. cit., p. 328.

ship as well, so as to vest the property in the possessor and leave to the original owner nothing but a *chose* in action" was the original thing called "special property"—the name still given to the rights of bailees. Thus when it became diminished and derivative (or secondary), it retained the dignity of this name and we have in the case of bailments two coexisting properties, the general and the special (the bailor's and the bailee's), of somewhat different nature.[268]

Before leaving the subject of land and chattels one general point seems worthy of note. The original sources of the distinction between real and personal property, the real actions, were abolished in the nineteenth century. In the meantime the distinctions in proprietary character and in heritability also disappeared. Present resemblances are far more important than differences. Holdsworth's analysis of the closely parallel roads along which the law has developed upon these two classes of property suggests that this resemblance has always been much closer than legal doctrine is accustomed to acknowledge. He says,[269] "That the common law has, throughout its history, applied to the possession of chattels the same general principles as it applied to the seisin of freehold interests in land, will be clear if we look at the following facts and rules of our law." These facts are: (1) that "seisin" and "possession" are used (originally at least) convertibly; (2) the rule that two persons cannot possess the same thing at the same time is applied to chattels as well as to land; (3) the person in possession is the one having all the rights of owner—"the converter of a chattel, like the disseisor of land had the power of present enjoyment and the power of alienation"; (4) the person out of possession had merely the right to recover—a chose in action which was inalienable; (5) "a delivery of possession was, in the thirteenth century, in all cases as necessary for the valid transfer of a chattel as a 'livery of seisin' was for the valid transfer of a freehold interest in land." If it is conceded that there is little evidence, in the case of chattels corporeal, of a right which might be called ownership, this parallelism supports the conclusion we have already reached that the same was true in the case of land.

[268] Dicey, *A Treatise on . . . Parties to an Action,* p. 377, Note q, calls special property some "sort of temporary or provisional ownership." Story, *Commentaries on the Laws of Bailments,* sec. 93, considers it some right in the thing, of the nature of property, which he calls "possessory interest." Terry, op. cit., p. 326, says it is "often used as synonymous with 'possessory interest,'" denoting any possession sufficient for the purpose and as distinguished from detention. Markby, op. cit., p. 192, calls it "possession through a representative," and seems to think that Savigny's interpretation of the Roman law which construes legal possession as not passing to the bailee, also applies to the English law.

[269] Holdsworth, op. cit., III, pp. 352-3.

3. *Voluntary Losses of Possession—Contract*

Glanville, writing at the end of the twelfth century, says: "But we briefly pass over the foregoing Contracts, arising as they do from the consent of private individuals; because . . . the King's Court does not usually take cognizance of them; nor, indeed, with such Contracts as may be considered in the light of private Agreements, does the King's Court intermeddle."[270] From this expression one may judge the stage at which the law of contract had arrived at the period when the land law was approaching the finished state heretofore described. At about this time the study of Roman law was being revived in Western Europe. Some of it had filtered through to England, so that Glanville used the Roman names for the only contracts he mentions. And Bracton, according to Maine, "put off on his countrymen as a compendium of pure English law a treatise of which the entire form and a third of the contents were directly borrowed from the Corpus Juris. . ."[271] Holdsworth states that these "Roman theories of contract never took root," for "the theory of the English law is contained in the doctrine of consideration,"[272] though he admits that, "even at the present day English writers who discuss the general theory of contract use Roman terms borrowed from Savigny. . ."[273] One may resolve this apparent contradiction. Legal theorists, off and on from the time of Bracton, have endeavoured to rationalize the English law of contract by fitting to it the perfectly logical Roman theory. The fit is not good, and it may be doubted whether it is possible at all to organize this legal chaos on rational lines, for it hardly seems to have been constructed on any theory whatever. It is for this reason that most of the light which we shall obtain on modern property in contract will come, not from any English theory of the law of contract or even from English practice, but from analogies with other English forms of property. For our modern Anglo-American law of contract has either a Roman theory, misfitting modern conditions by nearly twenty centuries, or it has none.

There are, however, certain points about the beginnings of the English contract law which are of interest for our purpose. The early view of debt characteristic of both Roman and English law is well evidenced by the English action of debt. It developed as if the failure to pay money owed was a tort and not a breach of contract. Or rather, it showed that, originally, what we now call breach of

[270] Glanville, X, 18.

[271] *Ancient Law*, p. 79. Maitland in the "Introduction" to his *Bracton and Azo*, warmly defends Bracton against this charge. It is my impression, however, that there is much truth in it.

[272] Op. cit., III, pp. 412-413.

[273] Holdsworth, op. cit., II, p. 276.

contract was a certain species of tort—a deprivation of rightful possession.[274] ". . . originally it [debt] was hardly distinguishable from detinue" (i.e. detention of a chattel). But in the course of time it tended (especially if brought "in the debet") to become more contractual, while detinue remained proprietary and delictual.[275] In respect of its seeming to sound in tort it resembled the early Roman action. In respect of its proprietary character it did not. And this indicates a much less hard and fast notion of property than existed in Rome. With the Romans an object could only 'belong' in one classification (genitive) at a time. In early England it could 'belong' in several. In Rome the *obligatio* was clear cut, even at first. It gave no property to the obligee. In early England money lent—or owed on an incompleted sale—was still, or already, regarded as belonging to the lender, or vendor,[276] as being his by right, though he had not possession. And this was even more true of other non-fungible chattels.

In part the explanation of this difference lies in the fact that the Roman obligation was so much more than a right of action. It was a personal power over the debtor. In other words Roman law successfully quashed the proprietary rights of the creditor by leaving him, or giving him, an adequate substitute. This English law failed to do. Hence the frequent phrase, "*mere* chose in action." One never hears of a "*mere* obligation" in Roman law.

By a remarkable and extrinsic process both these actions, debt and detinue, without changing form or even theory to any great extent, became the first English actions to be called both contractual and personal. Bracton applied the Roman rule that if an action is purely personal only damages can be secured. Damages in England at that time were money awards still conceived to be the means of composition of wrongs, and applicable to injuries sustained. This was a doubtful remedy for one who was voluntarily out of possession. On the other hand it was not yet the practice to enforce promises, particularly the specific performance of promises. This left some form of real action as the only means of securing possession of a specific

[274] In the action of debt "the defendant was conceived of as having in his possession something belonging to the plaintiff which he might not rightfully keep, but ought to surrender." Ames, "Parol Contracts prior to Assumpsit," 8 *Harvard Law Review* (1894), pp. 252, 260.

[275] Holdsworth, op. cit., III, p. 420. But "the proprietary traits of the action of debt survived to the end," and, "to the last the law was never quite clear as to whether detinue sounded in tort or in contract." Holdsworth, op. cit., II, p. 368.

[276] It is possible that, in view of Glanville's statement quoted above, it is a mistake to think of the early action of debt as even a beginning of a law of contract. It may have been wholly a proprietary action, not involving the notion of contract at all. From the similarity of its occasion contemporary lawyers, beginning to be learned in the Roman law, may have applied this classification to it and thus, in the course of time, have changed its nature.

object. In that case the "plaintiff got the *res* which he claimed."[277] Since all specific recovery must be by means of real actions, the Writ of Debt (and of Detinue) was almost identical with the Writ of Right (the prototype real action). For the idea was, as Jenks shows, that "'the very debt itself' [i.e. the money loaned] was to be recovered."[278] Money was then deemed to be a material object of the same order as other chattels. But money is fungible. So, in the course of time, the nature and form of the action, which seemed to the thirteenth century to be a means of specific restitution, came to appear to be no more than a limitation in its aim which prevented it from being used except for liquidated (i.e. ascertained) damages. In a somewhat different manner the same thing happened to detinue. There the *res* was not money. It was a non-fungible chattel. But it was found necessary to require that a price be put on the chattel to cover the contingency that the defendant might no longer have it. This resulted in money awards rather than specific restitution or performance. It converted the action, in this respect, into a personal one, and the usual award came to be, as in the case of debt, assimilated to damages for the composition of wrongs. Jenks[279] suggests that this change took place merely because "it was found convenient to substitute a money judgment for a decree of specific restoration." At any rate it resulted in closing the only avenue by which, at that time, specific restitution could be secured. And the two parallel processes succeeded in converting these two real actions into the origins of the procedural law of contract. But the change was a change in result only.

Eventually the English law, permeated and constrained by its own peculiar theory of possession, must—as it begins at a somewhat later period to take cognizance at all of those rights among others which are not capable, by hook or by crook, of being included in any of its various possessory categories—devise a residuary classification for them. This is the nondescript remainder—the choses in action. They consist of all less than present possessory rights which are nevertheless recognized at law. They are rights (and therefore 'things') of a most highly incorporeal nature because no present possession is conceived to adhere to them. Thus in actual fact they represent little more than a right to bring an action. On the other hand the very reason for the right of action is itself the basis of their status as 'things'—incorporeal 'things'—for, as a class, they are all conceived to represent the right of the dispossessed to be repossessed—his persisting property in an object, possession of which he has temporarily

[277] Holdsworth, op. cit., II, p. 247.
[278] Jenks, op. cit., pp. 58-59.
[279] Op. cit., p. 61.

surrendered or failed to gain. The recovery is of this object or its equivalent. Choses in action are thought of along somewhat the same lines as the future estates in land, which are at first included with them. They are slices of a right of possession which has been "projected upon the plane of time." They are rights of the plaintiff pertaining to a material, or quasi-material, object; not rights of the plaintiff over the person of the defendant. To this obdurately un-Romanized viewpoint we shall have occasion to advert later.

Gradually, as a law of contract appeared, "much of that miscellaneous mass of incorporeal things, which, as we have seen, is a peculiar characteristic of the law of the earlier Middle Ages, disappeared, because men found that they could effect their objects more easily by making a contract than by conveying a *res*."[280] But the change of these arrangements from such incorporeal 'things' to rights of contract placed them at the opposite extreme of the property system. For, as we have seen, almost all things (objects) not in possession had come to be 'things' (or choses) in action. And to these, or to most of them, were denied the two principal attributes of property rights. They were quite generally non-assignable and a surprisingly large proportion did not survive after death. The gradual breaking down or evasion of the restriction on alienability by means of novation, the power of attorney, and the adoption from the law merchant of the "negotiable instrument," was a subsequent development. But at first the creditor as to debts, the reversioner as to a reversion, and the remainderman as to a remainder had a non-transferable right. "A bailor was unable to transfer his interest in a chattel." "The disseisee of land or chattels could not invest another with the right to recover the 'res' or its value."[281] As to survival, Holdsworth suggests that Coke invented the maxim "*actio personalis moritur cum persona*," and that *personalis* may have been a copyist's mistake for *poenalis*.[282] For "generally the rule was applicable only to causes of action in tort;" and even with them it was Bracton's idea "that any obligation which is penal [*poena*] dies with the person; but that an obligation to restore something [*res persecutoria*] does not." So Holdsworth says the rule of survival of actions excluded "all causes of action in tort whether to person or property;" but probably always included cases where liability existed for a wrong done by the de-

[280] Holdsworth, op. cit., III, p. 454.

[281] Ames, "The Disseisin of Chattels," 3 *Harvard Law Review* (1890), p. 337.

[282] Hearn, *The Theory of Legal Duties and Rights*, p. 160, says, "Mr. Poste happily conjectures that the word *personalis* is a mere copyist's mistake for *poenalis*, a mistake I may add which might easily arise when the abridged form (*p. lis*) was the same for each of the two words." But it seems to the writer more likely that the primitive idea persisted and that, in early English law, *personalis* was synonymous with *poenalis*.

ceased which had enriched his estate. This, however, is not certain since, at first, an executor could neither sue nor be sued on any grounds. About the end of the thirteenth century this fault was corrected.[283]

The most adequate explanation of this extraordinary process of expropriation seems to have been the excessive respect for possession and the excessive fear of "champerty and maintenance" that developed as the common law was getting under way.[284] As to the first, Jenks[285] suggests that "in early days, the precise situation of the border line between a chose in possession and a chose in action evidently depended on the extent to which self-help was permitted." In other words, if one did not or could not possess, one had nothing but a strictly personal life interest in a chose in action. Undoubtedly the analogous restriction on Roman obligations had some influence as well.

If the reader has carefully followed this presentation of the nature of the chose in action it must have seemed a bundle of inconsistencies. And so it was. But not so much so as it seems at first glance. The early chose in action was property in the sense of its being deemed a right to recover a specific object. It was not property in respect of alienability or survival. There are reasons back of this, sound for those times. In the first place it did not seem possible to convey the object to which the chose in action appertained. For how could one convey what he did not have? Or how could one convey again what he had already parted with, even if only temporarily? The whole concept of conveyance represented by "livery of seisin," and even the grant of occupation of incorporeal 'things,' was against it. In addition to the difficulties encountered also by choses in action dealing with land, those dealing with chattels faced still another difficulty. As a practical matter it was possible to create future estates in land because land would "stand without hitching." But "*meuble n'a suyte*" was a statement of fact. Chattels were difficult to identify or trace. And for that reason incorporeal interests in chattels were more difficult to conceive and to apply than those in land. The result was that if one wished to alienate a chattel which was "in action" (i.e. incorporeal) the first step was to recover it. For that purpose one had a right of action.

This process of development of law was taking place exactly at the time when the money economy was breaking down feudalism. It was this subtle revolution which helped to interpose the money

[283] See Holdsworth, op. cit., III, pp. 578-579.

[284] ". . . mediaeval Common Law had the greatest dislike to the assignment of rights which could only be enforced by legal proceedings. . ." Jenks, op. cit., p. 300.

[285] Op. cit., p. 279.

equivalent between the chose in action and the *res persecutoria.* As it did so debt and detinue became less specific. Then, too, the money award was indistinguishable from the thirteenth century relic of *wergeld.* Thus "damages" became an inclusive term for *res tanta* and for *poena.* This process brought these actions under the heading personal (or penal), without making them such in form or correctly so in Roman theory.

These original choses in action can be compared with three theoretical standards. In some respects they conform to, and in some respects they conflict with, each. They are property; and they are not property. They give rise to actions which are real in part and personal in part. And in some respects the actions appear to be founded on tort and in some upon contract. We cannot fit to them exactly either the Roman idea of the obligation and its personal action, or the English ideas of alienable rights of property, of possession, of specific recovery, or of damages for tort. They were a blend of all because they had grown up subject to the influence of all these conflicting ideas. But if we neglect these somewhat arbitrary and doctrinal labellings it remains possible realistically to analyse them. They were property in objects out of possession. Thus they were themselves incorporeal 'things.' It had not yet been discovered how, effectively and safely, to alienate such 'things' (except in land) without reference to the object to which they appertained. Later such a method was devised. When this was done the chose in action became full-fledged property. But in the meantime the object itself had become indeterminate instead of specific. Recovery of possession could be obtained, but only in other objects of an equal value taken out of the possessor's estate. Thus the original chose in action, or chattel incorporeal, became in its developed state true property, non-possessory, in indeterminate and fungible chattels.

F. *Summary*

The moving spirit of Roman law took effect as we have seen, in the *powers* accorded to the heads of *familiae* over other heads of *familiae* and over the members of their own *familiae.* The great bulk of the private law of Rome is given over to the provisions in regard to these two fields of authority, covered in the Law of Obligations and the Law of Persons respectively. In strong contrast to this we find the moving spirit of the common law to be the building up of barriers against domination by the feudal superiors. While it adopted a modified form of this feudal principle for its own peculiar property structure applied to land, nevertheless the whole tenor of the newer concept takes the form of protection against others, against those in authority as well as one's equals. English law is concerned primarily with protection in the undisturbed possession of physical objects. It deals only in the most rudimentary way, in its private law, with powers granted to certain persons over others.

The even more conspicuous difference between the English and the Roman systems of property has already been made quite apparent. To the classic Roman mind the absolute quality of *dominium* seemed so primordial, so fundamentally a part of the very nature of things, that it was taken for granted. The classificatory genitive was sufficient; and the technical terms for, and even the philosophy of, *dominium* are of later invention. From this point of view it appeared obvious that an object could not belong to more than one class at a time. It was either mine or yours unqualifiedly. There was no difference of degree. Nor did the idea permit two kinds of interest in an object to coexist.[286]

This simple and primitive prepossession coloured the Roman law of property. It led to the emphasis upon possession and delivery. Where a thing was, there it belonged. It led to the development of that outmoded masterpiece of Roman law, the law of contract. For presumptively a thing must change class when it changed place. In general it could not thereafter be recovered. Therefore some equivalent right must early be developed or trade would have been greatly hampered. This right was the right of the *obligatio*, conceived as a *iuris vinculum* long before *proprietas* was philosophized into a legal relation at all. But it was a bond to the person and not to his objects.[287] Thus each *familia* was a walled-in preserve, sufficient unto itself, within which objects were beyond the law. At each wall practically all external rights in objects terminated.

This was the spirit of the Roman law of property. We have called it the collateral system. Contrast it with the English, or lineal, system of landholding. There, ever since the law became self-conscious, lawyers have been trying to isolate the germ of this preconceived mode called ownership. But those who think they have succeeded in discovering something of the sort disagree as to its locus. Is it the right to the use inhering in the terre tenant; the *dominium* of the tenant in demesne; the *dominium* of some mesne lord; or that of the sovereign, of whom all land is, eventually and in the last anal-

[286] The coexisting titles of Quiritarian and Praetorian ownership ("*meum esse ex iure Quiritium*" and "*in bonis habere*") was but a tecnnical duplication because of two jurisdictions. "But where there was a bonitary owner the quiritary owner was entirely excluded. For all practical purposes there was but one owner. . ." Markby, op. cit., p. 169. There is also the minor inconsistency of the *iura in re aliena* which obviously puzzled the Romans themselves and which, in classic times, they did not know how to classify.

[287] In fact we do not find the word *ius* used with reference to objects in classic Roman law, except with the gerund, i.e. an act concerning them.

ysis, held? Among the estates, is it in the reversion, or in the present possessory freehold? Does this elusive relation move from rank to rank at different periods? Or does it, as a matter of fact, never exist at all? Is the lineal system a more highly evolved organization which simply defies the primitive classificatory genitive because it has progressed beyond that early stage? Does it represent the natural evolutionary process of differentiation under which numerous specialized relations may coexist at one and the same time simply because the original homogeneous whole has now been split into its integral and heterogeneous parts? Certainly there is more of a division among these tenures, and even among these estates, than is covered by the concept of quantum. They are simultaneous as well as successive divisions of the rights of property. All these interests, considered as present rights with reference to the land, have the same characteristic of summing up to a totality corresponding to the original unity, that they do when considered in the aspect of the period or duration of their enjoyment.[288] However the fact that the present rights to the land run to several persons at once, is more evident in respect of the differing qualities of their various interests than it is with regard to their differing quantities. In fact estates of different quantities are only strictly coexisting to the extent that they are maintained as present relations through various qualitative assortments of present rights.

True the Roman idea, considering itself sophisticated whereas it was in fact primitive, together with the self-assertion of certain classes of holders at later periods, has modified to some extent the original feudal, or lineal, plan and reduced it to something more nearly like Roman *dominium*.[289] But, on the other hand, through the system of estates, the tenant in fee simple himself, the *cestui que use* and the creditor have together created anew a large portion of the original dependent and derivative system, which in the normal and universal process of dispossession of landed proprietors, had fallen into desuetude.[290] It is also necessary to admit that the English emphasis upon possession is even greater than the Roman. But the fundamental idea of possession is different. It is an assorted lot of possessory rights, not a single simple 'thing.' In this respect the English law of personal property is a stunted or partial assimilation to the law of estates in land. There-

[288] This fact will appear more plainly in later chapters. But the early English "uses" make it plain enough.

[289] In certain respects, and entirely apart from this direct influence, it is true, as Maitland says, that England unconsciously reproduced Roman legal history. See Pollock and Maitland, op. cit., II, Chapter 9.

[290] Also, it should be noted, coexistent tenures of different quality have carried on in the case of copyhold, the one remaining survival of the organization based on status.

fore it is not on the whole an exaggeration to oppose the English to the Roman system, and to perceive as the spirit and essence of the former a concurrent and qualitative division of the various elemental relations which may exist between men with respect to the objects of property. It is the development of this modernized form—a development which has not yet seen its counterpart in legal theory—which is the great contribution of English land law to the institution of property.

CHAPTER IV

THE MODERN JURISTIC ANALYSIS OF PROPERTY — LEGAL THEORY

A. *Private Rights and Property*

1. *The Conflict of Schematizations*

We have now traced the more conspicuous developments of the institution of property in its legal aspects, as it evolved in both the principal strains which compose our institutional heritage. By way of preparation for our examination of the practical law of today in the United States it will be helpful to consider the dual background of legal theory upon which the modern institution may be said to be, in some degree, organized. For it is in juristic analysis rather than in the substance of the law itself that the merging of the two strains is found. English law is an indigenous growth. Influenced considerably in its earliest stages, and, perhaps, to some slight extent throughout its history, by Roman law, it has produced nevertheless its own concepts, its own classifications and its own structure.[1] The purest representation of this particular formulation appears in Blackstone who summarized this characteristic native growth about the middle of the eighteenth century and who thus represents the end of an era. With Bentham and, especially, Austin there began to reappear, soon after, the influence of the Roman strain imported immediately from the continental civilians of the period. With them began the modern era in Anglo-American law, and today most of our legal theory derives its manner of thought from this school and from these and contemporary continental sources. There is a curious result of this fact that English and American jurisprudence — a recent development — has so largely accepted from the civilians, or founded upon its own study of Roman law, its theoretical structure. For it has led to an endeavour to plaster the beautiful logic derived from an archaic

[1] As we have noted, Maitland speaks of English law "unconsciously reproducing" the course of development of the Roman law. And at various stages it was certainly submitted to the influence of imported ideas. Nevertheless there was no such "Reception" as took place upon the Continent. Pound appraises the effect at the earlier stages when, *Philosophy*, p. 41, he speaks of "the strict law made for feudal England out of Germanic materials, sometimes superficially Romanized. . ."

Roman system, or its philosophized medieval descendant, upon such highly evolved legal relations as the extraordinary and flexible English system of estates in land and the closely analogous modern system of holdings of personal property. Even where this has not been attempted, nevertheless the uncontested supremacy of Roman law in the theoretical field seems to have blinded the English legal philosophers to the peculiar merits of their own native specialties. Naturally the theory does not fit the facts. Wherever it has influenced the law or the lawyers during the last hundred years, its effect has been more constraining than developing. And this is the more unfortunate since the facts lend themselves to a theory quite alien to Rome, but one which would be most constructively useful in the Anglo-American economic world of today.

The great confusion of our law of property is at least partly due to this combination of indigenous structure with exotic theory. Neither is representative of the modern facts. We have, on the one hand, the classification of the forms of property peculiar to English law. While in most respects obsolete they nevertheless persist in current practice. On the other hand we have the Roman classification, an arrangement which not only does not agree with the first in grouping but which is not organized on the same principle.

The following scheme of property is based on Blackstone:

1. Things Real (Real Property: Wholly rights connected with, or originally connected with, immovables; but not all such rights)

   A. Corporeal Hereditaments

      Estates in land
      a. Freeholds of inheritance (Fee simple, fee tail)
      b. Freeholds not of inheritance (For life)

   B. Incorporeal Hereditaments

      a. Commons (Now assimilated to profits a prendre)
      b. Rights of Way (Now assimilated to easements)
      c. Franchises
         (And other feudal relics now generally unimportant)

2. Things Personal (Personal Property: All rights in movables and some in immovables)

   A. Chattels Real

      a. Terms for years in land (Probably all estates less than freehold)
      b. Certain conditional estates in land (Securities)
         (And other feudal relics now generally unimportant)

B. Chattels Personal[2]

a. Choses in possession (Chattels corporeal)
b. Choses in action (Chattels incorporeal)

Jurisprudence ignores this analysis of property. So far as it deals with the subject in this way at all, it approaches it from the Roman angle. But it is difficult to arrange a corresponding scheme upon the Roman basis. Strictly speaking the term property is, even in modern civilian doctrine, reserved for *dominium*, though it is at times stretched to include the *iura in re aliena.* There remain outside the pale the two forms of obligations, regarded as rights: those arising *ex contractu* and those *ex delicto.* Efforts are made to match the category of *dominium*, under the name "ownership," with the corporeal hereditaments and chattels personal in possession; that of the *iura in re aliena* (sometimes called by the name of its limited sub-class, the servitudes) with the incorporeal hereditaments, with special property, and even at times with the chattels real. Finally the obligations *ex contractu* are often identified with the class choses in action, which is doubtless partly responsible for the frequent inclusion thereunder of rights of action arising from tort (obligations *ex delicto*) in spite of the fact that the latter are specifically excluded by Blackstone and other authorities. In none of these cases is the resemblance between the two categories close. Therefore there is no single authoritative scheme available. It will, however, serve our purpose to present the germane parts of the theory of modern property law upon the following skeleton.

1. Complete Property
   With its subordinate attribute possession
2. Fractions of Property
3. Equitable Property
4. Contract

We cannot accurately apply this classification to the English system. The latter arranges the forms of property somewhat according to their objects and somewhat according to their historical sources and developing attributes and remedies (procedure). On the other hand, any arrangement that is analytical and Romish is based on the division between *meum* and *tuum* – the aboriginal classificatory genitive. Nevertheless there is some correspondence between the two, as will appear in due course.

[2] The special property created in the bailee by bailment, which we have already discussed, is not classified by Blackstone but is included by him in the class of "qualified" property – as opposed to absolute property – discussed under choses in possession.

2. *The Sources and Ingredients of Private Rights*

Before proceeding with this scheme it is necessary to consider some of the general attributes of the modern legal idea of property. If one accepts the construction that we have heretofore placed upon the word *ius*, as used in Roman law, it must appear evident that the modern concept of "a right" was almost unknown in classic Roman times. There was a positive power, a jurisdiction, appertaining to those in control, which gained gradually the sanction of the state and which was only slightly and gradually limited in the interests of those subject to it. Self-help long remained the implement through which these powers were exercised; a self-help permitted only as authorized, gradually restrained, and eventually displaced, but nevertheless the core of the power. *Ius* was a species of sanctioned or delegated authority.

It was in the parlous and oppressive period of the early Middle Ages that we find the beginnings of a different idea of a right, based, to be sure, on the revived Roman law, but being read into it rather than out of it. This is the concept of the negative right—the liberty or immunity gained by the individual through protection against the power of his superiors and the interferences of his fellows. This type of right is a *protection* not a *power*. Its orbit is defined, as Holland says, by the definition of its infringements. It is an area within which the individual is free from control of others. Out of this medieval-modern concept have chiefly grown the rights of possessory property and of person.[3] And, for the most part, only the rights arising from contract and from tort maintain even the form of the original Roman idea of powers, though they are now completely denuded of the sanction of self-help and, in fact, have become powers to call on the state to create protective rights and to enforce them.[4]

Valiant efforts have been made to find a definition for the modern legal concept of a right, which will include both these types—the power over others and the immunity from the power of others. But

[3] Thus Holland, op. cit., p. 193, says that the essence of property rights lies not so much in the enjoyment of the thing (i.e. the sanction of a power over an object) as in the legal power of excluding others from interfering with the enjoyment of it. This is a more realistic definition than Ihering's, *Geist*, III, p. 339, where he says, "Der Begriff des Rechts, beruht auf der rechtlichen Sicherheit des Genusses, Rechte sind rechtlich geschützte Interessen." Paulsen, *A System of Ethics*, Trans., p. 635, gives a good example of its application to the person. He says, "we may regard the laws which have been enacted for the protection of labor during the last half century as a continuation of the legislation in defense of individual liberty against new forms of slavery."

[4] Holland, op. cit., p. 129, says of private rights, ". . . the parties interested in or affected by the right have nothing to do with protecting it." This is the opposite of self-help—it is the helping of the helpless.

it seems to the writer that when this is done the essence of the idea, both historically and practically, escapes.[5] Rather than to attempt a theory of absolute rights – a sort of rationalization after the fact, on one hand, or an ethical goal, on the other – it is better for us to treat merely of the fact of those rights which are actually accorded. Of these we find that some are conceived to inhere in all, some to accrue as a result of arrangements men make among themselves and some to arise only when an existing right is infringed. Holland uses the term "antecedent" to apply to the first two classes and the term "remedial" to the last. "Actions," says Dalloz,[6] "are the particular rights which spring from the violation of other rights, and which aim either to stop this violation or to repair the effects of it." Here the action is itself the remedial right. But all rights have two aspects. Hearn,[7] who emphasizes the duty rather than the right, perceives that. "Thus a right has no independent existence. It denotes merely a certain course of proceeding taken by its donee upon the breach of a certain species of duty. When, therefore, we speak of the violation of a right or of its infringement, we really mean the violation or the infringement of a duty in respect of which a [relative] right exists, so far as such violation or infringement affects the donee of the right." In essence it is this concept of "duty," as the correlative of "a right," which represents the modern view. The change is well exemplified by the sense we now attach to the word obligation, which signified, in Rome, the bond of a power and which now signifies a duty.

Hohfeld[8] laid the foundation of the disintegration of any right into its component parts, or, better, of a bundle of rights into its elements. His analysis was qualitative and he does not seem to have carried the idea beyond the characterization of different kinds of rights; so that it remains to others to take apart the individual right, so-called, or bundle of rights, and determine its constituents.[9] The generic term,

[5] Pound, for instance, *Readings,* p. 413, defines rights as follows: "The chief means which the law adopts, however, in order to attain its end, is the recognition or definition of certain capacities in persons of influencing the actions of others. . . These capacities of influence are called rights."

Holland, op. cit., p. 82, says "It [a right] is one man's capacity of influencing the acts of another, by means, not of his own strength, but of the opinion or the force of society." A legal right is this when "with the assent and assistance of the state." In other words the law finds absolute rights *in a state of nature* and merely clothes them with the attribute of legality.

[6] *Répertoire,* s. v. No. 69.

[7] *Legal Duties,* p. 153.

[8] Hohfeld, *Fundamental Legal Conceptions.*

[9] This is being done to some extent in the process of preparing the various "Restatements of the Law," under the auspices of the American Law Institute, which may well attain the validity of the *responsa.* It is gratifying to note that Hohfeld's real contribution to American jurisprudence has been incorporated *in toto* in the *Restatement of the Law of Property.* See pp. 12-15.

he says (and I should say also the particular interest which is in itself always a complex bundle of rights), covers four different relations. There is the *claim* to a duty on the part of another or others; the *privilege*, which connotes the absence of any claim by others; the *power*, which involves a liability upon some other; and the *immunity*, which creates a disability in others. Generally speaking the first two have to do with existing static relations and the last two with existing dynamic relations; that is, rights to acts which will alter existing static relations. Thus the latter are vested potentialities as opposed to vested actualities. For example, the right of property in a lease, let us say, involves a claim corresponding to the duty of the lessee to pay sums of money at intervals; the privilege of transferring the lease along with the rest of the property, thus substituting a new lessor, against which privilege the lessee has no claim; the power of distraint involving a liability on the part of the lessee; and an immunity from accepting a new lessee, corresponding to the disability of the present one to sub-let without the owner's consent. All these and many other elements compose what is called the right of property (the interest) in this case. The same compound of qualitatively differing rights is found in all cases.[10]

In a frequently quoted passage the philosopher Kant says,[11] ". . . if a man were alone in the world he could properly hold or acquire nothing as his own; because between himself, as person, and all other outward objects, as things, there is no relation." "The relation," says Holland, "is between him and other people whom he excludes from the thing."[12] This is another characteristic of all rights. They are relations, negative or positive, between persons, though they may also exist *with reference to* 'things,' or to material objects.[13]

In our further considerations it will be useful to bear these three points in mind. The rights we will examine are the rights of property. Each bundle—or interest—consists of a complex mass of claims, privileges, powers and immunities, all of which are relations

[10] While Hohfeld himself, in his later work, and most of his followers have restricted their use of the word "right" to the narrower field which he originally designated as "claim," we are not able to follow this practice. The word "right" has come to be a generic term and, since we are referring to a literature which has generally imposed no such restriction upon itself, it would only be confusing to limit the coverage of the word to certain types of rights.

[11] *Rechtslehre*, I, 2, sec. 11.

[12] Op. cit., p. 193.

[13] ". . . property consists essentially of legal relations. Legal relations in our law exist only between persons. There cannot be a legal relation between a person and a thing or between two things." American Law Institute, *Restatement of the Law of Property*, p. 11.

with other persons with reference, perhaps, to the interest itself or to some material object. These relations may pre-exist a wrong or they may exist only consequent upon a wrong. And, to return to our historical derivations, these rights are bundles composed either of promised liberties from interference by others or of what still appear to be sanctioned powers (not in Hohfeld's sense) over others, or of mixtures of the two.

3. *The Inherence and Classification of Private Rights*

Legal rights accruing to individuals are held in common when they constitute the protection of social interests; corporately, or pseudo-corporately, when they represent the protection of public interests; and only directly when they are concerned with private interests. Pound[14] analyses the protection and sanction of the interests as follows: The social interests are maintained chiefly by criminal law—and, we might add, by restrictions on all other rights; which restrictions, when they are positive, are enforced by criminal law.

Public interests are maintained:

a. By private actions of the state on the analogy of those maintaining private rights.
b. Indirectly by private actions allowed to individuals.
c. By the prerogative writs such as "mandamus" and "quo warranto."
d. By criminal law.

Private interests are maintained:

a. By rights, powers and privileges vindicated by private actions.

In sophisticated law, then, the individual is conceived to be surrounded by this triplicate web of social, public and private rights, and a single wrong may infringe rights in each field.[15] A private wrong (breach or tort) is defined, according to Blackstone,[16] as an "infringement, or privation of the private or civil rights belonging to individuals, considered as individuals"; and a crime "is a breach and violation of public [social] rights and duties, which affect the whole community, considered as a community. . .". Therefore, as Holland says,[17] the right which is violated by a tort is always a different right from that which is violated by a crime. While this

[14] *Readings*, p. 410.
[15] Such, for instance, as damage wrought by riots.
[16] *Commentaries*, III, I, p. 2.
[17] Op. cit., p. 331.

view seems essential to legal theory – for the author of an action must be conceived to vindicate his own right only – the result is that many private rights receive the added protection of public law in so far as offences against the person or property are considered as likely to cause social inconvenience. The extent to which this new basis for the enforcement or protection of private rights is superimposed upon the primitive one, varies with time and place, and the end is not yet.[18]

There is another direction in which the inherence of rights – at least of property rights – is modified. There are five avenues through which benefits of this general order accrue ultimately to the individual. For the first we have no name. It may be called rights over "common resources" and corresponds in some respects to the Roman *res communes.* In this division objects are conceived to be held by the state in a sort of trusteeship for the benefit of all. Nevertheless the method of holding is not a form of property, because the objects so held (usually of a certain kind and always natural resources) are susceptible of appropriation by the state, as public property, as well as by corporations and individuals, as private property.[19] But such appropriation from the common stock is restricted to inconsequential quantities and is based on the assumption that supplies are so plentiful that no one suffers deprivation thereby. The essential protection of whatever joint right exists takes the form of protection of the right of access. The second division consists of the social subtractions from the rights of property which we will consider later. It comprises those benefits which are common or available to all because certain exercises with reference to appropriated objects are prohibited or not protected to the immediate property holders. Public property is the method of holding objects or other 'things' specifically appropriated to public use, title to which rests in governmental organizations. Such public use may consist in employment in the conduct of public business, or either in free or in economic service to the community so organized. It is identical in form with private property. Allied to this is property in private corporate bodies, another method

[18] Hearn, with his emphasis upon the duty rather than the right, escapes this dualism. He says, *Legal Duties*, p. 157, in effect, that when absolute duties (i.e. those with relation to no other person) are broken, "the consequence is a punishable offence"; that when particular relative duties (i.e. those which relate to definite persons) are broken, "the consequence is a breach of contract or other obligation;" and that when general relative duties (i.e. those which relate to indefinite persons) are broken, "the consequence is a tort or both a punishable offence and a tort."

[19] Pound, *Philosophy*, p. 199, says, ". . . in fact the so-called state ownership of *res communes* and *res nullius* is only a sort of guardianship for social purposes. It is *imperium*, not *dominium*."

by which the benefit ultimately accrues, though indirectly, to the individual member.[20] Finally there is private property of individuals. The route of inherence and the quantity of benefit varies in all these cases according to the relation of the individual to the group. But in all cases only individuals are the ultimate beneficiaries. Beyond the confines of these methods of holding there lies the no-man's land of property, the *res nullius* of Roman law, in which remain all objects neither restricted nor yet appropriated. Strictly speaking no such objects exist in a modern state. Natural resources are treated as "common resources," except as they are treated as attributes of particular sites and therefore as public or private property.[21]

To such an extent has the law of property monopolized the field of private law that Sohm goes so far as to define the first part of its persisting dichotomy, the Law of Persons, as "identical with the law of the *subject* of private [i.e. proprietary] rights, in other words, it is concerned with proprietary capacity, the capacity of holding property."[22] Others do not follow him to this extreme position. Holland will make the Law of Persons the definition of the various kinds and degrees of abnormality in respect of their differing legal capacities in every respect.[23] And Austin, still somewhat broader,[24] makes the matter of status embrace varying duties as well as rights, capacities and incapacities. Thus the title "Law of Persons" has come in the course of time to cover several different categories. In Rome it originated as the field of the intra-familial *ius* and became a description of status in respect of various kinds of control over persons. Blackstone uses it to describe the personal rights together with the organization of society, political and domestic. Finally the moderns conceive it primarily as an analysis of the modifications in the capacity of the persons of inherence to whom any rights run. It is, in this view, a description of the influence of special status upon the enjoyment of all private rights.

These private rights include not only the property rights but also the familial and personal rights. Blackstone[25] divides them into three

20 This includes the foundation. For the real beneficiaries of all artificial persons, see Ihering, *Geist*, III, p. 359. He says of foundations that they are "nichts als eine Form der Zuwendung und Bestimmung eines Vermögens für die Zwecke und Interessen unbestimmter Personen. . ."

21 Because the Romans, under different circumstances, defined wild animals as *res nullius*, some of our courts have been led into the error of calling them by this name, though they always treat them in part as "common resources" and in part as objects of "qualified property," in the English sense.

22 Sohm, op. cit., p. 159.

23 Op. cit., pp. 136-139.

24 Op. cit., Lectures XL-XLIII.

25 *Commentaries*, I, I, p. 129.

groups; personal security, personal liberty, and private property. Pound[26] carries the analysis further, in a way more generally acceptable to modern theory. In doing so, however, he evades the question whether any or all the rights which he defines as being *in personam* are property rights, and restricts the term "property" to its primitive civilian sense.

I. Rights *in rem*
  1. Personal Integrity
     Those against injuries to life, body, and health, either bodily or mental
  2. Personal Liberty
     Free motion and locomotion
  3. The society and control of one's family and dependents
  4. Private Property

II. Rights *in personam*
  1. Contractual, arising independently of pre-existing rights, out of the agreement of the parties
  2. Quasi-contractual. Rights to restitution or compensation for a benefit conferred, imposed by law to prevent the unjust enrichment of one party at the expense of another
  3. Fiduciary. Rights to have a trust or confidence executed specifically (in specie)
  4. Delictual. Rights to compensation arising from violations of pre-existing rights *in rem*

Terry would add to the rights *in rem* that of personal reputation, which might be included with personal integrity, and that of unimpaired pecuniary condition, which might be included under private property.[27] As to the latter his recognition of property in value, as well as of property in substance, while it treads dangerous ground,[28] may turn out to be the rationalization of much of the present

[26] *Readings*, p. 420.

[27] Op. cit., pp. 343-355. Terry's forward-looking reasons for giving this latter right a place by itself are therein given in full. He says, "The protected condition of fact which forms the content of the right is the holding of purchasing power, in whatever form it exists, or the being in such a situation that purchasing power in some form will come into one's hands, such an arrangement of circumstances as will bring it to one." It is "simply with regard to its value, whereas the rights of property . . . concern the specific qualities of things."

If this is to be included as a part right of property it must be more carefully discriminated than Terry does from what Pound, *Philosophy*, p. 192, calls the "claim to be secured against interference by outsiders with economically advantageous relations with others." The test would be, does the relation consist of property?

[28] For, as Hearn says, *Legal Duties*, p. 162, "The State does not undertake to insure people against loss; but provides that they shall enjoy their rights, whatever these rights may be worth."

fumbling of courts seeking to deal out justice without an adequate rule. Others prefer other modifications.

Inspecting Pound's scheme of rights, we find that, broadly speaking, those which he calls *in rem* seem now to have largely the character of the negative rights to protection – the protected field of freedom from interference – which we have found to be principally of medieval origin; while his rights *in personam* are, in form at least, the direct descendants of the positive rights (*iura*) of Roman law, which are, in effect, powers or controls over others. An exception to the first statement is found in the fact that he includes in the rights *in rem* the society and control of one's family and dependents. In respect of its element of *control* we will recognize here the private *ius* of Roman law, the legal embodiment of the original pre-property control over persons within the *familia*. In fact it is its direct descendant. So persistent has been this tacit assumption that the whole right retains the original savour of property simply because no subsequent introjection of the idea of independence within the field of the classificatory genitive has, even to this day, been capable of destroying the innate idea, of converting those subject to it into persons, or the rights over them into rights *in personam*. The protections against external interference with the familial rights are of course a direct relic of the early proprietory nature of these familial rights and as such naturally classified as *in rem*. An exception to our generalization of the source of the second group is the fiduciary right, a right largely of English origin, and in England in most respects a protection, but treated by Pound as though it were analogous to the Roman powers over others.[29]

The general use of the terms *in rem* and *in personam* we shall discuss later; as also the essential question, for us, as to which of these rights are properly to be included in the term property and which are not. As to the latter the principal questions are two. First, it is necessary to find a line of demarcation between the personal and familial rights, on the one hand, and the property rights, on the other. This is complicated by the fact that the protection given by the courts to property rights seems to have been more highly perfected than that given to personal rights, so that there is a constant effort to broaden the scope of property by including the personal rights thereunder – an easier task than to improve the protection accorded to personal rights. Second, it is necessary to determine the nature and extent of property in choses in action; in other words, to answer the question whether or not rights *in personam* can be brought within a general definition of property.

[29] The *ius obligationis quasi ex contractu.*

B. *Complete Property*

1. *"Dominium" and "Ownership"*

With this brief survey of the character and various types of private rights in general and, in particular, that limited class which is, strictly speaking, called property, we are now prepared to consider the first of our four categories, namely complete property.

This legal idea is often treated as if it were identical with what is called "absolute property," "absolute ownership," or merely "ownership" (assuming its absolute quality). In popular and even in legal usage the word "ownership" has another application, quite generally confused with this one, which we hope to succeed gradually in discriminating. And this *double entendre* exists for the reason that it is an English word, bred in the bone and incapable of accurate assimilation to the imported idea of absolute property. It is hardly necessary to remind the reader that this latter idea had its origin in the Roman term *dominium* (the classificatory genitive as applied to material objects). But the Romans did not develop the content of the idea. They named it only, and appear to have considered it as so original a fact, implicit in the very nature of things, that it was subject to no analysis either as to content or as to boundaries.[30] Just so we, until recently, have not considered it necessary to examine in what respects and to what extent a man's body is his own to do with as he wishes. The content of the term *dominium* has been supplied by medieval and modern analysis and speculation, concurrently with the development of the idea of a right of protection. But, as we have already noted, no such idea was indigenous in English law and there is no form to which it can be applied with certainty. It is true, as Holdsworth has said, that the common law structure of estates has been modified by the Roman concept of *dominium*.[31] But it is also true that the Roman concept had to be so modified that, when it came to be applied to the English system, it was hardly recognizable.

The highest reaches of the philosophic imputation of content to

[30] "The owner stands in a certain relation to the material thing which he owns; and neither the nature of such a relation, nor of the thing toward which it existed, was regarded by the earlier Roman jurists as a matter calling for analysis or explanation. Each was treated as a simple idea, one of the *praecognoscenda* of legal science." Terry, op. cit., p. 28.

[31] "The Roman conception of ownership, as an abstract right, was made familiar to English lawyers by the legal renaissance of the twelfth and thirteenth centuries; and though, as we have seen, that conception has never been completely acclimatized in the common law, yet the common law has acquired a conception of ownership which is different from that better right to possess which was the dominant theory in the Middle Ages." Holdsworth, op. cit., VII, 510.

complete property synchronized with the era of the *Social Contract* and the *Rights of Man*. When Blackstone defines property he seems to be thinking of *dominium*, for he calls it "that sole and despotic dominion which one man claims and exercises over the external things of the world, in total exclusion of the right of any other individual in the universe."[32] Today this seems to us so extravagant as to be laughable. But we must admit, in justice to the great British institutionalist, that elsewhere he qualifies this despotism by making it subject to "control and diminution" "by the laws of the land."[33] Sohm[34] says, "Ownership is a right, unlimited in respect of its contents, to exercise control over a thing." He concedes that it is subject to legal limitations, imposed by the rights of others or by the rules of public law, which subtract from it. But since, in default of them, it is complete, one may say it is intrinsically unlimited. Austin finds more difficulty in acclimatizing the foreign idea to English law. The theory does not fit the facts. The tailoring is not good, however much he seems to admire it. "But though the possible *modes* of property are infinite, and though the indefinite power of user is always restricted more or less, there is in every system of law, some one mode of property in which the restrictions to the power of user are fewer [the power of indefinite user more extensive] than in others. . . And to this mode of property, the term dominion, property, or ownership, is pre-eminently and emphatically applied."[35] But the "one mode" can only be applied, in English law, to "absolute property in a movable" or to "an estate in fee simple in land." And he denies that even the latter is "absolute property." The one mode must, therefore, be immediately altered to several and the "emphasis" considerably weakened to fit the complex facts of the English estates in land. Thus he must admit a distinction between absolute owners, owners and limited owners.[36] So that it becomes possible to have no

[32] *Commentaries*, II, I, p. 2.

[33] *Commentaries*, I, I, p. 138.

[34] Op. cit., p. 309.

[35] Op. cit., II, p. 824.

[36] Elsewhere, II, p. 866, he defines "absolute property, or *dominium* preeminently so called," as "a right indefinite in user, unlimited in duration (that is, capable of going over to a series of successors *ab intestato* which may possibly last for ever), and alienable by the actual owner from every successor who in default of alienation by him might take the right."

Since the owner "could not, by an alienation from his own heirs, affect the interest of the lord of the fee," "there is not in the law of England any absolute property in land, in case there be any mesne lord interposed between the tenant and the king." The rights of the sovereign as *ultimus heres*, is not treated as a reversion. Nevertheless he seems to assume a mesne lord in all cases, for he says there is no absolute property in land in England. "The mesne lord has not absolute property. He has merely *nuda proprietas*," because his right is "subject to a right of indefinite user . . . residing in the tenant" (p. 877).

Dominion or ownership seems, therefore, to be something less than absolute

more than the reversion or escheat remaining in the so-called absolute owner. Holland is more cautious and therefore more vague. He says that ownership is a "plenary" (*sic*) control over an object. But it is "unlimited only in comparison with other rights over objects . . . it must always be enjoyed in such a way as not to interfere with the rights of others," and the enjoyment and the fruits are limited by the rights of the state and of other individuals. To it adheres, in his view, the right of disposition, including destruction, alteration and alienation, though the last is subject to many legal disabilities. In its legal aspect it includes possession and vindication, except when the former is expressly severed, as in the case of a lease, loan or mortgage.[87]

In spite of the verbiage of these high-sounding definitions, it is always recognized that all these constituent attributes but one can be stripped off. It is possible to reduce this so-called "ownership" to the right to vindicate the "ownership" (*nuda proprietas*), so that its only content is the right to claim itself. And this I think accurately portrays the final legal concept of the only property which, in the original feudal sense, can be called absolute. It is that legal relation with respect to objects to which, when every constituent right is removed, something still remains. Thus in fact the one distinguishing characteristic of the notion of "absolute property" in modern law is that it is an artificial legal concept providing a very necessary vacuum for the law to abhor, in order that it may have some residual interest which will absorb all accretions accruing to no other, and all abandonments.[88] In this way "absolute property" can be reduced to a bare

property, for it includes estates in fee simple and perhaps also estates in tail (ibid., p. 863). It is described as any "right *in rem* (of limited or unlimited duration) as gives to the party in whom it resides an indefinite power or liberty of using or dealing with the subject [object] . . . which is not capable of exact circumscription or definition . . ." (ibid., p. 831). And this definition, in turn, permits the inclusion of certain limited estates, where the "right indefinite in user" exists, such as estates for life and for years. This is, however, not logical since the "power of user may extend to destruction" only "when there is merely a reverter to the state" (ibid., p. 868). The whole analytic system is inadequate and lacks the usual Austinian precision. Hearn, *Legal Duties*, p. 206, extends the use of the term limited owners to include "interests of limited duration, condominion, rights *in re alienâ*, and successive interests."

[87] Op. cit., p. 209.

[88] Markby, op. cit., p. 159, makes much of the re-merging of detached rights in the interest which he calls ownership – their extinction when they are "at home, as it were." He also says, "An owner may be described as the person whose rights over a thing are only limited by the rights which are detached from it." This Austinian "indefiniteness" makes it an interesting conceptual tool but adds nothing to the definition of the final characteristic residuum given above. If the magnetic feature did not exist we could as well make possession, or even control, use, or other benefit, the core of property. Thus we prefer this definition that, whatever is stripped off "it is the holder of this residuary right whom we always consider the owner" (i.e. the holder of the absolute property).

In the *Restatement of the Law of Property*, p. 23, ownership is also identified

hypothetical residuum and represents today, in many of its applications, a legal artifice – almost a fiction – rather than an economic fact. The simple social organization, for which the classificatory genitive sufficed, has passed. And now the varied natures of the interests to which the name "ownership" is commonly attached seem almost to justify the indefinite statement of Corbin interpreting Hohfeld.[39] "Ownership" is a "legal interest, consisting of various rights [claims], privileges, powers, and immunities." But it may be more definite than that. It may be used to indicate the particular interest to which *de jure* possession attaches; or it may mean the particular interest which always includes, among the assortment of whatever other separable rights have not been stripped off, that one residuum which may be called "absolute property."[40]

In the process of this analysis I think we have demonstrated that the notion of complete property is a wholly different one from that of "absolute property," "ownership," etc. The latter terms may be applied to a particular interest in an object, not necessarily exclusive but always characterized by a certain quality which is conceived to distinguish it from all others. But the concept of complete property is that of an all-embracing and therefore exclusive interest in an object; one that cannot be defined by a difference from the others because, by definition, there are no others.

2. *Possession*

The legal concept of possession is of a different order from that of "ownership." It approaches the object from a different angle though it arrives at much the same practical result. In spite of Ulpian's oft-

with the interest containing this core right. "It is characteristic of ownership of land that upon termination of any lesser interests in the land the interests of the owner of the land are thereby automatically increased."

[39] A. L. Corbin, "Legal Analysis and Terminology," 29 *Yale Law Review* (1919) p. 161, 173.

[40] In fact the identification of this remnant with the original ownership, or dominion, seems to be of value only in theory. "To just what extent either in the case of ownership of land or of any of the smaller aggregates of interests in land, the constituent interests can be parted with and the characteristics of 'ownership' . . . be still regarded as existing is not a matter upon which any precise rule can be laid down." *Restatement of the Law of Property*, p. 23.

In popular and sometimes in legal usage ownership is frequently identified with that particular interest to which appertains the title, so-called. But this is a mere begging of the question. In the first place this involves a misconception of the meaning of "title." Strictly speaking "title" is no more than the means by which any property – any interest – is established. In the second place the recording of the latest step in this chain, by which the nominal title of owner of any certain piece of land is established in any person, is not considered, as we shall see, to invest such person, if he be trustee or mortgagee, with an interest which can be recognized as ownership.

quoted dictum,[41] it is a similar kind of right, and is usually included in, or delegated by, the so-called "ownership." Developing in Rome – much as our equitable property developed – from the Praetorian law, it was originally there the method of holding developed for those who could not acquire property under the civil law, or for property over objects which could not be appropriated at all under that law.[42] In England it has been blended somewhat unsuccessfully and incompletely with those realest of the real rights based on seisin, which were the practical basis of property from the beginning. Thus to Blackstone, thinking in English terms, *de facto* possession and the right of possession *de jure*, when added to the *mere* right of property, make up the complete title to lands, etc.[43] On the other hand, Holland, with the civilian viewpoint, says, "In its lowest form it [property] is a right of Possession, in its highest form a right of Ownership."[44] Again Salmond,[45] thinking in English terms, says that possession "is in *fact* what ownership is in *right*." It "is the *de facto* exercise of a claim; ownership is the *de jure* recognition of one." Others, attempting to blend the two incompatible ideas, divide the complete property into Blackstone's three grades, and add even lower forms

[41] Ulpian says, *Dig.*, 41. 2. 12. 1, "*Proprietas* has nothing in common with *possessio.*"

[42] In general it appears to the writer that Hunter's view of the origin of possession is correct. See his *Roman Law*. His seems to include the Niebuhr-Savigny theory as a possible individual but wholly speculative instance. Moyle's objections, based on the latter theory, seem if anything to prove Hunter's case. Hunter uses the term "equitable ownership" to mean an ownership created by the Praetor (equity). Moyle seems to misunderstand him to mean that it was a dependent ownership like the interest of our cestui que trust.

The original *legis actiones* were proprietary not possessory actions (analogous to the English Writ of Right). Moreover they were accorded only to property held *ex iure Quiritium*. In the beginning of the equitable jurisdiction of the Praetor there were granted the possessory interdicts. Whether these were first used to protect the rights of possessors (i.e. squatters) upon the *ager publicus* – land not then subject to Quiritary dominion – or of those who were incapable of holding any property *ex iure Quiritium*, is unimportant. In either case possession was a substitute for dominion. It was an inferior (equitable) property, but not derivative, nor dependent, nor divided (as ours). By means of *usucapio* continued possession came to be capable of ripening in a certain period into ownership (Ulpian, 19. 8). Gradually possession acquired a legal province and general applicability of its own, owing to the increasing popularity of the Praetorian jurisdiction, and was recognized to be an element in all property, sometimes retained, sometimes separated.

In Rome the thing necessary to complete possession, besides the fact of possession, was called *animus domini*, not *animus possidendi* as in England. And this seems to clinch the argument. When that rule was laid down one intended to *own*, not merely, as in England, to *claim the best right to possess*. The "law of possession was originally a law of ownership." Hunter, op. cit., p. 377.

[43] *Commentaries*, II, XIII.

[44] Op. cit., p. 193.

[45] *Jurisprudence*, p. 322.

such as derivative possession and "detention." Pollock[46] defines these three grades as they are applied in English law: *De facto* possession, he says, "may be paraphrased as effective occupation or control." But much less than "occupation . . . is sufficient as a rule and for practical purposes to exclude strangers," and "will often amount to possession in the absence of any more effectual act in an adverse interest." "When the fact of control is coupled with a legal claim and right to exercise it in one's own name against the world at large, we have possession in law as well as in fact. We say as against the world at large, not as against all men without exception. For a perfectly exclusive right to the control of anything can belong only to the owner, or to someone invested with such right by the will of the owner or some authority ultimately derived therefrom, or, exceptionally, by an act of the law superseding the owner's will and his normal rights." Pollock also says, "Possession is single and exclusive."[47] The fact is that there are wide exceptions, past and present, to this broad rule. It has been possible to have different types of possession concurrently—or, perhaps better, to split possession into several elements.

3. *Social Reservations from Complete Property*

Both with property and with possession it is agreed that the privileges of the property holder can only be exercised "within limits fixed by law on grounds of social and economic policy."[48] These limits are set, as we have seen, both by the ending of protections and by the beginning of prohibitions. Ely, who has considered property from the social rather than the economic point of view, is particularly interested in this matter of limitations. He has pointed out the course of the continual progressive erosion of the absolute character of property. Both property in sovereignty and property in human beings were once integral parts of the institution and have been defended on the ground that to attack them was to undermine the whole institution of property. Yet both have "disappeared, and the institution of property is stronger even than it was, because that abuse of the idea has disappeared."[49] He describes the retractions from absolute rights of property in the German and French codes,[50] finds evidence of somewhat the same thing even in Roman law, and quotes the famous decision of the Supreme Court in the Slaughter House

[46] Pollock and Wright, op. cit., pp. 12-13 and 16.
[47] Pollock and Wright, op. cit., p. 20.
[48] Hohfeld, op. cit., p. 96.
[49] Op. cit., I, p. 257.
[50] Op. cit., I, pp. 140-141.

cases as to the warrant for this policy. ". . . persons and property are subjected to all kinds of restraints and burdens in order to secure the general comfort, health, and prosperity of the State. Of the perfect right of the legislature to do this, no question ever was, or, *upon acknowledged general principles, ever can be made*, so far as natural persons are concerned."[51] Along similar lines, the *Restatement of the Law of Property*[52] defines complete property by deducting what we have called the socially reserved rights from a theoretical whole. "The totality of these rights, powers, privileges and immunities which it is legally possible for a person to have with regard to a given piece of land that are other than those that all other members of society have as such, constitutes complete property in that land. This totality varies from time to time, and from place to place, either because of changes in the common law, or because of alterations by statute."

The legal grounds upon which this creeping abrogation of private rights of property are founded, are the doctrines of police power, public necessity, taxing power, and the right of eminent domain. All are of modern origin.[53] This question of the power of the state to diminish the content of particular elements of the various rights of property; the question of fixing its disabilities in that regard, if any; the question of its liability for compensation for such deprivations and the extent and method of measuring such liability; these are questions of great moment and urgency in America today. We call attention to them here merely for the purpose of getting rid, once and for all so far as we are concerned, of the notion that there is, in practice, any such thing as unlimited property of any kind.

[51] Op. cit., I, p. 218.

[52] P. 18.

[53] As Dwight, *Commentaries on the Law of Persons and Personal Property*, p. 425, points out, the modern doctrine of eminent domain is not of feudal origin for it applies to personal as well as to real property.

But Gierke finds its origin in medieval Romanizations. He holds, op. cit., p. 80, that "property had its roots in the *Ius Gentium*," and states that "all were agreed that there was Natural Law, which, on the one hand, radiated from a principle transcending earthly power, and, on the other hand, was true and perfectly binding Law" (p. 75). Nevertheless, because the least centralized theory of ownership of the time still admitted a "Superiority on the part of the State," "men developed the theory – a theory strange to archaic German law – of a Right of Expropriation. . ." But, because of the existence of Natural Law, "the history of the Theory of Expropriation takes, in the main, the form of a process whereby definite bounds are set to an expropriatory right" (p. 79). The power being strange to Roman law so too, of course, was this protection. These doctrines of compensation and of limits could be based on Natural not Positive Law because "the power of the State stood below the rules of Natural and above the rules of Positive Law" (p. 78). This is a part of the process of the development of protections which we have described elsewhere.

4. *The Disintegration of Complete Property, and the Core Right*

We have now arrived at the modern concept of complete property as given in the *Restatement of the Law of Property*. It is the totality of rights as to any specific object which are accorded by law, at any time and place, after deducting the social reservations. We have found the most generally acceptable definitions of possession to be a graded series of individual rights of a particular type which go to make up one element in this totality. And we have found that the only mark of identification which can with certainty be associated with the rather arbitrary legal concept which is called "absolute property," is that core right or residuum which remains the nucleus from which all other rights in the totality are derived, upon which they are dependent, from which they may be detached and to which they automatically return when liberated.

It is evident, then, that we are not dealing with synonyms when we discuss complete and absolute property, or "ownership" and *dominium.* Nor, if we treat "ownership" as synonymous with *dominium*, are we able to identify it with either complete or absolute property. For the principal characteristic of *dominium* was its qualitative indivisibility. But, by definition, the characteristic of complete property and of its core right, absolute property, is their divisibility or separability. It is also evident that complete property is a mere concept of totality rather than an actual phenomenon.[54] When we come to apply even the limited aggregate which has been defined above to English land law we find no instances. In feudal times each plot of land had built upon it a complex of tenures. As these were simplified a complex of estates came to divide the total property, and even today all land is conceived to be held of the crown.[55] It is true that we in America more nearly approach the possibility of complete property in land. But even here, as will appear in the next chapter, an undivided totality is not so common and the identification of any one who may indisputably be called an "owner" is often more or less a game of blind man's buff.

The realistic quality of the concept of complete property, then, lies not in its existence as such, but rather in the fact that it truly presents property as a complex which is divisible into many assortments of the component rights, rather than as an integer (dominion, "ownership"). Hearn,[56] while he confuses his statement by using

[54] There is almost always, in the case of land, at least a dower right outstanding.

[55] Blackstone says, even of his times, "Almost all the real property of this kingdom is . . . supposed to be granted by, dependent upon, and *holden* of, some superior lord. . ." *Commentaries*, II, V, p. 59.

[56] *Legal Duties*, p. 186. The interpretations in brackets are ours.

the word "ownership" and by using it to mean both complete property and absolute property indiscriminately, disintegrates complete property into its elements and illustrates their divisibility. He says, "Ownership [complete property] is merely a collective term denoting the aggregate of several independent rights. It has no meaning other than the sum of its component parts, and it admits of no other definition than an enumeration of these parts. . . The rights which collectively constitute ownership [complete property] are the right to possess, the right to use, the rights to the produce, the right to waste [use up], the right of disposition, whether during life or upon death, and the right to exclude all other persons from any interference with the thing owned. . . All these rights may, in the case of the same object, either co-exist in the same person or be enjoyed in varying degrees by different persons. . . If he have less than the full ownership [complete property], if he can exercise some but not all the rights that I have mentioned, he has a limited ownership of some kind; and he may or may not have the full ownership [in the other sense of ownership] of his interest, whatever that may be, in the property [i.e. the object]." And he continues,[57] "Each of the singular rights which collectively constitute ownership [complete property] may be enjoyed separately or in conjunction with one or more of the other rights. Thus the lessee of property has its possession, although he has not its ownership [absolute property]. A person who hires chattels for a temporary purpose has the use of these chattels, although he has not their possession. The purchaser of a growing crop may be said to have the right to the produce of the land, although he has neither its possession nor its use. The lessee of minerals has a right of abuser [use up], even though he may have no other right whatever to the surface. A secured creditor has the right of sale to enforce his security, although the ownership [absolute property] and even the possession be in another. The right of exclusion without any other rights is found in a mere trustee, as, for example, the trustee of a church. In like manner ownership [absolute property] may exist less by one or more of the singular rights. Thus the reversioner has the ownership [absolute property] but not the possession. . . A trustee has the ownership [absolute property] but not the use. A tenant for life may exercise all the powers of ownership [complete property] except sale and waste."

Among all these varied assortments of the rights composing complete property we have suggested that one may always be identified because it contains the core right. In connection with Anglo-American land and chattels voluntarily out of possession, this peculiarity

[57] *Legal Duties*, p. 207.

must logically be reserved for the single estate in land to which attaches the final reversion[58] and to the right of the bailor of a chattel. In all other cases the core right must be concealed in possession *de jure*.[59] This viewpoint suggests that we may regard the various fractions of complete property in a different aspect as well. They are, it is true, parts of a totality; but they are also segments stripped off from a core. And this points the conclusion that while other fractions may have no relation to each other, all must be related directly or indirectly to the core. The core is, therefore, not a mere disconnected residue. It is the skeleton, however emaciated, upon which the whole complex of complete property depends. Because it is that fraction from which ultimately the titles of all other fractions are derived, it is the apex of the system of derivative and dependent property into which the totality may have been divided. The rights remaining in that fraction may be insignificant. All the practically important rights may have been assigned to other fractions. But the whole complex hinges upon the fraction containing the core right. In it reposes the individuality. For the core right is the only property in the entire complex which complies essentially with the original notion of absolute property. Even for this right, in view of the relics of feudal law in the English version (the escheat of the sovereign) and the right of eminent domain in the American, it might be more appropriate to use the term "ultimate" than the term "absolute."

C. *Fractions of Property*

According to the time-honoured notion, when we leave the subject of dominion and possession and take up the lesser kinds of property we pass from the field of corporeal 'things' into that of the incorporeal. Therefore it behooves us to stop at this point to examine the legal meaning of the word "thing" and to reconsider the moot question of the validity of the ancient dichotomy, corporeal *vs.* incorporeal, in the hope that by this means we may more closely come at the true nature of property. We shall find, I believe, that the word "thing" is the prime example of what Hohfeld calls "chameleon-hued words"[60] – vague terms used to conceal intellectual vacua – and that this is the reason for the confusion its use engenders. And we shall

[58] In this we are disregarding, in the American case, the right of eminent domain residing in the state and, in the English case, with due consideration for the special effect of abandonment, the escheat to the sovereign.

[59] Thus Kocourek, op. cit., p. 328, calls ownership (i.e. absolute property) "*the most ultimate right of possession and nothing else.*"

[60] Hohfeld, op. cit., p. 35.

find great difficulty in applying the terms corporeal and incorporeal in any way which is appropriate to their sense.

1. *The Evolution of the Word "Thing"*

It is not necessary for us to review at this point the analysis we made, in our discussion of Roman law, of the classic Roman use of *res* and of the terms *corporalis* and *incorporalis*; nor the interpretation of the term "thing" and of the borrowed "corporeal" and "incorporeal" which we suggested in the chapter on early English law.[61] Nor is it necessary for our purpose to develop the sequence of thought by which medieval and modern legal theory, working through a philosophized *dominium*, came gradually to identify the words *res* and "thing" with material objects exclusively, in spite of the fact that such was not their original legal significance and that common usage has never limited them to so specific a sense. Nevertheless such a process of concretion did occur in the law, until Austin could say, "*Things* are such *permanent* objects, *not being persons*, as are sensible or perceptible through the senses."[62] And Salkowski,[63] "Thing in the juristic sense is, strictly, every portion of external nature which, limited in space, and subject to the control of the Person, has a money value. . ." He states that, according to the idea of the Romans, it was everything existing in space, not possessed of personality. Having accomplished this concretion, the use of the term "incorporeal" with respect to a "thing," in either Roman or English law, though it persisted, nevertheless seemed absurd. How can a thing which is a material object be "incorporeal"? Austin sees this error reproduced in the "jargon" of English law, where, he says,[64] "*rights* of a certain species [the "incorporeal things"] . . . are absurdly opposed to the *things* (strictly so called) ["corporeal things"] which are the *subjects* or *matter* of rights of another species" (i. e. dominion). He goes on to explain that, properly, "things [i.e. material objects] are opposed, on the one hand, to *persons* themselves; and . . . on the other, [distinguished] from the *acts* of the persons, and from . . . *facts* or *events*" (i.e. the *res incorporales—ius obligationis, ius successionis*, etc.).[65] A similar analysis leads Poste to conclude that, since all property consists of rights, and is therefore incorporeal, and since all things are material objects, and therefore corporeal, Roman law should have classed *dominium* among the former, and should not have

[61] For the first see pp. 177-184; for the second see pp. 268-270.
[62] Op. cit., I, p. 368.
[63] Op. cit., p. 333.
[64] Op. cit., I, p. 372.
[65] Ibid., I, p. 368.

classed other rights of property as "things" at all. And this, I think, shows how blinded jurisprudence has become to the original meaning of the words which it has gradually metamorphosed into the cornerstone of its new philosophy.

Meanwhile the public, and that everyday law which is in the closest contact with it, proceeds serenely today—as perhaps it did in Roman and early English times as well—to develop a quite different concept of the 'thing.' Starting with the procedural fact—the *res* or 'thing'—which signified a dispute, the substantive legal fact of property was gradually "secreted in the interstices of procedure." From being the matter of dispute it came thus to stand for something which pre-existed the action and which persisted after it. It became a word for any property interest—not an incident but a continuum. In this sense the popular concept of 'thing' is distinguished from the legal concept, in that when fully analysed the 'thing' is never material and never a personal attribute—that is, it is conceived to exist apart from the material object to which it has reference and apart from the person in whom it inheres. We may best describe it by diagrams. This 'thing' is conceived figuratively to be a composite of property rights which is so integrated that it behaves as a ganglion of property relations. The rights pertaining to, or included in, it are related in some one of many different ways to a material object because they have reference to that object. One kind of relation is that of the complete property; another that of conditional property, like pledge, for instance; another that of a lease held for a term of years, etc. This may be illustrated diagrammatically.

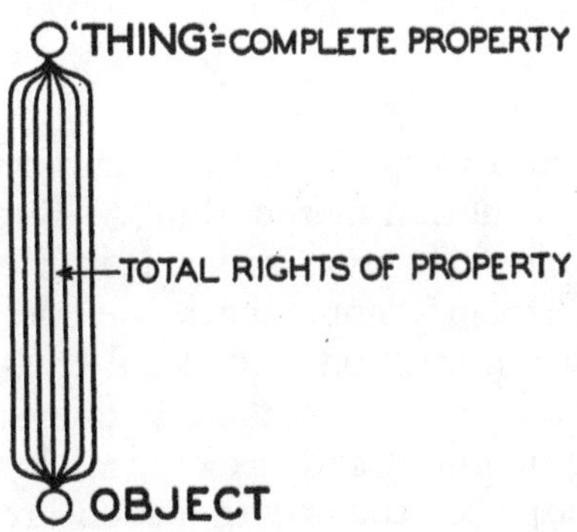

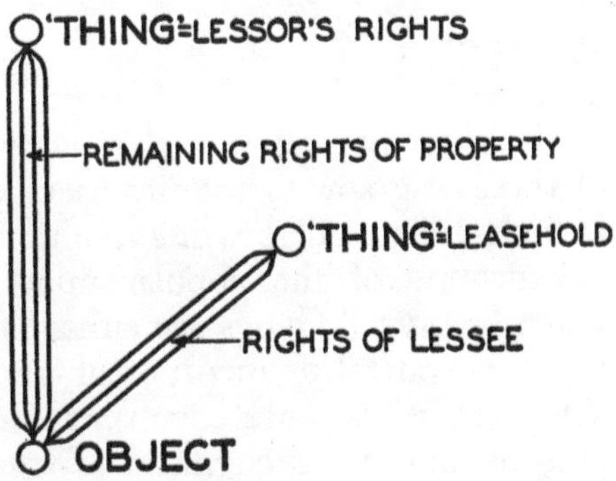

The owner of each of these 'things' is conceived to be attached to the respective 'thing'—or rather the 'thing' to the owner—in such a way that it is independent of him, persists when he ceases to be, and can be transferred to another without alteration in its nature. Let us represent this relation.

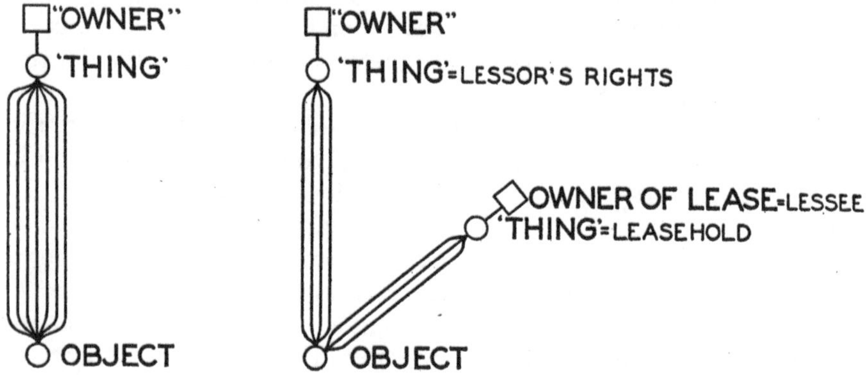

But the matter is subject to much greater complication, for many of the 'things' are capable of being themselves treated exactly like the original object; that is, as the basis for various new ganglia of rights, or 'things,' in turn. For instance:

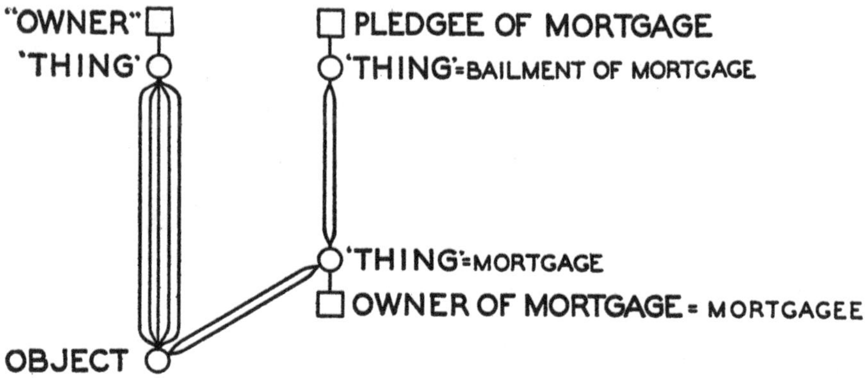

It is not necessary at this point to stop to question the accuracy of these diagrams or the propriety of this notion of the 'thing.' But I think most readers will agree that some such visualization is in the background of the popular mind. Ortolan[66] approaches the idea when he says, "Things are either of natural creation or of legal creation," corporeal or incorporeal, and the latter are "ranked as things, inasmuch as they are capable of being acquired and disposed of by persons, and are recognized as legal objects, attached to which are rights." One has only to eliminate the words "either of natural creation or" and the words "corporeal or"—which of course he did not intend to do—to make his statement fit our analysis exactly. Kocourek[67] also comes close to our analysis. He says, "*A jural*

[66] *The History of Roman Law,* p. 610.
[67] Op. cit., p. 309.

thing is a future protected infra-jural relation." The word future must be conceded to his highly legalistic and procedural point of view.[68]

On the basis of this interpretation of the ordinary usage of the legal term 'thing' what remains of the distinction between "corporeal" and "incorporeal" 'things'? Hohfeld[69] points out that "all legal interests are 'incorporeal'," consisting, as they do, of more or less limited aggregates of abstract legal relations. Why then is one particular aggregate, "ownership," singled out for corporeality? In Roman law the classificatory genitive is an adequate explanation. Always someone must be *dominus* even if he be *nullus*. Therefore, by ellipsis, the incorporeal 'thing' has, in this case, been overlooked or eliminated as an unnecessary duplication, and the object itself has appeared in its place. For it would seem a tautology to speak of the "owner of the ownership." And this point of view continues to this day. No better demonstration of this ellipsis can be given than to cite a passage from Professor W. W. Cook, interpreting Hohfeld's theories.[70] He says, "To say that A owns a piece of land is really to assert that he is vested by law with a complex—exceedingly complex, be it noted—aggregate of legal rights, privileges, powers and immunities—all relating of course to the land in question. He does not *own* the rights, etc., he *has* them; because he has them, he 'owns' in very truth the material object concerned; there is no 'convenient figure of speech'[71] about it." In other words this rather will-o'-the wisp 'thing,' called dominion or "ownership," which we have been seeking to identify, is said to represent a bundle of rights of a certain nature with reference to a certain object. Other kinds of bundle may exist with reference to the same object. In fact this particular kind of bundle, as we have seen, can only be distinguished from the

[68] Holland tries to compromise by using "thing" in both the Austinian and popular sense, substituting a new set of words. In his view "thing" is the object of a right; "whatever is treated by the law as the object over which one person exercises a right . . ." (op. cit., p. 101). They are material objects (i.e. physical things, *res corporales*) or intellectual objects (i.e. artificial things, *res incorporales*). The latter include patents, trade-marks, copyrights, easements, *hereditas, universitas,* etc. (and Gaius even included obligations) — cases where the right itself is *incorporeal* though it often relates to corporeal objects. Under this latter class all rights might be included, "though the Roman lawyers abstain from treating under it of *dominium*." Thus a right might be the object of a right. The reason for the class of intellectual objects is that it is convenient "to include among 'Things,' not only physical objects, but also certain groups of rights, which, for purposes of transfer and otherwise, are occasionally treated as if they were physical objects" (pp. 101-105). If Holland had unified his concepts by saying that 'things' were ganglia, or sets, of rights, pertaining to a material object or even to another 'thing' (i.e. another set of rights), his difficulties with Roman ideas and his inconsistencies would have been cleared up.

[69] Op. cit., p. 30.

[70] "Introduction" to Hohfeld, op. cit., p. 12.

[71] Referring to Salmond, *Jurisprudence*, p. 277.

others, if at all, because it is organized about a magnetic field as a core, a field which remains when all present rights are removed from it, and which attracts to itself all separate, part or future, rights as they become extinguished. It does not seem reasonable that we can own all the other bundles of rights as incorporeal 'things,' but that this one, because of its distinguishing core, we cannot own, or call an incorporeal 'thing.' Which leads us to the conclusion that "ownership" or dominion, if it exists, is also an incorporeal 'thing' which has been eliminated by ellipsis.[72]

Nothing remains, then, of the distinction between the so-called "corporeal" and "incorporeal" 'things' to which this terminology can be accurately applied. Nevertheless, as we have already suggested in considering the incorporeal 'things' of the English land law, it is clear that, both in Rome and in England, what was meant by the distinction was almost exactly what is meant today by the distinction between possessory and non-possessory interests—with the exact definition of which terms the *Restatement of the Law of Property* is now struggling.

A legal 'thing,' then, is any one of a great number of kinds of aggregate, or bundle, of property rights. It is simply what we have come to call a property *interest*. Each aggregate is subject to great variation in its particular composition, according to the particular rights entering into it. All the aggregates combined, which have reference to a single object, constitute complete property in that object. In turn from this originally complete property can be separated many fractions or interests. But there is always a remainder—one fraction, or interest, which contains the magnetic core and has exclusively the quality of *absolute* or ultimate property. If we have regard to each individual fraction or interest—an aggregate of rights—we see that it, too, is subject to being stripped of part of its rights, which may thereupon be used to create another coexisting legal 'thing,' more or less connected with or tributary to the first. This new 'thing' may exist with direct reference to the same material object as the first, or we may find that it can also exist with only indirect reference to the material object—that is, mediately through the first 'thing' only.[73]

Having established this concept of the legal 'thing' as any of the various possible bundles of rights (i.e. interests) with reference di-

[72] This view is confirmed in the aforementioned *Restatement of the Law of Property*, p. 22. "A person who has the totality of rights, powers, privileges, and immunities that constitute complete property in land . . . is the 'owner' of the 'land,' or owns the 'land.' The term 'land' is substituted in this connection for the term 'interests in the land,' that is, the ownership is predicated of the physical objects and not of the interests."

[73] A mortgage pledged as collateral, for instance.

rectly to an object, or to another 'thing,' and therefore indirectly to an object, we are now prepared to clear up the *double entendre* in the words "ownership" and "owner" to which we referred on p. 296. We have sought in vain for any particular interest which may be universally and therefore exactly described as "ownership." But if there is no certain interest which constitutes "ownership" of an object, then it is equally inappropriate to speak of the "owner" of an object. We can, however, revert to the English use of the word "owner." The term has been generally used to describe the relation of a person to any of these legal 'things.' One can own an estate, an easement, a profit, a mortgage, etc. But none of these estates, etc., constitute "ownership" of the object with reference to which they are interests. It is only by confusion with the Roman idea of *dominium* that the word has come to its double meaning. It seems necessary, therefore, to abandon the word "ownership" and also, tentatively, to confine the use of the word "owner" to designate him in whom any classified interest resides, and to describe his relation to that interest, not to the material object to which it has ultimate reference. If it remains necessary to identify the particular interest in which the recorded so-called *title* to an object resides, or that one which contains the right of present possession *de jure*, or that one which is residual (i.e. contains the magnetic core), it is better to call such interest by its class name and to add that it is in this case the titular, the present possessory, or the residual interest.

2. *Estates in Land*

The foregoing analysis leads us naturally to the consideration of the only actualities of modern property, namely the various interests which go to make up the complete property in a material object. These we have called the fractions of property. The first and most important class of these fractions is that which comprises the English estates in land. Only on the foregoing theory can such a character of interest be fitted into the concept of complete property. Or, it would be more correct to say that we have now adopted the doctrine of the English estates in place of that of *dominium*. The concept of the divisible complete estate is substituted for the hypothetical, but practically archaic, fact of integral "ownership." Once this is done the strictly defined concept of absolute property must shrink at best to a single element in the complex whole—the core right. Perhaps the core right goes with the reversion. Perhaps the practically unimportant contingency of abandonment points to the sovereign. What matter? We have the idea of infinitely variable portions of the totality of rights summing up to the complete property. And once we grasp the idea that these portions are not only "projected upon the plane of time," so that their incidence is successive, but that, to a considerable extent, they coexist as separate divisions of the various present rights, we apprehend not only their true nature, but also the applicability of the doctrine to all other 'things' (i.e. property aggregates) as well.[74]

To appreciate the elasticity[75] and complexity which such a doctrine permits in the subdivision of the complete property we have only to glance at Blackstone's table of estates in land – some of which in English law, and most of which in American law have no longer the practical importance they had, because forms of property, even more complex, in other objects have superseded them in economic pre-eminence.

- Real Property
  - Freeholds of Inheritance
    - Fee Simple
    - Fee Tail
  - Freeholds not of Inheritance
    - For Life
      - Conventional
        - Own
        - *Pur auter vie*
        - For more than one
      - Legal
        - In tail after possibility of issue extinct
        - By Courtesy (husband's)
        - In Dower (wife's)
- Personal Property (Chattels Real)
  - Less than Freehold
    - For years (Term)
    - At will (Copyhold)
    - By sufferance

[74] Holdsworth says, op. cit., VII, p. 469, "As we have seen, it was the nature and variety of these remedies [available to all interests] which, in the Middle Ages, gave to all these simultaneous estates in the land that reality, and that capacity for simultaneous coexistence, which is the distinguishing characteristic of the English doctrine of estates. The estate, whether in possession or not, was regarded, not as a mere chose in action, but as a very real thing; and this conception tended to increase the owner's power of disposition; for, though not entitled to the possession or seisin, he could be regarded as the owner of an actually existing interest, which was merely deferred in point of time."

[75] Markby, op. cit., p. 167, says, ". . . tricks have been played with the *ownership of an 'estate'* which could hardly have been ventured on with the ownership of the land itself." Our italics indicate the innate English concept of the estate as a legal 'thing' apart from the land, capable of being owned and thus of course itself incorporeal, though, because it may include physical possession at some time, it has usually, under the old English sense of corporeality, been called a "corporeal thing."

There are also the following, which Blackstone regards as rather "qualifications of other estates [including any of the foregoing], than a distinct species of themselves; seeing that any quantity of interest . . . may depend upon these provisional restrictions:" [75a]

Estates upon Condition
- Implied
- Express
  - In Gage
    - Vif gage (to be paid from use)
    - Mort gage (not the modern form)
  - Statute Staple and Statute Merchant } Chattels Real
  - By elegit }

Estates may also vary with respect to time of enjoyment:

In possession
Remainder
Reversion [76]

And they may vary with respect to the number and connections of the tenants: [77]

In Severalty
Joint Tenancy
Coparcenary
Common [78]

The several standardized types of estate, varying among themselves as to length and certainty of duration, are again subject to modification by "these provisional restrictions," and also as to time of enjoyment and as to the number of, and the relations among, the participating holders. To one, among the many estates which may coexist in a single piece of land, runs present possession *de jure*. The 'owner' of this estate is sometimes called the "limited owner" of the land, and Jenks [79] describes him "as virtually entitled to control, not merely the management and administration of the land, but the form which the investment of the settled capital shall take. . ." Fre-

[75a] *Commentaries*, II, X, p. 152.

[76] Though originally only used of the fee simple, this term is now frequently applied to the ultimate or residual rights to any property interest.

[77] An even greater complexity exists in modern law. The whole system is presented in the *Restatement of the Law of Property*, and the reader is referred to this document as evidence of what the law can do, given time, in working out special rules for individual classes of interest. When this same learning gathers around the modern "security" we will have a clarified and accepted theory of "choses in action."

[78] "Joint tenancy" accrues to survivor and is undivided: "Coparcenary" accrues to heirs of each and is in aliquot shares originated together: "Common" accrues to heirs of each and is in aliquot shares originated independently of each other.

[79] Op. cit., p. 251.

quently, however, in the case of a long term lease, "the power of alienation is detached from the ownership [possession] of the estate [land] when the estate [land] is parted with, and is either retained by the grantor, or given to someone else. Thus the ownership [possession] goes one way and the power of alienation goes another."[80] When the various essential attributes of complete property can be so divided it becomes necessary to conceive of two or more present estates in the same land as coexisting. It becomes almost a matter of indifference to which is applied the misnomer "ownership," since that depends upon which particular right is considered to identify this "ownership." The only enduring and the only ultimate interest is the reversion. To that attaches what we have chosen to call the core right. But as to the rest there is no fundamental distinction. Thus it is better to consider that all are fractions of the complete property; divided as to present rights as well as to successive enjoyment; and that each is a legal 'thing' which may, within limitations, be alienated, qualified or pledged without altering the rest of the property structure erected on that piece of land.

Blackstone gives the classic basis for the distinction between the estates which are chattels and those which are real property. He says these chattels – the chattels real – are real because they "concern, or savour of, the realty" but are chattels for want of a "sufficient, legal, indeterminate duration."[81] Like many other theories constructed after the fact, this is a brave effort to find a logical reason for a distinction which really grew out of their different historical origins and their different procedural histories.[82] That this persisting distinction makes much trouble in America today we will perceive in the next chapter.

3. *Servitudes and Securities*

The term fractions of complete property, which we have been using, is borrowed from Bentham who, in turn, adapted it from the French. It was his term for the "servitudes," etc. – the *démem-*

[80] Markby, op. cit., p. 166. The interpretations in brackets are ours.

[81] *Commentaries*, II, XXIV, p. 386. The utmost period during which they can last is fixed and definite. It is a "space of time certain, or till such a particular sum of money be raised out of such a particular income." Though the period may be of any duration it is nevertheless contrasted with the "lowest freehold," *pur auter vie*. For the law does not conclude that limited until death occurs. It is therefore uncertain.

[82] While the freehold estates were devices for keeping the land in the family and therefore of a dignified status, representing a "perpetual succession" of interests in the land, the term of years was the device to accommodate a "renter" and therefore one who had no great interest in the capital, or principal, value of the land.

bremens du droit de propriété" of the civil law, which came in the post-Roman period of Roman law to be analysed as *iura in re aliena.* It is curious that we should have come to apply the term "property," which, in effect, means *iura in re propria,* to its opposite, *iura in re aliena.* But so we do. Austin, whom we may follow on this particular subject, defines a servitude as "a definite subtraction or exception (accruing to the party having the right of servitude) from the indefinite rights of user or exclusion which reside in the proprietor of the thing."[83] Elsewhere he goes even further and defines any member of that more inclusive class, the *iura in re aliena,* as a "fraction or particle (residing in one party) of dominion, strictly so called, residing in another determinate party."[84] Nevertheless the character of these bundles or 'things,' separations of *iura in re propria,* is supposed to be differentiated from that of dominion by the existence in the latter of the magnetic core right to which we have alluded.[85] Austin's proof of the character of the *iura in re aliena* as subtractions, which is based on this differentiation, is the rule, "*nulli res sua servit.*" This Markby[86] explains as follows: when "one or more of the rights of ownership have been detached and given to another," so long as these rights "are in the hands of any other person, they have a separate existence, but as soon as they get back into the hands of the person from whom they are derived, as soon as they are 'at home' as it were, they lose their separate existence, and merge in the general right ownership." This is the basis for our ascription of magnetism to the core right. Others have limited the application of the term *iura in re aliena* to this special class of fractions of complete property,[87] but Austin points out that in England estates in land shade into servitudes. The line of distinction is not sharp. Recognizing the resemblance, though he does not combine the two, he reserves his concept of absolute property,

[83] Op. cit., II, p. 843.

[84] Op. cit., II, p. 878.

[85] Austin, op. cit., II, p. 832, maintains this distinction as to servitudes. ". . . the subject [i.e. object] of a right of servitude is also at the same time the subject [object] of property [i.e. dominion] residing in another or others." The parenthetic interpretations are ours. Austin's use of "property" is synonymous with "dominion." If it were not for that his statement might seem less arbitrary and more realistically flexible than it is. For, in the case of estates we have found it almost impossible to determine that one which is dominion. Holland, op. cit., p. 223, is even more arbitrary. "One or more of the subordinate elements of ownership, such as a right of possession, or user, may be granted out while the residuary right of ownership . . . remains unimpaired."

[86] Op. cit., pp. 158 and 159.

[87] Civilian law limited *iura in re aliena* to the servitudes and to use and usufruct (later including pledge) and construed them as subtractions. Thus Hearn, *Legal Duties,* p. 216, says, "The furthest advance that the Romans made in the direction of divided ownership was to treat all minor interests as *jura in re alienâ,* or, as we should say, as burthens upon the property."

(dominion or "ownership") for movables, and, when referring to land, speaks only of estates.

In this sub-class of fractions of property, the modern servitudes strictly speaking, we find two interesting and instructive points. In the first place these specialties, which are now confined to application to land, retain the ancient terminology. In Rome, as we have seen, they were derived from, or upon analogy with, slavery—probably debtor slavery. So the land to which the right of servitude is appurtenant is still called "dominant," and the object-land is called "servient." In the second place, for the sake of convenience in transfer, so that all tributary rights may automatically pass with the entitled estate, a fiction is maintained which makes this dominant land the subject of a right. This is the only case, I believe, where a material object is personified and treated as the subject rather than the object of a right.[88] The fiction, made easy by the antiquity and authority of the form, is only rendered necessary by that peculiar legal blindness which, in all cases capable of being considered as dominion, identifies the legal 'thing' with the material object. If the complete property in the land were seen as an independent entity—a legal 'thing' by itself—as it undoubtedly is, then such special rights in other land would attach naturally to this 'thing' along with all the general rights as to its own locus, and would pass with the 'thing' as a whole or with any fraction in which it should practically be included. Since, as we shall see, the most important kinds of modern easements are in reality rights of access to common resources or to objects held in public property, and are therefore general rights inherent in all property in land and not special rights created by grant, such a view would greatly simplify the law. On the other hand, in the obverse (i.e. as to the servient land) servitudes are restrictions on, or subtractions from, complete property. But in that respect, if they are general, they are no different in kind from the social reservations from property rights, nor even from the general restrictions on liberty. The difference exists only when they are deductions which are special and limited, rather than general and unlimited, in their inherence in abutting property only. To oppose "dominion" to "servitus," as Austin does, in that the former is only limited by social restrictions and by the subtractions of the servitudes to which it is subject, while the latter is definitely circumscribed, is a quantitative rather than a qualitative distinction.

In Anglo-American law the term servitude is now applied to the more recent analogues of the ancient "commons" and "ways," two of

[88] Ships, in Admiralty law, are treated as the subjects of duties, but not, I believe, as the subjects of rights.

the incorporeal hereditaments.[89] The successor of the former is the profit a prendre (or profit) and, of the latter, the easement. None of the other forms mentioned by Blackstone have become naturalized in America. His advowsons, tithes, offices, dignities, pensions, and annuities were, or are, feudal survivals. His rents were of a different sort from ours, for they were feudal and permanent charges on the soil. Of his franchises, we have transferred the name to a different order of interest which, as a class, is neither "of indeterminate duration" nor is it found "issuing out of a thing corporate (whether real or personal) or concerning, or annexed to, or exercisable within, the same."[90] The surviving remnant of these original special privileges (freedoms) in regard to land – the public service franchise – so far as it still relates to land, has been assimilated partly to easements and partly to eminent domain.

We find a useful tabulation of the modern servitudes and the remaining class which are usually treated as fractions of property in Pound's "Scheme of Rights in Another's Property in Anglo-American Law."[91]

a. Servitudes
   1. Profits
   2. Easements
   3. Covenants Running with the Land
   4. Equitable Servitudes
b. Securities (Collateral)
   1. Pledge
   2. Mortgage
   3. Common Law Liens
   4. Statutory Liens
   5. Equitable Liens

Pound's definition of pledge as "a bailment of property [i.e. chattels] by way of security" serves to identify this fraction of property with the class which we are about to describe. The mortgage is defined as "a conveyance upon condition subsequent – subject to equitable right to redeem unless foreclosed." This final form of many experiments is a successful anomaly. In form it is a registered transfer of a conditional present right without title and without possession. In fact it is a conditional future interest. In form the condition is subsequent; in fact it is precedent. The liens are varied

[89] Blackstone, *Commentaries*, II, VII, p. 106, says of them that "their owner hath no property, *dominicum*, or demesne, in the *thing* itself, but hath only something derived out of it; resembling the *servitutes*, or services, of the civil law."

[90] *Commentaries*, II, III, p. 20.

[91] *Readings*, p. 605.

forms of fractions of property which we shall examine more fully in the next chapter.

4. *Bailments*

In the previous chapter we discussed the origins of "special property." At first, when possession was, in practice, the most complete property one could have, what remained to the bailor, voluntarily out of possession, was little more than a chose in action. Later, with the development of the idea of a residual right of property superior to possession, the possession of the bailee was construed as a derivative possession. But even at the time of Blackstone neither party to this anomalous arrangement was considered to have an absolute right of property (i.e. "dominion" so-called) in the object bailed. Bailment is to Blackstone a species of contract, and contracts are means of acquiring title to property—in fact, in the case of a contract to sell, do actually execute the sale and transfer property at such time as the parties intend. But in the case of bailment "there is no absolute property[92] in either the bailor or the bailee . . . for the bailor hath only the right, and not the immediate possession; the bailee hath the possession, and only a temporary right."[93] The bailee has a "special qualified property" and possession. His property is not absolute because of his contract for restitution. "And, on account of this qualified property of the bailee, he may . . . maintain an action against such as injure or take away these chattels." The bailor also has these same rights of action against others and there is "still left in him the right to a *chose* in action" against the bailee, grounded upon the contract, which is evidently considered to be as definite a right of property as any other.[94] Today this right of the bailor, which would otherwise have degenerated, with the Romanization of the chose in action since Blackstone's time, into a mere obligation, has been maintained in full. And this because, under the modern theory, the bailor retains "the same right of ownership that he had before, or . . . so much of the dominion as he has not transferred with the possession to the bailee."[95] Thus, in both terminologies there is conceded to be a division between the bailor and the bailee of the totality of the rights of property, or the complete property, in the material object.

The fundamental difference between the truly indigeneous viewpoints of Roman and of English law is perhaps most clearly demon-

[92] Except in the stipend in the case of hire—which he does not treat as bailment.
[93] *Commentaries*, II, XXV, p. 396.
[94] *Commentaries*, II, XXX, p. 453.
[95] Terry, op. cit., p. 325, citing American decisions.

strated in the case of bailment. Today the general classes of bailment are (1) for carriage, (2) for storage and custody, (3) consignment for sale, (4) to do work thereon, (5) for hire, (6) for free use and (7) for pledge. Of these the second is nearly identical with the Roman *depositum*, the sixth with the Roman *commodatum*, and the seventh with the Roman *pignus* – all of which were among the contracts *re* – while the fifth is part of the Roman *locatio et conductio*, which was, in the Roman law, a consensual contract. In these very differences of classification we perceive a difference in the root idea. In developed English law the emphasis was upon the property, the relation of both the bailor and the bailee to the object. The bailor surrendered the possessory interest, true, but he was conceived to retain a certain right in the object, which may be described as a "repossessory interest," to be asserted by means of an action rather than by self-help. This view persisted even when the composition of a wrong to this property became an award of damages. And, in the end, the interest itself grew to be capable of possession so that it became possible to bail in turn the bailment itself. The bailee, on the other hand, always had a "special property." In Roman law, we meet no such modifications of property. The Roman replicas of these bailments were contracts pure and simple. The emphasis was upon performance. Neither the possessory nor the proprietary rights were considerably disturbed by the dislocation of the object. It remained in the same classification by the genitive. Possession did not pass. English law was based upon divided property in objects and little or no control over persons. Roman law passed sharply from a complete property in objects to its only alternative, a substituted control over the person. The Roman equivalents of bailments were wholly the latter.

D. *Equitable Property*

1. *The Origin of Trusts*

The servitudes and the collateral securities are the classic exemplars of this concept of fractions of property. In so analysing them we coincide with the most legalistic legal theory. In fact we adopt that theory. But whereas we purpose to continue to apply it to the next class, equitable property, we must here part company with accepted theory, if there can be said to be such a thing as accepted theory on this debated subject. By equitable property we intend the rights of the beneficiary (cestui que trust) under an Anglo-American trust. Sometimes the term is applied, in retrospect, to "bonitarian" dominion in Roman law. Except that the latter was another example of a type of property developed by the equitable jurisdiction—for the Praetor was in many respects an analogue of the Chancellor—there is no resemblance between the two. Both are cases of "conflict of laws" (i.e. conflicting jurisdictions). But, while in English law the essence of the matter is some sort of derivative or dependent tenure[96]—a persisting relation between trustee and beneficiary—in Rome the problem lay in the very fact that not only such a persisting relation but even a transfer between a legal person and a technical outlaw as to property rights was impossible, so that a novation, or creation of new and independent rights, was necessary. Much the same is true of the Roman trust, *fidei commissa*. This too, according to Poste,[97] had as its original object the enablement of legacies to those legally incapacitated to receive them. But, by the time it became fully validated in equity, it had become a species of general executorship, and thus of a transient nature involving few, if any, problems in the way of coexisting rights of property.[98] Wholly different from these two expedients, the original trust, the English "use," was an artifice to escape from feudal burdens and restraints. A straw man was set up as feoffee, from whom the cestui que use held in trust.[99] The Statute of Uses tried to close this avenue of escape by eliminating the nominal feoffee. But instead, except in a few cases, it only succeeded in strengthening the cestui who became thereafter the effective possessor, with a very real "equity." Thus Holland says of trusts that "their history is a curious one, beginning, like that of the Roman 'fideicommissa,' with an attempt to evade the law."[100] And it might be added that, since he wrote, the sudden leap into popularity of the more modern form of trust is also considerably due to an "attempt to evade the law"—the super-tax on incomes and the inheritance taxes.

While this modern form, the trust of personal property, so general

[96] "A true equitable right is always derivative and dependent, i.e., it is derived from, and dependent upon, a legal right." Langdell, "A Brief Survey of Equity Jurisdiction," 1 *Harvard Law Review* (1887), p. 55, 59.

[97] Op. cit., p. 250.

[98] Hearn, *Legal Duties*, p. 215, calls the *fidei-commissarius* a "conduit-pipe."

[99] As a matter of fact the original practice, which defeated the incidence of the feudal casualties, was a feoffment in joint tenancy of a party of friends, even as many as ten, who thereby, by accrual to survivor, insured the longest possible avoidance of succession and its charges. So far as the name is concerned this joint party of friends would account for it. Maitland, in his "Introduction" to Gierke, op. cit., p. xxxiii, notes that in the Lex Salica the "*trustis* is a group of comrades." And Justice Holmes, "Early English Equity," 1 *Law Quarterly Review* (1885), pp. 162, 163, says, "The feoffee to uses of the early English law corresponds point by point to the Salman of the early German law, as described by Beseler fifty years ago." We have already suggested that the word is another case of "third party," functioning in an active or guaranteeing way, like *testis, tiers* and *dritte.*

[100] Op. cit., p. 250.

in American practice, is not identical with the English "use"—the former usually being a special and independent body of property and the latter a kind of estate in land—nevertheless the two are generally treated as one legal form. Therefore, with the elimination of many of the elements of conflict of jurisdiction resulting from the consolidation of equity and law in England and in most American states, it has become more than ever necessary to incorporate the complete structure into the theory of the now unified system. The trust can no longer be treated as one thing at law and another in equity.[101] In fact it has become so much an integral part of the property system that the courts have used it as a model upon which to create many types of so-called resulting and constructive (construed) trusts.[102]

2. *The Conflict of Laws and the Misfits of Theory*

When Chancery treated the cestui as owner and the law courts treated the feoffee as owner each had protection for his particular rights.[103] And there was surprisingly little conflict. Then, so far as any theory of the relation between the two was necessary, it was sufficient to imply a contract, or obligation, resting upon the feoffee in favor of the cestui. This is the basis of the more generally held Eng-

[101] Nevertheless the remaining conflict of rules is almost as confusing as was the prior conflict of jurisdiction. Thus Hohfeld, op. cit., p. 121, says of the present, ". . . a large part of the rules of equity . . . conflict with legal rules and, as a matter of substance, annul or negative the latter *pro tanto*." ". . . the equitable rule is, in the last analysis, paramount and determinative." The "legal rule in every such case has, *to that extent*, only an apparent validity and operation as a matter of *genuine* law." Naturally this would be true since equity is, in its nature, a detailed qualification, or modification, of the broad generalities of law.

[102] Thus, in America, of the property of an intestate, the legal title is construed to be in the government (escheat) and the equitable title in the creditors and next of kin. Bankruptcy and insolvency practice are also modelled on trusts.

[103] Markby, op. cit., pp. 170 and 171, says, "The Court of Chancery, had it confined itself to compelling owners of property either to fulfil certain fiduciary relations, such as those of guardian and ward, or to fulfil the wishes of persons from whose bounty they had received the ownership, would have kept within the limits of analogous institutions in other systems of jurisprudence" (i.e. property in the *pupillus* under guardianship, or in the trustee, as *fidei commissarius*). Instead "It has created an entirely new interest in land; an interest as comprehensive, as general, as beneficial, as transferable, as ownership itself—which *is* ownership in fact, only the rights of the owner are somewhat clumsily exercised; and so it is frequently called."

Hearn, *Legal Duties*, p. 214, says that in the "use" the cestui "had, with some trifling exceptions, the same powers of dealing with the property that he would have had if he were in possession of the legal estate." He defines the "use" as a *ius in re aliena* (the same classification that he makes of estates). "It is a right in another person's property, but that right is so extensive as to smother the rights of the nominal owner." Yet he conceives that the trustee "has all the rights of ownership (see page 447) save one," the right of user. "Against him a perpetual usufruct" is held.

lish theory of trusts.[104] But when, in the preponderating number of instances with the modern trust, the "donor" and "cestui"—or as we should say, the "settlor" and "beneficiary"—ceased to be one and the same person this theory of contract runs head-on into the doctrine of "privity of contract." Under this doctrine it is not possible for the settlor to impose upon the trustee an obligation which runs, not to him, but to a third party, the beneficiary; nor to confer upon the beneficiary a right of action against the trustee.[105]

Representing the older point of view and with a "use" of land in mind, Ames[106] says, "A *cestui que trust* is frequently spoken of as an equitable owner of the land. This, though a convenient form of expression, is clearly inaccurate. The trustee is the owner of the land, and, of course, two persons with adverse interests cannot be owners of the same thing [sic]. What the *cestui que trust* really owns is the obligation of the trustee. . ." Langdell[107] says of trusts that the law does not permit imposing a real obligation on the property, and subjecting the title of the donee (trustee) to a condition subsequent is inadequate. So equity imposes on the donee a personal obligation with respect to the property. In his lectures on *Equity*, Maitland takes a similar stand. ". . . the thesis that I have to maintain is this, that equitable estates and interests are not *jura in rem*."[108] "The trustee is the owner, the full owner of the thing, while the *cestui*

[104] "The Courts of Chancery, however, ingeniously contrived to avoid a direct conflict with Courts of Law by giving decrees which were in form in personam only." Markby, op. cit., p. 173, Note 2.

"In the origin of trusts and of uses out of which the modern trust has developed, the emphasis was laid on the personal relation; but in the course of time the emphasis has shifted and is now laid on the aspect of a trust as a disposition of property." *Restatement of the Law of Trusts*, p. 12.

[105] Thus Anson, up to the 6th Eng. ed. (1892) of his *Contract*, said, p. 218, "A man cannot incur liabilities, and again, a man cannot acquire rights, from a contract to which he was not a party." (Substance still continued in section headings.) For this reason the subject of trusts is omitted from his work. But he devotes a good many pages, 5th Amer. ed., pp. 345 ff., to what seems to me a vain effort to reconcile the changing facts as to third party beneficiaries with the doctrine of privity of contract.

It is to be noted, however, that the necessities of modern business and particularly of the corporate form, have decidedly modified this doctrine in America. Thus, in the *Restatement of the Law of Contract*, the creation of rights in third parties, the assignment of rights and the delegation of duties (performance) under a contract are all admitted, but each under its own conditions and rules of law. See *Restatement*, Chapters 6 and 7 and notes thereon.

It is also interesting to note that, in England, the courts are using the constructive trust as a device to escape the doctrine of privity of contract and enable them to award benefits to third parties to contracts. See Corbin, "Contracts for the Benefit of Third Persons," 46 *Law Quarterly Review* (1930), p. 12.

[106] "Purchase for Value without Notice," 1 *Harvard Law Review* (1887), p. 1, 9.

[107] "A Brief Survey of Equity Jurisdiction," 1 *Harvard Law Review*, p. 55, 65.

[108] *Equity*, p. 112.

que trust has no rights in the thing."[109] But the trustee is "bound to exercise [his rights] for the benefit of"[110] the beneficiary. Thus he comes to the conclusion that trusts were originally *in fact* contracts, but having rules of their own.[111] Then he takes one long step away from this position; ". . . a *cestui que trust* has rights which in many ways are treated as analogous to true proprietary rights. . ."[112] In his later studies he came to the more realistic conclusion that, while one cannot say that the right of the English cestui is either *dinglich* or *obligatorisch*, "people habitually speak . . . of it as a kind" of ownership. The land is conveyed to the trustee in a "thing-like" right. He has the ownership. But the cestui has rights that are treated as ownership, "or as some of those modalities of *Eigenthum* in which our medieval law is so rich." The cestui's estate is in the use not in the land. "We might say that 'the use' is turned into an incorporeal thing, an incorporeal piece of land; and in this incorporeal thing you may have all those rights, those 'estates,' which you could have in a real, tangible piece of land."[113] As representing the opposite extreme from Ames we may quote Salmond:[114] "If we have regard to the essence of the matter rather than to the form of it, a trustee is not effectively an owner at all, but in essence a mere agent, upon whom the law has conferred the power and imposed the duty of administering the property of another person. In legal theory, however, he is not a mere agent, but an owner. He is a person to whom property substantially that of some one else is technically attributed by the law, albeit on the footing that the rights and powers thus vested in a nominal owner are to be used by him on behalf of the real owner."

These authorities are cited to show the extent to which, as Justice Holmes has remarked, "ideas become encysted in phrases and thereafter for a long time cease to provoke further analysis."[115] The rigid concept of "ownership" is inapplicable here, as elsewhere. So too is the concept of a contractual obligation.[116] "A trust still is only a trust, although according to the orthodox it creates merely a personal obligation."[117]

[109] Ibid., p. 47.
[110] Ibid., p. 48.
[111] Ibid., pp. 115-116.
[112] Ibid., p. 115.
[113] *The Collected Papers*, III, pp. 326 ff.
[114] *Jurisprudence*, p. 285.
[115] Dissent in Hyde v. U.S., 225 U. S. 347, 391 (1911).
[116] "Trusteeship," says Hearn, *Legal Duties*, p. 215, "follows the analogy not of a contract but of an office. It may involve for an indefinite period active duties and increasing responsibilities."
[117] Holmes, *Papers*, p. 218.

3. *A Special Type of Fraction of Property*

In respect of the strictly proprietary rights concerned, a trust is merely one among many methods of dividing complete property. Its first essential quality is that the titular interest is in the trustee. This may be bare. Or to it may be added, in varying degrees, those rights which pertain to the control of the 'thing.' But the beneficial rights (except perhaps for compensation) and what rights of control are not vested in the trustee, are in certain respects in the beneficiary. So far it is not unlike many other cases of divided interests, such as coexisting estates in land. The quality that makes it *sui generis*, however, is the personal relation that exists between the trustee and the beneficiary with reference to, and only with reference to, the proprietary interests concerned. Analogies to this personal relation are not to be found in the realm of obligations, though for want of any adequate concept similar relations were so classified in Roman law.[118] Rather they appear in those substitutes for the familial relation, which because they were not concealed within the *familia* as their prototypes had been, required not only that the law accord control to one party, but also protection to the other.[119] These are the fiduciary relations. "A person in a fiduciary relation to another is under a duty to act for the benefit of the other as to matters within the scope of the relation." Thus a trust is a "fiduciary relationship

[118] Such relations were those of wardship, of curatorship, of certain partnerships, of joint heirs, etc. "Here the defendant cannot be said to be bound by contract, for there has been no contract made between the parties; but as his obligation is not based on delict, it may be said to be quasi-contractual." Justinian, *Inst.*, 3. 27. 3. Classing it by default!

These relations cannot even properly be called quasi-contractual obligations because, as is stated in the *Restatement of the Law of Trusts*, "an obligor cannot be trustee either of his own duties or of the obligee's rights under the obligation" (p. 49). "Although the obligee can be trustee of the rights under the obligation . . . the obligor, not having them, cannot be trustee of them. The obligor has duties under the obligation but one cannot be trustee of duties owed by himself" (p. 139).

[119] Agency, partnership, heirship were of course projections of the original familial relationships. Wardship and curatorship were substitutions *in loco parentis*. These latter were the harbingers of future change in all familial relations in which "the old relation of *ownership* has given way to one of *reciprocal duties*." Hunter, op. cit., p. 140. *Pupilli* "were secured against loss from the dishonesty or negligence of their tutors or curators." Moyle, op. cit., I, p. 164. "The duties which the pupillus could enforce against the guardian . . . were, in general those of maintaining the full value of his property." Moyle, op. cit., I, p. 444. A tutor must do anything that a prudent man would do and do nothing that such a one would not do (see *Dig.*, 26. 7. 33). But the *pupillus* retained title. "His patrimony still vested in him, though he was deprived of its administration." Poste, op. cit., p. 90. And the curator was an administrator of property only. Moyle, op. cit., I, p. 159. Such an arrangement corresponds more realistically, if not more practically, to the purposes of the modern trust, than does its own inherited form.

with respect to property," in which the beneficiary has a so-called equitable interest and the trustee a legal interest.[120]

The property rights are variously separated. In the original "use" the position of trustee was nominal, whereas in the modern trust of personal property all the rights inhering in the beneficiary may require to be exercised through the medium and the instrumentality of the fiduciary. The "use," the "driest" trust, is at one extreme. The modern trust of personal property reaches to the other. At the first pole only technically, but at the opposite pole very practically, the tenure of the beneficiary, as to those particular sub-rights separated from the complete property which compose his equitable interest, is not direct but rather of a dependent and derivative nature. In many respects they are "held of" the trustee, or rather, of the body of property, the legal interest to which is vested in him. On the other hand, the fiduciary relationship confers the beneficial interest upon the beneficiary and exacts that the benefit derived must match the hypothetical benefits which would accrue if the beneficiary were administering his property himself. Nothing must be lost in the process of passing through the trustee's hands, unless "it is so nominated in the bond." Therefore, in many cases of a trust of personal property, it is difficult to apply the concept of the usual division of the complete property in specific 'things' or objects. Rather the equitable interest seems to be a subordinate and indirect property in the *corpus*, while it may be an exclusive and direct property in the *fructus*. It is obvious too that in such case the property of the beneficiary is construed to be in the *corpus* as a whole and in the *fructus* as a whole, rather than in the particular embodiments for the moment of the value of the former or the particular sources of the latter. Therefore it is not so much a dependent and derivative interest in specific 'things' or their yield, as it is an interest in a body of property.

Both in respect of the fiduciary relation with reference to property and in respect of this peculiar suspended or generalized interest in a fund, or body of property, rather than in determinate objects or 'things', the law of trusts is to us an especially interesting transition from the more direct and immediate rights of property, with which we have been dealing, to the indirect and mediate rights which we will now examine. In one respect – that of form – the transition is sharp. The English system of estates, strictly so-called, has been applied as a whole to the fractional and the dependent interests represented both by the incorporeal hereditaments and equitable property. In other words it is possible to divide the hereditament or the equitable prop-

120 *Restatement of the Law of Trusts*, pp. 11 and 14.

erty into the same varieties of estate as it is with legal property in land itself. And this practice, penetrating the domain of trusts through the "use," now applies *in toto* to the modern trust of personal property. Thus the same forms persist throughout these transitional types of property. But thereafter a complete change of form occurs.

E. *Property in Contract*

1. *The Chose in Action in General*

In the highly rarified jurisprudence of the nineteenth century we now step from the domain of the rights of property, as interests in material objects, to the domain of rights under contract which are, in this dynamic theory, rights to an act or event with no reference to a material object. Since our method of attack has been to explore the relation of property to material objects, our chief purpose in investigating the subject of contract must be to determine whether this step is, in fact, one so radical as has been pictured. Let us for the moment confound rights under contract with the chose in action,[121] which certainly includes them. Let us also try out the assumption that a succession of small steps may demonstrate that the same organization of property, which we have heretofore described, penetrates for quite a distance into this *terra incognita*. For such, in many respects, the field of the chose in action seems to be—the uncharted field of property rights; a region of more or less uncertain boundaries in which each new form of property remains until, in the gradual extension of the boundaries of the known, they are one by one reclaimed; a sphere in which, in the meantime, nothing is conceived to persist but only to happen; in which there are no material objects but only persons.

Bailor's rights, equitable property and even future estates in land are themselves retrievals from this twilight region of inchoate things. Another form which has until recently been classed with the choses in action, and by the orthodox as a contract and no more, is the share of stock in a corporation. Following the course of the trust, this is

[121] "As its name implies, a thing in action was, originally, a claim which could only be enforced by legal proceedings, as contrasted with a right or interest which could be enforced by actual seizure or possession of a tangible object." Jenks, op. cit., p. 279.

". . . the concept 'chose in action' has been gradually and continuously extended by analogy, until it has come to include so many heterogeneous rights that it is a work of some difficulty to discover any resemblance between certain classes of them." Holdsworth, op. cit., VII, p. 530. "'All personal things are either in possession or action. The law knows no *tertium quid* between the two.' It follows from this that the category of choses in action is in English law enormously wide, and that it can only be defined in very general terms." Ibid., p. 515.

beginning now to have a status of its own, to be treated as a 'thing' *sui generis.* In several respects it must remind us of its immediate predecessor in the process of admission to "state-hood." For the share of stock too is some sort of beneficial interest in the property held by another. It has something of the nature of derivative and dependent tenure – which tenure, we are coming to perceive, is not merely of antiquarian interest after all. Moreover, like the trust of personal property, it is decidedly not an interest in the several specific 'things' to which the corporation holds title, but is rather an interest in the totality of these 'things' in the aspect of their value – an interest in a body of property. But since this form of property has become, in recent years, the most important of all we shall reserve examination of it until we can give it the space and the background it deserves.

So too with the protected monopolies, which, for want of analysis, have been, like the Roman fiduciary relation, tossed into the hotch-pot of choses in action. Specifically these are franchises, patents, copyrights, trade-marks and names, memberships, and goodwill. These, too, belong in a class by themselves and have even less resemblance to contract than have shares of stock. But, again, we have not yet reached the point in our exploration at which we can satisfactorily place and analyse them, so that it is necessary to defer consideration of them as well.[122]

2. *The Origin and Nature of Credit-debt*

Perhaps the region of pure contract that lies nearest to our approach is debt. This is itself a vague term, but not so vague as chose in action, nor so broad as contract. Perhaps it can be defined and limited to describe a particular portion of contractual rights in such a way that it can be separated from the rest, just as has been done with trusts, shares of stock and the monopolies. The word itself is a pitfall. Let us amend it before proceeding. When we speak of debt we refer to a specific type of express or implied (and sometimes

[122] Jenks, op. cit., p. 280, says, "It is not, in fact, till we depart still further from the notions both of a mere right of action, and of a concrete object to be reached by means of it [Blackstone's concept], that we arrive at the most important classes of modern choses in action." Patent and copyrights, stocks and shares "could not possibly be regarded as mere rights of action." Yet the original view clings on in the French term for a share – *action.*

Holdsworth, op. cit., VII, p. 530, makes this suggestive comment: "Probably if these forms of property [patents and copyrights] had arisen at an earlier stage in the history of the law, they would have been regarded as franchises, and therefore as incorporeal hereditaments; for it is obvious that, in the case of the patent, and of that species of copyright which depended upon royal grant, the analogy to the franchise is close. . ." And, in general, ". . . in our modern law, the incidents of many of these things classed as choses in action show that they are in substance property of an incorporeal kind."

a quasi-) contractual obligation which upon the side of its inherence is a credit of the creditor. To avoid confusion we must therefore refer to it as a *credit-debt.*

In his *Summary of the Law of Contracts,*[123] Langdell remarks that, "A debt, therefore, according to the popular conception of the term, is a sum of money belonging to one person (the creditor), but in the possession of another (the debtor)." As we have assumed in the case of early Roman law, under simple economic conditions debt arises always from incompleted exchanges.[124] Such exchanges may be either sales not paid for or loans not repaid. When the settlement is to be made in kind it is a loan; when not in kind, a sale. But when in the maturity of the law the *nexum*, or obligation, so established, comes to be regarded as a legal 'thing', then the exchange is in itself complete at once, the seller or lender receiving the obligation in payment.[125] But though complete, this settlement is not final. The first exchange necessitates a second, the liquidation of the obligation. Thus the law, for the sake of convenience and to avoid miscarriage, construes the obligation, except in minor cases, to have been sub-

[123] P. 124.

[124] With the facts of early English law in mind Langdell, loc. cit., finds the origin of debt in a loan of money. Other loans are bailments. At first the two are not distinguished. Bailments are regarded as debts and are sued under the Writ of Debt. But later, since bailment does not transfer "ownership," it is distinguished from debt, and only the loan of money creates debt. Nevertheless the lender continues to feel that the borrower has "his money." The original and only remedy for breach of contract was the Action of Debt, which "was, at first in truth an action to recover a specific object. . ." Jenks, op. cit., p. 134.

[125] Ames, "Parol Contracts prior to Assumpsit," 8 *Harvard Law Review,* p. 252, 259, speaking of the rule as to transfer of property in a sale, which was at first effected by delivery and then by payment of purchase money, says, "It was hardly an extension of principle to treat the delivery of the buyer's sealed obligation for the amount of the purchase-money as equivalent to actual payment of money, or delivery of a chattel. . ." And Williston, *Sales,* sec. 260, notes that already, "Before the seventeenth century it was possible for the seller to transfer the property, not only without delivery, but without payment of the price or earnest money. This could probably only be done, however, if credit was expressly given by the seller."

The present status of incomplete exchanges is even more complex. Williston, *Sales,* sec. 2, says, "Whether a bargain between parties is a contract to sell or an actual sale depends upon whether the property in the goods is transferred. If it is transferred there is a sale, an executed sale, even though the price be not paid. Conversely, though the price be paid there is but a contract to sell . . . if the property in the goods has not passed." And in sec. 259 – provision of the Uniform Sales Act, sec. 18 – he says, "Property in specific goods passes when parties so intend. – (1) Where there is a contract to sell specific or ascertained goods, the property in them is transferred to the buyer at such time as the parties to the contract intend it to be transferred. (2) For the purpose of ascertaining the intention of the parties, regard shall be had to the terms of the contract, the conduct of the parties, usages of trade, and the circumstances of the case." But (sec. 3) "a parol gift is not valid without delivery, whereas a gift by deed transfers property without delivery." And in general, "the delivery of possession is necessary in a conveyance of personal chattels, as against everyone but the vendor." Lanfear v. Sumner, 17 Mass. 110, 113 (1821).

stituted in the hands of the seller or lender for the property rights in the objects he surrendered, and it converts his right under the obligation from a right to the restoration of these objects into a right to their equivalent in money—which, for reasons arising from the evolution of procedure, is identified with the *damnum* (damages) or thing *given* in punishment or composition. In this way the *iuris vinculum* is cut between the obligee and his object, and a new one substituted between the obligee and the obligor. In general this specific process gives rise to the particular form of obligation called credit-debt.

The transition stage in this development is well represented by Blackstone's contrast between property in possession and property in action. He confines the latter to contract, but he is thinking mainly of debt.[126] Such property in action exists "where a man hath not the occupation, but merely a bare right to occupy the thing in question; the possession whereof may however be recovered by a suit or action at law. . ." "But while the thing, or its equivalent, remains in suspense, and the injured party has only the right and not the occupation, it is called a *chose* in action; being a thing rather in *potentia* [in possibility] than in *esse* [in being]; though the owner may have as absolute a property in, and be as well entitled to, such things in action, as to things in possession."[127] In other words it is a case of recovery of an object of which the owner has lost, or surrendered, possession. As he says, the distinction between property in possession and in action is a distinction as to "the different *degree* or *quantity* of *dominion* or *property* to which things personal are subject."[128] Even Sohm is only a step beyond this idea. He says,[129] "Obligatory rights have this peculiarity that, prior to the fulfilment of the obligation, the creditor can never be said to be exercising his right, and that

126 And of bailor's rights, then still choses in action. He is thinking of the original objectives of debt and detinue.

127 *Commentaries*, II, XXV, pp. 396-398.

128 Commentaries, II, XXV, p. 398.

129 Op. cit., p. 224. Elsewhere, op. cit., p. 159, he presents this point of view still more clearly. He says, "On the other hand, in private law the thing [material object] is always the object of a legal right. But it may be subjected to the will of the person invested with the right in one of two ways: either directly, the right existing over the thing itself (real rights [*Sachenrechte*]); or indirectly, i.e. through the medium of the act of another, the debtor (obligatory rights). The purpose of real rights (such as ownership) is to enlarge, at once and definitively, the scope within which the person entitled may exercise his power. Real rights are thus the *final end* of proprietary dealings. On the other hand the purpose of obligatory rights is to make over to the creditor, by means of the act of the debtor, at some future time, a thing or that which has the value of a thing. Obligatory rights are thus the *means* of proprietary dealings."

This is also Ihering's view. He says, *Geist*, III, p. 365, ". . . der Besitz ist ein rechtlich geschütztes Interesse. Da dies Interesse aber die Sache zum Gegenstande hat, und zwar unmittelbar (nicht wie bei der Obligation mittelbar). . ."

his right is never . . . against a thing, but always only against the person of the debtor." He evidently conceives the possession of an object to be the only means of "exercising" a right. The right is, in this view, a suspended one.[180]

By the time theory has completely divorced the right of the obligee from the object which he has surrendered it is possible to say, "The liability of the promisor to fulfill his promise is a thing; and from its being capable of being bought and sold, assigned and transferred like other things, and also from its having a money value, it is looked upon as the object of ownership."[181] ". . . for an obligation is as truly the subject-matter of property as any physical *res*. The most striking difference between property in a thing [object] and property in an obligation is in the mode of enjoyment. The owner of a house or a horse enjoys the fruits of ownership without the aid of any other person. The only way in which the owner of an obligation can realize his ownership is by compelling its performance by the obligor.[182] Hence, in the one case, the owner is said to have a right *in rem*, and, in the other, a right *in personam*. In other respects the common rules of property apply equally to ownership of things and ownership of obligations. For example, what may be called the passive rights of ownership are the same in both cases. The general duty resting on all mankind not to destroy the property of another, is as cogent in favor of an obligee as it is in favor of the owner of a horse. And the violation of this duty is as pure a tort in the one case as in the other."[183] Thus "a legal duty rests upon persons, though extraneous to the obligation, not to interfere, without sufficient justification, with its due performance."[184] "It is because the liability or obligation is the object of ownership that contract is said to create a [the foregoing] right 'in rem' as well as a right 'in personam.'"[185]

In the foregoing the dynamic theory begins to show its origin. "Obligation then is a [right of] control exercisable by definite persons over definite persons for the purpose of definite acts or forbearances

[180] An early term for choses in action was "chattels incorporeal." Perhaps this demonstrates the original sense even more clearly since incorporeal property was, in England, property in objects of any order less than possessory.

[181] Markby, op. cit., p. 320.

[182] Again the idea of suspended ownership.

[183] Ames, "Purchase for Value without Notice," 1 *Harvard Law Review*, p. 1, 9-10.

[184] Anson, op. cit., p. 349. ". . . procuring a breach of contract [is] . . . an independent tort, which treats the contract, not as the cause, but as the mere subject-matter of the offence." Jenks, op. cit., p. 333.

[185] Markby, op. cit., p. 506, Note 1. But the means by which the law does this is not by attaching the ordinary rights of property to the obligation,—the legal 'thing'—but rather under the doctrine of "master and servant" or under a generalized "right of contract." Such a tort is not an injury to property. It is an injury to personal rights.

reducible to a money value."[186] And acts or forbearances (negative acts) are "determinations of the will which produce an effect upon the world of sense. . ."[187] By this time we are back where we started in early Rome. Is this a case where English law has succumbed to the superior prestige of a highly philosophized and self-conscious civilian law, the principles of which are, in the main, relics of primitive society? Or is it evidence that both independent developments attained similar doctrines at similar stages of maturity? The recognition of this surviving prepossession of the classificatory genitive, which cannot admit of divided dominion in the object in spite of all facts to the contrary, suggests the former. And this is reinforced by the obvious derivation of the terms "obligation" and "control" from that particular form of the rights of property which we have called the powers—originally the *ius*. In Rome, we have seen, the right of the creditor was for a long time a *ius* over the person of the debtor, to be exercised physically against his person—*in personam*. But during the evolution of the English idea of debt which has, in modern times, brought it back to the point at which it started in early Roman law, the whole basis of this original conception has disappeared. Gradually in later Rome and again in England, the person of the debtor has been freed and the incidence of the debt has been transferred to his property. It is true that this later developed incidence has not restored the original and primitive condition. It does not constitute a repossessory right, for it is no longer attached to a specific 'thing.' Rather it has become a claim to an equivalent in value—a floating charge against the generality of 'things' which are the property of the debtor—an incidence similar to that which we found existing in the case of the trust of personal property.[188] Therefore it is in many respects, as we shall develop later, of the nature of coexisting property rights. As such it has become more closely allied with the newer protections than with the older powers, though it still retains the form of the latter.

When we analyse this process of development it becomes evident that, in this field, the early powers and the later protections have grown together at their centres—the one growing down from above, the other up from below—so that in respect of certain powers there has been an anastomosis and they have been gradually metamorphosed

[186] Anson, op. cit., p. 11.

[187] Holland, op. cit., p. 108.

[188] The closeness of the resemblance of the chose in action to equitable property is well evidenced by the frequent introjection of the concept of a fiduciary relation, borrowed from the latter form, into the field of choses in action. Thus it is frequently said that the corporation, as to its stockholders, and the debtor, as to his creditors, is in the status of a trustee. This is not the law. But there is an analogy of which the courts occasionally make use.

from a control over another man to a protection with respect to certain portions of his 'things' – indeterminate, unspecified, nevertheless purely 'thing'-like – and in no remaining respect to be exercised over his person but only over his property. Debtor slavery is now a thing of the past, though it still casts its ghostly shadow over the modern survival of the archaic Roman theory of the *obligatio* – that *iuris vinculum* which pictures the debtor in chains. Today the chain is very insubstantial, "consisting only of right," but it has not yet been found possible to modify legal theory to bring the incidence of the right past the debtor to his property, where it actually rests in fact and law and where it is exclusively applied.

These considerations lead us to revert to the question whether the contractual obligations *re* – broadly so-called – are not more nearly what the naïve think them than what the nineteenth century jurists thought them.[189] Is it possible to view contracts of a class which establish the credit-debt relations as something more than promises, something which establish rights of property in the body of property of the debtor?[140] And is it due to the recognition of such property that, in spite of theory or through the medium of theoretical fictions, the rights of the creditors against voluntary dissipations of the debtor's fund and the rights of exclusion inhering in these credit-debt relations, have been granted? In general are the incompleted exchanges (sales on credit and loans) more nearly a parting with possession and certain other property rights, with the retention of a "string" on the 'things' surrendered – or rather on their equivalent, an aliquot part of the generalized mass of 'things' appertaining to the debtor?

While we are not yet prepared to determine all these questions it is worth while, before leaving this preliminary discussion, to discriminate between credit-debts and all other contractual rights, since our points have been made only with reference to the former as a particular class. Such a definition is difficult and probably cannot be made exact. It seems that the term "credit-debt" should be limited to cases of unilateral contracts where a property right, arising from a

[189] It would, perhaps, represent the juristic viewpoint to say that proof of the *re* is merely evidence of the promise.

[140] Anson, op. cit., p. 75, speaks of the two leading ideas, one that a promise is binding if given in a certain form, the other that "the acceptance of benefits of a certain kind imports a duty to repay them." The second involves "the readjustment of proprietary right" and results in an informal liability "arising from sale and delivery of goods, or loan of money, in which the property has been transferred, and the duty to return or repay [which] was enforced in the action of debt."

And Langdell, op. cit., p. 60, states that "debt" in English law existed only where legal consideration on one side had passed. "The consideration, therefore, was of the very essence of a debt,– was in fact what created it." In "assumpsit" only a nominal consideration was required. In "debt" the contract was *re*.

promise, express or implied, comes to exist, which should result in the transfer by the promisor, or promisors, of an ascertained or readily ascertainable sum of money, or other property of determined value, equivalent to the disequilibrium created by the failure of the promisor to perform, and due at a time certain or on demand; or to cases of bilateral contracts, after full or part performance by one promisor, where a property right, arising from a promise, express or implied, comes to exist which should result in the transfer of an equivalent *pro tanto*, measured by the disequilibrium due to the deficiency in performance by the other promisor or promisors, in the form of a readily ascertainable sum of money or other property of determined value and due under above conditions; or of imposed, or quasi-contractual, obligations assimilable to the foregoing.

3. *Unliquidated and Quasi-debt*

There remain other contracts where the net liability is either not readily ascertainable in terms of money value or where the liability itself is in doubt. This leads us to recognize two other criteria. The liability [141] under a contract can be conceived as passing through two principal stages among many. Having sprung into being *re*, or through a promise with consideration or performance, it may be acknowledged by the obligor in a certain money value. Thereupon it becomes assimilated to the preceding definition of a credit-debt. Or it may never become so liquidated [142] until adjudication, when it becomes a judgment debt. And this either because the fact or the amount of the liability is disputed. In the extremely legalistic view, all antecedent contractual rights may thus be regarded as inchoate until the remedial right to which a breach gives birth is reduced to judgment. Nevertheless here, as in the case of personalty in possession, the question is rarely raised and adjudication rarely required, although such property is not registered or recorded and so has not ordinarily a formal title to support it. Thus the stages of progress classify the rights under contract into four groups. First, there are those which have not yet become property in the aggregate

[141] In law "liability" means legal responsibility to do, pay or make good something (*dare, facere, praestare*). In business and accounting it is usually limited to a debt.

[142] In business the word "liquidated" means converted into money. Therefore a liability that is liquidated is one that is paid or settled. In law "liquidated" means ascertained or determined in terms of money value. "A demand is not liquidated . . . unless it appears how much is due." Nassoiy v. Tomlinson, 148 N. Y. 326, 330 (1896). In law the term "due," as used of debt, merely means certainly "owing" or "payable." It has no reference to time of payment. Thus is lost the useful distinction, which is preserved in business, between debts not due, debts due and debts past due, or overdue.

of an obligor's 'things' because no net liability against either party has yet arisen. They have not entered the first stage. Second, there are those in which a liability may have arisen but is not yet admitted or ascertained. These are in the first stage. Third, there are those in which a liability exists which is admitted and ascertained. Fourth, there are those in which a certain liability is adjudicated – judgment debts. The last two have arrived at the second stage, and only they resemble the aforementioned complete but semi-final exchanges which make of the obligation a part of the property structure. Only they can be called credit-debts. The immature liabilities may involve future changes in the structure. We do not know. At their present stage they are but "stresses and strains." [143]

This differentiation is based on the stage of development rather than on an intrinsic difference in character. It assumes in other respects a unity not usually conceded. It assumes that the property lies in the lack of balance resulting from a deficiency in mutual performance or consideration, and not in the promise or its performance itself. And it therefore assumes that the true root of the English doctrine of contract is not the promise but the consideration, the theory of "quid pro quo." [144] It would seem to be on this theory that

[143] It seems to a layman that it is the effort of the law to assimilate debt to the unliquidated damages wrought by mere non-feasance of a promise, in order to bring both under one form of action (assumpsit) and to make possible the construction of a homogeneous law of contract, that has occasioned the loss of the fundamental distinction between those so-called rights of action which include a definite present property right (debt) and those where the property is literally in action or potential (damages).

"It appears somewhat difficult to class a mere expectation of damages among property, and if it is not property it is not a chose in action;" Elphinstone, "What is a Chose in Action?," 9 *Law Quarterly Review* (1893), p. 311, 315.

[144] Justice Holmes seems to hold that the doctrine of consideration is a rather non-essential derivative of the original *secta* of the simple contracts arising from incomplete exchanges (sales on credit and loans) and which was used as evidence in the Writ of Debt. *Common Law*, Lecture 7.

But its resemblance to the *causa debendi* of medieval continental law seems to indicate for it a greater generality than this would account for. In the Middle Ages "religiously sanctioned undertakings by promissory oath and real transactions of pledge of person or property and of exchange gave rise to a simple system of formal undertakings. Out of these came a theory of *causa debendi*, or reason for owing the promised performance, which has had a profound influence upon subsequent thinking." Pound, *Philosophy*, p. 251. This German *causa* was the reason for making the pact, not, like the Roman *causa*, a legal reason for enforcing it; "Where something was exchanged for a promise that something was a 'causa debendi'" (p. 254). But the idea of consideration has persisted, in English law, as the idea of the *causa debendi* has not, in civilian. And the former idea seems more likely to be responsible for modern American attempts at a complete theory of equivalence, such as Langdell's system of "conditions implied in law, or dependent promises" (p. 259), than that they are derived from a rationalization of the *causa debendi*, "influenced by canon law and casuist writings" (p. 255). The notion of equivalence arises directly from experience and from the notion of justice – *aequitas*, equity, equality.

the courts have come, in the course of time, to their general assumption that all contracts involve an exchange until proved otherwise; in the doctrine of consideration, that men do not as a rule promise something for nothing; and in the doctrine of implied contract, on the other hand, that men do not as a rule give something for nothing.

Yet does this unity actually exist? Is there not still another criterion by which to differentiate the liability represented by credit-debt from all others? We have seen that the economic credit-debt does truly arise from an exchange – a purchase of the obligation, in fact; payment being made either prior to the contract, as consideration, or during its existence, as part or total performance on one side. Is this always true of the other contractual rights? Certainly not. It is only true of such others as have been excluded from being classed as debts only because they are disputed either as to the fact of the *re*, or as to the amount of the liability therefor. As to all others the reciprocal element put forward and adjudicated is not based on the claim that the plaintiff furnished the defendent with a consideration, or a performance, the value of which is now to be recovered, but that the plaintiff has, because of a breach of the contract, sustained an injury or a detriment – perhaps not even to the benefit of the defendant – for which he demands compensatory damages. This group includes all unilateral contracts where there is not and does not pretend to be an equivalent consideration.[145] When such damages are admitted or adjudged and become thereby acknowledged (or judgment) debts, they may resemble true debts, but they have arisen differently. They are not the result of exchanges and it is always possible that by the contract the defendant has gained no property and is the poorer for the one-sided debt thus created. An obligation has been created against him, but he did not sell it, nor necessarily receive any value for it. To the extent that such one-sided obligations give rise to debt without mutual benefit it is important to distinguish them from true debts, since their economic effects are quite different. We shall call such obligations, or the non-reciprocal part of them, *quasi-debt.*

4. *A Fraction of Property in a Body of Property, Terminate and Subject to Discharge*

Having examined the evolution of the legal practice with regard to debt it becomes possible to define true credit-debt as a purchase by

[145] Such as, for instance, gifts. It does not include, I think, the accessory contracts such as letters of credit, etc., nor insurance. Strictly speaking these are, it is true, unilateral. Actually they are individual portions of trilateral or multilateral arrangements which balance the *quid* and the *quo* – or are supposed to – as much as any contract of the first class.

the creditor of an interest of a certain kind in the aggregate of the property of the debtor, which interest is to be liquidated at a certain time by means of a process which is, in effect, the repurchase of this interest. A quasi credit-debt is the creation of such an interest other than by purchase. It is in respect of the repurchase agreement that both differ most radically from any of the previous classes of property discussed. This kind of property interest has a limited duration. The same is true of many other kinds of property interest, some of which are for time certain and some for time uncertain. But whereas in all other cases, at the due date, the property either terminates by expiry or is discharged by the surrender of the specific 'things' to which it has directly or indirectly attached, in this case such means of discharge is only a last resort. What is provided for is discharge by means of a repurchase of this 'thing' itself (the credit-debt) by the debtor. In respect of the interest which subsists in the meantime the whole is an arrangement of property relations, a real or fictitious complete exchange. In respect of the agreement to repurchase it is temporary. We might regard the latter as a separate element, conforming to the doctrine of pure contract and merely secured by the former as a kind of inchoate lien. But it seems more sensible to regard it, as it is regarded in practice, as an inseparable part of the whole, which whole in turn is an interest, to be terminated at a time certain by due process of law and then to be converted into another interest of the same kind (renewal), or one of two other kinds of property (money or an aliquot share in the 'things' of the debtor). And we arrive at this conclusion for the especial reason that, either this credit-debt must be perceived to be something more than a personal relation and to have legal existence as a 'thing' independent both of the person of inherence and of the person of incidence, or in order to explain its alienability and its survivability, we must adopt the alternative and archaic Roman idea of perpetual succession, under which the *persona* is conceived to persist from generation to generation. But, as applied to modern conditions, the return to such a doctrine would lead us into other difficulties because we have now admitted these so-called personal obligations to every form of succession as *res singulae*, which the Roman concept of the personal quality of this relation, and of the limited cases where a succession of personality could occur, would not permit. If we were to continue to conceive debt as running from person to person it would then be necessary for us to devise a legal doctrine of "split personality." But if we choose to regard the debt as independent of both persons and running rather from the body of property of the debtor to that of the creditor, then such an interest is not personal, nor does it consist of rights which can any longer properly be called *in personam*.

By way of summary at this point, let us say that all contracts, after a certain stage is reached—and some, at once—give rise to acknowledged or adjudicated credit-debts (or quasi credit-debts) and thus to a kind of interest in the aggregate of the property of another; a floating charge which should be discharged (repurchased) at a certain time and in a certain medium, but which in default of that, may have to be discharged by occupation of an equivalent part of the total property itself; which exists, in the meantime, as an indirect, or mediate, beneficial interest in the indeterminate 'things' composing the debtor's aggregate—attended perhaps with a share of the total fruits and with some protections, at least, as to the maintenance of the aggregate and as to exclusion of others from interference with the relation. This interest is of the nature of a fraction of the complete property of the debtor in his body of property as a whole. It is therefore more closely related to the fraction which we have found to exist in the case of the trust fund of personal property than it is to the various fractions described as part of the complete property in specific objects or even specific 'things.'

To some extent this preliminary statement will require to be modified, as we proceed, because we have hardly at all discriminated between the antecedent and the remedial rights constituting property in contract. We have treated the incidence of the antecedent right as if it were the damages eventually to be collected. But for this clarification we will have to await the further development of our analysis.

F. *The Boundaries of Property*

1. *The Right of Action in Tort*

Upon the far side of the land of contract we enter the wholly inchoate region of the "right of action sounding in tort," which according to various views held among the geographers is, or is not, a part of the *terra incognita*—choses in action. Four stages may be distinguished in this case. There is first the general and potential remedial right attaching to all persons to bring an action if and when their personal, familial or property rights are infringed. Such a right becomes specific and precipitated when a cause of action arises; that is, when any personal, familial or property right is actually infringed.[146] In the case of action for tort no property could possibly

[146] In the case of breach of contract we have ignored this step, though technically the occasion is supposed to bring into existence a new and remedial right which, at that point, is substituted for the antecedent contractual right. We shall have occasion to refer to this later.

be conceived to exist in the right of action until the tort is committed. Thereafter the third stage begins when the action is commenced. Finally the action may result in judgment. At this fourth stage the right has certainly become property—a judgment debt. As to whether it becomes so at the second or third stage there is much difference of opinion and of statute. For certain purposes it does and for others it does not. And practice varies. Certainly for our purposes it is inchoate until ascertained damages are admitted—or until judgment—and it should be left among the "stresses and strains" which may be about to change the property structure and may not. So may the "shopper." But as in the case of the "shopper" the question is not yet decided.[147]

It is even more obvious in this case than in the case of contract that only those torts which have enriched the tortfeasor to the extent of the damages admitted or awarded can be regarded as an exchange—albeit a forcible one. Only to this extent is the obligation finally incurred by him a true credit-debt. For the rest, and in all other cases, the obligation is a quasi credit-debt—not one which restores the *status quo ante* but one which compensates the injured party *at the expense* of the injuror.[148]

2. *So-called Rights "in rem" and "in personam"*

At some point in our recent progress we have passed out of the region of property; just where it is difficult to say. But the charac-

[147] To apply Hohfeld's analysis of rights it would appear that legal theory, for procedural purposes, attempts to lump together as choses in action the relations of claim-duty, exemplified by liquidated credit-debts, with the relation of power-liability, exemplified by unliquidated damages in tort. The remaining class of unadjudicated or unliquidated damages arising from breach of contract resembles the latter. It is considered as being founded upon a claim-duty relation, but the duty, or its extent, has not yet been ascertained. The right to have it ascertained is rather a power than a claim, for until it is so fixed it is not strictly to be construed as a debt.

[148] Blackstone, *Commentaries*, II, XXIX, pp. 436-437, makes a similar distinction as to torts, but does not carry it into the field of contract. "A judgment, in consequence of some suit or action in a court of justice, is frequently the means of vesting the right and property of chattel interests in the prevailing party. And here we must be careful to distinguish between property, the *right* of which is before vested in the party, and of which only *possession* is recovered by suit or action; and the property, to which a man before had no determinate title or certain claim, but he gains as well the right as the possession by the process and judgment of the law. Of the former sort are all debts and *choses in action*. . . But there is also a species of property to which a man has not any claim or title whatsoever, till after suit commenced and judgment obtained in a court of law; where the right and the remedy do not follow each other, as in common cases, but accrue at one and the same time; and where, before judgment had, no man can say that he has any absolute property, either in possession or in action." These are principally judgments in tort.

ter of the verdure has changed so that, either because it is not yet matured sufficiently to be useful, or because it is of parasitic and not symbiotic growth, it is of no economic interest. Some may object to the hardly noticed transition from contract to tort. Yet a legal historian has remarked that "one of the most striking lessons to be learned from a study of legal history is, that ideas which to us now seem absolutely distinct, and even opposed, are found originally to have been blended in a common stock, from which they have subsequently split off by a process of specialization." "As a matter of historical fact, the simple [breach of] contract and the ordinary tort spring from the same stock; and the wonder would be if they did not, in some points, betray signs of their common origin."[149] Even today the line of distinction is not sharp. "The only common feature," says Markby, "of the torts enumerated that I can discover is that they are acts forbidden by the law which cause damage." And this definition, he finds, includes as well all breaches of contract.[150]

In legal theory the distinction as to the basis of these two types of action is established upon the basis of the dichotomy, *in rem* and *in personam.* Not as to the actions directly; for both torts and breaches of contract give rise only to personal actions. But as to the rights; the tort is an infringement of an antecedent right *in rem* and the breach an infringement of one *in personam;* the one a right good "against the world," the other, against a certain person or persons only; the one, in Hohfeld's terminology, "multital" (or "multiple"), the other "unital," or "paucital." By way of interpretation of this classification let us say that torts are deemed to be violation of duties imposed on all by reason of their status, and that breaches of contract (together with breaches of trust) are deemed to be the violation of duties imposed on individuals because of particular circumstances.[151] In this view the individual is conceived as being surrounded by a complex web of duties, general and particular, involuntary and voluntary. The breach of any one of these duties establishes or precipitates a right of action in the individual beneficiary of the duty. Whether the breach constitutes a breach of contract or not depends finally on whether, in the particular case, a contract exists, or is

[149] Jenks, op. cit., p. 133. And he notes that, even now, legal theorists cannot agree on the question whether the Writ of Detinue for the recovery of a specific chattel is an action on contract or in tort. Assumpsit originated as an action in tort and it was only in its later stages that a contract began to be implied. See Holmes, *Common Law*, pp. 275-285.

[150] Op. cit., p. 338.

[151] This is on the theory of Hohfeld who calls a right *in rem* "multital" because it is a "right possessed by A against B when it happens to be one of innumerable similar rights possessed by A against all (or nearly all) other members of organized society, each one of whom is under a correlative duty to A. . ." See Corbin, "Legal Analysis and Terminology," 29 *Yale Law Review*, p. 163, 170.

implied or construed from the facts, or is construed from the relation (quasi-), as the occasion of the obligation.

However, the nature and consequences of the distinction involved in the terms *in rem* and *in personam* cannot be passed over so lightly. It reaches far further than the question of breaches and torts. We have already noted that the terms have come to mean respectively "against the world" and "against a particular person." And we promised ourselves an examination of this remarkable development in sense. In the beautiful but primitive logic of classic Roman law the structure of property was erected upon two simple and wholly corporeal concepts—the intrinsic necessity that a material object 'belonged' exclusively in one class or another (i.e. to one *persona* or another), and the complementary idea of the obligation as a physical control over the body of the debtor. As evolving facts came to make it necessary, the idea of the material object was extended to include those 'things' which seemed immaterial and nevertheless analogous to material possessions. But the assimilation of the *res incorporalis* was never completed. It remained incapable of *traditio*, of *possessio* and of *dominium*—three obstinately physical ideas—and so of the actions to support them. Thus actions *in rem* remained limited, with a few exceptions, to the vindication of *dominium*, or its subordinate rights in material objects. So, too, the body of the debtor became immaterialized to a degree. The person was gradually spiritualized; came to be independent of the man and immanent, rather, in the body of 'things' which appertained to any "part" or "character" in the world of property. The legal doctrine of the soul (*persona*) and its immortality (*successio*) paralleled and was based upon the theological doctrine. But this process, as well, was never completed. The obligation continued to impinge, in theory, upon the *persona*, although, in fact, it impinged upon the body of 'things' which had, in this normally circuitous way, become personified. Thus the actions *in personam*, at first against the body of the debtor, came to be composed for a share in his body of property. His *corpus* became impersonal. But to this day the theory of law has retained the primitive distinction originating in the objective of the Roman *actio*. And the dichotomy *in rem* and *in personam* is now used most inappropriately to cover, not only the original distinction as to actions,—the substance of which has been almost wholly altered—but also other distinctions not at all parallel to the first. The result is great confusion.

In our examination of the difference between the property interests of the beneficiaries in trusts of personal property and those of creditors in credit-debt, on the one hand, and all the previously discussed types of 'thing,' or interest, on the other, we have developed the thesis that property may be either an interest in a specific material object – or directly dependent upon such an interest and therefore an interest in a specific legal 'thing' – or it may be an interest in a body of property as a whole, in which case its specific incidence on 'things' certain is not yet determined. Thus we may say that an interest of the latter type is an interest in indeterminate objects or 'things.'

Every property interest of any kind has certain protections. As a part of each 'thing' – any interest or aggregate of property rights, whether in a specific object or in a body of property as a whole – there are always these certain adjunct or component remedial rights of action which enable the holder to bring an action against anyone interfering illegally with the rights composing his interest. Such rights are included as parts of even the 'thing' called contract. So long as they are potential they remain indeterminate as to both the person and the 'things' which will constitute their objective. But only until a specific cause of action occurs. Then they are precipitated and become determinate as to the person (body of property) against which they are to be brought, though they still remain indeterminate as to the specific 'things' which they seek to recover. Let us call these component remedial rights, rights of action of the first class.

As a part of these 'things,' which represent interests in specific objects or even in other specific 'things,' the protections accorded extend to component remedial rights of action for the recovery of this specific object or 'thing.' While they remain potential they are of course specific as to the object which will be their objective, but indeterminate as to the person or body of property. When a cause of action occurs they become also specific as to the person. Let us call these remedial rights, rights of action of the second class.

Finally, in case of all interests in indeterminate 'things' and in many of the dependent interests in specific 'things' there are included remedial rights of action which, whether potential or actual, are nevertheless always specific as to the person (or body of property) against which they must be brought and always indeterminate as to the object or 'thing.' Let us call these remedial rights, rights of action of the third class.

In the extravagant rhetoric of jurisprudence rights of action of the second class, and those of the first class while they remain potential, are "against the world," or *in rem*. Those of the third class, and those of the first class after a cause of action has arisen, are "against a person," or *in personam*. Again the rights of action of the second class are the original protections which have maintained their form intact. Those of the third class are the original powers.

Today the distinction between powers and protections is largely traditional, due to their origins, and exists principally in differences of form. It is difficult to distinguish among current rights as to which are protections and which powers. The component rights which retain the form of powers are in reality, as we shall see, inchoate protections; that is, protections which have not yet arrived at the state of being relations to specific objects or 'things' and are only as yet suspended over a body of 'things.' So too the component rights of action which have the form of the original protections are only indeterminate as to the person or body of property while they remain potential and until a cause of action gives them a specific person as defendant.

It has become the custom to misuse the original Roman terminology and, in barbarous Latin, to consider that all interests in specific objects are rights in *in rem* and all interests in indeterminate objects are rights *in personam.*[152] But, in the first place, be it noted that all property interests include rights of action of the first class, which may give rise to interests in indeterminate objects. And, in the second place, while both these and the rights of action of the third class begin in the form of claims to indeterminate objects, they are really directed toward, and in the end become, rights to specific objects or 'things.' For the actual process of the judicial realization of property interests consists in a series of steps. Of these the first step is the action. If the right of action is of the second class it gives rise to an action *in rem,* so-called. If it is of the first or third class it gives rise to one *in personam.* Actions of the second class are in form *in rem;* the others are in form *in personam.* The result of each class of action may be a judgment or decree by the court, which follows the same form as the action itself. An action *in rem* gives rise to a judgment *in rem.* An action *in personam* gives rise to a judgment, or decree, *in personam.* But in the final enforcement, in spite of fictions of form to the contrary, the incidence of all actions alike is upon specific 'things' or objects[153] and never upon the body of the debtor, as the term originally connoted. Executions against the body of the debtor (*in personam*) are now considered bar-

[152] *In* with the accusative indicates the objective of an action. In this case the sense is "against" rather than "into." If *ius in rem* and *ius in personam* are used as ellipses for *ius actionis in rem,* or *ius actionis in personam,* they may be grammatical though they do not represent the Roman law. But if they are used to represent the pre-existing property rights they are not only subsequent readings into Roman law but are ungrammatical – or, as Poste says, op. cit., 3d ed., p. 7, "barbarous." *In rem* was used as an adverb at times, Markby, op. cit., p. 99, but never as an adjective. And *ius* took the genitive, not even *in* with the ablative.

[153] Where a judgment aims at establishing the inherence of a specific property interest (i.e. 'thing') without the co-operation of the defendant it is in form *in rem.* All judgments do so. But only these do so openly.

barous.[154] Thus the final goal is the same in all cases, though the aim of the action called *in personam* is not specifically determined until execution.[155]

The differences in method, aim, and form according as to whether the objective is from the beginning specific, or at the beginning indeterminate, are probably essential. But the two trajectories merge in the end. And in no way do the differences correspond to any "fundamental difference in the nature of private rights." [156] The differences are in the method of attack not in the character of the right. For this reason it is far better not to use the confusing and confused distinctions *in rem* and *in personam*, but to confine ourselves to more exact distinctions in the nature of the component rights of interests

154 Only in criminal procedure has the execution against the body been retained. Equity originally adopted this same procedure. But it rapidly relegated execution upon the body to the position of a tentative or preliminary step and it has now practically discarded this method of enforcing its decrees and has been authorized to use the methods of the law courts, which are wholly against the property.

The early English phrase, "Equity acts only *in personam*," signified that the method of giving effect to the decree was, in the hands of the Chancellor, exactly the same power, or instrumentality, that had been delegated to the obligee in early Rome; namely a taking possession of his person and of his property and a sale of the latter under the principles of an equitable lien – which has been likened to distress (*pignoris capio*). Thus it is a combination of punishment and satisfaction – the debtor slavery of early times. Under this fiction the proprietary rights of the debtor were not interfered with. Property was sacrosanct. He was merely being compelled to pay his debt.

155 The technical part of this statement is based upon the admirable and illuminating analysis of the terms *in rem* and *in personam*, by W. W. Cook, in "The Powers of Courts of Equity," 15 *Columbia Law Review* (1915), p. 37, 106, 228. It should be noted that Professor Cook approximates our theory in several places. "Our classification of actions, then, turns upon their principal object – the assertion against the defendant of a power *in personam* or of a power *in rem*; of a general personal liability or of a liability to lose a particular *res*" (p. 49). "Judgment *in personam* . . . means a judgment of such character that by means of it the plaintiff can, as a means of attaining the principal object of the action, subject the general assets of the defendant, as distinguished from some specific property interest, to the payment of his claim . . ." (p. 120).

156 Sohm, op. cit., p. 263. The result of classifying a bundle of rights according to the presence or absence among its components of the so-called rights *in rem* or those *in personam*, and of the effort to create an antithesis between property and obligation, is well shown in an argument given in Anson *On Contract* (p. 10). In pointing out the specific personal incidence of rights *in personam* he says, "Nor can the whole community be under an *obligation* to him: the rights on his part correlative to the duties owed to him would be rights *in rem*, would be in the nature of property as opposed to obligation."

In the first place, every bundle of rights composing an obligation also contains rights *in rem*, so-called, of the first class described above. Then such a 'thing' is property. Thus all obligations are property. In the second place, not every bundle of rights which includes rights "against the world" – *in rem*, so-called – is on that account property. Familial, personal, and especially occupational rights are rights against the world. But they are not property.

The criterion is a false one.

(or 'things'), rights of action and of other procedure, by which the incidence of these interests is made ultimately to reach, as in all cases it does and must, specific material objects or 'things.' Actions or procedure may properly be described as *against the person* when they are, as in criminal law, against his physical person; but they should be described as being *against indeterminate objects or 'things'* when they are so directed, without specific incidence, until some portion of the objective body of property is taken, or the property, in part or as a whole, is liquidated and the proceeds taken; and as being *against specific objects or 'things'* if they are immediately directed against a specific object or 'thing.' To these categories of action we may fit corresponding portions of the rights going to make up various property interests.[157]

When it comes to the division of property interests as a whole we see that such interests are composed in all cases of certain rights which are or may be specific as to persons and that all component remedial rights, as well as the antecedent rights, have as their ultimate object a specific 'thing.' It is therefore unrealistic to follow the traditional legal arrangement and to treat a bundle of rights as if it were a single right and to classify the whole bundle according to the character of that particular member of the bundle which happens to be uppermost in the mind of the commentator. It was on this basis that property—in the older sense, including "ownership," possession and *iura in re aliena*,—was conceived to be a right *in rem*, and contract, or obligation, to be a right *in personam*. Such classification is not valid. The distinction must be reserved for the component rights of action. For contract, as we have seen, includes many multiple rights in its make-up. And the assertion of most of the rights of action appertaining to "ownership," so-called,[159] instantly converts them into rights against a single person.[160]

[157] In the *Restatement of the Law of Property*, the American Law Institute has concluded to dispense with the use of the terms *right in rem* and *right in personam* because the "term *right in rem* has no single fixed meaning" such as would be necessary if the former were to be used in antithesis to the latter (pp. 18-19).

[159] A "right *in rem* is a name for a large number of [identical] rights *in personam*, actual or potential. A violation of a right *in rem* is always a violation of a definite one of these rights *in personam*." Cook, loc. cit., p. 53, Note 49.

[160] We can summarize these statements by an illustration. A promissory note is a 'thing' (i.e. an aggregate of property rights). It has reference to indeterminate 'things' (i.e. an aliquot part of the debtor's aggregate of 'things'). It is treated, as will hereafter be shown, as a present interest in that aggregate. In this respect is it to be considered as composed of rights *in rem?* The note itself is protected against theft. This is generally conceded to be a right *in rem*. But it gives rise to a right of action *in personam*. Yet this cannot be enforced against the person of the debtor. It does not include rights against his body but only against his body of property. Do they remain rights *in personam?* Eventually the rights must be executed

3. *The Distinction between Property and Personal Rights*

Because of the origin of the term *in rem;* because its use has emphasized the general, or multiple, character of certain rights adjunct to certain types of interest in objects or 'things'; and because its use as an antithesis to rights *in personam* has identified it with the older idea of property as opposed to contract; there has been a disposition to consider all rights *in rem* (general or multiple rights) as identifying property. We have already considered the determination of the boundary of property in the region of contract. This leads us to consider its boundary upon the other frontier. In the Roman system that concept, which is the basis of our idea of a right *in rem,* involved the primitive, familial identification of governance with property. Relations giving rise to such rights were not contracted by the free will, but existed so to speak in the nature of things; they were the rights of a person over all that which is inherently subject to him – his body; his name and reputation; his occupation; his wife, children, dependents and slaves; his land and goods. These matters he dominated. He was both their lord and master and their owner. They were the *corpus* of his *persona.* Against these were opposed the rights now called *in personam,* which resulted either from a voluntary relation or one imposed by authority, as between person and person; that is, heads of *familiae.* These latter rights, in so far as the liability is certain and admitted or adjudicated, are now generally included in the domain of property. In fact we are proceeding on the theory that they represent in law interests in the debtor body of property. But as to the limits of property in the former group there is more question. Can a line be drawn among these rights *in rem* by which some will be classified as *property* and the rest as *personal* or *familial* rights? We shall proceed to try to work out a criterion for the division which will discriminate, according to Pound's scheme, the rights of personal integrity, of personal liberty and of the society and control of one's family and dependents, on the one hand, from the rights of property on the other. Thus we will attempt to recognize the completion of the process which has been taking place since the days of the early house community, in releasing from all tinge of property the personal relations created by the domestic organization. The practical importance of this distinction, both for law and economics, will appear in the next chapter.

It is clear that the rights of personal integrity and personal liberty

against specific 'things.' Are they nevertheless *in personam?* Finally almost every action in defense of any property rights must be brought against some person. Are some of such actions nevertheless *in rem?*

—which latter should include the general right of contract and of otherwise acquiring property—are common to all "normal" persons. Thus if we should exclude from the definition of property the rights which are common to all, except by reason of differences in legal personality, we would eliminate the strictly personal rights.[161] But this criterion does not successfully exclude those other rights *in rem* arising from the familial relation, for they accrue only when one assumes this particular relation, and are therefore not common to all. And if we try to discriminate these latter by regarding them as results of status we shall be faced with the imperfect distinction between status and contract. Is not marriage a contract? That difficulty has already appeared in dividing torts from breaches of contract.

Another proposed criterion is that of *value*. In law this is popular. But in economics no content is admitted for the term value other than that of "exchange value." And rightly.[162] The idea must then be re-examined under the precise prerequisite of value, namely "alienability." Obviously it is impossible to attribute exchange value to any right of a kind which is incapable of exchange. On this basis can we define property as all rights which are themselves transferable or of which the benefits are transferable? In this way we successfully exclude all the personal rights and the familial rights as well—except perhaps as the latter may be delegated. The difficulty is that such a test would also eliminate a part—in the past a great part and even today a considerable part—of those rights which are in every other respect regarded as property.

As we have noted, the chose in action was the catch-all of English law. Starting as a right of action pure and simple it was held to be, for the reasons already given, non-transferable. Thus it came to be opposed to "property" which, in the old sense meant hardly more than possession, but which was essentially transferable. And this contrast was sharpened by the resemblance of the chose in action and of seisin to the Roman obligation and dominion, respectively. As each new form of chose in action developed it was congenitally incapable of alienation and only with much difficulty and in the course of time were various of the forms successively released from this impossible handicap. One finds a perhaps unconscious assumption, based, I believe, on this test, that when a particular chose in action becomes transferable, it *thereby* becomes property. Thus alienability

[161] If these, which seem to be covered by the constitutional terms "life" and "liberty," are recognized as being distinct from "property" but nevertheless in every respect as fully entitled to protection, it should not be necessary to confuse the issue by attempting to bring them under the wing of the term "property" to secure to them as adequate protection as property now receives.

[162] Nevertheless Ely, op. cit., I, p. 132, gives value as one of the necessary attributes of property.

is made the criterion. However, viewing the history of the species, a layman would conclude that the actual process was the reverse of this assumption. It appears that when any form called a chose in action began to be treated by the public as property the attribute of alienability had eventually to be granted to it. Gradually, by statute or by equity or by a laggard and grudging common law, the right of an owner out of possession; the right to recover a tortious enrichment; various instruments negotiable under the law merchant;[163] patents and copyrights, stocks and shares; contingent, executory and future interests in land; rights to an ascertained sum of money (i.e. debts); the fruits of an action arising from tort; the mortgagor's equity of redemption; and various others were, subject to various conditions and in various degrees, made transferable.

Nevertheless there still remain so many varieties of interest that are inalienable – or only to be transferred by one or two of the several varieties of succession – and which are at the same time subject to treatment as property in the hands of the holder, that the criterion of alienability does not seem to fit our needs.[164] Perhaps one by one these too will be granted this distinguishing attribute. Nevertheless, heretofore and now no such exact test has actually been followed.

There is another angle of approach to this problem which, though it will require that we retrace our steps to some extent, is sufficiently representative of legal theory to require exposition at this point. Holland defines proprietary rights as "extensions of the power of a person over portions of the physical world."[165] But within this field he limits them closely. They may only vary from "absolute

[163] Beginning with the fourteenth century negotiable instruments or paper to bearer, if in a form prescribed by the law merchant, passed by delivery or endorsement. Holland, op. cit., p. 316, says, "It has been acutely remarked [probably referring to Savigny, *Obligations*, II, p. 99] that the assignability of a negotiable instrument is due to its being in point of fact a material object, and so capable of actual delivery." This is an excellent example of the crudely material form into which the legal idea of the "thing" as the object of property has arrived. It seems to assume that, if a *res incorporalis*, representing a *ius obligationis*, is condensed into a quasi-corporeal object, its obligatory character disappears and the representation becomes itself property. If this were the true reason all documentary evidence of agreements should follow suit. It is much better to reason with Holroyd, J., in Wookey v. Pole, "But the Courts have considered these instruments either promises or orders for the payment of money, or instruments entitling the holder to a sum of money – as being appendages to money and following in the nature of their principle." In other words, since negotiable instruments were introduced full-fledged into England, they were at once regarded as representatives or equivalents of money – or, in the case of bills of lading, of specific goods – like floating titles, so to speak – and thus capable of possession and delivery as if they were identical with the objects they represented; as if they were all bailments, not credit-debts.

[164] Many beneficial interests in trusts, contracts closely connected with personal characteristics, rights of action for unliquidated damages for tort, etc., are incapable of some or all kinds of transfer.

[165] Op. cit., p. 191.

ownership to a narrowly limited power of user."[166] On similar principles Maine states that the proprietary right "is sharply distinguished by the analyst of mature jurisprudence from the . . . right *in personam* . . . or Obligation. Now Conveyances transfer Proprietary Rights, Contracts create Obligations—how then can the two be included under the same name or same general conception?"[167] Corbin would confine them just as closely. He limits legal interests to "the aggregate of the legal relations of a person with respect to some specific physical object or the physical relations of specific objects."[168]

The way of approach of both Holland and Corbin suggests the ground for regarding relations of persons with respect to material objects as the criterion of property. But here, if we follow Maine, we find our way barred by the already noted hurdle between "property" and "obligation." The law, to be consistent with its theory and perhaps even with its procedural forms, must conceive the rights of an obligee, not as property, but as means of acquiring property, just as the Roman institutionalists regarded them.[169] The substitution of payment in fungibles, by way of damages, for the specific performance agreed to has seemed to convert what had previously resembled a future or executory conveyance into a mere personal obligation. Thereby it ceases to be an interest in material objects. But to this objection we may suggest that, if such is the orthodox view, then in that view limping legal theory stands alone. Legal practice has long since established the very real interest of the creditor in the 'things' of the debtor, as we shall later demonstrate. The French Code includes obligations and actions (legal) in "*mobiles*." The English Conveyancy Acts include, under property, any debt and any thing in action and any other right or interest. The common definition in American law is equally broad.

In spite of its narrow confines this criterion seems to afford the best possibilities of all those considered, for it directs attention specifically to the fact that property consists of relations of persons with reference to physical objects or with reference to the inter-relations of physical objects. Obviously this excludes the aforementioned personal and familial rights if human beings are excluded from the category of material objects. Whether we can justify, in this light, the boundaries of property, which we have previously established well inside the limits of contract, must remain unsettled until we can fully determine the exact nature of the relation of the creditor to the

[166] Op. cit., p. 193.

[167] *Ancient Law*, p. 305.

[168] Corbin, "Legal Analysis and Terminology," 29 *Yale Law Review* (1919), p. 163, 173.

[169] See Sohm's analysis, supra, pp. 329-330 and Note 129.

'things' in the body of property of the debtor; the question whether there are 'things' that are neither directly nor indirectly interests in material objects; and the question of what we mean by the term "material objects." These questions must be reserved for later chapters.

4. *The Law and the Facts*

It must now be evident to the reader that the tendency of the theory of Anglo-American law, as of the Roman law which preceded, paralleled and finally greatly modified it, has been to build from procedure to procedure. To understand the principles today one must understand the genealogy of the procedure. It is not the evolution of the social, political and economic institutions alone which determines the present legal structure. It is more particularly the special, and usually not cognate, evolution of juridical practice. This may be a necessity; nevertheless it is a defect. For it results in producing a body of legal principles and legal doctrines which are, in many respects, artificial from the standpoint of the practices to which they are today applied.

Moreover it leads to the complacent belief that the law is by necessity composed to a considerable extent of conventions which are fictions rather than truths. As Salmond says,[170] "Nor does the existence of a legal principle imply or involve any belief in its truth. To accept a principle as true for the purposes of action is a different thing from believing it to be true; for though a principle be not true, it may be expedient to act upon it as if it were. . . "We have ever to distinguish between that which is in deed and in truth from that which is in law."

Certainly it is true that legal philosophy, to some extent a guide and to some extent a rationalization of existing practice, is particularly subject to this defect. Jurisprudence, confirmed in its habit of mind, always classifies and analyses the rights which the law is intended to confer or confirm, not so much according to their nature or to that of the transaction out of which they spring, as according to the remedy which by tradition is applicable to an infringement of these rights. And the more the body of the law becomes organized and crystallized by such theory, the more it seems to present this contrast. Early law in its relatively inchoate form is relatively free from this defect. It has, at least, no theory of rights. But the theory of mature law is, as a result and in many respects, thoroughly artificial.

170 *First Principles of Jurisprudence*, p. 83.

CHAPTER V

PROPERTY IN MODERN AMERICAN LAW – LEGAL PRACTICE

A. *Modern Legal Idea of the Nature of Property*

In these preliminary studies of the facts and forms of the institution of property as it existed in the two sources of our inheritance, and as it is conceived in the theory projected from their confluence, we have endeavoured to prepare ourselves for an analysis of the institution as it stands today in its most highly evolved state, in America. This preparation has been essential. For at no previous stage have the facts and the forms appeared so disparate. This complex modern structure is still clothed in great measure with an antique legal costume, patched, misfitting, outgrown. If we did not fully understand the origin of this costume in the facts and fashions of other days we might fail to perceive what remains to it of design. Or if, as antiquarian legalists, we saw that too clearly, we might let imagination deceive us into seeing in place of the present facts an illusory restoration of the harmonious original. In either case, confused or deluded, we should fail to see through these outlandish habiliments to the actual anatomy of the structure they conceal.

Since this costume makes the present structure of property appear to be so different from what it really is, we shall perhaps come at the facts most readily by unravelling bit by bit its most glaring disguises and inconsistencies. To this end we must go to the law as it is applied and theorized about by the modern American courts themselves – to the decisions on actual cases. In separating these brief citations from their context it is necessary to make clear that much of the time the courts are making rulings only intended to fit a special case or special circumstances, or an interpretation of some limited meaning or application of particular constitutional or statutory provisions. One cannot safely make indiscriminate generalizations from these citations. In the second place these are not "authorities." They are selected as fair samples of the way the law is being construed in the courts of the various states and of the United States. They are not weighted. They would not serve for purposes of instruction. Nevertheless they are the facts – good, bad and indifferent

– representing what the law is, rather than what it should be. For our purpose they serve better than selected material taken from text-books or commentaries. It will be noted, however, that, in many cases, the judges themselves are but handing down the words of the "authorities," old and new, private and judicial.

The terminology of American law is a mongrel jargon of medieval English, French and Latin terms, derived through many channels and over a long period of time. The concepts they express are far from precise, for they represent many strata of overlaid schemes and classifications which are not congruous with one another, and which have undergone varying degrees of adaptation. Upon the English stock – which is itself, as we have seen, no model of order and consistency – has been grafted, over large portions of the South and West, parts of the civilian law of France and Spain. We have fifty jurisdictions – which, except for the first, are almost wholly independent of each other – each in some degree expressing its own ideas and traditions; we have fifty legislatures, all – again with the exception of the first – independently constructing statute law at a record pace; and we have fifty constitutions and almost as many codes. Perhaps it is more remarkable, in view of these conditions, that American law is as intelligible as it is, rather than that it is at present beyond the powers of any jurisprudence to reduce it to an ordered and rational *corpus juris.*

Moreover the economic subject matter with which it so largely deals has been evolving more rapidly than at any prior time in the history of the world. Again, except for sporadic and private efforts, no attempt has been made to rationalize its ideas and language. What improvement there has been consists in a slow accretion of authority and voluntary acceptance. The profession itself seems content to have the conceptual structure remain irrational and vague.

Such diverse usage in terminology and such anachronistic concepts make it necessary for us to interpret and sometimes to translate the language of the jurists as we proceed. We shall do this by means of comment and by inserting in brackets (which are always ours) after certain words a translation into the terminology we have adopted.

1. *General Definitions of Property*

In order to come at the nature of property it is necessary to be able to distinguish it from that which is not property. It must be defined. And this, not for intellectual exercise, but simply because until one achieves a complete separation into its pure and elemental state no qualitative analysis of property is possible. The courts struggle to meet this need. The favourite definition is that the term property "is a 'nomen generalissimum,' extending to every species of valuable right and interest." [1][1] This is so vague that it is safe. It means nothing. Another court adds the attribute of the relation to the person of inherence. Property is "everything that . . . goes to make up a man's wealth—every interest or estate which the law regards of sufficient value for judicial recognition." [2] But inclusively to define this relation is difficult. One attempts to define it by stating that property is "anything of value of which exclusive possession may possibly and lawfully be had." [3] The truth of this dictum depends on what is meant by "thing" and by "possession." Is "thing" always a material object? If so is the object the property? If the "thing" is not always material but can be incorporeal as well, can it be capable of "possession"? All these citations agree in requiring the attribute of value. We have already suggested the pitfall in that vague idea. However, the issue is met squarely by converting the vague term "value" into the economic term "exchange value." Property "is everything which has an exchangeable value." [4] If that is true it is necessary that the term be confined to "all rights and claims having a pecuniary value, and which could be transferred by the party or parties entitled." [5] Or, combining and making specific both these attributes—that of inherence in a holder by a definite relation, and that of alienability and therefore of exchange value—property is "anything of value, anything that may be owned or possessed," "anything which has debt-paying or debt-securing power." [6] And since "'assets' . . . is equivalent in its common acceptation to the term 'property'," [7] this term comes to the same thing. "The term 'assets,' as applied to decedents' estates," means "property, real or personal, tangible or intangible, legal or equitable, which can be made available for, or may be appropriated to, payment of debts." [8] Thus, through this series of refinements, such an attempt at defining "value" has now led us into an impasse. For we have already seen that, both in the past and at present, much that is for many purposes treated as property is not capable of voluntary or involuntary transfer. Alienability is not, therefore, an adequate criterion. Nor is it followed in practice. And that fact renders useless the criterion of value as the identifying characteristic of property. The fact or manner of inherence is equally useless as a criterion, for this is but a definition in terms of itself.

Rarely do we find a suggestion of the criterion which we have already proposed as an alternative. "Man's rights in respect to things constitute property." [9] If, as is reasonable to suppose, this West

[1] The numbers inserted in brackets in the text and notes in this chapter refer to the case citations used here which are listed by these numbers in Appendix II.

Virginian judge used the word "thing" in its legally accepted and wholly material sense we may translate this dictum as follows: "Property consists of man's rights with respect to material objects." Let us keep this in mind as we proceed.

2. *Property Rights Distinguished from Personal and Familial Rights*

While the use of the term value, in the sense of exchange value, in connection with the foregoing definitions, does not withstand precise analysis, it is possible that the indefinite idea intended to be expressed by this word is that of economic benefit – the so-called "use value." As Marshall well says the experience of economists "has shown that it is not well to use the word" in this sense.[2] For there is no determinant nor measure of such value. Nevertheless there may be an ulterior motive in this definition. The great advantage of the perfectly vague definition of property as "every species of valuable right and interest" is the wide latitude it gives the courts in the interpretation of the constitution and statutes. Thus, by somewhat of a fiction, it seems to justify according to many other rights the same protection they are specifically authorized to give to property rights. Later we shall examine the results of this policy. At this point let us see if we can penetrate this perhaps intentional confusion and discover any valid basis for a discrimination between property and other private rights.

The constitutional phrase "life, liberty and property" is conceived to be all-inclusive so far as private rights are concerned. This is generally conceded. For instance: "The terms, 'life, liberty, and property' are representative terms, and intended to cover every right, to which a member of the body politic is entitled under the law. These terms include the right of self-defense, freedom of speech, religious and political freedom, exemption from arbitrary arrest, the right freely to buy and sell as others may. Indeed, they embrace all our liberties, personal, civil and political, including the rights to labor, to contract, to terminate contracts, and to acquire property." [10] In this decision no separation is attempted within the general class. Let us proceed. In the first place we find that certain of these rights are conceived to be included both under the category of liberty and that of property. Property "necessarily includes the right to contract. . . This right . . . inheres in property, and, in connection with its possession and use, forms its chief element of value. It is only by contract that its ownership can be acquired or transferred." [11] And again, "property does not consist merely of the title and possession. It includes the right to make any legal use of it, and

[2] *Principles of Economics*, p. 61.

the right to pledge or mortgage it or to sell and transfer it. The right to contract a debt or other personal obligation is included in the right to liberty; and the right to contract a debt, or to enter into a bond or other writing or obligation, is also a right of property." [12] Thus "the privilege of contracting is both a liberty, and a property right." [13] From which we may conclude that the right to contract is construed both as a personal right, or liberty, inhering in every person, and also as one of the component, or part, rights of property attaching to every specific bundle of rights, or interests, in material objects. If this right is exercised with reference to such specific interests it seems to be exercised as a property right. If, on the other hand, it is exercised with reference to economic services, since these concern ephemeral acts and not material objects, it is exercised as a liberty.

So, in general, we may assume that the freedom to carry on such economic activities as do not involve the actor in the delivery of specific interests in existing material objects is, strictly speaking, not an element of property but is embraced in the term liberty—a term which is sufficiently inclusive for this purpose. "Liberty [as used in the Constitution of the United States] means, not only the right of the citizen to be free from the mere physical restraint of his person, as by incarceration, but the term is deemed to embrace the right . . . to be free in the enjoyment of all his faculties . . . to live and work where he will; to earn his livelihood by any lawful calling; to pursue any livelihood or avocation . . ." [14] and "for that purpose to enter into all contracts which may be proper, necessary and essential to his carrying out to a successful conclusion the purposes above mentioned." [15] [8] If it were not for the different constructions placed by the courts upon the meaning of the same terms where they are used in the fifth and in the fourteenth amendments to the Constitution, "life and liberty" representing the personal rights, would be as adequately protected as "property," and it would be much easier for us to find authority for discriminating the two. The tendency to try to stretch the term property to include the right to work, to carry on business or a profession, etc., might then be corrected.

The foregoing is evidence of a considerable tendency to erect a structure of fully differentiated personal rights upon the foundation of the common law rights of personal security and personal liberty,

[8] It has been frequently held that this includes the right of the employee to work and to choose employment. It also includes the liberty of the employer. "Every person has a right, as between his fellow citizens and himself, to carry on his business, within legal limits, according to his own discretion and choice, with any means which are safe and healthful, and to employ therein such persons as he may select:" and with such absolute right third persons may not interfere with intent to injure if their demands are not complied with. [16]

broadened in scope by all readings into the constitutional terms "life and liberty." In order to complete the structure there should be added to it the familial rights. We would then have a clearly defined organization of rights corresponding to Pound's three classes of rights *in rem*, personal integrity, personal liberty and the right to the society and control of one's family and dependents.

At common law the right of personal security covers a "person's legal and uninterrupted enjoyment of his life, his limbs, his body, his health, and his reputation." [17] And that of "personal liberty . . . consists of the right of locomotion – to go where one pleases, and when, and to do that which may lead to one's business or pleasure, only so far restrained as the rights of others may make it necessary for the welfare of all other citizens." [18] Using the terminology of modern practice let us attempt a synopsis of the personal and familial rights in order to segregate these from property rights. It is evident that none of the antecedent rights in the following cases are "rights with respect to material objects."

Personal Security
(Defined by the following standard classification of infringements)
- Assault
- Cruel and Inhuman Treatment
- Deceit
- Death or Disease (Inflicted)
- False Imprisonment
- Fraud or Injury to Person
- Libel or Slander
- Malicious Prosecution
- Mental Injury
- Personal Injury (Strict)
- And, perhaps, Injury to Credit (Financial)

Personal Liberty
(Defined, less exactly, as certain positive rights)
- Right of Free Locomotion
- Right to Labour
- Right to Pursue Lawful Business or Profession
- Right to Contract (Including Right to Acquire Property)

Familial Rights
(Defined by the following standard classification of infringements)
- Alienation of Affections
- Breach of Promise of Marriage

Criminal Conversation
Injury to Consortium
Loss of Services of Dependents
Seduction

If these personal and familial rights are definitely distinguished from property rights we shall find that American practice submits itself quite readily to a definition of property which will be utilizable for our further purposes.

3. *Is Property the Right or the Object?*

In order to perceive the utter confusion with which the courts are confounded – not only as to words but as to ideas as well – it is necessary to remind ourselves of the duplicity of four of their chief terms. "Property" was originally synonymous with *dominium.* The word seems now to be used quite generally to cover any kind of interest with reference to material objects. On the other hand, it is used by the public, as well as frequently in legal parlance, to mean the object of this property interest rather than the interest itself; i.e. the rights with reference to that object. Again "ownership" is still conceived as equivalent to *dominium.* Therefore the term "owner" should indicate the holder of that particular type of interest identified as "ownership" or *dominium.* But "owner" is generally used instead to denote a person who has a certain kind of relation to any property interest whatever – that called "ownership" as well as many others. Thus we can have an owner – and through that perhaps "ownership"– of a mortgage, which is a certain kind of interest in specific land. Yet this owner and this "ownership" are not the owner and the "ownership" of the land. Finally there is the word "thing," which usually to the legal mind signifies a material object but which sometimes refers to the aggregate of rights composing some certain interest in such material object. No one of the following citations is quite clear on all these points. But we shall use them as best we can to demonstrate the uncertain and the exact usage as to each of the terms in turn.

When it is stated that property is "everything that is the subject of ownership" [19] it is clear that the court is thinking of the object as the property. This is very common. In certain cases the word is allowed to do double duty. "Property . . . is any object of value that a person may lawfully acquire and hold, or any valuable interest therein or thereto." [20] The word "means not only the thing [object] owned, but also every right which accompanies ownership and is its incident." [21] But the term "property," "although frequently applied to the thing [object] itself, in strictness means only the rights of the owner in relation to it." [22] The following citation is still more clear on the point we are examining, although it limits "property" to "dominion": Property is defined as "the dominion or indefinite right of user, or disposition which one may exercise over particular things or subjects [objects]. This is its appropriate meaning, and that which it has in the constitution, although it is not infrequently used to indicate the thing [object], rather than the right, and much of the uncertainty and confusion, observable in the decisions, have arisen from overlooking this distinction." [23] Or this; property "is not the physical thing [object] which may be the subject [object] of ownership, but is the right of dominion, possession, and power of disposition which may be acquired over it." [24] Once only I find an unexceptionable statement. "The term 'property' may be defined to be the interest which can be acquired in external objects or things. The things themselves are not, in a true sense, property, but they constitute its foundation and material, and the idea of property springs out of the connection, or control, or interest which, according to law, may be acquired in them, or over them." [25] This definition may be taken as our thesis.

4. *What is a "Thing"?*

In most cases the American courts use the word "thing" as a synonym for material object. Nevertheless, when the medieval term "incorporeal" is used, the thing seems to be a non-possessory interest — or an interest less than *dominium* — in some material object. And, unfortunately the newer term "intangible" is in process of being spoiled in the same way, referring not to immaterial wealth or services but to non-possessory interests, as if it were synonymous with the legal term "incorporeal." The standard usage is shown in this quotation. Thing "in common parlance may intend all matters or substances, in contradistinction to *person*." [26] Nevertheless the older idea persists, confounded now, as it was in Blackstone's time, with the newer objectivity. "Credits are 'choses in action'— things 'incorporeal'— consisting in the right of one person to demand and recover from another, a sum of money or other things in possession. The value of a credit grows out of the right to have and receive property in possession, either by a sale and transfer of the claim to another person in exchange for money or other things, or by requiring or enforcing payment from the debtor. Credits, therefore, although fictitious, nevertheless constitute property — substantial, convertible and productive property." [27] In other words an incorporeal thing is still regarded as the right to recover a corporeal thing. And "thing" either stands both for "rights" and for "material objects," or it always refers to one and the same material object which, when it is out of the possession of its claimant, is called incorporeal. With this exception there is little or no legal authority for popular usage which treats all property interests in material objects, direct or indirect, and from what is called ownership down to the most insignificant fraction, as themselves 'things' and as such capable of being acquired, owned and transferred independently of the possession of the ultimate material base. Nevertheless, under cover of an inconsistent conceptual structure, that is the way in which property interests are treated and considered even at law.

B. Property Identified with "Ownership"— The Complete Property

Following out this analysis we frequently see the tendency to identify all property with "ownership." This may be done by using "ownership" to describe the inherence, so that "property" comes to mean "anything capable of beneficial ownership," [28] or "everything which is the subject of ownership." [29] In these cases we have perhaps the native English idea of "ownership" as the fixed point, and the term "thing" is immaterialized and made the variable—presumably thereby becoming any interest of either a corporeal or incorporeal nature. Or the word "property" may be used to cover both the object and the right in such a way as to leave us in doubt whether "ownership" is a relation of inherence or a specific type of interest. "Property is a general term to designate the right of ownership; and includes every subject [object], of whatever nature, upon which such a right can legally attach." [30] Or the word "property" may be limited to the particular interest conceived as "ownership," and the word "thing" limited to material objects. Property does not properly mean the material thing—the land or chattel owned—but "means only the right of the owner in relation to it." "It denotes a right . . . over a determinate thing." [31] "Property, in a legal sense, consists in the domination which is rightfully and lawfully obtained over a material thing." [32] In these two cases we find the original sense of the term property (*proprietas*) confined to the original *dominium* over material objects. Finally, escaping this *double entendre* of "thing," as signifying both interest and object, the point of view may seesaw the other way. "Thing" may be materialized and become fixed, while "property" becomes the variable. Thus property "includes every interest any one may have in any and every thing [object] that is the subject [object] of ownership by man . . ." (i.e. appropriable). [33] Property "includes every right and interest which a person has in lands and chattels, and is broad enough to include everything [interest] which one person can own and transfer to another." [34] Here we return to the citation presented above which seems to be almost unique in its accuracy. "The term 'property' may be defined to be the interest which can be acquired in external objects or things. The things [objects] themselves are not, in a true sense, property, but they constitute its foundation and material, and the idea of property springs out of the connection, or control, or interest which, according to law, may be acquired in them, or over them. This interest may be absolute [complete], or it may be limited and qualified. It is absolute [complete] when a thing [object] is objectively and lawfully appropriated by one to his own use in exclusion of all others. It is limited or qualified when the control acquired falls short of the absolute." [35]

1. *Property as a Bundle of Rights*

This same identification of all property with the vague antique concept of "ownership" continues when the courts attempt to define the component rights which go to make up property. Property includes "every right which accompanies ownership [complete property] and is its incident." [36] The assortment of rights are somewhat varied. They consist of the "indefinite right of user and disposition;" [37] or "the right to freely possess, use, enjoy and dispose of;" [38] or "the exclusive right to possess, enjoy and dispose of, a thing;" [39] or even "the unrestricted right of use, enjoyment, and disposal." [40] But this last is qualified in a way reminiscent of Blackstone. For property "consists in the free use, enjoyment, and disposal [by a person] of all his acquisitions, without any control or diminution, save only by the laws of the land." [41] Perhaps the constituents of complete property are more accurately summed up as "certain rights in and over the thing, those rights being: 1, user; 2, exclusion; 3, disposition." [42] But when one undertakes to discover the exact content of any of these terms they prove baffling, because they represent physical concepts often applied to non-physical 'things.' For instance "use means the act of employing anything, or of applying it to one's services;" [43] the terms "use, occupancy, and enjoyment . . . are practically synonymous." [44] According to this the owner frequently has not the use. But since this would be inconsistent with the fixed idea of "ownership," another judge will have "'use' . . . include the person who had the actual, though not physical, control." [45] Eventually, in order to avoid this break with tradition it becomes necessary to state that "the use of a thing does not mean the thing itself [i.e. possession], but means that the user is to enjoy, hold, occupy, or have in some manner the benefit thereof. If . . . real estate, the use thereof is its occupancy or cultivation, etc., or the rent which can be obtained for its use. If it is money or its equivalent . . . it is the interest which it will earn." [46] In other words, in order to make the fixed and traditional definition of "ownership" and its attributes fit the varied facts, it becomes necessary to make "use" cover most of the beneficial relations that can subsist between men with regard to material objects.

One perceives in all these citations this persistent, traditional and simple concept – an undefined possessory interest, called "ownership." Such phrases do not indicate a recognition of the present fact of property – a complex and varied assortment of limited protections and qualified permissions. The details are blinked. Because of this failure to resolve the complex bundle into its elements the general addition or subtraction of any individual part rights to or from the property in any object are still apt to be conceived, not to be modifications of this property along the lines of the detailed definitions of its boundaries in the direction of the social reservations, but rather to be independent 'things' by themselves. For instance, we find it said that, "the owners of lots abutting or adjacent to a public street of a city, even if not owners of a fee therein, have the right of access and 'the right of quiet enjoyment,' and such rights are property . . . that is, they have an interest in the street not common to all the people of the state, but personal and peculiar to themselves." [47] Such an interest extends to the "character of street" and is as such protected against "even partially sentimental objections, such as the noise of electric cars or the unsightliness of elevated structures." [47] But the only way to fit this protection to the archaic concept of "ownership" as an integral and standardized 'thing,' is to conceive that "the right to the circulation of air, the undiminished radiation of light, an unobstructed view, and a surrounding relatively harmonious" with the abutting lots, is an incorporeal hereditament attaching to such abutting lots. [48] In other words such rights are treated as an implied easement granted by the municipal corporation, the street being the servient tenement and the abutting land, to which the easement is appurtenant, the dominant tenement. The insufficiency of this viewpoint is demonstrated where the servient land is in private ownership and where, with or without the implication of an easement, the same protection is nevertheless accorded. A property owner is entitled to recover from a railroad "if, by the construction of its tracks so near the residence [of the appellee] . . . and the operation . . . of its locomotives thereon, and the escape of noise, smoke, cinders, and gas therefrom, his property was damaged." [49] In actual fact these protections all constitute part rights of property and are included in varying degrees in all real property. A true easement, properly speaking, is the result of grant or prescription, and only that.

Such attribute rights of access to air, light, view, etc., *via* public property are similar in nature to the rights of access to common resources. The latter is properly defined in the following: "The riparian proprietor . . . has a right to the flow of the water of the natural stream passing through or by his land; such right being inseparably annexed to the soil and passing with it, not as an easement or appurtenance, but as a part and parcel of the land." [50] This definition holds good for both classes, for the two are closely similar in nature. In this respect there is also much confusion between the objects of public property, which are appropriated to public use, and common resources, which are not appropriated at all, but to which access is protected and of which limited appropriation is permitted, as well as between, on the one hand, the right of access to common resources, such as light, air, water, etc., *via* land held either in public or private property or as common resources (navigable streams) and, on the other hand, the right to appropriate such common resources. This confusion is shown in the following Federal court decision. "The state, as trustee for its citizens, owns the beds of all the tidewaters in its jurisdiction. . . The right to fish is a property right and not a mere privilege of citizenship . . . the state can impose any conditions [on the right] it sees fit." [51] And another refers to the right of an owner of land "to take fish and wild game upon his own land . . . bounded by this limitation, that it must always yield to the State's ownership and title, held for the purposes of regulation and preservation for public use." [52] The fact is that, like the riparian's right defined above, access to common resources is a part right or attribute of the property in all abutting land. But the privilege of appropriating any part of such resources is a license granted by the state upon a wholly independent sanction, though it may be, by the nature of the terrain, only available to persons whose property includes the right of access to such resources.

When the composition of any complex bundle of part rights, which together constitute a property interest, is analysed, it will be found that the law does not define property or any type of interest as a whole. It defines each component right specifically. Upon this basis not only must we construe as part rights the foregoing limited protections without and within the boundaries of the locus of the property itself, but we must perceive that the permissions as to user and disposition are also strictly qualified. The right of user is confined to "the right to acquire [property], possess and enjoy it in any way consistent with the equal rights of others and the just exactions and demands of the state." [53] Such limitations are specified and constantly modified by the state in the exercise of its police power. Again wherever the right of eminent domain exists, "whatever exists in any form, whether tangible or intangible, may be subjected to the exercise of its power and may be seized and appropriated to public uses when necessity demands it." [54] Finally, as one example among many, even the right of disposition is limited in its present control, by the common law rule against perpetuities, which provides that no interest is good unless it must vest, if at all, within the period of a "life or lives in being, and 21 years, and a fraction thereafter for a term of gestation in case of posthumous birth."

2. *Identifying the "Owner"*

The difficulty of fitting the strict and strait concept of property as "ownership" (dominion) to the diverse and complex facts is well exemplified by the quandary in which the courts find themselves when they attempt to identify the owner. One says "ownership implies occupancy." [55] But since occupancy "indicates always actual and corporeal possession . . . [as] distinguished from 'possession' . . . [which] may be partially actual and partially constructive," [56] this will obviously not do. The criterion of possession is also tried—"'own' is synonymous with 'possess.'" [57] This permits the inclusion of both actual and constructive possession. "The possession of the lessee is the possession of his lessor." [58] "The possession by a tenant is sufficient." [59] In other cases it is enough to identify the owner by "some extrinsic circumstance that gives him the right to possession, and therefore the right to control." [60] Thus, in a vicious circle, the owner is identified by possession, which is defined as the right of (constructive) possession inhering in the owner.

In default of any other way of distinguishing the owner he may be held in practice to be the one charged with an "active duty with reference to the property." [61] On this basis we find that, for all police purposes, the "owner" is construed to be whoever is in immediate control. This has been identified in various cases with such diverse relations as that of "occupier," "indorsee" (of note), "whoever has right of possession," "agent in full control," "all persons having an interest," "agister," "one who employs a contractor," "equitable owner," "homestead entryman," "any having a usufruct, control or occupation," "tenants of a term," "remaindermen," "lessee," "vendee under contract," "vendor under contract," and even "shareholders." In the face of this demonstration of the quicksilverish nature of the idea, but desperately clinging to the antique notion, one judge defines ownership as "any valid interest 'in rem.'" [62] That is as far as he can stretch his conscience. But another continues the process of stretching so that it is at two different stages in two succeeding sentences. "An owner [*dominus*] is not necessarily one owning [English] the fee simple or one having in the property the highest estate it will admit of. One having a lesser estate may be an owner [*dominus*], and indeed, there may be different estates in the same property, vested in different persons and each be an owner [English] thereof." [63]

C. *The Recognition of Fractions of Property*

1. *Legal Estates in Land*

The effort to lump together a variety of different relations to objects under the *a priori* concept of "ownership," and even, in many cases, the effort to distinguish one relation to each object by that name, is, as we have seen, an almost complete failure. It is only attempted because of the persistence of an antique theory of jurisprudence, quite recently borrowed from civil law, and because it seems to fit common phraseology, though the concept expressed by the latter is quite discrete from that of the former. As soon as it gets down to cases in one particular field, American law quite readily abandons these superimposed and mutually inconsistent ideas of "ownership" and utilizes the indigenous English idea of varied divisions of the complete property into interests or estates. That field is of course the field of real property, the modern patchwork built around the remains of old English land law.

The term "estate" is properly held to mean "the state, condition, or circumstances in which the owner stands with regard to his property," (or better, the holder in regard to the object of his property). [64] Some hold that "estate" means "the kind and quantum of interest therein," [65] and others that "estate . . . imports merely the relation that a party has to the land, not the quantity of interest." [66] But in either case "the word *estate* refers rather to the interest than the subject [object]." [67] Thus we find at least this pair of terms, estate and interest, which, in legal parlance, are strictly confined to the kind or quantity of property—that is the rights with respect to an object—and are practically never used of the object itself. It would have been useful if the word "estate" had been confined to its original sense of the quality of a relation (status) with regard to land. And so we shall use it. Nevertheless we have gained much. For while some try to destroy the exactness of this older term "estate,"[4] there has been coined, in the effort to describe what an estate is, a new term, "interest," which represents today the purest and most exact idea of the nature of the unit of property which we have. "Interest" is now what "thing" and *res* were in their respective terminologies, before they were concreted. It is a generic term for any kind or size of fraction of complete property in an object, or even indirectly, in some other interest or interests in an object.

We have already noted the analysis of the variety of estates in land contained in Blackstone's synopsis and have referred to the fact that an even more complex classification is being found necessary in the *Restatement of the Law of Property*. However, the importance of this system for our purposes lies in the theory of property interest it presented to us rather than in the detail. And we have already sufficiently examined that theory, so that it is for the most part unnecessary to review the facts of modern American land law at this point. Nevertheless, in two respects difficulties in construing the theory confront our courts – difficulties which did not appear in our previous treatment. Examination of these two points will prove useful to us.

2. *Lesser Interests in Land, or in Regard to Land*

The first difficulty is to determine how far the concept of "interest," or the less inclusive concept of "estate," reach in describing any fraction of property. Do these terms cover all or only certain bundles of rights with reference to land? In this respect the first difficulty is presented by the very ancient practice of describing any estate less than one feudally heritable as a lease and its holder as a lessee. An estate for life is strictly a lease. But so is a mere estate at sufferance. Yet, in the former case the land is held in the name of the lessee while, in the latter, it is *in nomine alieno*. In the former case the possessory interest has been raised to a level which has been called "limited ownership." In the latter it is reduced to a subordinate, or derivative, possession little higher than detention. Thus the question arises whether a lease is a conveyance or a contract. For, as we have seen, the attempt is made to draw a hard and fast procedural line between these twin descendants of a single process, in spite of the fact that they are still hardly distinguishable means of creating interests in objects.

[4] Property is defined "to mean 'estate' and 'estate' to mean 'property.'" [68] Estate is also frequently used to mean a complex of interests, or body of property, as in the phrases "estate of decedent," "trust estate," etc.

Let us see how the courts are dealing with these questions. "The elements of a lease [are] the creation of a lesser estate from the greater; the reservation of rent, the retention of some interest or estate after the termination of the term and the recognition by the terms of the lease of the ownership of the demised property by the lessor [while] . . . an assignment . . . transfers the whole and entire estate . . . makes no reservation of rent and reserves no interest in the property assigned." [69] Or again a "lease refers to a deed of a less interest than the lessor has, for, as Blackstone says, if it is of the whole interest it is more properly an assignment than a lease." [70] An assignment is here taken to mean a deed conveying the whole of an existing estate rather than one creating and conveying a new and lesser one. The distinction is valid as far as it goes. But both these definitions would include as leases the conveyance of anything less than the bare reservation after a fee tail. So the term "lease" is construed in the following: "A lease is properly a conveyance of a particular estate in lands whether for life or for years or at will where reversion is left in the grantor." [71] The modern usage of "tenant" as equivalent to "lessee,"[5] enables us to use the following citation to demonstrate that any interest which is dependent upon that estate which we have defined as the absolute, or ultimate, property is held to be a lease. "A tenant [lessee] . . . [is] one who occupies the lands or premises of another in subordination to that other's title, and with his assent, express or implied." [72] This "subordination" is the old line drawn half way down the series of derivative and dependent tenures and estates where holding *in nomine alieno* began. It excludes estates for life which are still called leases. The "assent" suggests a contract. This raises the question whether a lease is in all cases a conveyance of a possessory interest, or estate, or merely a contract. "A lease . . . is a contract by which the owner divests himself of the possession and use of his property, for a valuable consideration, for a definite term, at the end of which he has the absolute right to re-enter." [73] And again "a lease is defined [by the Revised Civil Code of Louisiana] to be a contract by which 'one party gives to the other the enjoyment of a thing' at a fixed price." [74] But sometimes the transaction is conceived to be metamorphosed from one status to another at a certain stage. "A lease is a contract between the lessor and lessee, vesting in the latter a right to the possession of the land for a term of years. It becomes an estate when it takes effect in possession." [75] On the other hand a Federal court holds that "a lease . . . is a conveyance of lands or tenements. . . A lease creates an estate for years

[5] But the term "tenant" is still used in its original sense as well. "A tenant is one who holds or possesses lands or tenements by any kind of title, either in fee, for life, for years or at will." [77]

or for a less period. . . A lease is something more than a mere contract." [76] The nub of the question is, in which of all these interests, less than the reversion, that are called leases — and, in each case, when and how far — is there vested in the lessee a present or prospective possessory interest in the land, and to what extent is he conveyed merely a liability, or indeterminate interest in the body of property of the lessor?

This question resolves itself into a second one, that of determining whether a certain interest can be conceived to be a "real" right — that is, an interest in the land — or merely a "personal" one — that is, an interest with regard to the land. Decision on this point determines whether the remedy is to be specific restitution or merely damages. In the *Restatement of the Law of Property* an effort is made to divide all interests with regard to land into three classes. The first is estates. This includes any "interest in land that is or may become 'possessory.' "[6] The second includes all "interests in land in which there is neither a present nor a potential future possessory interest."[6] These are easements, profits, etc. The third is "interests with regard to the land,"[7] such as licenses, etc., which do not come within the first two classifications and are, nevertheless, "other than interests of members of society in general."[8] This seems a useful basis of analysis, for it is quite general to treat the first two as one and to confuse the term "interest in" with "possessory interest in," as in the following example: An easement "comprises no interest in the thing itself. It supposes that different rights in the use of the same thing may coexist in different persons." [78] Or, on the other hand, it is common to consider that the distinction between estates and other non-possessory interests is sufficient. For instance, "a lease is a contract for possession and profit of land by the lessee, and a recompense of rent or increase to the lessor, and is grant of an estate in the land. . . A license is an authority to do some act or series of acts on the land of another, for the benefit of the licensee, without passing any estate in land." [79]

The second difficulty arises in determining the stage of development at which an interest becomes subject to recognition as property. Are rights with reference to objects to be considered interests in the objects only when they have vested? Or are all rights, such as those subject to a condition, to be considered as a kind of interest in the object? This question applies, of course, to any variety of interest. Rights are "vested when the right to enjoyment, present or prospec-

[6] *Restatement of the Law of Property*, p. 37.

[7] Ibid., p. 19.

[8] Ibid., p. 17. The criteria by which these three classes are divided are described therein on p. 19 ff. and p. 33 ff.

tive, has become [in the case of real property] the property of some particular person or persons as a present interest [i.e. one subject to no condition except the expiration of preceding freehold estates]. They are expectant when they depend upon the continued existence of the present condition of things until the happening of some future event [before they shall become vested, as above]. They are contingent when they are only to come into existence [as vested interests] on an event or condition which may not happen or be performed until some other event may prevent their vesting." [80] Among the future estates in land there is, on the one hand, the reversion which, however indefinitely its right to possession may be postponed, "is a present vested interest, to be enjoyed at some future time upon the happening of some particular event." It commonly exists where the grantor has conveyed less than his whole interest, or estate." [81] It is therefore the "residue of [his former] estate left in the grantor, to commence in possession after the termination of some particular estate granted out by him." [82] [9] On the other hand there are many interests in land which are executory and are not vested because they are subject to a condition precedent.[10] Nevertheless they too are treated as prop-

[9] The reversion "is that present, vested, alienable, inheritable and devisable residue of an estate remaining in grantor or his successors, or in the successors of a testator, to be enjoyed in possession, from and after the happening of a particular [future] event." [84] But the event is only the determination of the estates of which this is the residue. A remainder "is an estate limited to take effect in possession immediately after the expiration of a prior estate created at the same time and by the same instrument." [85] And therefore granted to some other than the grantor or his heirs.

[10] Gray, *The Rule Against Perpetuities*, p. 589, analyses the question of vesting and of conditions as applied to interests in land.

Estates are either present or future.
Future estates are either vested or executory.
Vested future estates are those which become possessory when the preceding possessory estate is determined.
Executory future estates are those which may thus become possessory only when something else occurs first.
This something else may be certain or uncertain.
1 a. If certain it may be something certain to happen at time certain.
b. Or it may be something certain to happen but at uncertain time.
2. If uncertain, the estate is contingent;
a. To become possessory, if at all, on termination of preceding estates;
b. To become possessory, if at all, at other time.

In this analysis the question whether an estate is vested or not depends on whether the condition is precedent or subsequent. Thus all reversions are vested. "A remainder is vested in A, when, throughout its continuance, A, or A and his heirs, have the right to immediate possession, whenever and however the preceding freehold estates may determine. A remainder is contingent if, in order for it to come into possession, the fulfilment of some condition precedent other than the determination of the preceding freehold estate is necessary" (p. 80). But it is "none the less vested because it may terminate before the remainder-man comes into possession" (p. 81). In other words the vesting is not affected by the fact that it may divest on a condition subsequent (see p. 93). For the condition of every conditional

erty and as some sort of interest in the object. In fact it is held that even an "interest to be acquired by the complainant in the future" [83] is subject to protection as property.

The same question arises in connection with inchoate rights. An "inchoate right is that which is not yet completed or finished. It is merely the beginning of a right" that has not yet ripened. The term covers, among others, those rights for which the completion of certain legal proceedings is required. For instance a judgment is an inchoate lien from the date of entry. It does not become consummate until the motion for a new trial is overruled. Legal instruments are inchoate before registration, if the law requires that they be registered. Nevertheless such rights are treated as property. Title need not have been completed. Property as used in the statute by which Louisiana was acquired by the United States "comprehends every species of title, inchoate or complete . . . those rights which lie in contract . . . executory as well as . . . executed." [86] "Bare possession [occupation] of anything of value of which exclusive possession may possibly and lawfully be had is property." [87] "The locator of a mining claim has a 'possessory title;' [interest] . . . it is property, in the highest sense of that term." [88] The term "property" includes "the possession of and claim to public land" (belonging to the United States). [89]

On the whole the law seems to be aiming at recognition as property, and therefore as interests with regard to objects, of every variety of fraction of complete property in land or other objects, however deferred, however uncertain, however limited the physical contact, and however incomplete the basis of the claim. Uncertainty exists as to the nature of the rights belonging in each particular type of bundle. But all are regarded as in some wise property.

3. *Security and Special Property*

In spite of the fact that in theory the collateral securities form a part, though not an original part, of that group, the *iura in re aliena*, which is the basis for the civilian concept of fractions of property, American law as often as not treats them as representing no interest in the object pledged. Perhaps this is because in no case except one – and that one special property – is there attached any present unconditional possessory right, which right seems to be conceived as an essential attribute of any true property interest.

We have seen that the mortgage, a 'thing' *sui generis*, while it is

estate is always both precedent and subsequent; it is precedent as to itself and subsequent as to the estate which now exists and will continue to exist if the condition is not fulfilled (see p. 93).

in form a registered conveyance of a conditional present interest in land, though without title and without possession, is in fact the creator of a conditional future interest in the mortgaged land; and that in form the condition is subsequent, whereas in fact it is precedent. Its technical form is well described in the following: "A 'mortgage' . . . – first, it is a covenant to pay a sum of money upon an expressed consideration [and as such is an executory contract], and, second, it is an [executed] conveyance of land to secure the debt . . . with a defeasance, and liable to be defeated if at the time it is sought to be enforced there is nothing due upon the executory contract it was given to secure." [90] Because it purports to convey title without actually doing so it can be said, "while a mortgage at law does carry the legal title, it is not, either at law or in equity, an absolute, unconditional, and indefeasible title. It becomes such only after the mortgagor has breached the condition of the mortgage and his equity of redemption has been foreclosed." [91] On the other hand, because it does not actually convey title, it is sometimes conceived presently to do nothing. "A mortgage of real property . . . does not convey the title nor does it create an interest or an estate in the mortgaged property. It merely creates a lien or an incumbrance against the property as security for the payment of a debt or the fulfillment of an obligation, and becomes void on payment of the debt or the fulfillment of the obligation. Equity regards the debt as the principal thing, and the land as a mere incident to it." [92] But the more accurate view is that, "although the mortgagee has no rights of possession or title to the land, he certainly has an interest in it, and under the statutory definition a mortgagee has property in the land mortgaged." [93] The similar expedient, the trust deed, "is a conveyance in trust for the purpose of securing a debt, subject to a condition of defeasance." [94] Therefore, " a deed of trust . . . is simply a mortgage with power of sale." [95]

The class of securities which is comprised under the general term "lien" includes the equitable lien; the maritime lien, which closely follows the equitable; the common law lien, which is a pledge or bailment; and the statutory lien, which is based upon the common law lien. In general "a lien is a charge upon property." [96] "A lien necessarily excludes any idea of ownership by the party claiming it. 'A lien, whether implied or by contract, confers no right of property upon the holder. . .'" [97] It "is not a property in the thing itself, nor does it constitute a right of action for the thing. It rather constitutes a charge upon the thing." [98] Frequently the words "hold" or "claim" are substituted for "charge." Thus a popular definition is that a lien is "a hold or claim . . . upon the property of another." [99] Nevertheless, in another and equally authoritative view, a "lien is a right of property, and not a mere matter of procedure." [100]

It appears, when we examine the two prototype liens that the reason for this difference of opinion rests largely in the fact that the one is conferred by a jurisdiction which is conceived to have no power except over the person and which cannot create property, and that the other is historically defined to confer, not property, but rather that viable abortion, special property. The result is some remarkable circumlocutions. An equitable lien, when "possession is not essential to its validity," is said to be "a right to have a debt satisfied out of a particular thing." [101] Or, more elaborately, "An equitable lien, strictly speaking, is not a 'ius in re' or a 'ius ad rem,' but is the right to have the property subjected in a court of equity to the payment of the claim. It is a *floating* equity until action by the court is invoked." [102] But when an attempt is made to reason it out, certain difficulties are met. "An equitable lien is not an estate of property in the thing itself nor a right to recover the thing,—that is, a right which may be the basis of a possessory action; it is neither a 'ius ad rem' nor a 'ius in re.' It is simply a right of a special nature over a thing, which constitutes a charge or encumbrance upon the thing, so that the very thing itself may be proceeded against in an equitable action. . ." [103] In other words it is that peculiar right to bring an action which is in form *in personam* and in effect *in rem.* Another says, equitable liens are "a right of a special nature over the thing, which may, by proper process, be sold or sequestered under a judicial decree, and the proceeds in the one case, or the rents and profits in the other, applied upon the demand of the party holding the lien. But such party is not entitled to the possession of the thing, nor to the rents and profits, except under a judicial decree. This is a distinguishing feature between equitable and legal liens." [104] Since the object itself can be reached for sequestration or sale only under judicial decree we may be excused if we fail to perceive the sharp distinction noted between these rights and those of possession or beneficial use which may alternatively be obtained in the same way. As a matter of fact an equitable lien is, in general, a property right which *commences* by being a non-possessory right to indeterminate objects in a specific body of property and develops into any one of a variety of possessory rights to specific 'things.'

A common law lien is "the right of an apparent pledgee to retain the articles pledged as security for his loan." [105] There must be an "immediate delivery and . . . an actual, and continued change of possession." [106] Here again it "does not transfer the title." "The title remains in the pledgor until it is divested either by a foreclosure in equity or a sale on due notice." [107] "It was for a long time doubted whether incorporeal things, like debts, money in stocks, etc., which cannot be manually delivered, were proper subjects of a pledge. It is now held that they are." [108] More elaborately, such a pledge is "a transfer of personal property as security for a debt or other obligation . . . a bailment of personal property by a debtor to his creditor, to be kept by him until his debt is discharged. . . The three elements necessary to constitute a contract one of pledge are: (1) the possession of the pledged property must pass from the pledgor to the pledgee or to some one for him; (2) the legal title to the pledged property must remain in the pledgor; (3) the pledgee must have a lien on the property for the payment of a debt or performance of an obligation due him by the pledgor or some other person." [109] To which should be added that the law requires the pledgee to hold the property exclusively as a security. [110] "Statutory liens, [including judgment liens] . . . have, without possession, the same operation and efficiency that existed in common law liens where possession was delivered." [111] This peculiarity, the necessity of vindication by possession, leads us, as before, from the common law lien into that general class of special interests in objects to which it belongs, the bailments.

Bailments are limited to personalty, but they can take place as well with choses in action as with choses in possession. If a chose not in possession can be bailed, the *thing* is obviously not the object ultimately to be recovered but only the present interest in that object. "Bailment is the delivery of goods for some purpose, upon a contract express or implied, that after the purpose has been fulfilled they should be re-delivered to the bailor, or otherwise dealt with according to his directions, or kept until he claims them." [112] "In bailment the identical thing delivered is to be restored." [113][11] The pledge (or a bailment in general) vests "a special property interest in the thing pledged." [114] "The general property in the thing pledged remains in the pledgor, and only a special property vests in the pledgee." [115] These terms are usually defined rather vaguely. Special property in a 'thing' is a "special fixed interest or right therein distinct from, and subordinate to, the absolute property or interest in the general owner" (Judge Story); it "is where he who has the possession holds it subject to the claims of other persons" (Justice Lawrence). [116] In other

[11] "The passing of the legal title from the owner to the party to whom personal property is delivered distinguishes a 'trust' from a mere bailment." [118]

"One of the principal tests by which to determine whether any particular contract creates a mere bailment or is a sale on credit is this: was there a binding promise on the part of the person to whom the possession was given to pay for the article?" [119]

"A general deposit in a bank creates the relation of debtor and creditor between the bank and the depositor, and although it is called a deposit it is a loan and not a bailment." [120]

words, to define it in terms of itself, "special property is a qualified or limited right, such as a bailee of it has." [117]

One other, and a new, type of security has been developed of recent years. This is the conditional sale. It takes two forms. In one the "vendor of personal property reserves title in himself until the payment in full of the purchase price." [121] The other is "a purchase accompanied by an agreement to resell upon particular terms." [122] In both cases possession passes with delivery and reverts upon the occurrence of the condition (i.e. non-payment). In the first case the condition is precedent; in the second subsequent. But the retention of the title in the seller, in the first case, or the cloud upon the title of the purchaser, in the second, does not prevent the law from treating the purchaser as "owner" in fact. Thus "there must be a delivery of possession to the purchaser, with the intention of passing immediate ownership, subject only to the reservation of title to the seller, as security for the purchase money." [123] As in the case of mortgages the retained title, subject to defeasance, does not correspond to the ordinary title of "ownership" for "contracts which reserve the title absolutely in the vendor are not conditional sales." [124] Here is further evidence of the statement already made that the criterion of title is not in fact an exact method of identifying any particular interest as "ownership." [12] This new form of commercial lien has largely taken the place of the chattel mortgage which was an effort to apply the principle of the modern real estate mortgage to personal property as a non-possessory lien given by way of security for debt.

Each of these varied types of security has a particular relation to some determinate object or the documentary evidence of an interest in indeterminate objects (chose in action). They may be possessory or non-possessory. But all, directly or indirectly, have abstracted some element of control or enjoyment from the complete property or the interest subjected to the lien. In this respect the securities resemble the trusts. Wherefore, as we have seen, the latter are sometimes used in the shape of trust deeds to obtain the same results. The mortgage, the trust deed, the pledge, or common law lien, and the conditional sale are used as security for credit-debt relations. They are therefore antecedent, and accessories to contracts. The equitable (and maritime) and the statutory liens are

[12] The right of the buyer resembles equitable property similar to an equity of redemption. Williston, *Sales*, sec. 579, says of the conditional sale that "such a transaction is in its essence analogous to a transfer of title to the buyer, and a mortgage back by the buyer to the seller in order to secure the price." The seller retains title (legal property). "He retains it, however, merely as security. The beneficial interest in the property, so far as is not inconsistent with the security of the seller, is vested in the buyer." Savouring of the trust!

methods of collecting debts. They are therefore remedial, and accessories to rights of action. In fact the general equitable lien bears the same relation to a decree that a judgment lien bears to a judgment.

Certain and carefully defined property rights in the object or 'thing' given as security are universally granted in all these cases to the holder of the security. The facts of the law are clear. Otherwise the forms would not serve their purposes or be used. It is only theory, which in these particular cases is more than usually incompetent to describe in its simple and antiquated terms facts that are nevertheless quite clearly recognized, which occasionally denies the condition of true property interests.

4. *Equitable Property*

In contrast with the confusion introduced by the application of the theory of *dominium*, as "ownership" or property, evidenced in the citations adduced in the first part of this chapter, it is interesting to note, when we come to examine the American law of trusts, that none of the puzzlements disturbing the theorists seem to have communicated themselves to our courts. They hold, as Justice Holmes puts it, that "a trust still is only a trust." One, to be sure, is afflicted with the notion of obligation. But in other respects his description is adequate and justifies its popularity. "A trust is an obligation arising out of a confidence reposed in the trustee, or person who has the legal title to property conveyed to him, that he will faithfully apply the property according to the confidence reposed; in other words, according to the wishes of the creator of the trust." [125] Perhaps the generally accurate understanding is due to the peculiar continuity and insulation of the active tradition from its very beginning until today. For even now the rules laid down by the Statute of Uses determine the fact of a trust, if of freehold. Such "a trust is . . . a use not executed by the statute." [126] This is explained as follows: "The test, which determines whether the device or conveyance is governed by the statute of uses, whereby the legal title is transferred, or whether a trust is created . . . is very plain and simple. If the party who takes the beneficial interest has the full and uncontrolled use of the property, he takes the legal as well as the equitable title. If anything remains for the trustees to do concerning the property, such as may require them to retain control of it to any extent or for any purpose, in such a case they retain the legal estate, and the cestui que trust has only an equitable interest." [127]

In respect of the division of the complete property between the trustee and the beneficiary, trusts may range from the "dry," or simple, trust, which, in the case of freehold is just over the line from a use which would have to be executed by legal conveyance to the beneficiary, to the other extreme of a spendthrift trust which creates property in the beneficiary which is not alienable. In the case of property other than freehold, from the standpoint of the beneficiary, "a simple trust gives the beneficiary the right to possession and control, and power of disposal for his own use." [128] From the standpoint of the trustee such a trust is said to be " 'simple,' 'passive,' or 'dry' when the trustee has no active duty to perform, or when the trust serves no purpose, or none that would not be equally served without it, the trustee being the mere depository of the naked title, charged with no duty and without power to take possession or manage, or exercise any control over the property." [129] But " 'active or special trusts' [including those of freehold] are those in which . . . trustees are charged with the performance of active and substantial duties with respect to the control, management and disposition of the property." [130] And "a special trust . . . maintains the legal estate in the trustee, to enable him to perform the duties devolved on him by the donor; and gives to the cestui que trust only a right in equity to enforce the performance." [131] Finally, a spendthrift trust is described as a trust which "vests no estate in the beneficiary [at least not an alienable estate] . . . or, more correctly speaking, the estate is a terminable one, and ceases upon the occurrence of insolvency in the beneficiary, or of other specified act or event which, but for such restriction, might expose the estate to seizure for his debt." [132]

The favourite statement of the property thus created in the beneficiary describes it as "an equitable right, title, or interest in property real or personal, distinct from the legal ownership thereof." [133] When applied to land the term equitable estate includes "the estate or title of a person for whose use or benefit lands are held in trust by another" or "of a mortgagor after the mortgage has become forfeited by non-payment and before foreclosure." [134] Upon the side of the trustee it is clearly recognized that "the legal estate is . . . no more than the shadow always following the equitable estate which is the substance." [135] Thus "absolute control and power of disposition [upon the part of the trustee] are inconsistent with the idea of a trust." [136] For the distinguishing characteristic of, and inherent limitations upon, the rights of a trustee is that these rights are not to be exercised for his own benefit. "A trustee may be defined generally as a person in whom some estate, interest or power in or affecting property is vested for the benefit of another." [137] He has legal title and perhaps control. But this fraction of property is subjected to a special disability in favor of the derivative equitable property dependent upon it. The relation between the two fractions, much like feudal fealty, is a species of fiduciary relationship which, in general, "exists where confidence is reposed on one side and resulting in superiority and influence on the other." [138]

While such a relationship seems at first sight to be a personal and not a property relation, such is not the case. There is no confusion between the status of the trustee as trustee and that as an individual. Or, rather, the trust fund is conceived as one entity and the trustee's own property as a wholly separate matter. The two must never be confused. In the case of a bankrupt his body of property is conceived to include "only the property to which the bankrupt is beneficially entitled" and not "property to which he has only a bare legal title." [139] For the same reason the courts find it necessary to deny to this "bare legal title" the name of "ownership." Ownership "is an inherent right to the dominion over, and beneficial enjoyment of, some valuable right, or interest [which cannot be predicated of the estate of a trustee]." [140] This and the provisions for replacing deceased or discharged trustees are further evidence of the fact, which we have already suspected, that a body of property is treated as something which exists independently of the persons to whom it is related.[18]

We have now briefly examined the way modern American legal practice recognizes the fractions of property; that uncertain 'thing' called "ownership" and, in the case of lands, the estates which vary from fee simple to tenancy at sufferance; the subordinate rights in land and the varieties of perfection of title; the division of complete property between lienor and lienee, bailor and bailee, and trustee and beneficiary. In all cases these are conceded at law to be rights with regard to objects, though some are not dignified by being termed interests. In so far as this last is the case it is apparent that it is due to the fact that such subordinate interests have not yet been fully recognized to be—what they are—fractions subtracted from the whole. There is another fractional property relation which is as yet not accurately appraised in American practice. That is the relation of the stockholder to the corporation or its assets. The character of this relation is defined as you please. But we must reserve our examination of this question. Finally there is that large and ill-defined mass of rights known as choses in action, into which group

[18] This was already dimly apprehended in Roman law. One man might wear several *personae*. But while the personality concept has retained some of its original application when used in connection with the *person* of inherence, it has become almost completely depersonalized, except in form, when used in connection with the *person* of incidence. The word *corpus*, curiously enough, although it originated as the physical fact, has been continuously employed more purely in this sense of a depersonalized body of property from the time that Roman law came to its maturity. We still distinguish the *body*, or principal, of a trust fund as its *corpus*.

is thrown everything for which a place cannot be found in the trational classifications. Since these are not now conceded to be relations between men in regard to objects at all, but wholly between men with regard to acts, they are not treated as fractions. Therefore we must defer their examination until we come to the general classifications of property.

D. *The Border Lines of Property*

1. *Different Boundaries for Different Purposes*

We have already referred to the serious impediments to accurate generalization which hamper the American judge. The diversities of terminology and of jurisdiction and the novelty of economic facts are well-nigh insuperable obstacles to a rational conceptual structure. In view of these considerations one is impressed with the ability of the courts to deal as unerringly as they do with these linguistic and conceptual confusions. It is done by means of rules of statutory construction; by means of shrewdly applied appraisals of the intent of legislatures and even of parties; a deal of common sense; and a proud arrogation of the privilege and duty of dealing justice regardless of technicalities and the duplicity of words. In all these citations it would be necessary to examine the details of the case and all the qualifications of the dictum, before we could rightly assume to know the particular application to which the learned judge intended, and intended only, to apply his definition. Space does not permit such detailed study. Nor is it necessary for our purpose, provided we remind ourselves that for each separate application the term property and its analogues may be given slightly different boundaries.

In order to make this qualification more definite it seems desirable to give a few examples of the major differences of application to which we refer. Let us take, for example, that rather nebulous concept a "calling, business, or profession." Within the meaning of the constitutional provision prohibiting the taking of property without compensation, "property" includes, as a whole, a "calling, business or profession chosen and followed." [141] But "it generally has been assumed . . . that injury to a business is not an appropriation of property which must be paid for [i.e. under the exercise of the right of eminent domain]." [142] And, under an act in connection with the prevention of routs, riots, etc., the term "property" meant "only tangible property." "Business losses were not considered as property in such statutes." [143] Nevertheless "a person's occupation or calling . . . is 'property' entitled to protection as such from boycotts or unlawful interferences by others." [144] On the other hand, "while the right to pursue any lawful occupation or calling is generally if not universally recognized as 'property,' within the 'due process' clause of the Federal Constitution, yet on the other hand the right of the State to regulate such a business when its unregulated operation may injuriously affect the welfare of others is equally well settled." [145] And the character of the protection is limited. "The right to labour in any calling or profession in the future may be considered a property right, for the purpose of protection, but no right exists as to labor or services already rendered." It is "quite another [thing] to assert that [the latter are] . . . property, in order to enlarge or change the ordinary remedies by which the debt due [therefor] . . . may be recovered." [146] The word property "as used in the constitution [in connection with taxation] cannot by any forced construction be tortured into meaning an occupation, calling or profession." [147] For "'business,' in the sense in which it is used in taxing laws [and elsewhere], does not generally mean property," [148] so that "a tax upon business is not a tax upon 'property.'" [149]

Franchises for public service are construed to be property in connection with the right of eminent domain [14] and also for purposes of taxation. But the general franchise of a corporation secured "upon complying with the requirements of the statute and the payment of the incorporation tax . . . the 'right to be,' to 'exist,' would not be an element of property that could be taxed." [150] So, too, goodwill is not "property," within the meaning of the "Tax law." [151] But "as . . . used in connection with fraud and defamation . . . it [property] may include good will." [152] And labour "is not property in the sense that it can be liable to a property tax." [153]

In general "property is not necessarily a taxable thing any more than it is always a tangible thing." [154] But when it comes to "protection of 'property' . . . it has been uniformly held that the term 'property' embraces all rights, whether legal, equitable or imperfect." [155] So that, as an extreme case, even "mail is 'property'" within a statute authorizing the head of each department to prescribe regulations for the preservation of the property appertaining to the department, and "it belongs for certain purposes to the United States." [156] The extent to which the courts are thus compelled, in the interests of justice, to take liberties with such laws as are expressed in general rather than in specific terms, and the basis upon which they go about doing it, are well exemplified in this citation. The court says, "It is true, the general term 'property' may often embrace mere debts and choses in action. Whether, in a particular

[14] *See* Metropolitan City Ry. Co. v. Chi. W. D. Ry. Co., 87 Ill. 317, 324 (1877).

statute, it is to be construed as having that broad meaning, or a more limited one, must be determined by the aid of the familiar rules relating to statutory construction." [157] [15]

2. *Interests Generally Treated as Property*

The extent to which American courts have gone in expanding the concept of property to include practically all rights, however attenuated, which immediately or ultimately concern relations with respect to specific material objects can be well demonstrated by a few citations. Certainly any right pertaining to land, whether it be real or personal, is property, for the term is authoritatively said to include "all rights and interest in real and personal property, and also in easements, franchises, and incorporeal hereditaments." [158] The "term 'property in lands' . . . include[s] any usufructuary interest, whether it be leasehold or mere right of possession." [159] It covers even "a leasehold interest in premises for a definite term," [160] for "a tenant has a property in land." [161]

"Ores and minerals contained in land are 'property' . . . [which] by proper conveyance, can be severed from the land by the owner thereof." [162] So, on the other hand, the term includes the owner's reservation of "the minerals and the right to mine the same; also a right of way over the land, or any part, for mining purposes." [163] "The mining right [to drill for oil and gas] . . . is property." [164] So too are mining leases even though they do not "convey title to the unextracted ore deposits," [165] and "a turpentine lease." [166] "A priority to the use of water is a 'property right' which is the subject of purchase and sale." [167] One creates property even by granting "an exclusive right to hunt on game preserves." [168] "An equity in incumbered real estate" [169] remains property even after the mortgage is in default and, as such, may be sold.

The term includes "a 'bona fide' equitable interest in property, of which the legal title is in another." [170] This interest is not merely an obligation of the trustee, for "an ordinary cestui que trust has a property in a fund held for his benefit." [171] Nor is it deprived of its character as property because the attribute of alienability has been removed. "A trust fund . . . is property . . . though . . . the beneficiary cannot 'assign, or convey or devise' it." [172]. Property "includes a mortgage," [173] and even an equitable "lien . . . upon bonds." [174] It includes "shares of stock," [175] held directly,

[15] Under which the court declined to permit the garnishment of accounts assigned to a referee in bankruptcy for benefit of creditors, though the law positively stated that a "garnishee summons may be issued against any person who has property . . . in his hands or under his control belonging to the defendant in any action for the recovery of money."

or even an indirect "interest in the pool property" of a stock pool to advance the market in a certain stock. [176]

The question whether the enjoyment is present or prospective, or whether the right is present or future makes no difference. "A vested remainder is 'property'." [177] So is "a vested interest in a contingent right, being more than a mere possibility." [178] And, while "a contingent remainder is not technically an estate, but a mere possibility of an estate in the future, . . . that is very far from saying it is not property." [179]

Certain choses in action are generally conceded to be property. The term "includes also credits." [180] In fact so often is it stated that "a debt is property," [181] that it becomes necessary for one court to proclaim that "debts are far from being the 'property' of the debtor." [182] Property "includes money," [183] for "the payment of money works a transfer of property from debtor to creditor." [184] It includes "a promissory note. . . The fact that the maker may be irresponsible does not change the rule that one buying a note buys property." [185] It includes "bonds," [186] "a check," [187] and even an undelivered check. [188] Express company checks, which had not been signed or countersigned by original payee, have been held to be 'property,' being evidence of debt. [189] A "draft is . . . property." [190] "Outstanding uncollected accounts" are property. [191] So is "a judgment debt," [192] and even a dormant judgment. [193] Contracts other than debts are also held to be property in many cases. Thus "a contract between a water-supply company and a city to supply water to it," [194] and "contract rights transferred to a corporation in payment for stock" [196] have been held to be property. The Chancellor of New Jersey has referred to options for the purchase of manufacturing plants as "undoubtedly property," [197] in spite of the fact that an option is frequently not conceded even to be a contract.

We have already seen that the quality of the title is not a determinant. Thus "the locator of a mining claim has a 'possessory title'; . . . it is property." [198] Nor is it limited to rights in objects already appropriated. It covers permits to appropriate common resources. Thus "the right to fish is a 'property right' and not a mere privilege of citizenship." [199] "Leasehold interests in the tide-lands of the state" are property, [200] as well as ice on a floatable stream, formed over land belonging in fee to the owner. [201]

3. *Doubtful Cases—By Reason of the Nature of the Right*

When we come to examine certain other classes of rights we find a real difference of opinion as to whether or not they are properly to be classed as property. The first group of doubtful cases consists of those in which the question is whether the nature of the right permits it to be classed as property; and in the second group the question is whether the nature of the object permits it to be so classed. As to the first group there are two questions. What, if any, rights in regard to material objects are to be denied the status of rights of property? Is the term to be limited to interests *in* objects, rejecting all which exist only *with regard to* objects? And, second, where is the line to be drawn between personal, familial and property rights? Let us examine a few typical cases.

It has been frequently held that property does not include "a right of way [which] is no estate or interest in land, but an easement." [202] But this view seems to be based on a theory, which most courts are not willing to follow, that the rights of property are limited to possessory interests in objects, or, rather, that they include only the complete possessions. In opposition to this theory it is generally asserted that "an easement is property." [203] Thus, specifically, "a right of way . . . is property," [204] so that "a railroad's right of way" is an interest in the land having "the substantiality of the fee." [205] For this reason, in the case of railroad rights of way at least, the superimposing of one right of way over another is a deprivation of property. The laying out of public streets across the right of way of a railroad constitutes the taking of property. [206] This view also applies to other types of easement. Thus "an easement . . . for ingress and egress . . . and also for the free and uninterrupted passage and circulation of light and air" is property. [207] Perhaps, as we shall see later, the courts are groping for a classification of the several different property relations which have been lumped together as easements because they find it necessary to accord somewhat different groups of rights to each.

Because they find it necessary to distinguish between beneficial and non-beneficial interests, just as between possessory and non-possessory, there is the same inclination to deny the name property to the legal title of a trustee. Thus, in the citations already given, this method is used to protect trust funds against the personal liabilities of the trustee. This circumlocution and the distinction upon which it is based would be rendered unnecessary if the law recognized the facts and regarded the trust fund and the personal fund of the trustee as two separate entities with no relation, except the fiduciary one, existing between them.

The same reason, that they are non-beneficial, is sometimes given as grounds for refusing the name of property to liens in general. In the case of common law liens there is the additional reason that they do not possess the attribute of alienability which is often assumed to be a necessary element of property. A lien "is neither property nor is it a debt, but a right to retain property as security for the debt." It "is a personal right and cannot be transferred to another." [208] In other words it is a bare right of possession subject to defeasance. The time-honoured and well defined status of this particular fraction as "special property" seems here to have been forgotten.

Another criterion often misleads. The courts are apt to conceive that the distinction between rights *in rem* and rights *in personam*, so-called, is the basis for the distinction between property and personal or familial rights. Thus a married woman's right to the affections of her husband is a "property right," and the loss thereof constitutes an injury to the consortium. [209] And again, the reciprocal rights possessed by each, husband and wife, "to the society and companionship of the other" are regarded as "the 'property' of the respective parties." [210] But it is more generally held that the consortium to which a wife is entitled is not property, [211] for "the right [of a wife] to the society of her husband" is a personal right. [212] The reason for this view is that a wife's marital companionship is purely personal to the husband and possesses none of the attributes of property. [213]

In passing we may note one minor form of contract which has occasioned considerable difficulty. Railroad tickets are property and may be the subject of larceny. [214] On the other hand "a non-transferable passenger ticket . . . is not property." [215] And again, "at most a railroad passenger ticket is mere evidence of a contract" and is not property. [216]

We have seen that "choses in action" is the classification into which the law throws all relations for which it has found no place in its settled property structure. In it first appear most of the new forms and contrivances of business. For this reason it is a very heterogeneous mass. While the courts attempt to generalize in regard to it, such generalizations do not work. They result from failure to analyse the wide differences in the several species of this genus. It will therefore be more profitable for us to defer consideration of the disputes as to whether, or how far, choses in action come within the domain of property, until we are prepared to analyse and classify each variety for itself. Suffice it to say at this point that this represents the chief field of dispute as to what interests are and what are not property.

4. *Doubtful Cases—By Reason of the Nature of the Object*

Hitherto we have dealt exclusively with property rights, direct or indirect, in or with regard to material objects. But there is another class of object which furnishes many puzzles for the law. These are the franchises, patents, copyrights, etc. They are sometimes called incorporeal, though this term, on account of its specific use in connection with a certain kind of right, is inapplicable to objects. They are frequently called intangible. In business and in accounting this is the correct usage of the term. They might be called immaterial, for they are carefully defined to be entirely separate from material objects to which they relate but which are factually as well as legally separable from them. But, inasmuch as they behave in law and in economics much as if they were themselves material objects and inasmuch as they occupy almost identical positions in the structure, the term "quasi-material objects" seems to be the most descriptive. These objects are the exclusive processes, capable of being appropriated and protected; processes which, while immaterial, are, in spite of that fact, capable of transfer; processes which are special and not general, and therefore distinguishable and identifiable; and processes which persist independently of persons.

A franchise is a special authority conferred by government. The privilege of securing a corporate charter by complying with statutory requirements is general and in no respect exclusive. Therefore "a corporate franchise . . . [is] a mere privilege, or grant of authority by the government, and is not 'property of any description'." [217] Nevertheless, such "a franchise is valuable, and in that sense has sometimes been held to be property." [217] In general the term is used of franchises for the exclusive performance of some public service. Such "a franchise [is] a vested right, peculiar in its nature; [and is] a quasi-property." [218] Others go further; "A franchise is property, and it cannot wantonly or of whim be taken away." [219] On the other hand, "Although, technically speaking, franchises are property, they are property of a peculiar character, arising only from legislative grant, and are not, in ordinary cases, subject to execution or to sale and transfer, even in payment of the debts of the corporation." [220] The franchise does not include the objects with which the process deals. "It does not . . . embrace the property acquired by the exercise of the franchise." [221] Therefore it is a purely immaterial process. It may be positive. So privileges to use streets and public places for the purposes of a public utility business constitute a special franchise which is property. [222] Or it may be negative. A franchise granting "immunity from taxation . . . is a property right." [223]

It is said that "a patent . . . which vests the sole and exclusive right of making, using, and vending the invention . . . in the person to whom it has been granted by the government, as against all persons not deriving title through him, is property, capable of being assigned by him at his pleasure." [224] So "a patent-right is the subject of assignment, sale or inheritance," [225] and contributions to capital in property may be made by the transfer of patent rights. [226] Because it is a special privilege conferred by government the question of its susceptibility to involuntary transfer is moot. One court holds that "the right acquired by the patentee by the issue of a valid patent, is property which is subject to the claims of a creditor." [227] But the weight of authority is that it "cannot be sold under a common execution." [228] Whether this is due to its nature or to a special rule as to jurisdiction is a question. "A patent is . . . 'a property in notion . . .' and cannot be levied on and sold under execution issuing from the state courts, and whether . . . from the federal courts is . . . doubtful." [229] It is recognized that "a trade-mark is a species of property which may be sold or transmitted by death with the business in which it has been used." [230] Copyrights have both common law and statutory character as property. "Copyright . . . is an incorporeal right, not a corporeal thing. At the same time it is property, capable of being assigned. . ." [231] And, perhaps upon the basis of the common law copyright, "the quotations, [of the stock exchange], when collected and tabulated by the exchange, constitute its 'private property'." [232]

Other special privileges conferred by government have to an even less extent the attributes of property. For instance, "a license is in no sense property. It is a mere temporary permit to do what would otherwise be illegal, issued in the exercise of the police power." [233] Or, more specifically, "a license to operate a motor vehicle is a permit to do that which would otherwise be unlawful. Although the privilege may be valuable, it is not property in any legal or constitutional sense." [234] And yet even licenses, while revocable, may be transferable. A considerable traffic takes place in such are are. And in that respect they are treated as property. "Though a [liquor] 'license' is technically not property in the sense that it can be taken away by the state without compensation, yet under the statute, it is a valuable right and possesses all other characteristics of property." [235] In one case a special license, revocable for cause, was, when it was condemned for other reasons, treated as an easement. The court stated that "a vault constructed under the sidewalk with the permission of the city, by an abutting owner, is an easement . . . and is in itself a species of property," under an act defining property as including "any 'such' real estate and any rights . . . privileges, franchises and easements." [236]

Perhaps because the feudal offices, along with all other kinds of status in the social organization, were regarded as incorporeal hereditaments it is still frequently contended that public offices are property. Occasionally a court will rule that "under the term 'property' is included the right to hold public office." [237] But usually it is stated that "a public office is not property," [238] and "the right of an incumbent to his office is not a right of property." [239] The salary earned during the term of office is however a debt, so that "the salary of an office is property, the right to which depends on the right to the office." [240] And "a teacher's salary is a property . . . to use . . . as he sees fit." [241]

So much for the special privileges conferred by government. There are some other exclusive processes capable of being appropriated, protected and transferred, which are identifiable and capable of being regarded separately from the material objects with which they are concerned and of existing independently of particular persons. Of these the chief are business goodwill and memberships in market organizations. The courts have some difficulty with both. "The good will of a business is the expectation of continued public patronage" and "is property, transferable like any other property." [242] It is therefore "an advantage and benefit that is acquired by business establishments beyond the value of the money or property invested therein." [243] And though it is not conferred by government, "good will, like a franchise, is a privilege which the courts will protect as a right of value. As such it is property, though intangible." [244] But, being only a quasi-material object "good will" is not property within the meaning of the "Tax Law." [245] Sometimes goodwill is concreted and comes to be spoken of as if it existed in material form. In this way one court is led to state that property includes the subscription list of a newspaper. [246]

So great a difference of opinion exists as to memberships in exchanges that one might suspect a geographical discrimination. A membership in the New York Stock Exchange is property. [247] But "a certificate of membership in the board of trade of the City of Chicago . . . is not property." [248] Membership in the San Francisco Stock and Exchange Board is property. [249] But in Pennsylvania a seat in a board of brokers is "not property." [250] One says "It is a mere personal privilege, perhaps more accurately, a license to buy and sell at the meetings of the board." [251] But another retorts, "A seat or membership in a stock exchange is property, and should be applied in the same manner as other property of a debtor to the payment of his debts." [252] An excellent statement of the case is this: "Although of a character somewhat peculiar, its use restricted, its range of purchasers narrow, and its ownership clogged with conditions, it [is] nevertheless a valuable right, capable of transfer and correctly decided to be property." [253]

Because the right of contract does not seem to have been authoritatively established to be a personal right as well as an element in all property, and because protection of freedom from interference with employment, as a personal liberty, does not seem to have been adequate, both are frequently claimed to be property rights. We are forced to conclude, however, that the right to free and undisturbed employment is incapable of existing independently of the person; is a right of all citizens equally; is therefore a personal right and as such should be fully protected. It is partly the peculiar twist given the wording of the Constitution, partly insufficient emphasis on the personal rights, and partly mere demagoguery which leads the courts to assert that "labor is property;" [254] to compare the "property that a man has in his labor" to that of the capitalist in his "gold" or the merchant in his goods; [255] to say that "the laborer has the same right to sell his labor, and to contract with reference thereto, as any other property owner;" [256] that labour "lies, to a large extent at the foundation of most other forms of property;" [257] or that "labor is property, and as such merits protection. The right to make it available is next in importance to the rights of life and liberty." [258] If rights were conceived to inhere in a particular person as to a particular job, then such rights might be regarded as property, even though not heritable or otherwise transferable. But of course no such right is at present conceded. And we may say, without in the least diminishing its importance, that the generalized right to work is not property under any definition of that term which will bear analysis. Such a right is inseparable from the person and in no respect exclusive. It is a personal right.

Certain personal businesses and professions, where the only employer is in fact the customer, may be conceived to be in some respects the objects of property, much in the same way that a going concern and goodwill are conceived to be quasi-material objects. But the analogy can only be pushed far enough to include the goodwill of a professional or personal service "practice." More broadly property is frequently held to include "a calling, business, or profession, chosen and followed." [259] In this respect it would seem to have to be limited to a right to a particular job for which one is not beholden to another. So, specifically, "the right to practice medicine is, like the right to practice any other profession, a valuable 'property' right." [260] And "the office of an attorney is his property." [261] But such occupations or professions as require special and revocable authorizations are in this respect not treated as property. Thus it is stated that the office of attorney at law is not a "property right," but an extraordinary privilege, conferred on one in possession of certain moral and educational qualifications, and after admission he stands as an officer of the court, of which office he may not be deprived, except in the exercise of a sound judicial discretion and upon strict proof of professional unfitness. [262] Since it covers the chief point which leads to the claim that a business has some other vague existence as property, aside from its transferable assets and its transferable goodwill, we quote an excellent judgment on the subject *in extenso*. "It generally has been assumed, we think, that injury to a business is not an appropriation of property which must be paid for. . . No doubt a business may be property in a broad sense of the word, and property of great value. But a business is less tangible in nature, and more uncertain in its vicissitudes than the rights which the Constitution undertakes absolutely to protect . . . the diminution of its value is a vaguer injury than . . . appropriation. . . A business might be destroyed by the construction of a more popular street . . . as well as by competition." [263]

There is another vexed question which is constantly assuming more importance. In some cases financial standing, or "credit," [264] is defined as property. In others it is regretted that it is not practicable so to regard it. Thus "a man's financial standing or credit may not be 'property' within the technical meaning of that term, but it is something often more valuable." [265] If the personal rights received equal recognition and protection as such this question could not arise, at least in regard to individuals. Financial standing, or credit, would then be classed as a part—the vital part perhaps—of personal reputation. For such it is, since it is wholly personal and inseparable from the person. On the other hand, where it was identified with a non-personal going concern—a body of property—such as a corporation, it might require to be treated as an object of property.

Some rights seem to have as their object the identity of the person, represented by the individual name, along lines analogous to the identifications of a business individuality (viz. trade names and goodwill). New Jersey courts of equity have held that an injunction will lie to restrain the unauthorized use of one's name by another as a part of its corporate title, or, in connection with its business or advertisements, his picture or his pretended certificate; [266] and even that "a man's name is his own 'property,' and he has the same right to its use and enjoyment as he has to that of any other species of property." But each "has no exclusive right in the name as against others of the same name." [267] Perhaps this species of property should be included under trade names since it follows much the same rules.

Inchoate patents or copyrights, that is, inventions or ideas still in the shape of personal or trade secrets or secret processes, are regarded as, in certain respects, objects of property and, as such, are granted a measure of protection. The difficulty is that the only occasion for protecting them arises when they are no longer secrets. It is then too late. Moreover the very fact of publication, which destroys their value, is the essential requirement of a patent or copyright. Thus, instead of being exclusive privileges granted in return for publication, such protections consist merely in rights against breach of trust. "Secret processes and formulas are property, and rights in them are . . . recognized as entitled to protection as property rights." [268] The owner of a secret process, not patented, has no exclusive right to make, use, and vend the article to which it relates, but he has the right to keep his own knowledge to himself, and to protection of same, as a property right against one who, in violation of a contract or through a breach of trust, or confidence, undertakes to apply the secret to his own use or to impart it to others. [269] "Equity recognizes a secret in trade as property, and will protect trade secrets by injunction as against those who seek to disclose or use them by a violation of confidential relations, or contract stipulations, express or implied." [270] Apart from this "an invention, a painting, a book is the property of its creator. He may keep it for his own exclusive use or enjoyment if he sees fit. . . But if once he publishes it, his property right in it is gone and every one may make use of it." [271] For a mere idea, unprotected by contract or statute, is not property. [272] So one cannot claim property in knowledge. "It is not exactly accurate to say that the mere abstract knowledge, acquired in the study of a special employment, is of itself property. It is the right to apply that knowledge to the accomplishment of a particular result, which constitutes property." [273] And then only if the process of so applying it is a protected process.

5. *Rights Conceded not to be Property*

It is generally agreed that rights in regard to persons, even when they are recognized in other ways, are not to be treated as property rights. And this includes the rights one has in his own person. Thus "By no possible intendment could 'property' . . . be made to include a human life." [274] The taking of life is a tort, an injury to the person, as well as a crime; but it is not an injury to property. A "child is not property."[275] The services of a wife are not property,[276] for "the domestic services of a wife possess none of the attributes of 'property'" and are "purely personal to the husband."[277] Thus one can no longer have property rights in, or in regard to, another person, even though one has, in regard to them, rights still traditionally called rights *in rem*. One might gather from the tendency to regard the marriage relation itself (the consortium) as property, while the wife's domestic services are treated as not property, that, since the Nineteenth Amendment, the contract to "love and honour" retained its primitive nature while that to "obey" had been modernized.

A claim for alimony, made by a married woman, is not property which she could dispose of, such as would vest in her trustee. A right to alimony creates no interest in the husband's property.[278] This and allowances for maintenance of minor children are allowances by the court and not even quasi-contractual credit-debts. While it may receive protection as a tentative right, "a bare possibility or mere expectation of acquiring property does not constitute property or a title to property; nor can it be transferred or levied upon."[279] Possession and use of any object are not property when they are in any respect illegal. For instance, a slot machine "only capable of use in violating the laws of this state" [the anti-gambling laws] is not "property."[280] Constitutional provisions against the impairment of the obligation of a contract are part rights of property. But this does not apply to restoring such obligation. "We are unable to see how a man can be said to have property in the bar of the statute of limitations as a defense to his promise to pay."[281] In general, advantages of a non-economic nature are denied the protections accorded to property, unless they are purely incidental to an economic purpose. Thus "the moral, intellectual, and social privileges, [of members of a fraternal order] are mere incidents of membership . . . and constitute no . . . property right."[282]

When they deal with income the courts are often in difficulties. Obviously this is because their concept of income is by no means precise. Before the income is received it is held not property. The word "property" does not mean earning capacity.[283] "Anticipated profits are not, and can not, be held and regarded as property in the ownership or possession of him who owns the article out of which profits are expected to flow. The property is one thing, and remains untouched—the profits are not 'in esse,' and can not be claimed as property."[284] After receipt of the income the question becomes puzzling. One decision argues it thus: "Money or any other thing of value, acquired as gain or profit from capital or labor, is 'property'; in the aggregate these acquisitions constitute income

. . . income includes 'property' and nothing but 'property,' and therefore is itself property." [285] We are left wondering when such acquisitions begin to be and cease to be income. By way of justifying taxes on income it is frequently held that "income is property," so that a legislature had authority to enact an income tax law. [286] In view of the enabling amendment this theory seems quite unnecessary. The fact that the beneficiary of a trust fund may have rights in the income thereof also causes trouble. The right to receive the income from a trust estate is property, within a statute providing for the appointment of a conservator over a person having property, who is incapable of managing his affairs. [287] In such cases the receipt of income is the enjoyment or benefit of the property interest, not itself that interest. For, if there ceased to be any income it would not be held that the beneficiary had sustained a deprivation of property.

E. *The Classifications of Property*

Considerable further light on the question of the nature and forms of modern property is gained by examining the classifications by which it is commonly analysed – and particularly that class of the unclassified, choses in action.

Following the example of the Roman Institutes we find it desirable before proceeding to the main system of classification to examine briefly certain preliminary divisions. While the terminology, and perhaps the distinctions, are not exact there is nevertheless a fairly definite concept of common resources, a body of objects not appropriated and only subject to limited and regulated appropriation. These are sometimes spoken of as if they were subject to the property of the state and sometimes as if held by the state as a sort of trustee for its citizens, but only in respect of the regulation of appropriation or enjoyment. The idea is a confused one. It is compounded of the antique *res communes*, and perhaps *res publicae* and *res nullius*, as well as English "qualified" property; of the theory and fact of the original grants to, and purchases by, the colonies and the federal government from various sources, of the national domain; and of a confusion of the idea of the *state*, taken from political theory, with the federated states, of which the resemblance is largely confined to the name. This is an interesting subject, for it lies at the foundations of various theories and practices of property. However, space does not permit its complete examination here. We may cite a few selected decisions indicating the general view. "The wild game in the State belongs to the people of the State in their collective and sovereign capacity, and not in their individual and private capacity, except so far as private ownership may be acquired therein under the Constitution [authorizing inhabitants] . . . in seasonable times to hunt and fowl on the lands they hold, and other lands not inclosed, under proper regulations to be thereafter made by the General Assembly." [288] "Water, when reduced to possession, is property, and may be bought and sold and have a market value, but it must be in actual possession, subject to control and management. Running water in natural streams is not property, and never was." [289] "That the natural gas found within the territorial limits of the state is the common heritage of the people of the state, which may be conserved and preserved by the state as trustee of those things in which the people have a common interest, as flowing streams, wild animal life, etc., is unsound and must be denied." [290] These well describe the present concept of common resources. As to natural gas, the first tendency was to place it with minerals as a part of the soil of individual holdings of land (as illustrated by the decision quoted). However, the recognition of its special nature, existing as a pool, perhaps under a large number of holdings, is tending to change its status to that of common resources. The fact that the same condition exists with regard to oil suggests that we may eventually secure a sound basis for conservation of that important natural resource.

Objects definitely appropriated by, or otherwise become the property of, the state and dedicated to public use are subject to public property. For some purposes such property is divided into two classes according as to whether the objects are used for governmental purposes or for other public service. Thus "property used [by a city] for carrying on its municipal government" is exempt, but whatever is used "in its social or commercial capacity as a private corporation . . . is subject to taxation." [291] This puts municipal ventures in the field of private enterprise, for hire, into a different category from the conventional functions of police and protection. The former are treated as private property; "private property of municipal corporations—i.e., that which is not necessary to performance of the functions of Government." [292] But sometimes it is held that all the property of municipal corporations is private as against the state. [293] This rule gives rise to some difficulties. For instance in the State of Louisiana, the special immunity not only applies to all public property used for governmental purposes, owned or held in trust by the sister states of the Union, [294] but "property dedicated to a public use, the revenues of which serve a public purpose, is public property, although the title be not in the public. The property of a quasi public corporation is public property." [295] In general, however, it is the auspices, rather than the purpose to which it is dedicated, which determines the public or private character of property. The property of a private eleemosynary corporation is private property, [296] "private property [meaning] property belonging to a private individual . . . as distinguished from the property of the State or of a municipality, which is public property. Property held for pious or charitable uses . . . for a limited portion of the public, is private property." [297]

The law has unfortunately adopted from accounting the terms "tangible" and "intangible," and is in process of rapidly spoiling them by using them to cover much the same ground as its own terms "corporeal" and "incorporeal." In accounting, intangibles are property nuclei around which are centred capitalizations of surplus earning power. The dichotomy is a useful distinction to differentiate interests in material objects, direct and indirect, from interests in processes. For the intangibles are none other than the protected processes heretofore discussed. But in law the term "intangible" is now being used to describe non-possessory interests in objects, or even possessory interests if the object is located outside the jurisdiction. Thus real estate within the state is held to be tangible property. [298] A lease of land is not "intangible personal property." [299] But a vendor's right in an executory installment contract for the sale of realty providing for possession in purchaser, title to be transferred on full payment, "is intangible and not tangible property." [300] In these citations the terms are being used to cover the identical ground covered by the old legal terms "corporeal" and "incorporeal." Sometimes the distinction is still vaguer because it is applied to a mixture of the old and the new. "Intangible property includes franchises, credits, choses in action, and the like." [301] Or, worse still, "intangible property [is] incorporeal property, including money, deposits in banks, shares of stock, bonds, notes, credits, evidences of an interest in property and evidences of debt." [302]

1. *Real Property*

The principal classification by which private property is commonly divided represents a wholly antiquated and unsatisfactory analysis of the subject. The classes are in fact no more than remnants of distinctions which may have been valid in other days but are almost without significance today. Our task will be to determine, from the mass of conflicting statements, to what extent these ancient categories are being modified to restore them to usefulness and from this to proceed to an analysis which will serve our purpose.

The general division is that between real and personal property and, as to the latter, between choses in possession and choses in action. The word "property" is "a generic term including all the others." [303] It "includes both real and personal property." [304] Since "every kind of property that is not real is personal," [305] it becomes necessary first to determine what the law intends by the term "real property."

The principal sources of confusion in the law are two. In the first place the term has to do with an antique conception of real property which originally confined it to the subjects of seisin and therefore the interests to which the original real actions were available; later extended it to include all interests which were feudally heritable; and finally extended it to everything which was not "less than freehold." Such a criterion is of almost no importance today. But the rules of law are derived from it. In the second place the term fails to distinguish correctly and thoroughly between the land itself, as the object of rights, and the interests in, or with regard to, land which are the various bundles of rights with respect to it. Actually the law only deals with these interests, not with the land itself. It is these which are exercised, protected and transferred under its auspices. But it continually talks about the land itself, much to its own discomfiture. A definition of what is comprised in the totality of this object, land – that is, what accessory objects are included therein – together with detailed definitions of the complete property therein and of the various types of interest into which it can be subdivided, would successfully clarify this muddle. In attempting to read out of the decisions, or construct out of the facts, something of this kind, let us begin by tentatively assigning to the land itself, as object, the term "realty" and to the interests therein the term "real property." There is some precedent for this terminology, though the usage is by no means exact.

The antique definition is that " 'real estate' means an estate in fee or for life in land, and does not comprehend terms for years or any interest short of a freehold." [306] On this basis "a lease of real estate [realty] for a term of years is personal property." [307] Thus a lessee of a 99 year lease has no *real* property in the land. His estate is not a *real* estate. This fine distinction is prettily put in one decision. "A lease for years, though a chattel real, is personal property, and therefore, though it may be an estate or interest in real property [realty], it is not . . . 'real estate'." [308] The remaining validity of this distinction is based on the following tenuous considerations: "Leases for years have a definite legal character as chattels. Although called estates in land they have none of its characteristics. Originally the only remedy for ouster was an action for damages. They did not formerly, nor do they now, pass to the heir, but to the personal representatives. In the absence of statute they may be transferred without any of the formalities required for the conveyance of realty."

[309] This is the strict interpretation of the statutes, and to this the courts must for some purposes adhere. "A lease for years is a chattel real, and, being less than freehold . . . is considered as personal estate or property . . . and under our statute is not included under the word 'land,' or the phrases 'real estate' or 'real property' . . . but is included in the phrase 'personal property'. . ." [310] But only for these purposes. "A lease for years is a 'chattel real.' It conveys an interest in land. While it has some of the attributes of personalty [personal property], it is treated in many respects as real estate." [311] Having taken that first step some attempt is made to distinguish according to the length of term. "'Real property' . . . includes leasehold property, where the lessee . . . is possessed . . . of at least five years' unexpired term." [312] Other courts may be found including in real estate "all 'chattels real' [which are] such as concern or savor of the realty, as terms of years of land." [313] And an authority declares that real property "comprehends leases." [314] It is even held that a lessee, having an option to purchase the premises, is entitled to compensation for the value of the option, on condemnation of the property as being an "owner" of "real property." [315] While rents not due are part of the estate of the lessor and pass with transfer, "rent past due [is] personal property," [316] and does not so pass. Nor, as such, is it a "rent," in the old sense, but only a debt of the lessee. Having gone so far it is but a step further to include as real property leases of access to common resources. "A leasehold [in tide and submerged lands from the state] . . . is . . . 'real property' . . . " [317] Moreover certain other interests in land are commonly held to be real property. Thus, "in the case of a contract for the purchase and sale of real property . . . the interest of the vendee is real estate [real property]." [318] This is one type of equitable interest, and such an "equitable interest in land to that extent [part of purchase price paid]" is real property. [319] On the other hand another type of equitable interest is not so construed. "An interest as cestui que trust in land can never be called realty in the cestui." [320]

Interests may be created in separable material portions of the realty. Thus "growing trees constituted a part of the realty, and their conveyance . . . was a conveyance of an interest in the land itself." [321] Such "a right . . . to remove and appropriate . . . any part of the soil belonging to another man, or anything growing in or attached to, or subsisting upon his land, for the purpose of the profit to be gained from the property thereby acquired in the thing removed . . . is commonly called a 'profit a prendre'." [322] Such interests may be temporary. Thus leases of mineral rights occupy in the class chattels real the same position that profits a prendre occupy in the incorporeal hereditaments. They are temporary part possessions. But they too come to be regarded as real property. An oil and gas lease for a period of five years conveys real property. [323] And even a conveyance of an interest in an oil and gas lease on land is a conveyance "affecting real estate." [324] They may be inchoate and still be real property. " 'Real estate' or 'real property' [shall be deemed] to include mining claims." [325]

On the other hand interests may be created which consist of a use of land only in its spatial aspect, or a restriction upon such use. Such interests, if perpetual, are styled easements and constitute the other existing variety of the old incorporeal hereditament, now modified by the lore of the Roman servitude. An easement "is a mere use of the land of another without taking anything from it." [326] It is "a permanent privilege," [327] and is "distinct from the ownership of the soil," [328] whatever that may be. It is "appurtenant when it is for the benefit of a grantee's estate, and in that case it passes with the estate to all subsequent grantees and is inheritable." [329] So that if an easement granted "be in its nature an appropriate and useful adjunct of the land conveyed . . . it will be held to be an easement appurtenant," [330] and passes with the dominant tenement. [331] Such an easement is "not attached to the person; it is part of the estate [property] and passes with it." [332] Here is a summary of the "essential qualities. . . First. They are incorporeal. Second. They are imposed on corporeal property, and not on the owner thereof. Third. They confer no right to a participation in the profits . . . and, Fourth. There must be two distinct tenements, the 'dominant' to which the right belongs, and the 'servient' upon which the obligation rests." [333] All these definitions are above reproach. The difficulty arises in that the courts are firmly convinced that they mean by "estate" or "tenement" the land itself, rather than a particular interest, or several interests, in the land. So they construe easements as running to the land which is the object of the dominant estate. Land thus becomes the owner of property in Anglo-American as it was in Roman law. Easements take various forms. "A right of way over the land of another is designated in the common law as an 'easement'." [334] Other kinds are easements of light and air. It has also become the custom, as we have already noted, to include in this class such parts right of all complete real property as right of access to streets and other advantages available by means of public property, as well as rights of access to contiguous common resources. Within the last may be included the general right of access to light and air and such special rights as riparian right, water rights, etc. "A water right is 'real property' appurtenant to, and passes with a conveyance of, the land." [335] But strictly an easement should be confined to those certain permanent rights to the spatial use of any piece of land, which are subtracted from the complete property in that land and are added by grant or prescription to the complete property in certain other land.[16]

As to the definition of the totality of the land itself, as object, it is generally agreed that "a crop . . . not detached from the soil . . . is a part of the realty;" [336] "minerals in place are 'realty';" [337] "oil and gas in place are a part of the 'realty'." [338] Extravagant statements are frequently made as to the spatial dimensions above and below the surface. Defining this totality which we have called realty, one court states that it is "the land itself, and all buildings, structures, and improvements or other fixtures of whatsoever kind thereon, and all rights and privileges thereto belonging or in any wise appertaining, [i.e. appurtenant easements, etc.] and all mines, minerals, quarries and trees on or under the same." [339] Unfortunately the court finds it necessary to mix in some rights with these objects, assuming in the classic fashion that easements are appurtenant to the land and not to certain estates in the land.

There is considerable dispute in current legal theory as to the nature of land. One view is that it is spatial; the other that it is material. The truth should be obvious that it is both. And it is highly desirable to recognize the existence of these two aspects and to keep them separate. In respect of its spatial aspect it is immovable. In respect of its material aspect it is not wholly irremovable. But the law attaches all presently removable portions to the realty and also arbitrarily classifies therewith many "improvements." Thus the whole mass is frequently treated as immovable, though it is so only in certain legal respects. Because the objects of the property are thus to some extent immovable the rights thereto have been conceived, both in English and in civilian law, as if permanently anchored and thus themselves immovable. Such a jumbled concept of the object, half of a material and half of an immaterial or spatial nature, half immovable and half more or less removable, seems to reflect its characteristics upon the rights thereto, and leads to Blackstone's viewpoint, from which such definitions as the following still result: Real property "consists of such things as are permanent, fixed, and immovable, as lands, tenements and hereditaments of all kinds which are not annexed to the person, or cannot be moved from the place in which they subsist." [340] The law of real property will be upon a firmer foundation when the process of clarification, which the fore-

[16] Even then it is hard to distinguish rights covered by appurtenant easements from those implicit as part rights of any present possessory estate in land, and imposed by law by way of restriction upon the complete property in contiguous land.

going citations demonstrate to be already under way, has succeeded in adjusting itself to a definition such as we now proceed to set up for our own purposes.

Land consists of any definite site, regarded as a portion of the earth's surface and extending in both vertical directions as defined by law; together with such natural resources as are conceded to it by law, while they remain *in situ*, on, under, or above the surface, and together with such "improvements" as are defined by law to be irremovable by the holder of any subordinate interest without the consent of the holder of the interest from which his is ultimately derived. The totality of rights in such aggregates of objects are defined by law and usually include rights of access to common resources contiguous to such land, as well as to adjoining land held as public property. This totality may also include, by grant or prescription, similar appurtenant rights of use or removal with respect to other sites, held under private property. Such complete property may be divided into any variety of fraction. Fractions, usually of standard types, are recognized as property *in* land if they include rights protected as to the relation with the land itself and not to be fundamentally changed by changes in the other interests. All other interests with reference to specific sites are property *with regard to land*. The two classes combined, which include all property having land as its object, may be covered by the term for the wider classification. With this definition we can well substitute the term "land" for the equivocal term "realty," and the term "property with regard to land" for the partial terms "real property" or "real estate."

2. *Personal Property and the Chose in Action*

Personal property, as we have seen, is defined as all property that is not real property. If, then, real property is confined to freehold interests in land, personal property consists of a conglomerate and nondescript medley. If, on the other hand, we seek some term for all property in objects other than land, as we have defined it, we find no such term available in law. The term "chattel" with its curious history would seem to be suitable. But in fact it has been used as if it were identical with the term "personal property." So we have chattels real, chattels personal and, under the latter, chattels corporeal, corresponding to choses in possession, and chattels incorporeal, corresponding to choses in action. "There is no term broader than 'chattel.'" It includes "all kinds of property, except the freehold and things which are parcel of it" (i.e. real property in its strict sense). [341] It is true that in colloquial legal phraseology the term "chattel" is coming, by a process of elimination, to refer only to the particular class of chattels corporeal. As real property is stretched to include chattels real, and as choses in action take in everything not in possession, the term "chattel" is narrowed down to cover only direct property in objects other than land. However, the term is still too loose for our purpose. Moreover, though it is usually a term for property it is also used loosely to cover the objects of property. If we seek to approach the distinction from the angle of the object we find at hand the term "movables" as contrasted with "immovables," which is borrowed from the civilian *mobilia*, vs. *immobilia*. But as we have seen, the characteristic of immobility exists only in law, is subject to many qualifications and has, therefore, a misleading connotation. Also these words as well have come to stand both for the property and its object. Finally they have never come into general use in Anglo-American law. Perhaps the best term to stand in an antithesis to "land," is the term "goods." And this in spite of its different significance in economics. Here at least we have legal usage with us. Then the classification opposed to property with regard to land will be property with regard to goods.

There remains the general class called choses in action, or incorporeal chattels. We discussed the legal theories with reference to this class in the last chapter, but have hitherto postponed the examination of the legal practice in this one. First, as to the nature of the *chose* or *thing*. We have seen that, when the term "chose in action" was introduced into English law, the words *thing* and *chose* had already acquired in legal usage the meaning of material objects. But to the laity, and therefore to some extent also in the law, they continued as well to designate the bundles of rights in these objects. In the case of a debt, for instance, "chose" in its first meaning referred to the money (i.e. coin) owed. In its second it referred to the debt, or its evidence. Thus it was both the material object out of possession, of which possession was to be sought, and it was the present rights of property which would be cancelled and disappear when settlement was effected. It stood both for the object and the property. This dual usage, together with the conceptual confusion to which it gives rise, continues and leads to strange results. The original legal view is represented by Blackstone's definition already quoted. The *double entendre* is well shown in an argument to a court in which the chose (in action) was said to be "a thing not in occupation or enjoyment, but merely a bare right to be recovered by an action." [342] Here it is conceived to be both object and right. In another case a judge plays the same trick. He says it is "a personal right not reduced into possession, but recoverable by a suit at law." [343] If one modified this statement to read, "It is a property right, not itself possessory but through which a possessory right is recoverable by a suit at law," one would have successfully eliminated the entanglement with the idea of the object. But usually we are left wondering which is the "chose," the obligation of the contract, or the object. This dilemma is successfully escaped in the purely procedural definitions. One of the standard definitions is that the class of choses in action "includes the infinite variety of contracts, covenants, and promises, which confer on one party a right to recover a personal chattel or a sum of money from another by action." [344] Or, more broadly, "If the relief sought is the recovery of money or other personal property, the cause of action is designated 'a thing in action.'" [345]

Another point which causes trouble, on account of the old materialistic notion conveyed in the term "recovery," is the explanation of what a chose in action is before it is a right to sue immediately for possession. In this *dinglich* view the chose in action "is property distinguished from a thing of which the owner has actual or constructive possession but for which an action may be brought to reduce it to possession. . . A present right of action is not necessary. . . There must be a fixed present right" (that is, not a future right, as an unearned commission). [346] *"A present right of action is not necessary," but "there must be a fixed present right."* In general it is said that it does not require a present right of action. [347] But on the other hand only a "vested right of action is property." [348] What is meant, of course, is that the right must be vested, not merely expectant, or conditional or contingent. But it need not be ripe. In other words it is already a chose in action while it is a right to a potential action and before it is due to be converted into an interest of some other kind. All of which circumlocution is of course only caused by the refusal to recognize the true nature of the property in the meantime. For it is in fact this very attribute of being suspended, so far as it is a present right to a future conveyance (the repurchase agreement), which makes the chose in action property and has resulted in according to it protection in the interim as an interest in the aggregate of 'things' of the debtor. The debtor must maintain his ability to discharge the liability at maturity, else he is insolvent. His rights in his own body of property are to this extent limited or temporary. There is an analogy to the case of land where the future interest must be protected against certain forms of waste by the occupier.

It will be noted that in the foregoing the object to be recovered has always been referred to as personal property. This statement is common. It is again due to the confusion of the right with the object. The right is personal property. The object need not be goods or even personalty. Choses in action are "not confined to claims to personalty." [349] They include actions for recovery of realty, such as "a suit to enforce specific performance of a contract (even if such contract relate to real estate)," [350] and "suit [by assignee] . . . for specific performance of covenants of the lease" of realty. [351] However, we have already seen that "rent . . . which was to accrue, does not fall within any of the definitions of a part of the realty, and passed as such, with the estate." [352]

There are practically no characteristics common to all the forms of property which it has been the habit of the past to lump together as choses in action. The term has served as a residuum of the unclassified, not as a true class. Therefore what is needed for our purposes is to examine the various forms so included and to endeavour to arrange some general system of classification with regard to them. While the rights in quasi-material objects, such as patents, copyright, etc., which we have already discussed, have been included in choses in action, this tendency is passing. They are now treated as a special class of property by themselves. Even such border line protected processes as memberships in marketing organizations are coming to be included in this new grouping, though the old idea still persists to some extent. It is still said, for example, that a membership in the New York Stock Exchange is property in the nature of a chose in action. [353] This group of objects of property will be discussed more fully in the next chapter as a class by themselves.

Shares of stock in corporations are in process of reaching this same condition of independence. We see the gradual change of view in the following excerpts. "Shares of stock in a corporation are generally held to be choses in action." [354] "A share of stock is an intangible thing, technically known as a chose in action." [355] As such, the content of the property is "the interest or right which the owner . . . has in the management of the corporation, in its surplus profits, and, on a dissolution, in all of its assets remaining after the payment of debts." [355] In general, "such property [shares of stock] is personalty, and not realty." [356] As such, however, "shares of stock are not chattels, but are in the nature of choses in action;" [357] or "shares of stock, as such, are not chattels; they bear a closer resemblance to choses in action." [358] Here we see a less positive statement of their nature. But within the class of personal property they are distinguished from certain other forms. "Shares of stock were considered [at common law] . . . neither a specific chattel nor a debt. . . 'They have more resemblance to choses in action, being merely evidence of property.'" [359] "Shares of stock in a corporation are not regarded as money or securities, but constitute title to the stock, and confer proportionate rights in the entity and in the corporate income." [360] But more and more they come to be recognized as a special class of personal property, *sui generis*. "Corporate stock is 'personal property' and not a mere 'chose in action.'" [361] Assuming the authority of the most modern views we shall hereafter consider that the class of choses in action does not include either franchises, etc. or corporate stock.

It is said that the class of choses in action also includes "a bill of lading." [362] That statement is not accurate. As a matter of fact the bill of lading fits very neatly into three separate categories. It is a receipt for the bailment of a specific object, and as such is a negotiable instrument which is said to be the symbol or representative, or to stand for, the object consigned. It is a contract for the service of carriage; also negotiable. Thereby it becomes in that aspect a chose in action. And the document itself, being the evidence of a contract, is treated as personal property in possession.

The segregation of the foregoing groups, however, only eliminates part of the heterogeneity of our class. Let us begin again at the simplest form. In general, contracts giving rise to what we have called true credit-debt are choses in action. The prototype idea is that "a contract for the delivery of goods and chattels is a chose in action." [363] But with the substitution of money damages, without distinction as to whether the latter are *poena* or *res persecutoria*, the idea of the "chose" comes to be stretched to include almost any claim for money under a contract, express or implied. [364] Thus the connection with the object is severed and the "chose" itself comes to represent any "demand for damages for breach of contract." [365] Nevertheless it continues to cover as well specific deliveries and even services. Having achieved this metamorphosis it is not a far cry to certain torts.[17] On this basis it is held that the term chose in action includes "all debts, and all claims for damages for breach of contract, or for torts connected with the contract." [366] In order to discriminate, the criterion of survival is introduced. It is said that the term "choses in action" "refers to a particular species of property, recognized by the law, and which, upon the death of the owner, would be inventoried as such by his legal representatives." [367] This rule limits the variety of actions for tort which are admitted. The class "only includes rights of action founded on contracts, or for injuries to property, and not rights of action for torts, which are

[17] The way the tort slips in to the subject of contract is shown in these citations. "A tort is one's disturbance of another in rights which the law has created either in the absence of contract, or in consequence of a relation which a contract had established between the parties." [373] As to the latter, "in certain relations duties are imposed, the breach of which is regarded as a tort, though the relations themselves are formed by contract, and the contract may cover the same ground," [374] and "the party injured by the non-fulfillment of the duty [imposed by law] may proceed against the other for its breach, or for the breach of the contract, at his election." [375] Nevertheless even here a tort "denotes an injury inflicted otherwise than by a mere breach of contract." [376]

purely personal, such as the action for slander, which dies with the person." [368] But, because of the introduction of the tort to property and because of the substitution of damages in place of the claim to the object sought, the way is wide open to permit the concept of chose in action to be stretched to include "a demand arising . . . on wrong or injury to the . . . person," [369] or even to related persons. Thus the "right to sue for damages for a tort [injuring wife] is a chose in action and property." [370] So, in general, "the term 'choses in action' includes rights of action for tort." [371] Finally the definition comes to be extended so that "a chose in action is a right to damages arising either from the commission of a tort, the omission of a duty, or the breach of a contract." [372] In this last, which presents a view very generally held, we see the final stage in the progression of the idea of a chose in action from its simple and specific origin as an object voluntarily out of possession to any claim for damages on whatever grounds. By this time the term, while it has been improved by conversion from the concrete to the abstract sense, has nevertheless been enlarged to include so many discrete bundles of rights that it has lost all value for analytical purposes.

It is sometimes customary to introduce another term, the "right of action," as if it had a more specific meaning than "chose in action" and might serve as a basis for dividing remedial from antecedent rights—rights which may become property from those which are already property rights. But, lest we think that the distinction between these two is held to determine the boundaries of property for which we have been searching, it is well to note that "a right of action is property." [377] In fact "a right of action is as much property as is a corporeal possession." [378] Some refine this generalization. Thus only "a vested right of action is 'property'." [379] Or again: "There is no doubt that a right in action, where it comes into existence under common-law principles, and is not given by statute as a mere penalty or without equitable basis, is as much property as any tangible possession." [380] However, the fact of property may hinge on the criterion of alienability. Specifically it is held that a claim in action of tort for personal injuries is not property. "It is not assignable, and it cannot be appropriated by creditors in proceedings in bankruptcy or insolvency." [381] Seeming to admit this last rule as to rights of action in tort, other decisions determine the question according to the stage at which the proceedings have arrived. Where statutes make a distinction between a plaintiff's interest in a pending action and his cause of action before suit brought, making the one assignable in cases where the other is not, the interest of a bankrupt in a pending action, which he might sell and assign, and of which his creditors might obtain the benefit on administration of his estate, is to be held property within the purview of the bankruptcy act rather than a right of action. [382] And property does not include "a right of action in tort," but does include "a judgment in tort." [383] Here again, as in the case of the term "chose in action" there seems to exist no fundamental agreement either as to the usage of terms or as to the rules of law.

Let us look closer. Is it possible that, without refining their points and expressing them in sufficiently explicit and accurate statements, the courts are endeavouring to establish a classification of choses and rights of action along some such lines as the following? Commencing again at the beginning we may define the original chose in action, strictly limited to true credit-debt, to be non-possessory property in indeterminate material objects or in other 'things,' created by contract or by a legally imposed obligation. The benefits conferred by this property may be rendered voluntarily but they are otherwise assured at law almost wholly by resort to action, positively, and hardly at all by protection, negatively, because enjoyment is *via* the body of property of another rather than direct. Nevertheless the right is antecedent to any breach and the property in the aggregate of 'things' of the debtor is antecedent to the action to support it. Whatever one wishes to call it, this is the original chose in action and is the modern 'thing' which contains what we call property in contract (to which must be added property in obligations legally imposed). As opposed to this we find a wholly different category, which through loose thinking and looser wording has become merged with the first. When a breach of contract rights occurs, or when a tort is committed either to these or to any other property or personal rights, the breach or the tort constitutes a cause of action. It is the wrong and not the antecedent right which is the cause of action. And it is this cause which brings into being, or precipitates from its potential condition, the ensuing right of action. Since, then, the right of action springs always from a wrong which is the cause, when this wrong is a tort to person or property it is closely assimilated to the wrong which is a breach of contract. In fact it is not always easy to distinguish between them. Such a right of action is wholly remedial. It is not a continuation of the antecedent right which was disturbed.

It is evident that the courts wish to establish the rule that such a right of action, given a cause which brings it into being, and to whatever degree the claim is a mere possibility of being validated as property, is entitled during the process of adjudication to certain protections as such. But only in special cases is it subject to the other general privileges and liabilities of property. So, for instance, when certain rights of action acquire the attribute of survival, another characteristic of property is added. Once suit is brought, though the property rights involved are still not established, a certain vested interest in the action – as a claim – is developed which in various cases becomes, by law or by statute, alienable. Such an interest then possesses even more the attributes of property. But during this process, whatever attributes accrue, the right of action is never more than potential property. That part of it which consists of the right to sue may have become vested, but the right to damages, which is the element of potential property perhaps corresponding to and measuring the antecedent right, is still uncertain, conditional or contingent. Eventually the right of action may be adjudicated and be assimilated to the original type of chose in action. For, if and when it becomes a judgment – a legally imposed obligation ready for execution – it is in reality, except for the elimination of subsequent procedure, in the same status as that particular form of antecedent non-possessory property in contract which is called credit-debt. Thereupon it has become full-fledged property. But at no time is the remedial right of action to be identified with the antecedent property, from a wrong to which it sprang. The judgment itself, while it displaces them, has no true identity with the original rights disturbed, either in the case of tort or breach of contract. It is an award of damages as a recognition of the deprivation of, or injury to, pre-existing property or other rights. But it is a substitution for, and not a restoration of, that property or those rights. Whether the term "chose in action" can be reserved strictly for antecedent property in contract and that of "right of action" restricted to the remedial right only is questionable. But the terminology is not important. Call these two classes of things what you will. The essential is exact discrimination between them.

While this analysis may satisfactorily dispose of the question of the character of property in a right of action, confining this term to the remedial right which springs into existence upon commission of a tort or breach of contract, it does not fully cover the antecedent right existing in contract. Such property, whether or not we apply thereto the term chose in action in its strict sense, is property in contract. It remains to determine to what extent true property exists in contract. We must inquire further.

3. *Credit-debt*

In general the further difficulty arises that the law, even in its classification of the antecedent rights represented by choses in action, does not distinguish, according to the stage of development which we described in the last chapter, between those interests which, as present claims and duties, are already parts of the present property structure and those which are merely powers and liabilities to future changes in that structure. It is led into this error by viewing all of them, according to the antique version, as belonging in the latter class and consisting of rights to the redistribution of possessory interests in objects. Such a fallacious analysis is the result of blinking the present proprietary rights with which the law itself clothes the first class (which we will examine in some detail in Appendix III) and of treating all together as if they existed only as rights to future payments.

The law should discriminate between present interests and future interests in contracts just as it has done between present and future estates in land. This refers to the distinction between present and future interests, not to that between interests due to be extinguished by purchase now and those to be extinguished later. The present antecedent interest of either party to a contract is measured by the disequilibrium resulting from a deficiency in the consideration or performance rendered to him in exchange for his consideration or performance. This interest is an interest to that extent in the body of property of the debtor. Such present interest is of course always a present right to a conveyance, or repurchase, at due date, regardless of whether that due date is now or later. The future interest of either party, on the other hand, is the *equivalent* of what remains due *by him* in performance. By rendering what remains due by him he may convert this future interest into a present interest. In the case of present interests the debtor has obtained additional assets, not paid for, by reason of the contract, and the right of the creditor constitutes a present modification of the property structure. In the case of future interests the right of each party is to a future modification when he establishes his right by further performance, thus exercising his power to create a liability to himself. Upon this basis it makes no difference whether the render by either party is of other present interests in contract, or of extant material objects, or of services. And in the case of future interests the objects may not as yet be in existence or the services not as yet performed.

In its practice, however, as opposed to its theory, the law does make such a distinction. If between two bodies of property there runs a bilateral but wholly executory and unperformed contract, which is, in legal terms, "in the same right," each has some sort of reciprocal power over and liability to the body of property of the other. The contract is in some respects future property to each. But the assumption implicit in dealing with such a contract is that it represents an equal exchange. Therefore it is usually treated as a complete set-off, and neither party sets up the contract either as a liability or as an asset, until performance begins on one side or the other. Occasionally, after making the contract and prior to any performance, the value of either side of the exchange may be altered by unforeseen circumstances, and thus alter the liability of one and the asset of the other in terms of value. In such cases it is becoming accepted practice to set up such contract – or, at least, the gain or loss involved – as asset and liability. In fact, more and more, credit information is demanded as to "commitments," so-called. This is clear recognition that in enforcible exchanges some sort of future property is created at the moment the commitment is legally made.

In general this confirms our original analysis of credit-debt as based upon the notion of equivalents. We may say that the law regards the mutual powers and liabilities of the parties to a contract, each in the body of property of the other, as set-offs to the extent that the failure to perform on each side is equal to that of the other. If it can be shown that failure by either party to perform this remainder will occasion a loss to the other greater than the cost of performance of his own part, then damages or even specific performance may be awarded. In other words this situation is closely related to the above-mentioned treatment of a change of value of either part prior to performance. The one is the accounting aspect; the other the legal aspect. With these exceptions, set-offs "in the same right" are not regarded or treated as present property either in law or accounting, if they arise from the same transaction.

As against these types of future property we find in practical affairs a sharply differentiated present property. Some effort to define as a definite class such antecedent present interests in contract may be found in the law under the terms "credit" or "debt." But, again, confusion is introduced by failure to distinguish between the antecedent property in contract, which takes the form of credit-debt, and the remedial rights of action which cannot take this form until they are finally adjudicated and become judgment debts. Strictly the term "debt" is applied to any such present interests only when the value of them is ascertained, or "liquidated," in terms of money. In general "credit is the correlative of debt." [384] The favourite definition is that "a debt is a sum of money due by certain and express agreement. It originates in, and is founded upon contract express or implied." [385] This is taken from Blackstone, as adapted by Bouvier. It is completed therein by the qualification, "where the amount is fixed and specific, and does not depend on any future valuation to settle it." This covers cases where "the precise sum due may be ascertained by simple mathematical calculations from known facts . . . [but does not comprehend unascertained damages for] the breach of an executory contract." [386] Nor does it include liability for torts, [387] because a claim for damages "founded on a tort or breach of covenant" is not a "liquidated claim," [388] and "damages are no debt till they are liquidated." [389] Thus "every debt . . . is an obligation, but every obligation is not a debt. 'Obligation' is the broader term; 'debt,' the narrower." [390] This distinction is accurately adhered to. For instance, if finding of jury in action of tort that an executory contract was broken by defendant, was conclusive as to plaintiff's right to damages, "no debt was created thereby, nor could be until the wholly unliquidated damages arising from the breach of the contract were determined and the precise amount ascertained by the verdict of a jury and the entry of judgment thereon." [391] Thereupon it becomes a debt regardless of its origin. "A judgment on a claim for negligent injury constitutes a 'debt,'" [392] and a judgment in favour of a widow for damages for the killing of her husband is held a debt. [393]

Even if a liability is fixed in amount but only due upon contingency or condition, it is not a debt until the contingency occurs or the condition is fulfilled. For example it has been held that the obligation of stockholders to pay the amount remaining unpaid on par value of capital stock, since it is contingent until formal call, is not such debt to the corporation that extinguishment of contingency by transfer to capital account from profit and loss account would amount to income to stockholders within Income Tax Act. [394] Nor is it usual to hold that a strictly unilateral agreement such as a gift or an option can create a debt. An option to purchase "created no enforceable indebtedness . . . and therefore the amount still due and unpaid [after first payment] is not a 'credit.'" [395]

This antecedent credit-debt relation, however, even when most strictly defined, includes the four major classes of commercial instruments; notes, etc.; bonds, etc.; accounts receivable; and bank deposits.[18] But, though the antecedent right may be a true debt, the remedial right, even if it spring from a debt, is always damages and

[18] An account stated in effect converts an account receivable into a promissory note. "An 'account stated' is an agreement, express or implied, between parties who have had previous transactions with each other, fixing and determining the amounts due in respect to such transactions, and, when made, such account stated becomes a new agreement and takes the place of the obligations resting upon either party by reason of the prior account." [403] "And where a plaintiff is able to show that the mutual dealings which have occurred between the parties have been adjusted, settled, and a balance struck, the law implies a promise to pay that balance," [404] "so that the demand is essentially the same as if a promissory note had been given for the balance." [405]

An "account current" is the antithesis of an "account stated," and is an account not stated, but running, open, and unsettled, and in which no balance has been agreed upon or struck. [406]

"A bond is . . . an obligation to pay a fixed sum, with stated interest," [407] and "a promise under the seal of the corporation" issuing it. [408]

cannot become a debt until it is converted into that legally imposed obligation, a judgment debt for damages. On the basis of the old English actions the distinction between the antecedent and remedial may be made, and it is sometimes still held that "debt does not mean damages, and an action to recover 'damages' is not an action to recover a 'debt.'" [396] But under the later and more general form, even "an action in assumpsit . . . for money had and received . . . is [an action] for damages." [397] So that the term "damages" is used in general of all money awards. In the case of the right of action arising from a breach of an antecedent debt "the detriment caused by the breach of an obligation to pay money only is deemed to be the amount due by the terms of the obligation, with interest thereon." [398] So that we may say the damages to be expected from a breach are the measure, and determine the legal character, of the antecedent property, though this antecedent property exists prior to the award of damages or even the breach. In other cases "damages for breaches of contract are only those which are incidental to, and directly caused by, the breach." [399] In general the theory "involves the idea of a loss that must be made good, and that the party injured shall be put in as good condition as he would have been if the injury had not been inflicted." [400] Thus damages are "a compensation given by the jury for an injury or a wrong done the party before action brought." [401] The Supreme Court has gone still further. "Damages are designed not only as a satisfaction to the injured person, but likewise as a punishment to the guilty, to deter from any such proceeding for the future, and as a proof of the detestation of the jury to the action itself." [402] Thus today, without using the exact terms, we see the idea of the *damnum* stretching from the exact *tanta res*, in the case of a debt, to *poena*, in the case of a tort.

Nevertheless, it is clear that not even in the case of debt is the final render, in theory at least, the enforcement of the antecedent and present interest in property in contract. It is damages for injury to that property right—"the breach of a duty arising out of contract." "An 'action in contract' is for the breach of a duty arising out of a contract, either express or implied, while an 'action for tort' is for a breach of duty imposed by law." [409] Nor are such antecedent and present interests always debts. They are only so regarded if the balance due can be readily determined, without appraisal, in terms of money. However the term "credit-debt" covers the larger part of such present interests.

By way of summary of this analysis of the present law, at this stage of our argument while we have still in mind the viewpoint of actual decisions, let us say that, of the antecedent property in contract—the chose in action strictly so-called—the disequilibrium resulting from exchange, where there remains a surplus of value in the consideration or performance on one side over that of the other, measures present property. Such property is credit-debt if this measure is legally of an ascertained or readily ascertainable value, or practically, if the value is agreed upon between the parties. Otherwise it is an unliquidated but present liability, and potential or inchoate property.

The rights of either party in those matched portions of a contract which exceed the consideration or performance on the side most nearly completed may be called future property. In practice they are only treated as property when the value of one of these matched and unrendered balances comes to exceed the other. In the meantime they remain respectively powers and liabilities.

Whether the interest in the debtor's body of property is present or only future (i.e. in the shape of a power to create a liability) and whether it is of determined or undetermined value, it is nevertheless treated by law as in some degree property. Both are protected from interference by others, and the restrictions upon disposition of his assets by the debtor favour both equally.

When we come to remedial rights—the right of action—the theory of jurisprudence envisages a substitution of a new right for all such antecedent property in contract, just as it does when the cause is an injury to other property, personal or familial rights. And the ideas and practices of the courts haltingly follow the same principle. The new right—the right of action—is of similar nature in the case of breach of contract or of tort. But it is dealt with somewhat differently according to the nature of the antecedent right infringed.

All rights of action, from the moment they come into being, are potential interests of determined or undetermined value in the debtor's body of property. As such they receive full protection as property and are coming to be, in almost all cases, alienable. But the interest is defeasible. It is terminated on condition subsequent (i.e. failure to secure judgment). Until then it is legally in some respects in the same position as an antecedent credit-debt not due, though in business practice the distinction is very definite between recognized debts and unadmitted claims or other contingent liabilities.

The nature of this property represented by the right of action is in practice conceived partly as if it savoured of the antecedent property replaced and partly as if it were determined by the award. The award goes by the name of damages, or, in a few cases, of specific performance. (1) If the antecedent right was a credit-debt and the cause of action a breach of contract, then the property represented by the right of action is a defeasible interest of an ascertained value in the body of property of the debtor. (2) If the antecedent right was other property in contract and there was an unliquidated surplus of performance or consideration upon one side, and the cause of action a breach of contract, then it is a defeasible interest of an unascertained value. (3) If the antecedent right was future property—that is, if it represented the future and reciprocal interests of both parties in the equally unperformed balance of the contract—it cannot give rise to a valid cause of action for breach of contract. This type of interest is recognized only when, broadly speaking, failure to perform this further equal exchange will involve a loss to either party. In this event the future property has already by that fact been converted into present property either of ascertained or unascertained value and thus falls under (1) or (2). (4) If the antecedent right was any property or personal right and the cause of action a tort, then the right of action represents a defeasible interest of an unascertained value. Damages are the general measure of the interest arising in all cases. In some cases of the last three types specific recovery (now called performance, in the case of contracts) is substituted. In other words the interest may be projected beyond the general body of property of the debtor to a specific 'thing' or object. Finally all such interests in the shape of rights of action may come to be converted into judgment debts, or decrees of specific performance. Thus, in the end, nearly all become assimilated to the antecedent interest defined as a credit-debt.

Antecedent recognized debts or remedial judgment debts may constitute the semi-final settlement of the balance upon an exchange of other property or services, which when the final settlement is made will represent a supposedly equal exchange. This is true debt for economic purposes. On the other hand the type of antecedent debt which arises out of future property in contract, and the judgment debt, in many cases, is not of this nature. It is not the result at the semi-final stage of an exchange which will be finally equal. Rather it is unilateral and a reapportionment of property interests. We have called these debts "quasi-debts." This term comprises those which grow out of contract or tort where the creditor has suffered or will suffer an injury or loss of some other kind than that due to the failure of consideration and performance by both parties to equal each other in money value. In the case of all quasi-debt, by the nature of the definition, the parties, in the final solution of the matter, cannot jointly be as well off in respect of this transaction as they were before. There has been a detriment to one or the other. The debt is either this detriment itself or its offset. A quasi-debt is, then, a reapportionment of property made for other purposes than to bring reciprocal renders in exchange into equivalence.

Only debt and quasi-debt constitute full-fledged present property.

All other interests in contract or in rights of action are present but unliquidated interests, or powers to create interests in the future, or potential (defeasible) interests, liquidated or unliquidated. They only become consummate property when they are defined as ascertained and, if necessary, adjudicated interests. Until then they are inchoate, to be treated tentatively as entitled to certain of the qualitative rights of property, but not to the full quantitative rights. Nor are they yet parts of the property structure.

The terms "creditor" and "debtor" are not confined to those who are parties to a credit-debt. In its broad sense the word "creditor" means one who has "any legal liability that may have been incurred upon a contract, express or implied, or in tort." [410] Thus creditors and debtors include all those who are parties to any of the foregoing property relations described in the general groupings of choses in action and of rights of action, if a distinction can be made between them. They cover the parties to the antecedent interests, whether ascertained or not and whether present or future. And they cover the parties to all remedial interests. The law still speaks as if these creditors and debtors were persons. But it acts as if they were bodies of property. It distinguishes in every respect between the various groups of property appertaining to any person, natural or artificial. It deals with each where it is domiciled. It exercises its control over them directly and not necessarily through the person to whom they appertain.

The same is true of the use of the term "liability"—the relation between the debtor and the creditor. The term "liability" is defined in the theory of law as the correlative of the power to alter a legal relation. Where it is used in connection with the law of property it seems to apply to a relation between two persons and to connote the old notion that it is the potential of a change in the property relation. But actually it is the common term for the correlative of all the foregoing interests in bodies of property, from the most inchoate to the most consummate, and it is itself the nether aspect of the property, present, future, or potential, inhering in the body of property of the creditor and incident upon the body of property of the debtor.

The final clarification and completion of this analysis must be reserved until the last chapter.

F. *Summary*

In the course of sampling the actual application of the law in these numerous citations one gets the impression of an unusually shrewd and sagacious group of men penetrating quite unerringly, in most cases, to the inner substance of the subject of property, but impeded in the expression of the reasons for their decisions by an archaic formulary – a very limited assortment of classifications, concepts and definitions which are largely a relic of "pastoral" times and which have already been stretched beyond rhyme or reason. In spite of much confusion in language and some in thought, it seems possible to set out a summary of some of the general points they seem to be trying to express in this poverty-stricken vocabulary.

The term "property" is used in such a way that it has a great variety of different contents and extents. In applying the provisions of the constitutions, the statutes and the law, its sense in each case must therefore be specially construed.

In general the courts seem to define as property at law whatever is treated as property in the economic life of the time. Since persons may no longer be the objects of property, the law confines property to rights with reference to material objects and to a variety of intangible (quasi-material) objects, such as patents and other protected processes, which relate to tangible objects but are distinct from them. All property is conceived to relate ultimately, in some obscure way and directly or indirectly, to these two classes of objects. In fact the idea of property is so difficult to conceive apart from a material object that the word is used more than half the time to signify the object rather than the rights or interests with regard to it.

Property – these interests with regard to objects – is seen as by no means a uniform matter. The assortment of rights composing various types of interest is almost as varied as is the number of subjects or the multiplicity of objects of property. Nevertheless the one word "ownership" is made to suffice for a very large proportion of this nearly infinite variety of different composites. When they have regard to the ultimate material object of property, the courts tend to consider "ownership" – thought of as "dominion" over an object – as a generic term covering a limited number of the possessory interests out of the many forms of property – "valuable rights and interests" – which may pertain to it. But when they have regard, rather, to these various interests themselves, then each interest seems to be held by an "owner" in a sort of "ownership," on the presumption – taken from common thought and common speech – that "ownership" is a relation to a 'thing' (interest) rather than one to an object. Thus they spring from one horn of the dilemma to the other and naturally involve themselves in all sorts of inconsistencies. Frequently too the courts are merely searching for that person who is in control and who is also frequently described under the alias of "owner." Then they may identify as "owner" any lessee, occupier, entryman, agent, trustee, consignee, etc., who seems to be the one responsible, regardless of the nature or source of his power of control.

In spite of this apparent prestige of the term "ownership" it is evident that the courts do not attach undue importance to the mere legal title. In the cases of mortgagees and trustees what is set up at law in the form of "ownership" is seen clearly to be no more than an empty shell. It seems to be of the essence of the matter that "ownership" is, or ought to be, a beneficial relation.

In general it seems to be an assumption that property has as a universal attribute the capacity for being voluntarily or involuntarily separated from the person so that if rights persist independently of the holder, and thus are capable of transfer *inter vivos* or of succession, they are property of a person—and not otherwise.

There are rights which because of immaturity have not yet secured this essential attribute. But the courts hold that all rights which may be on the way to becoming property are entitled, during their period of gestation, to be treated as potential or future property and to be accorded the protections, if not all of the privileges or liabilities, of property.

Finally, in spite of the fact that the classification of personal and familial rights as rights *in rem* tends to confusion and leads to their identification as property rights, an effort is made to discriminate between them on the grounds that these have a personal and not a non-personal object. Certain rights exist both in an irrelevant and generalized form as personal rights and in a specifically relevant form as component rights of any property interest. And this seems to the courts to justify rendering them as good protection in the one condition as in the other.

CHAPTER VI

THE SUBSTANCE AND STRUCTURE OF MODERN PROPERTY

A. *The Place of Property in the Social Order*

1. *Results of Procedural Development*

THE brief and summary studies, in the foregoing chapters, of the legal concepts and clothing of the institution of property have given us a view of the sources of our modern Anglo-American legal ideas; the Roman strain from early times through to its classic development supplying a small part of the modern law and practically all the modern theory, and the English strain supplying the greater part of the law and but little of the theory. We have seen these rules and viewpoints of the law clashing with the economic facts and these theories clashing with the legal facts, both together producing considerable bewilderment in the current application of the law to modern American conditions. It now remains to complete the process of stripping off the legal clothing in order to see through to the substance of modern property, as a social institution, and thereafter to endeavour to complete our analysis of the degree to which the scheme of legal facts and legal theories of the present day offers a true picture, or to what extent and in what ways, on the other hand, this picture requires modification or new development in order to represent reality. Nor is this a too presumptuous undertaking, for it will generally be agreed that at all times and places both the theory and the practice of law have lagged to a greater or less extent behind the practices of society with which they attempted to deal.

In this endeavour to submit the chaos of property, as it exists in the law, to some degree of new analysis and ordering so that we may establish a basis for its inclusion in the field of economics, it should be clearly understood that we are not attempting to instruct or reform the law upon the basis of some economic theory. We recognize that the financial relations of men with regard to objects operate through the medium of the property structure and have always done so. In order to understand these relations one must understand the structure. In the beginning this structure may have been simple though doubtless vague. Today it is highly complex but also extremely precise. If one attempts to simplify its design he is in danger of misrepresenting it, for there is nothing simple about it. Nevertheless it seems that there is more rhyme and reason to its arrangement than is allowed to appear. Because of gradual growth from many sources; because of concentration upon procedural relations and forms; because of the necessity of dealing with each case as it arises as a more or less special instance; and because of the advisedly conservative character of the law; the legal clothing of the substance of property has come to be much more of a patchwork than the skeleton itself really requires. A little study in the anatomy will soon demonstrate that, while there exists an enormous diversity and many fine shades of distinction, nevertheless certain general essentials and fundamentals exist and can be brought out by X-ray methods. Such methods will not reproduce the minutiae of the substance but they will make the broader outlines of the structure clear. The requirement of any such representation is that it shall not be inconsistent in any respect with the essential facts of law, though here and there it may differ from the traditional arrangement, the background of theory, upon which these facts have been customarily organized.

In general the criticism seems justified that the law fails fully to apprehend the fact that property is an inherent part of the social structure and its functioning. It retains the procedural point of view—a practical one to be sure, but not one which leads to a correct appraisal of the character and connotations of the institution. For instance it still holds that a chose in action is a pending something, not an actual present interest in the body of property of the debtor. It still builds its double structure of rights upon the primitive distinction between those which could be asserted directly against the object and those which were at one time only to be asserted against the person. Substantive law still maintains the look which Maine detected in its early forms—"the look of being gradually secreted in the interstices of procedure"—in the frame of a system of actions.[1]

At the outset certain general statements were made as to the manner of growth of the *corpus juris*. In the course of our examination we have seen many instances of these inborn habits. But let us remind ourselves that these habits have their beneficial as well as their detrimental effects; that, in regard to them, our critical viewpoint must be emotionally ambivalent if it is correctly to evaluate the state of the law of property. For the law arrives very slowly at

[1] *E. L. and C.*, p. 389.

consistency and unanimity on any point. And it is wiser that this should be so. It grows only by the inductive method, by fitting its decisions to individual cases. Its principles and rules are but hypotheses, developed in their early stages by such induction, and serving as labour-saving devices for unifying the practice and deducing the particular application. But, no sooner are they developed and agreed upon than some new fact of a constantly changing economic life arises to break the charmed circle. Then they are found not to fit or they seem to work injustice in many cases. And gradually such tentative generalizations must be modified by further induction. Eventually, as the body of the law itself becomes crystallized, some other agency like the Praetorian edicts or equity must come into existence to carry on the process of growth. This continuity of growth, which is the antithesis of a code – of consistency and unanimity – is a particular virtue of the English law, in which it excels the continental systems founded upon the Roman law. Though it is a principal reason for the chaotic condition, let us hope the process will continue in America. If lack of consistency and unanimity in the law can be taken as an indication, it is certainly doing so.

While we have heretofore followed the historical method and have viewed the institution of property as evolved and evolving – which is natural in the case of all institutions, since they are particularly a process of growth rather than a creation – we will now undertake to see the phase that subsists at this time in America, viewing it in the light of its past, but discounting the inherited traditions in which it is disguised, and attempting to detect, wherever such has occurred, a "substitution of the content," as Rathenau called it. And with this viewpoint we will do well to remember that American institutions are peculiar. Our political organization actually arose in the form of an agreement, an expressed constitution, which, so far as it affected the institution of property, supported a tacit understanding to take over bodily, to continue, and to develop the English common law, but which created by convention, so to speak, and out of the particular social philosophy of the times, a more or less formal and rigid body of principles to regulate its further evolution.

2. *The Organizations for Control*

To assume that the rise of the institution of pre-property, which was becoming converted into property at the stage at which the latter begins to appear in early Rome, was due to the expression of some urge or instinct common to human and animal nature – such as, for instance, the so-called acquisitive instinct – is completely to overlook the fact that the force working in this early institution was obviously not such an urge, but was rather a conventionalized and organized power over human groups determined by propinquity. If property were the natural outgrowth of an innate urge its benefits would have been generally distributed. On the contrary it was then highly centralized; far more so than it is today.

The animal likes and wants; man likes and wants. The force behind many of the idealistic movements of these days looking toward the diffusion of property is the recognition or feeling of these likes and wants. But the actual movements of history, the actual development of the social institutions – included in embryo in this early form – which today hedge us round with a web of intangible controls, these rise from another source and are brought into existence not by vague wishes (urges) but by effective practices hardened into customs and rules. Pre-property, when we first find it definitely presented in the western world, is a power or control vested in a few over all other animate and inanimate objects, including human beings.

All systems of organization of society may be said to take shape as a medium for the control, or power, yielded to, or attained by, some over the rest. It is, in fact, this method and means of dynamic co-operative functioning in which the fact of organization itself seems particularly to consist – a concentration of power by which men, and perhaps the units of any other organic aggregate, are taught, guided and impelled, or compelled, to co-operate.[2] If we take an objective view of the facts it appears that the movements which give rise to these changing and differentiating forms of organizations are not the results of – nor particularly responsive to – the will or the notions of men – even those of leaders. Rather they grow out of conditions in their entirety. Programs and doctrines are rationalizations after the fact, or illusory implements of a hardly self-conscious purpose. Organization is always a result of the necessity for it, and its forms develop out of past habit, modified by the reaction of different types of human nature and capacities among themselves and to circumstances, and by changing conditions.

Therefore to think of these systems of control as if they were in any sense artificial or deliberate creations is I think to misread the facts. They are not even imposed upon an unwilling humanity. It is rather these needs and demands of what is called human nature, in its reaction to its changing environment, which evolve them. True the systems may change. But they do not change by fiat. Changes which seem to be made by fiat, or to be imposed according to a

[2] One seems to find, in the lower strata of the animal world, organizations which appear to function without leaders. But all these seem to be strictly mechanical; i.e. incapable of modifying themselves or their actions to meet varying conditions.

theory, do not turn out to be changes of substance, but merely of name. Looking under the surface of doctrine and nomenclature I can find no case in history where the reality of social institutions seems certainly to be the result of a rational plan deliberately adopted by the human will either of leaders or of led. Instead the practical working of these institutions has always been the expression, in a limited variety of forms, of relatively unchanging human nature. It is said that human nature can be modified; that it is the product of a conditioning which may be deliberate. But in any deliberate conditioning we are again dealing with an institution – one of the systems of control – and usually that one which is the most intimate and intangible of all – the thing we call culture. Culture is a system, as Samuel Butler put it, which places the control in the hands of Mrs. Grundy. Who will say that even that system of compromise, enforced upon fundamental human urges, has ever been more than a product of general experience, or that the various propagandas by which it is maintained are reasons for it rather than rationalizations after the fact of its existence? All we can see is that, in what we call progressive societies, there are changes in this culture, changes apparently brought about by gradual experience and by alterations of environment, of which society itself is for itself the major element.

Organization then is leadership and subjection – a subjection of different degrees and kinds, but one of which the element of autonomous co-operation is at first slight and always minor. The control, which is partly assumed and partly delegated, consists always, therefore, partly of direction and partly of compulsion. In this aspect most of the movements and varieties in the form of our human institutions for control seem to me to resolve themselves into a change in the methods by which leaders acquire control; or, to put this in its not quite so realistic obverse, the method by which leaders are *selected*. Popular interest in, and change of heart in regard to, these various methods seems to be the result of the natural desire on the part of the led that control should be exercised for their benefit. But who shall judge benefit? Peoples have been led to destruction in the illusion that the objective was for their own good. Of course all such social benefit is not illusion. Nevertheless, to the general, the gauge of benefit seems to be relative, not absolute; and it is *relative* to other degrees of benefit within their own economy at the time, not relative to that of other times and places. Moreover, it remains among the most difficult of appraisals to discriminate the individual benefit and sanction of the leader's own interests from the general or individual benefit and sanction of the interests of subordinates. All types of social control have a general similarity, though they vary much in their force and firmness in different times and under different conditions. But, always, and in each field, it is the more capable and aggressive members of society who seek control for themselves and freedom from control by others—power and liberty; while it is the less capable and the docile who seek protection, at the same time demanding that the power which yields it shall serve only the general interest. Movements looking toward the reallocation of benefits take the form, for the most part, of efforts to change the organization and therefore the essential of organization, leadership. In the last analysis they are rivalries for leadership, or control.

It also seems evident that, so far as we can trace the origin and development of our own institution of property and its precursor, it did not first appear as a system, legal or customary, for the accumulation of external objects for immediate and later use as the product and reward of individual labour—along the lines of the classical economic descriptions of the beginnings of capital—nor even as one for the appropriation of land and natural resources.[8] Actually there are almost no early signs of the first—of the attribution of the results of work to him who performed it. And the second was a purely incidental and later development. Instead property grew out of that form of organization of persons which we have called preproperty, itself a welding of the social aggregate; a fundamental political, domestic and economic arrangement for the grouping of men and objects upon the land. That was the preceding, and perhaps the first, metazoic social fact. And the indications are that this aggregation of persons, the later beginnings of the accumulation of objects, and the final settlement upon the land, were all successively as much the result of the nucleating effect of a refuge, a protection, established by a man, or men, as they were of any reaching out for control. One suspects that the true origin and prerequisite of the forerunner as well as of the institution itself was security. Control inhered in him who could create and maintain some degree of security; a magnet to attract and retain persons; a *sine qua non* for a store of objects; and the ground of stability as to location.

Property is the term we now apply to the modern elaboration in the form of a legal institution of certain elements of the original single organization which served all purposes. Its prototype was, therefore, that somewhat despotic governance of persons which seems to have been the first form of control of matters external to himself which our cultural ancestors developed in such a way as

[8] Fustel, *Alleu*, p. 4, says, "Si les modernes font volontiers dériver la propriété du travail, et s'ils aiment à justifier l'appropriation du sol par la fiction d'une longue accumulation de labeurs mis dans ce sol, les jurisconsultes romains n'ont pas eu recours à cette théorie. Pour eux, la propriété était un droit antique et indiscutable, qui n'avait pas besoin d'être justifié."

to necessitate its institutionalization, on a basis so formal that it survived into historic times. But its field of exercise has since been narrowed down so as to exclude human beings. They have become subject exclusively to the other forms of control specially differentiated for their governance. Property is now confined to control over material objects. If, with this in mind, we look back upon the original homogeneous control we see in it a point of view, a psychology, of a political and domestic character, but a set of forms of a seemingly proprietary character. In reality all that observation means, when the order of succession is recalled, is that the subsequent political and domestic controls have inherited and liberalized the original point of view because they have continued to deal—as it primarily dealt—with human beings. In the process of liberalization they have gradually discarded the forms while they retain the purposes. Property seems to have retained the original forms—the shells of the early ideas—while converting the purpose. In its theory, at least, it also seems to have continued without liberalization the original ideas; almost at times to have allowed them to regress since they no longer deal with human beings. But actually the constitution of modern property is almost as far removed from its prototype as are the constitutions of the modern family and the modern state. For, in the last analysis, the institution of property rests, not upon what the law says, but upon what it does.

In the early social grouping from which, by way of both strains, our institutional inheritance seems to have descended, there was but a single system of organization and the one homogeneous control covered in its simple form the whole field of persons and objects. The unit of this organization was the house community, or *familia*. Upon the heads of these groups centred the entire power and at this stage the members were subject for all purposes, economic and political as well as domestic, to the power of the *pater* or ruler. This original homogeneous power was probably that of *manus-mund*. At a later stage, in Rome, the super-familial control was imposed upon the basic organization by the heads themselves, and this took over the specialized political functions of the now multiple grouping. This purely political system at first left the internal government—pre-property minus its external political element—still unified and more or less undisturbed. But gradually it came to assert a suzerainty over both the remaining elements in this internal government, without however changing their intra-familial character. And then its first business was to sanction and to modify the control over persons within the *familia*—the domestic power—and to distinguish it thereby from the control of objects—the property power. As a result property seems, in Roman law at least, to be the undifferentiated residue of the original control—the continuous and parent stem from which the others were differentiated and separated, leaving to property only its present limited scope. True this continuity is largely a matter of outward appearance. Actually property was the last to be recognized as a separate power and was slow in being specialized to its own function because it was for a long time a minor power. Perhaps this accounts for the failure of the newer substance to burst the old shell which still clings on in much of the theory and some of the forms.

In Rome the remaining original familial control was divided in this way into domestic and property power. But both continued to be exercised entirely by the *patrifamilias*. The group itself regressed into the domestic (or little political) organization—still called the *familia*, though that name seems to have stuck to the coterminous unit of property as well. In some respects the domestic and property relations of the household were subordinated to the political relations of the oligarchy. But in most respects the domestic power was absolute and property became a limited accessory or dependent of it, wholly in the hands of the domestic chiefs.

Feudalism was almost a reversion to pre-property, a reversion to type. There this combined domestic and proprietary organization merely expanded its field until it became, again, as well the political. As it enlarged into the macrocosm the new units dividing within it—the microcosms—acquired most of the domestic power, but in a subordinate capacity. Property remained with the macrocosm, being gradually submerged in the political function. In England property was at first an indistinguishable element in the broader field—the political organization upon the land. As the economic function became again gradually differentiated and separated, nevertheless the political organization still retained its foundation upon the land, and, in form, the stamp of its origin. The two prerogatives of the holders of land gradually became distinguished. But political rights continued to follow property in land and for political preferment property in land was deemed essential down to recent times, even when it had to be supplied by royal grant. Even now the empty form of a title newly created has usually a geographical locus. With this separation of function and the gradual taking over of the economic function by the subordinate domestic organization, the institution of property, which began to reappear as a separate matter, appertained to the newer and lesser domestic system.

Where property remained as an element in the domestic organization, as it did in Rome, it was so entirely an incidental part of the latter, and so entirely taken for granted (the classificatory genitive) that almost the only specialized and elaborated element in its legal portrayal consisted in the sanction which related it to the domestic system (succession) and in its expansion into the inter-familial field – the law of contract, the relic of inter-familial treaties. On the other hand, under feudalism, in its later stages, where the resurgence of property as an independent institution took place by way of its division from the political system, it was that combination which was taken for granted and, in the law, it was the encroachments upon this union, made by the domestic organization, which first appeared as a self-conscious and overt process.

Thus in all these cases – the single or dual organization of pre-property and of feudalism, and the triple organizations of classic Rome and post-feudal England – the development of the special economic organization, property, has received its most vital stimulus in association with the individualistic domestic power rather than with the less individualistic political. It was the domestic power which gradually usurped economic control (property) from the political power, as the familial estates in land gradually superseded the feudal tenures in England. And it was the domestic power which retained economic control, subject only to the support of the state, in Rome. Again in modern times, in the great Russian experiment, economic control is being reincorporated into the political – along somewhat similar lines to those of the feudal system; perhaps for similar reasons to those which brought its prototype into existence in the Dark Ages; and, possibly, with similar results.

In the beginning the direction of the economic activities of subject persons was included in the one control – pre-property. With its separation, in Rome, into three systems this control over economic activities remained with the domestic power, in association with its adjunct property. In feudal times the development of these two into the primarily political organization carried with it, to a large extent and at first, the direction of men's economic functioning. Again, as property began to attach itself to the new and subordinate domestic organization, this specific control of men's economic activities went with it. In this way, during the Middle Ages, alongside the older organizations for control of economic activities, there began to be developed a new and wholly economic organization of men as an appanage of the again specialized organization called property. This secondary organization we call "employment." It began as an expansion and outgrowth of the domestic labour system among the burgher families, who had succeeded in ridding themselves earliest of the feudal politico-economic control, and in a type of activity – trading and handicraft – which was both dissociated from the political control *via* the land and of a nature somewhat demeaning. But the new system was contagious and extended, in time, into the domestic organization which was replacing the feudal in the management of the land. In our time, and in the countries of higher economic civilization, it has almost wholly removed the control of the economic activity of persons from the political and domestic systems. It is a dependent of property, for it operates as an indirect control over men in their economic activities by means of the exercise of the remaining powers of the original property organization. However this subordination is no longer due, as it was in early Rome and under feudalism, to the assertion of a control savouring of property over men themselves, but only to the economic power over men which is a resultant of the property over objects.

Thus in modern societies we have come to have a triplicate organization, three principal social controls wielded separately by somewhat different groups of leaders. These are the domestic, or familial, organization; the political, or super-familial organization; and the economic or property organization with its recent satellite, employment—the management of objects with its derived management of men.

Occidental societies are now generally organized on these lines:

1. *Domestic.* The intra-familial control. Gradually coming to be of lesser importance as it is stripped of its political autonomy and its economic functions
2. *Political.* The super-familial and inter-familial control. With the disintegration of feudalism, under which political and economic control were united, this has been, from the fourteenth to the nineteenth centuries, very largely stripped of its economic power, and its economic functions have become highly specialized
3. *Economic*
   A. Property. The remains of the Indo-European social organization become a legal (super-familial) institution, and gradually reduced in its scope until it is confined to control over material objects
   B. Employment. Control over the economic activities of men. The latest development and an offshoot of property

These systems of organization now subsist co-ordinately. They are inter-related in certain respects—in some ways dependent upon and in others independent of each other. Each member of society is subject to control directly or indirectly in several or all these ways. Those possessing the various forms of control constitute more and more distinct groups, though several different varieties of power may inhere in the same persons. In individual cases the influence of one kind of organization upon the others is often marked. But in the aggregate the exercise of each type of power must be regarded as distinct and incident upon society in a different aspect of its life.

The source of the sanction of domestic power was the attribution of the inherent authority of pre-property which came later to be supported by and qualified by the super-familial control. As the tinge of property faded this authority has further been modified by relatively modern limitations which, viewed on the obverse side of the relation, have come to be the rights of the individual as against the power of the head of the family. The super-familial sanction of this parent's authority still lingers in the form of a positive right or power. The super-familial sanction of the individual's independence of this authority appears in the form of a negative right, or protection. Also there still persist certain familial rights, as well, which retain the stamp of property. These are the modern protections against infringements of familial rights from outside the family.

The source of the sanction of political power was also pre-property.[4] It has been exercised both through the joint contribution and action of the heads of all constituent households and through the attribution of a super-seniority (sovereignty = *superanus*) to one or a few. Against this power there has also developed a defense mechanism, the doctrine of the rights of the subject—a doctrine which at first merely limited the political power and protected the individual against its exercise. These limitations have become the negative rights of citizenship. To these were added later some positive rights enforcing the idea of an attribution of power to and, in turn, from the individual. The latter gave rise to the theory that all, not merely an oligarchy of heads of households, contribute the sanction of political power, though the power itself is a development of the original oligarchical sanction.

The source of the sanction of economic power in the aspect of property was also pre-property. As such it was limited to economic control over persons and objects within the household. But, as it came to be reinforced by the super-familial authority and thus to be converted into the legal institution of property, the arena of its control was extended, in certain cases, to persons beyond the confines of the household. Thus it was clothed, within and without, with positive rights or powers. In the course of time, with the limitation of property to material objects, the political organization has taken

[4] It is hardly too much to say that the foundation of government was pre-property, for, at least in the earlier evolved hierarchical forms, as opposed to the later oligarchical forms where there is more evidence of a convention or contract between equals, government was an expansion of that original social unit, the house community or *familia*. Certainly pre-property was the aboriginal Indo-European form of control over men, out of which grew the other forms.

over all these powers over persons. The result is to leave the property control supported only by negative rights, or protections. Incidentally all persons have thereby acquired negative rights, or protections, against the property power. They cannot be made, or make themselves, objects of property. In the meantime it has also come to be assumed that, by a process of devolution, all persons may share in property power.

The source of the sanction of economic power in its aspect of employment was originally derived from the domestic power (master and servant) and thence indirectly, like the others, from pre-property. But this sanction has now been practically eliminated, and the law no longer concedes any important positive rights, or powers, to the employer. On the other hand certain negative rights, or protections, are beginning to be accorded to the employee against the *de facto* exercise of this form of economic control. The newer relationship between the two is contractual—that is, upon each side, a property control, not over the person but over the property of the other. Because this is by the nature of the case unequal—the liability of the one being of fairly certain incidence and that of the other being of highly uncertain incidence—and because the nature of the relationship is relatively new, it can hardly be said that any sort of complete organization of reciprocal rights or of doctrines nucleating them, has as yet been developed.

Out of the early grouping have developed the four principal elements of social organization. Of these, property, which in form most nearly resembles the original, is but one. Nevertheless its history shows that, as one, it is a part of the fundamental system of government—of the institutional organization of society. It is confined to the control of objects—a control now somewhat limited, it is true. Through the control of objects it is, indirectly and in some respects, the control of the economic activities of men. The other controls over men subsist alongside of it. The domestic control is diminishing, with the economic enfranchisement of women and youth. The political control is growing. It seems at times and in some respects to be partially subservient to the economic. But, in turn, the economic control is entirely dependent upon the political. At all periods covered in our study control has existed in all three fields, and in most of them the forms of control have been independent of each other in varying degrees. The question of which form of control has been chief and which subordinate has depended at any particular time upon which of these three elements in the structure of society has conferred, upon those who held it, the greater power over the rest of the society. In Rome the power was at first chiefly domestic and later it was political. In England until recent times it was chiefly political. In America today it is chiefly economic. In Rome civil and economic power accrued to the domestic *patrifamilias*. In England economic and even domestic power accrued, in constantly lessening degree, to the political feudal aristocracy. In America domestic power is disappearing. But what remains of it together with some considerable, though not obvious, part of the political power appertains to economic control.

It seems necessary to recognize that property (not necessarily any particular form of property) has proved itself to be an essential condition of the social structure. Certainly it is not an idea; nor is it a creation. On the contrary it is, in one of its most important and not wholly separable aspects, the evolved organization of society itself. Certainly at all times and places it has in some form constituted the social organization for economic purposes. And, in times past, it has frequently been hardly distinguishable from the political and domestic aspects of that organization. Even now it is so intimately connected with the government and with the family that recent schools of thought in all the social sciences have been inclined to attribute to economic forces, working through this channel, a preponderant influence upon the developments in political and other social spheres.

The system of individual property, out of which has developed the so-called money economy, is a comparatively recent development. It is a system, by comparison with others, which has produced a decentralization of property control and its dissociation from domestic or political power with which, in former times, it was associated. And yet it too has a centripetal tendency of its own. It is essentially one out of several possible systems, whereby the determination of the volume of savings and the administration of these savings and of natural resources, is left primarily, under a certain degree of natural selection, to individual initiative. It has developed by an evolution, not by a theory. Where it has developed most highly, there men as a whole seem to enjoy a greater degree of material welfare than in the societies less developed in this respect. That is all that can be said about it. No part of it is essential. Russia is experimenting, under the guise of a created system declared to be based on revelation and authority. We will eventually learn whether this system is better or worse. But we cannot determine the result by argument. We must wait and see. True the test will only be definitive if Russia does not depend on the institution of individual property outside of its borders for any part of its supply of saving, or for any part of its technique. It must save all its own requirements and it must not borrow the technique worked out under a method perhaps more stimulating to individual initiative. But to assume that the Russian plan is new because its declared objectives, principles and doctrines are new, is only possible if one neglects to look beneath the surface and fails to detect the intimate resemblance to the combined politico-economic organization of the Middle Ages, called the feudal system. Thus it may quite well prove to be a retrogression to a lower state of society instead of a progression to a higher.

B. *The Substance of Property Rights*

1. *Replacement of Powers by Protections*

Consideration of the gradual differentiation of these several types of social organization from the single undifferentiated form makes clear to us the reason for the inevitable process of derogation in the nature of property rights which took place by reason of this process. The result of gradually confining the field of exercise, of the control inhering in that part of the social organization we call property, to objects other than human beings is to render no longer necessary the original autonomous powers nor the later grant of power by the super-familial political organization. For power is power over men; a positive authority to enforce control by sanctioned self-help. Therefore, as this process of denuding the powers continued, the character of rights accruing to the property system became more and more limited to the protections – protections against interference, by others, with a control over objects which required no other sanction or support from the state. The power to deal with objects is unrestricted self-help. True, in recent times, some limits have been put even on this exercise of self-help and we are acquiring a system of limitations which we have referred to as the system of limited permissions. Thus property has changed from a customary power over the *familia* and an analogous legal power over those outside the *familia* who voluntarily submitted themselves to it (contract and delict) – in both of which the emphasis was upon control over persons rather than that with respect to objects – to a limited protection as to objects.

In the end the private powers, which were the original sanctioned control of the property system, have almost wholly disappeared. In their place we have only protections. But, curiously enough, the form remains in the so-called rights *in personam*, and theory continues its attempt to explain this vestigial relic by inventing a new content for it.[5] A system of contract relations which has created a hier-

[5] Holmes, *Common Law*, p. 5, says, "A very common phenomenon, and one very familiar to the student of history, is this. The customs, beliefs, or needs of a primitive time establish a rule or a formula. In the course of centuries the custom, belief, or necessity disappears, but the rule remains. The reason which gave rise to the rule has been forgotten, and ingenious minds set themselves to inquire how it is to be accounted for. Some ground of policy is thought of, which seems to

archical organization of property, like all other modern property based solely upon the foundation of material objects and which requires and obtains from the law only protections in its relations to these objects, is nevertheless still today fitted as badly as may be into a practice and a theory which is the shell of the old system of powers, with its old content, the control *via* property in persons, entirely removed.[6]

But this process has gone far deeper than a mere change in the nature of private rights or the content of legal forms. Fundamentally it has consisted in a change in the organization of society. In the first chapter we undertook to describe the integral social unit of prehistoric times—an autonomous group—the house community. Within this group only the head had powers—those powers which we have called pre-property and which obtained over both persons and objects indiscriminately. The rest had protections; protections through him and perhaps, through the restraints of custom, against him. But the power of this head had no other sanction than its own strength and the protections conferred by him were delimited by his power, while those against him depended upon a vague ethic. No external force either supported or tempered this power.

Gradually the aggregation of these integral social units developed, through the agency of their respective heads, a super-familial government. With the sanction of this government, to which we first give the name of law, the powers of pre-property were converted into legal powers. Those over persons within the *familia* gave rise to the Law of Persons (familial law); those with respect to objects within the *familia* gave rise to the Law of Things, strictly speaking—the powers to acquire, convey and devise; those over persons outside the *familia*—a mere legalizing of the self-help to which resort had always been had—gave rise to the Law of Contract and Delict. These powers were sanctioned by the new external authority. But they remained only powers. The sanctions were not an implementing of the law. They only authorized the pre-existing exercise of control over persons within and without the limits of the immediate sphere of influence of the head. And these powers pertained only to such heads. Private law began with the function of sanctioning the authority of those who controlled the pre-existing integral and

explain it and to reconcile it with the present state of things; and then the rule adapts itself to the new reasons which have been found for it, and enters on a new career. The old form receives a new content, and in time even the form modifies itself to fit the meaning which it has received."

[6] What the law now calls powers (i.e. a sub-class of rights) are in reality no more than legal capacity to alter existing legal relations. They do not vest control over one human being in another, as did the original powers. They merely place the individual in a position to demand of the judicial authorities that they alter the area of the protections against others which they are according him.

autonomous units which came to compose the new super-familial organization.

Eventually and very gradually there began to appear the protections; that is, the assumption by the super-familial organization, through its deputies, of the exercise (enforcement) of many of these powers, and thus the substitution of protections, accorded in place of the powers formerly authorized to the now subordinated heads. This process of substitution began as to the powers of the head over those outside his immediate sphere of influence. But in time and slowly it invaded the régime of the *familia* itself, the field of the powers of the head over those within his sphere of influence (domestic power). Already in classic Roman law in a small way, and more completely in modern times, the super-familial government began to reach the individual and to accord protections to the subordinate members within the domestic circle against the authority of the head. In this process the original paternal power was gradually destroyed. Then, in the course of time, protections in a new form made their appearance. These were accorded to the heads of the now dwindling families against external authority. In the end, only the original powers over objects within the *familia* remained relatively untouched.

In the most recent stage of this evolution – during our own era – practically no powers remain to the individual as to persons. The state has assumed them all. Such authority, conferred by law, has become wholly an attribute of the political organization. Thereby the substitution of the super-familial control for that of the originally autonomous familial group – the sole organization of early times – has become almost complete. And in this way the autonomous subsidiary unit, the household, is in process of being finally dissolved into its constituent individuals, so far as the law is concerned. Thus the power sanctioned by the Law of Obligations has disappeared and has been replaced by a new system of property rights in bodies of property or indeterminate objects which, it is true, betrays us by retaining the old form of a power over the person. The power sanctioned by the Law of Persons has been converted, on the one hand, into a non-proprietary domestic relation, the power of which is fast disappearing, and, on the other, into the transition form of employment relation (master and servant) which is the seed out of which has grown the newest social organization for control. Thus the intra-familial power has remained to some extent a power over persons but has ceased to be property; inter-familial power has remained property but has ceased to be a power over persons. Around the third – the intra-familial power over objects – centres the whole system of property, as far removed as possible from the simple original classificatory genitive (*dominium*), so that it is hardly possible any longer to say of an object that it is *propria* to one or *aliena* to another. Beginning as a part of the system of powers it has been converted into a new system of protections. And it has become a prerogative of every individual.

The state has assumed practically all the powers formerly tacitly granted the heads of households and has conferred in their place protections for a complex web of interests in objects. It has developed a system of criminal law which is in part a support to the property organization, displacing to some extent the old reliance on the Law of Delict; and it itself asserts the enforcement of proven interests in objects arising alike from conveyance or contract. So that, in this last case, what was originally a sanctioned private power over the person of the debtor is now a protected property interest in his body of property, and therefore not even a public power over his person. As a result the only remnants of the original property powers over persons are the modified and disappearing familial control and the power of the state in the field of criminal law. Those empty forms of legal procedure which still call themselves *in personam* are not in any substantial respect powers over persons either in the hands of the holder of the right or of his protector, the state.

In the light of this analysis it becomes apparent that what has occurred is not in reality a substitution of protection for powers. Rather it is primarily the disintegration of the primitive social unit.[7] It is entirely due to the fact that what we call law represents only the rules of the super-familial government and not those of its predecessor, the familial government, that the interpolation of protections in the place of the former powers and the literal supersession of these powers by those of the state gives the impression of a creation *de novo*. Precisely the same set of relations probably existed within the *familia* as now exists within the state. Therefore, in essence, the movement has consisted in the extension of the upper poles of these bipolar powers to a broader and hierarchically higher agency for control; a general substitution of power over objects for power over persons; and an upward expansion of protection against all powers, whether authorized or unauthorized. So in a similar case, a future historian, who had available only the data as to the growth of our federal government, might be deceived by the process of centralization and fail to recognize that the intrusion into the affairs of these originally autonomous states—the taking over of parts of their administration and powers—has been, not an addition but only a supersession.

The disintegration of the subsidiary social unit and the concen-

[7] Ihering, *Geist*, I, p. 179, says that, at least so far as the external legal organization of the family is concerned, it is important in inverse proportion to the maturity of the political development.

tration of power in the state has been accompanied by a complete system of doctrinal rationalizations. It is obvious that the change in theory from one which placed upon the person of each integral group the responsibility for taking care of his own interests (self-help) to that of today, which is tending to place all responsibility for individuals in general upon society, is an extreme change. In fact the change is so great that it casts doubt on the feasibility of the enterprise, and the contrast between the two aims makes clear the fact that the new social theory is still more nearly theory than practice, even in the field of property.

2. *The Nature of Integral Rights*

We have found that property is that specialized organization of society which functions primarily for purposes we call economic. It consists of a system of functional relations between men with regard to material objects. These relations are defined in the philosophy of law as claims, privileges, powers and immunities, and their correlatives, duties, etc. Technically this analysis is doubtless correct and necessary. Practically the whole mass can be fairly described as, in the last analysis, a system of prohibitions. The modern rights themselves, as we have found, now consist largely of protections, or, viewed in another way, of limited permissions. But when we analyse these rights of property we find that they are bounded positively in some directions by the definitions of those acts which constitute infringements by others — in other words by the prohibitions against interference which hedge them round; and, in other directions, by the line beyond which their exercise constitutes an infringement upon the rights of others; and that they are bounded negatively in still other directions by the line beyond which their exercise is not protected, because interference or deprivation by others no longer constitutes an infringement of the right itself. Thus the orbit of a right is bounded by the presence or absence of prohibitions against others and by the presence of prohibitions against the holder. Within these boundaries there is a legal vacuum. One is left free to enjoy what benefits one can. The definition of the right is not that of a field. It is that of a fence. Strictly there is no legal content to it. The right is a system of protections, not a thing protected. Within the protections there may exist no value, no benefit, no enjoyment. Such is the general nature of the component rights of which property is constructed. Search where we may in this field for commands to do, as opposed to prohibitions — which are commands not to do — and we search almost in vain. Some retain the appearance of positive commands, but when they are followed through to the end one finds only negative commands. Even these prohibitions are enforced by prevention not by compulsion; and usually by punishment or compensation after the fact, not even by prevention before the fact.[8]

It is hardly necessary here to elaborate a point to which we have alluded in a previous chapter and which is a commonplace in jurisprudence. Property rights always define relations between men, not those between men and material objects. They have reference to material objects, but in no other respect than designation do they concern the object. The foregoing analysis goes to support this dictum.

These property rights come into existence largely through the arrangements men make among themselves according to prevailing customs, or according to practices which later are confirmed into customs. The law usually accepts what it finds and clothes it with legal sanction. Statute creates but a minor element. But from whatever source they come, these prohibitions are enforced by government, partly on its own initiative (criminal and regulatory) and partly on the appeal of the citizen (civil). Custom continues to reinforce and to out-reach the arm of government in maintaining these rights. For instance, verbal agreements between men whose "word is as good as their bond," constitute extra-legal property rights which may be fully as valid as legally enforcible rights. The largest business in the world, the New York Stock Exchange, deals in property rights which for a short time are—between the members—wholly in an extra-legal status. Yet they are "good."[9]

[8] The statements in terms of legal theory of the nature of a property right are often somewhat fanciful. In Professor Commons' terminology, which I think well represents this point of view (see "Institutional Economics," 21 *American Economic Review*, p. 648), they consist of "performance, avoidance, forbearance by individuals," established and controlled by the principal form of collective action. Actually, in the last analysis the law offers protections of a limited sort to property rights *which it recognizes.* But its enforcement (its execution of these offers) consists almost wholly of punishments after the fact (criminal) or damages for infringement (civil). To this extent "performances, avoidances and forbearances" are for the most part only induced by the threat of consequences. Actual prevention of interference, that is the enforcement of forbearances, is limited. And the actual enforcement of performances and avoidances is almost wholly nominal. These latter elements of property exist only in the field of contract. In almost all cases it is not performance or avoidance that is required by law, but an equivalent (damages) for non-performance or non-avoidance. And this equivalent, in the end, is discovered to be rendered by the law, rather than by the promisor, and entirely in the shape of an extension of the negative property rights above mentioned for the benefit of the promisee over equivalent property interests formerly protected for the benefit of the promisor. This is also true of almost all cases of so-called specific performance. The specificity is not as to an act, positive or negative, but as to certain of the promisor's property interests instead of an aliquot and indeterminate part of all of them.

[9] It seems to me that many writers on the subject come near to substituting the facts of law for the facts of economic life. But in reality law does not determine economic life. It trails along behind the developments in this field, endeavouring to interpret and codify developed customs. The social phenomenon, the thing

The Supreme Court of the United States seems to accept the theory that these bundles of rights constituting property have some inherent character which is sacred, inviolable and guaranteed under the Constitution. And yet in its decisions the court is constantly accepting legislative or instituting judicial changes in the shape of additions, subtractions and modifications of the particular component rights, as fast as conditions change and even in conformance with changes in current social philosophy. We might define the constitutional protection to property as a certain irreducible minimum existing in the honoured traditions and in the present minds of the Supreme Court.

This nature and this way of growth of property rights give special point to the importance of distinguishing between the property itself and the material objects with which it is directly concerned. For property, being composed of rights, and consisting in reality of bundles of prohibitions, can and does change without change in its objects. In spite of the Constitution, custom and law are constantly changing, for instance, the structure of private property upon the land. It is being continually redefined with important economic effects. New forms are devised. Component rights are qualified or abrogated. Others are added or enlarged. The institution is in a continuous state of change. But the underlying land persists through it all relatively unchanged.

There is a further important practical reason for insisting on this distinction between property and its objects. Today the greater proportion of transactions in economic life take place without affecting possession of material objects. They are transactions in property, by which interests are created, transferred or extinguished. And only in that small proportion of cases which alter *de facto* possession is there involved any physical change for the object or any change of relations among men with direct regard to objects. Whatever is the substance of this organization of property, it is necessary to perceive that it is the elements of its structure, the ganglia of these relations, which are dealt with in economic life, rather than, for the most part, the ultimate objects themselves.

3. *Distinction Between Property and Other Rights*

Most definitions of property, for purposes of discriminating them from other rights, simply beg the question. They either attempt to define them by description, merely listing the subdivisions; or they

that is, develops apart from the law; continues to exist apart from it; is only gradually apprehended by the law and then after the fact; and is never more than sanctioned, defined and supported by the law.

define property as that which can be appropriated, in other words as its object, and its object precisely circumscribed by a vicious circle; or they refer to the impossible criterion of value.[10]

We have already demonstrated that the criterion of exchange value implies the attribute of alienability. For value in exchange can only be attributed if one is permitted to exchange. In other words this test depends on the universality of alienability as an attribute of property. But, even aside from this requirement, there are many property rights which turn out to be valueless, yet remain property. Property may persist after value disappears, although it is true that it is rarely asserted except where value exists or while it persists. Nor has value in exchange entirely displaced value in use—however immeasurable the latter may be in economics. The protection to such rights as rights of access to market, certain rights against injury to exchange value, etc., which is now being accorded, has been a factor in leading some economists—Professor Commons, for instance—to identify property with exchange value. This seems to be going too far. As the number of types of property which are included in the exchange economy enlarges and the number of those retained exclusively in the domestic economy contracts, it is natural that the protections accorded against interference with freedom of exchange or against willful depreciation of exchange value require more emphasis and perhaps extension. But the rights of use and enjoyment still remain the origin and much of the content of property. Much property exists which, because exchange does not occur and is not contemplated, is not valued nor considered in the aspect of exchange value. It is better, therefore, to read this new movement in the light which Terry sheds upon it, as merely an addition of certain new protections to existing rights of property, which he groups together around the right to unimpaired pecuniary condition.

It is true that the attribute of alienability has come to be an almost universal attribute of property.[11] But since it was not by any means a universal one in the past and is not completely so at present, it cannot be made to supply the necessary criterion. All

[10] Anson, op. cit., p. 10, says, "The matter of the obligation, the thing to be done or forborne, must possess, at least in the eye of the law, a pecuniary value, otherwise it would be hard to distinguish legal from moral and social relations." The definition that property includes all relations with reference to material objects successfully includes many moral and social relations which are treated as or define property. But it excludes those which are not so treated because they do not concern interests in material objects.

[11] "In the United States generally all rights of action are assignable except those arising from a tort to the person or from a breach of promise to marry." Anson, op. cit., p. 395. Even the right of action arising from a tort to the person is, as we have noted, becoming by statute transferable at certain stages or in certain cases.

sorts of limitations have been and are placed both by law and by creators of property upon the privilege of alienation. When none is permitted it is obvious that the property dies with the person. But often a seeming deprivation does not really eliminate the attribute of alienability. For instance, in the case of the spendthrift trust, it might appear that since the beneficiary is deprived of the power of transfer this attribute is absent. But a moment's reflection corrects that. For it is by transfer of the interests of which such a trust fund is composed that the trust estate comes into being, and these will pass elsewhere by transfer at the expiration of the particular estate. It is not that the component interests are incapable of transfer, but that by the act of its creator the power of voluntary or involuntary transfer was expressly withheld from the interest created for the whilom beneficiary and was *exercised in advance* by the settlor. Nevertheless the spendthrift trust is property of the beneficiary. It is a non-transferable (by him) interest in a body of property. It is a mass of 'things' separate from his own and over it he has no control; nor can the law merge the two.

Another consideration which has tempted to making alienability the criterion of property is the fact that it would seem to serve as a means of distinguishing property rights from personal rights, which are inalienable. But this is not in reality the true contrast of these latter to property. It is true that these personal rights are constitutionally inalienable. A citizen is not permitted to deprive himself of them. Since each citizen already has his own complete quota he could derive no benefit in acquiring the rights of others except for the purpose of depriving those others of their liberty. The real effect then of this inalienability is to prevent the person from being made the object of property to anyone, even to himself. He is prevented from selling himself through the medium of selling his liberties. In this manner the person is ruled out from the class of material object. Rights with regard to persons (personal and familial rights) are rights with regard to inappropriable objects. And that, rather than the characteristic of inalienability, which is also frequently found in the case of property rights, is the correct point of contrast between the two classes of rights.

Survival is another criterion which has been proposed. With respect to the variety of interests of which it is an attribute it has almost but not quite the same coverage as alienability *inter vivos*.[12] In

[12] The use of the terms for transfer of property is very inexact. For instance: "The assignability or survivability of things in action have frequently been held to be convertible terms, and . . . furnish as clear and intelligible a rule to determine what injuries to property rights or interests [will survive to the personal representative of

this view property comprises all particular rights inhering in a person which do not disappear upon his death, but which pass thereupon to some other by will, by intestate succession, by the terms of settlement, or persist by any other mode ("by conveyance, devise, descent or act of law").[18] But the test is not adequate. Take, for instance, a life estate in land. Obviously it does not survive. It is extinguished by the death of the lessee. At that point a different and pre-existing estate becomes possessory. Yet both have been property. In reality the attribute of survival is one which attaches to the object and not necessarily to the property. If the object is consumed or destroyed the property disappears with it. The test of survival of its object is a true test of the persistence of property. But the test of survival of the particular interest is not a necessary attribute of property.

We have heretofore suggested that the only satisfactory basis of distinction between property and other rights is that the former cover all interests of whatever nature in appropriable material and quasi-material objects and that they are strictly limited to such. This clearly discriminates them from the familial rights, since members of families have come to be specifically excluded from the form of control called property. In other words human beings are no longer material objects in the legal sense. Upon the basis of this criterion it is possible, though with more difficulty, to draw the line between property and personal rights. The latter, sometimes called "liberties," bear no relation to any specific object or group of objects, unless perhaps they are conceived to relate to one's own person as an object. But one's own person cannot be made the object of property. In so far as they are rights relating to economic activities they seem to have some indefinite relation to material objects (i.e. the objects worked on, or the interests received in payment). But this is not true. For as soon as they become projected upon specific

the injured party]." Morenus v. Crawford, 51 Hun. 89, 95 (N. Y. 1889). This is certainly not true.

The newer word "transfer" was at first used of alienation *inter vivos* only. "Transfer is an act of the parties or of the law by which the title to property is conveyed from one living person to another." Codes of North Dakota, South Dakota, Montana and California. But it is now coming to mean "any act by which the property of one person is vested in another." Wallach v. Stein, 103 N.J.L. 470, 472 (1926). It "includes all transactions whereby property of one person becomes the property of another." Elwood v. Kan. Soldiers' Compensation Bd., 117 Kan. 753, 754 (1925). Thus "transferability" is the same as "alienability," and properly covers both survival and alienability *inter vivos*.

[18] It was in this view that the term "hereditament," which originally meant everything "capable of being 'inherited,' be it corporeal, incorporeal, real, personal, or mixed," 3 Kent *Comm.* 401, quoting Coke *On Littleton*, 6, a, came to mean "everything that may be holden."

material objects or specific bodies of property they no longer remain personal rights but are converted into property rights. Therefore they must be construed to remain liberties so long as—and only so long as—they do not concern the delivery of any particular interests in specific objects or bodies of property. Then too they are general attributes of all persons, only varying according to legal status; whereas property rights are particular attributes of individuals who have always *acquired* the rights from some source. Thus personal rights are neither peculiar as to subject (person of inherence) nor do they relate to a material object, while property rights are always peculiar as to subject and relate directly to specific material objects or indirectly to indeterminate material objects. The rights concerning economic activities, which we have already considered, must then be seen to exist both as personal and as property rights. They are originally generalized liberties, whence they are precipitated and included as part rights in most bundles of property rights. Such are the right to inherit or devise; the right to contract, or to acquire property by other means; the right personally to perform economic activities (labour, business, etc.). When these are exercised in connection with some material object in which one has an interest they become specific-particular and are part rights of property composing that interest. But in their generalized form they are not property rights. Such a distinction and such a narrowing of the rights to be called property may not satisfy those who, for practical social reasons, desire to retain and extend the specially effective protection accorded property rights for the benefit of the general personal rights of particular economic interest, known as the occupational rights. But for our purpose, in order to effect a qualitative separation which makes possible exact analysis, this is a necessary and accurate distinction.[14]

These considerations all lead us to the following definition and identification of those rights which are *property* rights. Property is any protected right or bundle of rights (interest, or 'thing') with direct or indirect regard to any external object (i.e. other than the person himself) which is material or quasi-material (i.e. a protected process) and which the then and there organization of society permits to be made the object of that form of control, either private or public, which is connoted by the legal concepts of occupying, possessing or using. The effective essence of these legal concepts seems to be the right to exclude all persons not legally entitled to

[14] There is plenty of precedent for this distinction. A good statement of it is made by Lord Holt in Keeble v. Hickeringill, 11 East 575 (1809). He says, "There are two sorts of acts for doing damage to a man's employment, for which an action lies; the one is in respect of a man's privilege; the other is in respect of his property."

entry or interference. They are protections in the form of prohibitions. So long as the object is so controlled by someone it may be subject as well to other interests which are not possessory *de facto*; that is, which do not involve any direct control by the holder of such interest, but rather a control by proxy through bailee, fiduciary, debtor, etc. And the object may be subject, by means of such other rights, to deputed or future or conditional control on various bases. Such rights may be held jointly or severally. The ultimate object may be related to an interest only through a series of intermediaries; which, viewed in the opposite aspect, means that each holder of an interest, beginning with the occupancy or use, in some respects and to the extent of the interest, "holds of" the holder next removed in the series. Such interests, or bundles of rights, may be varied endlessly in their composition; impaired in many respects; impeded in realization of enjoyment and, even, may be projected upon the object only as rights to an aliquot share in a group of such objects or other interests (a body of property) in such a way as to remain for the time being of indeterminate incidence as to specific objects. Nevertheless all such interests are composed of property rights because they relate ultimately or eventually to a possessed material or quasi-material object, with regard to which—or to the equivalent of which, or to a part or use of which—they are or may become possessory.

C. *Objects of Property Rights*

1. *Material Objects—Land and Goods*

The law of property is concerned almost exclusively with defining and dealing with these rights and the bundles of them (interests), and not with their objects. In one respect, however, the law must deal with material objects. For it is customary for mature societies to define under what circumstances, and what categories of, objects may be brought within that form of control called property; to define of what each particular object consists; and generally to prescribe the permissions and the limited protections, with reference to the physical use of material objects, which compose the interests having any degree of the quality of possession. With these details we need not concern ourselves. But it is now necessary for us to secure a sufficiently definite picture of what we mean by material objects so that we can have firmly in mind the nature and limits of this foundation upon which the property structure is erected.

Let us consider, first, the classes of strictly material objects. As we have seen, in general, the air, sunlight, the sea, running water, wild animals, and certain other manifestations of nature are treated as common resources. As such they are subject to limited appropriation only, under regulation by the state, and only by those who, on account of other property rights, public or private, have access to them. When so appropriated these resources become the objects of property and may enter the exchanges. These are the facts of modern law with reference to that which the economist has erroneously called "free goods." The fact that they can never be appropriated without effort removes them even further from such a theoretical category. In occidental societies human beings are no longer appropriable. All other physical manifestations capable of being detected, localized and identified are for the most part now the object of property.

Of these the two major classes are land and goods. We have, in the previous chapter, defined land. Let us repeat the definition. Land consists of any definite site, regarded as a portion of the earth's surface and extending in both vertical directions as defined by law; together with such natural resources as are conceded to it by law, while they remain *in situ* on, under or above the surface; and together with such "improvements" as are defined by law to be irremovable by the holder of any subordinate interest without the consent of the holder of the interest from which his is ultimately derived. The land as site consists of its spatial aspect only. The land as material is divided into two parts. It is, first, the store of natural resources in, under, or upon the surface. This includes growing things attached to the soil. Presumably it includes, as well, any material from time to time deposited upon the surface by the processes of nature. All these material resources are in fact removable from the land without altering it, in respect of its purely spatial aspect, as site. Therefore it must be obvious to anyone acquainted with modern agronomy that there is in fact no such attribute as is described in the old phrase "the inexhaustible resources of the soil." Such resources may be regenerated by nature or by man. But agriculture is at best a mining, as well as a manufacturing, operation, only peculiar in that it is conducted largely through an organic instrumentality. The land as material is, second, all artificial modifications in its above described material aspect, either in constitution or conformation, together with all additions, structures, and objects, produced by man and placed thereon which are, by legal definition, "part of the realty." As an object of property the term "land," then, defines a conglomerate legal artifact, consisting of a spatial element and a material element. The latter consists of identified manifestations of nature and works of man, located within that space and in certain respects legally attached thereto, which are commonly divided into its natural resources and its "improvements."

All other material objects capable of appropriation are, in the legal terminology we have adopted, called "goods." They are legally separate from the land though usually located thereon. Though they are referred to as tangible, they are certainly not always either tangible or visible. Perhaps they are almost always sensible; certainly they are always detectable as existing. The essential point is that they must be localized and identifiable in order to be capable of possession and thereby of becoming the objects of practically protectable rights.

We have then a definition of material objects. The definition is wide enough to include all the material and energic aspects of nature, even to electric currents, radio wave-lengths, etc.[15] This totality is then to be reduced to those material objects which, at any particular time and place, *may* be the objects of property. Here and now there is subtracted from the whole; first, all human beings; second, all so-called natural resources not yet appropriated; and, third, all other manifestations of nature which by reason of the practical impossibility of according to anyone protected possession thereof, are in that sense incapable of being made the objects of property.

Recognition of these present legal and practical limits upon the appropriability of the total class, material objects, leads us to remind ourselves that the definition of what objects may be subjected to private property has evolved gradually from primitive times, under the regulation of custom and law. The change has been complete.

In western Europe pre-property was primarily exercised over persons, the members of the *familia* including adopted members, clients and slaves. To this class were added, at a very early stage, domestic animals (cattle = chattels; *pecus* = *pecunia* = *peculium*; *vieh* = *feoh*) held to a considerable extent as a loan from the common or capital stock. Later, property in land appeared. It appears to have begun as a conversion, bit by bit, of political territory to economic use. Perhaps the individual house community acquired at first only a small plot, the site of the home, as its *alod*, and the waste remained political territory or common. When, in historical times in Rome, rights in the common, or *ager publicus*, began to be acquired by the *familiae*, the acquisition was at first in the form of *possessio*, or something less than *dominium*. Under the feudal system, all land having been acquired in *dominium*, all subordinate holdings came to be "held of" some superior title just as was at first the case with domestic animals. The products of materials obtained from animals and land and worked up by human labour—which, in the hand to mouth con-

[15] In the present viewpoint of physics it is impossible to discriminate between what was formerly called matter and what was called force.

dition of living, probably never existed at any particular moment in sufficient volume to make them of importance—came to be reserved or hoarded, if consumable, and erected or used, if durable, to an increasing extent. So long as production failed to exceed consumption it was natural that the agents of production, animals and land, loomed large, while the stock of products was almost insignificant. Once the accumulation got under way it grew until, in the end, such products came to constitute the largest element in the foundation of the property structure. When they had "arrived" the consumable products partook, as movables, of the legal nature of cattle (chattels), which are thus shown to be the prototype of economic capital in fact as well as in name. Finally, as persons were liberated from this form of control, the original object of property became generally inappropriable. Thus a complete revolution was accomplished and the property structure was wholly transferred from its original base—human beings—to these subsequent additions to the foundation.

2. *Quasi-material Objects—The Protected Processes*

There is, in addition to these two modern classes of material objects, land and goods, another class which we have called quasi-material objects. These are the protected processes which exist as objects of property entirely separate from the material objects with which they may deal. The physical matter upon which a process may operate and the process itself are two sharply distinguished legal facts. It is not possible to define, as a whole, the processes which are protected. For the first question, as to whether or not they can be protected, is a practical rather than a legal one and the second question, as to whether or not they may be protected, depends upon a constantly changing social policy. The nearest approximation to a general statement which can be made has already been given. Quasi-material objects may be defined as certain exclusive processes, capable of being appropriated and protected because, while immaterial, they are, in spite of that fact, capable of transfer; because they are special and not general, and therefore distinguishable and identifiable; and because they are processes which can persist independently of persons. When reduced to its essential element, the property in these protected processes becomes a composite of disembodied rights to do, disjoined from those rights associated together as part of the right to have, but in detail identical with certain of them. Analysed, the content of the right "to do," just as in the case of the right "to have," becomes a prohibition against others interfering with or imitating the doing—a prohibition rather than an authority. These rights to do are adjuncts to property in objects, for in practically all cases they require property in material objects for their exercise. But unlike property in material objects, they have no immediate or ultimate relation to a material object and they are by their nature separable from any particular set of material objects. Their only identification is with a process, to which objects may come and from which they may go.[16]

We shall tentatively define them all as property in protected processes. Some are granted, as rights to do, by statute. Some are organized by private persons and protected as rights to do by law. But all are identifiable to a particular process, are separable from property in material objects and do not inhere so indissolubly in the person that they are incapable of separation and transfer from person to person. Those other processes which are not identifiable (such as ideas); which are not separable from property in objects (such as going concern values), or which are incapable of separation from the person (such as occupation, business, profession, labour, personal financial standing, personal name, etc.), we shall have to exclude.

Some of these protected processes owe their legal status as objects of property wholly to legally created monopoly. Others are based on a temporary factual monopoly which the law merely recognizes. The latter kind of monopoly arises when a process is to some extent inimitable. Public service franchises, patents and copyrights belong in the former class exclusively, since the act of granting them involves their being made immediately inimitable. But goodwill, memberships in marketing organizations, etc., owe their monopolistic position not to grant but to the fact that they are relatively and temporarily inimitable except by false pretense.

In respect of its being a monopoly property in such quasi-material objects does not differ from that in material objects. All private property is a system of monopolies. One of the concurrent elements of possession which has been much emphasized in jurisprudence is the right of exclusion – a corollary of occupancy and use. This is of course the right to monopolize. The right to monopolize necessarily lies at the foundation of the institution of property. Thus the natural monopoly that exists in the relative inimitability of such processes as we have described as business individuality (goodwill)

16 "Property, even as distinguished from property in intellectual production, is not, in its modern sense, confined to that which may be touched by the hand, or seen by the eye. What is called 'tangible property' has come to be, in most great enterprises, but the embodiment, physically, of an underlying life – a life that, in its contribution to success, is immeasurably more effective than the mere physical embodiment. Such, for example, are properties built upon franchises, on grants of government, on good will, or on trade-names, and the like." Natl. Tel. News Co. v. Western Union T. Co., 119 Fed. 294, 299 (C. C. A. 7th, 1902).

and memberships, or that which is created by law in franchises, patents and copyrights, is not necessarily more obnoxious or less justifiable in its effects than those which exist *per se* in all other property, such, for instance, as the right to any or all particular stores of natural resources. The test by which to discriminate between normal and abnormal monopolies is not that between property in quasi-material objects specially permitted by statute, and all property in material objects—that is, according to the objects of the property. Rather it is entirely a question whether an artificial scarcity is created or, where competition cannot exist, whether advantage is being taken of the statutory monopoly to the injury of public welfare.

Some detailed examination of the protected processes is necessary in order to resolve the vague concepts into their elements and to learn which elements are in fact the real and only objects of property therein—to identify, in other words, the true quasi-material object. In each case we must note that the legal term is a name for the property and not, strictly speaking, for its quasi-material object. In fact we shall find considerable difficulty in determining exactly what is the process protected.

3. *Monopolies Created by Law*

Considering first the franchise, we will remember that it had its origin in the "freedom," or special privilege, granted by the lord to some other than the tenant, thus creating an incorporeal hereditament exercisable on certain land. Eventually the term was confined to the privileges granted by the sovereign, and the power to create them became vested solely in him. Upon this historical basis franchises are defined to be "special privileges conferred by government upon individuals, and which do not belong to the citizens of the country, generally, of common right."[17] "The right possessed must be . . . a privilege or immunity of a public nature, which cannot legally be exercised without legislative grant,"[18] and one, therefore, which "owes its existence to a grant, or, as at common law, to prescription, which presupposes a grant."[19]

"Corporations or bodies politic are the most usual franchises known to our law."[20] "To be a corporation is a franchise; the various powers conferred on corporations are franchises."[21] The

[17] Bank of Augusta v. Earle, 13 Pet. 519, 595 (U. S. 1839), and many others.
[18] State v. Minn. Thresher Mfg. Co., 40 Minn. 213, 225 (1889).
[19] Board of Trade of Chicago v. People, ex rel. Sturges, 91 Ill. 80, 82 (1878).
[20] Wilmington R. R. Co. v. Downward, 14 Atl. 720, 721 (Del. 1888).
[21] State of N. Y. v. Mayor and Aldermen of the City of N. Y., 3 Duer 119, 144 (N. Y. Super. Ct. 1854).

very "corporate capacity is a franchise."[22] But this charter, or corporate franchise, while for historical reasons it goes by the same name, is itself hardly to be included with the franchises which are protected processes. As a modern fact it is an authority to organize a "body politic" for specific purposes. The authority is granted to anyone upon prescribed terms, is not exclusive and therefore is not, as to itself alone, the object of property. This form is the only completely organized social unit which exists so far separately from its component members that it is legally in some respects independent of them and they in turn are in some respects relieved of responsibility for its acts. Thus it is essentially a political form though, as will be seen, the "specific purposes" for which it is organized, beginning as privileges and now become limitations, have, in relation to the state which grants them, come to be treated as if they were the objects of property rather than what they really are, a granting to a limited extent to a "body politic" of some of those personal rights which inhere as matter of constitutional liberty in every individual.[23]

This distinction between the two types of so-called franchise is made in law, but not usually with any degree of clarity. For instance: "There is a marked distinction between a franchise which is essential to the creation and continued existence of a corporation – a right to exist as an artificial being – a right conferred by the sovereignty of the state – and those rights subsidiary in their nature by which the corporation obtains privileges of more or less value,

[22] Central Pacific R. Co. v. People of State of Cal., 162 U. S. 91, 125 (1895).

[23] The term franchise is the direct descendant of that grant of the royal prerogative which in feudal times was the most important of the incorporeal hereditaments, being usually in fact a species of sub-government. But, with the changed political organization, its most important usage is now to cover a then nearly nonexistent type of economic group activity.

By far the commonest franchise is the purely formal one, granting a corporate charter. This, the direct descendant of the medieval, has retained the form of the body politic while transferring the field of its exercise to the economic sphere. It is created in this form upon the surviving, if obsolete, theory which the Germans call the "Concession Theory." Actually it does not assume a part of the prerogative of the state; it is not a body politic, but a body economic; it does not attain perpetual but only limited succession. It is merely one among many forms of group activity and group property and the only reason for its dominance is that it is convenient and open to all.

Since the British Act of 1862 that "Magna Charta of co-operative enterprise" as Palmer, *Company Law*, p. 1, calls it, and the later statutory grantings of charters in our various states, the "Concession Theory" is more honoured in the breach than it is in the observance. Nevertheless it has been the prevailing theory in Anglo-American law merely because the form was borrowed from another field where it was in fact a jurisdiction which was delegated by the state. To attach any meaning to the use of the word "franchise" in connection with a corporate charter only misleads us.

to the enjoyment of which corporate existence is not a prerequisite." [24] Or, "These are its [the corporation's] franchises. First, the franchise of existence as a corporation,—its life and being . . . But, with respect to the other franchises with which it is clothed . . . these it enjoys as an individual could . . . A franchise to be a corporation is distinct from a franchise, as a corporation, to maintain and operate a railroad." [25] The fact is that there are three different elements all called by the same name but of quite different character. There is first the right to corporate existence, to organize in this form a "body politic." This is now open to all citizens under statutory provisions and requirements. Second, there are the ordinary limited powers conferred by the charter. In so far as these are limited and merely part of the personal rights which all individuals enjoy, they constitute a discrimination against corporations, not special privileges to them. Finally there are the franchises, strictly so-called, and the only ones we include in the protected processes. These are the special privileges, "to the existence of which corporate existence is not a prerequisite" and which *do* grant powers and prerogatives not included in the personal liberties of every citizen.

These true franchises, whether granted to individuals or corporations, have a peculiar character of their own. In this sense the privilege of doing business as insurer is a franchise.[26] "Exemption from taxation being a special privilege granted by the government to an individual . . . is a franchise." [27] And again, "No one can exercise the right of eminent domain, or establish a highway or railway and charge tolls for the same, without a grant from the legislature. Such rights as inhere in the sovereign power can only be exercised by the individual or corporation by virtue of a grant from such sovereign power, and when the state grants such a right it is a franchise." [28] In other words these are not powers granted to corporations from among the personal rights inhering in every citizen. They are delegations of those powers reserved to the state or special immunities against the powers of the state. Originally the right to be a corporation, since it was conceived and largely used for the purpose of constituting subordinate bodies politic for purposes of self-government, was obviously of this class and conferred some element of the sovereign power upon the corporation. Even when first turned to economic or other uses it trailed along with it these political ele-

[24] State v. Topeka Water Co., 61 Kan. 547, 558 (1900).

[25] Central Trust Co. of N. Y. v. Western N. C. R. Co., 89 Fed. 24, 31 (C. C. W. D. N. C. 1898).

[26] People v. Loew, 19 Misc. 248, 250 (N. Y. Sup. Ct., 1896).

[27] State of N. J. v. Wright, 117 U. S. 648, 656 (1885).

[28] Lasher v. People, 183 Ill. 226, 233 (1899).

ments and was conceived as a form of self-government. But that situation can hardly be said to exist today.

Of true franchises it is held that "a franchise is a grant . . . conferring a special and usually a permanent right . . . and, when accepted, it becomes a contract and is irrevocable, unless the right to revoke is expressly reserved,"[29] so that "so long as the grantee [of a franchise] fulfills the conditions and performs the duties imposed upon him by the terms of the grant, he has a vested right, which cannot be taken away, or otherwise impaired by the government, any more than any other property."[30] As such, a franchise "cannot be transferred without the consent of the grantor."[31] The quasi-material object in the case of such franchises is difficult to define. It may at first sight seem to be the economic function of a public service, to the exclusive performance of which the right is granted. Yet this cannot be made to include immunity from taxation, etc. Its true nature can only be perceived when we come to examine it from the economic standpoint. Suffice it to say here that it is a process which in some essential respect would not be permitted to be performed without special legal sanction.

The word license has come to be used of certain minor privileges of the same order as franchises except that they never entail a grant of sovereign powers. Such licenses, differing from those of private grant but following the same lines, are special permissions to do what is otherwise prohibited. They extend over a wide field and cover a multitude of different processes. Usually the end in view is the enablement of regulation by the police power, rather than the establishment of a process not to be otherwise secured. The method of creation reduces itself to that of first abstracting from everyone a right generally enjoyed by all as a personal liberty or property right, and then regranting it subject to regulation and revocation for cause. It is thus a temporary and conditional minor franchise.

In certain respects such a specially permitted process is the object of property. Take, for example, a liquor license. "As between the state and the licensee no such [property] right does exist . . . But it does not follow that as to all the balance of the world the licensee has not a property right in the license."[32] "Where the statute recognizes the right of transfer [of a liquor license] . . . and where the right is a valuable right, capable of being surrendered and reduced to money . . . the license or right to do business becomes a valuable

[29] Trustees of Southampton v. Jessup, 162 N. Y. 122, 126 (1900).
[30] Cal. State Tel. Co. v. Alta Tel. Co., 22 Cal. 398, 423 (1863).
[31] Levy v. Reed, 69 Okl. 180, 183 (1918).
[32] Lane v. Hewgley, 155 S. W. 348, 350 (Tex. Civ. App. 1913).

'property right,' subject to barter and sale."[33] Because it is deprived of so many of the customary attributes of property, another court has difficulty with it. "The mere license represents a police regulation . . . [Since] it may be revoked without compensation, because it represents no vested right, it is not possible to regard it as property of itself . . . On the other hand . . . it . . . represents invested capital . . . (which) is property which the bankrupt is bound to assist in realizing for his creditors, so long as he can render practical aid thereto by merely giving his signature."[34]

The term "letters patent" was originally used of all such grants of special privilege as we have described above, and more particularly of those royal favours in the form of monopolies of special trades which have made the word monopoly a "red rag." The term is now reserved for the limited protection which is an outgrowth of these "monopolies," but which is now accorded exclusively to a published invention. It has no relation to the grants of sovereign powers. "A patent is a monopoly . . . the consideration for which is the disclosure by the patentee of something not then within the domain of public knowledge."[35] It is "a contract by which the government secures to the patentee the exclusive right to vend and use his invention for a few years, in consideration of the fact that he has perfected and described it, and has granted its use to the public forever after."[36] But it "is not a grant of a right to make, use or sell. It does not directly or indirectly imply any such right. It grants only the right to exclude others."[37] Thus a patent is "not a regulation of commerce, nor a license to sell the patented article, but a grant that no one else should manufacture or sell" it.[38] In other words it is negative like all other property. It is a fence not a field. The letters patent themselves are documentary evidence of property. They are "like a 'title deed,' a personal chattel," and a contract for the transfer of the patent right may require the delivery of the original letters patent.[39] But the process—the object of the property—is intangible. "A patent must be for a method detached from all physical existence whatever."[40] And it is an indivisible whole. "The monopoly . . . is one entire thing, and cannot be divided into parts, except as authorized by those laws. The patentee

[33] Degginger v. Seattle Brewing and Malting Co., 41 Wash. 385, 388 (1906).
[34] Fisher v. Cushman, 103 Fed. 860, 865 (C. C. A. 1st, 1900).
[35] Farmers' Mfg. Co. v. Spruks Mfg. Co., 119 Fed. 594, 596 (C. C. E. D. N. C. 1902).
[36] Nat'l Hollow B. B. Co. v. Interchangeable B. B. Co., 106 Fed. 693, 701 (C. C. A. 8th, 1901).
[37] Waterbury Buckle Co. v. G. E. Prentice Mfg. Co., 286 Fed. 358, 360 (C. C. A. 2nd, 1922).
[38] Minn. v. Barber, 136 U. S. 313, 327 (1890).
[39] Paine v. Parkhurst, 205 Fed. 740, 743 (C. C. A. 6th, 1913).
[40] Whitney v. Carter, Fed. Cas. No. 17,583 at 1071 (C. C. D. Ga. 1810).

or his assigns may, by instrument in writing, assign, grant, and convey, either (1st) the whole patent . . .; or (2d) an undivided part or share . . .; or (3d) the exclusive right under the patent within and throughout a specified part of the United States."[41] As we saw in the previous chapter, it is probably not subject to involuntary transfer. Here again the exact quasi-material object concerned is difficult to identify. A patent does not authorize the manufacture and sale of a product, or even the use of a process. It merely prohibits either to others than the patentee.

The property in the next protected process to be considered has a dual nature or, perhaps, a dual object. "'Copyright before publication' [the common law right of first publication] . . . is the exclusive privilege of first publishing any original material product of intellectual labor.'" "When once published . . . the right of an author or proprietor of literary work to multiply copies of it to the exclusion of others is the creature of statute ['copyright after publication']."[42] "'Play right' and copyright are quite distinct under the [old copyright] statute, in spite of the fact that printed publication will forfeit both, and that one statutory copyright will protect both. If so . . . [an author] was justified in reserving his common law play right from the original assignment to the . . . [publishers], and they could, by the necessary formalities on the printed play, create a statutory play right which they held in trust for him, and a statutory copyright which they held beneficially."[43] Gradually the field of copyright has been broadened until it now includes anything "evincing, in its make-up, that there has been underneath it, in some substantial way, the mind of a creator or originator."[44] "It is property capable of being assigned by the author at his pleasure," but "it cannot, like tangible property, be made the subject of seizure and sale on execution."[45] Thus, as in the previous cases, this property is not subject to involuntary transfer. When we come to determine the quasi-material object—the exact process involved—we are again in difficulties. It is commonly said that "a copyright gives to the owner the sole right to print, publish, and vend copies of a written composition."[46] But obviously this positive statement of the case is not correct since other legal agencies may deprive the author of the right to publish without deprivation of property. What is granted is strictly the common law right to prevent others from anticipating the publication by the author, and the statutory right to prevent others, for a certain term after his own

[41] Waterman v. Mackenzie, 138 U. S. 252, 255 (1890).
[42] Palmer v. De Witt, 47 N. Y. 532, 536, 537 (1872).
[43] Fitch v. Young, 230 Fed. 743, 744 (S. D. N. Y. 1916).
[44] Nat. Tel. News Co. v. W. U. Tel. Co., 119 Fed. 294, 297 (C. C. A. 7th, 1902).
[45] Werckmeister v. Springer L. Co., 63 Fed. 809, 810 (C. C. S. D. N. Y. 1894).
[46] Petition of Rider, 16 R. I. 271, 272 (1888).

publication, from publishing his work at all. Publication is the process of making public by any sensible means.

Between the copyright and property in goodwill, which we will examine next, and savouring of both, belong the trade-mark and the trade name.[47] In connection with these there are certain equitable rights arising by prescription which somewhat resemble common law copyright. There is also the statutory provision for registration and protection along the lines of patents and copyrights. On the other hand, in these cases, as in the case of goodwill, the thing itself is secondary to the prime intent which is the identification and preservation of business individuality. Trade-marks and trade names are means for preventing one economic process from utilizing the "acceptance" of another by using names or signs in a way which would be deceptive. The essence of the matter is the prohibition against "unfair competition"—against false pretence.

4. *Monopolies Recognized by Law*

The foregoing analyses prepare us for the fact that the legal definition of goodwill fails to put its finger on the fact. The favourite statement is that "good will is the advantage or benefit which is acquired by an establishment beyond the mere value of the . . . property employed therein, in consequence of the general public patronage and encouragement which it receives from constant or habitual customers, on account of its local position or common celebrity, or reputation for skill or affluence, or punctuality, or from other accidental circumstances or necessities, or even from ancient partialities or prejudices."[48] In short, "Good will is defined by Lord Eldon to be 'nothing more than the probability that the old customers will resort to the old place.'"[49] But the occasion for extending legal protection to this peculiar form of property arises almost exclusively when it is transferred. Under these circumstances it is construed to accord to the purchaser the privilege to hold "himself out to the public as succeeding to an enterprise;"[50] to continue an established

[47] The popular definition is that, "A 'trademark' is the name, symbol, figure, letter, form, or device, adopted and used by a manufacturer, or merchant, in order to designate the goods that he manufactures, or sells, and distinguish them from those manufactured or sold by another; to the end that they may be known in the market as his, and thus enable him to secure such profits as result from a reputation for superior skill, industry or enterprise (Upton, *Trademarks*, p. 9)." Moorman v. Hoge, Fed. Cas. No. 9,783, at 718 (C. C. D. Cal. 1871).

"A trade-name . . . is descriptive of the manufacturer or dealer himself." Cady v. Schultz, 19 R. I. 193, 195 (1895).

[48] Haverley v. Elliott, 39 Neb. 201, 204 (1894).

[49] Porter v. Gorman, 65 Ga. 11, 14 (1880).

[50] Knoedler v. Boussod, 47 Fed. 465, 466 (C. C. S. D. N. Y. 1891).

business under the old firm name;"[51] and to continue to enjoy all advantages "acquired by a firm in carrying on its business whether connected with premises or name or other matter."[52] To support this transfer and make it effective it is held that there is an implied covenant not to engage in the same business in the same locality,[53] nor "endeavor to draw off any of the customers,"[54] nor "to interfere with . . . the vendee . . . in his use of business house and control of the lease . . . and the exercise of the 'tenant right' [in respect to renewal of the lease]."[55]

Whatever the goodwill itself may be conceived to be it is clear that the property in it, which is usually called by the same name, is strictly limited by the extent of legal protection accorded it. Among the property rights in any going concern are rights protecting the owner against imitations of his name or attempts by others in many other ways to make use of his "acceptance." These rights are generally included together as rights against unfair competition, which is defined as "passing off or attempting to pass off upon the public the goods or business of one person as and for the goods or business of another."[56] The law permits the owner to sell the goodwill along with the tangible assets of a business; in other words, to effect a transfer of the whole going concern. It then enforces the agreement and compels the seller so to conduct himself that none of what he has sold will stick to his fingers. As part of his property there were included rights against unfair competition. These rights were against outsiders. When he sells these rights he simply puts himself outside the pale. Thereupon he becomes himself an "outsider," and these rights hold against him as well. This does not make of it, as Professor Commons seems to think it,[57] a sale of a part of the seller's liberty. He cannot sell his liberty, but only his property. The right to protection against unfair competition is a part of the property he has sold. A confusion of identity is more likely to arise between the old business of the seller and any new one he may establish, than between the old one and that of anyone else. If such confusion occurs because the seller so acts that any of the identity of the old business adheres to him, he is, in effect, converting such identity to his own use and abstracting it from the business he has

[51] Matter of Ulrici's Est., 111 Misc. 55, 59 (N. Y. Surr. Ct. 1920).

[52] Farwell v. Huling, 132 Ill. 112, 119 (1889).

[53] French v. Parker, 16 R. I. 219, 222 (1888), Dwight v. Hamilton, 113 Mass. 175 (1873), Angier v. Webber, 96 Mass. 211 (1867).

[54] Merchants' Ad-Sign Co. v. Sterling, 124 Cal. 429, 432 (1899).

[55] Fine v. Lawless, 139 Tenn. 160, 169, 172 (1917).

[56] Westminster Laundry Co. v. Hesse Envelope Co., 174 Mo. App. 238, 242 (1913).

[57] *Legal Foundations of Capitalism*, p. 264.

sold. So the courts must be stricter, in cases of the sale of goodwill, in construing the doctrine of "unfair competition" against the seller than they need to be against other competitors. The entity protected is not strictly the goodwill. That cannot be protected. It is the identity, the individuality. In other words, legally, goodwill is the *persona*, or personality, of a business. It is that which is injured by any infringement on its exclusive identity – by "unfair competition." So far as a purely legal analysis is capable of arriving at the nature of the quasi-material object in this case, it is this individuality.[58]

In the case of memberships in marketing organizations identification of the property and the object is even more difficult. A typical decision has stated that "the membership [in the New York Stock Exchange] is personal to the member, but the inchoate right of sale, if it may be so termed, and the right to the proceeds of the sale, if the Stock Exchange authorities shall permit a sale to be had, is a 'property right' and a valuable one."[59] Here the court is defining as the property that which, in connection with it, can be secured by involuntary transfer. In reality that is the proceeds of sale of the property, not the property itself. The property itself would be differently defined if the right of eminent domain were exercised against it, and, perhaps, in still another way if legal questions arose as to the rights of a member against fellow members, or against the organization as a whole. For the present we can best define the quasi-material object here involved as a participation in an economic process carried on by an exclusive but collective and formal organization of a definite type.

Summing up the general class of quasi-material objects, we find the following: –

[58] "Despite the almost universal recognition at the present day of good-will as in the nature of property, the law on this subject is of comparatively recent growth. The cases greatly confound the thing itself with the means of transferring it, and with the rights an assignee acquires in order to effect that transfer. . . As civilization became more complex, the realization was forced upon the courts that the right to carry on an established business, and to represent that it is the old business that is carried on, is often a thing of value, since men were willing to pay for the privilege and contended for it at the forum, and therefore the courts have, by evolutionary processes, so adjusted themselves to conditions as to treat such privileges, even where not connected with real estate, as in the nature of assets. The trend of authority is that they will be so regarded and protected, not only where they are made the subject of express contract in connection with the voluntary sale or the bequest of a business . . . but . . . in cases of compulsory sales. . . Some of the cases seem to treat good-will as property, while in other cases courts have attained the result by the exercise of control over the assignor. . . We regard it as clear, however, that good-will is not in and of itself property, but that it is an incident that may attach to, or, in some cases, be connected with it." Hart v. Smith, 159 Ind. 182, 185, 186 (1902).

[59] Wrede v. Gilley, 132 App. Div. 293, 295 (N. Y. 1st Dept. 1909).

Property created by statutory grant or authority
- Franchises
- Licenses
- Patents
- Copyrights, statutory
- Trade-marks, registered
- Trade names, special, registered

Property created by common law right
- Copyrights, common law

Property created by equitable right
- Trade-marks, not registered
- Trade names, special, not registered

Property created principally by contract
- Goodwill
- Memberships in exchanges

5. *Rights with no Separable Object*

Other rights have been improperly included in that class of property which we are calling property in protected processes, and which represent no interest in material objects but rather rights over quasi-material objects. We have already excluded from this class the right to be and the rights to do, conferred upon a corporation, which latter represent no more than an attribution of part of the personal rights running to every individual citizen.

Going concern value is often treated as an object by itself in which some sort of property exists. "It is not the value of the franchise and it is not the good will." [60] Sometimes it is said to be the "added value of the plant as a whole over the sum of the values of the component parts, which is attached to it because it is in active and successful operation and earning a return." [61] But this is not satisfactory. Here it is neither itself an exact idea nor is it distinct from goodwill. The following begins to approach the essence of the matter. Going concern value is "an element of value in an assembled and established plant, doing business and earning money, over one not thus advanced." [62] The correct statement is that "it is an allowance for losses during the lean years while business is being developed and the corporation was not receiving a fair return." [63]

[60] Appleton Water Works Co. v. Railroad Comm. of Wis., 154 Wis. 121, 146 (1913).

[61] People ex rel. Kings Co. Lighting Co. v. Willcox, 156 App. Div. 603, 607 (N. Y. 1st Dept., 1913).

[62] City of Huntington v. Public Service Comm., 101 W. Va. 378, 385 (1926).

[63] People ex rel. Adirondack Power and Light Corp. v. Pub. Serv. Comm., 200 App. Div. 268, 275 (N. Y. 3rd Dept., 1922).

This should include overhead charges allowed for promotion, organization, and development expenses,[64] and "the investment necessary to organizing and establishing the business which is not embraced in the value of its actual physical property."[65] A good analysis of the items composing such going concern value includes "loss of interest while the plant is in course of construction and is building up a paying business . . . and the loss while pipe lines are extended to await the coming of consumers as the city extends . . . the cost of securing and retaining customers, of encouraging the greater use of gas for fuel and for light by the introduction of new and improved appliances, the necessary loss attending experiments . . . the obsolescence of plant apart from that ordinary calculable depreciation . . . the expense that must attend and the additional value that arises from the uniting of separate concerns . . . with a view to economical production, and the cost of procuring capital for the original works or subsequent extensions."[66]

Going concern value, as thus defined, is doubtless an element of value, or a way of arriving at a certain surplus value in addition to physical values, which it is necessary and just to consider when the business is a public utility with rates fixed by order of a commission rather than by competition, and when the purpose is to determine its value for condemnation or as a basis for future rate making. But in the case of all other kinds of business concerns, and in the case of these when the market is valuing their securities or when the concern as a whole is to be bought by private interests, such going concern value does not exist except as an element of franchise value or goodwill. For it is not the expenses incurred in building up the business but only the present and prospective earnings—which may, it is true, be the result, in part, of such outlays—that are then taken into consideration in fixing a valuation of intangibles. Thus we confine our quasi-material objects of this general order to franchises and goodwill, two forms for which some degree of specially protected privilege or immunity exists and which together include all the elements actually recognized in general as constituting going concern value.

The right to public office, which as we have seen is sometimes, for historical reasons, claimed to be property, is today not different from any other arrangement for employment. It is a loose form of wholly executory contract which, as fast as it is performed by either party, becomes a credit-debt; which is not to be interfered with by

[64] Des Moines Gas Co. v. City of Des Moines, 238 U. S. 153, 166, 167 (1914).

[65] Kings Co. Lighting Co. v. Lewis, 180 N. Y. S. 570, 578 (N. Y. Sup. Ct. 1920).

[66] Public Service Gas Co. v. Bd. of Pub. Ut. Comm., 84 N. J. L. 463, 476, 477 (Sup. Ct. 1913).

third parties; but which is subject to alteration or cancellation by either party under certain terms and conditions.

It is doubtful if there is ever any right savouring of property either in services or in the opportunity to serve—that is, in either side of the relation of employment. Rights to the performance of services have come to be nullified by the elimination of property in persons and of action against the person, except as they can be enforced in the form of an equivalent in rights to objects (damages). Services are no longer susceptible of compulsion. The result is that the damages for non-performance have come in reality to be the only true object of any property which may exist in such cases, and only where there is a body of assets upon which such damages may be incident is property involved at all. The assets must be some interests in objects capable of involuntary transfer. It is true that the worker sells his services; that is, the effect of his work. It is construed at law that he has sold these effects on the basis of an agreement of employment. But since the law has exempted him from any form of compulsory performance he is only liable to damages for non-performance. And damages are only collectible against property, not against the person. Thus the customer or employer of persons selling their services who have no adequate body of property in which a resulting credit-debt might create an interest, have ceased to commit themselves on their side to what would be, for this reason, a unilateral liability. Now, therefore, the sale of labour, the contract of employment, is merely an arrangement as to the terms of an exchange which is construed to take place *pari passu* with performance. For this reason, it is clear that the worker's only property as a result of his labour arises in the form of unpaid wages, salaries, or fees for services *already* rendered. As to the future he has liberties but no property.

It is true that, as one passes from one extreme, where the buyer of the services is wholly an intermediary or employer, to the other, where the buyer is wholly a customer, one finds a gradually increasing degree of personal "acceptance" in the relation. Coincidently there appears an element of goodwill which leads us to differentiate and describe these more direct sales of services as businesses, professions, or occupations. In so far as the element of goodwill enters the personal service occupations it is of the same order as that accruing to a more complex and less personal organization. And the protection accorded this personal goodwill is upon the same lines. But strictly personal goodwill is difficult to transfer. Therefore the question of protecting its purchaser does not often arise. Special personal faculties and skills are by their nature inalienable and cannot be construed to be processes separable from the person. Personal financial standing and personal name, while certainly entitled to protection, are also very obviously inseparable from the person. Therefore they are not property. Occasionally one finds that certain rights of protection which can be accorded to such personal peculiarities, as well as the general rights to contract, to buy and sell services, etc., are spoken of as if they were property. But all these are properly defined as personal rights, not as property.

D. *Aggregates of Property Rights*

1. *The Nature of Interests*

With the modern analysis of property into its elements the *rôle* of the term "property right" has become atomic. Whereas one formerly spoke of the right of "ownership," one now conceives of any property relation as an aggregate of innumerable particular rights, each representing some particular provision of the law. For such a molecular aggregate we have been using the customary term, "interest." The substance of each interest is a highly complex mass of component rights (claims, privileges, powers and immunities). The assortments of individual rights composing the various property interests differ widely in form at one time and place (jurisdiction), and both these forms and the multitude of individual rights composing them, though they may go by the same name, differ widely in different places (jurisdictions) and at different times. Nevertheless there are a large number of more or less standardized types of aggregate which we shall undertake to list and classify as we proceed. The law seems to have lost sight of the continuing simplicity in this complexity. It imputes too much a totally different substance to the various different present types of interest. It is apt to treat each type, or at least each class, as if it were elemental. Through the failure to break down complete property into its integral component rights and then to rebuild the variety of more or less standardized interests, as if they were composed of different assortments of these rights and summed up to totality, it has missed an opportunity to secure a relatively simple system of classification and relationships. It needs a chemistry of property forms. Some of the bases for such a chemistry are suggested in these pages. But at this point we are concerned only with the nature of the integration of interests. The one universal characteristic of all of them is that they are compounds of property rights, so polarized that each has a single point of incidence and a single point of inherence, and so consolidated as to behave as a unit. That is to say, all are specific in their incidence upon material objects or upon the body of property which relates them to indeterminate objects. And all are specific as to the body of property of which they compose a part, though not necessarily so as to the so-called person of inherence. Therefore we must always think of an interest as a bipolarized relation.

The general type of definition of "interest" customary in the law is shown in the following examples. The term "includes any right, title or estate in, or lien upon, real estate,"[67] and "both legal and equitable rights."[68] "In fact, the word seems to be one of extreme elasticity, which may be used to include nearly everything legally connecting the claimant with the subject-matter."[69] This terminology is extremely vague. But the idea is there. In business "interest" is a term connoting capacity for quantitative measurement. We speak of a man having a large or small interest, of men's respective interests, etc. In other words the term "interest" suggests the idea of a "share." In law, however, its proper meaning is wholly qualitative. The interest is viewed in the aspect of its variety, its composition, its relation to other interests, but as if each of the forms were individual, disparate and incommensurable.

Elsewhere we have traced the process by which, in Roman and in Germanic law, the words *res* and *thing* (or *Ding*), commencing as a case or claim, have in strict legal terminology come to be concreted and to stand for the material object of property itself. When, in this terminology, or in the medieval and modern reading of it, the *res* or "thing" became wholly concrete it was necessary to find another term to replace the original sense. That term is the term "right." And, because the classic Romans, for other reasons, used their word *ius* to represent the incorporeal *res*, we have come to impute to *ius* the sense of "a right."[70] What the early Roman or English citizen originally claimed was only of course in all cases his "right." He called it a *res* or "thing" because the lawyers called it a "thing." And they called it a "thing" because they were thinking of it as his claim, his case, or, as we say, his reason for action.

In the meantime there subsisted, alongside the developing legal usage, in at least the English case, the original usage which was equivalent to the then idea of a right of property—a notion still molecular and not reduced to atomic proportions. Therefore we have today this alternative to the word "interest." We have adopted this popular usage and are using the word 'thing' not to represent the material object of a bundle of rights, but rather the aggregate

[67] Ormsby v. Ottman, 85 Fed. 492, 497 (C. C. 8th, 1898).
[68] Gibb v. Phila. Fire Ins. Co., 59 Minn. 267, 273 (1894).
[69] Church v. Young, 130 N. C. 8, 13 (1902).
[70] In Bracton's Medieval Latin, the word for a right is *rectus* not *ius*.

into which that bundle is assembled—the property which is represented by a bond, a share of stock, a lease, a mortgage, etc. Each of these is a 'thing' having reference to specific or indeterminate material objects, and all are composed of complex bundles of legal rights in various assortments. These 'things' are not themselves rights, for the individual rights included in them may be independently altered, improved, impaired or even rescinded. Nevertheless the 'thing' remains, changing its character, it is true, as the attached rights are modified, but not changing its identity.

A 'thing,' then, is any "piece of property"—an *interest.* Let us recognize that property law is not concerned with, and men are for the most part not dealing in, material objects. What is dealt with both in law and in economic life is one and the same. It is such 'things.' It is these 'things' which are bought and sold, treasured, protected, fought over. It is these 'things' which are measured against themselves in exchange and which give rise to the notion of economic value. The law hardly needs a term for material objects—the objects of rights. What it needs are terms for these immaterial 'things,' these bundles of rights, these pieces of property, these *interests.*

The term "estate" covers a certain limited group of legal or equitable interests in land which are or may become possessory of the whole or a part, together with their analogues among the beneficial interests in trust funds of personal property, which are almost never possessory.[71] It has been said that the definition of a particular estate is a quantitative one. But this is only true in a fanciful legal sense. Included in the definition of any estate may be two wholly temporal or quantitative elements. One is the duration of the possessory attribute, if present. The other, if the estate is non-possessory, is the period prior to its extinction as such, when it may be converted into some other estate in the same object, possessory or even still non-possessory. These periods may be certain or uncertain. But essentially the individual estate is qualitatively, more than it is quantitatively, determined. All come within the class defined above as interests. The sense of relation to those of whom the rights are held, the idea of status, has largely disappeared, though the structure is still erected upon this plan, so that estates are formally almost wholly dependent and derivative with reference to a single source in the case of each site or other body of property.

[71] As to the doctrine of estates in connection with personal chattels see Gray on *Perpetuities*, App. F.; D. T. Oliver, "Interests for Life and Quasi-remainders in Chattels Personal," 24 *Law Quarterly Review* (1908) p. 431; Williams, *Personal Property*, p. 438; Schouler, *Personal Property*, Pt. I, Ch. 7.

2. *Interests with Regard to Specific Objects*

We have previously analysed the objects which can be or are subject to appropriation; that is, which are practically and legally capable of being specified as parts of the foundation of the structure of relations which is called property. The first and indispensable stratum of interests immediately adjacent to the foundation of objects contains all those which have any of the attributes contained in the legal concept of possession. All property is built upon this foundation of objects. But only certain property interests – including, however, all those containing any of the attributes of possession – relate to specific individual objects. These certain interests we have called interests with regard to specific objects. But we may also and more conveniently call them *direct* interests in objects, because they are immediate with regard to the objects. In order to be direct, they must, in some one respect at least, contain rights which are part of the fence of prohibitions with reference to some specific object. All other interests are what we have called interests in indeterminate objects, or interests in bodies of property as a whole.

In the theory of law the term "interest" has been reserved for these direct interests with regard to specific objects. None of what we have classed as interests in indeterminate objects have been conceded in theory to be interests at all. As an example of the best statement of this limited application of the term "interest" we give a résumé of the description in the *Restatement of the Law of Property*. Therein it is stated, the word "interest" is used "generically to include varying aggregates of rights, privileges, powers and immunities and distributively to mean any one of them."[72] To which we must add, of course, that these rights, etc., must pertain to a specific object.

An interest is there stated to be *in* an object when it includes rights against persons in general to be not interfered with in respect to the object, or rights not fundamentally changed by a change in the person of the owner of the present possessory estate.[73] The latter is, I think, a questionable statement of the non-possessory interest *in*.

An interest *with regard to* an object (a wider term including interests *in*) is one existing only in a particular person but not complying with the definition of interests *in* the object. The precise line distinguishing interests *in* from the rest cannot be categorically defined.[74]

"If the interests [rights] in question are numerous and if they are

[72] P. 16.
[73] Ibid., p. 17.
[74] Ibid., pp. 17 and 19.

conventionally grouped under a single term, the person who has these interests is . . . the 'owner' of them."[75] That is, he is the owner of the interest, not of the object. But in the *Restatement of the Law of Trusts*[76] this is qualified. Therein it is stated that such holder is only an "owner" when the interest is vested in him "for his own benefit." With this qualification a trustee is not an owner. Neither is, strictly speaking, a corporation.

"These interests . . . in their totality constitute the complete property. . . A person who has complete property . . . may create in another person various rights. . . By so doing, he correspondingly diminishes the totality of his own interests [rights]." So too, when the original interest is less than totality it can be diminished. "A person who owns . . . an estate for years may part with some of the interests [rights]that compose" it. Just when such diminution of a total or partial interest causes the owner of what remains to cease to be classed as an "owner" "is not a matter upon which a precise rule can be laid down."[77]

3. *The Varieties of Direct Interests*

The characteristics of these direct interests in objects can best be grasped by arranging them successively according to the four attributes – kind of object, physical relation to the object, relation to the attributes of possession, and duration.

Classified according to the kind of object, they may be divided into interests with regard to land, interests with regard to goods and interests with regard to quasi-material objects. If we could confine the term "realty" to those objects included under our definition of land, it would be useful to be able to refer to all interests with regard to land as "real property." But, though the tendency in the law seems to be to do just this, it is still for historical reasons deterred from such consistency. At least we may say that all interests with regard to goods are personal property. So are the interests with regard to quasi-material objects. In examining these latter objects

[75] Ibid., p. 22.

[76] P. 16.

[77] *Restatement of the Law of Property*, pp. 19-23. It will be noted that in certain of these statements no distinction is made between the interest and its component rights. The concern with the question "when is an owner not an owner" is of great technical importance, for it largely determines the inherence of the various rights to possessory actions with reference to the object. We will discuss the use of the term at a later point. But it may be noted here that for our purposes we can better substitute the term "holder" in connection with all interests indiscriminately. Wherever it is more convenient we use the word 'thing' to denote a property interest of any kind.

themselves we have necessarily considered the nature of the property in them as well, since the two are difficult to distinguish. And since it is customary to denote them by the names of the property and not by the names which might be given to the objects or processes, it is not necessary to repeat or revise our previous analysis at this point.

Classified according to the physical relation to the object we have interests in:

Object and Physical Relation	*Interest*
Material Objects	
Land	
Occupancy, or complete *de facto* possession	All present possessory estates and leaseholds (including inchoate)
Uses, or partial *de facto* possessions (spatial or material)	Easements, profits, etc. Mineral, oil and timber leases, etc.
Goods	
De facto possession	Possession ("ownership") Bailments (bailee's)
Quasi-Material Objects	Possession ("ownership")

Classified according to the relation to the various other attributes of *de jure* possession (the right of possession) the direct interests with regard to land and goods appear as follows: –

Attributes of Possession	*Interest*
Land	
Possession *de jure*, present	Freehold estates
Possession *de jure*, future or conditional	All other estates, including mortgages and judgments *in rem*, which may become possessory *de jure* [78]
Uses, spatial or material. Actually partial possessions	Easements, profits, etc.
Derivative possession – exclusive only against others than the holder of rights of *de jure* possession	Leaseholds *in nomine alieno*, etc. Equitable estates with occupancy

[78] Even a contingent interest, since it may become possessory, is entitled to certain of the rights of *de jure* possession. "The owner of a contingent interest may protect that interest against deterioration or destruction by enjoining a threatened waste." Pavkovich v. So. Pac. R. R. Co., 150 Cal. 39, 50 (1906).

Attributes of Possession	*Interest*
Land (*cont.*)	
Derivative partial possessions or uses, also exclusive only against others than the holders of rights of *de jure* possession	Mineral, oil and timber leases, etc.
Non-possessory charges	Statutory and equitable liens upon specific land
Goods	
Possession *de jure*, present	"Ownership," so-called
Possession *de jure*, future or conditional	Other interests, such as judgments *in rem*, which may become possessory, including certain beneficial relations created on the analogy of estates in land
Derivative possession	Conditional sales Equitable interests with possession
Special property (Detention, etc.; also varieties of derivative possession)	Bailments, including pledges [79]
Non-possessory charges	Chattel mortgages Statutory and equitable liens upon specific goods

The final classification is according to duration.

Duration	*In Complete Land*	*In Spatial or Material parts of Land*	*In Goods*
Perpetual			
(Potentially) [80]	Estates in fee simple	Easements Profits [81]	Possession *de jure* ("ownership")
Temporary			
Terminated			
By uncertain event	Estates in fee tail Estates for life		

[79] The bailment for hire seems to give possessory rights against even the holder of the "right of possession," which may lift them from this class and place them upon a basis similar to a leasehold of land, *in nomine alieno*. For instance it was said, in Internat'l. Postal Supply Co. v. Bruce, 194 U. S. 601, 606 (1903), "In the case at bar the United States is not the owner of the machines, it is true, but it is a lessee in possession, for a term which has not expired. It has a property – a right 'in rem' – in the machines, which, though less extensive than absolute ownership, has the same incident of a right to use them while it lasts."

[80] Judgments *in rem* are in effect identified (though not in name or form) with the perpetual interest to which they give a new and original title.

[81] Profits include mineral rights, oil rights, timber rights, etc., which are perpetual or for the life of the supply. Sometimes these are erroneously called leases.

Duration	*In Complete Land*	*In Spatial or Material parts of Land*	*In Goods*
Temporary (*cont.*)			
Terminated (*cont.*)			
At time certain	Leaseholds for term	Mineral, oil- and timber leases	Bailments for hire for term
At will	Lesser leaseholds	Licenses	Most bailments for carriage, safe-keeping, etc.
By condition subsequent	Mortgages Liens upon specific land Vested remainders, if upon condition subsequent		Conditional purchase on condition subsequent Chattel mortgage Pledge (bailment) Liens upon specific goods
By failure of contingency	Contingent interests		
Converted			
By uncertain event	Reversions and vested remainders [82]		
By condition precedent	All conditional interests and mortgages		Chattel mortgage Pledge (bailment) Conditional purchase on condition precedent
By occurrence of contingency	Contingent interests		

4. *Interests with Regard to Indeterminate Objects*

In the course of the survey of modern legal theory and of modern legal practice we have concluded, both in the case of the trust of personal property and in that of credit-debt, that the property interests which exist in these cases are in reality in the nature of interests in indeterminate objects, or, in other words, interests in an aliquot part of the body of property of the trust fund or of the debtor

[82] A reversion is of course merely the fee simple during the time a derivative fee tail or life estate is possessory.

respectively. They are not so considered in legal theory nor even in the statements of legal practice. But this is the way they seem actually to work out. We are now prepared to analyse these putative interests more closely. Let us begin with the interests of the creditor in the aggregate of 'things'—the body of property—of the debtor.

We have found that the true credit-debt behaves as if it arose from the surrender of specific 'things' by the creditor to the debtor which thereupon become merged in the generality of 'things' in the debtor's total property, and that the creditor's rights thereto are then converted into a claim to an equivalent in value—a floating charge against this total of property. The ultimate incidence was proved to be upon specific objects or other 'things,' but we construed the incidence in the meantime as being upon objects or 'things' as yet indeterminate. If the debtor's body of property consists of interests of the class examined in the previous section (i. e. direct interests in objects) then the ultimate incidence of the creditor's interests may be conceived to be upon an aliquot part of these objects. But if, on the contrary, a part of his property consists of credits against some other debtor in turn, then the incidence of the interest of the first creditor may be, not upon objects but upon these other interests ('things'). In this way we see that the relation of the creditor's interest to objects is not only indeterminate but that even its indirect relation to objects may only be through one or many successive credit-debt relations. In place, then, of the phrase "interest in indeterminate objects or 'things,'" it is more convenient and more exact to speak of *indirect*, as opposed to *direct*, interests in objects.

The case of trusts of personal property seems somewhat similar. Here we find that, frequently, the interest of the beneficiary cannot be defined as a fraction of complete property in specific objects. For the trust fund does not usually consist of direct interests in objects at all; or, when it contains them, these interests may form a constantly changing mass upon which, only as a whole, the interest of the beneficiary rests. More often the immediate incidence is not even upon such indeterminate objects, but upon the indeterminate 'things' which compose the trust fund. The relation to objects is again better described as indirect.

There are other cases, which we have hardly touched upon hitherto, which share these characteristics of indeterminate incidence and of immediate incidence upon a mass of 'things' (interests) rather than upon specific objects themselves. These are of the nature of undivided property. In describing the English estates in land we found that one of the possible qualifications upon all of them had to do with the number and connections of the tenants. Joint tenants hold undivided the entire estate. The interest is not in shares, nor is the object of the estate divided in any respect. Each is interested in the whole. It is a crude idea. Several tenants stand together on precisely the same basis as would one alone. The second and third forms are coparcenary and tenancy in common. Here, in different respects, the interest of each is a share in the whole, but the whole is undivided. Now these methods of collective property are outgrowths from the various forms of Roman condominion, in which the undivided property in an object, or in a congeries of objects, was conceived to run to a group as a whole. The notion of definite shares pertained only to certain aspects of the rights and benefits accruing. It is clear that in none of these cases is the incidence or the interest of any individual exactly determinate. For, if it were so, it would be divided and not undivided, or shared, property. Such devices of joint or common property can be and are applied to the holding of other 'things' besides direct interests in objects. Where they are so used the incidence is still more indeterminate as to the ultimate object.

Along similar lines, and perhaps from the same source in the Roman *familia*, there has developed a still more elaborate system represented by the form of collective property known in Rome as *societas* and to us as "partnership." The property of the partnership is the property of the partners collectively but not individually. The interest of each partner is in a share of the undivided whole, not in a particular part. Thus the partners' interests are indeterminate in their incidence upon the 'things', constituting the whole and these 'things' in turn may quite as well consist of other indirect interests in indeterminate objects as of direct interests in specific objects.

In England, France and Germany there remain vestiges of the forms which collective property took in its evolution from the partnership to the corporation, before finally the corporate charter became free to all upon registration instead of only to be secured by legislative enactment. But these transitional forms are but adumbrations of the end-product and hardly appear in the United States. In the case of the fully evolved form—the corporation with paid up capital and limited liability—the property of the corporation is conceived to be entirely separate from the property of its stockholders and *vice versa*. The interest of the stockholder in the corporation is a legal anomaly. But again it is some sort of interest in a share of an undivided whole, not in a particular part. Therefore the incidence of this interest is upon an aliquot part of a mass of 'things.' The particular 'things' in which it is an interest are indeterminate, not specific, and these 'things' may either be direct interests in objects or they may be indirect interests in objects *via* some other body of property in turn.

In the case of both partnership and corporation the contributions made by partners or stockholders toward the formation of the collective body of property are made severally. Just as usually between the creditor and the debtor, the interest is acquired by the surrender of specific 'things.' But, once contributed, these 'things' become merged and amalgamated in the property of the partnership or corporation and the partner's or stockholder's rights are thereupon converted into a floating interest in the whole, in certain respects analogous to that of the creditor.

As a result of this preliminary analysis we are left somewhat dissatisfied with our discrimination. It is clear that certain property interests have regard to specific objects and may, therefore, be called direct interests with regard to objects. But in the course of the analysis of the class which we have opposed to this one—the class to which we have tentatively given the name "indirect interests with regard to objects," or "interests with regard to indeterminate objects"—we discover that, in all the various forms, these interests may be incident upon a mass composed of 'things' like themselves, so that even when they come to be extinguished their incidence may not be upon specific objects. Even then they may be converted into other similar interests still indeterminate as to the material objects to which they relate. Thus the ultimate material object recedes into the distance, and the interest may be so indirect as to any object that it never becomes specific. Nevertheless all such interests have a very definite specificity. This specificity exists as to the mass of 'things,' or body of property, upon which they are incident. The perception that the sole present specificity of these indeterminate or indirect interests is upon a determinate mass, leads us naturally to the examination of the next grouping in the series—the aggregation of property interests (themselves aggregates of rights) into bodies of property.

CHAPTER VII

THE SUBSTANCE AND STRUCTURE OF MODERN PROPERTY – [*Continued*]

A. *Aggregates of Property Interests*

1. *Development of the Ideas of Aggregates and of Offices*

In order adequately to come at the true nature of that aggregate of property interests to which we have hitherto given the name "body of property," and in order, at the same time, to discover the true centre in which property is in practice conceived to inhere, it is necessary for us to review and to reinterpret some of the ground over which we have travelled.

At the beginning of our research we found two relata, a chief and a congeries of subject persons and objects. Between these relata existed a system of relations which we called pre-property. At some stage it became possible for these relations to extend from one chief to another and thence, in some degree, to the persons or objects within the sphere of that other. Thus the chief was the focus or medium upon which all internal relations of this type converged and through which all such external relations were maintained. In the differentiated form of this prototype which we term political organization, these functional concepts were retained and elaborated. The ruler of the state occupied an office. "His" people constituted a body politic of ever-changing individuals and occupied a land as *his* and *their* territory. To the collectivity of changing persons upon the land there was connected a rulership which personalized the whole, though it was separate from it.

In the field of property the development was more diverse. The continuing stem of the flowing, branching community of persons came to be called the *corpus*, of which the house head was the *caput*. Because of its dual composition the concept of *corpus* had a dual evolution. Consisting originally principally of persons, it gave rise to that notion of collectivity which was distinguished as the *universitas personarum*, and thence became the source of the term for the body of persons which formed themselves into an artificial aggregate upon the model of the original and natural *familia*–

whence our corporation. But since, in the course of time, persons came more and more to be excluded from the status of objects of property, the remaining elements of the *familia* – land and goods – became differentiated as a *corpus* of another order, distinguished as the *universitas rerum.* Then, with the development of the fact, if not the theory, of non-possessory interests, there was incorporated in this *universitas* not only interests in objects in possession which seemed naïvely to be located within the strict circle of the classificatory genitive – the *res corporales* – but interests in the totality of objects possessed by others and actually located within other familial circles – the *res incorporales.* Finally, in the later terminology, we find included in the *universitas bonorum* not only all positive interests inhering therein, whether possessory or not – the *bona activa* – but also all negative interests incident upon such a *universitas* – the *bona passiva.* In these two steps we see the body of property changing from a congeries of objects to a congeries of interests in objects and thence to a collectivity which is so abstracted from either persons or objects that it itself can be conceived to have both plus and minus relations. But even the late Roman thought never quite succeeded in freeing this concept from that of personality. The *universitas bonorum* could not be seen to be *nothing but* an aggregate of 'things.'

Another and partially inconsistent conceptual development paralleled this one. More and more the position of the head – the headship, called *patrimonium* when occupied and *hereditas* when presumptive – came to be treated as something apart from, and investing but not identical with, the incumbent himself. Thus *caput* acquired the connotation of an office in the proprietary as it did in the political field. But always it described the attributes of the office rather than the office itself. As these attributes became conventionalized and derogated to a matter of general status, the term and notion of *persona* seems to have taken the place of the original *caput* and we have the beginnings of the idea of legal personality. In the *persona* rights inhered and upon the *persona* rights *in personam* were incident. But this concept also became divided, just as had the notion of *corpus.* One form of the notion suffered the same fate as had *caput.* It became generalized until it gave rise to the modern system of general legal capacities and liabilities involved in our Law of Persons.[1]

[1] The derogation that this concept suffered under is evidenced by the following, otherwise discerning, modern statement of its nature. "The word 'persona,' in its primitive sense, was applied to the masks worn by the actors in the dramatic performances of Rome and Greece, which masks were made to represent the character which the actor performed; and . . . in the same sense, it was subsequently employed in jurisprudence to signify the rôle or status which a man fills in the social organization. Thus the same man may, at different times, and even at the same time, represent different persons or rôles; as, in his youth he represents the person of a

On the other hand the other part of the notion of legal personality still retained its original content as the centre of inherence of the rights appertaining to a body of property, a sort of headship or office. The continuity and independence of this centre continued to be attributed to a *persona*. Then, as we have pointed out in a previous chapter, this intellectual implement proved insufficient to meet two difficulties and, in its original form, it tended to disappear. The first difficulty, which arose with the growing complexities of property, was that of multiple personality. In order adequately to segregate the numerous proprietary relationships to independent bodies of property which were possible to a single individual it would have been necessary to endow him with a distinct personality for each of his functions. He might be a trustee of several trusts, a member or officer of several corporations and at the same time the possessor of a body of property of his own. Each such position is separate and there must be no merger or confusion between the respective rights and duties belonging to the several capacities in which he acts. But a notion growing from the soil of the classificatory genitive and the bodily incidence of obligations was incapable of such abstractions. The second difficulty which the concept of *persona* could not meet was that of dividing. Gradually, as relations appertaining to *personae* became divisible and continued after division, and as they became individually transferable, a concept of "split personality" would have needed to be worked out. But this psychic possibility was unknown until too late. The legal notion of personality failed to meet this requirement because it was integral and could not rid itself of its anthropomorphism.

Thus in modern times the original concept of *persona* has become obsolete except in the one case of the artificial personality with which an antiquated legal philosophy still clothes the corporation – the only survival of the primitive household, or *familia*. And this is the one case, curiously enough, in which the original concept is least appropriate. For this philosophy has taken the Roman representation of the *head* of the *familia* and applied it to the *body* of the corporation. And it has taken the scheme for a focal point upon which all responsibility for the *familia* was concentrated and made it in many respects irresponsible.

To attempt to trace the rise and decay of the idea of artificial personality in so brief a compass is presumptuous. Nevertheless a résumé is necessary to complete this analysis. As we have seen, the form of the *familia*, as it developed its point of external contact in the individual *persona* of the head, gave rise, on the one hand, to a super-

minor, and after his maturity that of a major, each having different qualities, rights, and obligations." Brent v. City of New Orleans, 48 La. 1098, 1099 (1889).

organization of these familial heads and thus to the concept of the state and, on the other, to artificial *familiae* which grew into the medieval concept of the corporation. By the time this latter antique-modern concept, as Gierke calls it, became modern, the corporate organizations on the model of the *familia*, which was originally autonomous, had become degraded because of application to corporate communes definitely subordinate and owing their existence to a "concession" by the state.[2] "And then as the sphere of the State's Might on the one hand, and the sphere of the Individual's Liberty on the other, became the exclusive and all-sufficing starting-points for a Philosophy of Law, the end was that the Corporation could find a place in Public Law only as a part of the State and a place in Private Law only as an artificial Individual, while all in actual life that might seem to conflict with this doctrine was regarded as the outcome of privileges which the State had bestowed and in the interest of the public might at any time revoke."[3] And so grew the *persona ficta* out of the invention of Innocent IV and the prerogative which he retained that it could only attach where it was conceded by him. But, after a long life, the artificial *persona* is now merging in the corpus.[4] The concession theory is disappearing with statutory charters and, as Maitland suggests, the fiction theory may go with it because courts, particularly in America, are implying corporateness where no charter has been taken out.

In retrospect we see that the natural correspondent of the original *persona* should have invested the directors and officers of the corporation, rather than dwelling apart as a mystic immanence. Thus, as in the case of all other multiple legal personalities attaching to individuals, the responsibility for torts and crimes committed as acts of the group would have rested upon those in which the power really lies. Just so, in this way, the acts of trustees, etc., are acts of persons, not acts of bodies of property. And the liability therefor rests on the person. But the difficulty in the case of corporations lay in the fact that legal theory was struggling to retain the notion of the *persona* as the centre of inherence and incidence of property rights and the pattern would not conform to both purposes.

Coincident with these two continuing integrations, the *persona*—office or aggregate of offices—and the *corpus*—body of property—

[2] Though some contemporary authorities, according to Gierke, op. cit., p. 98, "sought to oppose a scientific statement of the idea of corporative articulation [i. e. decentralization]."

[3] Gierke, op. cit., pp. 99, 100.

[4] Maitland, in his introduction to Gierke, p. xxxviii, says, "Spectacles are to be had in Germany which, so it is said, enable the law to see personality wherever there is bodiliness [i. e. corporateness]." And, p. xxxiv, "If once we are allowed to see personality wherever we see bodiliness, the victory of Realism is secure, though an old superstition may die very hard."

there has persisted in a gradually widening differentiation a functional integration of material objects themselves. Originally coterminous with the *corpus* it seemed at first to be identical with it. But in the course of time it has become so distinct that the two must be distinguished. In the agricultural economy the original house community or *familia*, as it developed into an organization projected upon the land, became in turn, in its material and unfree human aspect, the early Roman *fundus*, the *villa* of the Roman Empire, the *domaine* or manor of the Middle Ages, and eventually the landed estate of England. And in the commercial and industrial economy the *fundus*—the Roman landed estate—developed into the old French *fonds* which designated, as well, a merchant's stock or capital; that is, his personal estate.

2. *The Nature of the Centre of Inherence—Funds*

In this whole process we see the development of a legal entity—the body of property—lying between the person or persons connected with it as incumbents of its offices and any groupings of material objects to which it may be related. This body of property is a wholly impersonal aggregate of 'things.' It may be defined as a legally segregated organic grouping of property interests to which persons are attached by means of offices—that is, places or *rôles* existing apart from the persons—which are occupied independently of their relations to other such groupings. The development of the concept of this body of property is summarized in the progressive changes in the usage of the word "estate." Commencing as a man's status, and thus representing much the same concept as *persona*, it has gradually become depersonalized, and today the term is quite generally used to describe the *universitas bonorum* of a man, more especially in the form in which it survives him after death. It has its agents, its executors or administrators, its heirs and legatees. And these are persons. But the estate itself has no personality and exists independently of all persons. The estate of a decedent is but one of many modern forms in which a body of property is conceived as *selbständig*. The trust fund, while not in form so independent of persons, is equally so in fact. When a trustee is removed for cause the property is not taken away from him. He is taken away from the property. He is removed from an office which is merely connected in administrative ways with the body of property. Finally, as we shall undertake to show more clearly, the corporation, which is the dominant novelty of our time, in so far as it is an element in the property structure is of exactly this order. But, while its history and the fact that it is commonly used for certain types of bodies of property make it seem appropriate, the term "estate" is not suitable as the general term for all such aggregates because its technical use covers a specific kind of interest in land and because its common use covers land itself. In spite of its concrete origin perhaps the word "fund" is the most satisfactory term available. True, it is frequently used of some part of a body of property set aside for a special purpose. Nevertheless it has the proper connotation of an entity independent of the personal relation thereto.

The fact is that the law has come to deal with all integral agglomerations of property as if they were such funds, individualized and segregated, and yet existing independently of the persons who may be connected with them in various capacities as owner, beneficiary, trustee, receiver, executor, or what-not. As in the case of primitive *dominium* where the concept of an interest was elided, so in the case of the fund which is a man's own (of which he is owner, so-called) the fund is not treated as an independent entity so long as he is alive, solvent, and not mentally or otherwise incapacitated. But as soon as the occasion arises in this particular case, and at all times in all other cases, funds of property are treated as something apart from the individuals related to them. The law does not deal with a corporation, or even in most respects with a partnership, as a group of individuals. Nor, except in theory, does it do so as a mock individual—an artificial personality. It deals with it as a fund—something which it is peculiarly capable of reaching because the fund is in no way gifted with personal attributes but is composed of a substance which is solely of the law's own creation, namely property.

Funds may be formal or informal in their organization. In most cases the fund is not formally organized. The interests composing such funds still stand in the name of an owner or a trustee, etc. And, in turn, the individual component rights making up these interests are conceived to inhere in this same person. Thus the fund of John Doe, Bankrupt, may nominally be vested in the trustee in bankruptcy; that of Richard Roe, Lunatic, in the committee in lunacy; that of the John Doe Trust in the trustee; and that of the Estate of Richard Roe, Dec'd., in the executor. But the fund (the component interests) of Doe, Roe and Co., a partnership, is vested in the partners collectively not individually (i. e. in the partnership); while that of the Roe Corporation and the Doe Foundation, Inc. is in the corporation or fund itself. It is necessarily true in all these cases, though it is only obvious in the last two, that the inherence of the interests composing the body of property cannot be directly in the persons occupying the offices, because these persons can be removed without changing the point of inherence. Neither can the inherence be in the offices themselves, for the state can alter the assortment of offices, apply new ones, etc., without changing the point of inherence. Therefore, actually, whether organized or not, both the whole fund and its component interest always inhere in some sort of centre or core of the fund itself. These interests belong *to* the fund as well as belonging *in* the fund.

This core is the nucleus or identity of the fund. The fund is composed of various property interests which inhere in it. Upon it in turn various other interests are incident. Such we have found to be the interests of the beneficiary in a trust fund of personal property, the interests of the stockholders in a corporation and all the modern rights which come under the classification *in personam.* Actually the personality against which is directed the right *in personam* has become merged into the fund itself. Finally we find that many persons may be connected with a fund in various capacities which are, or are analogous to, offices. This serves as a preliminary statement of the nature of the integral aggregate of interests which forms a body of property. And it explains the entity upon which, as we have stated, that type of interest is immediately incident which we have called an interest in indeterminate objects or, better, an indirect interest in objects.

This organized centre of property relations in which interests inhere and which is usually and traditionally referred to as if it were a person, but is in reality always a fund, may be called the "holder" of the property. Originating in the concept of physical possession, just as did the original equivalent word tenant, the word "hold" is now in quite general use to denote the act of having this relation. Thus we have property holders, stockholders, bondholders, holders "in due course" of negotiable instruments, leaseholders, and even the pleonastic lien holders. It is sometimes said that "'owner' and 'holder' are synonymous terms."[5] But this is not exactly true. By avoiding the term "owner" we escape its connotation of "ownership" of material objects, a concept which we have found inapplicable in general but which continues to cause confusion.

3. *Varieties of Relation of Persons to Funds*

The vast multiplicity of the funds of all sorts which have appeared in modern times, among which are included funds to which no determinate person is related as a beneficial owner (foundations), is the result of an unconscious process of depersonalizing the inherence of the property relation and has not yet been rationalized by the philosophy of the law. These funds go by all sorts of names. Those which are identified to an individual owner probably still outnumber

[5] Amer. Nat'l. Bk. of Tucumcari v. Tarpley, 31 N. M. 667, 673 (1926).

the rest. But those in which no one person maintains this simple relation are increasing far more rapidly. Trusts, estates of decedents, corporations, partnerships, unincorporated associations, foundations, etc., probably represent by far the largest holdings of direct property in objects at the present time. Thus, while we have spoken and will continue to speak of the holder of property, it should be clearly recognized that this immediate holder is more often impersonal than not, and that, in point of fact, the law has come to treat all property aggregates, even that of the individual owner, as if they were in some respects independent of the person. To be sure property is in the last analysis, as we have said, a system for the control by men of material and quasi-material objects. Also, in almost all cases, it ultimately accrues in the form of beneficial interests to someone. Nevertheless it will not do to cut through the complexity, to dissolve the intermediate relations between men in respect of these objects. For the elaboration of the system is very real, though entirely impalpable. In fact it is of the essence of social organization. It is itself the structure of property. As well ignore the successive steps from electrons and protons, through atoms and through molecules, to the cells themselves, all of which, except the last, we know only by inference from their behaviour.

One simplification we may permit ourselves. As we build these rights into bundles or interests, called 'things,' and the interests in turn into funds in which they inhere, we do not always separate the person from occupying the same relation, whatever that is, to every interest and every component right that he occupies to the fund as a whole. The introduction of the fund is not, in its unorganized form, so much a process of interpolation as it is one of aggregation. But the relation of the individual to the rights is determined by his relation to the fund, not *vice versa*. And the fund is always a more or less independent entity which need not change with changes in the relations of individuals thereto.

However many other funds an individual may be related to in various ways other than as sole owner, there is one fund which is conceived to aggregate all his transferable beneficial interests—his *own fund*. As to this he is 'owner,' though the interests composing the fund are not "ownerships." And only of this fund and of the interests composing this fund can he be said to be 'owner.' To other funds he may have administrative relations as trustee,[6] executor, officer, receiver, partner, agent, etc.; or lesser forms of beneficial relation

[6] The customary discrimination as to the so-called "bare legal title" of the trustee and the practice of refusing the name "owner" to a trustee because the interests in his name are not *beneficial* to him, are efforts to recognize the true nature of this purely administrative office which is concealed by the form of antique "ownership" in which it is still wrapped.

as beneficiary, legatee, etc. Such administrative and beneficial relations to other funds are also personal. They are part of the property structure and all may be described as interests. However, they do not appear as component interests in the 'own' fund, for either they are not beneficial or, if so, they have not yet been incorporated in his aggregate. Therefore they are final. The individual has all these other relations appertaining directly to himself, not *via* his 'own' fund. On the other hand many of the relations to other funds which seem to appertain to a person are in substance component interests of his 'own' fund. Such, for instance, are those represented by shares of stock or credit-debts. These relations, therefore, are not really final or personal. For this reason they are incorporated as parts of his semi-independent 'own' fund.

So long as a man retains the relation both of complete 'owner' and of administrator in every respect to his 'own' fund no one else has any immediate concern with it. He has with respect to the direct interests in objects and all other 'things' of which it is composed, something analogous to the complete property we have already discussed. He controls it and he enjoys it. Yet perhaps no one of the component interests is itself complete property in a material object.

Such a status as sole 'owner' and administrator of his 'own' fund is the only case where an analogue of complete property may be had in a fund. For if, for instance, such an 'owner' becomes "incompetent" some one else may legally assume control of his fund, leaving to him the beneficial relation only. Or if he dies or becomes insolvent, while the fund goes on,[7] both the relation of control and

[7] In the case of bankruptcy, under Federal statute, the situation is somewhat different. There at the time of adjudication in bankruptcy all of the property (as defined) of the bankrupt, in existence at the date of the filing of the bankruptcy petition, is divided into two portions. Out of that portion which is subject under the law to the claims of the general creditors a new fund is constituted which is wholly independent of the old one. The title to this new fund nominally vests in the trustee for the creditors, upon his appointment and qualification, but relating back to date of adjudication. In respect of this fund the trustee occupies a curiously dual relation. He is at once "a party litigant" (the trustee for general creditors) and "an officer of the court," or custodian (holding all property in his possession subject to the determination of the rights of the parties therein). Out of that portion of the bankrupt's property which is exempt or is not subject to the claims of the general creditors another fund is constituted which is in part independent of the old one and in part a continuation of it. As to the first new fund title rests by law (i. e. assignment is not necessary) in the trustee as a "party litigant" (i.e. as trustee for the creditors). As to the second, title, of course, continues in the person of the bankrupt. But custody of both portions remains, in whole or in part, in the hands of the trustee in bankruptcy as "an officer of the court," until determination by the court as to the division.

The status of the creditors' fund is not exactly the same as when it was the property of the bankrupt. In other words the trustee does not take the identical rights

that of enjoyment pass to others.[8] Those who, for these reasons, enter upon control do so in their personal capacities. Their funds do not become related. Yet they are conceived to have some sort of property relation to this fund. If property is a system of control over objects this relation of theirs would seem necessarily to be a property relation. We must revert to this question later. Again, those for whom the enjoyment is reserved seem to have a property interest in the 'owner's' fund after his death and before distribution. Yet, in this case too, their funds are not for the present related. Here is another question for further consideration.

We have, then, the complete or variously modified relation of the 'owner' to his 'own' fund; the relation of non-beneficial administrators to this fund; and the later relation of personal beneficial heirs and legatees to this fund. We have also the analogous relations of the trustee and the beneficiary of a trust fund. All of these are final or direct relations between a fund and persons – relations which do not consist of interests appertaining to, or composing parts of, other funds; and which are wholly personal, though they are obviously parts of the property structure. Such relations have their analogues in connection with all other types of funds. The non-beneficial administrations of all funds alike, organized or not, include

in the assets or the identical liabilities which were incident upon the bankrupt. The fund is a new fund created by law and defined in its nature by the Bankruptcy Act. The trustee does not only stand "in the bankrupt's shoes" but stands as a creditor "armed with process"; or rather, as Remington, *A Treatise on the Bankruptcy Laws of the U. S.*, secs. 1409 and 1507, puts it, he is both "successor to the bankrupt's title and rights" and "successor to the rights of creditors." From this second capacity it arises that the rights to certain assets may be enhanced or recovered and certain liabilities may be avoided. As to the first the chief change is the avoidance of liens and preferential or fraudulent transfers made within four months prior to the filing of the petition. As to the second the chief exception is the capacity of the trustee to accept or decline the unexpired term of a leasehold.

The status of the bankrupt's new fund may be said to be that it is a continuation of his old fund, in so far as exempt or undiscovered assets and non-dischargeable liabilities are concerned, but that it is a new fund so far as subsequently acquired or excess assets and liabilities actually discharged by bankruptcy are concerned. It is a survival in some respects and a fresh start in others.

Thus we see that in the case of bankruptcy it is not merely a question of the alteration of an old, or the addition of a new, administrative office, nor the substitution of a new beneficiary to an existing fund. The process is *sui generis*. It does not involve the legal death of the bankrupt as did the *cessio bonorum*; there is no question of any successor assuming his *persona*; the matter concerns the fund alone or that part of it of which the bankrupt is stripped.

[8] Obviously the installation of a trustee in bankruptcy, a receiver in equity receivership, an executor or administrator of the estate of a decedent, a committee of a lunatic, an assignee for creditors, a statutory receiver of an insolvent corporation, or a receiver of a bank, involves the deposition of the owner or others beneficially interested and the substitution of another who represents the creditors as a whole, as distributing officer.

executors, administrators, referees in bankruptcy, receivers,[9] trustees, agents, officers, attorneys, etc. But the beneficial interests which do not compose parts of other funds are limited to those of 'owners' of 'own' funds, those of personal heirs and legatees in estates and, if they are inalienable as such, those of personal beneficiaries in trusts. These several classes limit the types of relation of persons to funds, or to interests in funds, which are so purely personal that they do not merely relate fund to fund. All other property, or interests, in funds inheres in turn in other funds.

We have noted that all these personal relations to funds are treated by law as if they ran to offices rather than to individuals; that is, to places which may be filled by successive individuals without altering the office. This is obviously true of all the administrative relations. But the statement must be qualified in the case of many of the personal beneficial relations. Strictly speaking, the office of 'owner' can only be filled by one incumbent.[10] But its character is prescribed and defined by law and can only be altered or terminated by legal procedure. It is so altered, for instance, when a guardian is appointed, and then resembles that of the beneficiary of a trust fund except that the incumbency must be for life. The other personal beneficial relations may run to successive incumbents in the same office. But in these cases, too, the offices may be changed in nature by law. And, though not arbitrarily, only the law creates and terminates the incumbency or office of heir or legatee and beneficiary under a trust. Therefore, as with the Roman *caput* (*persona*), the law defines and determines the civil death of all these beneficial relations to personal funds. And the 'owner-ship,' the heirship, the cestui-ship, etc., are, at law and therefore in the institution of property, something apart from the individual incumbent and susceptible to change in character without a change in the individual.

[9] Receivership is a form of equitable execution upon any fund. The receiver is actually *amicus curiae* and the fund is regarded as being *in custodia legis*. However, the connection between the receiver and the creditors so closely resembles that between a trustee and a beneficiary, that, for the corporate form of fund, the doctrine has arisen that "the assets of a corporation represented by its capital stock are a trust fund for the payment of its debts." Spencer v. Smith, 201 Fed. 647, 652 (C. C. A. 8th, 1912). Strictly this applies only after "the Court of Equity, through its receiver, takes charge of the assets." Merchants Nat'l. Bk. of Richmond v. Newton Cotton Mills, 115 N. C. 507, 515 (1894).

[10] It is perhaps more exact to conceive of the office of 'owner' as having a dual nature – one beneficial and one administrative. In this view the latter can be modified as to nature and incumbency independently of the former. And, in this view, all generalizations, hereafter, which refer to administrative relations, apply as well to the administrative portion of the office of 'owner.'

4. *Chief Types of Fund*

We have taken as the prototype fund, that particular variety to which some individual stands in the relation of sole 'owner.' We have recognized that, even here, in the case of incompetents, certain of the elements of control may be parted with without depriving it of its character as a final unit immediate to the person; that in the case of an insolvent, even the beneficial relation may be removed from the so-called 'owner' without at once dissolving the fund; and that at death the fund continues as an estate during probate, the beneficial relations to which immediately pertain to the heirs and legatees but do not become parts of their funds until the estate is distributed and ceases to exist as an independent entity. These interests, if personal, together with interests of personal beneficiaries in trust funds inalienable as such and all the purely administrative non-beneficial relations, are the only property relations which do not inhere immediately in funds. These modified interests, be it noted, are all themselves interests incident upon funds, never direct interests in objects. All other relations are, at the pole of inherence, immediate to funds and only mediate to the person; although, in the end, all these others will be found also to project themselves upon persons indirectly, through the medium of funds and thence through these final relations of funds to persons.

The other principal types of funds are partnerships, trusts and corporations. In all these types the administrative functions relating thereto, while they are part of the property structure and are called at law interests of a certain sort, do not represent interests which go to compose other funds. They are of the order of the personal relations already noted. When we come to examine the beneficial relations to these other types of fund—that is, all relations to them except those which are administrative—we find wide differences among them. The partnership, as a fund, is a primitive and peculiar system of joint property which in one direction effects a partial merger with the 'own' funds of the individual partners, who are necessarily persons, and in the other direction does not. The 'own' funds of the partners are a secondary supplement to that of the partnership and are in that respect subordinated thereto. But that of the partnership does not consist of, nor is it merged with, the 'own' funds of the partners. In the latter respect the two are separate and the interests in the partnership fund inhere as inter-fund relations in the 'own' funds of the partners. The structural relation is loose and informal. Yet the distinction exists. It may be said, then, that all beneficial relations to a partnership fund are themselves formal interests which inhere in another fund and not directly in a person.

The trust, on the other hand, is quite different. Here the separation between the relation of the beneficiary to his 'own' fund and to the trust fund may be complete. But the beneficiary may be a person direct or may be another fund. The personal beneficial interest in the trust fund may be incorporated in the personal beneficiaries' 'own' funds or it may not be. The same is true of a non-personal beneficial interest in such fund. In neither case, however, is there any merger whatever between the trust fund and the beneficiaries' 'own' funds, nor any supplemental relation in the opposite direction, as in the case of partnerships. It is for this reason that it has been necessary to include the rights of personal beneficiaries in trusts among the previously described final beneficial relations of persons to funds.

We are not prepared to deal finally with corporations at this point. Suffice it to say that they resemble each of the foregoing in certain respects. All beneficial relations to corporations as funds are only mediate to persons through other funds. None are final. In this regard they resemble partnerships. But, unlike partnerships, the beneficial relations may run not only to the 'own' funds of individuals but also to any other type of fund. In this respect they are like trusts with non-personal beneficiaries. Also, unlike partnerships and like trusts, the fund of the corporation is almost wholly independent of those of its stockholders. Only in respect of unpaid subscriptions or excess liability does a remnant of the secondary supplementary relation of the partnership survive in this newer form. In every other way a corporate fund is as *selbständig* as a trust fund. The foundation is still further removed from the partnership or the trust. It is a corporate trust fund in which there are no stockholders, or an unincorporated trust fund in which there are no named beneficiaries. But in either case the fact that there is no equitable property is due only to the fact that the beneficiaries are indeterminate and merely incidental to its "settled" purposes.[11] It should also be noted that corporations and foundations may be among the heirs and legatees to personal estates of decedents as well as the beneficiaries of trust

[11] See Note 20, p. 293. The German view of the *selbständige Anstalt* or *Stiftung* defines the fund, in that particular case, as itself the centre of inherence; but it does so, curiously enough, by conceiving it as a real person. And it singles out this form of fund for such a view because there are neither legal interests incident upon it, as in the case of the ordinary corporation, nor equitable interests, because the beneficiaries are indeterminate. Buckland, *Principles*, pp. 16, 17, says, "German lawyers have evolved the idea of a pure 'Stiftung,' or Foundation, a fund destined to specific permanent applications, of which the various assets are regarded as vested in the Fund itself and not in its administrators. Thus the 'Stiftung' is itself a person, and as it is capable of obligations, its personality, at least for some thinkers, is in no way fictitious – it is a real personality."

funds. When this occurs the interests therein are not personal or final but rather impersonal and mediate and inhere in another fund.

5. *Dominant and Pre-dominant Interests in Funds*

We have now succeeded in discriminating the following types of interest in funds. Those which are personal and do not inhere in other funds we describe as final, or immediate, if they are beneficial, and as administrative, if they are not. Those which are beneficial but always inhere, in turn, in other funds, we term impersonal and intermediate.

Dominant (and Administrative) Interests in Funds

Personal (Immediate)	Of the nature of offices
Beneficial	Relation of 'Owner' to 'Own' Fund Relation of Personal Heir and Legatee to Estate Relation of Personal Beneficiary to Trust Fund, if Inalienable as such
Administrative (Non-beneficial)	Relation of Trustee, Executor, Officer, Attorney, etc., to any Fund
Impersonal (Intermediate)	
Beneficial	Partner's Interest in Partnership Stockholder's Interest in Corporation Impersonal Beneficiary's Interest in Trust Fund Personal Beneficiary's Interest in Trust Fund if Alienable as such Impersonal Heir's or Legatee's Interest in Estate of Decedent

The law regards all these relations as property interests but, nevertheless, it differentiates them in much the same way as we have done. All these types have been elaborated from, and are still closely allied to, the original superstrate of the property structure which has been variously denominated "dominion" or "ownership," but the only modern examplar of which is found in the final relation of the 'owner' to his 'own' fund.[12] For this reason we will find it conveniently

[12] It is obvious that the *societas*, or partnership, commenced as a form of familial condominion, and that the corporation is a modern derivative from the artificial replica of the *familia*, or household, the original body in which, or in the *persona*

descriptive to term the beneficial interests of this class, *dominant* interests. It is essential to discriminate between the personal and the impersonal interests of the dominant type; that is, between those which relate a fund directly to an individual and those which only relate it to another fund. Since, for the most part, this distinction depends upon and follows the type of the fund, and since in these types all the dominant interests in the fund must either be final, immediate and personal or intermediate and impersonal, the same distinction applies to the funds themselves. Only in the case of the trust fund and the estate of a decedent can the interests be partly personal and partly impersonal. Thus there is a class of wholly personal funds, and a class of wholly impersonal funds, and a class which may be mixed.

There is another type of relation, which exists only between funds and is therefore always of the intermediate type and which has arisen from an altogether different source and upon a different model. This is the 'thing' with which we have already become quite familiar – the credit-debt, its remedial analogue the judgment debt, and all the various interests which may be on the way to becoming credit-debts and in the meantime subsist as antecedent present or future property in contract, of unascertained value, or as the various remedial rights of action which are treated as potential property until disproved. All of such interests that survive or are transferable inhere immediately in some fund. And practically all do so. Those that do not are of such inchoate character, regarded as property interests, that we can safely ignore them in this connection. All of such interests are, like all the dominant and administrative interests, incident upon some other fund and never upon an object.

Thus all varieties of property interests, including those which only compose and inhere in funds, if they are regarded in the aspect of their incidence rather than in that of their inherence, divide themselves into three classes. There are, first, the class of direct interests in specific objects already discussed. There are, second, the two classes of interests – those personal and impersonal which are built upon the original *dominium*, and those impersonal which are built upon the original *obligatio* – both of which are of the order we have described as interests with regard to indeterminate objects or interests in bodies

of which, property inhered. The trust was, as we have seen, derived from the "use," a legal evasion intended to secure the benefits of the completest possible property without its burdens. It is for that reason that today the law tends to look through the form and see therein something almost exactly like its idea of "ownership." "'Cestuis que trustent' are those for whose benefit others are seized of real or personal property. . . The cestui que trust is the real, substantial and beneficial owner of an estate which is held in trust as distinguished from the trustee in whom the mere legal title is vested." Larkin v. Wikoff, 75 N. J. Eq. 462, 474 (Ch. 1909).

of property and which are therefore only indirectly, indeterminately and ultimately, through one or many successive steps, interests in specific material or quasi-material objects. Besides the procedural differences in these two latter classes of indirect interest, arising from their independent origins – which differences are constantly becoming of less practical importance – there are fundamental distinctions between them. Actual or potential credit-debt, as a class, is preferred to the dominant interests, as a class. It is for a fixed term or at will. And it is fixed in amount in terms of value. The term *pre-dominant* seems therefore well adapted to indicate the essential quality of this class. In contrast to these, all those interests modelled upon *dominium*, which we have called dominant interests, are, as a class, residual; are not necessarily for a fixed term or at will; and, if they are divided, are measured by shares not by fixed values. To be sure, certain of the latter may be preferred and fixed in value as they relate among themselves to the other residual interests. Such hybrids are legacies and preferred stocks, for instance. However, this latter preference and fixity of value does not pertain to the fund as a whole, but only to the residue of the fund after deducting the fixed value of the pre-dominant interests. Still another distinction exists in the scope of these two types of indirect interest (in funds). Those of the credit-debt, or pre-dominant, type can be incident upon any fund, an 'own' fund as well as upon those derived from the 'own' fund as a model – the other personal and the impersonal or the mixed funds. But the derivative dominant types of indirect interest cannot be incident upon 'own' funds. The fund of John Doe can be a debtor. An interest of the type of a credit-debt can be incident upon it. But an interest of the type of a beneficiary, a partner, or of a stockholder cannot. Neither can any of these other types of dominant interest be held in a fund of a different type. Moreover, in every respect the incidence of a credit-debt is the same when it is incident upon an 'own' fund, as it is when it is incident upon any other type of fund. In other words the pre-dominant interest ignores the special structure of the fund, while the dominant interests *are* themselves that special structure – they constitute that which differentiates these types of fund among themselves.

We have seen that the interest of an 'owner' in his 'own' fund may be complete property therein. Or, without altering its legal nature, this complete property may be divided, since pre-dominant or administrative relations may become incident upon it. On the other hand, in the case of all other types of funds, the beneficial or dominant interests therein are never complete property. Always there is subtracted from complete property of the dominant interests therein at least the rights of the administrators, running to persons more or less different from those holding beneficial interests and always an essential part of the organization of such funds. In these cases too pre-dominant interests may exist and impair the complete property of the dominant interests still further.

Where interests of the nature we have called pre-dominant are incident upon any fund, the law, endeavouring to maintain its ancient illusion as to the incidence of such interests, has usually selected one or another related person—or office—upon whom these rights *in personam*, so-called, might be conceived to be projected. It has sometimes selected the person—or fund—holding the beneficial or dominant interests, and frequently the person—or office—related in an administrative capacity. But the legal formula has no consistency. Finally, in the case of the corporate fund, it has nominally created a personality with which to invest the corporation. But this fiction, when examined, turns out to be in fact none other than the corporate fund itself. And even in the other cases, where it has succeeded in finding a natural person to be the butt for its antique humour, it is always in reality the fund which it has in mind and against which it directs its actions. The layman is either ignorant of, or ignores, these legal fictions and looks through the form to the facts. It is certainly true that all those who obtain dominant interests in a fund, by exchange, consider themselves as purchasing an interest in the fund. And this is true, in most cases, of holders of pre-dominant interests as well. The investing creditor, at least, regards himself as the purchaser of an interest, fixed in extent, in yield and in duration, but nevertheless an interest in the property of the debtor. Neither thinks of himself as holding some sort of right over the person or persons, natural or artificial.

6. *The Composition and Projection within a Fund*

We have noted that the interests incident upon a fund constitute its organization, the method by which the rights of property over it are apportioned and according to which it functions. To be sure only the dominant interests in it—those which give to it its special type or character—represent the relatively fixed organization of the fund. The organization of the pre-dominant interests is more temporary, more fluctuating, and subject to the possibility of a periodic partial division of the fund. On the other hand, the interests inhering in the fund are those which compose it. These components may be direct interests in objects of the varieties we have described, or they may be interests in other funds, as also described. But there is nothing fixed about this composition, as there is about the organization. The content of the fund is a perpetual succession of 'things,' regarded *en masse*, of which the only characteristic which is expected to endure is the stable reflection, in terms of total value, which the interests composing the fund cast on those incident upon it. And this because changes in its composition are expected to be confined to *exchanges* or *divisions*.[18]

In so far, however, as interests in funds, of any kind and either dominant or pre-dominant, may be conceived to be projected upon the 'things' which in turn compose the fund, the *interests in* the fund are indeterminate as to their incidence upon these specific 'things' composing the fund. They float upon the aggregate. When any of these interests in a fund are discharged and the organization of the fund is thereby rearranged, the specific 'things' so used to repurchase the discharged interest, if it is pre-dominant, or to liquidate it, if it is dominant, will be at that time part of the corpus of the fund. All such interests, except 'owner's' interests in 'own' funds, contemplate that they shall be so repurchased or liquidated at some definite or indefinite future time, and that such payment will be made out of corpus – out of a division – not out of income. No such distribution can be made out of income. Or rather, if income is accumulated for such purpose, it has become part of the corpus (even if a special segregated part) before it can be so used.

Thus all interests in funds are in reality undivided interests in the 'things' composing it. Such undivided interests are the oldest form of property. In some respects they resemble joint or common property. But in other respects they are more like reversions and remainders. For the reversioner and the remainderman are parties at interest in regard to the land, and yet the holder of an estate in tail or for life has possession *de jure* in his own name, with all the rights which have been called "limited ownership." The interests composing a fund are, in this indirect way, "held of" those persons or other funds, in turn, who hold the interests incident upon the fund; that is, the interests which inhere in the fund are – by the fund – "held of" those which are incident upon it. The connection is indirect, for such interests incident upon the fund can only consist of unprojected rights to parts of the whole, as yet unidentified. And this fact makes it possible that the administrators of the fund can dispose of the underlying 'things' as independent units – free assets – and give title to them better than they as sellers have, free of

[18] The law has to deal with other masses of this constantly changing order. For instance, in the case of insurance, "under . . . 'floating policies' or 'shifting risks,' the property insured is the property of a class and kind described, in the place described, which the insured may have on hand at the time of the fire, whether it is or is not identical in items with that which he had on hand at the time that the insurance was written." Bloch v. Amer. Ins. Co., 132 Wis. 150, 160 (1907).

attachment by the interests incident upon the fund except on constructive notice.

Pre-dominant interests in funds, as indirect interests in indeterminate 'things,' will presently be liquidated by exchange. That is, the debtor will buy his debt, and usually cancel it. It may then cease to be property according to the old rule, *nulli res sua servit.* But, until so repurchased and cancelled, it exists as an undivided interest in the whole conglomerate of 'things.' Thus the particular 'thing' to which each such interest pertains is not only undetermined but will always remain so. For, when the specific component 'thing' used to repurchase it is delivered, the interest in the fund is thereby extinguished as such, and a new property in the means of repurchase takes its place in the fund of the creditor. If all creditors find it necessary to enforce their property in the 'things' of the debtor their interests remain undivided until they are liquidated; whereupon again these properties (credits) are extinguished and the 'things' received, whatever they may be, take their place. Exactly the same situation exists with respect to the liquidation of dominant interests. It is true therefore of all interests in funds, dominant and pre-dominant, that they always remain, as long as they exist, indirect floating rights over indeterminate 'things.' The only determinate rights are the direct interests in specific objects. And these rights always inhere in funds—never directly in persons.

7. *Peculiarities of Pre-dominant Interests*

In the case of pre-dominant interests in funds there are two peculiarities, not common to dominant interests, which we must examine. The first is the existence of that special type of property known as accessory property, or security. Separate from, but by way of security for, many of these pre-dominant interests there are various types of liens. Of these we need only stop to consider those liens which are antecedent and therefore voluntary, or which, though remedial and involuntary, support judgment debts or certain decrees. For all others are part of the process of validating an unsecured interest or of protecting a potential interest prior to adjudication. They are processes of projection of interests in funds upon specific component 'things' rather than accessories to these interests.

In the first group of accessory interests to be considered are pledge, mortgage, chattel mortgage,[14] trust deed (as mortgage), conditional sale, etc. In these cases the debtor fund assigns to the creditor a defeasible interest in specific objects or even in other specific 'things'

[14] The chattel mortgage is not literally an interest in specific objects, for here the objects are constantly shifting.

(i. e. specific component interests which are incident upon other funds). These are conditional interests, which are as little as possible a deprivation of direct property in the object or 'thing,' and which vary from that type of possession called special property (detention, etc.) down to a mere floating hold upon a constantly changing mass of objects, as in the chattel mortgage. But they largely determine the eventual incidence of the pre-dominant interests in the fund to which they are accessory. If repurchase of the pre-dominant interests so secured is not effected when due, it is these specific objects or 'things' which can thus be divided off from the fund and become the satisfaction of the creditor. And, up to the value of the pre-dominant interest, it is only these particular objects or 'things.' There is a complex body of rules as to each variety of these antecedent accessory direct interests and their relation to the pre-dominant interests they support. These incumbrances, as they are called, to some extent exclude the underlying objects or 'things' they cover from having projected upon them any of the other interests in the fund. Also to some extent the interests supported by these incumbrances are limited to being projected upon the particular objects or 'things' they so cover. The rules are elaborate and it is not necessary for our purpose to examine them. Suffice it to say that this practice makes the incidence of pre-dominant interests upon funds a very complex matter, subject to many priorities and peculiarities both at law and in equity.[15] It must also be noted that, while we have included these antecedent or voluntary securities among the direct interests in objects, they are today applied as well to 'hold' in this way all specific 'things.' Thus the pledgee of a bond does not really 'hold' an accessory direct interest in an object. He holds, by way of security for his interest in his debtor's fund, a specific 'thing' composing that fund which is, in turn, a pre-dominant interest in some other fund with accessory property in specific material objects in that second fund. Thus the relations may be, and are, endlessly complicated – a chain leading from one to another fund, so that the ultimate objects may be far distant and only connected through many links.

The other group of accessory interests, those which support judgment debts or decrees for specific restitution, consist of equitable liens and attachments resulting from such decrees, and of execution processes, garnishments, etc. Here the incidence of the remedial credit-debt has been removed from a fund and directed *pro tem*, upon a specific 'thing' or object. Sale and delivery of the proceeds,

[15] For example there is the doctrine of the marshalling of assets, by which each secured creditor is required to satisfy his interest out of the security peculiar to him, so far as possible, before reaching for other 'things.'

or delivery of the 'thing' itself, extinguishes or converts the property. But the interest in the fund remains in existence as a potential and secondary resort until the debt is satisfied. Thus this type of remedial security is truly accessory.

The second peculiarity of pre-dominant interests is the repurchase agreement. It may seem to the reader that we have been beating the devil about the bush in insisting heretofore that the general class of rights which are called in law rights *in personam*, in so far as they have become credit-debts, constitute interests in debtors' funds, rather than mere rights to future personal acts in the shape of repayment, and in then admitting that they involve repurchase agreements. It may well be asked what is the difference between an agreement to repay and an agreement to repurchase. Let us attempt to clear up this question. The subject is dealt with more fully in Appendix III. Here we briefly present a few points only.

1. Treating such rights as if they involved no more than a duty to repay at a certain time does not explain the fact that they are protected against interference by third parties (rights *in rem* in a contract) as if they were property of the same order as other non-possessory interests.

2. Nor does it explain the various ways in which the debtor is required to maintain his fund, as if there were an adverse interest in it, both against involuntary shrinkage in value beyond a certain point (insolvency) and against voluntary dissipation (in fraud of creditors), and in other ways.

3. Nor is it entirely consistent with the personal view that, when the rights of the creditor are due to be extinguished, "repayment" may not be made to him but rather to another, if in the meantime these rights have been transferred by the original creditor to that other. It is this hurdle which at first prevented alienation of choses in action. Admitting the practice should strictly have produced an alteration in the theory. If debt is not personal at both ends, can it be held to be so at either?

4. In certain cases, such as insolvency, such rights can be enforced and transmuted into rights to a portion of the 'things' of the debtor even before the debt is due. If they constituted a mere promise they could have no such incidence before the debt was due, because the promise cannot then be held to be in default, except by means of the pure fiction of "anticipatory breach."

5. If the repurchase agreement is not carried out when due, the interest in the debtor's fund remains intact and unchanged. Merely one attribute of it is affected. If it were only a promise to pay this would not be the case.

6. In the most highly developed forms of credit-debt the debtor

may and often does repurchase his obligations before maturity, hold them for a time and then resell them. They are not repaid by such repurchase prior to maturity nor even necessarily retired. Nevertheless they cease for the time to be adverse interests.

Thus the repurchase agreement is not the essential feature. It is merely the means agreed upon for the extinction of a subsisting interest which in many respects is not unlike the general class of dominant interests in funds. It corresponds to the liquidating dividend of the dominant interests in corporate funds. The legal theory of rights *in personam* is almost wholly obsolete—a lingering convention derived from the ancient organization of society and the resulting form of action. It conceals the true nature of the rights involved, for, when they are enforced at all, such rights are enforced, in every detail, as rights *in rem.* There are certain differences in procedure which may still be distinguished by the inappropriate name *in personam.* But the real distinctions in law are of a different order. There is, first, that between direct interests in material and quasi-material objects and interests in funds. There is, second, that between the dominant interests in funds and the pre-dominant.

8. *Discrepancies between Theory and Facts as to Pre-dominant Interests*

We have already devoted much attention to developing a distinction, within the field of pre-dominant interests in funds, between that antecedent property called credit-debt and all other antecedent or remedial rights which may be on the way to becoming such. We have seen that, if they are true debt, such antecedent rights grow out of exchanges at a semi-final stage and constitute the offset to the disequilibrium resulting from a deficiency in mutual consideration plus performance. When such a balance is of ascertained value it is credit-debt. Until then it is some sort of interest of uncertain magnitude and therefore not yet consummate. Also the power-liability relation, which may create a further balance due under the agreement, is in the meantime future property which may later graduate into credit-debt, directly or through the intermediate unliquidated stage. Quasi-debt covers a relation in the same form which is not arrived at by exchange but which covers the preliminary stage of a unilateral transfer.

The remedial rights can never be said to be full-fledged property until they become judgment debts. Until then they are tentative and defeasible, though safe-guarded by certain protections accorded to true property. And this latter on the quite proper theory that they are potentially property because they may ripen into ascertained interests upon the adjudication of the claim. But all these inchoate interests, existing in the form of rights of action for breach of contract or for tort, and even the consummate interests which arise when and if they ripen into judgment debt, have this radical general difference from antecedent interests in funds. They are transitory. When and as they ripen into judgment debts it is only to be shortly executed against specific 'things' in the debtor fund. In other words all remedial rights in funds are in process of becoming. And as rapidly as possible, after they succeed in passing through the various stages one after another and have become true credit-debt, they are converted into the end-product, which end-product is not a pre-dominant interest in the debtor's fund at all, but a withdrawal from his fund of some 'thing,' or 'things,' which was one of its components. Therefore a remedial right is only an interest in the debtor's fund *en passant*.

This difference is of course only a matter of degree. The same statement may be made as to all short term antecedent credit-debts. These do not, of course, pass through the same stages as remedial rights. But they subsist only briefly as interests in the debtor's fund. Nevertheless even here the distinction is important. For it will be found that, in practice, there is a more or less constant mass of such short term antecedent credit-debts succeeding each other in series, whereas the judgment debt is occasional and fortuitous only. In general it may be said that, while antecedent credit-debt contemplates conversion into other forms of property at some future (perhaps distant) date, all remedial claims—and especially when they become true interests, as judgment debts—contemplate immediate reallocations of the component 'things' in funds.

While jurisprudence has invented the distinction between antecedent and remedial rights, it has treated the antecedent rights in contract as if they were rights to the promised performance and has conceived both these and the remedial rights springing from breach thereof to be rights against the person and not of the nature of property, strictly speaking. In other words the theory of contract in jurisprudence does not admit that contract gives rise to antecedent property in the nature of what we have called pre-dominant interests in funds. The theory of the legal practitioner goes even further. It ignores and almost denies the existence of the antecedent right in the case of contract. The general reason for this second extremely legalistic view is principally fixed habit. The law is apt to take cognizance of rights only as they come within its purview. Usually they only do so when they are contested or infringed. Then jural relations are apt to be classified and analysed by their appropriate procedural (i. e. remedial) character. Thus a credit-debt, if it is regarded as a property right at all, is still largely treated as a property right as yet unadjudicated (a chose in action); that is, as one to which no true property is attached until and unless by review.

This treatment of credit-debt as if it were nothing until it has been adjudicated has also resulted, to a large extent, from the fact that all awards, whether they arise from breach of contract or from tort, have been lumped together indiscriminately as "damages." All claims to such awards from either source are called rights of action; and, since when they come before the court they are thus on much the same footing, the difference in their antecedent condition has not been given proper attention. The very restriction on claims to specific performance is evidence that the theory of legal practice goes further than that of jurisprudence and that it does not regard the right of action arising from a breach of contract to be identical with any putative antecedent right in the contract which has been violated, and certainly not with any right to the performance of a promise. Rather the right of action is conceived to be a right to a sum of value, by way of composition of a wrong. True, there are cases where only specific performance of a service, or delivery of a specific material object or of other 'things,' will serve the ends of justice. And here the incidence of the legally created obligation is not in terms of value but in terms of specific 'things.' Nevertheless, this equitable right is, in fact, a legal anomaly. Of course such specific performance always grows out of a contract or out of the relations imposed by law as the result of a contract. Sometimes "the remedy at law by damages is inadequate."[16] Then justice requires and equity can allow an award of specific performance, which is "the actual accomplishment of a contract by the party bound to fulfill it."[17] But the decision "rests in judicial discretion, exercised according to the principles of equity, and with reference to the facts of the case."[18] So it is the exception and is "never a matter of right, but always of grace."[19]

Though jurisprudence and the theory of legal practitioners disagree on the nature, or even the existence, of the antecedent right in contract, they both agree that such right, if it exists, is not a property right in the strict sense of that term and certainly not a predominant interest in the fund of the debtor. By neither is any such property admitted, in this case, except through the medium of security. In other words the theory of law says, in effect, "bring this claim before the court *in personam*—as against the individual,

[16] Dow v. Northern R. R., 67 N.H. 1, 65 (1886).

[17] D. S. I Co. v. Todd, 6 Del. Ch. 163, 176 (1888).

[18] Wolf v. Great Falls Water Power and Townsite Co., 15 Mont. 49, 57 (1894).

[19] Appeal of Alexander, 4 Montgomery Co. (Pa.) Law Rep'r. 33, 36 (Sup. Ct. 1888).

not against the property of which he is the holder—and, if it be proved, a right will be established by the court in the shape of a judgment which can then be asserted by execution and become a property right." It is clear that the end-product of the process is that either the court or the plaintiff has obtained a right *in rem*, and that the defendant has been deprived of one. And it seems to me that the legal practices can only be construed on the basis that, in the case of credit-debt at least, the creditor is considered to have held all along a certain kind of antecedent undivided property interest in the fund of the debtor—a something which pre-existed the cause of action.

It appears that the reason for the legal position is threefold. The law dislikes to project the rights of individual creditors because it is jealous of the rights of other unknown creditors, as is shown by its dislike of the general lien.[20] It also jealously preserves the freedom of action of the administrator or 'owner' of the debtor fund.[21] Again it is probable that it chooses to hold that no such interests exist at all until they are adjudicated (become remedial), in order to avoid defining and classifying them in all the detail that has been found necessary with the similarly complex analogous estates in land. The same attitude was prevalent of old as to future estates in land, until out of the bewildering confusion of actions it became necessary to weave some sort of definite pattern. When that was done future estates stood forth as present vested rights.[22] The analogy between the half-completed development of property in contract and the history of the early stages of English land law is close. In so far as old theory has prevented the full scope of this modern elaboration of rights from being proclaimed and exercised, their projection can well be expanded upon the precedent of estates in land. But the analogy is in fact broader in respect of both its relata. It applies to the whole field of interests in funds as contrasted to the whole field of direct interests in objects. The law has in the past consolidated into a complex but definite system the whole of the great number of somewhat formal types of direct interests in material objects and

[20] "General liens are looked at with jealousy, because they encroach upon the common law, and destroy the equal distribution of the debtor's estate among his creditors." 2 Kent, *Comm.* II. 637.

[21] It is true that, in the past, progress in equity, at least, seems always to have been in the direction of relieving debtors. On this ground it may be urged that the assertion of any real interest of creditors in the 'things' of the debtor is retrogressive. On the other hand requirements as to maintenance of aggregate value intact (analogous to waste) can hardly be retrogressive.

[22] Jenks, op. cit., p. 85, says of the development of the law of future estates in land that "The real difficulty had been, to persuade the courts that an interest in land could be conferred otherwise than by way of corporal investiture or delivery—a mode of creation obviously inapplicable to a future interest."

their analogues over specific 'things.' But, though it has come to define and to discriminate among all these part rights over specific objects (i. e. to discriminate servitudes, or specific securities, and the various non-possessory estates and interests from "possessions") it has not yet succeeded in bringing within its doctrinal horizon the corresponding system covering all indirect rights to indeterminate things (i. e. a sufficient part of the value of the defendant's fund to cover a specific debt, or a certain share in an impersonal fund.) These newer forms of property in funds are far more elastic, varied and informal. It may be more difficult to find the ways and means to assert and protect these floating interests in changing masses of 'things.' Yet it can be done. And there is a practical necessity that the various administrative and the active dominant interests in funds be not accorded the same degree of liberty in dealing with those funds that is and can be accorded to the 'owner' as to his 'own' fund when he has complete property therein.

The distinction between true and quasi-debt is another matter. Whether claims arise from true credit-debt relations, existing prior to a breach of contract and resulting from exchanges or loans at the semi-final stage, or, on the other hand, whether they arise from interferences with the property or the person, matters not so much to the practice of law. But it matters greatly to the study of the institution and the structure of property. For such purposes we are in fact only concerned with those relations which can be termed property relations before the occasion when they may give rise to a remedial right, or, on the other hand, after the remedial right has been adjudicated and become full-fledged property. All others are merely potential redistributions of existing interests—claims not yet ascertained—rather than themselves new and additional elements in the structure of property now existing. Financial economics is therefore vitally concerned with the distinction between true and quasi-credit-debt. Practically all remedial rights arising from tort yield only quasi-credit-debt. The same is true of strictly unilateral contracts, such as gifts, as well as of those awards which leave the aggregate of the parties to the contract less well off than before. To a considerable degree the distinction between antecedent and remedial rights is the basis for the distinction between true debt and quasi-debt. It, too, is therefore essential for financial economics. But, I believe it is also necessary for the background of legal theory. The name "choses in action" in effect lumps together the two varieties of right because it implies that both can only be asserted by suit. In this way it gives to the antecedent rights a name which sounds as if they were only remedial rights. This tends to confusion. Then, again, to the ultimate incidence of practically all remedial rights, regardless of the particular kind of antecedent right from which they spring, it gives the one name, "damages." And this tends to increase the confusion. This confusion can only be eliminated by recognizing that the relation of the creditor to the debtor (or to his fund) which arises from an incompleted sale or a loan of value (paid in money or other property transferred) is, from the moment it arrives at what we have called its semi-final stage and until it is finally discharged by repurchase, an antecedent property interest. True, it can only be asserted in law by an action. But that is also the case with all other rights of those out of possession. The facts are that it is already, grudgingly and in certain ways only, recognized by the law as an interest—and even a pre-dominant interest—in the fund of the debtor.[23] Theory must digest these facts.

9. *Fusion of the Old Theory and the New Facts as to Property in Contract*

It is essential as well as possible still more accurately to adapt the theory of the law of contract to the facts of modern law as to property in contract, which we have hitherto presented, and in that way to make our propositions for the most part additions to, rather than alterations of, the present theory of contract. This we do by starting again at the primitive oneness of contract and conveyance.

The definition of contract given in the *Restatement of the Law of Contract*[24] is as follows: "A contract is a promise or a set of promises for the breach of which the law gives a remedy, or the performance of which the law in some way recognizes as a duty." And, "A promise is an undertaking, however expressed, either that something shall happen, or that something shall not happen, in the future." This is a satisfactory definition broad enough to include everything the law construes as a contract. It will be noted that the contract is the promise and that performance is the carrying out of the undertaking. In early English forms this performance was most usually a conveyance. Thus contract seemed to be nothing but a conveyance for future delivery. And, in effect, so it was regarded. As a chose in action it was originally therefore a claim to this delivery in the future which could only be enforced by an action. And such, in much of the theory of law, it still remains. But since the chose has been forced to lose its *Dinglichkeit* in order to cover cases where this now concreted thing has become a service rather than the delivery of an object, the law now lumps together

[23] See Appendix III.

[24] Secs. 1 and 2.

services and delivery in one formula and treats them, in the Roman style, as an act or event, a happening or non-happening. In this way, to be all-inclusive, the theory envisages two immaterial acts or events, a promise at the beginning and a happening or non-happening at the end. Nor does it greatly concern itself with what exists between the beginning and the end.

So far as this goes it is satisfactory. But it does not describe property in contract, the relation with which we have concerned ourselves in our previous analysis. It is true that the legal theory admits property in the document itself, just as it does in conveyancing documents. It is also true that it admits, in a vague way, a right in the performance as against interference by third parties. But it does not satisfactorily incorporate either in its theories.

We have heretofore determined that contract (promise) may give rise to immediate and antecedent property—an interest in the debtor's fund; and that breaches of contract may give rise to immediate and remedial property of an inchoate sort, which, when and if it matures into a definite interest in the debtor's fund, displaces and succeeds the first. We have described the stages and degrees through which this antecedent or remedial property passes as it ripens and have noted that when it becomes ripe it is always credit-debt or quasi credit-debt. Now we must note that this property results from the promise, or its breach, not from the performance. Nor, judging by its measure and incidence, is it property in the performance. Rather it is property in the fund of the debtor, occasioned by the lack of performance on his part.[25] Balancing the bilateral performance (including consideration), on the other hand, which may or may not itself be accomplished by a conveyance of some other property, extinguishes this property in contract. In other words, as we have said, such a balancing of performance effects, in fact, the repurchase of that interest in the debtor's fund which may have sprung from the promise (contract) and the previous lack of performance. Damages, of course, always consist in a conveyance of other property and always extinguish property in contract by such a repurchase, though here the result is accomplished by first converting the antecedent property in contract into remedial damages.

To the extent that contract does, during its life, give rise in this way to an interest in the fund of the debtor, it is incidentally itself a conveyance of this interest. However, it conveys no other

[25] Williston, *Sales*, sec. 576, says, "Strictly the consideration of the buyer's promise is not the seller's performance but the seller's promise. The parties [to a contract of sale] contemplate a double exchange. They exchange promises when the contract is made and they plan to exchange performances later. The fact that the performances are not to be simultaneous does not alter the fact that one performance is regarded as the price or exchange of the other."

form of interest than a credit-debt. Contract originates, though it does not measure, this interest. Other forms of conveyance or delivery, by way of performance, may extinguish it. But the contract, as conveyance, and a true conveyance, as performance, are two separate and distinct legal forms. Thus the naïve view of the contract as a conveyance for future delivery is no longer true to the legal facts. In so far as it is a conveyance at all it is but a conveyance of a potential credit-debt.

No one would hold that a conveyance is itself the property which it creates or conveys. Neither is a contract the property which it may create. Both are but causes of title and give rise to property. Therefore, just as we differentiate between a conveyance and the estate, let us say, so created, we must also distinguish between a contract and the property which the contract creates. The difficulty is that, while the theory of the law makes conveyance subordinate to property in the first case, it considers the contract, as promise, to be the only effect of itself in the second. Nevertheless, though the promise or contract is all that the law talks about, the property—or interest in the debtor fund—is practically all that it enforces. Our supplement to the theory of contract is therefore a reflection of legal facts even though it may be opposed to antique legal ideas. As an example of this construction we may cite two parallel cases. A 99 year lease is an interest in land created by conveyance and extinguished by its expiry. A 99 year bond (disregarding its security) is theoretically nothing but a promise until it expires in performance at the end of the period. It is hardly necessary to recite, however, that, in practice, it is much more. The whole difficulty is that the theory of law has failed to envisage the property created by its contracts, property which it actually protects and enforces and which fits quite consistently into most of its theory of contract.

We may define a conveyance as the means of transferring existing, or creating new, direct interests in objects or dominant interests in funds, and of transferring existing pre-dominant interests in funds. Contract, on the other hand, is the only antecedent means of creating new pre-dominant interests in funds. True, as we have seen, it does not create them *per se*. But the means by which they are created are determined by, or construed from, the terms of the contract. Nor does such property spring into being full-fledged. It may begin as future property (power-liability), pass through the stage of unliquidated present property, and only finally become antecedent credit-debt. And at any point it may be converted by a breach into a right of action to damages and thus, perhaps, eventuate as a remedial credit-debt. It is measured at all times by the disequilibrium resulting from the lack of balance in performance plus consideration. In all cases property in contract does not expire. It is always converted; for it is only extinguished by a balancing of performance or by the collection of damages. To the extent that it seems sometimes merely to expire it is because the contract has not been construed to give rise to property at all, or because the contract has not been enforced.[26]

There is one further point to consider. In our original discussion of the nature of true property in contract, as typified by credit-debt, we demonstrated that it is actually an interest in indeterminate 'things' in the debtor's fund (i.e. an indirect interest in objects) because, while it is called a right *in personam* and the proceedings follow the old form against the person, its ultimate incidence and manner of execution is upon specific 'things,' in the debtor's fund. This viewpoint, which we have followed throughout and which interprets the incidence of the antecedent right as if it were determined by the incidence of its remedial right, suggests that the realistic view may be the same as the legalistic view. It casts doubt on the existence of any antecedent right? The antecedent right may be merely that one which has received no legal recognition because it has not yet required to be adjudicated. Where adjudication is unnecessary the result is performance. After performance the property

[26] Let us analyse this analogy further. The creation of a new property interest is effected by the selection of a particular assortment of the component rights of the grantor's existing interest and their incorporation into a new grouping, thus reducing to that extent the grantor's interest. Obviously this new interest only comes into being when it is alienated. Until then it remains a part of that from which it is made.

A conveyance effects such an alienation *inter vivos*. Succession effects it *causa mortis*. At the same time both methods may effect either the transfer of the entire interest of the transferor or the transfer of only a part of his interest, and therefore the creation of a new interest. The two cases must be carefully distinguished. Transfers of complete interests do not increase property; do not elaborate the complexity of the property structure. Transfers (creations) of new (partial) interests do.

Contract is only the frame in which a new property interest is to be created. But this interest is only created when, as and if the excess consideration plus performance of the creditor principal brings it into being. At that point the new interest comes into being.

It is probably true that direct interests in objects can be created new, or, if existing, can be transferred, only by conveyance or delivery. And, of all other existing interests – including those which are negotiable – only conveyance effects transfer. This is also true as well of certain new interests in funds. But the rest of the new interests in funds are all created by contract. And contract never transfers an existing interest of any kind. It is true that, when specific performance is required, there appears to be an exception. But, actually, specific performance is a compulsory conveyance. It is the result of an adjudication of the contract, not the contract itself.

Leaving aside, then, succession, which is wholly a continuance, and non-economic, we may say that the business of exchanges consists in the conveyance of new (partial) or of existing property interests, both direct and indirect, and in the creation of new indirect interests arising from the surplus consideration or performance of the creditor principal under contract.

is in the result of performance. Before performance, where was it; in the possible performance which could not be legally enforced; or in the damages which could be (i. e. in the potential remedial right)? In other words is the remedial right the only legal right in contract?

Let us attempt to answer this objection. In the first place, as to the antecedent quality of property in contract. In the case of direct interests in objects the state creates only the complete property in the objects, by means of its fence of prohibitions against others and of its limited permissions to the holder. The direct interests as they actually exist are apportionments of this complete property. These apportionments are wholly the acts of parties, not of the state. The titles to the various interests consist of the series of conveyances or successions from which each interest has arisen or through which it has been transmitted. The rights of action which attach to the complete property, and which are granted by the state, are therefore distributed among the fractional interests by acts of parties. Thus the rights of action which pertain to a particular interest are grounded on the title to, and the nature of, the particular interest. It is clear, then, that such a fractional interest is necessarily antecedent to the remedial rights which are assigned to and are potential within it, and that the acts of parties which created it are the very basis of the remedial right which springs upon the infringement of the antecedent rights which compose it. In the case of those actions which are wholly between parties at interest this is even more obviously true. For such actions have no reference whatever to the complete property granted by the state nor to the remedial rights against non-interested parties attaching thereto. They are rather concerned wholly with the internal division of this complete property and depend entirely upon the title to, and the nature of, the particular interest. Since the title to, and the origin of, a particular interest is necessarily prior to an infringement of its component rights, it is therefore antecedent to the springing of a remedial right.

In the case of property in contract there is certain property in the documents and there are rights against interference by third parties which are analogous to the foregoing complete property, in that they are rights against others than the parties at interest. But as to all other elements in property in contract the resemblance is confined to the apportionment of complete property in an object. For the whole ground of the claim is the contract; just as, in the other, it is the grounds of title (i. e. the conveyance or succession) to the particular fractional interest. Both are exclusively due to the acts of parties and what remedial rights spring are against, and the resulting actions are between, parties at interest only. Since, in the first case, the interest is antecedent to its remedial right, it is necessarily equally so in the second case.

When we come to consider the question of incidence we may limit the parallel between property in contract and direct interests in objects to the relations among the parties at interest in the same object, within the latter class. Necessarily the incidence of all the latter interests is upon the object itself. Perhaps a remedial right of one interested party against another may eventually rest on that other's fund. But the antecedent rights in all cases and the remedial rights in most cases rest on the object; that is, they are in some respect and at some time possessory. At first blush the incidence of the corresponding property in contract would seem to be upon the performance or upon that which is to be delivered or done. But since this is frequently not yet in existence it cannot then be an object of incidence. Furthermore such incidence is rarely asserted, and then only as a matter of grace and when it is possible. So we may say that the antecedent rights prior to performance can only be construed to rest where the remedial rights are almost always made to rest; that is, not upon a specific performance or a specific object, but upon an equivalent portion of indeterminate 'things' in the debtor's fund.

The basis for the determination of the measure of the interest in the case of direct interests in objects, is either the object itself which is pointed to, or the value, or the loss of value, of this object. The measure in the case of contract has already been fully discussed. In this respect and in practice, Anglo-American law seems to have tended to be governed by the economic facts behind the promise, rather than by the promise itself. It has treated contract as giving rise to a property interest measured by these economic facts, rather than one measured by the promised performance. It seems to have been guided by a desire to restore the balance — the *status quo ante* — of value, rather than by a desire to enforce, or penalize the failure to perform, promises.

Thus it seems most realistic to construe the facts of property in contract in the following way: The final determinant of the property in the case of credit-debt is the incidence of the potential remedial right which attaches to it. If the antecedent right is not disputed it will usually be valued and treated only within this limit of legal liability. Therefore, in reality, the obligee's property in the contract before performance is not in the promise nor even in the performance, but in what would be the incidence of the remedial right if it became necessary to adjudicate. If, on the other hand, the antecedent right is disputed the remedial right which displaces it will, within the rules of law, reflect it. The former continues, as a measure or standard, if not as a 'thing.' The antecedent and remedial right, therefore, each determine the other. The antecedent, when the remedial springs, becomes merely a set of facts which determines the nominal or maximal extent of the remedial right. But the remedial right, while it remained potential, had always in reality determined the actual or minimal extent as well as the true incidence of the antecedent property. Thus the only legal content of any property right, either of direct or indirect property, is finally determined by the potential effective remedies for its infringement; and the only incidence and measure of any interest is, as to incidence, that to which the aggregate of its remedies point and, as to measure, the area which they circumscribe.

10. *Varieties of Pre-dominant Interest*

In passing we should perhaps call attention to the fact that, in one respect, interests in funds (indirect interests in objects) are theoretically and practically confused with interests in material objects. This occurs as a result of property in documents. The document representing a property interest, which is often considered to be itself the property and which often goes by the same name as the interest, is never more than evidence of the character and inherence of the property. But where it is negotiable, or nearly negotiable, the holder of the document may automatically become the holder of the interest and it then incorporates in itself the value of the property it represents. In this respect it seems itself to become the object. For, if it is lost or stolen, the property is lost or stolen. But a bond is, nevertheless, not the credit-debt; a check is not the bank deposit; a stock certificate is not the shares of stock; a contract is not the obligation; any more than a bill of sale is possession of an automobile, or a deed the estate in a house and lot. All are merely evidence of title. In those cases where titles are customarily registered the document is not so important. But where they are not and the document is almost the only evidence of right, then possession of the document is nine points of the law. It is for this reason that documents representing interests in funds have come to be regarded in some respects as themselves material objects. And this, at times, has led to such interests being treated as if they were possessory interests in such material objects rather than what they really are. It is therefore necessary to recall the fact that the law treats all documents, for themselves, as personalty, i. e. as objects of personal property in possession.

It is also necessary, at this point, to call attention to one small and relatively unimportant class of indirect interests in objects which are the only ones that are not, at the same time, interests in funds. These are modeled upon a certain class of direct interest in objects and go so far as to treat an evidence of property interest much as if it were an object. They are a particular kind of security—bailments of 'things,' which 'things' in turn are almost always interests in funds, though occasionally they may be documents representing direct interests in objects. Such bailments are the rights of bailees in the pledge, deposit, carriage, etc., of what are popularly called "securities." It may also be possible for non-possessory but specific liens to be directed against such specific 'things' just as is done in the case of a specific lot of land or goods, and thus to come within this special class.

Let us now attempt to tabulate the chief varieties of pre-dominant interests in funds, just as we have already done with direct interests in objects and with dominant and administrative interests in funds.

Pre-dominant Interests in Funds[27]

1. Antecedent Property in Contract
   - A. Credit-debt. Present Interests, Admitted and of Ascertained Value (Liquidated)
     - a. Currency
     - b. Bank Deposit
     - c. Promissory Note
     - d. Bond
     - e. Mortgage (as note or contract)
     - f. Account Stated
     - g. Account Current
     - h. Liquidated Liability on Other Contracts
   - B. Other Property in Contract. Potential or Inchoate
     - a. Present Interests. Admitted, Unliquidated. Such as work in process, etc. (usually only the margin is unliquidated)
     - b. Future Interests. Admitted power-liabilities on mutually executory contracts.
       - Purchase and Sale
       - Interest on Loans
       - Lessor's Interest in Lease, etc.
2. Remedial Property in Obligations Legally Imposed
   - A. Credit-debt
     - a. Judgment Debt (same as 1A)
       Present Consummate Interests arising from Rights of Action
3. Potential Remedial Property. Inchoate Interests, Defeasible
   - A. Rights of Action for Breach of Contract Claimed
   - B. Rights of Action for Tort Claimed

[27] The most precise definition of the constitution of the fund as a body of property is provided by bankruptcy practice. The rules which determine what

4. Contingent Property in Contract

A. Accessory to other Property

a. Suretyship	Primary but Substitute
b. Warranty	Primary
c. Guaranty	Secondary
d. Indorsement	Secondary [28]

B. Principal

a. Insurance Policies

b. Miscellaneous

5. Accessory Antecedent Property. Voluntary and Usually Possessory

A. Pledge, etc., of 'Things' not themselves Direct Interests in Objects

6. Accessory Remedial Property. Involuntary and Non-possessory
In transition between remedial property and dominant interests in some specific 'things' composing the fund, or other equivalent

A. Liens, Equitable, Statutory and Maritime, not upon Specific 'Things'

B. Executions, Attachments, Garnishments, etc., of the Same Order

assets and liabilities the trustee in bankruptcy assumes (i.e. the content of the trustee's fund) circumscribe the exact kinds of pre-dominant interest which may be deemed to be incident upon the bankrupt's old fund, together with all interests which are deemed to compose it at that moment; and they discriminate, as to both, between property and personal rights and, within the field of property, between beneficial and administrative and between present and future or contingent interests. The cut-off is complete. Those assets and liabilities which are construed as belonging with the bankrupt's new fund, which is segregated at the same moment, cannot be defined as having composed or as having been incident upon his old fund. This with the exception of his exempt assets, which are of a privileged status – a transferred nest-egg – and of his non-dischargeable debts.

In general the interests composing the bankrupt's old fund are defined as consisting of all transferable or leviable property except such as the trustee promptly rejects. There is some limitation among the powers, rights and documents, such as books, deeds, instruments and papers. Interests in patents, patent rights, pending applications for patents, copyrights, trade-marks, trade names, franchises, licenses (if not personal) and goodwill are included. Rights and powers which the bankrupt could have exercised for his own benefit are included. But those he could have exercised only for the benefit of others are not. His own beneficial interests in trusts are part of the fund, if the trust was passive or dry, or if consisting of surplus income or a fixed sum from a testamentary trust. So too property receivable by legacy or inheritance, if the claim thereto was valid at the time of petition. Other interests composing the fund are stock exchange memberships (though contingent on the election of the purchaser) ; liability (if a corporation) on unpaid stock subscriptions ; debts or claims due the bankrupt ; rights of action on contract or for unlawful taking, detention or injury to bankrupt's property (i. e. torts to property) ; rights to rents or reversionary interest as landlord ; estate in leased premises as tenant ; the cash surrender value of life insurance policies, not exempt, and payable to the bankrupt, his estate, or, personal representative, or where the beneficiary may be changed by the bankrupt ; and, finally, the assets which are exempt or construed as not being subject to the claims of, or rejected by the trustee for, the general creditors. [*cont. on next page.*]

The interests composing this old fund do not include expectancies nor inchoate interests at the time of application, even if in the latter case the "bankrupt by joining in a deed or otherwise, might be able to estop himself from afterwards claiming title to the property when the inchoate interest should actually become consummated and vested" (Remington, *A Treatise on the Elements of Bankruptcy Law*, sec. 52) ; nor the future property in incompleted contracts for personal services by the bankrupt where personal trust or confidence was reposed for the exercise of his skill; nor rights of action for tort for injury to the bankrupt's person (including slander, libel, malicious prosecution, etc.), (Black *On Bankruptcy*, sec. 194, says that rights of action for torts which occasion injury to person, do not, and for those which occasion injury to property, do vest in trustee in bankruptcy) ; nor life insurance policies, except for cash surrender value – which gives a sort of lien on the policy.

The pre-dominant interests which are incident upon the bankrupt's old fund include:

1. Fixed liabilities at time of filing.
   a. On contract, evidenced by an instrument in writing, if absolutely owing, (though not necessarily due) with interest, or with rebate of discount, including unliquidated claims if liquidated by direction of court.
   b. Unpaid rent, accrued up to date of filing.
   c. Judgments without regard to cause of action (including those for personal injury and other similar torts) if claim reduced to judgment before filing.
2. Liabilities on open accounts or on contracts express or implied (or on quasi-contract) executory, or executed, or for damages in breach of contract, if the liability is accrued and definite at time of filing.
   Including,
   a. Liability on note to payee or indorsee and liability as indorser, if it is fixed at commencement of proceedings or becomes fixed within time for proving claims.
   b. Stockholders' liability on unpaid subscriptions, but not double or other statutory liability unless reduced to judgment or definitely ascertained and fixed at time of bankruptcy.
   c. Liability for breach of covenant, like warranty, etc., if breach occurred before filing.
   d. Liability for breach of contract, though time of performance has not expired, if bankruptcy constitutes an anticipatory breach or if contract is repudiated or renounced.
   e. Liability on contract though induced by fraud, if creditor waives fraud.
3. Taxes and court costs (preferred claims).
   Including,
   a. Costs as plaintiff in pending suits, if trustee declines to prosecute.
   b. Costs incurred by creditors in prior actions to recover provable claims.

The potential pre-dominant interests, both antecedent and remedial, which are not construed as being incident upon the bankrupt's old fund are:

1. Unliquidated claims *ex delicto*.
2. Contingent claims, except if, during period of proving, liability as or to indorser or surety becomes fixed.
3. Rents not accrued, if trustee does not assume lease, or if lease does not provide that in case of default remaining installments become immediately due and payable.
4. Claims not owing, whether on judgments, written instruments, open accounts or contracts express and implied (such as interest not accrued, etc.).
5. Usually judgments for penal fines, alimony, support of wife, child, etc. (because imposed on person, under public, and not on property, under private, law).

[*cont. on next page.*]

B. *The Property Structure*

1. *The Substance and Pattern of the Structure*

The presentation of the composition and design of that structure of relations called property, which we have gradually worked out in the foregoing pages has necessarily resulted in a somewhat confused picture. And this for two reasons. The first is a difficulty inherent in the historical method. In tracing the course of development of anything whatever we are necessarily describing a succession of changes affecting, perhaps, both its composition and its relations. Each such thing is not a fixed fact to be readily identified throughout its history and to be fitted precisely into its proper place at each phase, all neatly labelled. It is on the contrary a flow streaming from the past into the present, meandering, branching, anastomosing, and only identifiable at all because we somewhat arbitrarily invest it with a certain species of continuity. An equal difficulty arises when it is necessary to proceed by the method of analysing each part and its relation to other parts. For then, since at each stage some of the other parts have not yet been described, it is impossible until the last

Such interests may be construed to be incident upon the bankrupt's new fund. And the unpaid balance of certain non-dischargeable claims, which were provable and therefore incident upon his old fund, may be construed as being also incident upon his new fund. The cases of these two kinds are:

1. Taxes.
2. Liability for obtaining property under false pretences.
3. Liability for wilful or malicious injury to person or property.
4. Liability for alimony, due or to become due.
5. Liability for maintenance of wife and child.
6. Liability for seduction or breach of promise.
7. Debts not scheduled by bankrupt, unless creditor had an opportunity to prove claim.
8. Debts, demands and claims on account of fraud, embezzlement, etc., as officer or fiduciary.
9. Wages of employees for previous three months.
10. Debts for guaranty money from employees.
11. Liability of partners for partnership debts if they have not been discharged as individuals.
12. Debts or claims not provable in the bankruptcy proceedings either because of their nature or because they had not matured or attached at time of filing.
13. Balance of non-dischargeable debts, in excess of trustee's dividends.
14. Liens against property not divested by bankrupt and not foreclosed or administered in bankruptcy court.
15. Liens on judgments attaching more than four months before petition, if the claim was not proved or the property did not become an asset of the trustee.

[28] "An indorsement [of a negotiable instrument] is not merely a transfer of title, but a new and substantive contract by which the indorser becomes a party to the instrument and liable, on certain conditions, for its payment." Johnson v. Beickey, 64 Utah 43, 48 (1924).

step is completed to merge the discontinuous parts into a continuous whole. For these reasons we have deferred until the end any effort to present as a whole a picture of this property structure to which we have frequently alluded.

We have not attempted in this study to deal with the functioning of property, but have confined ourselves to examining its growth and the development and design of its structure. We have examined the anatomy rather than the physiology. Strictly speaking this structure consists not of substance but of relations. Today prohibitions and their obverse, limited permissions, define, in the capacity of a sort of interface, the unit of the property structure, the property right. But other similar units, namely all other civil rights, exist outside the property structure. We are enabled to distinguish between the classes of rights by means of one criterion. Property rights relate, directly or indirectly, to material or quasi-material objects appropriable in law, and are defined by prohibitions and permissions with ultimate reference to these objects. Other civil rights are either personal, familial or political. They are the rights of a person with reference to himself, to his family, or to his status in the body politic. Similarly these rights are defined in terms of prohibitions against others and limited permissions to oneself. The state confirms property as the rights of one person, against other persons and against itself, with reference to objects. It confirms the other civil rights as rights of all persons, modified by status, against other persons and against itself with reference to the person, the family, and the body politic. In both cases what is not permitted to the holder of the right or what is not prohibited to others and to itself, constitutes the reservation of liberties and powers, specifically to the state, or generally, in common, to all persons.

Thus the personal liberties accorded the individual and the sovereign powers, so-called, accorded to the community (or state) define what is permissible to do by means usually of stating what is not permissible to do. In so far as property rights legally confer, on persons holding them, rights to do, it is because there is usually condensed within and applied to each property interest all of the general personal liberties which are thereby given specific reference to this 'thing.' The rights to contract, etc., included in specific properties are derived from the personal liberties and not *vice versa*. Occasionally we also find some of the sovereign powers conferred on persons, or funds, by inclusion in specific properties (franchises, etc.). And we find personal liberties conferred in a limited way upon funds (corporations). The peculiar attributes of property, not derived from these sources, consist exclusively of definitions, not of what the holder can do but of what he and others cannot do with reference to a specific object or fund. They are prohibitions, exclusions and monopolies defined and limited by law.

Personal, political and familial rights are acquired by birth or by entrance into a status such as citizenship or marriage. Sovereign powers are acquired by private persons or funds only through grant from the sovereign. Personal rights can only be acquired by impersonal funds through grant from the same source. Property rights, on the other hand, are acquired, for the most part, by transfer from other persons. This may occur through the voluntary acts of parties, as in most succession (testamentary inheritance, legacy, gift) and in final or semi-final exchanges of one set for another. It may also occur through the force of law, as in titles derived from law, from judgments and from decrees. Only in the case of appropriation or prescription does property arise other than by transfer. Thus the elaboration of the property structure consists primarily of the subdivision and rearrangement of the existing system of interests.

An attempt has been made to depict the broad outlines of this general structure in a diagram, as shown on the following page. This diagram presents the various connections between the persons (natural) in which all property ultimately inheres, and the material or quasi-material objects to which it ultimately refers. We have used the term incidence to indicate this latter reference. All such connections are bipolar. Their inherence is in the direction of persons, and their incidence is in the direction of objects. We therefore present the superstrate of the structure as if it were composed of persons and the substrate as if it were composed of material (and quasi-material) objects. From the standpoint of persons the proximate beneficial relation is that final connection that is had with the immediate or personal funds—'own' funds, estates, trusts, etc. From this same standpoint the ultimate relation, that immediate to the substrate, is the class of direct interests in objects. To some extent the personal funds are composed of these direct interests in objects. But for the most part such direct interests run to the intermediate or impersonal funds (partnerships, corporations and foundations), which constitute the system of ganglia interposed between the upper and lower strata, and which are inter-connected among themselves by a vast network of inter-fund relations. In turn, an equally complex web of interests, both dominant and predominant, run up from these intermediate funds to the personal ones. There is one other type of connection which, in the diagram, appears to run in the reverse direction. That consists of the predominant interests *only* which are incident upon personal funds and which may inhere either in other personal or in impersonal funds. In spite of this interposition of intermediate funds and the cross

THE STRUCTURE OF PROPERTY

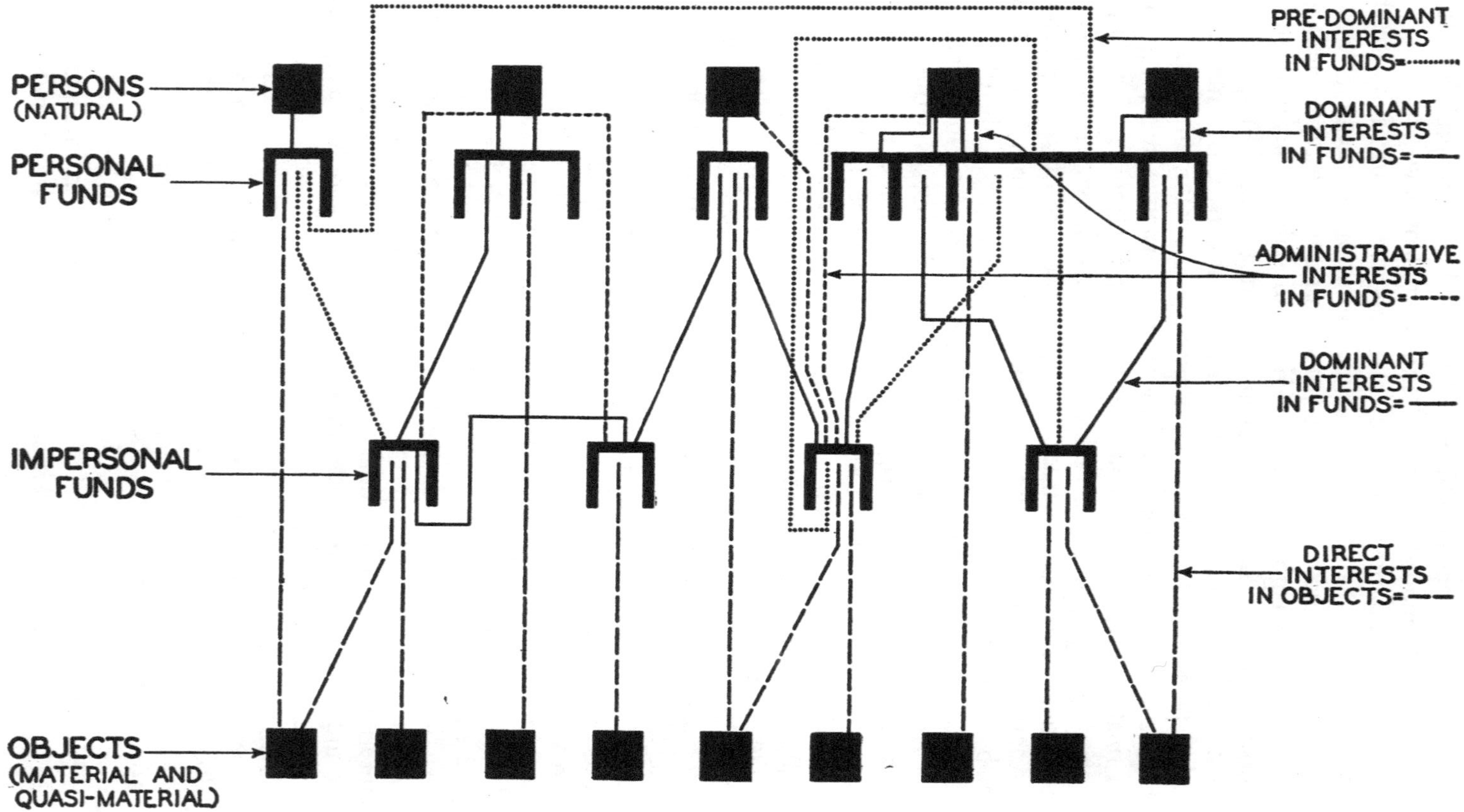

currents which to some extent this sets up, it is a fact that ultimately – through many steps – the complete property in the material base is distributed among the persons to whom run the final beneficial and the administrative relations.

Thus we may conceive the structure of property as an intricate framework of relations, summing up to complete property in, or control of, the whole material base in the hands of the aggregate of all persons connected. The individual strands of the whole system of relations, where they issue from the lower margin of the complex and connect with objects, not only relate always to some definite one among the whole cosmogony of specific objects, according to a system of units defined by law, but they are infinitely varied among themselves in respect of the particular, perhaps minute, fraction of complete property which they represent therein. So too, when they issue from the upper margin and connect with persons, they run always to some individual person among the millions concerned though they may be varied according to the type of personal relation that exists. Between these two margins the interlacing complexities and the variety of character of the inter-fund relations is even more elaborated. But here as well all interests connect with but one fund at each pole.

Now that we have envisaged the structure of property as a whole we are in better position finally to discriminate between those interests which are already parts of the structure and those which are only in process, or have the possibility, of becoming parts of the structure. In other words we are prepared to distinguish vested property from mere claims. It is true that the difference is one of degree; for in certain respects all property is tentative until it has been finally confirmed by judicial proceedings. Nevertheless, in general, property subsists because it is acknowledged by the parties thereto. Even then it is of course subject to modification and extinction in unforeseen ways. But when we project the whole organization of relations upon its base we find that mere claims do not appear. Unliquidated or future property in contract must develop into credit-debt before it is consolidated into the structure as an additional relation between two funds. And all rights of action must develop into similar remedial credit-debts before they are definitely a part of the system. Even then the latter are but transitory because, being immediately due, the debtor fund is promptly modified and sufficient of its component 'things' are transferred to repurchase the transient interest. Thus the result is a reallocation of 'things' between funds, not the establishment of a lasting interest inhering in one and incident upon the other. It is of course true, however, that since the parts of the structure are delicately equilibrated *inter se* and interests are piled upon interests in series and are therefore dependent upon each other, any major modification of one fund, from extrinsic causes, which removes a considerable portion of the interests composing it without replacing them with others, may cause a collapse of the particular superstructure of interests incident upon it, and thus involve by repercussion a considerable part of the whole organization. This is the very real difference in effect between what we have called true debt, which results only from exchanges, and quasi-debt, which is by definition a mere unilateral reallocation.

It is this framework of relations, principally, among the various social institutions, in which the so-called economic activities take place. This is itself, in fact, the fundamental economic institution, to which that other which we call employment is only an adjunct. In modern societies there are practically no persons, except a majority of infants, who do not participate in some way and in some degree in the so-called beneficial or administrative relations to the property structure. The various elements in control are so minutely divided and so highly organized, and the various forms of compensation, derived from those to whom is conceded dependent beneficial interests or paid to those to whom is conceded administrative interests, flow so generally among the adult members of society that the whole structure must be regarded as representing the organization of society in one of its chief aspects.

All of which is in striking contrast to the primitive concentration of property in the single head of each *familia*, and to its original development in propinquity. No longer is it necessary to "sit near" one's possessions. In fact most persons have no means of knowing where the objects are located which constitute the point of ultimate physical incidence of their rights of property. Nor would it be possible to trace the various interests in most objects to particular individuals to whom these objects, in a sense, still *belong*. This whole complex structure of property intrudes between persons and objects. By as much as the legal relations which are interposed are complex, so are the physical relations attenuated and disjunctive. Nevertheless the property relation—that which lies between—is as real and as definite as the original relation of propinquity.

This visualization of the structure of property aids in clarifying one common legal problem. In the administration of law, both for purposes of jurisdiction and for purposes of taxation, the question of the *locus* of property is a constant source of trouble. It is amusing to watch the judiciary and other political officials attempting to settle this question. Where is a bond? Does it reside with the creditor; or with the documentary evidence of the debt; or with the mortgaged objects; or, according to the old notion of the personal incidence of debt, is it quartered upon the person of the debtor? Now property is a relation and, of course, a relation can have no locus. Only the relata have loci. The relata of property are material objects, persons, and those seemingly concreted foci of their inter-relations, called funds. Obviously material objects have definite loci. Land is controlled by the law of the jurisdiction in which it is located. Goods are conceived to accompany the person of the *de jure* possessor and are thus controlled by the law of the jurisdiction where he is domiciled. As to the person himself he is of course subject to the law of his domicile, as well as to that of the state from which he derives his civil rights. Personal funds usually follow the domicile or allegiance of the person. As to impersonal funds, they will be found on examination always to have no other "local habitation" than the office of their chief, or at least their nominally official, administration. It is there that impersonal funds are domiciled. Since the loci of the relata are frequently different it is of course impossible to assign a locus to the relation – the property interest. It is only possible to determine what it is one wishes to reach; the object of incidence of a direct interest in objects, or the fund of inherence or incidence of any interest whatever. Which end of the bipolar relation is one seeking to locate? There may, at times, be occasion to reach as well the person in whom the administrative, or even the final beneficial, interests in a fund are vested. But this is a simple problem.

When we review the process of development and the final nature of this structure, which represents the modern institution of property, it becomes a matter for surprise that the concept of property could have become concreted. How is it possible that the term for an institutionalized arrangement of society – which was originally compounded of a range of notions running from governance through patronage and mastery to the right of the parent, and which now consists of this complex web of relations – has come eventually to be transferred, in its most naïve usage, to cover a material object in its aspect of 'belonging' (whatever that may be)? So complete has been the transubstantiation of the term that it has been quite a general practice to overlook its beginnings and the continuing institution which it covered, and to seek the origin of property – on the basis of its concreted meaning – in a *primitive instinct*,[29] an imputed desire to possess material objects. Not only is such an origin quite imaginary and unrelated to the actual facts, but it is objectionable because it reflects and reinforces a view of even the present institution which blinds us to its historic and true present nature.

[29] I have deliberately used here two words which are in the Index Expurgatorius of the psychologists.

The heredity of the customs of our modern property system seems to have originated in what we have called pre-property—the simple unitary organization of the human group. The vestigial relics of this early government of persons survive to our day in the remaining familial rights. At the dawn of Roman history this organization had become projected upon the land. While, at first, this relation to the land was territorial (i. e. of a political character) it was the source of what we now treat as "real property." The form in which it has been transmitted to us was greatly modified when, in the Dark Ages, this organization upon the land became three-dimensional—a hierarchy. From the time of pre-property the nature of the relations with regard to the flocks seems to have been differentiated, and to have been the first property to be diffused—individual. It served as the prototype, and perhaps one of the sources, of the form of the feudal hierarchy upon the land. But, as the law of chattels, it lost that dependent character which "real" property was just then acquiring. This secondary and less mature system has survived to us as our organization upon goods—"personal" as contrasted with "real" property. In modern times these two systems of property have become partly merged and a modified type of structure has developed following the model, though not the forms, of the earliest "personal" property—*peculium* and *cheptel*—and of the medieval "real" property—the feudal hierarchy and the estates. But this structure, which represents the major element in the economic organization of society, no longer consists of a grouping of human beings. Nor, though it succeeds the early *familia* and the successive arrangements of *fundus*, *villa*, *domaine* and "estate," does the new system of grouping attach itself directly or especially to the land. Instead it is founded—with little or no geographical projection—upon the substratum of land and goods, now merged. The grouping, now, is in the *fund*.

The fund itself is not new except in name. We have already pointed out the direct descent of the corporate fund from the original property organization, the household or *familia*, and the fact, no less true though not so obvious, that all[80] the other modern forms of funds are similarly descended. As the original group—composed almost wholly of persons and controlled by a leader who held what we have called the pre-property power over them—gradually added to itself material objects—animals, land and goods—the original property power came in the end to control only these accessions. Thus the household was metamorphosed into an aggregate of objects. All persons were removed from it. In the end the various forms of relation which had developed within the *familia* were converted into

[80] Except the trust.

the various types of dominant interests in funds which, because they give its organic character to the fund, determine in turn its type. Single dominion gave rise to the own fund; single dominion in transition or in liquidation (the *hereditas iacens* and *bonorum cessio*, or *venditio*, of Roman law)gave rise to the estate of a decedent or bankrupt; the trust has to some extent amalgamated itself with the projected substitutions of artificial parents *in loco parentis*. The relations upon which all these funds were organized remained personal and final. Other funds, such as partnerships and corporations, developed out of the secondary relations which existed within the original *familiae*. And, because they were secondary, they came to relate fund to fund only – to be impersonal and mediate. The partnership, or *societas*, probably grew from the same stem as agency – the special relation of the chief with one of his subject persons; and the corporation seems to have been originally an artificial *familia* – formed usually for political or religious purposes – related most closely to that special type of familial organization which has come down to us as the *consortium*. Thus the funds, though derived from the same source, now divide themselves into two strata.

In these various ways the form of the major aggregate which now appears in the property organization has become multiplied and variegated. The dominant relations of fund to fund, connecting the impersonal funds among themselves and to the personal, have gradually developed out of the secondary intra-familial relations. And the pre-dominant relations of fund to fund have gradually developed out of the original inter-familial relations. The influence of this structural resemblance has gone so far as to modify, and in some respects amalgamate, some even among those inter-fund relations which are dominant, such as shareholding, with the pure stock of the pre-dominant relations – to make hybrids of them.

If we were to describe the property structure of today in terms of its primitive elements, we would say that there are now more *familiae* than there are persons; that each *familia* has a *dominus* or *quasi-dominus* (single or multiple) ; that the contents of any *familia* are limited to various intra-familial relations to material objects and to other *familiae*, or to various inter-familial relations to other *familiae*, which inhere in it; and that these inter-familial relations have now been converted, in all cases in fact and in most cases in form as well, from powers over the head (*persona*) of such other *familia*, into protections as to participation in the benefits derived from its contents.

Upon this framework society in this aspect is organized. To each individual, regardless of age or sex, may be attached, by any of several types of final personal relation, one or more personal or immediate funds. And, in addition, each active participant may be attached, in an infinite variety of administrative property relations, to one or to many funds, both personal and impersonal. Society in this aspect is thus ordered upon a skeleton of funds – no longer upon a chequer-board of land. This organization *is* modern property. The controls and the benefits conferred by place in this social structure are the chief incentives for the competitive struggle in the sphere of economic activities. This scheme represents a functional dynamic order. Possession is a minor incident. Position is the major objective. That which is "real," in the economic sense, may be regarded as the foundation of the whole. But it is no more the essence of the matter than was the land the essence of feudalism. In both cases it is only possible to describe the institution of property itself – feudal or modern – as a system of relations among men which projects, or reflects, itself upon the substrate. To identify the term property with the pattern of this ultimate reflection exclusively is almost as naïve as it is to identify it with the substrate – land and goods – itself. And yet one or the other naïveté is the necessary consequence of the concreted notion.

This presentation of the facts as to the composition and arrangement of the property structure should now have clarified and fully supported the preliminary statements made in the Introduction. It is necessary to recognize that the major part of modern economic activity consists in and depends upon the processes of creating, transferring, inheriting and extinguishing the elements in this financial structure; that the great bulk of transactions deal with these – the relations – rather than with the relata (i. e. the material objects and human services); that the nature of these elements cannot be described and lightly passed over as "titles to ownership," "claims," or "credit"; and that the study of the behaviour of this system may well be, because it has been neglected, a branch of the science of economics in which investigation is more immediately essential than is the further exploration of the behaviour of the material field to which economics has hitherto so largely limited itself.

2. *The Functional Elements of Property and their Distribution*

While we have hitherto confined ourselves to the structural aspect of property it is necessary at this point to touch briefly upon one feature of its functioning which largely explains the very existence, in so complicated a form, of the structure itself. We have continually been at some pains to point out, in the course of examining modern property, the difficulties which the law lets itself in for by regarding various types of interest as if they were uniform and integral things. It must be recognized that all such property interests vary not only according as they deal with the whole or some part of an object, or as they bestow only certain parts of the complete property, but that they vary in many minutiae according to the exact definition of the individual rights of which they are composed and of the particular and complex assortment of these rights. On account of the vagueness and duplicity of the terms used, and on account of the more or less general failure to disintegrate each interest into this multiplicity of rights which compose it, great confusion results. Of course, the study of the individual rights and their inclusion in one or another bundle is the whole study of the law of property and of contract. We cannot undertake here even a digression into that vast field.

There are, however, several somewhat different ends which these individual component rights serve; some specifically and some more generally or jointly. And, in so far as legal theory or doctrine has resolved the various species of property into their components at all, it has usually confined itself to analysing them according to which of these ends are served. Hearn, for instance, has divided complete property into the right to possess, to use, to the produce, to waste (use up), to disposition and to exclusion. In our quotations from American decisions we found a tendency to agree on the division into possession, exclusion, disposal, use, and enjoyment. Of these, use and enjoyment are practically synonymous. As to the content of the term "possession" tomes have been written. The more exactly it is defined the more uncertain it becomes. "Exclusion" is obviously a corollary of "possession" and of "use." And "use" itself is an almost thoroughly ruined word.[81]

We have approached this subject from an historical angle. Perhaps from this point of view we can see behind these confusions to the points that are being driven at. All property, we have seen, is a form and method of control which in these times ultimately pertains, directly or indirectly, to material objects. We should expect to find, therefore, the basis for the means of analysis the law is seeking, in this fact. Let us take first, as the simplest example, a single object. Into what elements can we resolve the control over this object? The lessor of a piece of land controls it in certain respects and the lessee controls it in other respects. To the lessor pertains all the control over changes in the property in the land. And to the lessee pertains

[81] The favorite kind of description of "use" is shown in the following: "The use of a thing does not mean the thing itself [i. e. possession], but means that the user is to enjoy, hold, occupy, or have in some manner the benefit thereof. If . . . real estate [land], the use thereof is its occupancy or cultivation . . . or the rent which can be obtained for its use. If it is money or its equivalent . . . it is the interest which it will earn." Elwell v. Stewart, 110 Kan. 218, 219 (1922).

most of the control over the land in its physical aspects. The former is principally control of the property, that is, the rights; the latter principally the control of the object itself. With the former go the right to transfer (disposal) and the right to create, or to permit the creation of, new interests in the land by imposing upon it other estates subtracted from his own or his tenant's, such as remainders, sub-leases, mortgages, etc. With the latter go the rights which are literally the use. This division is not hard and fast nor exact. Moreover in all direct interests in objects there pertain to the property control some various physical controls and *vice versa.* Nevertheless we have here a reasonably thorough basis for the separation of two major elements of property control over material objects. These are control proper (control of the property in the object) and use (physical control of the object).[32]

So far so good. But to what end is it desired to exercise either of these controls? Clearly for the benefit of the controller. And this consideration brings in the element which, as we have heretofore noted, is distinguished by the term "beneficial." In what respect does this element add to or cut across the divisions of control? It is evident that the benefits of use go, or are permitted to go, to the lessee. And use of material objects is, as a form of physical control, hypothetically beneficial. For this reason there must supposedly be some compensation to the lessor for parting with this beneficial use to the lessee. Let us call this rent the *return* to the property control. It is the substitute for—or, indirectly, the part of—the beneficial aspect (result) of the use which induces the controller of the property to separate from himself the physical control.

We have now divided the functional relations of direct property in material objects into three component elements; control, use and return. Under this definition of use it is improper to continue to apply the term when we leave the field of direct interests in objects; for one can neither physically control nor enjoy property as such. We have remaining at that stage only control (property) and return. But when we leave this field we are arrived in that of indirect interests in objects, which is another way of describing interests in funds. And, here, we find appearing another division in the remaining control, somewhat analogous to the first separation. For when one transfers any property interest whatever into some fund in exchange for an interest, dominant or pre-dominant, in that fund, one retains no rights whatever specifically in the 'thing' so transferred. One has surrendered both the functional relations, that of control therein and

[32] I think this is the distinction Ihering has in mind when, *Geist*, III, pp. 345 ff., he describes "die freie Dispositionsbefugnis" as "die Wahl der Genussformen," in contrast to "die Benutzung."

that of return therefrom. Thus, for the same reason as in the first case, it is necessary that these surrenders must be compensated. They are respectively replaced by some one of many forms of control over the fund as a whole, on one hand, and by a secondary return from that fund, on the other, which may be either preferred – fixed and contractual – or residual.

Finally, as applied both to material objects, to property in material objects and to property in funds, we have the various forms of control which we have called administrative. These are non-beneficial – that is they include neither use nor return – and they are limited in their powers. This difference is so radical that, when administrative forms of control are established, the administrator must usually be compensated for his services, rather than having to pay for the privilege of securing a part of the total control, as in all other cases.

In the foregoing we have merely sketched in the basis for the distinction between these different functional relations to property. The details vary widely in the different types of relation. But here again the exact nature of each control, each use, or each return is the subject matter of encyclopaedic treatises on law and is too vast to be dealt with here. In the broad we find, over all objects and kinds of property, many types of restricted or administrative control and of physical control (use). And, over funds, we find many types of control over the fund as a whole which do not reach to the control of the interests composing the fund. Finally there is the functional relation that we have called the return, which exists wherever the physical control, or use, of material objects, or the immediate property control in other 'things,' is divorced from one whom it is "held of." Return is thus, from the sophisticated standpoint, the direct or indirect benefit flowing up by way of substitute or compensation for the alienated beneficial use which has flowed down. From the primitive standpoint the return was itself considered to be a part of the yield, "issuing out of things corporeal." In either view the right to the return is a beneficial interest as much as is the use.

In the light of this analysis let us re-examine briefly certain of the funds which we have found typical. First as to an 'owner's' 'own' fund. In so far as no one else has an interest in it he may be said to have complete property in it; that is, he has entire control of all kinds and he has all the benefits. But as to the 'things' composing it he has only those controls and those benefits which are accorded to the particular variety of each interest. Any alteration he makes in the organization of his fund, such as placing its administration in the hands of an agent or creating pre-dominant interests (debts) against it, does not alter the aggregate of control over and return from his fund. It merely reapportions such functional relations among others as well as himself.

In the case of a trust, the trustee has some degree of limited control over the fund, and in his office there vest immediately such controls as the component interests accord their holder. In exercising both, however, he is acting as a fiduciary or officer and not in his own behalf. For all the beneficial functional relations accorded to the fund accrue, in turn, personally and finally to the beneficiary. While the latter may be deprived of all control, nevertheless, by the very organization of the trust, there is reserved from the limited power given the trustee certain elements of control not accorded to either but prescribed, and therefore exercised, by the settlor in advance in the deed of trust itself.

With a corporation we find officers acting as administrators and possessing, as such, very limited control over the fund as a whole. Creditors – those possessing pre-dominant interests in the fund – are, in fact if not in theory, accorded some limited degree of control and a fixed return by way of benefit. And the stockholders, acting through their directors as administrators and constituting the dominant interest, exercise all the rest of the control and secure all the rest of the return or benefit. Thus to the last two classes accrue all the return or benefit. So much for the fund as a whole. But when it comes to dealing with the component 'things' of the fund the division is much more complex. For title to all such controls as are accorded with these 'things' is deemed to vest in the corporation. And here the officers have much wider authority to exercise powers in behalf of the corporate entity. In fact in this case the administrators are deemed to represent the corporation, to act for it and to wield the control vested in it.

From these three tests it is evident that the distribution of the various functional relations described is not in general made uniformly nor limited according to the character or division of interests in a fund. Rather they are distributed in various ways throughout the system.

C. *Implications in Theory and Practice*

1. *The Lineal Architecture of the Property Structure*

The superimposition of an elaborately complex series of layers of property interests upon the foundation of material objects, which we have described as the pattern of the modern property structure, is not new. It was also, as we have often noted, the implicit pattern of the feudal system and its adjunct, medieval law. So, in the broad, we may find this modern plan simplified and partially analysed for us by stretching it upon the already familiar framework of the old English system of estates in land. The nineteenth century has worked out through the medium of credit and of corporations an intricate system of interests in funds similar to that which the fourteenth century created in land. Both developed in the same way as a variety of expedients invented to enable a rising group of the more aggressive, capable and resourceful members of society, who had not, to take over the control and administration of productive facilities from those who had.

In the fourteenth century there were subjoined to, or interposed between, existing tenures in land many new forms called estates. The basis of both tenures and of estates in land was the lineal or feudal relation—a relation in series. It consisted in passing down from one holder to another the physical control (use) of the land, and in reserving to each in the series some part of the property control and, perhaps, of the benefit. The partition was in some degree successive (temporal) and in some degree coexistent. And in various ways this use was made to return the way it had come, upon termination of the subordinate tenures or estates by events certain or uncertain. Thus the forms of the medieval structure came into existence by reason of the fact that these transfers were neither complete nor permanent. In that fact lay their characteristics of dependence and derivitativeness.

The modern system of interests in funds, both dominant and predominant, is similar. In this case, too, the power of property control is being passed down from one holder to another—persons or funds—each retaining an interest which, for want of any exact appraisal, is still for the most part relegated to the chaotic region of choses in action—the no-name interests that are at law deemed to be nothing until they require a remedy. But, when they are analysed, we find that this system of interests also consists in essence of a method of delegation under which there is passed down something which at first sight bears the look of complete property but which is seen, on closer examination, to be in reality a dependent and derivative holding. This system is arranged in series, and consists of interests which are defined as to their duration, which have provisions for their retraction at times certain or uncertain and which have behind them some not yet clearly defined elements of control in all those *of whom* in series the property is held. Today, however, the difference exists that in modern economic life, at least in form, the relation is based upon a power of property in the abstract and is in terms of a general measure of all fungible forms of property, called money value, while formerly it was based upon a certain non-fungible but specific piece of land, and was in terms of some use of, or benefit from, this land. And this difference complicates matters.

It is very obviously this lineal form of organization, descended originally from the internal organization of the household and thence, through the personal organization of the feudal system, from the English system of property in land, which has been the perhaps unconscious model toward which modern economic organization has tended. This tendency may mean no more than that the possibility of such hierarchical relations as now prove convenient in the field of property had already been demonstrated in that of status, or that the prior existence of such relations indicates that they are a natural mode of thought and of operation. Such a recognition of consanguinity does point sharply, however, to the inconsistency of endeavouring by transplantation to apply rules derived from the collateral, or extra-familial, system of early Roman times to practices inherited from the lineal, or feudal, system of early England.

Once we grasp this resemblance and this difference it becomes clear that the legal philosophy of Rome is, at least in this respect, no longer applicable to the modern institution of property. On the other hand it is also evident that the common law of England has in it the germs of a philosophy which will fit the facts of today. The English method of organization of property was confined to land because, when the genius of the common law was at its height, land constituted nearly all of wealth. Romanism choked off the native growth of this theory before the same principles could be applied to those other objects of property which later became of greater importance. Nevertheless economic relations continued to grow on these English lines. As the early English erected a hierarchy of rights upon the substrate of the land, so their successors have erected one upon the substrate of all material objects. The modern applications of the lineal system are *faits accomplis* waiting only to be construed upon the medieval rather than upon the antique basis. It is impossible to avoid this issue and still to bring theory into any reasonable degree of harmony with the facts of law and the necessities of economic life. And until it is settled the law will continue to restrict the natural freedom of motion and to fail adequately to protect the special and novel instrumental forms developed, because it is intellectually constrained by the antique and outworn Roman theories to which it clings. It seems necessary to admit that we must abandon the notion of absolute ownership founded on the Roman classificatory genitive. We must abandon the notions of the Roman Law of Contract, or their subsequent elaborations, which conceive its substance to be a personal relation with reference to an act (not a 'thing') and pertaining to a future moment in time. We must abandon the notion of the fixed, integral and mutually discrete character of the various modes of property. For all these we must substitute notions founded on the principles and structure of the English law of landed estates, which recognizes no such relation as absolute ownership but which relates many persons simultaneously, although in different modes, to the same object; which has gradually transformed the originally personal and political *status* into a purely impersonal and economic "estate"; and the most salient characteristic of whose development has been the extraordinary flexibility and mutuality of its dismemberments of complete property.

2. *The Concept of "Ownership"*

In certain respects modern legal ideas of property continue to reduce themselves to a philosophic statement of the most primitive property notion of all—the classificatory genitive. The concept is still contaminated by the naïve assumption that every object of property must, by the nature of things, 'belong' somewhere and to someone, and moreover that, under a sort of Euclidean axiom, it cannot 'belong' in different respects to two persons or in two groupings at the same time. In other respects these ideas have also been constrained in their development through the influence of the continental civilians, who themselves had as intellectual heritage a certain medieval legal scholasticism which has come to be confused with the Roman law upon which it was founded, but which finally resembled the latter as little as the theology of the medieval church did the Gospels. The transplantation of such decrepit notions and their application to the indigenous common law of England, so far as might be, has only served to stunt the growth of a native jurisprudence, so far as property law was concerned, and to cause men to overlook the fact that English law had innate in its fundamental conception the true nature of modern property, the line along which the major developments of the future were to take place.

However much we may admire the Roman philosophy of law and wonder at the high stage of development which their economic law reached, in comparison with other civilizations of their time, it is obvious that the Romans, hampered by their innate idea of the classificatory genitive, were prevented from utilizing their economic resources to the full. Either the objects of property had to be disposed of altogether or they had to be kept. This notion of property was a strait jacket on economic development. True the Romans sprang two small openings by inventing the transfer of the *ius* without the transfer of the *res*—the servitudes—and by the use of leases; and they made some progress in the conditional conveyance of money.

But on the whole their system appears not to have permitted more than two layers of lineal—or derived—property in objects and only a limited variety of collateral interests.

The English, however, developed a much more flexible property system for land and some of its analogues. Here the classificatory genitive did not exist. It was impossible even in feudal times to identify any one of the variety of coexisting tenures as "ownership." By the time the feudal system reached its apogee the sovereign was conceived as the apex of the system for holding land. For the benefit of all who held in various degrees of subordination (infeudation) the various rights in regard thereto were pared off step by step until at the end came the right "paravail," the right of use. To each holder in the series there was extended a different character of interest, and with respect to each character some legalist could now be found to claim for it the title of "ownership"—*de facto* if not *de jure*. Actually there was no true "ownership." Later there appeared the system of appended estates to elaborate the complexity of the various different interests, both simultaneous and successive, which could exist in the same object at the same time. By such inventions *de facto* possession of these objects was made to pass from hand to hand, not only irrevocably as by sale, but also with a great variety of strings attached. A property relation could be established to suit almost any need. The result was a freedom of motion and an activity—tending, in the case of land at least, to shuffle it into the hands of those who could use it best—which has hardly been equalled. But, with this flexibility, the various interests were removed still further from any resemblance to the exotic legal concept of "ownership."

The very word "estate" suggests, as we have already noted, that the inter-relation between these ranked holders was, at first, a matter of status rather than of property—a matter of control over persons rather than over objects—and that, although it was applied on a far larger scale, it was originally derived from the system of the internal relations of the *familia*—the source of the Law of Persons (status)—not from the external relations of the *familia*, from which most of the original concepts and procedures associated with the Law of Things (property) had risen. It is natural that, because of this origin, the land system took the form of a lineal organization rather than the intrinsically collateral system of classic Roman property.

Markby,[88] in attempting to reconcile the fact of the lineally derived estate with the collateral and absolute concept of "ownership," says: "By an extremely bold effort of imagination, he [the English lawyer] first detaches the ownership from the land itself, and then

[88] Op. cit., pp. 165-166.

attaches it to an imaginary thing which he calls an estate." And, again: "If I give an estate in my land to you for your life . . . according to the language and ideas of English lawyers the land is in one sense yours, but still remains in another sense mine; and with what is mine I may deal." But this is merely a straddle. The fact is that the English lawyer, inheriting from the beginning of the common law the medieval concept of things corporeal and incorporeal, was compelled to continue more or less consciously to conceive of a great variety of somewhat standardized coexisting legal groups of rights and privileges, localized as to their "territorial ambit"; and that it is these various bundles of rights of property, or interests, in the land, their locus, which are called estates. The foreign notion of "ownership" only intruded when the question of primacy arose. Now, this question of primacy among the various interests does not often arise. When it does there is no rational system of identification which brings the various tests of primacy which have been proposed into unanimity.

In another respect this arrangement has been preserved in the dependent character of our whole property system, especially as it relates to land. As Ely points out,[84] the English legal concept of estates in land is not far removed from the present concept of private property in general. The patrimonial, or absolute, system of property disappeared during the so-called Dark Ages. Theoretically, at first, the chief lord occupied the same position as had formerly the *dominus*, or still further back, the *paterfamilias*. But practically, no such corollary of his succession was recognized at the time, nor until much later when the sovereign was established at the apex of the structure. Finally, one may say, society as a whole was substituted for the sovereign and came to be regarded as holding the only absolute right in a sort of perpetual succession. For property is now, in practice, a limited group of protections and permissions afforded by the state, from which much has been withheld as a sort of social reservation, from which more can be reserved in the interests of others, and of which, under the power of eminent domain, the net of the whole can be retaken in the public interest with adequate compensation. It is for this reason that, in modern American land law, although the theory of property has been at times allodial (collateral), the practice as regards the power of the state has been, in substance if not in form, almost exactly feudal (lineal).

In addition to the impossibility of reconciling the idea of "ownership" with the English estate in land, we may also remind ourselves that, at the lowest layer of property—that layer, immediate to the material foundation, which we have called direct interests in objects—

[84] Op. cit., I, pp. 124-126.

we had difficulty in finding any modern interest which could be called "ownership," in the sense of complete property in any kind of object whatever. The fact is that complete property in material objects is largely a thing of the past. Where we do find a direct interest that appears to be complete property, such as that which sometimes subsists in goods, it will be found to inhere in all cases in a fund. The fund may then be deemed to be "owner," but unless it is a completely free 'own' fund, the property is in reality qualified. Is such an interest then "ownership"?

If we attempt any definition of the terms "owner" and "ownership" with a content less than complete property we are also in difficulties, as has already been shown. The courts sway from one definition to another as seems fitting in any particular case.[35] For there has arisen such an infinite variety of interlacing interests in the material basis of property that even the law itself can no longer apply its simple primitive concept with its somewhat arrogant content. It may seem necessary to define the difference between those estates in land which are freehold and those which are not, as if something akin to "ownership" belonged with the first and not with the second. But when we apply this technical line between a life tenant and a tenant for a term of 99 years we see that, while formally correct, it is substantially absurd. The real difference in estates is not a sharp distinction between those which hold "*in nomine suo*" and those which hold "*in nomine alieno*," but rather it is a graduated difference according to the duration and security of tenure and the degree of freedom in dealing with the land. Here even the special concept of "ownership," which has been modified to fit a certain series of estates that are called freehold on account of the dignity of their origin, is found inappropriate.

It is therefore clearly impossible to identify anything resembling that which has been defined as "ownership" in any of these cases. The fund—the successor to the estate, the manor, the *villa* and the *familia*—is still the only entity over which we may be said to hold something savouring of dominion. And even then it is only true of the relation of the 'owner' to his 'own' fund as a whole. He, in fact, is also the only person who can correctly be called 'owner.' In that sense he owns the 'things' in his fund, though these 'things' are rarely themselves complete property in any object or any other 'thing.'

Almost the same difficulties arise with the concept of possession. It becomes necessary, in using the term, always to define precisely what variety of possession is referred to. Thus we find, both from

[35] "The word 'owner,' as applied to land, has no fixed meaning which can be declared to be applicable under all circumstances and as to any and every enactment." Coombs v. People, 198 Ill. 586, 588 (1902).

our historical studies and from our study of modern law, that the legal concepts of "ownership" and of possession are of very little use in analysing property. They are by far too indefinite. And this objection is by no means a matter merely of academic or theoretical interest. The fact is that the devious devices of modern economic life have escaped from the grasp of these primitive legal ideas. If we are to comprehend these facts at all we need to submit them to the much less vague and indeterminate method of qualitative analysis which we have outlined in the foregoing pages.[36]

[36] It may clarify matters to review at this point the various now analysed relations to which the term "owner," and its derivative "ownership," are commonly applied.

(1) The relation of a person to his 'own' fund is that of an 'owner,' strictly speaking.

(2) No relation to the fund of a decedent is described as that of an "owner."

(3) The relation of a trustee to a trust fund is described as that of a "legal owner" and the relation of a beneficiary as that of an "equitable owner."

(4) The relation of a person, *via* 'own' fund or trust fund, to those 'things' which inhere in and compose 'own' funds and trust funds is described in the same way as in cases (1) and (3). This by ellipsis ignoring the fund. In reality the fund is holder.

For exceptions see (7).

(5) The relation of a partnership (partnership fund) and a corporation (corporate fund) to those 'things' which inhere in and compose the funds is described as that of "owner." This by personification of the fund.

For exceptions see (7).

(6) In most of these cases the relation of the so-called "owner" to the fund or 'thing' is also described as "ownership."

For exceptions see (7).

(7) In cases (4), (5), and (6) it is not common to speak of "owning" (or "ownership" in) security or special property, except in the case of mortgage. The bailee or lienor of a 'thing' are usually said to hold, not to "own," their interest in the thing.

(8) Among direct interests in objects:

(a) Certain freehold estates in land have been described as "ownership," or "limited ownership."

(b) The possessory (*de jure*) interest in goods has been described as "ownership."

(c) The holder of such interests (which holder is always a fund) has been described as the "*owner*" *of the object itself*.

(d) By ellipsis again, the person personifying the fund, in the case of 'own' funds and trust funds, has been described as the "*owner*" *of the object itself*.

In only one instance is it possible for complete property in an object to inhere in one person, and then it occurs only indirectly. If no pre-dominant interest is incident upon a person's 'own' fund; if in that fund there inheres an interest in an object; and if there is no other property interest in that object; then complete property in that object inheres indirectly in that person. Such instances are rare. Therefore the concept of complete property is rarely capable of practical application and serves only as a conceptual representation of the summation of divided interests. Nor is there any practical possibility of identifying the term "ownership," as commonly used, with such a concept. What it has always been used to mean is something else.

We have no other term than 'owner' to describe the relation that exists in case (1). As used in this case "ownership" might be defined as that single dominant relation existing between one person and the personal, immediate fund which we have called

3. *The Distinction between Property and Contract*

The distinction between property, in its strict legal sense, and property in contract is primarily historical and secondarily, as a result of that, procedural. The latter seems to have been the first Roman form to develop definitely into an interest in a fund.[87] If then we briefly summarize at this point the history of its development it will become apparent not only how far removed from the present were the conditions under which the distinction originally arose, but, also, in what manner that other strain of interests—those which we have called dominant—as they branched out from the stem of the original direct interests in objects, tended to close the gap and became themselves interests in funds of a not altogether separable class. As we consider this curious divergence and subsequent convergence of type, the resemblance between the end-products forcibly reminds us that,

his 'own' fund. He is 'owner' of that fund. But such 'owning' and 'ownership' is not necessarily complete property even in the fund, for it does not preclude the incidence of pre-dominant interests therein, though it does preclude other dominant interests. The result is to abandon the content as well as the application of the old terminology.

For the sake of clear thinking it is best to eliminate, except in this case, the terms "own," "owner" and "ownership," and to eliminate all connotation of complete property even there. If we need a set of general terms for the fact and function of a person or fund of inherence we have the terms "hold," "holder" and "holding," which are commonly used. In many of the cases described above there is a special and suitable term which describes that particular relation or interest and no other. As to the remaining personal relations to funds, we have the executors and the heirs and legatees of an estate; and we have the trustees and beneficiaries of a trust. As to the dominant inter-fund relations we have partners, stockholders; and as to the predominant we have bondholders, note-holders, or the more general term creditors. Some of these "offices" have also special terms for the nature of the interest which binds them to the fund. As to the direct interests in objects we have a fairly complete terminology for the interests themselves, though they are not always conjoined with special terms for the holder of the interest. Describing the holders of the various interests in land, the terms fee-holder, life tenant, lessee (or termor), reversioner, remainderman, etc., are somewhat unsystematic. Nevertheless they serve the purpose. The description of the interests in goods is not so satisfactory. As to that one which is commonly called "ownership" (of goods) we are completely lacking a satisfactory term both for holder and for interest. We have used the term "possessor" and "possession *de jure*" as the only accurate descriptive terms with a reasonably definite content.

The *de facto* possessor of land or goods is generally said to *hold* the *land* or *goods* as lessee or pledgee, for instance, or *in* or *by* a certain specific interest. Strictly speaking what he holds is some direct interest in the object, which gives him *de facto* possession, and not the object itself. And this is an important distinction, for otherwise one comes readily to overlook the other holders with interests in the same object.

[87] *Consortium* and *societas* may not have been far behind. However the notion which came to be termed *bona passiva* seems to me to have been earlier than the elevation of the concept of condominion, from its application directly to individual 'things' to its application to an aggregate of 'things.' Believers in early communal property may not agree with me.

while both processes of growth of interests in funds have been developments of increasing mediacy, nevertheless, in one case as truly as in the other, these final pinnacles in the elaboration of the property structure are now clearly demonstrated to retain, as their ultimate and necessary basis, material and quasi-material objects, and that in somewhat different ways both are, indirectly, interests in this foundation.

Having regard to the historical evidence as to Roman and English law it would appear that the only original distinction, in these systems of property at their earliest stages, concerned the object and its classification. Ordinarily the subject persons and objects within one classification were located there. But even when removed the natural *manus* continued over them. When a loan was made the thing lent remained a 'belonging' of the lender, but out of possession (*cf.* vestiges in *commodatum* and *detinue*). When an injury was done the idea of vengeance gave a sort of claim which lay against the body of the tortfeasor—to possess it as one's own and usually to destroy it. As a further step in the complication of classification there were developed practices under which rights could arise in other men's land or goods without changing the *manus* over the object. One might consider such rights as property, but as property *in re aliena.* All such rights remained of an order which later came to be called "rights *in rem*"; the distinction being that they were rights supported by actions directly against subject persons or material objects.

With the development, in both civilizations, of the monetary economy, the result was to substitute a composition for vengeance in the case of wrongs; to dissociate gradually those voluntary obligations which were incurred before the fact from those which were incurred after the fact, and in that manner to discriminate breach of contract from its original oneness with tort; and to convert, alike in delict and in contract, the thing that was to be paid, whether as penalty, price or repayment, and usually the thing that was lent, from a non-fungible person or material object to a fungible material object. Always the penalty or price paid, and usually the object lent and repaid, took the form of a generalized chattel serving as money. No longer was it necessary, convenient or even practicable for the avenger, the seller, or the lender to put his finger on the particular object he was to receive and claim it as his property. The *Dinglichkeit* had faded. With this change, because of the early incapacity of the law to take the initiative in altering the classification by the genitive; because, perhaps, of the personal nature of security (hostage); and because a large part of such transactions continued to be supported by their original incidence upon the *noxa* or, as a substitute, upon the *persona* of the household; one seemed, in all these cases, to have left only a claim against a person rather than any longer one against an object. The early history of the Roman *obligatio* seems to bear the earmarks of this process of growth. Certainly Maitland makes it clear that early English law reflects the same change as the Roman seems to, when he says that, in the thirteenth century, "we may see the action [for debt] gradually losing some of its proprietary traits; we may see the notion of personal obligation slowly emerging."[88]

Thus the property right which came to be called a "right *in personam*" was differentiated and evolved from the so-called "right *in rem.*" The penalty or price due and the money lent, seemed no longer to be *my* property. They were not specific objects, out of possession but *owned by me;* they were a sum of fungible objects *owed to me.* Viewed as rights, however, they remained mine; but rights now always against a certain person, and never against a certain 'thing.' More and more these non-possessory or incorporeal rights tended themselves to become a new type of *res* or 'thing.' Nevertheless the difference between *owning* something out of possession and being *owed* it, resulted solely from the fungibility of the object owed and the consequent freedom of the debtor to treat the specific objects borrowed or owed as his own and to pay or repay in "specie," as the Roman lawyers said.

In this way, at a very early stage, the obligation lost, in the eyes of the law, all contact with specific material objects. Nevertheless it retained for a long time its contact with the debtor's person. It had originally consisted of a liability against his person which he could buy off with some of his property. So long as it remained so — so long as the obligation could be taken out on his hide, so to speak — its incidence clearly, and the objective of the action naturally, were against his person. Ultimately, however, with the gradual release from liability of the Roman debtor's person, though the objective of the action remained the same, the incidence of the obligation was imperceptibly shifted to his property.

Because of this change of incidence the later philosophers of civilian law, over a period of many centuries, were compelled to recognize that the distinction which they were coining, upon the basis of the Roman classification of actions, between the rights which came to be called *in rem* and those which came to be called *in personam,* could not logically be based on a difference in the object of the rights. In neither case was the object any longer a person. On the other hand, it was impossible for them to resolve the logical

[88] Pollock and Maitland, op. cit., II, p. 206.

contradiction presented by supposing the objects of the debtor's property to have two 'belongings' at the same time. Therefore they eventually devised a theory that the phrase *in rem*, in the original action, meant, not what it said – "against the object" – but rather a claim good "against the world" with respect to an object; and conversely that *in personam* meant, not what it said – "against the person" (i. e. the person or *persona* of the debtor) – but rather a claim good only "against a certain individual" not "against the world." By way of a first step away from incidence directly upon the person without returning to incidence upon material objects, this second class of claims had – already at an early stage of this philosophizing – been conceived to have reference to an immaterial act or happening only – the act of payment or any other positive or negative act (*dandum, faciendum, praestandum*) – rather than to a material object. This solution, which transferred the incidence of the obligation to the performance, seemed logical and helped to consolidate in the one theory the newer developments of contract, where frequently the performance had no relation to a material object but consisted only in happenings of the type called, in economics, services – positive or negative – which might be accomplished by voluntary acts of the person.

It was considerably due to the conceptual confusion, which resulted from its origin and the consequent maintenance of the original objective of the action as well as the conception of this fictitious substitute for the old incidence of the right, that the obligation was so long considered a purely personal relation, inalienable except through the subterfuge of attornment, dying with the creditor and even, at times, with the debtor. This *idée fixe* produced the centuries of resistance to the legal acceptance of negotiability which had, so to speak, to slip in through the back door of equity and to be borrowed from, and fathered upon, the exogenous law merchant.

In the meantime the change in the true incidence of the obligation failed to follow theory. It was gradually removed from the debtor's person (or *persona*). But in practically no cases was the promised act enforced – or even enforcible. Nevertheless the theory was maintained; so that even when the act consisted in the payment of a material object such as metallic money it was grasped by its heels instead of its head and was thrown into the realm of the immaterial. In practice the law diverged in another direction. The promised act did not even serve as measure of the liability; nor did the deficiency between the promise and the performance of the act. The measure became – at least in English law and most usually – the disequilibrium resulting from this deficiency between the consideration plus performance on each of the two sides – a sort of compensation to restore the balance. The incidence, itself, of the obligation – the object of the creditor's rights – was transferred from the debtor's person to his property in general – his fund – and thus returned again to a projection, now indirect, over the base of material objects which underlie all property rights. With punishment for failure to perform or compulsory performance practically eliminated, how could it be otherwise? For, then, obligations, whether they constituted a nominal liability for the performance of a service only or even a nominal liability for the delivery of a material object, had only one recourse. They were only valid as property if the fund of the debtor, representing interests which ultimately concern material objects, was good for the equivalent of this disequilibrium resulting from lack of balance in performance. It was only the claim against this underlying property, enforcible either through pledge or through judgment, that validated the antecedent obligation. That became its only incidence. It is by this route that the claim itself has become a new kind of property interest.

At the end of this process of change all forms of property, including contract, again stand out from an objective viewpoint, stripped of every remaining appearance of immateriality of object, as various kinds and degrees of rights in objects which are, almost without exception, perceptible to the senses. Nevertheless the incidence upon the material object is, in this new form, different from the original. It is no longer specific. And this not because its ultimate object is fungible, but because it is indeterminate. In the meantime the law has interposed a creature of its own making – the fund – in place of the natural person, to act as the proximate holder of all property. In arrogating the power to apportion the interests in this new creature, it has derogated the formerly absolute power of the person. It has thus arrogated the incidence of contract near to the level of the derogated incidence of property – in the strict legal sense. Today they both impinge, as interests of a somewhat similar character, upon these ganglia of the property structure through which their incidence is ultimately and indirectly transmitted to an indeterminate section of the principally non-fungible material and quasi-material objects which form the base. It is this new manner of incidence which has been substituted for the original property in the object out of possession (*commodatum*, for instance, or the "chose in action") or in the person of the debtor, which formerly constituted the property in contract. It is an incidence which the practice of law has introduced but which its theory has not yet envisaged. And it is this new manner of incidence which has brought property in contract into so close a resemblance, in so many respects, to the modern derivatives of the original *dominium.*

4. *The Tradition of Standardized Interests*

Once we free our minds from the notion of a 'thing' called "ownership" and from the hard and fast distinction between two classes of rights—those *in rem* and those *in personam*—we have accomplished two important steps forward. In the first place we are then prepared to see clearly the extent to which all property interests, in spite of congenital inhibitions, have already evolved in the direction of a single graduated system. And in the second place, we are then prepared to discard the old and to formulate realistic and forward-looking categories which will permit continued and freer evolution in compliance with economic needs.

The modern system of dominant interests in trust and corporate funds has already paralleled the medieval system of estates in land. It is varied, flexible, progressing. In fact, if not in theory, these multifarious imagos have shed the uniform chrysalids from which they all developed. Dominance is divided, qualified, delegated and postponed almost at will, to suit the fads and fancies of a fickle market, or to meet the changing requirements of economic and political conditions. Types of interest are developed, discarded and forgotten. The freedom from conventionalized form has reached a stage where almost nothing is determined by a name. The deed creating each interest must be consulted in order to determine its exact content.

To some extent a similar development has taken place within the field of pre-dominant interests in all kinds of funds. The tendency has clearly been to adapt old types of interest to new requirements until it has become frequently difficult to find the resemblance of the modern exemplar to that interest whose name it bears.

Finally, in the case of impersonal funds, there has been a marked tendency in the development of the class of dominant and the class of pre-dominant interests to converge. The junior obligation and the senior equity, while they are still separated by a fundamental procedural difference, are in practical effect distinguishable rather in degree than in kind. The line between the income debenture for the life of a corporation and the prior preference stock is a shadowy line. Rather one progresses from being a preferred creditor to being the holder of the final equity by almost imperceptible gradations.

Essentially, then, the classification of present day property interests must become, like classifications of other natural phenomena, a system of somewhat arbitrary divisions established for the sake of convenience. To some extent such classifications may continue to conform to the different sources from which the interests have developed; to some extent they may be based upon a selected salient characteristic. But it will probably be continually more difficult to determine the proper classification of the more novel of the hybrids which are continually appearing. And the infinite variety of the blends and shadings of species and genera suggests that, at best, the whole system can only be conceived as a compound of graduations from one extreme to another according to several different and disparate scales.

The classification we have hitherto made is of this nature. It distinguishes direct interests in objects from interests in funds. It distinguishes these direct interests in objects according to the nature of the objects, according to the physical relation to this object, according to the relation to *de jure* possession of the object and, finally, according to the duration of the interest. It distinguishes interests in funds, according to their descent, as dominant or pre-dominant. As to the former it separates the beneficial (primarily) from the administrative (primarily); and in each class it classifies according to certain traditional and more or less distinct types of fund. As to the latter it grades the interests according to their stage of development and according to the character of the steps upon which their development is predicated. It is not a "periodic" system. But for the purpose for which it is intended—that is, the clarification of the structure of property for use in economic analysis—it may serve. At any rate it permits of unlimited interpolation of new forms because it abandons the notion of standardization of interests into any fixed categories according to an archaic nomenclature; it eliminates the completely obsolete concept of "ownership"; and it relegates to its properly secondary position the perhaps obsolescing distinction between property and contract.

5. *Protection of Non-possessory vs. Possessory Interests*

While the sole purpose of this study has been to prepare an accurate groundwork for the examination of the structural and functional aspects of property which so largely determine economic life in modern societies, nevertheless it seems appropriate, in this and the closing section, to suggest two practical ways in which this point of view of the institution as a whole might advantageously lead to some modification in the legal point of view which should reflect itself in legal practice. Our presentation of the character of property in contract and the allied remedial rights has been almost unmitigated heresy so far as general legal theory is concerned. The doctrine, still almost universally followed in practice—however much it may seem a mere fiction—is that all such rights are merely choses in action. And a chose in action is a claim against the obligor (*in personam*) which is conceived to be in no sense property in his 'things.' In effect the doctrine, overtly or implicitly, denies the existence of any antecedent right except that universal personal right, the right of action for a wrong. When it is necessary to identify it at all, it identifies the "chose" with the remedial right—the right to damages. But, of course, a remedial right can only come into existence when a true antecedent right has been infringed. This has led to another doctrine. Out of the theoretical necessity of imputing rights to be infringed, has arisen the juristic concepts of antecedent rights *in rem* (property, personal and familial rights) and of antecedent rights *in personam* (contract rights) and of the distinction between them. But this concession of the theoretical existence of antecedent rights *in personam*, has never been consistently developed in practice.

There is an essential practical advantage which has been served by these doctrines of the suspended or wholly remedial right of the chose in action and of the antecedent right *in personam*, although neither is realistic. Under the old view, which envisages something called "ownership" or complete property, any subtractions of fractions of this property for the benefit of others qualify the naturally complete rights of the "owner." In some or several respects they impair his freedom of control or use by making him partly answerable to others to whom he has assigned part rights. Most of these separations of fractions of property are given in exchange for a return or consideration, viz. easements, leases, etc. The impairment is compensated by other rights received in exchange. Only in the case of the general class of what is called security is this not true. So in this latter group we find that an evolution has taken place for the very purpose of escaping the unintended impairment. Compare the most primitive common law lien which requires possession—almost a denial of the benefit of ownership—with the more modern forms of mortgage and equitable liens, trust deeds, etc., which are designed to lighten this burden just as far as possible. In this respect it seems that the evolution of the "security" is in the direction of leaving the debtor as free as possible to exercise his rights of property—of reducing a right *in rem* as nearly as possible to the practical effect of a right *in personam*.

Exactly the same trend has been exemplified by the development of English property in contract. In the field of contract the modern chose in action has largely developed as an unsecured credit-debt, having freed itself from the early necessity of specific security. This was fortunately made possible because the obligation was early distinguished from the pledge which supported it. So the unsecured credit-debt has been free to develop commercial standing on its own legs, so to speak. And the principal reason which has encouraged this development is that, in this way, the desirable end is accomplished of leaving the debtor with an unimpaired control, free to act without the slightest impediment of an asserted string to any particular part of his property.

It must be admitted that the theoretical distinction, which has been erected upon the antiquated foundation of the *actio in personam* and the legal fictions adjunct thereto, has, in this way, had an important influence in maintaining the principle of the freedom of the debtor's property and thus in permitting to a constantly greater degree the free informal exchanges which are the permissive basis of modern commerce and finance. And this example has led to the gradual impairment of the creditor's right *in rem* in the security. But, though these civilian doctrines as to what might be called property in promises have been imported into English law and have had their influence in shaping the legal ideas in regard to the various types of property out of possession – the general class of choses in action – as well as in regard to trusts, they have not in all respects worked so beneficially, nor are they solely responsible for this result. For the most part the native forms are not well fitted to the exotic legal doctrine and the application of this doctrine has had the result that their true nature has been largely blinked. It is, therefore, enlightening to examine the process by which, in varying degrees, the rights and interests of those concerned have, in each of these native forms, been defined – the more accurately the longer the time during which the instrument has been in use – and to note how much more often these definitions have followed the conveniences and precedents of practice than they have the imported theory. In all cases the necessary practical degree of freedom of action has been accorded the active holder. But that result has as often been impeded as it has been helped by the misfitting Romanisms.

English jurisprudence has attempted to conform the native institution, the trust, to foreign categories by conceiving it to create complete property in the trustee and only a personal obligation running to the beneficiary. But since the trust is really a contract between the settlor and the trustee and the law formerly held that no contract can affect third parties, this view has presented difficulties which have caused interminable disputes. The view of equity has been that the beneficiary is the "equitable owner" and the trustee the "legal owner." Two "ownerships" in one aggregate of property is shocking to the views of the legalists, is hard to digest and results in an insoluble case of conflict of laws (jurisdictions) one being "owner" in one court and the other "owner" in another. Therefore the view of the most modern law – if it can be said to have *a* view – is that the trustee is "owner" and the beneficiary holds some personal relation to him which falls in none of the recognized categories and is therefore *sui generis.*

In fact, though the property of a beneficiary in a trust of personal property varies over a wide extent, it is the oldest of the modern forms which relate holders of property to definitely constituted funds and which give them something in the nature of undivided but complementary interests in an aggregate of 'things.' And because it is the oldest, and because the trustee in general has never been in any respect intended to derive the benefits of the property, it has gone furthest in limiting the beneficial rights, while enforcing the powers and duties, of the nominal holder as well as in protecting the rights and restricting the powers of the beneficial holder.

The most recent form of property to develop along similar lines is the interest of the stockholder in a corporation. In this comparatively recent development we have retained the Roman form, but perplexed with new problems. For we have turned the fraternal replica of the original familial agency for property holding to a new use – the use of profit – and upon an internal basis of lineal grades (preferences) and collateral inequalities (varying shares). Therefore we need to define and relate these internal rights as the Romans did not. And to do this we need to intrude upon this supposedly independent jurisdiction as the Romans could not. The corporation can no longer be conveniently disposed of as the eventual beneficiary of its own property, a final unit in the body economic. It must in some way be resolved into its constituent elements, without at the same time losing sight of the necessary facts of its semi-independent existence. Here, as with the trust, it is now recognized that the artificial person who is conceived to be "owner" – the corporation – is itself incapable of enjoying the benefits of "ownership" so-called. It can only withhold them; eventually the benefits should accrue to the stockholders. But on what basis? Although shares of stock have until recently been defined as choses in action, they have never been, so far as I know, treated as personal obligations of the corporation, in spite of the fact that these two have been treated as somewhat equivalent in other cases. Instead they have never been defined at all. Therefore, both because the courts do not seem as yet to have had time to clarify and to determine the extent of the limitations to be imposed upon the freedom of the corporation in dealing with its property, and because it is desired to avoid all incumbrances to the free exercise of the control over this property, the as yet inchoate theory detaches the property of the stockholder in the corporation from the property of the corporation and treats that of the stockholder, apart from his internal political rights, almost as if he had made a gift to the corporation for the term of the corporate life. There is almost entirely lacking the fine definition of respective rights which has been accumulated in the case of the trust. By this silence the freedom of the active holder, who is construed as "owner," is more than fully safeguarded. It is the interest of the inactive stockholder which fails of adequate protection. And this is a problem, not merely for the theory of law and of economics, but one of pressing necessity for the administrators of the law, who must presently do what they did with the land law and thread their way through a maze of conflicting interests to devise a consistent body of principles for determining, as well as may be, where the right lies.

Between these first two cases we have the chose in action, strictly speaking. Here the courts have had time to work out a *modus operandi*, but they have done it largely under Roman influence. The claim is treated as a claim *in personam;* the rights of the debtor to control his property are left free and unimpaired; relatively speaking, no cloud hangs over titles; no impediment exists to the free movement of individual 'things' or objects; no interest is held to run to the creditor in the 'things' of the debtor. But let the debtor's assets shrink to less than his liabilities; let him attempt to prefer one creditor to another; or let him try to dispose of all or part of his property in such a way as to defeat the incidence of the rights of all creditors; and some sort of antecedent interest, suspended or denied in fair weather, is asserted by the law itself and vigorously sustained. The fact of the adverse interest is there, as it was in later Rome, though theory screens it from view and impedes its adequate protection.

Obviously the existing pattern of legal fictions and these curious compromises between misfitting theories and experimental practices have accomplished a useful purpose in greasing the wheels of commerce. We would not wish to see them altered unless it should prove possible to find an intellectually honest way to achieve as good or better results. It is apparent that the law has, in the course of centuries, discovered fairly well how to control the trustee of a trust fund in the interests of the holders of dominant interests in such funds, and at the same time without unduly impairing the freedom of the trustee in dealing with the property nominally vested in him. The motive for this judicial control may be that it is assumed that the beneficiary of a trust is incapable of protecting his own interests. While the wide dissemination of the trust plan is constantly making this assumption less sound, it makes its results no less beneficial. At any rate the rigours of the law in dealing with trustees have inculcated a wholesome sense of responsibility upon those undertaking such offices.

In practical fact, in modern times, the non-controlling stockholders in a corporate fund and the holders of pre-dominant interests in any fund are hardly more capable of safe-guarding their interests in these funds than is the present day beneficiary of a trust fund. Corporations, particularly, are rapidly becoming the means for a degree of socialization of property of which the so-called capitalistic system never dreamed itself to be capable. And on the whole the process seems desirable and worth encouraging. But the power of self-protection left in the hands of either the non-controlling stockholders or the creditors is rapidly diminishing. Their practical disabilities are becoming so much alike that the dual nature of their interests seems to be blending into a single one and the need for a more adequate definition of the safe-guards to the rights of a beneficiary of property in 'things' out of possession seems to be common to both. The essence of the attitude of the law toward trustees is that they shall deal with the trust *quasi bonus paterfamilias*, and that in matters within the scope of the relation they shall act for the benefit of the beneficiary; that they shall have no personal dealings with the fund; and that their 'own' funds are liable for any breach of trust. Yet within these limits they are free to act and, provided the fund is maintained intact, to act without interference from the beneficiary. Once the resemblance between the organization of different funds, their composition and the relation among the different interests in them, are fully grasped in all their relative simplicity, it seems quite within the reach of practical possibilities to accord to the inactive dominant interests in corporate funds and to the pre-dominant interests in all funds much the same varieties of protection, without seriously hampering the freedom of action of the administrators of such funds. The protections to be accorded the former would seem to be appropriately modelled upon the protections now given beneficiaries of trusts. To be sure the stockholder in a corporate fund voluntarily assumes a risk not associated with trust funds. And for that reason somewhat greater latitude must be allowed to management. In the case of creditors' interests in the funds of debtors, the essential safe-guards are true statements as the basis of "credit," the maintenance of a reasonable margin over liabilities, the maintenance of a sufficient degree or prospect of liquidity to insure the repurchase or refunding of all obligations as they become due and, in case of failure to meet these conditions, a vesting of conditional control in the creditors. The courts seem quite generally already to be making a beginning at carrying out such a program, but perhaps not so completely as would be done if the nature of the stockholders' and creditors' interests were more clearly recognized.

If events do not follow these lines, history may repeat itself and the expropriation of the corporate creditor and stockholder by the management, or by the "control," may gradually come about. The history of the early development of the law of English estates in land indicates that this is much more to be feared than is the growth of too great impediments upon the freedom of action of the active holders. That history provides a satisfactory answer to the objection of modern law against treating the credit, in our modern lineal system of corporate credit-debt, as an interest in the body of property of the debtor, and against supporting these rights and those of the inactive stockholders on the ground that such a course would cause an impairment of the freedom of "ownership" of the corporation in its 'things,' and thus constrain commerce. The efforts to protect the original rights of the feudal superior, who had himself conferred the land upon the dependent holder, were far from producing such an effect in the analogous property structure on English land. In fact it was these superior rights, and not those of the derived tenures and estates, which proved most difficult of protection. It was, as we have seen, the tenant in demesne, the user of the land, to whom was first and most freely accorded the right of alienation. It was he, at the lowest rung in the ladder, who created the system of estates beneath him. So free was he that it became necessary for the lords to secure the statute *Quia Emptores* in order to find means to assert the continuity of their dues running against a new owner after alienation of the present possessory estate. Even then the process of attrition continued until it accomplished an almost complete dispossession of the successors at interest to the original landlords. In that period the superior holdings from which those of the active users were derived originated in a military aristocracy – the big fellows. Today the analogous superior holdings originate in the saving *bourgeoisie* – the little fellows. Therefore the wind of public favour may now blow in the other direction and economic need for capital may require the protection of the saver. Nevertheless the road of absentee landlordism has always been hard.

6. *The Determination of Property*

The other practical way in which theory and practice might be modified to advantage would come about as a result of a definitive segregation of the various applications of the word "property" for its several purposes.

It is apparent that the term "property" as used and conceived at the time the system of general property taxation was inaugurated meant no more than appropriated material objects.[39] For the most part it is still such objects that are listed and assessed for the purpose of real and personal property taxation. But because the term at one time means the object and at others the property in the object, or even property of certain sorts in funds, the practice of applying such taxes has become a serious evil. Not only are the objects themselves completely taxed, but we have duplicate and triplicate taxation upon them if the interests in the objects, direct or indirect, exist in certain forms. And the fact that such interests are only in small part a matter of public record leads to a still more serious abuse. The result is to burden such a minute fraction of these interests as can be got at—and particularly those of the dependents of decedents where the record is available in the probate proceedings—with a confiscatory tax on face values because the rate is calculated to fit low rates of assessed valuation on material objects.[40]

It is unfortunate that the legal notion of property has become so

[39] It was evidently not intended to include the quasi-material objects, for these being processes concerning material objects are already taxed once as to these material objects and should not be taxed again. Moreover, at that time, the rights to these processes were treated as choses in action.

[40] On the subject of duplicate taxation I find an interesting decision. It is evident that this court clearly grasps the nature of the structure of property, as we have presented it, in so far as it concerns credits. "Credits are not 'property,' in the sense in which the word 'property' is used in the thirteenth section of the eleventh article of the Constitution [all property shall be taxed in proportion to its value]. That credits are correctly designated as 'property,' in a general sense, no one of course will deny; and that they fall within the true meaning of that word as employed in other portions of the Constitution is readily conceded."

"But . . . it does not follow either logically or grammatically that because a word occurs in one section with a definite sense, that therefore the same sense is to be adopted in every other section in which it occurs." The Constitution provides, in effect, that all the common wealth within the state shall be uniformly taxed. "Mere credits are a false quantity in ascertaining the sum of wealth which is subject to taxation as property and . . . in so far as that sum is attempted to be increased by the addition of those credits, property taxation, based thereon, is not only merely fanciful, but necessarily the unconstitutional imposition of an additional tax upon a portion of the property already once taxed," and "to hold . . . that 'credits' constitute 'property' . . . would be to attribute a meaning to the word property . . . which would not promote, but would utterly defeat the uniformity of property taxation . . . which it was the principal purpose of that section to secure." People v. Hibernia Savings & Loan Society, 51 Cal. 243, 250, 252, 253 (1876).

concreted. But that seems to be a weakness of the human mind. It starts with a term for a category defined by its relations and then comes to use it as if it meant the physical objects subject to these relations. Just so economics has concreted the concept of capital. The law needs a term for the material and quasi-material objects of property.

The term "property," when used for the purpose of defining the incidence of debt, must be limited to such interests only as are beneficial and usually to those only which are already vested and capable of transfer. This points the necessity of clearly grasping the fact that debt is not truly incident upon a person, but always and only upon a specific fund. Only those who, according to law, have the administration of a fund have the power of creating these pre-dominant interests in it—the power of incurring debt for it. The rules of law as to the different degrees of such power are well defined. But the debt so incurred is not incident upon the person who incurs it. Nor is it even incident upon the beneficial interests which exist in the fund. Instead it comes to occupy a position alongside of these and analogous to them. Both together have their incidence upon those other interests which inhere in and compose the fund. It is these latter which must be divided into the class which are subject to both and those which are, as yet, subject only to the dominant interests. It is only necessary to recognize that the power is actually exercised for and in regard to the fund, rather than a person, and that this fund has certain bipolarized interests incident upon it, and others inhering in it, completely to rationalize present practices.

In this connection the law needs a nomenclature which definitely acknowledges the existence of the fund apart from the persons related thereto, which discriminates beneficial from administrative interests therein and which frankly recognizes that, in the former class, what we have called the pre-dominant beneficial interests occupy a position which is at least analogous to that occupied by those which we have called dominant beneficial interests.

On the other hand the term "property" should be extended to the limit when it comes to according various degrees of protection, either against others or against the state. For that purpose it should include every interest, direct or indirect, in material or quasi-material objects, whether vested or contingent or merely expectant, whether of inchoate or consummate title; every unliquidated or potential or future right in contract; and every remedial right resulting from a cause of action which is, or may be on the way to becoming, a credit-debt. *But* it should not be made to include the personal and familial rights. They are not property, though their infringements are causes of action which may give rise to property. Instead, if the present doctrines upon which are based the protections accorded to personal or familial rights, as such, offer less adequate protection to these than is rendered to property rights, then the scope and dignity of these rights need to be ameliorated. That will never be accomplished so long as they claim protection under a borrowed prerogative which disguises their true nature and conceals their real and inherent primacy.

APPENDIX I

ETYMOLOGY OF EARLY TERMINOLOGY

Introductory

In the following pages I have undertaken to lay out for the reader the background which "linguistic palaeontology," as Schrader calls it, has uncovered for some of the more important features of the ancient and medieval legal terminology. In so far as this is dependable it is, perhaps, the surest way of coming at the early point of view. The danger in using it is that we tend to short cut very gradual processes of growth of form and meaning which extended over thousands of years, and thereby to impute to some developing usage connotations which had been forgotten centuries before. Moreover most of the etymological and semantic chains that have been proposed by philologists are highly speculative. In many respects they are no more than enlightened guesses. For this reason the material must be taken as suggestive rather than as definitive.

So much for the purposes of the general reader. For the etymologist, the anthropologist and the legal historian there is a secondary purpose as well. The writer is impressed with the fact that a vicious circle now exists in this particular field, at least, of etymological research. Etymologists have been much influenced by their views as to early customs and ideas in determining the older senses of words. Then they have limited themselves to etymologies which seem semantically possible and in conformity with these imputed meanings and with their views of the ideas and customs prevalent at the time. On the other hand, historians and their ilk have attempted, in turn, to reconstruct the picture of the ideas and customs in large part upon the basis of the etymologies of the terminology. Thus each group is accepting the inferences of the other as if they were arrived at independently, whereas to a large extent they are but inferences from their own inferences. This being apparently the case it seems worth while to venture outside this vicious (or charmed) circle and to suggest certain etymological possibilities, for which there is at least some warrant in the authorities and which conform in sense to the somewhat heterodox notions of the early institutions which we have set forth. This is done in the hope that it may suggest new investigations and lead to interesting results.

A. *Terms for the House, or Village, Community and for the House Master*

1. "*Familia*"

Obviously the closest cognates to the Latin *familia* and *famulus* are to be found in the other Italic dialects. Walde (*Latin*) takes *famulus* (Old Latin *famul*) as the basic form and ascribes to it the sense of "servant."[1] Thence he derives *familia*, at first as "the domestics" and thence as "the entire house-company, or household, free and slave—the family." *Famulus* equals Pelignian and Oscan *famel*. Therefore, *familia* is cognate with Oscan (Bant.) *famelo* and with Umbrian *fameřias* (*familiae*).[2] Buck (*Grammar*), as well as Conway (*Italic Dialects*) and Zvetaieff in his work on the inscriptions, connect the Osc. *faamat* with this group of words. They translate the latter as *habitat* (or *tendit*).[3] Walde, to whom changes in vowel quantities always seem to be more insuperable than to others, rejects the association of *famel* and *faamat* entirely.[4] He interprets (Latin) *famel*, etc., partly as "belonging to the house, from **dhə-mo-* (house), compare Skt. *dhāman-* (dwelling place); partly one goes from the meaning *Schar* (*der Diener*) on account of Gr. θήμων (*Haufe*), θαμά (*dicht*), whose relation to **dhe-* is very questionable." Both, he says, are very uncertain.[5] Muller (op. cit.) carries this second

[1] So too Ernout and Meillet, op. cit.

[2] Buck, *Grammar*, Conway, op. cit., and others also identify Osc. *famel* with Lat. *famulus*, and Osc. *famelo* and Umb. *fameřias*, with Lat. *familiae*. As to the sense of the first equation Buck, *Grammar*, cites Festus, *De Verborum Significatu*, p. 62, ed. Thewrewk, "Famuli origo ab Oscis dependet, apud quos servus famel nominabatur, unde et familia vocata." As to that of the second he translates, Tabula Bantina, 4. 22, *famelo in. ei.* as *familia et pecunia*, and states that in the Iguvinian Tables the Umbrian *fameřias* (nom. pl.) has to do with families as subdivisions of gens.

[3] So do Bréal and Bailly, *Dictionnaire étymologique Latin*, p. 84. Conway, op. cit., II, p. 620, says that *faamat* clearly contains a strong form of the root of Osc. *famel*, Lat. *famulus*, etc. Buck, *Vocalismus*, p. 24, takes the same view, saying that *famel*, etc., are built from the reduced grade of the root of *faamat*. Von Planta, *Grammatik der oskisch-umbrischen Diälecte*, I, p. 458, groups the words together, but he gives to the word *faamat* the sense *commandirt* or *habitat* (II, p. 682). On account of the long *ā* in *faamat*, von Planta, I, p. 458, finds it difficult to accept the older derivation—cognate with Skt. *dhā-man-* (*Wohnung*), Gr. θαιμός (οἰκία)—from the root **dhē-* (*setzen, stellen*). Buck, *Vocalismus*, p. 26, says this connection "ist naturlich nicht aufrecht zu erhalten." But on account of the *ă* in *famel*, von Planta finds equal objections to the proposed derivation from the stem **bhăg-mo-*. He throws out the suggestion that the group may come from **bhuā-mo-* (root **bheu-*) to which Walde, *Idg.*, gives the original sense of *wachsen* and the developed sense of *wohnen*.

[4] He connects the latter, with *fās, fārī, fātum, fāma, fābula*, etc., to **bhā* (*sprechen*). This necessitates a different interpretation of the sense. He says it has approximately the sense of "call," presumably connecting it thereby to von Planta's sense of "command."

[5] Elsewhere, *Idg.*, he explains this. From **dhē* (*setzen, stellen, legen*) are derived the Skt. *dhāman-* (*Satzung, Gesetz*) and Gr. θέμις; and from **dhə-mo* are derived, in one sense (*Niederlassung, Wohnstätte*), Gr. θαιμός (= οἰκία, Hesychius) and Skt. *dhāman-* (*Wohnstätte*), and in another sense (*Haufe, Schar—der Diener*), "viel-

source in Walde's speculation to the extreme. To him the Prim. Ital. *þămelŏ-s* is *Diener* and *þămĕl-iā* is *Dienerschaft.*[6] Ernout and Meillet (op. cit.) suggest that *famulus* seems to contain a suffix of agency (*cf. baiulus*) indicating a slave charged with a special function. Nevertheless they find no connection with other Indo-European languages and suggest—as they frequently do—the possibility that the word was borrowed from the Etruscan. On the other hand Clark (*Regal,* p. 213) suspects that *familia* is not derived directly from *famulus,* but rather that the latter is a secondary derivative from the same source as *familia.* And this, I take it, is Bonfante's view. He says (op. cit., I, p. 204), "*Familia* semble plûtot dériver d'un radical, *dhăman-,* qui signifie la demeure, d'où est aussi dérivé *domus,* et la signification de *famuli* est un sens dérivé, comme celui de notre mot *domestiques.*" This interpretation seems the most reasonable to me and is entirely consistent with the best etymological views. It is also supported by the analogy of the Greek *δμώς* (captive, prisoner of war) and *οἰκέτης* (domestic).

The evidence is of the slenderest and the conclusions are very uncertain. But we may gather that the sense of the German *gewohnen—wohnen,* which pervades most of these suggested sources, appears the most credible core idea for the group—the idea of "settled." The term *familia* seems to have developed, therefore, in a channel which gave it the sense of "those who customarily dwelt together," or "a settlement," and perhaps conveyed, *via* the suffix, the sense of *belonging to* or of *functioning in connection with* the settlement or dwelling.[7] It also suggests the extent to which all subject persons, free or slave, were lumped together into one class of "domestics," or even "servants."

2. "*Vicus*"

The terms for such settlements, which are most generally represented in all the southern Indo-European tongues, are the cognates of the Lat. *vicus,* which Walde (*Latin*) defines as "Haüsergruppe, Dorf, Flecken, Fr. quartier." It is derived from Prim. Ital. **ueikos,* equivalent, with the vowel alternation *ei* instead of *oi,* to Umb. *uocu-com* (or *vuku*). The Greek representatives are *οἶκος* from *ϝοῖκος* (house), *οἰκέω* (dwell),

leicht mit Recht," Lat. *famulus,* etc. Thus he avoids von Planta's difficulty but does so by a route which makes the connection between *famulus* and *faamat* even more difficult. In the new edition of Walde, *Latin,* Hoffmann casts some doubt on the earlier interpretation.

[6] In support of this he cites Paul, 77L, "famuletium dicebatur quod nunc servitium." He does not explain how thence *familia* could come to mean *Gesinde, Hausgenossenschaft,* nor why his etymology leads particularly to the idea of "servant." He says that *famĕ-lo-s—*fa-mo-s* < *IE. *dhə-mo-s*—perhaps especially *Herdstelle,* from the root **dhē-* (*stellen* > *Wohnung*) as *aedēs,* originally *Herdstelle,* developed into *Wohnung* (**aiþēs, Feuerherd* > *Wohnstätte*) from root **aidh-* (*brennen*).

[7] In this connection it is worthy of note that Hubert, *Les Celtes,* II, p. 245, considers that the word Ir. *fine,* Gaulish *veni-* was replaced in Gaulish as a designation of the house community by the word *toullu* "qui signifie à proprement parler 'les occupants de la maison' (*ty,* maison; *llu,* hôte)."

οἰκέτης (*Hausegenosse*); the Sanskrit is *viç* (residence), plural *viçaḥ* (mankind, subjects); the Avestan is *vīs* (house, village, clan); the Gothic is *weihs* (*Dorf, Flecken*); the Albanian are *vise* (pl., *Orte, Plätze*) and *amvise* (*amε* = mother) (*Hausfrau*, esp. *materfamilias*). The Indo-European root is given as **u̯eik̑- — *u̯ik̑-*, and the stem as *u̯oik̑i-* (house, settlement).[8] The inference from these equations seems to me obvious; and we shall see further evidence as we proceed. In spite of the effort which has been made to squeeze them all into a fixed place in a preconceived pattern, this family of terms had no definite structural significance as to the organization of society. They were simply words for settlements in general, with the vaguest of boundaries, which in certain cases came to refer to specific types of settlement because in these cases settlements came, for economic and political reasons, to conform to a somewhat standardized pattern. The same root developed in different lands into terms to designate variously a farmstead, a village, or an extensive neighbourhood; sometimes conforming and sometimes not conforming to the outline of the unit of governance. Moreover we see it applied somewhat indiscriminately to the buildings, the district and the persons dwelling therein.

3. "*Domus*"

The most general term for the house (the building) itself, though this too comes to be applied to the household and even to the family connection, is represented in Latin by *domus* (house).[9] It is cognate with Skt. *dáma-ḥ* and Gr. δόμος, and is usually allied to δέμω (to build). All are

[8] Perhaps these definitions of Walde indicate too narrow a coverage. Schrader, op. cit., p. 399, says that these are the original terms for *sib* "so far as it required to be designated as a settlement on a common pasture ground." He so construes Avestan *vīs*; Gr. *ϝικ-, Lat. *vīcus*, Goth. *weihs*, and Skt. *viç-*, to the last of which he gives the sense "enter, settle." Ihering, along the same lines, *Aryan*, pp. 19 and 25, considers the Hindu *jana* as a tribe ruled over by a *rā-jan*, divided into provinces, or *viç-*, and these into villages, or *grāma*. So, too, Ernout and Meillet, op. cit., think that the root **weik-* had a "sens précis dans l'organisation politique indo-européenne; . . . indiquant l'unité sociale immédiatement supérieure à la maison du 'chef de famille'." AS. *wīc* had the wider sense of *vīcus*. And the English *vill* was a hamlet or village. But its source, Lat. *villa*, probably contracted from *vicula*, had like the Germ. *Dorf*, the general sense of a single estate. See Schrader, op. cit., p. 17. So did Skt. *vēçá-* (house or yard). Finally the Gr. οἶκος (house) and its derivatives, οἰκέτης, οἰκέται, οἰκετεία (household), pertain to a somewhat more definite and circumscribed settlement or group resembling, perhaps, the Lat. *familia*. Nevertheless, even the latter, like Gr. πάτρα (the society under the power of the πατήρ) shows a tendency, according to Schrader, op. cit., p. 396, to widen its coverage to include the tribe.

[9] Ernout and Meillet, op. cit., class *domus* with Gr. οἶκος as designating "la maison en tant que symbole de la famille." They deny its relationship to δέμω because of the disyllabic root of the latter, but elsewhere seem to contradict this by assuming for *domāre*, which is related to *domus*, a disyllabic root as well, namely **demə-*domə-*dmā-* (s.v. *veto*). Further, they consider that the Indo-European name for *maison* (**dem-*) seems isolated like the name, **weik-*, of the "clan." Both their *exact* translations and their imputation of isolation seem not to accord with the general view.

derived by Walde from IE. **dem-*demā* (*bauen*, orig. "fit together") (see his *Idg.*).

4. "*Pater*"

When we come to deal with the organization for governance we see the various terms for the "chief" formed as compounds from the foregoing terms for settlements, groups of persons, or buildings. The Skt. *jāspatiḥ* (chief of the tribe) and perhaps the OCS. *gospodĭ* (master) seem to be based on the root of Skt. *jánaḥ* (the tribe) [10] Skt. *viç-páti-ḥ* (which Walde translates as *Hausherr, Gemeindehaupt*) and Lith. *viẽšpat(i)s*, are obviously based on the root of *viç-;* while Skt. *pátir dán*, Avestan *dəng paitiš*, Skt. *dám-pati-ḥ* and Gr. δεσ-πότης, all meaning "master of the house," are held by Schrader, Walde, and others to arise from IE. **dems-poti-s* – that is, from the root for *domus.*[11] Finally we have the Lat. *paterfamilias*, from *familia.*[12]

The personal parts of all these compounds present a curious and important problem. Though they seem to have a nearly uniform use, they are no longer ascribed to a single source. For the series Skt. *pitár-*, Gr. πατήρ, Lat. *pater*, Osc. *patír*, Goth. *fadar*, AS. *fæder*, OHG. *fater*, Walde gives the source IE. **pətér-* from the onomatopœic *pa(pa)*, and defines them all as "father." For the series Skt. *páti-ḥ*, Avestan *paiti-*, Gr. πόσις, Lat. *potis* (in *hospes, hospitis, *ghosti-potis*),[13] Goth. *-faþs* (in *brūþ-faþs* – bridegroom – and *hunda-faþs* – commander of one hundred men), Lith. *patìs* or *pàts*, he gives the source IE. **poti-s*, and defines them variously as "master," "husband," and, in Baltic and Iranian (Avestan *xvaē-pati* = *erselbst*), also as "self." The older etymology threw these all together into relation, with Skt. *pāti-*, to the root **pā-* or **pō-*, expressing the idea of "protection." But even these two roots Walde separates, though the meaning of both is the same.

The personal part, then, of these compound terms for the chief (or protector) are variously ascribed to three sources. Is the distinction valid? In the first group, to which Walde assigns the sense of "father," we find the Latin *paterfamilias, patres*, and *patronus*. It is quite evident, whatever the sense of *familias*, that the *paterfamilias* was not the "father" of a large portion of it; the *patres* were not the "fathers" of Rome – they were the heads (or chiefs) of the *familiae;* and *patronus* has no sense of

[10] See Schrader, op. cit. Boisacq, *Dictionnaire étymologique de la langue grecque*, takes *gos-*, in the latter, from **gu̯os-* "feminine domesticity"; Walde, *Idg.*, takes it from **ghosti-* (stranger, guest).

[11] Ihering derives δεσ-πότης from the cognate of Skt. *dāsá-ḥ* (presumably as slaves) and the root **pa-*po-* (to maintain). See *Aryan*, p. 395.

[12] Ernout and Meillet, op. cit., s. v. *potis*, state: "A l'état isolé, l'indo-européen avait, pour désigner le chef d'un groupe de toute dimension – famille, clan, tribu – un thème **poti-*." To which I would add that, at this stage, he seems to have had no systematic nomenclature for groups of different dimensions or place in an organized social hierarchy.

[13] This has, according to Ernout and Meillet, op. cit., the "sens premier 'maitre de.'"

"father" but wholly that of "patron," or "chief."[14] In many languages the IE. **diḙu pəter*, Lat. *Juppiter, Jūpiter* (voc. used for the nom. *Diēspiter*) stood for the "chief of the day" (or "of the heavens," or "of the gods").[15] Jupiter and Zeus, even in the confused divine genealogy of myth, were not "fathers" of the gods. They were lords of the gods or the heavens; rulers rather than parents.[16]

When we turn to the second group we find Skt. *páti-ḥ* as the basis of the aforementioned *jāspati-ḥ, viç-pátiḥ* and *dám-pati-ḥ* (various kinds of "lord"); Gr. *πόσις* (spouse) and *δεσπότης* (usually **δεμσ-πότ-ā*—as house-lord); Lat. *hospes* (gen. *hospitis*, **ghosti-potis*, as guest-lord) and *potestās*, as the power of the *paterfamilias*—from *potis* (able, capable) like *potis est* (he can), *possum* (I can), *compos* (having the mastery of); Goth. *-faþs* (indiscriminately as the "lord of a bride" and the "lord of a hundred men"); and Lith. *patìs* (as spouse or self).

Whether or not this double etymology will prove tenable,[17] the construction placed upon it seems untenable. It presumes a division between the terms for what we may call the biological and the societal "fathers." But when we examine the evidence, in the absence of preconceived notions, both groups seem to refer almost indiscriminately to a general kind of relation of superiority (or to those so superior) which is equally applicable to that of fathers to their children, to that of husbands to their wives, as well as to that of all those *over* all other subject or inferior persons. This merging into one vague but undifferentiated notion seems best to represent the point of view of prehistoric Indo-Europeans. We can make no valid semantic distinction between the early *pater* and *potestas*.

5. "*Tribus*"

In support of this breaking down of the imputation of system and of exactitude to the early terminology for groups and their rulers we may cite the vagaries of certain other etymological equations. Into early historical material is usually read the notion of a fixed social arrangement in three or more ascending classifications. Then the systematic organization is imputed to prehistoric times because the terminology is found to be

[14] Ihering, *Entw.-Gesch.*, p. 64, calls attention to the fact that the *pater-* and *mater-familias* might well not be father or mother. Ernout and Meillet say "Ce qu'indique *pater*, ce n'est pas la paternitè physique, qui est plutôt indiquée par *parēns* et par *genitor*. *Pater* a une valeur sociale. C'est le chef de la maison, le *dominus*, le *pater-familias*; c'est l'homme qui est un des représentants de la suite des générations, et l'on parle ainsi de *patrēs*."

[15] Thus Prim. Ital. **dịoú-păter* = Lat. *Jūpiter* = Umb. *Iu-pater* = Gr. Ζεῦ πάτερ (all vocatives) = Skt. *Dyāuš pitā* (nom.).

[16] Ernout and Meillet say, "On lit πατὴρ Ζεύς hors de toute idée de génération; on voit aussi que πατὴρ est une désignation du chef d'un groupe, ici le groupe des dieux."

[17] Schrader, op. cit., p. 372, thinks IE. **p(ĕ)-ter* (father) goes back to the same root as Skt. *pá-ti-* and Gr. πόσις, which is perhaps preserved in Skt. *pā-* (protect).

somewhat cognate among the different Indo-European peoples. We question this entire construction.

The largest usual grouping seems to have been represented by the notion of folk or people (*populus*), whatever that was. Perhaps it defined the group who fought or moved together ("das Folk ist Heer").[18] But the largest subdivision is generally assumed to have been the tribe. Walde (*Latin*) adopts the conventional legendary notion and defines *tribus* as "one of three stocks, divisions of the Roman *cives*." But he says that it was originally a district (citing Mommsen, *Rom. Staatsr.* III, p. 95) and explains it as **tri-bhu-* (a "third," or Fr. *quartier*).[19] "That the entire common territory is thus designated [by Umbr. *trifu-*] does not speak against the notion of a canton, which for its inhabitants also appears as a complete whole." This is hardly convincing. He connects the words with Old Bret. *treb* (a subdivision of the people), *trebou* (*turma*) and Old Ir. *treb* (tribe), and finds for all the same source as the Italic root **tribhu-* (originally "a third," then "a quarter," as part of a settlement) as the base.[20] In support of this view Muller (op. cit.), who gives the Prim. Ital. word as **trifŭs*, from **tri-* + **fu-* (root **bhĕu̯-*), cites the Gr. *τριχά-(ϝ)ῖκες*, and *τρί-φύλοι* (Hes.) and *τριφυόν* = *τριπλοῦν* (Hes.). To Walde (*Idg.*) the first, a byword of the Dorians, means "*in drei Phylen zerfallend.*" Muller, however, says they all mean divisions of the folk (*Stamm*). It seems a strange coincidence that among all these people the folk should have been divided into three tribes. And it is this difficulty, perhaps, which leads Muller to point out our almost equally strange use of "quarter," Fr. *quartier*, Germ. *Stadt-viertel*. Upon this Greek analogy and in this view, it seems more reasonable to conceive the term as referring to the territory than to the people (Mommsen's view). Even then it would be a curious sign that the people thought in terms of three directions instead of – perhaps only since the compass – in terms of

18 As Ihering, *Geist*, I, p. 248, describes it. Parenthetically, and in support of this interpretation, it may be excusable to revive a suggestive hypothesis as to the etymology of *populus*. *Spolium*, originally an animal hide, came to mean warlike equipment taken from the enemy, or booty. It is related to Gr. ἀσπαλον (σκῦτος) and σπολάς (skinned hide, also a throw-on of leather or pelt, breastplate). *Populo* and *-or* means "devastate" (*verheeren*). Vaniček connected it with *spolium* and *spoliare* (to plunder). Walde, *Latin*, calls this uncertain because to him *populus* does not seem to contain the idea of an army. But it is just this idea which, in our interpretation, is to be given to the body of citizens as opposed to the heads of the house communities – the (members of) government. As Walde suggests, *po* (< **apo-*, *cf.* ἀπὸ = *ab*) + *(*s*)*polāre* may underlie *populo*. Or the formation may have been a reduplication of **spol-*, as **spospol-* > *(*s*)*po*(*s*)*pol-*, with loss of medial *s* like *spo*(*s*)*pondi* and loss of initial *s* as some authorities indicate for *populor*. Thus, either to designate the body of men who carried shields or wore breastplates – the **popoli* – or allied with a sort of battle cry as the "harriers" – directly with *populo* – may have arisen the collective term for "the people as army."

19 The cognate Umb. *trifu-* he takes to mean community, "as it appears also with the very explicit connotation of 'common' (*Gemeindeflur*)."

20 It is composed of **tri-* (three) and **bhū-* (to be). Ernout and Meillet call this a "simple supposition."

four. Otherwise, whence the occult three? Or was it perhaps but a practical means of avoiding impasses between two equal halves—like our committees of three?

It has evidently been tempting to connect this *tribus* and the related Umb. *trifu-* with a group of words in Italic dialects which are phonetically similar. This group includes Osc. *triíbúm* (*domum*), *tríbarakkiuf* (*aedificium*), *triíbarakavúm* (*aedificare*), Umb. *trebeit* (*versatur*) and *tremnu* (*tabernaculo*).[21] But the authorities differ. Summarizing the views cited in the foregoing note we may say that we have Walde's authority for connecting Lat. *tribus* and Umb. *trifu-* or *trefu-*, with Bret. *treb* or *tref*; that of d'Arbois for combining it with the family of *trebo*, from **trbho*; and that of Buck and von Planta for identifying a phonetically identical member, Old Ir. *treb*, with Osc. *triíbúm* and thus perhaps with Lat. *trabs*. Thus the consensus of these different opinions, all opposing the end result, nevertheless seems rather to confirm it. They unite on a root **tr*(*i* or *e*)*bh*(*o*, *u*, or *eu*), to explain the Umbrian *f*, on one side, and, except for d'Arbois, on a root **tr-b-*, to explain the universal *b* on the other. Actually all but *trifu-* can be explained on the latter root.

[21] Buck, *Grammar*, p. 13, assigns them to the root *treb-* (*habitare*). He says (p. 62) the "Latin *trabs* (trunk of tree), if related, has a reduced grade." The group is connected by him with Old Ir. *treb*, which he translates as "dwelling place," to Lith. *trobà* (building), Goth. *þaúrp* (field), Germ. *Dorf*, etc. Von Planta, op. cit., I, p. 458, Note, does the same, but he adds that Umb. *trifu-* and Lat. *tribus* have nothing to do with Osc. *triíbúm*, Lat. *trabs*, Old Ir. *treb*, etc. And Curtius, op. cit., p. 280 (Root 250, τύρ-βη), says, "The Umbr. form *trefu* . . . is opposed to the supposition of a relationship with *tribu-s*, which Zeuss . . . compares with the Brit. *treb*, 'vicus,' as the *f* of the Umbrian word cannot be reconciled with that *b* which = the Goth. *p*." D'Arbois, *Les Premiers Habitants de l'Europe*, has still a different view. He says, II, p. 358, "Le celtique avait un thème *trebo-* (village, groupe d'habitations sans enceinte de muraille)." It is shown in proper names. It "se rencontre en irlandais sous la forme *treb* (habitation), et le verbe *trebaim* (j'habite, je cultive). Le même mot existe en gallois et en breton : *tref* en gallois veut dire 'habitation' ou 'groupe d'habitations'; *trev* en breton est une subdivision de la paroisse et peut être rendu par 'succursale.'" He presupposes for all the Celtic words a form **trbho-*. Having lost the aspiration of the *bh* in Celtic it accords with his thesis to suppose it passed thence—not direct—into the Germanic languages as *thorpo* (Goth. *þaúrp*) and, after the second consonant shift, Germ. *Dorf* (village, assembly). For **trbho* he assigns the same root as Gr. τρέφω. Obviously this explanation of the German *p* eliminates Curtius' objection, for *bh* would be converted into *f* in Umbrian. However, d'Arbois perceived some other objection which he does not state. He says, ibid., II, p. 369, Note I, "One cannot admit that the Irish *treb* is identical with the Latin *tribus*. The phonetics are opposed." Walde, *Latin*, s.v. *trabs*, connects the group Osc. *triíbúm*, etc., with Old Welsh *treb* (*Wohnung*), Old Bret. *treb* (same), and assigns them to an uncertain root **tr-b-*. He does it by dividing the Celtic group into two parts. Then he reserves *treb* (*Volksabteilung*) and *trebou* (*turma*) for *tribus*. If the phonetic objection is compelling in one case it should be in the other. The true objection, therefore, seems to be preconceived notions as to meaning.

Hubert, op. cit., II, p. 256, speaks of "un mot commun aux langues italo-celtiques représenté par le latin, *tribus*, par le gaulois *tref*, portion de la tribu, et l'irlandais *treb*, maison : ce mot désigne essentiellement un groupe d'hommes qui défriche une certaine quantité de territoire, il designe aussi le territoire occupé par lui. En vieux slave *trĕbiti* signifie, il défriche. La tribu habite une clairière, elle est entourée d'une marche." This is to me by far the most convincing interpretation.

The real difficulty seems to be with the semantics. If, in spite of the denials, all should be related, then Buck's root sense *habitare* would give to all the notion of "dwelling" or "settlement" which we have already found behind *familia* and *vicus*. Or possibly a more original meaning of "trunk of tree," lying behind all, would give the sense of "clearing" in a forest. Thus we have several possible original meanings, that of "settlement," that of a "division of the whole," and that of a "clearing" or a "district." At least we must conclude, from all this interpretation of the term, that there is no reason to suppose that its application was systematic or that the early tribe was a regularly constituted group.

6. *"Curia," "Gens" and "Civis"*

The next subdivision, as a part of the tribe, was supposed, under the Roman system, to have been the *cūria*. The older etymology, which related it—and also *Quirītēs*—to the Sabinian *quiris* or *curis* (spear), imputed the military idea of "the spearmen." Walde, Muller and others interpret it as **co-viriā* (the gathering of the men). Muller relates it to Volscian *co-uehriu* (< **co-vīrio-* = *conventu*), and to *Quirīnus*, etc., and gives it the sense of *Sippegenosse*. Walde derives the proper name *Quirītēs* from **couirītēs* = a member of the citizenry.[22] At any rate the term meant a "gathering." There is nothing here to support the legend that a *curia* had been a tenth part of a tribe or that in any way it had represented a part of a permanent organization, until, perhaps, it came to be applied to a district of the city (or a meeting of the citizens) smaller than the *tribus*, the two being analogous to our wards and precincts.

The next smaller subdivision appears in the word *gēns*, upon which so much supposition has been made to hang. I doubt that it ever covered a prehistoric political organization of any kind.[23] Rather it seems to have been a term, corresponding somewhat to the wider use of *familia* (the *Grossfamilie*) which, prior to settled times, described a large house com-

[22] Wood, *Post-Consonantal 'w' in Indo-European Languages*, p. 77, has a curious and interesting thesis. He suggests a root **kuwer-* for *Quirīnus* (mighty, lordly, the epithet of deity), *Quirītēs* (Roman citizens). "Here also, in spite of Volsc. *couehriu*, the meaning of which is doubtful, and may itself be ultimately related, **kowīri̯ā-* (a massing together, a gathering), Skt. *çávīraḥ* (mighty), Lat. *cūria* (assembly, place of assembly); with which compare Lith. *szurai* (*Tross*, *Gefolge*) Gr. κύριος (having power or validity; lord, master)."

To my mind a more plausible connection may be made with Old Lat. *uruus*. See Hubert, op. cit., I, pp. 53-54. He finds the sense of "close" or "protect," in the root, developing into "trench" or "dike" and thence to "boundary." Viz. ὅρος (*ϝορϝο-), Old Lat. *uruus* (*circuitus civitatis*), *amburuāre* (surround with a dike), *ueruactum* (fallow), Umb. *uruvú* (frontier). From the same root Osc. *ueru* (gate), Umb. *uerofe* (towards the gate), *uerisco* (gate, little gate), Lat. *uestibulum*. Thence, like θυραῖος (public, literally that which is outside the gate), the Czech adjective *veřejný* (public) and the Osc. *uerehia* ("l'ensemble du public"). So perhaps, with prefix *co-*, the Volsc. *couehriu* and Lat. *cūria* (as **co-uer-ia* or **co-ur-ia*) merely as "assembly."

[23] The term *Sippe* which is usually held to correspond with it is a member of a family of words which run all the way from the reflexive pronoun corresponding to "self," to many proper names for entire peoples; Sabelli, Suebi, Swedes, etc.

munity or a group of house communities divided from a common source which had not lost contact or forgotten their origin—a group which might also call themselves a tribe.[24] After the adoption of surnames it seems to have denoted the *familiae* descended from a common source who retained a common surname; though even then the term extends vaguely to the whole of the patrician caste or the whole people.[25] *Gēns* seems to have stood, not for an element in the organization but for a "relationship" or "birth" that was worth claiming.

Finally we come to the later unit of the Roman political organization the *cīvis*.[26] Schrader (op. cit., p. 396) points out that the Germanic stem **hīw-* gives rise to words meaning house-master, family, marrying, man and wife, servants of the house, family servants, menials, married couple, domestics, and is the exact equivalent of *cīvis*. He suggests as the original meaning of *civis* itself "the individual *paterfamilias* in his relation to the *civitas*."[27] Walde gives, as the basic meaning of the whole family of words, "belonging to the sib, trusted, *liebreich*." It appears to me that *cīvis* means "one who belongs"—a member, in this case, of the *cīvitās*.

The general impressions which I receive from these authoritative views on the etymology and uses of all the foregoing terms connected with Indo-European social organization may be summarized in two statements. In the first place the variety of sense in which they came to be used in the post-ethnic stage seems to me to indicate a fluctuating and unsystematic early usage which corresponded to a fluctuating and unsystematic organization, or to reflect little organization of any kind above the simplest physical grouping. In the second place it seems to me a striking fact that there is no evidence connecting the sources of these words—with the exception of *gens* and cognates—with the fact of generation, and considerable evidence for other connections. Certainly the later sense of biological relationship must not be imputed to the earlier stages. In turn this impression suggests that the organization of prehistoric Indo-European societies and their immediate forerunner at the pre-ethnic stage, was not based on birth or kinship, in the sense of consanguinity, according either to a patrilineal or to a matrilineal reckoning. And the fact that *gens* and its cognates seem to be marked exceptions makes one wonder if the relationship they covered prior to historic times was not of a different order from the rest—as different as the status

[24] Ernout and Meillet, s.v. *genō*, define it as "proprement . . . le groupe de tous ceux qui se rattachent par les mâles à un ancêtre mâle (et libre) commun."

[25] Walde, *Latin*, defines the term as "Geschlecht, Stamm, aber seit alter Zeit auch Völkerschaft, Menge." He takes it from root of *gigno* through a base **ĝenti-s* and connects it with Avestan *fra-zaintiš* (posterity), Germanic **kindi-* in Goth. *kindins* (governor) and with Skt. *jāti-ḥ* (birth, caste), and with a different grade and suffix, to Skt. *jana-* (tribe).

[26] It is cognate with Osc. *ceus* (*cīvis*), Goth. *heiwa-frauja* (*Hausherr*), OHG. *hīwo* (*Gatte*), AS. *hīwan* (*Hausgesinde*), Skt. *çēvá-* (*traut, freundlich, lieb, wert*).

[27] Ernout and Meillet note that in Latin this element of the household vocabulary was peculiar in that it took on an official character and so gave the name *cīvitās* to the people as a whole. The ancient name for the people was Osc. *touto*, Umb. *totam* (acc. sg.), Ir. *túath*, Gaulish *teuto-*, Goth. *þiuda*, Lith. *tautà*, which is, perhaps, preserved only in a generalized sense in Lat. *tōtus*.

in the army appears to have been from the status in the house community — developing out of customs with reference to exogamy and endogamy and not out of governance, and, except in certain cases as a later development, entirely outside the pattern of the political organization.[28]

7. *The Locus*

There are two other pervasive sets of terms which refer, at the lowest level, to the unit of the house community itself as if it were a general, permanent and well defined organization. The first is the term for enclosure or farmyard — the locus of the house community itself even from the migrant pastoral days — the original nature of which is accurately described by its various eventual meanings. This family of words derived from the IE. root **ĝher-* (*greifen, fassen, umfassen, einfassen*). We have already referred to it (see Note 240, p. 93), but we may give Walde's more complete equation here: Lat. *hortus* (garden), *cohors* (farmyard, crowd), Osc. *húrz* (garden), Gr. *χόρτος* (enclosure, pasture), Old Ir. *gort* (sown field), Bret. *garz* (hedge, garden), Old Welsh *garth* (garden), Goth. *gards* (house), Old Ice. *garđr* (fence, yard), AS. *geard* (garden, dwelling), Old Sax. *gard* (enclosure, dwelling), OHG. *gart* (circle), Lith. *gar̃das* (wattle), OCS. *gradŭ* (enclosure), OHG. *garto*, Old Sax. *gardo* (garden), Goth. *garda* (stable). Here is the universal dwelling of the pastoral period where the residence and such slight agriculture, or horticulture, as was practised, needed to be protected against the herds. It was — to judge by the various eventual meanings of this family of words — a combined house, farmyard and garden, and was probably circular and enclosed with a wattle fence or hedge.[29]

8. *The Heirship*

The second set of terms is that which covers the inheritance and the heir. Here we find no general correspondence among the various languages, but the near universality of such terms indicates that the unit inherited was also nearly universal. Muller gives the Prim. Ital. **χēr(o)-* + *ē-d-* as the basis of the Lat. *hērēs*. The stem is cognate with that of Gr. *χῆρος* (bereaved) and *χῶρος* (empty space).[30] The only known

[28] It is worthy of note that the distinguished French Celticist, Henri Hubert, op. cit., II, pp. 241-242, concludes that among the Celts, as in my view among the Romans, the Irish term *clan* (or its Welsh equivalent *cenedl*) no longer reflected a particular type of unit in the social organization nor had a status in law between *fine* and *túath* (*familia* and *tribus*) but was a name used for both and perhaps for something else. It means "descent" or "descendants."

[29] Hubert, op. cit., II, p. 258, says, "Les relevés topographiques d'Irlande montrent précisément à l'intérieur des quartiers (of the *baile*) des cercles qui pouvaient avoir été l'habitation commune des gens de la baile ou du quartier."

[30] This, according to Walde, arises from IE. **ĝhēro-*, an extension of the root *ĝhē(i)- ĝhī- ĝhə-* (forsaken, to be empty). The second syllable *ēd-*, according to Brugmann, is from *ē-d(o)*, so that the term means "he who receives (or is given) the bereaved (person's) or vacant (position, land)." Boisacq dilates on this. He

synonymous cognate is χηρωστής which Bosaicq analyses in the same way as he does *hērēs*.[31] The Goth. *arbi* (inheritance), OHG. *arbi, erbi* (inheritance), and Germ. *Erbe* (m. heir, n. inheritance) are, according to Walde (*Latin*), cognates of Lat. *orbus* (bereft, orphan) and Gr. ὀρφανός (orphan).[32] All these he interprets as "to be bereft of something."

The general idea of "bereft" or "empty" seems to have placed difficulties in the way of these etymologies.[33] All these difficulties seem to vanish in the light of the thesis presented in our text. That which was bereft or orphaned was a group of persons, the house community, not a body of property. Certainly this was true before property in land appeared. We may conjecture that the eldest or strongest male replaced the chief automatically when the latter became decrepit or when he died. And this being a matter of internal and universal custom – the concept of perpetual succession – required no definitive terminology. However, there might be no male of age left. Then it became the duty (hardly the prerogative) of the nearest agnate to adopt and protect the bereft group.[34] Evidently the old terminology discriminated between external and internal heirs, or confined itself to the former. Since *hērēs* appears capable of being an exact cognate of χηρωστής it would have to be presumed that it too was originally applied only to external heirs. And in support of this thesis, it is worthy of note that, if this were not the case – if the original *hērēs* had been the internal heir – it would not have been natural to add the designation *suus* specifically to distinguish him. Instead the distinguishing adjective would have been given to the external heir. OHG. *arbi*, or *erbi*, seems to have been from the beginning "the bereft – and therefore inherited – group" itself. Thence, by transference, it became the term for heir as well.

When the inheritance first began to be thought of as something other than succession to an office of command over a group of people we may distinguish the stage when *arbi, erbi*, signified particularly cattle (See Note

says IE. **ĝhērēd-* comes from **ĝhēro-* + **ē-d-* like Skt. *dāyādá-h* (one who receives the inheritance or part of it), that is to say **dāyá-* (share, part of an inheritance) + *ā-da-* (one who receives), *á dā-* (to receive) with *ā* from IE. **ē* **ō*. This last Walde, *Idg.*, interprets as an adnominal and adverbial particle, "near by, close by, together with" and in this case, with -**d(ō)*-, as *empfangend*.

[31] He translates it literally (largely gratuitously) as "qui reçoit (en propriété ou en gérance) le (bien devenu) vacant." χηρωστής is formed on *ὤ-δ-τά ("le fait de reçevoir") like the Skt. *ā-tta-*, IE. **ō-d-to-s* in Skt. *dévá-tta-h* (given by the gods), root **dō-***də*, from IE. *ĝhērōd-* (*ĝhēro-* + *ō-d-*).

[32] Hubert, op. cit., I, p. 81, suggests that the Germanic group are borrowed from the Celtic source of Irish *orbe* (heritage).

[33] Walde, *Latin*, s. v. *hērēs*, attempts to get round them. He says, "Against this connection of *hērēs* with χῆρος some oppose the fact that the *hērēditās*, according to the Roman concept, was never deserted. The objection is not compelling for the very oldest word was certainly much older than the building up of the historic Roman concept of *hereditas*." He translates, *Idg.*, *hērēs* as "das verwaiste (Gut) an sich nehmend" and shows the development of meaning of *Erbe* thus : "the orphaned = the heir ; the orphaned property = the inheritance."

[34] Boisacq translates the term χηρωστής (Homer, Hesiod) as "a collateral who inherits in default of closer relatives." But, be it noted this was not the general Greek word for heir. That was the doubtless later κληρονόμος.

266, quoting Sievers, p. 103). For, then, cattle were practically the only objects other than persons to be so transferred. Later, with the development of property in land, and the general rule by which this, along with the government of the house community, followed the male line, *erbi* came to apply particularly to land (see also Walde, *Latin*). Then in Latin the word *hērēdium* appeared to distinguish such property. At this stage too, we may suspect, there appeared the terminology which covers the general Greek system of inheritance. The basis is the word κλῆρος.[85] Vinogradoff (*Jurisprudence*, II, p. 212) says, "In theory every private estate in Greece was considered an allotment by the State. Nor was this theory a mere judicial fiction or antiquarian speculation." "The complex of estates in Attika was regarded as a set of κλῆροι distributed as far as possible permanently among a set of citizen households (οἶκοι)." Upon it were built the general terms for heir (κληρονόμος = κλῆρος + νέμομαι = to take the lot, or domain) and thence the term for inheritance (κληρονομία) and that for inherit, "to be an heir" and "to have an heir" (κληρονομέω). By associating this with the Lat. *sors*, of the same meaning – which came also to stand for a plot of land and thence, as *cōnsortium* for a joint holding of a (landed) estate – and with the Teutonic method of dividing the land by lot among the citizens, the whole system seems to be related. Apparently it was the attachment of land to the house community which converted the bereaved group from a liability into an asset, and which converted a terminology expressing the duty of helping the helpless into one expressing the privilege of helping oneself.[86] The term *heres* certainly derived from the earlier period, probably as the "receiver of the vacant place (the *patrimonium*) – or the bereaved persons." Whether associated at different stages with persons, with cattle, or with land, it is clear that this set of terms indicates that a definite unit with a continuing headship was a pervasive social institution among all the western peoples of Indo-European culture.

B. *The Etymology of "Manus-Mund" and of the "Manus"-System*

When one begins to investigate the etymology of the two words *manus* and *mund* he has the sensation of peering into a psychological gloaming which almost conceals behind its shadows the central region of the beginnings of social abstractions. Perhaps more than in any other group of putative roots, the essentials lie here, and continued exploration at this particular point should yield results of great interest. At present, there is not much that can be said, and examination of the current interpretation must be more critical than constructive.

Upon the assumption that *manus* and *mund* meant originally "hand"

[85] The original meaning of this word (from **qel-*, **qelā*) was *Holzstückchen* and thus *Los, Anteil.* Boisacq defines it as a "morceau de bois dont on se sert pour tirer au sort ; lot, part, héritage ; bien, domaine."

[86] For this thesis the two kinds of rule of inheritance given in the Lex Salica – the older one and the later one as to land which was superimposed thereon – offer support.

and in order to account as well for the Gr. *μάρη* (hand), etymologists have set up an IE. **mə-r*, **mə-n-és*, **mn̥-tóς* (hand) a heteroclitic r/n-stem, "possibly as the 'grasping, gripping thing,' from **amē-* **amə-* (to grasp)." Gr. *μάρη* rests on the r-nominative, *manus* on **mə-n-* (casus obliquus), and *munt* on **mn̥t-*. Walde (*Idg.*) objects to Hempl's linking with Goth. *manna* (man), and Wood's with **mē-* (measure) as they "do not satisfy in the meaning." He admits, however, that the root **am*(*ē*)- is a doubtful one. "Of the words referred to this root, those designating vessels probably meet the test, so that it has a certain amount of support." "Yet the highly hypothetical character of this link is to be emphasized." Thus it is proper to say that this etymology is more than usually doubtful.

Hempl's ("Etymologies," 22 *American Journal of Philology* (1901), p. 426) curious suggestion is as follows: "English 'man' is known to be the same word as Skt. *manus* (man). The idea that the word is derived from *√*man* (think), and originally meant 'the thinker,' is so sophisticated and so contrary to what we know to be primitive man's conception of his relation to other animals, that no one could successfully defend it today. Skt. *manus* (man) is phonetically identical with Lat. *manus* (hand) and it is not difficult to show that the words are really one and the same." His demonstration is by means of the analogy of the modern use of "hands" to mean "men" ("farm-hand," "all hands," etc.).

Whatever we may think of this—and Walde rejects it—it leads us into the interesting and related question of the source of the Germanic and Indo-Iranian words for "man." They are generally ascribed to the root **men-* which is given the sense "to think." To my notion this raises not so much the question of what primitive men thought of themselves as it does that of their idea of the thinking process.

Current hypothetical Indo-European contains five phonetically identical roots **men-*.

(1) **men-* (*emporragen*), Lat. *ēmineo*, *immineo*, presumably as a prominent corner, *mentum* (chin), perhaps *mentula* (penis) and (?) **mono-* (neck, nape). Fick attributes *manus* (hand) to this stem.

(2) **men-* (*treten, zertreten, zusammendrücken*).

(3) **men-* (think), Goth. *muns, man, munum*, Gr. *μέμονα*, Lat. *memini*. Here too Walde places the words for "man." He says, "To our root probably also Skt. *mánu, manuš*, Germ. *Mensch, Mann*, also OHG. *Mannus* (Tacitus' first man, as the ancestor of the Germans), and *mennisc* (human). Probably the word for 'man' was already differentiated in Idg."

(4) **men-* (*klein, verkleinen, vereinzelt*), Lat. *minuo*, etc.

(5) **men-* (remain, stand still), Skt. *man-* (hesitate, stand still), Avestan *man-* (remain, wait), Gr. *μένω* (remain), Lat. *maneo* (remain). "Primitive identity with **men-* (think) is not to be doubted." (Walde, *Idg.*).

A large number of explanations of the union of "man," with "think" or with "remain" have been offered, most of which seem incredible. The identification of "think" and "remain" is, however, on firmer ground. Curtius connects the above, under (3) **men-* as well as Skt. *man* (remember), Gr. μένος, Lat. *mens* (mind), with (5) **men-* (remain), and believes that, "starting with what may be clearly recognized as a metaphysical application," the same root is then "employed to denote ideas, which lie rather in the region of the senses;" and that "language derived the idea of remaining and persisting first from that of reflective hesitant thinking and bethinking, as the opposite of hasty action."[87]

Presumably as an extension of (1) **men-* there is set up a base **menth-* (*Kauen, Gebiss, Mund*).[88] And the IE. **men-dh-* is expressly explained by Walde as a dh-extension from (3) **men-* (think), more exactly as **men-dhē-* (to set the mind upon something).[89]

In the foregoing we see Walde, perhaps the present "last word," placing our words *manus* and *mund*, as if they meant only or originally "hand," in a purely hypothetical class by themselves, partly in order to relate them to Gr. μάρη. If, on the other hand, *manus* is close to the words for "man," as Hempl and others have suggested, it may be more reasonable to relate it to the **men-* family. If it meant only "hand" it might go, as Fick suggested (*Vergleichendes Wörterbuch der indogermanischen Sprachen*), to (1) **men-*. But perhaps it was more closely related to "man" and belongs with (3) **men-* or (5) **men-*.[40] Is it only preconceived notions of semantics which prevent such a rearrangement?

As to *mund* or *munt*, Osthoff placed it, in the sense *Schutz*, as from the stem **mendh-*. Etymologically this is much simpler than Walde's supposition. If the word originally meant "hand" and the derived meaning was *Schutz*, such a placing would seem impossible. But if it originally meant *Schutz* and the derived meaning was "hand," this connection is far more reasonable than the other, though it requires a change in our notion of the sense which has been translated *Schutz*.[41] Finally there is

87 Op. cit., pp. 126-127. It should be noted that most of the thinking described in this family of words has to do with remembering. Thus Gr. μνᾶσθαι, Goth. *munan* or *gamunan*, Lat. *meminisse*, perhaps (Walde, *Idg.*) Osc. *memnim* (*monumentum, memoriam*), Lat. *memor*, and (Walde, *Latin*) Lat. *mora* (delay, hesitation, originally "to remain thinking"). It even extends to terms for "love" and "souvenirs" ("mementos").

88 Whence Lat. *mando* (chew), Goth. *munþs*, Old Ice. *mūđr*, AS. *mūđ*, OHG. *mund* (mouth). Another root **menth-*(*meth-*) is taken to mean *quirlen, drehend bewegen.*

89 Here are placed Goth. *mundōn* (*einen besehen*), *mundrei* (*Ziel*), Old Ice. *munda* (*zielen*), OHG. *muntar* (*munter*), OHG. *mendī* (*Freude*), *menden*, Old Sax. *mendian* (*sich freuen*), Lett. *mûdu* (*erwecken*), Lit. *mundrùs, mandrùs* (*munter*), OCS. *mądrŭ* (*weise*). It is evident from these, and the words included under (3) **men-*, that the thought processes involved are assumed to have been then—as perhaps they actually are still—principally the emotions, joy, love, desire, etc.

40 If so, μάρη might appear to belong with Lat. *mās* (< **măr-*, Muller), *marītus*, Skt. *már-yaḥ*, etc. But, if the latter (Ernout and Meillet) is from **merio*, this would not be possible.

41 Walde, *Idg.*, assumes the first when he derives from **mn̥-t(ós)* the Old Ice. *mund* (hand), *mundr* ("price of the bride and tutelage acquired over her by the purchase"), AS. *mund* (hand, protection, placing under guardianship), OHG. *munt* (same sense), Germ. *Vormund*. On this assumption he says there is no need of putting this word, in the sense of protection, with the Goth. *mundōn* (to keep an eye on someone) < **mendh-* (to direct one's mind upon something). There is no necessity, if the first alternative is right. But what of the second?

the possibility that these are two different words, *mund* (hand) and *mund* (protection?), as separate as is *mund* (mouth). There is much to warrant this last view.[42] Taking Schade (op. cit.) as a basis and adding the interpretation of other authorities as indicated, we find the following forms appearing in the various Germanic dialects.

NOUNS

	MOUTH	HAND	PROTECTION	AIM
Goth.	*munþs*, M. (Walde)	*mund*, F. (Kluge)		*mundrei* (Walde)
Old Ice.	*mūđr*, M. (Walde)	*mund*, F.	*mundr*, M. (price of bride)	*munda* (Walde)
OHG.	*mund*, M. *munth*, M. *munt*, M.	*munt*, F.	*munt*, F. *munt*, M. (protector)	
AS.	*mūđ*	*mund*, F.	*mund*, F.	
Old Fris.			*mund*, M. *mond*, M. (also as protector)	

VERBS

	PROTECT	TO KEEP AN EYE ON	THINK, ETC.
Goth.	*mundôn* (Schröder)	*mundôn* (Walde)	*munan*, *man*, *munum*, *munda*, *munds*
Old Norse	*munda* (Schröder)		
OHG.	*muntôn*		
Old Sax.	*mundôn*		
AS.	*mundjan*		

Let us make several observations on this analysis:

1. As a group these words, disregarding the meaning, are nearly indistinguishable. All might come from the same source. Distinctons must then be based on meanings.

2. There are as many differences in form between columns 1 and 3 as there are between columns 1 and 2; therefore, as much reason to assume that "protection" and "hand" are separate words, as that "hand" and "mouth" are separate.

[42] As Schröder, op. cit., p. 60, Note, puts it, "die in den früheren Auflagen nach Grimm vertretene Ableitung des ahd. masc. *munt* (mlat. *mundius*, *mundium*) von fem. *munt* (*manus*) ist nach Osthoff zu verwerfen. Die Grundbedeutung ist Scheu, schirmen, schützen, wie in got. *mundôn*, altn. *munda*, ahd. *muntọn*, alts. *mundọn*, ags. *mundian*."

3. All the words for "hand" are feminine; all but two of those for "protection" are masculine.

4. Of the verbs for "protect," all of which seem identical in form with Goth. *mundôn* (to keep an eye on something), none appear to have any connection with "hand," "handle," etc., except the possible one derived through the symbolism of protection.

5. Obviously these words, if different, had become somewhat confused in the languages themselves. The lines of cleavage are no longer clear cut.[48]

For the general class *munder*, *muntar*, etc., Schade assumes a root **man-* (as in *munan*) and a stem **mandh-*. This accords with Walde (**mendh-*). But we have to suggest that this stem **mandh-* or **mendh-*, may be of broader interest in this case.[44] It seems also most reasonably to account for all the nouns in columns 3 and 4 above and for all the verbs in column 1. It may thus be the source of an independent word for "protection"; or it may be the source of the original word for "protection" of which the sense "hand" was an offshoot.

This leads us to a possible connection with the Roman *manus*-system. The Latin verb *mandō*, formerly explained as *man-dō*, is now credited to Prim. Ital. **man-þāi̯ō*, with **-þāi̯ō* < IE. **dhē-*; *cf.* Gr. τίθημι (< **dhē-*), and *facio* < **dhē-* + *k-* (*stellen*). On this basis it is possible to explain, with some construction, the corresponding Osc. *aa-manaffed* (*mandavit*) and *manafum* (*mandavi*) as **man*(*a*)-*fefed* and **-fefom* respectively. Thus Buck, Muller, and others. But this "fe, fi, fo, fum" may be omitted if the verbal stem is considered to be **mandh-* (or **mendh-*), instead of **man-dh*(*ē*)-, directly.[45] **Mandh-* would become *manf-* or *man*(*a*)*f-* in

[48] Another evidence of this confusion, somewhat contradicting the other indications, is that OHG. *muntboro*, M. (protector), from *munt*, F. + **bëran* (*hervorbringen, tragen*) is converted in Old French into *mainbour*. This, Schade thinks, occurred through confusion with Fr. *main* (*manus*). But obviously the Latinized French would construe this institution in terms of *manus*. The other terms for the same, *muntwaltâ* (presumably *-walter*), *munthêrro* and *muntporto* are even less plausibly connected with the sense of hand.

[44] This same stem frequently occurs in proper names. In Icelandic *-mundr* appears frequently as a suffix in proper names. In Gaulish, Holder (*Altceltischer Sprachschatz*), gives *mandú-* as a frequent prefix in proper names. The pre-Celtic form **m̥dh-ú-s* is given and it is interpreted by d'Arbois to be from **mendh-* and to mean "who is preoccupied with." This interpretation is not very satisfactory for *Mandu-benos* (Old Ir. *ben* = wife), *Mandu-bii* (Old Ir. *bil* = *sûr, bon*), *Mandu-bracios* (*braci* < -**mraci* = malt), *Mandu-essĕdum* (*essedum* = *char de guerre*). There is also the old place-name *Mandū-rĭa*, in Italy. In spite of d'Arbois, all these proper names seem difficult to construe on the basis of the original sense assigned to **mendh-* by Walde. It is tempting to ascribe to it the sense of "family" or "house." D'Arbois, *Droit Celtique*, translated Old Ir. *muinter* as "family," *cêt-muinter* as *materfamilias*, and *muin* as *dot*, all words which seem to belong to this family. It should be noticed that in this group *muin-* seems the foundation, which relates it to Walde's interpretation of Old Ice. *mundr*.

[45] Brugmann, *Grundriss*, Eng. trans. IV, pp. 218-219, points out other cases which suggest that the consonant which began the second part of the compound stem (**man-dh*(*ē*)-) may have practically become the root ending (**mandh-*).

Oscan, and *mand-* in Latin.[46] In this way too the minor difficulty is eliminated, that *mando* is of the first conjugation,[47] not like *facio* nor even like *do.* At the same time this reading of the Oscan enables the verb to fit perfectly the first conjugation there as well. The sense of both words, which is "commend," "commit," or "command," fits the concept of *mund*, if not as "protect" then in a more general sense as the verbal idea covering the whole relation. The *Mündling* was commended to a protector who commanded him, and perhaps in turn committed him to a *Vormund.* The notion may even stretch to the counter-action of the *Mündling* to his protector. For he prayed where the other commanded. And this may explain the appearance of the word in the Oscan curse as an appeal to Ceres Ultrix—translated by Buck as, "*Cereri Ultrici mandavi,*" and, "*Id tibi mandavi.*"

It must be admitted that there is no evidence connecting either the Latin noun *manus* or any of the compounds directly based on it with this stem **mandh-*. Obviously the stem of *manus* is **man-* (or **men-*) not **mandh-*. But it is also true that **man-* (or **men-*) is the root of **mandh-*, or **mendh-*. It is this point that has seemed to bear out the suspicion that, at an early stage, either two words from the same or different sources, meaning two different things, became in Primitive Italic confused and blended, just as, it appears, may have partially occurred in German; or that the Latin *manus* had originally the sense which we have ascribed to it in the text and that the sense of "hand" was derived from its symbolism. There is to support this second possibility the fact that *manus* is feminine, which suggests that it was an abstract noun before it was concreted.[48]

What the content of this institution of *manus-mund* was we have undertaken to conjecture from other evidence as presented in the text. From the probable associations and sources of the terms we can only

[46] The rule, for Oscan and Umbrian, as stated by Buck, *Grammar*, p. 8, is, "Representation of original *bh* and *dh* by *f*, not only initially as in Latin, but also medially, when Latin has *b* or *d*; Osc. *mefiaí* = *in media*."

[47] Ernout and Meillet say that *mandō* as **man(um)dō* (see Pliny, *mandāre* = *in manūs dare*) accords with the sense and is like the Gr. ἐγχειρίζω. But they also suggest that one would expect **mandere* like *vendere*, etc. Has there been a change of conjugation like *fodāre* in face of *fodere?* It is difficult to admit that *mandāre* is due to an attempt to avoid a homonym with *mandere*, and the hypothesis of a denominative drawn from a compound adjective **man-do-s* is "en l'air."

[48] At any rate the stem which enters the Latin compounds is, except in the case of *manumissio*, *man-* not *manu-*. The earlier compounds were certainly formed at a stage when the thought was not "to take, etc., by, or with, the hand," but rather "to take, etc., this thing which was called **man-*." *Man-ceps* is the "**man*-taker," *manubiae* is "**man*-havings" (if from *man-hibeo*). The Osco-Umbrian case endings make that clear. *Manf, mani, manim* are not based on *manu.* Ernout and Meillet sum up the usual interpretation as follows: "Le mot est italique, en partie thème en *-u-* comme en latin: ombr. *manuv-e* (*in manu*), en partie thème en *-i-*: osq. *manim* (*manum*), en partie thème consonantique: ombr. *manf* (acc. pl.). L'ablatif ombr. *mani* (*manu*) est ambigu, parce que les thèmes ombriens en *-u-* ont tous l'ablatif en *-i-*." The non-Italic forms, they say, exhibit the "thème consonantique **mn̥-* élargi par un suffixe." One inclines to accept this as the correct interpretation throughout.

hazard the guess that they expressed the various habits and relations and activities of a many-sided system which had its roots in the social necessities of "thinking and remaining men," not in one of its symbols, the hand. Of all constructions the most plausible seems to be that which would assume the sense of "man" as an almost proper (house community or race) name, growing out of the association of ideas of "fellow" with (3) **men-* (remember) and (5) **men-* (dwell), so that a "man" was one who belonged to the race of "man" (*Manu, Mannus*). Therefrom *manus-mund* might arise as the fact of *belonging* to the group—the basis of propinquity—gradually shift its emphasis to the ground of the power which held the group together and finally become *control* in the Latin derivative and *protection* in the German. And at the beginning of this last stage the verbal form, from **mandh-*, might arise.

C. *The "Vindex"*

For our representation of the social structure and the beginnings of the processes of law, the accepted etymology of the term *vindex* is an excellent and vivid support. Walde traces the word to the IE. **u̯en-*, to which he gives the basic meaning "strive, or reach out," "whence there can result, on the one side, the meaning *wünschen, lieben* and thence *befriedigt sein*, or *sich gewöhnen*; and on the other, *arbeiten, Mühe haben* and, as a perfective, *erreichen, gewinnen, siegen*."[49] The steps in this semantic development are similar to those underlying the probable etymology of our word "belong," which is allied with "long for"; and it is this close analogy which has led to the use of the term 'belong' in our text, as the English term which corresponds most closely to that which seems to lie behind the institution of *manus-mund*.

Walde (*Latin*) defines the *vindex* as one "who, before a judge, lays claim to something (or someone) or takes it (or him) under his protection —*Bürge, Befreier, Rächer*."[50] Thus **u̯en- + dico- > *veni-dic-s*, "wer vor dem als Schiedsrichter gedachten Könige auf die Sippe hinweist, indem er jemanden als zu dieser gehörig bezeichnet und dadurch schützt

[49] See his *Idg.* From the root he takes directly Lat. *venus* (*Liebe, Anmut, Liebreiz*) and Old Ir. *fine* (*Verwandtschaft, Stamm, Familie*), *fin-galach* (*parricidalis*). From IE. **u̯eni-s* comes the Old Norse *vinr* (friend). "Haufig und allgemein verbreitet ist der Übergang zu, 'befriedigt sein,'" and a further development leads in turn to AS. *wennan*, etc., (*gewöhnen*).

[50] On the ground of this three-fold meaning he derives the first syllable from **u̯en*—whence Old Ir. *fine* (*Grossfamilie*) *fin-gal* ("Mörder eines Familiengenossen"), Gaulish *Venicarus* ("seiner Familie wert"), OHG. *wini* ("zur Familie gehörig, Freund") and Lat. *venus*. Ernout and Meillet consider these "rapprochements . . . séduisants."

Hubert, op. cit., II, p. 245, accepts this equation. *Fine* belongs "au groupe indo-européen occidental." *Fine* "designe à la fois en Irlande la grande famille de plusieurs maisonnées et la petite famille ou maisonnée. . . Cette famille . . . presente les caractères généraux de la famille agnatique indivisé et de la famille patriarcale indo-européenne." This is our "house community."

"*Dex = deik* (zeigen, mit Worten auf etwas hinweisen, mehrfach auch zum gerichtlichen, sagen, Sinn 'auf den Täter hinweisen, beschuldigen' entwickelt)." Walde, *Idg.*

(Bürge), oder etwas als Sippeneigentum beansprucht, oder die Verfolgung einer Tat durch die Familie ansagt (Blutrache)." We have then from the beginning of social organization the representative of the house community – usually the chief – who defends or demands any portions of his group, animate or inanimate, which has become separated from it. At some stage, when such disputes begin to take place before the representative or chief of larger groups including several house communities, this intercessor or claimant, who speaks for the *familia* (or shows the *vin* = familial connection) and claims *manus*, comes to be called *vindex*. And he who is chosen to arbitrate between the two house communities involved – who comes in the course of time to represent the whole as against its parts – receives the name *iudex*. He speaks or shows the right (or binding) as to a disputed *manus*, or as to a responsibility assumed by the *vindex* for an act of a member of his group. Walde says that these two nouns, not the verbs, are the original forms. Literally the one is the "friend" – or *familia-Fürsprecher*"; the other the "right-speaker, or -shower."

D. *Absolute and Dependent Property*

We have, in the text, outlined the suggestive indications that a general distinction existed among Indo-European peoples between, on the one hand, the rulership of the autonomous house community – an absolute right passing by a particular kind of succession (heritable) – to which house community came to be attached the land and its accessories; and, on the other, the control, original or subordinate, over the lesser elements, the prototype of which class was the cattle. Our entire analysis of the *familia*, and of the antithesis which evidently existed between that and *pecunia*, supports this supposition.

Patrimonium was, in the end, synonymous with *familia*. It appears that, just as *patrimonium* gave rise to *dominium* which crystallized in itself the Roman notion of absolute and original property, so the Germanic term for patrimony was the source of the northern word *alodium*, which expressed there the corresponding idea. The hypothetical etymology which would confirm this correspondence derives *alodium* from the Germanic *alōd*, and attributes to *al-* the sense of *pro* or "fore" and to *-ōd* the sense of "paternal" (from *atta* = father). *Ōd* is related to *adal* (nobility, birth, etc.) and perhaps to **audh-* (lucky, rich).[51]

[51] The Germanic words for patrimony are interpreted by Schade, op. cit., as follows: "OHG. *uodal*, *uodil*, *ôdhil*; Old Sax. *uodhil*, *ôdhil*, *ôthil*, st. N. (angestammtes Gut, Erbgut, Heimat); AS. *ôdhel*, usually *êdhel*, also *aedhel*, *oedhel*, st. M., [the same]; Old Norse *ôdhal* (Pl. *ôdhul*, later *ôdhöl*), st. N. (Landeigentum einer Familie, und zwar ihr freier erblicher unveraüsslicher Besitz, Stammgut)" – related to *adal*. Vinogradoff, *Jurisprudence*, I, p. 278, thinks that the Old Welsh *wale* may be cognate with *uodil*.

Walde, *Idg.*, also associates these words with *adal*. OHG. *adal* (race), Germ. *Adel*; Old Sax. *athali*, AS. *æđelu*, n. pl. (noble descent); Old Norse *ađal* (race); Adj. OHG. *edili*, Old Sax. *ethili*, AS. *æđele* (noble); OHG. *uodal*, Old Sax. *ōthil*, AS. *ēđel*, Old Norse *ōđal* (patrimony, paternal heritage). Compare also OHG.

Fustel (*Institutions Politiques de l'Ancienne France*, Ch. V) holds that the word *alodium* was not German, for, in the Middle Ages, one read it only in the texts written in Latin, and in the later form, *alleu*, it appears only in the neo-Latin or Romance languages, French, Italian and Spanish. But the etymology is fairly certain and Fustel seems later to contradict himself. Elsewhere (*Alleu*, p. 149 ff.) he speaks of the frequency with which one meets in the records of the Merovingian epoch the word *alodis* or *alotis*, "which is later changed to *alodium* and which becomes still later the French *aleu* or *alleu*." He thinks *ex alode* means *ex successione* (by inheritance) for where the text says *hereditas* the rubric says *alodis*. Later, as *alodium*, it came to mean *propriété patrimoniale*, and finally all *propriété*. But he considers it neither classic Latin nor German for, in the sixth century, one finds it only in Gaul. Nevertheless, in spite of his denial of its origin, everything he says confirms our interpretation.

If we detach the material notions from the later ideas of "patrimony,"

fater-uodal, Old Sax. *fader-ōđil* (patrimony). All of these he relates, citing Schrader (Kluge agreeing), to IE. *atta* (infantile for father, mother). Kluge, *Etymologisches Wörterbuch der deutschen Sprache*, cites Gothic *atta* (same), from the Germanic root **ath-* or **oth-*; Schrader, op. cit., supposes an **ăto-s* (paternal); Walde supports by OHG. *Uota* (*Urgrossmutter*) and Old Fris. *ēdila* (*Urgrossvater*).

Another set of words which seem closely related are ascribed by Walde, *Idg.*, to the root **au̯* (plait, weave) with dh-extension **au-dh-*, *(*a*)*u-ĕdh*, **u-dh*, on the basis of the idea of the weaving or spinning goddesses (Fates) and what was allotted by them (see Fick, op. cit., III, 4, 6, and Falk-Torp, *Norwegisch-dänisches etymologisches Wörterbuch*, under *Klenodie*). These are Old Sax. *ōdan*, AS. *ēaden*, Old Norse *auđinn* (granted by fortune), *auđna* (fate, luck); *auđr* (riches), AS. *ēad* (property, riches, luck), Old Sax. *ōd* (possession, prosperity, wealth, welfare), OHG. *al-ōd* (full and free property), M.Lat. *allodium*, Goth. *audahafts* (lucky), *audags* (blessed), *ōtac* (lucky, rich).

Unless the second syllable of the first group is considered more than a suffix – and that is contradicted by the derivation of the first syllable from the root *atta* – the separation of some of the second group away from the first seems far-fetched. At least AS. *ēad* and Old Sax. *ōd* appear to belong with the words based on the idea of patrimony. As for OHG. *al-ōd* this seems practically certain. Walde defines it as "full and free property." Fustel found the earliest appearance of the Latinized word in the phrase *ex alode*, always meaning "by inheritance" – i. e. "patrimony." And obviously it is by this avenue that it attained the connotation of "full and free." There is nothing of the idea of "luck" in this.

Finally we have to explain the first syllable of *alōd*. Either *al-* must be taken as "the whole" (the *universitas rerum*), or adverbially as *all* – the old etymology (Grimm's version) – or one must conclude that *alōd* is *uodal* inverted; in other words that the suffix (vowel + *l*) was, in the language of the Franks, used as a prefix. The words *ēad* and *ōd* lend some support to this possibility. In the case of the word *all-mende* or *allmeinde*, which was the term for *communitas* or *fundus communis*, it has been suggested that it referred to the *Alamannen*. Grimm, *Rechtsalterthümer*, II, p. 11. Or we might conceive this to have been the pronominal stem **al-*, whence IE. **alios* = other, according to Brugmann, 2^D^ Germ. ed., II, 1, p. 154 and II, 2, p. 340, from an adverb **ali* (*jenseits*) like the Ir. *al* (*jenseits, über – hinaus*). We find it used in Old Ir. both as a suffix and as a prefix. The vowel seems to be indiscriminately *a*, *e*, or *o*. It is also possible that it had the general sense of "fore" in "forefathers" and of the *pro* in **pro-patrios* (see infra) – in other words of a paternal line extending *hinaus*.

and even of "riches," and think of them as attributes—like the associated "race" and "nobility"—which are passed down from the chief to his successor, we class *alōd* with Walde's suggested **pro-p(a)trios* (property).[52] Before the time of property in land and of extensive property of any kind, such attributes, standing, relations, and the office which pertained to them—the position—were the inheritance. With the appearance of property in land the inheritance of the rule (*rex*, *rig*) developed into the inheritance of a domain (*Reich*) and made a man mighty (*reich*) and rich (*reich*). He may have been considered fortunate because he was rich, but I doubt—at that stage and in spite of the gambling instinct which Tacitus records—that his riches were attributed to his luck, or to the Fates, or to anyone but his forefathers.[53]

It is also to be noted that *odal*, the system of succession in Norse law was, according to Vinogradoff (*Jurisprudence*, I, p. 277) the method by which the "organic unity of the estate is guaranteed." In the Lex Salica (Title LIX) which provides for inheritance regardless of sex, the land—or at least *terra salica*—is permitted to pass only to the male sex. Both seem to be survivals, in what has come to be *Erbrecht*, of a prior distinction which allied the rules for succession, in the governance of the group and its land, to that of Rome.

As contrasted with the patrimony we have the cattle and, later, all *catalla*, or chattels, which represented the personalty of the chief, not passing to his successor. As this *pecunia* was the source of derivative and dependent holdings—*peculia*—in Rome, so apparently was the *feoh* of the north property of a special type and the medium there as well for the development of the dependent notion—the fundamental plan of organization of *feudalism*. The etymological chain is, of course, familiar.[54]

It is not necessary here to dilate on this apparent resurgence in the medieval land system of a terminology seeming to arise from an age-old

[52] See Walde, Latin, under *proprius*. Ernout and Meillet give an old adjective, *patrius*, ("qui appartient au père") which was later supplanted by *paternus*. But they do not accept "l'explication par **pro-ptrios* (= **p(a)trios*) proposée par M. Wackernagel." Instead they hold that *proprietas* was built up from the phrase *prŏ prīvō* ("à titre particulier"). Although "*proprietās* n'apparait pas avant Cicéron," this older view would identify *proprietās* with the Ciceronian successors of *pecunia* and *peculium*, not with *patrimonium*. From the standpoint of institutional evolution that derivation is not acceptable because the notion of *proprietās* is identified with the *patrimonium* not with the *pecunia*.

[53] A hint as to the possible limitations on such patrimonies and their restriction to the nobility, which Schröder suggests, would furnish an even more definite association of *adel* and *ôdhil*, and of both with the Roman patrician *patrimonium*. He says, op. cit., p. 62, "It is not probable that the kings and *Gaufürsten* participated in the annual division of arable. It was permitted to these to have lands as *Edelgüter*, which were at first perhaps the endowment of office, but at all times appeared to assume the character of family property."

[54] In general Schrader, op. cit., p. 260, gives the equation as Germ. *Vieh*, OHG. *fihu*, Goth. *faíhu*, Lat. *pecus*, Skt. *paçú-*, Avestan *pasu*. Diez, *Etymologisches Wörterbuch der romanischen Sprachen*, ascribes French *fief* to old *fieu*, a borrowing from Lombard *fiu*, related to OHG. *fihu* or *fehu* (cattle), Goth. *faíhu* (property) and Old Fris. *fia* (with both meanings). Littré, op. cit., adds AS. *feoh*, whence *feudum*, *feud*, *fee*, etc.

and ubiquitous practice for the dispersion of the capital herd. Maine (*E. L. and C.*) described it in early Ireland as "giving stock." Laveleye uses the early French term *en cheptel* in referring to Ireland. But the Irish term was *turcreic*; or at least it was this which the vassal paid the lord. *Turcreic* seems to be a compound word from *tor-* (or *tur-*) and *crîch* (a division or parcel) which d'Arbois translates as "prix d'achat." He finds the same system at the root of Caesar's *ambacti* and *clientes* in Gaul. Certainly it was a pervasive institution in Gaul and, under the name *en cheptel*, in early France.[55] Whether or not the Germanic term carried the same notion of derivative and dependent property into the Middle Ages as these Celtic terms did, we have, so far as I know, no evidence. It merely seems probable, since the system of capital herds with temporary or permanent sub-herds seems to have been prevalent among all the western branches of the Indo-European stock.[56] D'Arbois (*Droit Celtique*, I, p. 118 ff.) thinks that it did. He considers that "le fief immobilier français date seulement des temps où la théorie antique de la vassalité expulsée de Gaule par la conquête romaine, y a été ramenée par les Germains. Ceux-ci, en Gaule, ont trouvé établi le système impérial romain de la propriété foncière qui alors a changé les conditions de la vassalité primitive et lui a donné une base immobilière originairement inconnue."

One other family of words, not related to these, lends credence to this hypothesis. We have seen that *pecunia* and *peculia* were essentially the same word. Thus the chief's (or chief) and the subordinate's (or subordinate) herds were both, at an early time, simply "flocks"; the dependent and derivative "flock" being designated merely as the "little flock," but with the out-growing sense that it was *peculiaris* to one—namely private property, special, *peculiar*, *singular*. But the Oscan and Marrucian terms for *pecunia* apparently introduce another idea which

[55] Godefroy, op. cit., gives the following variants of Old Fr. *chief: cief, kief, quief, chep, chept, chieup, chup, chier, cap,* (*tête, capitale*) all from *caput*. *En cheptel* (in its old form *chatel, catel,* etc.) either meant "of the capital herd," or it meant "from the chief." Apparently this was a general Celtic practice long before feudal times. It is generally held, I believe, that the words "cattle," "chattel," and "capital" (in the sense of stock) have all derived from this source and, probably, from this practice.

[56] The Lombard term *faderfiu* (patrimony of the bride; see Schade, op. cit.) suggests the possibility that by that time the distinction had been lost. And there is something to be said for the old idea that the M.Lat. *feodum* (whence *feud*) was a compound of *fe-* (at a rent) + *ōd* (property). Nevertheless the same explanation will not do for the French *fief* and the German *Lehn*. The latter, which was the basis of the Germanic feudal terminology could only have meant "loan" or "borrow" and thus necessarily ties itself in with the general notion of "derivative and dependent" property. *Pecunia* indicated a special type of property, but without the connotation of dependence. Apparently *ōd* was used as a general term for property, often without the special connotation of "paternal." Certainly the Germanic *faihu, fehu,* etc., also meant property in general. Nevertheless there seems to have persisted in most cases alongside of these general meanings, special or technical senses which correspond to the very definite OHG. *suntarscaz* ("*peculium*, besonders Vermögen über das man frei verfugen kann"; see Schade, op. cit.).

in turn relates them to many terms of Roman law and helps to interpret the whole institution.

Walde relates Osc. *eítiuvam* (*pecuniam*), *eituas* (*pecuniae*) and Marr. *eituam* (*pecuniam*) to Lat. *ūtor* (to use) and thus, in turn, to Greek words meaning "share."[57] This general connection of other Italic words for *pecunia* with the idea of "share" seems to place them in a class with Lat. *peculium.* Moreover, as we have suggested in the text, the Lat. *usus* (share) as a special kind of property, may also have developed *via* this same channel as a kind of *peculium.*[58]

E. *The Terms of Law*

1. "*Ius*"

Some of the older writers on Roman law to the contrary notwithstanding,[59] it has become the rule to derive the word *ius* from the IE. root **i̯eu-* (to bind).[60] This construction is very satisfying to those

[57] Buck, *Grammar,* p. 14, considers the etymology uncertain. *Ūtor* (whence *ūsus*) = Old Lat. *oitier,* Osc. *úíttiuf* (*usio*), Pel. *oisa* (*usa*). Fick relates *utor* to *οἶτος* which he translates as "*Los, Geschick,*" but which Bartholomae takes as "*Zugeteiltes, Anteil.*" Walde thinks that perhaps *utor* is closest to *αἶσα* (*Anteil*), Osc. *aeteis* (*partis*). "Of these connections the vowel relation with *οἶτος* (Germ. *Eid* = oath) is phonetically closest. But the relation with Osc. *aeteis* (*αἶσα*) comes nearer in meaning and, disregarding Osc. *eítiuva-*, the vocalism is consistent."

[58] In the Irish institution, *en cheptel,* Maine says, *E. L. and C.,* p. 159, that the chief received "the growth and increase and milk" – the *fructus,* in other words. This suggests a general, not local, origin for the Roman distinction between the perhaps earlier *usus* and *usus fructus.* Maine also says, ibid., p. 162, "After food, rent and service had been rendered for seven years, if the chief died, the tenant became entitled to the stock." Laveleye, op. cit., p. 236, has it that, "In theory, the tenant after seven years became owner of the cattle." Here, perhaps, we see the route by which *usus* (as *usucapio*) became a method of acquiring property by prescription, the period becoming reduced in historic times at Rome to two years. Maine, *E. L. and C.,* p. 339, suggested many years ago that the oldest servitudes were a relic of the "shifting severalties" (shares, *sortes*) in which he conceived all Roman land to have been held in the beginning. In other words he imputed "prescription" as the basis of title to all Roman land. See *Ancient Law,* p. 255. At least prescription by uses of shares bears the earmarks of a very ancient and general process.

[59] See Muirhead, *Roman Law,* p. 18, who says, "the original idea conveyed was a 'rule of action' derived from the notion of the 'divine will.'"

[60] Walde, *Idg.,* gives **i̯eu̯os* (approximately statute, *Fug,* perhaps, earlier, an obligation or liability) from **i̯eu-* (bind), Skt. *yōḥ* (*Heil*), Avestan *yaoždađaiti* (purifies ritually), Lat. *iūs* (statute, *Verordnung,* right), *iūro* (swear), Alb. *jē* (permission), Old Ir. *huisse* (just). He says, *Latin,* "this, rather than directly to IE. **ieu̯e-* (bind, *iungo*)," whence *iugum,* yoke, etc. Wood, *Post-consonantal w,* p. 19, takes the latter line direct, interprets *iūs* as "that which is binding or fitting," *iūrāre* as "to bind oneself, band together, swear, take oath, conspire," relates them to Skt. *yujyáte* (*wird zu teil, passt zu*), *yuktáḥ* (*angespannt, verbunden*), and rejects *yóḥ* as nearer in meaning to Lat. *iuvo.* It is evident that both have in mind the analogy of Germ. *Fug* (1) aptness, convenience, (2) right, authority, *fügen* (1) join, unite, (2) ordain, dispose of, and *sich fügen* (to conform oneself to), from (Kluge) the Germ. root **fag-* in Goth. *fagrs* (fitting, suitable).

who view the subject from the angle of sophisticated law. Ihering (*Geist*, I, p. 304) accepts this notion of *ius* and bases his interpretation of *iuro* upon it. He says, "Sie stammen von *ius* (Band, Recht), *iurare* würde also wörtlich übersetzt bedeuten: ein Band, einen Bund, ein Recht begründen, *juramentum*: ein Bindemittel, ein Mittel des Rechts." And, "dass sich verbinden, ein Recht begründen und schwören lange Zeit hindurch für gleichbedeutend gegolten haben muss."

As to this, in the first place, Walde, Muller and others seem to think that *iuro* was the original word, or that the original sense of *ius* had to do with the oath. In the second place, as suggested in the text, when we first begin to meet these terms in law, *ius* has the sense of "right," but never of "a right"; *iustus* and *iniustus*, have the sense of "true" and "false," or "right" and "wrong"; and there is nothing in the use of *iuro* to connote binding. Rather it is a swearing as to facts. The simple prototypes of the application of justice were the determination of where a person or an object 'belonged,' whether or not an injury had been done, and what was to be done about it. Unless we assume that the "peace" (*pax*) of the household and of the folk was conceived to be a pact (*pactum* =, according to Ihering, Skt. *pāça*-—the fetters) under which the members were explicitly *bound*, or had *bound* themselves, to do no wrong, it is difficult to see how the idea of a *band* or *bund* entered as the general original sanction of this justice. Also *ius* was at first a criterion, not a code. Finally it is hard to reconcile this interpretation with the delayed appearance of the promise as contract in the law. The first Roman contract seems to have been *nexum* and that was a far from figurative bondage. The other words conveying the idea of binding, such as *obligatio*, *contractus* (*contrahere*), *solutio* (*solvere*), and *liberatio*, are later terms, apply to contract only and seem to be derived from the concept of this original physical bondage, which only eventually became a *iuris vinculum*.

The early content of this word *ius* has such a fundamental bearing on the question of the beginnings of Roman law that it is worthy of a thorough analysis. Let us begin with an analysis of the family of words built upon the general stem, whether through the noun or verb we do not know.

Ius (right, law), *iustus* (just, right), *iniustus* (unjust, wrong), *iuste* (justly, rightly), *iniuste* (unjustly, wrongly), *iustitia* (justice), *iniustitia* (injustice).

Iudex (judge), *iudicatum* (adjudged, decided case), *iudicatus* (office of judge), *iudicialis* (judicial), *iudicium* (trial), *iudico* (to be a judge, to judge).

Iurisdictio (judicial authority = the speaking of the law or right), *iuridicialis* (relating to right or justice), *iurgo* (*iure-ago* = lead into court, quarrel), *iustitium* (*iuris-stitium* = suspension of court), *iurisperitus* (one learned in (of) law), *iuris consultus* (lawyer).

Iuro (swear, take an oath; call the gods to witness—with *deos*), *iurandum* (oath, a swearing), *iureiuro* (swear by an oath), *iusiurandum* (oath), *iuror* (be sworn), *iniuratus* (unsworn).

Deiuro, or *deiero* (swear solemnly); *eiro*, or *eiuro* (deny on oath, abjure), *iniurius* (wrongful, unjust), *iniuria* (injury, injustice, wrong), *peiero*, or *periero*, or *periuro* (forswear, perjure); *ius perieratum* (false oath); *peiurus*, or *periurus*, or *periuriosus* (perjured), *periurium* (perjury).

The words of the first group, based directly on *ius*, seem to be reducible to the general notions of justice and injustice. Those of the second, based on *iudex*, have to do with the court. Those of the third, based on oblique cases of *ius*, have to do with the law or the courts. Those of the fourth, based on *iuro* or *ius-iuro*, have to do with the taking of oaths, the calling of the gods to witness. Finally the fifth group, also based on *iuro*, presents certain anomalies. *Deiuro* has in it none of the sense of the preposition *de*. It refers to an especially solemn swearing. And, on the analogy of *periurium*, *iniuria* should mean an "unswearing," or a false swearing, instead of an injury or wrong. We should also note that the more general forms are *iuro* and *ius*, which are obviously related directly, but that the alternative forms of the verb, *-iero* or *-iro*, in *diero*, *eiro*, *peiero* or *periero*, are forms reduced through loss of accent. The compounds *iureiuro* and *iusiurandum* are themselves peculiar. Why the duplication? Did these terms originally mean "right-swearing" or "to swear by right—or in court?" Or did *ius* also have the sense of "oath," so that the usual translation "to swear by an oath," or "an oath-swearing," contains the literal idea. Finally, in *iuro deos* (in the Duenos Inscription) why *deos* in the accusative? Does that indicate that the process of swearing was originally literally "calling the gods to witness?"

The evidence as to the old forms of these words is very incomplete. But that which we have is most interesting. The reconstruction by Muller is as follows: Of *ius* we have *ious* in *lex Acilia*, whence the original form is established as **i̯ŏu̯os*, which Muller and Juret take from **i̯eu̯-os*. For *iustus* the older form is **iou̯estos* and, in the Forum Inscription, *IOVESTOD* (= *iūstō*, abl.sing.). *Iuste* was *ioviste*, composed according to Paul (93L), "*a Iove et iuste.*" This proposal is unimportant etymologically but important psychologically for it shows the survival of a feeling of connection with the name of the god Jupiter. Etymologically, whence the *ioves*—in these two latter forms—and why the necessity of adding the *iuste?* Could not **iovestos* and *ioviste* be based simply on the same stem as **i̯ŏu̯os?* For *iūro* Muller gives the primitive form **i̯ŏu̯ezāi̯ō—*i̯(o)u̯ezāi̯ō* though the earliest known appearance is *iouesat* (*iūrat*) (Duenos Inscription).[61] Thus we have the earliest

[61] The contractions are traced for *ēiĕro* and *pēiero*. For the former, with the notion of *ex*, he gives the peculiar interpretation "mache mich vom Bande, vom so bindenden Eide, los." On the contrary it would seem that the term always meant "to swear oneself out of, or away from, something." He distinguishes *pēiĕro*, (= *periĕro* = *periūro*) and *periūrus* in that the latter is a new formation on the analogy of *peiiūrus*: "Hypostase aus *per ius* (*iūrandum*) genau wie *perfĭdus* aus *per fĭdem*." The verbs he traces as from è, or *pèr*, + **i̯(ò)u̯ezâi̯ō* > **péri̯(u̯)ezō* > *periĕro*, and *pér* + **i̯ĕu(e)s-ŏ* > *pe(r)i̯ūro*.

known stems of the adjective and adverb as **ioues-* or **iouis-*, of the noun as *ious*, and of the verb as **ioueso*. For these may be supposed an earlier **i(o)u(e)s-*, whence *ioueso* (< **i̯ŏu̯ezāi̯ō* > **iou(e)ro* > *iūro*) and **ious-s*(> *iūs* gen. **ius-e/os* > *iūr-is*, etc.).

This whole system seems very closely related to another. Muller gives the early form of *Iūpĭter*, (*Iuppĭter*, gen. *Iŏvis*) as **Di̯oú-păter*. *Di-* was the original initial; *cf. Diovem, Diovos*, etc. *Jupĭter* is from the vocative < IE. *Di̯éu-pəter*. The name itself also was *Diēs-piter*. So Osc. *Diúvei*, or *Iuveí* or *Διουϝει*; Umb. *Iuve* (*Iovi*). All, like **di̯éu̯-s*, **di̯e(u̯)i*, **dĭu̯(e)s* (by day), from **di̯ē(u̯)s* (day) = Lat. *diēs*. "*Diūs* und *diem* sind identisch mit Gr. *Ζεύς* (aus **diē(u̯)s*) und *Ζήν* (aus **di̯ē(u̯)m*)." Perhaps here, too, belongs the series of Old Lat. *deiuos* (the shining one, god).[62] It is evident that in a good many of these words the initial *d* was dropped. It is also evident that the vocative **Diou* (**Dieu*) or **Iou-* (**Ieu-*) is exactly like the stem of our first group, while *Diēs*, or **Dieus-*, or **Dious-* might give **ie-s(>r)-* or **i-eu(<ou)-s(>r)-*.

It might seem a far cry from the term for the "day-god," or for "day," to the oath, if it were not for the Osc. *deiuatud* (*iurato*) which Muller and others connect with **deiuos* ("the shining one"), a seemingly compelling etymology.[63] Here, it seems, is a proven case where the term for oath, or for swearing, is connected with the very name of the god to whom the oath is addressed (vocative or, in the third person, accusative) or by whom the statements of fact are presumed to be attested (ablative).[64]

In a very interesting and recent study of the family of words derived from IE. **dei̯eu̯-* (disyllabic ablaut base) G. S. Hopkins (Language Dissertation, No. 12, *Linguistic Society of America*, 1932) has summarized the present authoritative etymology of this family. On the basis of her presentation it is possible to reinforce the suggestion that *ius* comes from this source. From the IE. base **dei̯eu̯-* (sky) arose the noun **diēús* (sky); the adjective **dei̯u̯os* (of the sky) which became the IE. noun for "god"; the adjective **di̯u̯iós* (of the sky), formed to replace the prior adjective after it became a noun; and the form *-*di̯u̯o-* appearing in compounds. "At a comparatively late period, after **di̯u̯ios* had become an established word, it became customary to use **diēus* (and the form *-*di̯u̯o-*) to represent also the periods of time marked by the phases of the sky, that is, days." From the adjective **dei̯u̯os* (the earli-

62 Nom. sg. **dẹi̯u̯os* > **dẹi(u̯)os* > *dẹ(i̯)os* > *dẹus*; gen sg. **dẹi̯u̯ī* > *dīvī*; nom. pl. **dẹi̯u̯oi* > **dẹi̯u̯ẹi* >**dīu̯ī* > *dī*; Osc. *Deívaí* (*Divae*). Walde, *Latin*, takes this from IE. **deieuo-* (*leuchtend*, as "heaven" or "day") from **deia-* (*leuchten, scheinen*).

63 Other occurrences are (Buck, *Grammar*) pres. subj. third sing. Osc. *deiuaid* (*iuret*) fut. third sing. Osc. *deiuast* (*iurabit*) perf. past part. nom. pl. *deiuatuns* (*iurati*).

64 It is possible, as well, that in the Latin word *deiuro*, we have not *de-iuro* but rather one of the original forms of the address or oath itself, **deiu-s*(> *r*)*-o* = *deiur-o*.

est to have the sense of "god") arose Lat. *deus* and *divus*[65] and Osc. *deívaí* (*divae*). From the noun **diēus* came a number of Latin words.[66] We have then, in Latin, the noun *deus*, the proper noun *Diūs* (the earliest name for *Iupiter*, and also *Vedius* or *Veiovis*, *Diūs Fidius*, *Me-Diūs Fidius*, *Dium Fulgur*, *Iupiter*, *Iove*) and the noun *diēs* (*Diēspiter*), all of which signify "god," at least at some stage, though the latter two evidently retain the meaning "sky" or even "day" as well through various stages.

Now we can assume a verbal suffix **-s-o*, (*cf. gero* beside *ago*; αὔζω beside *augeo*) which, when attached to the root, gives the literal sense "to god."[67] For this we find three possible attachments. The first and oldest — which antiquity might account for the especial solemnity of the term — would arise from the stem **deiu̯-* shown in the form **deiu̯-os* (**deiu̯-s*(>*r*)*-o* > *deiuro*) and would be an almost exact parallel of Osc. *deíu-aí* (*divae*) > *deiu-atuđ* (*iurato*). The next in order and more regular and surviving would arise from the stem **diēu-* shown in the form **diḗus* (> (**d*)*iou-s* > *r*)*-o* > *iouro*. Finally would appear another, perhaps as a dialect form, arising from the stem **diē-* shown in the form *Diēs* (>*(*d*)*ie-s* (> *r*)*-o* > *iero*).[68] From the second, as **ious-o*, would be constructed a noun, meaning "godding," thus **ious-s* > *ius*, (*iūs-e/os* > *iur-is*, etc.). However, parallel phonetic developments cast some doubt upon this possibility.

Therefore so simple a building may be an hypothesis which needs refinement. It does not seem to account for the *e* which appears in the early form of the verb **ioues-o*, and also in the adjective **ioues-tos* and the adverb **iou*(*e*)*is-te*, though not in the noun **ious-s* as we have it. There is, however, a perfect parallel, which seems to solve this difficulty. It is as follows:

[65] *Deiu̯os* > **deios* > **dẹ̄os* > *deus*; *deiu̯ĭ* (gen.) > *dīvī*.

[66] The paradigms are reconstructed as follows:

	IE.	Lat.
Nom.	**diēús*	*Diūs*
Acc.	**diē* (*u̯*)*m*	**diēm* > *diem* (and from this, in Italo-Celtic, the paradigm based on *diēs* (day)
Gen.	**diu̯és, -ós*	
Dat.	**diu̯aí* (*-eí*)	
Loc.	**diéu̯i*	*Iove* (and other oblique cases of *Iupiter*)
	**diēu*	
Voc.	**dieu*	*Iū* (*piter*)

[67] Dr. Stefan Einarsson, Associate in English at the Johns Hopkins University, has called my attention to a very pertinent analogy in modern Icelandic. There is a custom in Iceland that, when one comes to a farmstead after darkness has fallen, one does not knock on the door as usual but goes to the window and bespeaks the people within with the following greeting: "*Hér sé guđ*" ("Here be God"). This act is called "*ađ guđa á gluggann*," literally "to *god* at the window." See also Cleasby-Vigfússon, *Icelandic English Dict.*, and Blöndal, *Islandsk-Dansk Ordbog*, s. v. *guđa*.

It is worthy of note that Falk-Torp, op. cit., s.v., derive this word *gud* from an IE. **ghutó-* which gives it the sense of "the invoked one." This suggests for this word a reversal of the process which we are suggesting for the word *ius*.

[68] The stem in the last was assumed to be *diĕ-* not **diē-*, viz. the oblique cases of *diēs*.

**Op-*
Op-s
**Op-es/os-s* > *Opus*
Oblique cases
**Op-es/os-is* > *op-er-is*, etc.
**Op-es-o* > *op-er-o*

**Dieu-* (> *Diou*)
**Diou-s* (> *Diu-s*)
*(*D*)*iou-es/os-s* > **iou-es/os-s*
Oblique cases
**iou-es/os-is* > *iu-r-is*, etc.
*(*D*)*iou-es-o* > **iou-er-o* > *iu-r-o* or >*i-er-o*
*(*D*)*iou-es-tos* > *iu-s-tus*
*(*D*)*iou-es-te* >*iou-is-te* = *iu-s-te*

The *-es-* is the noun suffix which appeared in usually neuter substantives, generally with an abstract sense denoting an activity or state (*nomen actionis*), as root + *es/os* (See Brugmann, *Grundriss*, Eng. trans. II, pp. 411 ff.). Since it seems to have been an *es/os* suffix (*cf. nemor-*, *tempor- corpor-*)[69] we may note in passing that it includes Muller's **iou-os*.[70] By this means we account for all the forms, but we do so by finding the abstract noun, from the word for "god," as the origin. Was this noun the word for "godding" (i. e. a *nomen actionis* like *opus*; Ernout and Meillet), thus reversing the etymological order of our "divine" (verb) – "divination" (noun of action)? Or did it rather have the sense of an adjective (and, therefore, arrive through the sense of "acts, or ceremonials, having to do with the god," and finally exclusively of this one act) thus following exactly that semantic order (i. e. "divine" (adj.) and "divine" (verb)?[71]

At least such a connection is demonstrated to be sufficiently plausible from an etymological viewpoint to warrant us in setting up the following partly hypothetical sequence as to the development of the word *ius*. From the word "sky" or "heavens" came those for "god" and for "day." From (probably) the original "heavens" came also *Iuppiter*, the name of the "master of the heavens" (presumed to be allied to the sun-god). Perhaps *ius* (early *ious* and (?) originally **iouos*) was formed from the name of this "god," who was called upon or addressed in the oath (in the vocative, **Iou*, like our "Oh Jove," or "By Jove"), either through the verb "to god," or directly as the act (*nomen actionis* "godding"), or the ceremony (adjectival) of calling upon Jupiter. Thus

[69] Brugmann, *Grundriss*, Eng. trans., II, p. 418, says, "The vowel gradation which belonged to the *-es-* suffix in the pre-Italic period (preserved e.g. in *gen-us*, *gen-er-is*) was superseded in many words in favor of the form *-os-* which prevailed over the other forms." Viz. *tempus* (*temp-or-is* beside *temp-er-ī*, *temp-es-tus*, *temp-er-āre*).

[70] He also gives *op-os* for *opus*. Brugmann gives Lat. *op-os* (*ops*), *op-us op-er-is*, *op-er-a*, Umb. *ose* (*opere*) and Skt. *áp-as*, *ápas*, as examples and notes that the Lat. *mod-es-tu-s* and *mod-er-ārī* like the Umb. *meř-s* (from *med*(*o*)*s*, the *o* being lost by syncope) are from Prim. Ital. **med-os*. Since Umb. *meřs* = *ius* and Osc. *meddíss* = *iudex*, this bears on our point. *Operō* and the other verbs, like *iūrō*, are of the first conjugation. There are, in the other Italic languages, a series of denominative verbs homologous to Lat. *operō*, *-āre*, such as Osc. *úpsannam* (*operandum*), *upsed* (*fecit*), Umb. *osatu* (*operato*), Pel. *upsaseter* (*operaretur*), all of which have retained the original *s* and the same meaning.

[71] For the developments of meaning of the verbal abstract nouns, see Brugmann, *Grundriss*, Eng. trans., II, pp. 466-7.

it became the word for swearing and for the oath itself. That would account for *iuro* and for the later pleonasm *iuro deos.* Then perhaps, by a process of abstraction related to the purpose of the oath, it became the criterion which the oath was used to establish; the criterion of truth or falsity. It would be necessary to assume that the idea of the oath became that of "a true asseveration." Thus *iuro* = "make a true asseveration;" *iniuria* = "an untrue asseveration;" *periuro* = "asseverate falsely" (literally excessively—beyond the truth); *iustus* and *iniustus* = true and false. As such I read its appearance in the earliest Roman legal formula, the *sacramentum* (*legis actio,* also "oath"). One participant accuses the other of vindicating by an *iniuria;* that is, not an injustice but "an oath contrary to the facts." And the court declares the *sacramentum* (oath) of one *iustum* and that of the other *iniustum*—that is "true" and "false." Thence the criterion was transferred to the crude antithesis of "right" and "wrong." With reference to statements we say that they are "right" or "wrong" when we mean "true" or "false." Thus, perhaps, the general adjectival ideas of right and wrong, or just and unjust, sprang from the source of the factual correctness or incorrectness of a statement when assumed to be deliberate. *Ius,* starting as "an oath"—that is, an asseveration with the connotation of truth—came to stand for the abstract notion of truth or right. As such it became the criterion of law and came thence to stand for the law itself and the place in which this criterion, in its combined sense, was applied—the court. Thence *iudex* as the "determiner and indicator of the truth, or right." It is in these two senses only, the law, in the sense of a double criterion, and the court, that the word appears in the text of the XII Tables. The later legal content (justice, law, in the sense of code) and the development therefrom of the notion of *soke,* or authority, (jurisdiction) is obviously entirely secondary. It is also possible, though not in my judgment probable, that the notion of right, justice, and even of authority might have been carried along—parallel and independent—as attributes of the divinity from which the word derived.

P.S. As this goes to press my attention has been called to the fact that the Forum Inscription actually reads *DIOVESTOD.* Whereas the authorities I have followed have construed the first *D* to be the last letter of a preceding word, of which nothing else remains, it may well be the initial of *IOVESTOD.* Considering the fact that, at the date of this inscription, such an initial *would have* been retained, this reading is weighty support for the etymology I have suggested; and, in turn, this etymology renders such a reading more plausible.

2. *"Lex"*

Walde (*Latin*) rejects the connection of Lat. *lēx* with Old Ice. *lǫg,* AS. *lagu,* Eng. *law* (*Gesetz*), Old Ice. *lōga* (to let lie), AS. *lōgian* (*disponere*), Old Fris. *lōgia* (*sich verheiraten*) and also with the IE. root **legh-* (as in *lectus*) through which the sense would be the same as Gr. *θέμις* (from *τίθημι*) which is interpreted as *οἱ κείμενοι* [passive of *τίθημι*] *νόμοι*, as the "set-up, or laid down, or established rules." He says that a connection is phonetically permissible with IE. **lĕĝ*-, the source of *legere*, which would permit interpretations as "*Zusammenfassung, Ordnung, Festlegung, Bindung*."

In his *Idg. Dict.* he makes this the probable connection, giving it a special interpretation, "**leĝ*- (zusammenlesen, sammeln), Gr. *λέγω* (sammle, lese zs., zähle, rede, sage, vgl. z. Bed. Engl. *to tell* = erzählen, zählen), Lat. *lĕgo* (zslesen, auflesen; auslesen, wählen; lesen), *legio* (ausgehobene Mannschaft, Legion) = Osk. *leginum* (legionem), *legulus* aufleser), Päl. *lexe* (*legistis*)." To this he attaches, as probably also connected, Lat. *lēx* (*Gesetz*), *lēgāre, lēgātus*, Osc. *ligud* (*lege*), *lígatúis* (*legatis*) as "Sammlung der Vorschriften."

This seems a perfectly plausible reading, giving somewhat the sense of "code" (written). But it seems to me to accord better with the various derivatives and the earlier use of the term to give it the sense of "collective declaration, or vote," or even that of "choice." Thus the notion of the assembly (viz. *legio* and *collegium*), or of its means of expression (the *collectio* of its votes) may have given rise to the term for that which was so expressed; that which was done by collective authority. Thus *legatus* (legate) and *lēgo* (appoint as ambassador). Or the fact that the declaration was determined by a "yes or no" vote may have indicated that it was a "choice." This interpretation argues that the use of *lēgo* to cover as well the making of a private *lex*, or legacy, indicates that at first such acts required the approval of the assembly, differing from other kinds of *lex* only in being concerned with individual rather than collective business, and, perhaps, in being proposed to the assembly by the individual concerned instead of by the official representing the *res publica*. In fact, if one conceives the earliest *legatum* to have been the appointment of an external guardian, as against the adverse rights of the gentiles or agnates, and if one also conceives the earliest *lex* to have been most usually a "resolution" or "verdict" as to specific business or a particular question, then the assimilation of the two becomes very close. I suspect that the nearer we come to the view that in the earliest times an action at law, a contract, the making of a will, a conveyance, an adoption, and legislation were in form indistinguishable, the nearer will we grasp the reality. Perhaps a *thing* (that is an assembly of the folk) transacted all "things" (*res*) by one mode; the proposal (motion) by one authorized; the affirmation or rejection (vote) by the assembly; resulting in a verdict (resolution) which not only permitted or denied, but guaranteed the transaction, though it did nothing in the direction of executing it. And this general proceeding was, perhaps, among the Indo-Europeans the second manifestation of organized large-scale collective action, the first having been the organization of the business of fighting.

3. "*Antiquo*" and "*Veto*"

Helpful light on the original sense of *lex* may be gained from consideration of these two other words which were earlier or later associated with it. The early historic Roman process, which developed into what we call law-making, was operated as follows: The consul, and presumably before him the *rex* or *pontifex*, proposed to the *comitia* a resolution dealing perhaps with any *res publica*. The form of submission or *rogatio* was "*Velitis, iubeatis, Quirites? Rogo vos, Quirites?*" The decision, or choice, was then made by vote. The affirmative was "*Uti rogas*;" the negative, "*Antiquo* [or *antiqua*] *probo*." (See Bonfante, op. cit., I, p. 100). This formula indicates that a resolution was only offered when consent to an exception to the rule was desired. Bonfante (loc. cit.) holds that the proper sense of *iubeo* was "consent," though it came to signify the power of the *comitia*. Thus the term *lex* ("choice") seems at first to have designated only a consent to make an exception—to do something differently. The formula also implies that proposed actions in accordance with custom (the rule) required no submission, and that rejection of the resolution left things as they were *ab antiquo*. In either case custom prevailed. But I think other terms suggest that this "custom" consisted of another (or two other) and prior set of rules, somewhat analogous to the new *ius*. The most probable etymology (Muller) of *mōs* relates it to *modus*, *medeor*, *moderor*, *modestus*, etc., and also to Umb. *meřs* (*ius*) and Osc. *meddíss* (*iudex*). In Rome *mōs* seems to have had only a lay (or intra-familial) sanction. The most probable etymology of *fās* connects it with *fārī*, *fātum*, etc., and thus gives it, as "the spoken," a sense similar to Gr. *θέμις*. Its sanction was, in Rome, religious, but that may have meant no more than that it represented the traditions handed down from the "Dī Mānēs," just as the *sacra* were their service. This construction would bring it within the domain of the *pontifices*. A double prior system of rules, one Sabine (*mōs*) and one Latin (*fās*) would be quite consonant with present suppositions as to the origins of Rome. (See Bonfante, op. cit. and Cornil, op. cit.)

Probō is a very early word exactly cognate to Osc. *prúfatted* (*probavit*). Its original sense seems to have been "I hold good, or admirable," and it is allied with the term of respect for honest men. *Probus* (*pro-bho-s) means "that grows straight." *Probō* took the accusative. Therefore the formula for rejection must be construed as, "(*rem ?*) *antiquo* (*modo*) *probo*," in order to account for the ablative (of manner). The origin of the word *antīquus* is uncertain. It is sometimes given as *antīcus* (from *ante*—earlier *anti*—plus suffix) on the analogy of *postīcus*. But Ernout and Meillet note that *postīcus* applied to space, not to time—the temporal word was *posterus*—whereas *antīquus* applied only to time. This is an objection to this systematic etymology. Nevertheless *anti* itself was a locative (see Muller). Ernout and Meillet speak of *antīquus* as an isolated formation. Muller says it was probably formed with the IE. suffix *-*qo*- and gives the older form as *antiquos*. But it is interesting to speculate. *Antiquus* may have been built from *anti* with the IE. formative **-quo-* giving the adjectival sense of the "-wise" or "manner" (*cf. reciprocus*, Brugmann, *Grundriss*, 2d Germ. ed. II, 1, p. 480-481). But since *anti* originally took the ablative (Ernout and Meillet) it is possible that this old legal phrase was "*anti quo* (i. e. the relative). As "(*rem* or *modum*) *anti quo probo*" it would require less construction, being equivalent to "I approve (the matter or mode which was) before that (or now)." But on either of these constructions *antiquus* (adjective or noun) would mean "before-now-ish" or "before-now-ness."

From this early legal process of the *rogatio* there appeared in later times a verb *antiquo*, meaning "reject" or, literally, "leave in its former state." This development suggests the possibility that, by a prior and analogous process, the verb *veto*, used in connection with a similar rejection by anyone having the *collegium* (co-choice or colleagueship), arose from the same source as, or an early form of, *vetus*.[72] The etymology of *vetus* is established; that usually given for *veto* is conjectural and unconvincing. Ernout and Meillet say, "Neither the one nor the other connection explains either the form, which is of the type of *domāre* (disyllabic root), nor the sense." *Domō – domāre – domuī – domitum* (*vetō – vetāre – vetuī – vetitum*) like *domus*, is from the disyllabic root **demə – domə – dmā*. It suggests a *vetə – votə – vtā*, which would cover the difficulty that *veto* was originally *voto*.

The antithesis of *vetus* and *novus* is exact – a typical Roman dichotomy. Thus *novus* meant both "new" and "young" and *vetus* meant "old" in both senses. Ernout and Meillet are impressed with the derogatory connotation of *vetus*, which they take to indicate that its principal or earliest sense was opposite to "new" rather than to "young." But it seems to me that in prehistoric times "old" may have been complimentary in both senses. The special sense of the verb *novo* is given by Ernout and Meillet as "innovate" or "change," though it also had the sense of "renew." If *novo* was originally "innovate" then *veto* was perhaps its antithesis – i. e., "leave things as they are." That being the exact sense of the verb *antiquo*, which through the law-making process came to mean "reject," it seems plausible to ascribe a place in a similar but prior legal process (perhaps magisterial) to *veto*, and to found thereon its sense of "forbid" or "prohibit" which is indicated by the fact that the veto power was also called the *ius prohibendi*.

4. "*Res*," "*Chose*," "*Sache*," and "*Thing*"

a. "*Chose*"

The genealogy of the word *chose* is, to say the least, extraordinary. Its Latin progenitor *causa* is derived by Walde (*Latin*) and by Muller from the IE. **qāu- *qəu-* (*hauen, schlagen*) whence *cūdō* (*schlagen*,

[72] *Cf.* Gr. ἔτος. In Brugmann's (*Grundriss*, Eng. trans., II, p. 418) construction *veto* may have come from the root direct, independently of the suffix *-es-* which gave rise to the genitive *vet-es*(>*er*)*-is*, etc.

klopfen, stampfen, prägen), from **caudō*. Thence, too, *caudex* (codex) as "Baumstamm, Klotz, zu Schreibtafeln gespaltenes Holz, Notizbuch," and *incūs* (*Amboss*).[73] In his *Idg. Dict.*, Walde abandons this relation and refers *causa* to IE. "**qeud-* (schreien; anschreien, schelten, höhnen, spotten)."[74]

These derivations are both possible. But when one takes into consideration the specialized legal use of *causa* it seems well to suggest the possibility of an alternative semantic development along the lines which *codex* followed; in other words that a **kaud-ta* was originally some sort of documentary evidence, or means of presentation, of a claim or title, perhaps also a "*Runentäfelchen*" of a sort. At any rate it came technically to mean "ground," at law. Thence, *via* the sense of pleading, it came by the time of Cicero to mean the entire "case at law." At this stage, if we have in the text correctly interpreted the sense of *res*, *causa* had already begun to displace it. And it was about this time too that its form was changing from *caussa* to *causa*.[75]

In the early Medieval Latin the process of substitution shows itself completely accomplished. As de Sainte-Palaye puts it (*Dictionnaire historique de l'ancien langage françois*, s. v. *chose*, Note 5) "*Causa* a le sens de chose (*res*) dans le bas-latin de la Loi Salique, etc." And he points out that even Pliny the Elder used "*quam ob causam*" for "*quam ob rem*." Diez, op. cit., shows that the same semantic development has taken place in the modern Greek *πρᾶγμα*, as also in *Sache*.[76]

[73] Muller gives the Prim. Ital. **kaussā* (*Schlag*), Lat. *caussa, causa* (*Tat-sache, Gerichtssache, Sache, Ursache*) which, he says, appears originally to have had the meaning of criminal delict ((*Tot*)*schlag*), and which as < **kaud-tā* he connects with Prim. Ital. **kaudō* and **kaudeks*. For his assignment to it of the sense of delict he cites the ideas expressed by *causa recēns* and by "*manu asserere alqm, liberali causa* (urspr. mit der *festuca*, bzw. *alapa!*)" in manumission, and the analogy of *culpā* cognate with Gr. *κόλαφος* – thus deriving the sense of "guilt" or "crime" from that of "blow" – and also the OHG. *sahha* as *Streit*(*sache*) coming as *Sache* to mean "thing." Muller's explanation of the semantic development of the sense of *causa* by way of a play on the various senses of *Sache* and its compounds is suggestive. So too, for our purpose, is his interpretation of *kaudā* as "*abgeschnittenes Ende*," whence *cauda* (tail) and of **kaud-ek-s* as "abgeschnittenes (*Holz*)," whence *codex* as "*Baumstamm, Holztäfelchen, Buch*." He explains that *caudex* is originally the "*surculus amputatus* (Tac. Germ. 10), das Runentäfelchen."

[74] Gr. *κυδάζω* (*schmähe, beschimpfe*), *κύδος*, Norw. *huta* (*schreien, lärmen*), AS. *hūsc* (*Schmähung, Spott, Hohn*). He says, "Lat. *causa*, das Holthausen anreiht (vgl. *crīmen* (eig. Geschrei), as. *inca* (Klage, Groll, Ursache), widerspricht dem Vok. von mhd. *hiuzen* und kann auch andere Grundbedeutung haben."

[75] See Grandgent, *Vulgar Latin*, p. 69. Ernout and Meillet, on the contrary, hold that the etymology is unknown; that the sense of "cause or motive" is the most ancient; and that, "C'est sans doute en pénétrant dans la langue du droit que *causa* s'est spécialisé dans le sens de 'procès.'"

[76] DuCange, op. cit., gives "cosa, pro Causa, Res." And for the original word and its derivatives he gives the following senses:

Causa

1. *Morbus*
2. *Res*
3. *Poena propter solennia non servata*
4. *Causae, causa, judicia, placita, malla*

In the formation of the Romance languages, Körting says (*Lateinisch-romanisches Wörterbuch*), "durch *causa* ist *res* nahezu verdrängt worden." But, curiously enough, it leads to two sets of words. Diez (op. cit.) says that It. and Span. *cosa* and Fr. *chose* continued that sense of *causa* as *Sache, Ding*, which had already appeared in the Low Latin.[77] But for the original sense (i. e. classic) there was continued the original form, It. and Span. *causa*, Fr. *cause*.[78]

In the meantime *res* had come in Vulgar Latin to be used of persons, and alone, or as *res nata*, to mean *anyone* or *anything* (Grandgent, op. cit., p. 8 and 38). And this meaning is also carried over into *chose*. When, then, Godefroy interprets the Old Fr. *chose* or *cose*, he gives only the sense *personne; créature*. De Sainte-Palaye, though he admits that this meaning is most frequent, says that the words also stand for "bien de toutes espèces, comme terre ou autre héritage." Already, in the *Grand Coutoumier*, *droit à la chose* and *droit en la chose* were said to correspond to *ius ad rem* and *ius in re* respectively. *Chose* is becoming a "mot indéterminé qui tient la place de plusieurs autres" and already "servoit aussi à exprimer ce qui n'a point de nom, ou suppléoit à l'expression propre de ce qu'on ne peut définer, faute de mémoire, ou de connaissance, ou par pudeur." In the end this impersonal use, as a "mot indéterminé," supersedes all others and only in law does *chose* maintain a certain connotation of property, the legal 'thing,' and very rarely, in phrases only, the late Roman sense of *causa*, like the English "cause" or case at law.

In modern French, *chose* is practically equivalent to the late classic Roman *res*, while *cause* has preserved most of the late Roman content of

Causalis = *litigiosus*
Causales or *causalicii* = *qui litigant de re aliqua*
Causare, or *causas agere*, or *in causam ducere*
1 = *litigare*
2 = *calumniare, repetere*
3 = *fabricare, facere*
Causatio = *lis, controversia, placitum*

And he shows that *res* had become (1) a kind of measure (*sextarium*), (2) an herb, (3) power, wealth. Of the last he says, "Hinc, ni fallor, vox Gallica *Resechable* (cui satis ampla res est)." But there are remaining phrases in which the old sense appears. "Res dotalis = donatio, quae a parente filiae fit propter nuptias aut intuitu matrimonii; res religiosae = sepulcra; res terrae = segetes; res soli = res immobilis."

[77] ". . . das bereits in der L. Sal., bei Gregor v. Tours u. a. diese Bedeutung zeigt, recht handgreiflich im *Capitulare de villis*."

[78] Only the Prov. *causa* "vertritt auch den neueren sinn." De Sainte-Palaye supposes this was because "en provençal *au* ne se transforme pas en *o*, comme en français." But Diez gives a Prov. *cosa*. The connection is more confused in the verbs. Diez says that It. *cusare* (*behaupten*) Prov. *chausar*, and Old Fr. *choser* (*zanken*) are from *causare*; that Fr. *causer* (*plaudern*) and Germ. *kosen* (OHG. *chôsôn*) may come either from *causare* or *choser*. And, in phrases, *chose* was sometimes used where *cause* is used now. For instance, *ob eam rem*, or *quam ob rem* = *quam ob causam* = *chose que* (Old Fr.) = *à cause que* (Fr.) (Godefroy).

causa, covering most of the ground of the English legal "cause." The early French verb, *choser* (*coser, cozer, chosser, choseir*), successor of *causare,* which meant "to reprimand" or "to make accusations," has practically disappeared and only *causer* remains to signify the mildest and least litigious conversation.

Thus the word, *causa-chose,* beginning with the significance either of a blow as the cause of action or of a record as the grounds of title or claim, came successively to mean in law the pleading, then the entire case or action, then the property concerned and eventually at law the notion of material things as the object of property. In the course of this progress it has given off dozens of other special senses into the common speech.

b. "*Sache*"

From a somewhat different source *Sache,* and its cognates, came to have, in the Germanic languages, the same sense as the early medieval *causa,* though here the "cause," or case, was more informal. Walde (*Idg.*) assigns it to the IE. **sāg* (*witternd nachspuren*). The most direct development of meaning is that of "following the scent."[79] This general notion of "hunting," which lies behind the later legal sense, is well shown by the Old Norse *rannsaka* ("*Hausuntersuchung nach gestohlenem Gut*"), a pre-legal process which also left surviving traces in early Roman law. Goth. *sōkjan* (= Lat. *sāgio*) meant *suchen, disputieren,* and *sōkns* meant *Untersuchung, Streitfrage.* Thus the AS. *sōcn* developed into "soke" or "jurisdiction," and AS. *sacu* developed into "sake" or *Rechtshandel.* The OHG. *sahhan* (which like the Old Fr. *choser* meant *tadeln, schelten*) is associated with OHG. *sahha* which (as *Gerichtshandel, Sache*) covers both the ground of Fr. *cause* and *chose.* Thus the contentious or litigious connotation of these and allied words (viz. Goth. *gasakan* = *drohen; sōk* = *zanken*) may well have arisen at the stage when the "seeking" or "search" comes before a tribunal. Eventually, as Kluge puts it, the general sense of "thing" appears as a "jüngere Entwicklung aus *Rechtssache, Streit,* die noch in nhd. *Sachwalter* (*Rechtsverteidiger*) (s. noch *Widersacher*) erhalten blieb. Die alte Rechtssprache ergab aus der juristischen Bedeutung die allgemeine."

c. "*Thing*"

Walde (*Idg.*) assigns *thing* to the IE. **tenq-* ("ziehen, dehnen, spannen: Zeitspanne?"). Thence, *via* Goth. *þeihs* (*Zeit*), he finds the Old Ice. and AS. *þing,* Old Sax. *thing,* OHG. *ding* and Germ. *Ding,* etc., as "zu bestimmten Zeiten stattfindende Gerichtsversammlung." Not only did these words come generally to have the sense of *Volksversammlung,* but they gave rise to others covering all sorts of "öffentliche Ver-

[79] Thus Lat. *sāgio* (*acute sentire*), Gr. ἡγέομαι (*gehe voran, fuhre*), Old Ir. *sāigim* (*suche*), Old Norse *skia* (*suchen, angreifen*), AS. *sēcan* (same), OHG. *suohhan* (*suchen*).

handlung vor der Volksgemeinde," such as AS. *þingan* (*einen Vertrag machen*), *þingian* (*beilegen, schlichten*), *þingung* (*Vermittlung*), MHG. *dingen* (*Gericht halten, Vertrag machen*), whence Germ. *Bedingung* and *dingen.* From this early secondary sense of a transaction *in iure* this whole group of words came to have the derived meaning of *Eigentum* and thence finally of *Gegenstand.*

d. "*Res*"

These three words, *Sache*, *chose*, and *Ding* or *thing*, have thus followed the same course from the point at which they came to mean "a matter, or case, at law." As the first step they came to mean a "right of action," then a "piece of property" as a "right of action," and finally the object of this property, or right, itself. All this is, of course, the reverse of what one would expect if property were in fact "an instinct in the human breast," and indicates on the contrary that it was a gradual realization through the slow development of a legal institution.

The general terms for property or wealth in two other languages have come from a wholly different source, apparently not connected with legal processes. The Osc. *egmo* is tentatively assigned by Walde (*Latin*) to the same stem as Lat. *egeō.* This suggests the same development of sense as in the case of Gr. *χϱῆμα.*[80] Thus a "want" (lacked) becomes a "want" (desired) ; a "need" (lack), as something required, becomes a "necessity" or "requisite." Only, in English, we do not have the German bridge from "lack," or "need," to "use," by which this Greek chain is interpreted.

In spite of these two exceptions it seems possible to make a plausible case for attributing to *res* a development of meaning parallel to the general rule appearing in *chose*, *Sache* and *thing.*[81] Muller gives the Primitive Italic word as **rē(i)s*, morphologically **rĕ-i̯o-s.*[82] Walde (*Idg.*) takes the same form **rē-i-os* (as an old genitive) to be the source of *rēus*, "a participant" and later "the defendant in a law suit." [83] Thus we should say that he assumed **rē(i)s* or *rē-io-s* to have meant the *matter* of a legal dispute, or the case itself, like the later *causa.* If so it is worth while to see what other words of similar form suggest this same origin.

Muller gives the Prim. Ital. form of *rĕor* (*rērī*, *rătus sum*) as **rĕi̯ōr*, morphologically the verb form of the foregoing **rē-i̯o-s.*[84] This he

[80] Which, with *χρῆσθαι* (*gebrauchen, benutzen*), *χρέως* (*Bedürfnis, Verlangen, Schuld*), *χρή* (*es ist nötig*), *χερείων* (*geringer*), is assigned to IE. *ĝher-* (*kurz, klein, gering*, also "*knapp werden, fehlen, nötigsein*").

[81] See W. Corssen, *Über Aussprache, Vokalismus und Betonung der lateinischen Sprache*, I, 477-8, for the whole relationship. He also connects *res* with *reor.*

[82] Umb. *ri*, dat.-abl. sg.

[83] " **Rēi̯os ; *rēi̯os est* bedeutete 'er ist am Prozess beteiligt.' " Ernout and Meillet, curiously enough, find that "le sens de *rēs* est éloigné" from *reus.*

[84] The objection of a possible difference in quantity may force the connection into the pre-Italic stage. Stolz, *Historische Grammatik der lateinischen Sprache*, holds the Lat. *-ē-* in *rēri* is IE. **-ē-*, while the Lat. *-ē-* in *rēs* is IE. **-ēi-* (through

translates as usual as "*(be)rechne: meine.*" He places *ratiō* there, and gives as perhaps the oldest meaning "*schichten, aufeinander legen: aufzählen,*" which seems to be connected in sense to the related Lat. *rēte* and *rătis.* Walde (*Idg.*) interprets *reor* as "count, think, opine" and explains that the most primitive counting was accompanied by laying or piling the counted pieces in series, thus connecting it with **ar-* (join, fit). Thus *ratus* means "of the opinion," but also "counted, settled, valid, legally valid," and *ratio* means "computation, consideration, reason, motive, ground." Schrader suggests (op. cit., p. 244) that *ratio* "did not mean to the peasants of the Appennine peninsula what later philosophers and still later jurists put into it." And this suggestion is supported by the association which Walde makes with cognate Goth. *urrēdan* (judge, settle), OHG. *rātan* (counsel, consult) and *rāt* (corresponding noun).

Upon the IE. root **ar-* there are based certain direct derivatives; others upon a t-formation, such as Skt. *ṛtá-*, Lat. *artus*, etc.; and still others upon an m-formation, such as Gr. *ἀρμός*, Lat. *arma*, etc. In addition there are two other root forms, the seṭ-Base **(a)rē-* and the i-Base **(a)rēi-*. The latter is either developed from a *-i̯o-* present, **(a)rē-i̯ō*, or is original, so that **(a)rē-* is a preconsonantal development therefrom. It will be noted that Muller's *rēs*, as **rē-i̯o-s*, exactly conforms to the first alternative above and makes his **rē-i̯ō-r* the corresponding verb.[85]

Of the words included by both Walde and Wood (see Note 85 above) under the root forms **rē- rēi-*, we find *reor* with a possible sense

reduction). But Corssen, Wood and others combine these two, and at some stage they are linked by nearly all authorities, since the root forms, *rē* and *rēi̯*, are intimately related.

[85] Wood, in a monograph entitled *Indo-European* a^x *:* a^xi *:* a^xu, p. 43, has presented the suggestion of four groups based on this root **rēi—rē*, which he interprets to mean "spread out, arrange, put in order, etc."

226. a. (rē̆) Lat. *rērī* (reckon, calculate: believe, think), *ratus* (fixed, settled, firm), *ratio* (account; list; number; manner, method; reason; rule, order), OHG. *redea* (*rechenschaft*), *rede* (*erzählung*), MLG. *rām* (*ziel, absicht; bestimmung, beschluss*), OE. *rōmian* (*besitzen*), Skt. *rā̂ti*, *rā̂satē* (*gibt, verleiht, gewährt*), *rātá-s* (*dargebracht*), *rātí-ṣ* (*bereitwillig, günstig; gunst, gabe*), *rās* (*gut, reichtum*), Lat. *rēs*, Ir. *rath* (*gerade*), Skt. *rátna-m* (*habe, besitz, gut*), *rā̂dha-s* (*gunst, gabe*), OHG. *rāt* (*vorrat*).

b. (*rēi*) Lat. *reor*, OHG. *rīm* (*reihe, reihenfolge, zahl*), OE. *rīm* (number), OHG. *rīmen* (*zählem*), Skt. *rayí-s* (*habe, besitz*), *rēvánt-* (*reich, reichlich, prächtig*), OE. *rīf* (abundant, frequent, rife).

227. a. (*rē̆*) Goth. *ur-rēdan* (*bestimmen, urteilen*), Goth, *rōdjan* (*reden, sprechen*), OE. *rǣdan* (discuss, deliberate; decide, decree; provide for; guess, interpret; read), OHG. *rātan* (*raten, beraten; auf etwas sinnen; mutmassen, erraten; bereiten, verschaffen*), Skt. *rā̂dhyati* (*kommt zu recht, bring zustande, gewinnt*), Skt. *rā̂dhas* (*gunst, freigebigkeit, gabe*).

b. (*rēi*) Goth. *raidjan* (*anordnen, festsetzen*), OHG. *antreita* (*ordnung*), MHG. *gereite* (*fertig*), *bereite* (*bereit*), OE. *gerǣde* (ready; armor), *gerād* (reckoning; wisdom, prudence), *gerādian* (arrange), *rǣdan* (rule, government).

228. a. (*rē̆*) Skt. *racáyati* (*ordnet*), Goth. *rahnjan* (*rechnen*), OE. *racu* (*rede, rechenschaft, sache*).

b. (*rēi*) MHG. *rīhe* (*reihe, linie*), *reige* (*reigen, art tanz*).

of judging and almost identical in form with *res*. We also find Goth. *urrēdan*, OHG. *rātan* and *rāt*, OE. *rǣdan*, Goth. *raidjan*, with a definite relation to the judicial process.[86] But it is more especially in the group which Walde bases on **reĝ-* that we find an abundance of relation with the process of government which was, as we have noted, at one period primarily a judicial or arbitral process.

Finally it is obvious from our examination of the histories of *chose*, *Sache* and *thing* that these actual semantic progressions have been neither

229. a. (*rē̆*) Skt. *ṛñjáti* (*streckt sich*), *ṛjú-s* (*gerade, recht, richtig*), *rājā* (*könig*), Lat. *rego* (keep straight, guide, direct; rule, govern), *rectus* (straight, right), Gr. ὀρέγω (reach, stretch), Goth. *rahtōn* (*darreichen*), *raihts* (*recht*), OHG. *recchen* (*ausstrecken*).

b. (*rēi*) OHG. *reihhen* (*darreichen*), OE. *rǣcan* (stretch forth, give), *gerǣcan* (reach, take, seize), Gr. ὀριγνάομαι (stretch, grasp at).

The outline is included here almost complete. Much of this Walde (*Idg.*) does not accept. *Reor, reri, ratus* and *ratio*, and some of the dh-extensions, given by Wood under 227 a, are included by Walde under **(a)rē-*, and he transfers Wood's suggestion of *rēs* (interpreting the sense as "piled up goods and chattels," which reminds us of his explanation of *reor* as well as of the Lat. *rogus*, Goth. *rikan*, etc., which he places under **reĝ-*) to **(a)rēi-* where it is included with Gr. ἀριθμός (number), Lat. *rītus* (traditional religious practice, custom, fashion, usage, manner), *rīte* (in fitting manner, in accordance with the proper religious custom). There too he places as dh-extensions, most of Wood's 227 b.

It will be noted that Wood has included under 229 many of the words that Walde and others base on an IE. **reĝ-* (*gerade, gerade richten, lenken, recken*, etc.) as follows: Skt. *ṛjyati* (*streckt sich*), *ṛjú* (*gerade*), Gr. ὀρεκτός, Lat. *rēctus*, Goth. *raíhts* (*in gerader Richtung*); Skt. *rāj-*, Lat. *rēx*, Old Ir. *rī*, Goth. *reiks* (ruler); Gr. ὀρέγω (stretch), Lat. *rego* (*geraderichten, herrschen*), *ērigo* (*richte auf*), *pergo, porrigo, surgo*, (*corgō, ergō, ergā*), *regio* (*Richtung, Gegend*), *regula* (*Richtholz*), *rogo* (*wornach langen, ersuchen, bitten, fragen*); Old Ir. *rigid* (*streckt aus*), Welsh *rhaith* (*Gesetz*), Bret. *reiz* (*Ordnung, Recht*), Old Ir. *rī-*(gen. *rig-*) (*König*), Welsh *rhi* (*Fürst*), Gaulish *-rīx* (*König*); Goth. *raíhts*, Old. Ice. *rēttr*, AS. *riht*, Old Sax. and OHG. *reht* (*recht, gerade*), *rahtôn* (*darreichen*), OHG. *recchen* (*ausstrecken, sagen*), AS. *reccam* (same); AS. *racu* (*Spur*), Eng. *rake* (*Bahn, Weg*), AS. *racu* (*Erzählung, Rechnung*), Old Sax. *rekōn* (*richten, ordnen*), Old Ice. *folk-rekr* (*Fürst*), *land-reki* (*König*). He adds, "durch Entlehnung aus dem Kelt. vor der Mediaverschiebung," Goth. *reiks* (*Herrscher*) (< Celt. **rīg-s*), Old Ice. *rīkr* (*mächtig*), Germ. *reich*. Whence also AS. *ríce*, M. Eng. *riche*, Eng. *rich*, MHG. *ríche*, Fr. *riche*.

There are certain striking facts noticeable as to these two series, Wood's 226-7-8-9, on the one hand, and Walde's **reĝ-* series, on the other. Judging by meanings only it would be quite impossible to separate the two. It is notable how many times Wood uses, as definitions of the words in the first group, words that appear as members of Walde's group, and also that the definition which gives the key to **reĝ-* is *gerade*, itself a member of the first group.

[86] Corssen, op. cit., I, 477, systematizes the relationship as follows:

	ă	ā	ē
Skt.	*ṛ-tá-s* (*wahr*)		
OHG.	*ra-d-ja* (*Rede*)	*rā-t* (*Berathschlagung*) *rā-t-an* (*sinnen*)	
Goth.	*ră-þ-jō* (*Zahl*)		*ga-rē-d-an* (*bedenken*) *ur-rē-d-an* (*bestimmen*)
Lat.	*ra-tu-s* (*berechnet*) *ra-ti-o* (*Berechnung*)		*rē-s* (*Gerichtssache*) *rē-us* (*in einen Rechtshandel verwickelt*)

precise nor logical; that what we should look for in the case of *res* is a vague connection built upon an association, in the life of the time, of the facts named rather than upon an identity of idea. On this basis we have to suggest that, at the beginning of Roman legal processes, *res* (as **rē-i-s* or **rē-io-s*) had come to mean something between "cause of action" and "cause" (as the action itself); that *reus* (as **rē-i-os* or **rē-io-os*) referred to the participants in the action; and that *reor* (as **rē-io-r*) (which, be it noted, is a deponent verb) had, at perhaps a prior stage, expressed or been associated in some way with the process by which the predecessor of the action had been determined. Independent of this hypothesis a secondary one may also be suggested, namely that the root **rē-*, which is the basis of this group, had some connection with early leadership, or the function of early leadership, and thus gave rise to the family of words based on **reĝ-*. It is difficult to dissociate from the judicial process the idea of direction behind the history of *rex;* an idea which corresponds so closely to the history of the allied *Richter.* It is even difficult to dissociate the word *rex* itself (or *rece-s;* dat. sg. in Forum Inscription is *rece-i*) from this early proceeding. If *thing,* the tribunal, became *thing,* the matter before the tribunal; if *Sache* the matter before the tribunal gave rise to OHG. *widersacho* (or *-er*), AS. *andsaca,* Old Franconian *gesakjo,* etc., as the counterclaimant, then it is reasonable to associate some word formed from **rē-* as the tribunal, with *res,* as the matter before the tribunal, and with *reus,* as the term for the counterclaimant. It is true that we have no verb from *causa, chose, Sache, thing,* or *Ding* which describes the act of the tribunal. Rather they all gave rise to verbs describing the acts of the claimants. But we must remember that *reor* is a deponent verb; that is, it probably expresses some notion that was originally passive, like Goth. *gadōmjan* in connection with *deem* and *doom.*

The purpose of the foregoing is to suggest an etymological hypothesis for the word *res* which makes necessary a different interpretation of this word in early and even in classic Roman law. Such slender evidence as is now available is assembled here. But the case is far from proved. Perhaps further investigation, conducted in the light of this point of view, may go to confirm it. And perhaps it may replace it. But, at least of one thing I feel certain; it will never confirm the theory that the original fundamental notion of *res* was that of "wealth."

F. *The Feudal Terms*

Godefroy gives the various spellings of the Old Fr. word *domaine* as follows: *demaine, demeine, demeyne, demoine, demoinne, demaigne, demeigne, demainne, demeinne, demenie, domaine, domane, damoene, demeisne, demesne.*

As a noun he translates it as "power." As an adjective he translates it as "seignorial, domanial," the equivalent of the M.Lat. *dominicus,* which was also an adjective. Another term for this power, which was also used to cover the seignory, was *demainement.* And the seigneur of any fief or other "*bien propre*" was sometimes called a *demainier* (=*dominus*). The adjective is said to be the original form. "*En demaine*" then meant originally "as lord." DuCange supposes that Old Fr. *domaine* (n.) was Lat. *dominium* or, as it sometimes appeared in M.Lat., *demanium*, the synonym of *dominicum*. He says it also meant concretely the *principale manerium* ("*chef lieu du fief*"). *Dominicum* he translates as, "quod ad Dominum spectat, quo Dominus ad propriam alendam familiam fruitur."

It seems likely, both from the varied spellings and the varied meanings, that this supposed single word was, as a matter of fact, a confusion of two different words with different origins and meanings which became partially blended and were in general translated by the medieval clerks into the M.Lat. *dominicum* (n. and adj.).

Evidently, Lat. *dominium* became converted in Old Fr. into *domane*, *domaine*, *demaine*, *demeine*, and possibly *damoene*. As the original adjective it meant simply *in dominio* or "as lord" (proprietor). As a noun this covered the proprietorship of the early provincial estates and came to refer to the land itself.

But there is another family of words which cannot be overlooked in this connection. It is composed of the descendants of the verb *maneo*, traced through some ten centuries or more. It will be noted from the diagram on the following page that in the case of all the Old Fr. derivatives from M.Lat. *mansura*, **mansuaticum*, *mansionile*, *mansionaticum*, and even *mansio-n-*, the *n* preceding the *s* was usually dropped. Thus in Old Fr. we have *ma(n)sure*, *ma(n)suage*, *ma(n)s(io)nil*, *ma(n)s(io)nage*, *ma(n)s(i)on(-)*. As a result of this vernacular change there were also direct or indirect M.Lat, corruptions of the same order; *messuagium* from *masuage* or *ma(n)suaticum; masnilium*, *masnile* and *mesnillum* from *mesnil* or from *mansionile; masnaticum* from *mansionaticum; masnagium*, *mesnagium* and *managium* from *mesnage* or *masnaticum*. In other words all the derivatives of *manere* which came from the participle tended to take the Old Fr. form *masn-* or *mesn-* (or *masu-*) and to be paralleled in M.Lat. on that stem.

Now it is obvious that, at the stage when this corruption was taking place, the *s* was not silent; for otherwise the *n* would not have been dropped. The new stem must have been pronounced *măs·n-* or *mĕs·n-*. There are old place names in France which still preserve this pronunciation. Later the *s* as well became silent before an *n* and, as it did so, caused a change in vowel quantity so that, when it disappeared, it was replaced by a long vowel as in *mainier* or in *ménage*. But even when it continued to appear in the written word, the *s* was a silent survival and itself the cause of, rather than merely a means of indicating, the long vowel.

In this family tree we find the most important of the fundamental terms for the manorial system—or rather for the social organization of the sixth to twelfth centuries. On the one hand the standard M.Lat. term, during most of the period, for a house or landholding was *mansus* (Fr. *manse*); and on the other hand, for the latter half of the period at least,

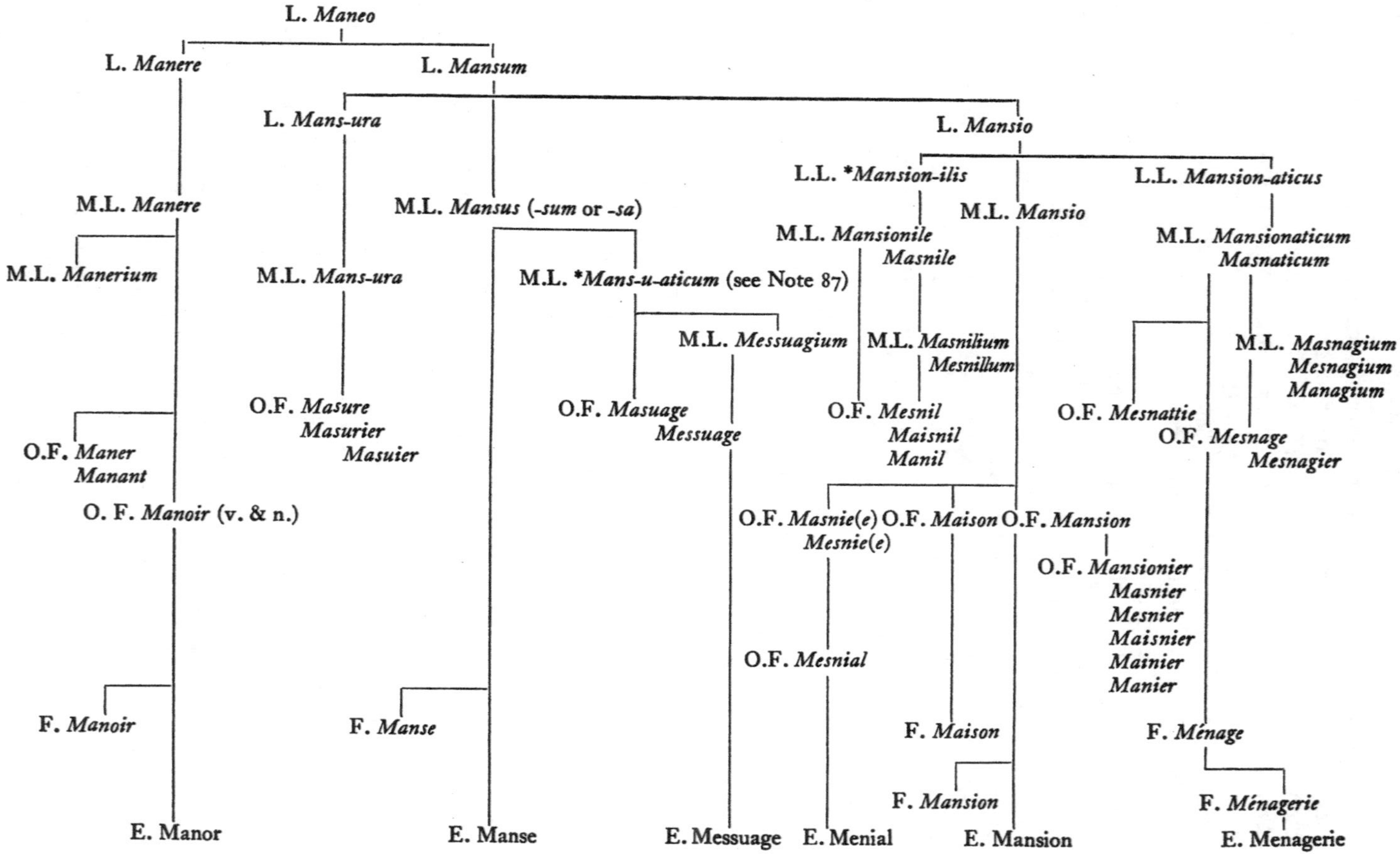
L. Maneo
L. Manere
L. Mansum
L. Mans-ura
L. Mansio
L.L. *Mansion-ilis
L.L. Mansion-aticus
M.L. Manere
M.L. Mansus (-sum or -sa)
M.L. Mansio
M.L. Mansionile Masnile
M.L. Mansionaticum Masnaticum
M.L. Manerium
M.L. Mans-ura
M.L. *Mans-u-aticum (see Note 87)
M.L. Messuagium
M.L. Masnilium Mesnillum
M.L. Masnagium Mesnagium Managium
O.F. Masure Masurier Masuier
O.F. Masuage Messuage
O.F. Mesnil Maisnil Manil
O.F. Mesnattie
O.F. Mesnage Mesnagier
O.F. Maner Manant
O. F. Manoir (v. & n.)
O.F. Masnie(e) Mesnie(e)
O.F. Maison
O.F. Mansion
O.F. Mansionier Masnier Mesnier Maisnier Mainier Manier
O.F. Mesnial
F. Manoir
F. Manse
F. Maison
F. Ménage
F. Mansion
F. Ménagerie
E. Manor
E. Manse
E. Messuage
E. Menial
E. Mansion
E. Menagerie

the standard Old Fr. term for the most important house community of the time—the household of the seigneur—was *masnie(e)* or, more commonly, *mesnie(e)*.[88] During the formative period of the feudal system this was the stem of the chief words for house, house-holding and household.

Since the term *demesne* is constantly used in two puzzlingly inconsistent senses it seems to me quite probable that the sense of the word when it means "home farm" might well have come from *terre de mesne*, literally "land of the house." And this *de-mesne* might well have become blended with the other *demaine*. Nevertheless, because of the separate origins, the word continued to mean, at one time, merely the home farm which pertained immediately to the manor house as in the phrases *en terre damoene, en demainne, en demesne*, etc. as if it were derived from *de-mesne;* and at other times to refer to the entire extent of tributary land, the whole domain or manor, as if it were derived from *domaine* (*dominium*).[89] Such a thesis also goes to explain the variety of spellings of *domaine*. It accounts for the most disparate, leaving a number which might have arisen from either of these sources.

The thesis offered here also affords an explanation for the English term *mesne* as applied to a lord. This word was always rendered into the M.Lat. *medius*. However, perhaps, this was not a literal translation but wholly a substitution by way of designating the place in the structural scheme into which the clerics were struggling to convert the highly unsystematic social organization of the time.[90] Nevertheless the result has been that, curiously enough, *mesne* has been assumed to be derived from *medius*. Now L.Lat, *medianus*, from *medius*, gave rise to It. *mezzano* (a mean man, i.e. one between great and little). But in

87 A M.Lat. stem **mansu-* is definitely indicated. This may be accounted for as a late analogical formation (*cf.* Lat. *censu-alis*—late and juris. as adj., also noun). As support we have M.Lat. *mansuagium* (Du Cange) which, according to accepted etymological views, must have arisen from an Old Fr. **mansuage* and that in turn from a M.Lat. **mansu-aticum*. As additional evidence of the existence of such a stem there are also M.Lat. *mansu-arius* and M.Lat. *mansu-alis* (noun and adjective). The alternative explanation, that a whole set of vernacular terms in *masu-* or *messu-* are due to a misreading of the *n* in *mesn-* (see *New Oxford Dict.*) seems to me preposterous.

It should be noted that, while Du Cange records M.Lat. *mansionaticum, mansionile* and *mansuarius*, Meyer-Lübke and Körting give these as hypothetical.

88 Flach, *Origines de l'ancienne France*, II, p. 462 ff., chooses it to describe that unit, the "family, real or fictive," which he claims in the eleventh and twelfth centuries "took the place of the state."

89 It is surprising that *demesne*, often spelled *demaine*, has not more often been interpreted to mean "held from the hand of." In Coke *On Littleton*, I. I. 10, Coke seems to ascribe to Littleton the thought that *demesne* meant "of the hand." Civilians ancient and modern should never have let such an opportunity escape. However, such a theory seems untenable.

90 The word *medius* was used to describe the *tenens medius*, or the *medietate teneri feuda*, or the *medietaria* (DuCange). As contrasted with the *dominus capitalis* (*chef seigneur*), the *dominus intermedius* (*seigneur entremoiens*) was one "*super minore domino feudali*" and "*sub alio majore*."

French *medianus* did not become *mesne*. It became Old Fr. *moien* or *moyen*, *meien*, *meen*, *mean*. It is much more satisfactory to derive *mesne* from *manere*. On this theory "mesne lord" would be an early designation equivalent to "lord of the manor" (literally the "manor lord"). Thus the intermediate (*medius*) feature would not be primary, but would have resulted from the fact that the beginnings of the feudal system upon the Continent centered around the tenants in chief of the *dominus*, or *seigneur*, or consisted of a superstructure erected upon the manorial system. So the "mesne lords" were perhaps originally the "lords of the manor" (or household) with reference to their sub-tenants, or were interposed as such;[91] and, in the process of sub-infeudation, the term continued to stick to the feudal position of any who had ever held the *mesne land* "in demesne" and thus, as well, to those who yielded themselves to a suzerain or who were interposed above that level.

In turn this would explain the phrase *in capite*. "*In capite esse*" or "*tenere in capite*" came to describe one who was subjected to no middle lord "*ratione feudi*." So Maitland conceives it in thirteenth century England. He says it "is merely equivalent to 'immediately,' *sine medio*" (Pollock & Maitland, op. cit., I, p. 212, Note). But when tenures were described as "held of," the preposition was Lat. or Fr. *de*, or Eng. "of." Such a concept would have been expressed as *de capite* (or *capitis*, or *capitale* or *-is*). However tenures were usually described rather on the basis of the right or prerogative *by* which, or the condition *in* which, they were held. Thus it seems more likely that the term *en chef* or *in capite* at first signified the fact that these men of the lord were being recognized or interposed *as* themselves chiefs or lords (*domini*), and thus distinguished from tenants holding by servile tenures, rather than the fact that they held *of* some other *chef seigneur* or *dominus capitalis*.[92] For, in the early stages, as the feudal structure was being built from the ground up and there were still at the most but three rungs to the ladder, the position of the lord of the manor would have been that of a chief to his servile tenants, so that he would have held his land *in capite*, though, as well, he might have been a "mean man" to his superior, if he had one. Upon this construction it would seem that one of the terms for such an early manorial holding continued to stick to this latter relation and, with the later elaboration of the superstructure by sub-infeudation, came to designate the place in the hierarchical system that was next to the top.[93]

[91] The surviving use of the adjective *mesne* in connection with land, otherwise so puzzling, is thus explained. "Mesne land" becomes "*terre de mesne*."

[92] Which also suggests a possible alternative interpretation for the term *en cheptel* to which we have previously referred. Did this term stress, not the dependent and derivative feature of the property but rather the aspect in which it was held, as by a "sub-chief"?

[93] It seems to me that the Old Fr. terms *chiefmasage*, *chiefmeisnaȝe*, *chiefmes -mais -mois -moys*, or *chef-*, *cheesmois*, *chiermois*, *quiefmez*, *chymois*, *chemois* – all of which are translated by Godefroy as "*principal manoir*," go to support this suggestion. Certainly they were not used of a feudal position but rather of a physical place; either of any *mansus indominicatus* or of some special class of such.

APPENDIX II

CASE CITATIONS FOR CHAPTER V

(1) Dissent in Scranton *v.* Wheeler, 179 U. S. 141, 170 (1900), and many others.
(2) Samet *v.* F. & M. Nat'l. Bk. of Baltimore, 247 Fed. 669, 671 (C. C. A. 4th, 1917).
(3) Burch *v.* McDaniel, 2 Wash. T. 58, 60 (1881).
(4) In re Tiburcio Parrott, 1 Fed. 481, 506 (C. C. D. Cal. 1880).
(5) In re Burnstine, 131 Fed. 828, 831 (E. D. Mich. 1903).
(6) In re Louisville Nat. Banking Co., 158 Fed. 403, 404 (C. C. A. 6th, 1908).
(7) Lowber *v.* Le Roy, 2 Sandford, 202, 217 (1848).
(8) Mutual Life Ins. Co. of N. Y. *v.* Farmers' & Mechs. Nat'l. Bk. of Cadiz, O., 173 Fed. 390, 397 (C. C. S. D. Ohio, 1909).
(9) Harvey Coal and Coke Co. *v.* Dillon, 59 W. Va. 605, 609 (1905).
(10) Gillespie *v.* People, 188 Ill. 176, 182, 183 (1900) (adapted from 2 Story, Const. sec. 1950).
(11) Dugger *v.* Insurance Co., 95 Tenn. 245, 252 (1895).
(12) Kuhn *v.* Common Council, 70 Mich. 534, 537 (1888).
(13) Mathews *v.* People, 202 Ill. 389, 401 (1903).
(14) Allgeyer *v.* State of Louisiana, 165 U. S. 578, 589 (1896), and many others.
(15) State *v.* Wilson, 101 Kan. 789, 796 (1917).
(16) Purvis *v.* Local 500, U. B. of C. & J., 214 Pa. 348, 358 (1906).
(17) Ketterer *v.* Armour & Co., 247 Fed. 921, 923 (C. C. A. 2nd, 1917).
(18) Pinkerton *v.* Verberg, 78 Mich. 573, 584 (1889).
(19) Stanton *v.* Lewis, 26 Conn. 444, 449 (1857), and many citations.
(20) State *v.* Frusha, 150 La. 995, 997 (1922).
(21) Gulf, C. & S. F. Ry. Co. *v.* Fuller, 63 Tex. 467, 469 (1885).
(22) Wynehamer *v.* People, 13 N. Y. 378, 433 (1856).
(23) Waters *v.* Wolf, 162 Pa. 153, 169 (1894).
(24) Low *v.* Rees Ptg. Co., 41 Neb. 127, 146 (1894).
(25) Griffith *v.* Charlotte, C. & A. R. R. Co., 23 S. C. 25, 38 (1884).
(26) Ingell *v.* Nooney, 19 Mass. 362, 367 (1824).
(27) Exch. Bk. of Columbus *v.* Hines, 3 Ohio St. 1, 25 (1853).
(28) Harvey Coal and Coke Co. *v.* Dillon, 59 W. Va. 605, 609 (1905).
(29) Dissent in Scranton *v.* Wheeler, 179 U. S. 141, 170 (1900), and many citations.
(30) Pell *v.* Ball, Speer's Eq. Rep. 48, 83 (1843).

(31) Eaton *v.* Boston, C. & M. R. Co., 51 N. H. 504, 511 (1872).
(32) Tatum Bros. R. E. & I. Co. *v.* Watson, 92 Fla. 278, 289 (1926).
(33) Bailey *v.* People, 190 Ill. 28, 33 (1901).
(34) Hamilton *v.* Rathbone, 175 U. S. 414, 421 (1899).
(35) Griffith *v.* Charlotte, C. & A. R. R. Co., 23 S. C. 25, 38 (1884).
(36) Gulf C. & S. F. Ry. Co. *v.* Fuller, 63 Tex. 467, 469 (1885).
(37) Rigney *v.* City of Chi., 102 Ill. 64, 77 (1882).
(38) Bailey *v.* People, 190 Ill. 28, 33 (1901).
(39) Groenendyke *v.* Fowler, 204 Iowa 598, 600 (1927).
(40) Spann *v.* City of Dallas, 111 Tex. 350, 355 (1921).
(41) Wynehamer *v.* People, 13 N. Y. 378, 396 (Quoting 1 Blackstone, Comm. 138).
(42) Dixon *v.* People, 168 Ill. 179, 190 (1897), (citing Lewis, Em. Dom. sec. 54).
(43) Coal & Delivery Co. *v.* Howard, 265 Fed. 566, 570 (C. C. A. 3rd, 1920).
(44) Jackson *v.* Sewell, 284 S. W. 197, 198 (Mo. App. 1926).
(45) Feitelberg *v.* Matuson, 124 Misc. 595, 598 (N. Y. City Cts. 1925).
(46) Elwell *v.* Stewart, 110 Kan. 218, 219 (1922).
(47) Holst *v.* Sav. El. Co., 131 Fed. 931, 943 (C. C. S. D. Ga. 1904).
(48) Village of Port Clinton *v.* Fall, 99 Ohio St. 153, 161 (1919).
(49) Missouri, K. & T. Ry. Co. of Texas *v.* Calkins, 79 S. W. 852, 853 (Tex. Civ. App. 1904).
(50) Crawford Co. *v.* Hathaway, 67 Neb. 325, 340 (1903).
(51) Leong Mow *v.* Bd. of Com'rs., 185 Fed. 223 (C. C. E. D. La. 1911).
(52) State *v.* Mallory, 73 Ark. 236, 248 (1904).
(53) Bertholf *v.* O'Reilly, 74 N. Y. 509, 575 (1878).
(54) Metropolitan City Ry. Co. *v.* Chi. W. D. Ry. Co., 87 Ill. 317, 324 (1877).
(55) Price *v.* State, 58 S. W. 83, 85 (Tex. Cr. Rep. 1900).
(56) Davis *v.* State, 20 Ga. App. 68, 70 (1917).
(57) Melvin *v.* Scowley, 213 Ala. 414, 418 (1925).
(58) Rawson *v.* Brown, 104 Ohio St. 537, 545 (1922).
(59) Mulkins *v.* Snow, 106 Misc. 556, 559 (N. Y. Sup. Ct. 1919).
(60) Lupico *v.* State, 157 N. E. 576, 577 (Ohio, 1927).
(61) McKee *v.* McCardell, 22 R. I. 71, 72, 73 (1900).
(62) Catts *v.* Sipsey C. W. Co., 212 Ala. 421, 423 (1925).
(63) B. & O. R. R. Co. *v.* Walker, 45 Ohio St. 577, 585 (1888).
(64) In re Rash's Estate, 2 Parsons' Eq. Cas. 160, 162 (Pa. 1850).
(65) Cutts *v.* Commonwealth, 2 Mass. 284, 288 (1807).
(66) McLaren *v.* Stone, 9 Ohio Cir. Decisions 794, 795 (1899).
(67) Jackson *v.* Merrill, 6 Johns. 185, 191 (N. Y. Sup. Ct. 1810).
(68) Stanley *v.* Stanley, 26 Me. 191, 199 (1846).
(69) Williams *v.* Randolph and Cumberland Ry. Co., 182 N. C. 267, 272 (1921).
(70) Kavanaugh *v.* Cohoes Power and Light Corp., 114 Misc. 590, 607 (N. Y. Sup. Ct. 1921).
(71) Chittim *v.* Gossett, 228 S. W. 393, 397 (Ark. 1921).

(72) Columbia Ry. Gas & Electric Co. *v.* Jones, 119 S. C. 480, 490 (1921), and others.
(73) In re Ass. of Aurora G. C. & C. Co., 64 Ind. App. 690, 697, 698 (1917).
(74) Viterbo *v.* Friendlander, 120 U. S. 707, 716 (1886).
(75) Howard *v.* Manning, 79 Okl. 165, 167 (1920).
(76) In re Barnett, 12 Fed. (2d.) 73, 76 (C. C. A. 2nd, 1926).
(77) Clift *v.* White, 12 N. Y. 519, 527 (1855).
(78) Peck *v.* Smith, 1 Conn. 103, 135 (1814).
(79) Holt *v.* City of Mont., 212 Ala. 235, 237 (1924).
(80) Pearsall *v.* Great Northern R. R. Co., 161 U. S. 646, 673 (1895).
(81) Wingate *v.* James, 121 Ind. 69, 72 (1889).
(82) Keogh *v.* Peck, 316 Ill. 318, 326 (1925).
(83) Vanderbilt *v.* Mitchell, 72 N. J. Eq. 927, 928 (1907).
(84) Johnson *v.* Palmer, 118 Me. 226, 230 (1919).
(85) Carolina Power Co. *v.* Haywood, 186 N. C. 313, 317 (1923).
(86) Soulard *v.* U. S., 4 Peters 511 (U. S. 1830).
(87) Burch *v.* McDaniel, 2 Wash. T. 58, 60 (1881).
(88) Black *v.* Elkhorn Min. Co., 49 Fed. 549, 551 (C. C. D. Mont. 1892).
(89) People *v.* Black Diamond Coal M. Co., 37 Cal. 54 (1869).
(90) Wilbur *v.* Jones, 80 N. J. Eq. 520, 524 (1912).
(91) Moore *v.* Tillman, 170 Ark. 895, 900 (1926).
(92) Schleef *v.* Purdy, 214 Pac. 137, 140 (Ore. 1923).
(93) Bodwell *v.* Heaton, 40 Kan. 36, 38 (1888).
(94) Union Nat. Bk. *v.* Bank of Chi., 136 U. S. 223, 232 (1889).
(95) Conn. Mut. Life Ins. Co. *v.* Jones, 8 Fed. 303, 305 (C. C. E. D. Mo. 1880).
(96) Marshall *v.* C. S. Young C. Co., 94 Fla. 11, 15 (1927), and many others.
(97) Fallon *v.* Worthington, 13 Colo. 559, 568 (1889).
(98) The Poznan, 9 F. (2nd) 838, 846 (C. C. A. 2nd, 1925).
(99) State *v.* Davis, 111 Ohio St. 569, 574 (1924), and many others.
(100) Britton *v.* W. Iowa Co., 9 F. (2d) 488, 490 (C. C. A. 8th, 1925).
(101) Bank of Florala *v.* Smith, 11 Ala. App. 358, 360 (1914).
(102) Milam *v.* Milam, 138 Tenn. 686, 691 (1917).
(103) Internat'l. Realty Ass'n. *v.* McAdoo, 87 Fla. 1, 8 (1924).
(104) Field *v.* Lang, 87 Me. 441, 443 (1895).
(105) People ex rel. R. Simpson Co. *v.* Kempner, 154 App. Div. 674, 678 (N. Y. 2d Dept., 1913).
(106) Jackson *v.* Kincaid, 4 Okl. 554, 560 (1896).
(107) Mitchell *v.* Roberts, 17 Fed. 776, 778 (C. C. E. D. Ark. 1883).
(108) Campbell *v.* Parker, 9 Bosworth 322, 329 (N. Y. Super. Ct. 1862).
(109) Rolfe *v.* Huntsville Lumber Co., 8 Ala. App. 487, 495, 496 (1913).
(110) Jackson *v.* Kincaid, 4 Okl. 554, 564, 565, 569 (1896).
(111) Becker and Degen *v.* Brown, 65 Neb. 264, 269 (1902).
(112) Firestone T. & R. Co. *v.* Cross, 17 F .(2d) 417, 418 (C. C. A. 4th, 1927).
(113) In re Galt, 120 Fed. 64, 67 (C. A. A. 7th, 1903).

(114) Averill Machine Co. *v.* Bain, 50 Mont. 512, 514, 515 (1915).
(115) McAndrews *v.* Idawa Gold Mining Co., 54 N. D. 734, 747, 748 (1926).
(116) Moulton *v.* Witherell, 52 Me. 237, 242, 243 (1863).
(117) Phelps *v.* People, 72 N. Y. 334, 357 (1878).
(118) Nat'l. Cattle Loan Co. *v.* Ward, 113 Tex. 312, 319 (1923).
(119) People *v.* Baker, 64 Cal. App. 336, 341 (1923).
(120) Pendleton *v.* Commonwealth, 110 Va. 229, 234 (1909).
(121) Fred. W. Wolf Co. *v.* Hermann Savings Bk., 168 Mo. App. 549, 552 (1912).
(122) Schneider *v.* Daniel, 191 Ind. 59, 62 (1921).
(123) Firestone T. & R. Co. *v.* Anderson, 190 Iowa 439, 442 (1920).
(124) Emerson B. I. Co. *v.* Lawson, 237 Fed. 877, 881, 882 (S. D. Iowa, 1916).
(125) Beers *v.* Lyon, 21 Conn. 604, 613 (1852).
(126) Farmers' L. & T. Co. *v.* Carroll, 5 Barb. 613, 643 (N. Y. 1849).
(127) Appeal of Tappan, 55 N. H. 317, 320 (1875).
(128) Austin-Nichols & Co. *v.* Union Trust Co., 289 Pa. 341, 347 (1927).
(129) Craven *v.* Dominguez Estate Co., 72 Cal. App. 713, 720 (1925).
(130) In re Buch's Estate, 278 Pa. 185, 188 (1923).
(131) Dodson *v.* Ball, 60 Pa. 492, 496 (1869).
(132) Keating *v.* Keating, 182 Iowa 1056, 1075 (1918).
(133) Pratt *v.* Thornton, 28 Me. 355, 360 (1848), and many others.
(134) Brown *v.* Freed, 43 Ind. 253, 256 (1873).
(135) Town of Cascade *v.* Cascade Co., 75 Mont. 304, 311 (1925).
(136) Hospes *v.* N. W. M. & C. Co., 48 Minn. 174, 192 (1892).
(137) Taylor *v.* Davis, 110 U. S. 330, 335 (1883).
(138) Rubin *v.* Midlinsky, 321 Ill. 436, 440 (1926).
(139) First Nat. Bk. of Baltimore *v.* Staake, 202 U. S. 141, 149 (1905).
(140) Metcalfe *v.* Union Trust Co. of N. Y., 181 N. Y. 39, 44 (1905).
(141) State *v.* Chapman, 69 N. J. L. 464, 469 (Sup. Ct. 1903).
(142) Sawyer *v.* Commonwealth, 182 Mass. 245, 247 (1902).
(143) Wells Fargo & Co. *v.* Mayor . . . of Jersey City, 207 Fed. 871, 877, 880 (D. N. J. 1913).
(144) Parker Paint & Wall Paper Co. *v.* Local Union No. 813, 87 W. Va. 631, 641 (1921).
(145) Wight *v.* B. & O. Ry. Co., 146 Md. 66, 73 (1925).
(146) Gleason *v.* Thaw, 185 Fed. 345, 347 (C. C. A. 3rd, 1911).
(147) In re Lipschitz, 14 N. D. 622, 627 (1903).
(148) Sullivan *v.* Ass. B. P. & D. of U. S. & Can., 6 F. (2d.) 1000, 1010, (C. C. A. 2nd, 1925).
(149) Adams Motor Co. *v.* Cler, 149 Ga. 818, 820 (1919).
(150) Commonwealth *v.* Ledman, 127 Ky. 603, 616 (1907).
(151) Matter of Dun's Est., 39 Misc. 616 (N. Y. Surr. Ct. 1903).
(152) Hansen Mercantile Co. *v.* W. P. Co., 105 Minn. 491, 495 (1909).
(153) State *v.* Wheeler, 141 N. C. 773, 777 (1906).
(154) Munden *v.* Harris, 153 Mo. App. 652, 658 (1910).

(155) State *v.* Russell, 38 Tex. Civ. App. 13, 19 (1905).
(156) Pakas *v.* U. S., 240 Fed. 350, 352 (C. C. A. 2d, 1917).
(157) Ide *v.* Harwood, 30 Minn. 191, 195 (1883).
(158) Met. City Ry. Co. *v.* Chi. W. D. Ry. Co., 87 Ill. 317, 324 (1877).
(159) Harvey Coal and Coke Co. *v.* Dillon, 59 W. Va. 605, 616 (1905).
(160) Pause *v.* City of Atlanta, 98 Ga. 92, 97 (1895).
(161) Walther *v.* Sierra R. R. Co., 141 Cal. 288, 290 (1903).
(162) State *v.* Downman, 134 S. W. 787, 793 (Tex. Civ. App. 1911).
(163) Anaconda Copper Mining Co. *v.* Ravalli Co., 52 Mont. 422, 424 (1916).
(164) People ex rel Carrel *v.* Bell, 237 Ill. 332, 338 (1908).
(165) Lynch *v.* Alworth-Stephens Co., 267 U. S. 364, 369 (1924).
(166) Thompson *v.* McLeod, 112 Miss. 383, 389 (1916).
(167) Seven Lakes Reservoir Co. *v.* New Loveland & G. I. & L. Co., 40 Colo. 382, 385 (1907).
(168) Guaranty Realty Co. *v.* Recreation Gun Club, 12 Cal. App. 383, 389 (1910).
(169) State ex rel. Deems *v.* Holtcamp, 245 Mo. 655, 670 (1912).
(170) Locke *v.* North Amer. Ins. Co., 13 Mass. 61, 67 (1816).
(171) Williston Seminary *v.* County Com'rs., 147 Mass. 427, 430 (1889).
(172) Meyer *v.* Meyer, 123 Wis. 538, 546 (1905).
(173) Stebbins *v.* Stebbins, 86 Mich. 474, 481 (1891).
(174) Hovey *v.* Elliott, 21 Jones and Spencer 331, 341 (N. Y. Super. Ct. 1886).
(175) People *v.* Williams, 60 Cal. 1, 2 (1881).
(176) In re Lathrop H. & Co., 184 Fed. 534, 536 (S. D. N. Y. 1910).
(177) Thompson *v.* Manhattan Ry. Co., 15 Daly 438, 440 (N. Y. Common Pleas, 1889).
(178) Clarke *v.* Fay, 205 Mass. 228, 235, 236 (1910).
(179) Earle *v.* Maxwell, 86 S. C. 1, 7 (1910).
(180) Lancaster County *v.* McDonald, 73 Neb. 453, 457 (1905).
(181) Matter of Daly's Est., 100 App. Div. 373, 380 (N. Y. 1st Dept. 1905).
(182) Dibert *v.* D'Arcy, 248 Mo. 617, 659 (1912).
(183) Commonwealth *v.* Morrison, 9 Ky. 75, 90 (1819).
(184) In re Ft. Wayne El. Corp., 96 Fed. 803, 804 (D. Ind. 1899).
(185) Crampton *v.* Newton's Estate, 132 Mich. 149, 152 (1903).
(186) Hall *v.* Miller, 102 Tex. 289, 294, 295 (1909).
(187) Roll *v.* People, 78 Colo. 589, 593 (1926).
(188) Worsham *v.* State, 56 Tex. Cr. 253, 256, 257 (1909).
(189) People *v.* Cohen, 71 Cal. App. 367, 370, 371 (1925).
(190) Wash. Brick Lime & Mfg. Co. *v.* Traders' Nat. Bk., 46 Wash. 23, 27 (1907).
(191) Standard Marine Ins. Co. *v.* Bd. of Ass., 123 La. 717, 720 (1909).
(192) Shipman Coal Co. *v.* Delaware and Hudson Co., 219 App. Div. 312, 314 (N. Y. 1st Dept. 1927).
(193) Armstrong *v.* Harper, 25 Ga. App. 71 (1920).

(194) Wood *v.* City of Millville, 89 N. J. L. 646, 651 (1916).
(196) General Bonding and Casualty Ins. Co. *v.* Moseley, 110 Tex. 529, 531 (1920).
(197) Haskins *v.* Ryan, 75 N. J. Eq. 330, 332 (Ch. 1909).
(198) Black *v.* Elkhorn Min. Co., 49 Fed. 549, 551 (D. Mont. 1892).
(199) Leong Mow *v.* Bd. of Com., 185 Fed. 223 (C. C. E. D. La. 1911).
(200) San Pedro, L. A. & S. L. R. Co. *v.* City of L. A., 180 Cal. 18, 20 (1919).
(201) Auburn Crystal Ice Co. *v.* City of Lewiston, 109 Me. 489 (1912).
(202) Snyder *v.* Warford, 11 Mo. 513, 516 (1848), and others.
(203) City of Springfield *v.* S. C. Ry. Co., 295 Ill. 234, 240 (1920).
(204) Durgin *v.* Minot, 203 Mass. 26, 29 (1910).
(205) Western U. Tel. Co. *v.* Penn. R. Co., 195 U. S. 540, 570 (1904).
(206) Old Colony and Fall River R. Corp. *v.* Inhabitants of Plymouth Co., 80 Mass. 155, 160, 161 (1859), and many others.
(207) Thompson *v.* Manhattan Ry. Co., 130 N. Y. 360, 365 (1891).
(208) Glascock *v.* Lemp, 26 Ind. App. 175, 178 (1900).
(209) Eliason *v.* Draper, 2 Boyce 1 (Dela. Super. Ct. 1910).
(210) Jaynes *v.* Jaynes, 39 Hun. 40, 41 (N. Y. 1886).
(211) Hodge *v.* Wetzler, 69 N. J. L. 490, 494 (Sup. Ct. 1903).
(212) Duffies *v.* Duffies, 76 Wis. 374, 379 (1890).
(213) Billingsley *v.* St. L. I. M. & S. R. Co., 84 Ark. 617 (1907).
(214) Patrick *v.* State, 50 Tex. Cr. 496, 499 (1906).
(215) Samuelson *v.* State, 116 Tenn. 470, 490 (1906).
(216) Kirby *v.* U. P. R. Co., 51 Colo. 509, 538 (1911).
(217) State *v.* Ferris, 53 Ohio St. 314, 329 (1895).
(218) J. Tome Inst. of P. D. *v.* Crothers, 87 Md. 569, 585 (1898).
(219) Wilmington & R. R. Co. *v.* Downward, 14 Atl. 720, 723 (Del. 1888).
(220) Randolph *v.* Larned, 27 N. J. Eq. 557, 561 (1876).
(221) City of Bridgeport *v.* N. Y. & N. H. R. Co., 36 Conn. 255, 266 (1869).
(222) Public Service Gas Co. *v.* Bd. of Public Utility Com'rs., 87 N. J. L. 581, 587 (1915).
(223) People ex rel. Interborough Rapid Transit Co. *v.* Williams, 138 App. Div. 612, 615 (N. Y. 3d. Dept. 1910).
(224) Ager *v.* Murray, 105 U. S. 126, 127, 128 (1881).
(225) Rehfuss *v.* Moore, 134 Pa. 462, 471 (1890).
(226) Rehfuss *v.* Moore, 134 Pa. 462, 472 (1890).
(227) Vail *v.* Hammond, 60 Conn. 374, 383 (1891).
(228) Peterson *v.* Sheriff of C. & C. of San Francisco, 115 Cal. 211, 213 (1896).
(229) Chisholm *v.* Forny, 65 Iowa 333, 335 (1884).
(230) Baldwin *v.* Von Micheroux, 5 Misc. 386, 389 (N. Y. Sup. Ct. 1893).
(231) Werckmeister *v.* Springer L. Co., 63 Fed. 808, 810 (C. C. S. D. N. Y. 1894).
(232) Western Union Tel. Co. *v.* Foster, 224 Mass. 365, 369 (1916).

(233) Voight *v.* Bd. of Excise Com'rs. of City of Newark, 59 N. J. L. 358, 360 (1896).
(234) La Plante *v.* State Board of Public Roads, 47 R. I. 258, 261 (1926).
(235) State *v.* Corron, 73 N. H. 434, 459 (1905).
(236) Matter of Low, 199 App. Div. 738, 741 (N. Y. 2d Dept. 1922).
(237) Dissent in State ex rel. Quion *v.* Miles, 210 Mo. 127, 181.
(238) State *v.* Crumbaugh, 26 Tex. Civ. App. 521, 526 (1901).
(239) State *v.* Henderson, 145 Iowa 657, 663 (1910).
(240) Greene *v.* Knox, 175 N. Y. 432, 437 (1903).
(241) Hibbard *v.* State, 64 N. E. 109, 114 (Ohio Sup. Ct. 1901).
(242) Merchants' Ad-Sign Co. *v.* Sterling, 124 Cal. 429, 431 (1899).
(243) Haugen *v.* Sundseth, 106 Minn. 129, 133 (1908).
(244) People *v.* Dederick, 161 N. Y. 195, 210 (1900).
(245) Matter of Dun's Est., 39 Misc. 616 (N. Y. Surr. Ct. 1903).
(246) Holden's Administrators *v.* M'Makin, 1 Parsons' Eq. Cas. 270, 298, 299 (Pa. 1847).
(247) Anderson *v.* Durr, 10 Ohio App. 329 (1919).
(248) Barclay *v.* Smith, 107 Ill. 349, 353 (1883).
(249) Hyde *v.* Woods, 94 U. S. 523, 525 (1876).
(250) Thompson *v.* Adams, 93 Pa. 55, 66 (1880).
(251) Pancoast *v.* Gowen, 93 Pa. 66, 71 (1881).
(252) Habenicht *v.* Lissak, 78 Cal. 351, 357 (1889).
(253) Powell *v.* Waldron, 89 N. Y. 328, 331 (1882).
(254) In re Tiburcio Parrott, 1 Fed. 481 (C. C. D. Cal. 1880).
(255) Jones *v.* Leslie, 61 Wash. 107, 110 (1910).
(256) Gillespie *v.* People, 188 Ill. 176, 183 (1900).
(257) In re Marshall, 102 Fed. 323, 324 (C. C. N. D. Cal. 1900).
(258) Justice Swayne dissenting in Slaughter-House Cases, 16 Wall., 36, 127 (1872).
(259) State *v.* Chapman, 69 N. J. L. 464, 466 (Sup. Ct. 1903), and others.
(260) Hewitt *v.* State Bd. of Med. Exam., 84 Pac. 39, 40 (Cal. 1906).
(261) Ex parte Steinman, 95 Pa. 220, 237 (1880).
(262) In re Thatcher, 190 Fed. 969 (N. D. Ohio, 1911).
(263) Sawyer *v.* Commonwealth, 182 Mass. 245, 247 (1902).
(264) Hansen Mercantile Co., *v.* W. P. Co., 105 Minn. 491, 494 (1909).
(265) Tootle *v.* Kent, 12 Okl. 674, 689 (1903).
(266) Edison *v.* Edison Polyform & Mfg. Co., 73 N. J. Eq. 136, 143 (Ch. 1907).
(267) Internt'l. Silver Co. *v.* Rogers, 71 N. J. Eq., 560, 567, 569 (Ch. 1906).
(268) Burand *v.* Brown, 236 Fed. 609, 614 (C. C. A. 6th, 1916).
(269) Hartman *v.* J. D. Park & Sons Co., 145 Fed. 358 (C. C. E. D. Ky. 1906).
(270) Elaterite Paint & Mfg. Co. *v.* S. E. Frost Co., 105 Minn. 239, 240 (1908).
(271) Jewelers' Mercantile Agency *v.* Jewelers' W. P. Co., 155 N. Y. 241, 247 (1898).

(272) Haskins *v.* Ryan, 71 N. J. Eq. 575, 580 (Ch. 1906).
(273) Dixon *v.* People, 168 Ill. 179, 190, 191 (1897).
(274) Gianfortone *v.* City of N. O., 61 Fed. 64, 67 (C. C. E. D. La. 1894).
(275) Anthony *v.* Tarpley, 45 Cal. App. 72, 79 (1919).
(276) Roberts *v.* City of Detroit, 102 Mich. 64, 67 (1894).
(277) Billingsley *v.* St. L. I. M. &. S. R. Co., 84 Ark. 617, 619 (1907).
(278) In re Le Claire, 124 Fed. 654 (N. D. Iowa, 1903).
(279) In re Wetmore, 108 Fed. 520, 523 (C. C. A. 3rd, 1901).
(280) J. B. Mullen & Co. *v.* Moseley, 13 Idaho 457, 464, 469 (1907).
(281) People ex rel. Eckerson *v.* Bd. of Educ. of Haverstraw, 126 App. Div. 414, 420 (N. Y. 2d. Dept. 1908).
(282) Lone Star Lodge, No. 1,935 K. & L. of Honor *v.* Cole, 131 S. W. 1180, 1185 (Tex. Civ. App. 1910).
(283) Jackson *v.* Burns, 116 La. 695 (1906).
(284) Munn *v.* People, 69 Ill. 80, 91 (1873).
(285) Hattiesburg Grocery Co. *v.* Robertson, 126 Miss. 34, 54, 55 (1921).
(286) State *v.* Pinder, 7 Boyce 416 (Del. Ct. Gen. Sess. 1919).
(287) Appeal of Beach, 107 Conn. 1 (1927).
(288) Zanetta *v.* Bolles, 80 Vt. 345, 347 (1907).
(289) City of Syracuse *v.* Stacey, 169 N. Y. 231, 245 (1901).
(290) Kans. Nat. Gas Co. *v.* Haskell, 172 Fed. 545, 564 (C. C. E. D. Okl. 1909).
(291) City of Owensboro *v.* Commonwealth, 105 Ky. 344, 346 (1899).
(292) Shamrock T. Co. *v.* City of N. Y., 20 F. (2d) 444, 445 (E. D. N. Y. 1927).
(293) Coyle *v.* Gray, 7 Houst. 44, 95, 96 (Dela. 1894).
(294) City of New Orleans *v.* Salmen B. & L. Co., 135 La. 828 (First opinion).
(295) Martin *v.* Louisiana Central Lumber Co., 90 So. 553, 562 (La. 1920).
(296) State *v.* Neff, 52 Ohio St. 375, 404 (1895).
(297) Thompson *v.* Bowes, 115 Me. 6, 8 (1916).
(298) Matter of Matthiessen's Est., 109 Misc. 297 (N. Y. Surr. Ct. 1919).
(299) Moulton *v.* Long, 243 Mass. 129 (1922).
(300) Matter of Boshart's Est., 107 Misc. 697, 705 (N. Y. Surr. Ct. 1919).
(301) Standard Oil Co. *v.* Howe, 257 Fed. 481, 486 (C. C. A. 9th, 1919).
(302) Matter of Matthiessen's Est., 109 Misc. 297, 299 (N. Y. Surr. Ct. 1919).
(303) Bates *v.* Robinson, 8 Iowa 318, 320 (1859).
(304) Cal. Code Civ. Pro. (1931) sec. 17 (1), and many other codes and decisions.
(305) Travis *v.* Dickey, 96 Okl. 256, 257 (1924).
(306) Sox *v.* Miracle, 35 N. D. 458, 470 (1916).

(307) Primos Chem. Co. *v.* Fulton Steel Corp., 254 Fed. 454, 460 (N. D. N. Y. 1918).
(308) Guy *v.* Breman, 60 Cal. App. 452, 455 (1923).
(309) Matter of Althause's Est., 63 App. Div. 252, 255 (N. Y. 1st Dept. 1901).
(310) Meni *v.* Rathbone, 21 Ind. 454, 467 (1863).
(311) Chi. Aud. Assn. *v.* Cramer, 8 F. (2d.) 998, 1005 (N. D. Ill. 1925).
(312) N. Y. Code Civ. Proc. (1920), sec. 1430.
(313) Kohring *v.* Bowman, 137 N. E. 767, 768 (Ind. 1923).
(314) Moulton *v.* Long, 243 Mass. 129, 132 (1922).
(315) Matter of City of New York, 219 App. Div. 387, 392, 393 (N. Y. 2d Dept. 1927).
(316) Park Bldg. Co. *v.* Geo. P. Yost Fur Co., 208 Mich. 349, 358 (1919).
(317) San Pedro, L. A. & S. L. R. Co. *v.* City of L. A., 180 Cal. 18, 20 (1919).
(318) Neponsit Realty Co. *v.* Judge, 106 Misc. 445, 447 (N. Y. Sup. Ct. 1919).
(319) Burney *v.* Burney, 261 S. W. 182, 184 (Tex. Civ. App. 1924).
(320) Hammond *v.* Carthage S. P. & P. Co., 8 F. (2d) 35, 39 (C. C. A. 2nd, 1925).
(321) Chi. Land Timber Co. *v.* Dorris, 139 Ark. 333, 339, 340 (1919).
(322) Walker *v.* Dwelle, 187 Iowa 1384, 1387 (1920).
(323) Terry *v.* Humphreys, 27 N. M. 564, 575, 576 (1922).
(324) Bentley *v.* Zelma Oil Co., 76 Okl. 116, 126 (1919).
(325) Nev. Comp. Laws (1900) sec. 3687 (Cutting).
(326) Kennedy S. & C. Co. *v.* Sloss-Sheffield S. & I. Co., 137 Ala. 401, 409 (1902).
(327) Long Island R. R. Co. *v.* Garvey, 159 N. Y. 334, 338 (1899).
(328) Harrison *v.* Boring, 44 Tex. 255, 267 (1875).
(329) Plattsburg Gas and Electric Co. *v.* Miller, 123 Misc. 651, 653 (N. Y. Sup. Ct. 1924).
(330) Jones *v.* Island Creek Coal Co., 79 W. Va. 532, 537, 538 (1917).
(331) Wolfe *v.* Frost, 4 Sandf. Ch. 72, 95 (N. Y. 1846).
(332) Ross *v.* Thompson, 78 Ind. 90, 91 (1881).
(333) Pierce *v.* Keator, 70 N. Y. 419, 421 (1877).
(334) Manbeck *v.* Jones, 21 Pa. County Ct. 300, 302 (1898), and many others.
(335) Tedford *v.* Wenatchee R. D., 127 Wash. 495, 499 (1923).
(336) Williams *v.* Mitchem, 25 Ga. App. 138, 139 (1920).
(337) Hager *v.* Stakes, 116 Tex. 453, 471 (1927).
(338) Sibley *v.* Pickens, 273 S. W. 897, 898 (Tex. Civ. App. 1925).
(339) In re Inglis, 69 Okl. 64, 66 (1917).
(340) Ralston S. C. Co. *v.* Ralston, 112 Ohio St. 306, 314, 315 (1925).
(341) People *v.* Maloney, 1 Parker's Cr. R. 593, 595 (N. Y. 1825).
(342) U. S. *v.* Moulton, 27 Fed. Cas. 1, 12 (C. C. D. Mass. 1830).
(343) St. Louis & S. F. R. Co. *v.* Crews, 151 Pac. 879, 882 (Okl. 1915).

(344) Sheldon *v.* Sill, 8 How. 441, 449 (U. S. 1850), and many others.
(345) State ex rel Coffey *v.* District Court, 74 Mont. 355, 358 (1925).
(346) Tumy *v.* Mayer, 289 Ill. 458, 460 (1919).
(347) Haskell *v.* Blair, 57 Mass. 534 (1849).
(348) Cody *v.* Dempsey, 86 App. Div. 335, 340 (N. Y. 2d. Dept. 1903).
(349) Hall *v.* Bartlett, 9 Barb. 297, 299 (N. Y. 1850).
(350) Realty Holding Co. *v.* Donaldson, 294 Fed. 541, 543 (E. D. Mich. 1923).
(351) Realty Holding Co. *v.* Donaldson, 268 U. S. 398, 401 (1924).
(352) Van Wicklen *v.* Paulson, 14 Barb. 654, 657 (N. Y. 1853).
(353) Anderson *v.* Durr, 10 Ohio App. 329 (1919).
(354) Leffingwell *v.* Evans, 185 Ky. 351, 355 (1919).
(355) Hook *v.* Hoffman, 16 Ariz. 540, 546 (1915).
(356) Cummings *v.* People, 211 Ill. 392, 403 (1904).
(357) Vidal *v.* S. A. Sec. Co., 276 Fed. 855, 868 (C. C. A. 2nd, 1921).
(358) Small *v.* Wilson, 20 Ga. App. 674, 677 (1917).
(359) Fowler *v.* Dickson, 1 Boyce 113, 121, 122 (Dela. Super. Ct. 1909) (quoting Howe *v.* Starkweather, 17 Mass. 240).
(360) In re Sutherland, 21 F. (2d) 667, 670 (W. D. N. Y. 1927).
(361) Koelling *v.* Citizens' Bk. of Warrenton, 237 S. W. 176, 181 (Mo. App. 1922).
(362) State Bk. of Swea City, Iowa, *v.* C. & N. W. Ry. Co., 281 Fed. 345, 346 (N. D. Iowa, 1922).
(363) Gulf C. & S. F. Ry. Co. *v.* Cities Service Co., 273 Fed. 946, 949 (D. Dela. 1921).
(364) Phillips *v.* City of Portsmouth, 115 Va. 180, 190 (1913); Suhr *v.* Metcalfe, 33 Cal. App. 59, 63 (1917); Power and I. Co. of Clear Lake *v.* Bank of Woodland, 213 Fed. 109, 111 (N. D. Cal. 1914).
(365) Hammond *v.* Carthage S. P. & P. Co., 8 F. (2d) 35, 38 (C. C. A. 2nd., 1925).
(366) Bushnell *v.* Kennedy, 9 Wall. 387, 390 (U. S. 1869), and many others.
(367) Dry Dock Bank *v.* Amer. Life. Ins. & Tr. Co., 3 N. Y. 344, 356 (1850).
(368) Wilson *v.* Schrader, 73 W. Va. 105, 110 (1913).
(369) People *v.* Tioga, 19 Wend. 73, 75 (N. Y. 1837), and others.
(370) Northern Texas Traction Co. *v.* Hill, 297 S. W. 778, 779 (Tex. Civ. App. 1927).
(371) Sharp *v.* Cincinnati N. O. & T. P. Ry. Co., 133 Tenn. 1, 6 (1915).
(372) Browne *v.* King, 196 S. W. 884, 887 (Tex. Civ. App. 1917).
(373) Louisville & Nashville R. Co. *v.* Spinks, 104 Ga. 692 694 (1898).
(374) Hoehle *v.* Alleghany Heating Co., 5 Pa. Super. Ct. 21, 24 (1897).
(375) Western Union Tel. Co. *v.* Taylor, 84 Ga. 408, 417 (1889).
(376) Barkley *v.* Williams, 30 Misc. 687, 688 (N. Y. Sup. Ct. 1900).
(377) Appeal of Wentz, 76 Conn. 405, 409 (1904).
(378) Power *v.* Harlow, 57 Mich. 107, 111 (1887).
(379) Williams *v.* Atl. Coast Line R. R. Co., 153 N. C. 360, 363 (1910).

(380) Dunlap *v.* Toledo, A. A. & G. T. Ry. Co., 50 Mich. 470, 474 (1883).
(381) Mulvey *v.* City of Boston, 197 Mass. 178, 183 (1908).
(382) Cleland *v.* Anderson, 66 Neb. 252 (1902).
(383) Gibson *v.* Gibson, 43 Wis. 23, 33 (1877).
(384) Mountain State Motor Car Co. *v.* Solof, 97 W. Va. 196, 199 (1924).
(385) City of Camden *v.* Allen, 26 N. J. L. 398, 399 (Sup. Ct. 1857), and many others.
(386) H. G. Kilbourne Co. *v.* St. S. A. Co., 216 Mass. 118, 121 (1914).
(387) Bovee *v.* Boyle, 25 Colo. App. 165, 173 (1913).
(388) Worley *v.* Smith, 26 Tex. Civ. App. 270, 272 (1901).
(389) Day *v.* Bennett, 18 N. J. L. 287, 288 (Sup. Ct. 1841).
(390) Lindstrom *v.* Spicher, 53 N. D. 195, 201 (1925).
(391) Stone, Timlow & Co., *v.* Stryker, 230 Mass. 67, 72 (1918).
(392) Ex parte Harrison, 272 Fed. 543, 544 (D. Mass. 1921).
(393) Rayborn *v.* Reid, 139 S. C. 529 (1927).
(394) Michaels *v.* McLaughlin, 20 F. (2d.) 959 (N. D. Cal. 1927).
(395) Read *v.* Lewis & Clark Co., 55 Mont. 412, 418 (1919).
(396) Millington *v.* Texas & Pacific Ry. Co., 2 Willson Civ. Cases 148 (Tex. Ct. App. 1884).
(397) Harp. *v.* Pease, 52 Cal. App. 744, 745 (1921).
(398) Security Nat. Bank of Tulsa *v.* Geck, 96 Okl. 89, 92 (1923).
(399) Hamilton *v.* McPherson, 28 N. Y. 72, 76 (1863).
(400) Bremhorst *v.* Phillips C. Co., 202 Iowa 1251, 1255 (1927).
(401) City of N. Y. *v.* Lord, 17 Wend. 285, 293 (N. Y. 1837) (Citing Co. Litt. 257).
(402) Lake Shore & Michigan S. Ry. Co. *v.* Prentice, 147 U. S. 101, 107 (1892).
(403) Dettmer *v.* Fulls, 122 Kan. 98, 99 (1927).
(404) Thomasma *v.* Carpenter, 175 Mich. 428, 437 (1913).
(405) Leonard *v.* Greenleaf, 21 N. M. 180, 184 (1915).
(406) Watson *v.* Gillespie, 205 App. Div. 613, 623 (N. Y. 1st Dept. 1923).
(407) Matter of Collier's Est., 112 Misc. 70, 73 (N. Y. Surr. Ct. 1920).
(408) Bd. of County Comm'rs. of the City & County of Denver *v.* Home Savings Bk., 236 U. S. 101, 105 (1914).
(409) Gearin *v.* Marion Co., 110 Ore. 390, 397 (1924).
(410) Superior Plating Works *v.* Art M. C. Co., 218 Ill. App. 148, 150 (1920).

APPENDIX III

THE NATURE OF CREDITORS' RIGHTS IN PRACTICE

Introductory

It may, I think, be safely stated that the classical doctrine as to general creditors' rights[1] differentiates them sharply from property rights, strictly speaking (i. e. so-called rights *in rem*) on the ground that they do not pertain directly or indirectly to material objects and in that they are of dynamic not static character. The antecedent rights arising from contract are, from the abstract legal viewpoint, rights to an act or event (positive or negative) and, from the economic point of view, rights to a future payment in some form or other. The remedial rights resulting either from breach of contract or from tort spring from the antecedent right in both cases; that is, the remedial right based on breach of contract results from, and partakes of the nature and limitations of, the antecedent right, and that based on tort results from infringement of a property, personal or familial right.[2] But, in most respects, the two varieties of remedial right then become merged in one class—rights of action—which, as to their incidence, take a form similar to the antecedent right under contract. They are then conceived as rights to damages—namely a payment of money—or, rarely, to specific performance or restitution—namely payment in another form. They are, in other words, represented as rights to an act or event (payment or conveyance) and are therefore still treated by the purists as rights *in personam* along with the antecedent rights under contract. In fact the older English jurisprudence as well as the common viewpoint of the practical jurists of today tends in theory to ignore all such rights except in the aspect of rights of action. They are classed and considered as *choses in action.*

As against this view we are presenting the thesis that actual modern legal practice is proceeding—somewhat covertly and under the guise of this doctrine—along quite other lines. A realistic doctrine of

[1] The rights of creditors here are what is called in legal practice the rights of *unsecured* or general creditors. But it should be noted that, in legal theory, the right of a secured creditor is, in reality, a compound of his right *in personam* as a creditor and his right *in rem* as a lienor. Thus, apart from security and the property rights involved therein, all creditors' rights are of one general nature.

[2] This is subject to the inconsistency, already noted, that certain torts arise from interference with or even breaches of contractual rights, which are not, in the strict view, property rights. This has led to some strange legal fictions or evasions.

creditors' rights would seem to call for recognition of the fact that they are coming to resemble far more closely, for instance, the rights of a stockholder in a corporation; that they are generally regarded by the law in their static rather than in their dynamic aspect; and that their nature can be far better defined, according to actual incidence rather than according to theoretical derivation, as existing interests in the fund of the debtor, only differing from the strict older classification of property rights (which did not include shares of stock) in that their incidence upon the specific 'things' of the debtor's fund is as yet indeterminate.

In this view, then, the rights of creditors are subsisting interests in the debtor's fund, not merely rights *in personam*, or to an act or event, or to a payment of money or equivalent. The repurchase agreement is not the essential feature but rather the means agreed upon for the reacquisition, merger and extinction of this interest. Hence the protection against interference by third parties becomes a tort against this property interest of the same nature as any other tort against property. Hence the requirement of maintenance of the fund against involuntary shrinkage of value (insolvency) or voluntary dissipation (fraud of creditors) becomes a recognition of an adverse interest in the fund. Hence the restrictions on disposing of assets or incurring liabilities, under such conditions. Hence the acceleration of maturity and the ripening of debt under such conditions. Hence the treatment of overdue debts as continuing interests. And only in this view can the repurchase of such interests by corporations and the holding, resale or reissue of same be made consistent.

The law may eventually have to devise a doctrine which conforms to this realistic view of the credit-debt relation, a view which is gradually displacing the older notion in modern business. And this seems necessary because the relation has come to occupy so essential and major a place in the financial structure of today. But the process will doubtless be a tedious one for the reason that the principles of law have been built up to protect the petty debtor, whose payments for current expenses in arrears and whose repayments of money lent are to be made out of income. Now that the same system has been taken over by productive enterprise, so that credit-debt behaves in a large measure as if it were capital and must be continually refunded, or repaid out of principal, and so that the relation between the creditors as the strong and the debtors as the weak has been reversed, these principles must be modified. But they can only be modified in a way that will permit their serving the now dual social purpose. And this duality presents a real dilemma.

The following pages attempt briefly to outline the evidence for this thesis by pointing out the ways in which the law seems to construe the creditors' rights as *interests*, in respect of the impairment of the rights of debtors, in respect of the projection of the rights of creditors within or over the debtors' funds; and as existing or *present and antecedent interests* in respect of their incidence prior to default or prior to judgment.

A. *Impairments of the Rights of Debtors*

"All other things being equal, a debtor holds his property free from any right of his creditors to specifically claim it or give directions with regard to its application; they have no title thereto, nor any equity therein."[3] This *ceteris paribus* strikes a familiar note to economists who are in the habit of setting up a norm and then qualifying it out of existence. In this case the principle serves as a means of resistance, a way of making the creditors' rights, which are pared off, deductions or exceptions, and thus of minimizing them. The burden of proof is put on the side of the creditor. But the principle does not envisage the facts.

1. *Impairments of Alienability*

a. *Fraudulent Transfer*

"Where the debtor has so dealt with the title to property as to put it beyond the reach of the creditor's remedy unless, on some principle other than those governing the devolution of title, the courts can allow the creditor to realize on the property despite the transfer";[4] if the transaction "will deprive the creditors of an ample fund for the payment of their debts";[5] if "when the operation is completed the debtor has less of a property right than he had before . . . [and] as a result, the debtor's estate has been diminished";[6] and if the grantee had knowledge of these circumstances or that intent;[7] then, "creditors whose claims existed at the time when the transfer was made,"[8] may void the transfer or other transaction or proceeding.

Glenn[9] considers that such conveyance is voided as a fraudulent transfer because it is a wrong by the debtor upon the right of the creditor to collect, and not because it is an invalid act by reason of the fact that the debtor's rights are impaired by the existence of the debt. And elsewhere the usual reason given for avoidance is that the act is intended or operative to delay, hinder and defraud the creditors. Nevertheless the fact remains that, under these circumstances, the debtor's complete rights of property are impaired, whatever the reason therefor. The reality of the general incidence of debt upon his 'things' is proven, and the fraud consists in exercising a normal right of property in such a way as to defeat this incidence.

[3] Glenn, *The Rights and Remedies of Creditors Respecting their Debtor's Property*, sec. 1.

[4] Glenn, op. cit., sec. 61.

[5] Verplank v. Sterry, 12 Johns. 536, 557 (N. Y. 1815). See also Williston, *Sales*, sec. 641.

[6] Glenn, op. cit., sec. 102.

[7] Williston, *Sales*, sec. 639.

[8] Williston, *Sales*, sec. 642.

[9] Op. cit., sec. 61.

b. *Fraudulent Preferences*

A preference among creditors is fraudulent and void if the debtor (a) procures or suffers an adverse judgment, or (b) transfers property during the four months prior to the filing of a petition in bankruptcy or between the petition and adjudication; "if the effect of such judgment or transfer is to enable one creditor to obtain a greater percentage of his debt than any others of the same class";[10] if the result was a diminution of the debtor's assets; and if the transferor intended to prefer and the transferee had reasonable cause to believe a preference was thus to be created. A preference is not created and the sale is not invalidated by a mere preference, for "a debtor has a right to prefer one creditor over another, even if he is insolvent; . . . if he does so in good faith;"[11] or merely by "a fraudulent intent on the part of the vendor to defeat his other creditors . . . although . . . [as a result] the remaining creditors of the vendor would be unable to obtain the payment of their debts";[12] but only when the vendee participates in the fraud. In other words we have here an assertion, not only of a certain disability upon the part of the debtor in respect of his normal property rights, but of the indeterminacy of the general creditors' rights in their projection upon an equivalent mass of the debtor's 'things.' Under these circumstances one creditor cannot knowingly subtract from the mass more than his share. He is in the position of a stockholder upon dissolution of the corporation.

c. *Sales in Bulk*

In order to secure a "limitation of the practice by dealers of selling all, or substantially all, of their merchandise at once, since frauds upon creditors have frequently been committed by a dealer making such a sale and departing with the consideration received without paying his creditors," the Uniform Sales Law or, in some states a Bulk Sales Law, provides "that a sale by a dealer of his merchandise in bulk is presumed to be fraudulent in the absence of certain formalities." The essential formality is that the seller must "give a list of his creditors to the buyer with the amount due each one of them, and thereupon the buyer is required to notify these creditors of the proposed sale." Here the disability is wholly upon the seller both in respect of the freedom of his right of alienation and in the respect of the necessary notice, through the buyer, of the substitution of assets (like the exchange of collateral in a trust deed), for "it is probable that an innocent purchaser for value from a buyer who has failed to comply with the bulk sales law, would be protected."[13]

[10] Glenn, op. cit., sec. 418.
[11] Strauss v. Abrahams, 32 Fed. 310, 313 (C. C. E. D. Mo. 1887).
[12] Bamberger v. Schoolfield, 160 U. S. 149, 158, 159 (1895).
[13] Williston, *Sales*, sec. 643.

2. *Initial Fraud*

"The law is well settled that where the buyer at the time of the purchase was insolvent and intended not to pay for the goods, it is a fraud which will render the purchaser's title voidable." As to this it is Williston's judgment that the intention not to pay is the only material circumstance. He holds that this view "seems correct on principle and would doubtless generally be reached, but not perhaps everywhere." He gives as the grounds of this rule that "the purchase of goods implies a promise to pay for them even if there is no express promise; and a promise to pay, whether express or implied, involves a representation that the buyer intends to keep his promise."[14] The intention not to pay is construed elsewhere to indicate that "there was therefore no meeting of minds [contract] and no passing of title."[15] Property so received and "converted by the bankrupt may be reclaimed; so may its proceeds if they can be identified and traced; but if neither the property nor its proceeds can be identified, . . . the owner will simply have the right to waive the tort and present his claim [for dividends] as on contract."[16] The intent to deceive and the innocence of the seller are essential. This rule may be adequately explained, as in these quotations, under the most refined of the classical doctrines of promise. But it may also be explained on the grounds of our thesis. A sale on credit is an exchange of which one side is an interest of a sort in the debtor's fund. If, knowingly upon the part of the debtor and innocently upon the part of the creditor, a seeming exchange is effected of which this one side (the interest) is in reality elsewise non-existent, it is construed to be not an exchange so long as the other side, or its equivalent, remains identifiable. Thus the debtor's right to grant interests of this type in his fund, his power of contracting, is limited and his ability to acquire property by such methods impaired.

3. *Injunctive Relief in Favour of the Creditors of a Corporation*

While the courts have shown great reluctance to interfere in the conduct of the affairs of a corporation for the protection of its creditors, there are already a limited number of instances and there will doubtless be more in future.

A creditor may attack corporate transactions as *ultra vires* if he can show that (a) the corporation was insolvent at the time of entering the transaction, or (b) that the contract made it so, or (c) that the intent or effect of the transaction is fraudulently to divert or destroy the corporate assets that are subject to payment of debts.[17] In general, injunc-

[14] Williston, *Sales*, sec. 637.

[15] Remington, *On Bankruptcy*, sec. 2456.

[16] *Student's Remington*, sec. 104.

[17] See Brent v. Simpson, 238 Fed. 285, 291 (C. C. A. 5th, 1916); Force v. Age Herald Co., 136 Ala. 271, 279 (1902); Wash. Mill Co. v. Sprague Lumber Co., 19 Wash. 165, 173 (1898).

tion has been held to be available to creditors against contracts or transfers by a corporation if fraud or breach of trust against them can be shown.[18] A bondholder is entitled to recovery and accounting in case of fraudulent misappropriation of corporate assets.[19] Bondholders have successfully required "a holder of a majority of the shares in the company to account for income which he had fraudulently diverted to his own use," and have enjoined a "company from complying with unreasonable schedules of rates prescribed by a railroad commission in violation of the constitutional rights of the railway company."[20] Machen concludes that "the company will certainly be restrained by injunction from doing any act for the purpose of injuring the security of the bondholders."[21] As to security, bondholders certainly have recognized property rights superior to the rights of general creditors. But in the cases cited as examples it is clear that the right protected is that of a general creditor and that such creditor is held to be entitled to relief, though perhaps only when the corporate equity approaches zero, if through the acts of an agent, a stockholder or even an outside authority, his interest in the assets may be defeated. Obviously such acts can only be construed as fraudulent if the supposedly absolute title of the corporation is in reality qualified and if the creditor is presumed to have a right or interest therein.

B. *Projection of the Rights of Creditors upon the Funds of Debtors*

1. *General Statement*

The nature of the projection of the beneficial rights of creditors upon the funds of debtors may be described as a "floating charge" upon the fund as a whole which impairs only the capacity of the debtor to deal with his fund as a whole[22] so long as the shadow of this charge does not cover, or threaten to cover, the entire mass of the fund. Until that time the interests of the creditors are discrete and separate, except in respect of being aggregated to measure the total debt, and are strictly indeterminate as to their incidence upon individual 'things' composing the fund.[23] Until that time, therefore, any individual creditor whose

[18] See Gay v. Hudson River Electric Power Co., 187 Fed. 12, 16 (C. C. A. 2d, 1911); Pond v. Framingham etc. R. Co., 130 Mass. 194, 195 (1880).

[19] See Edwards v. Bay State Gas Co., 91 Fed. 946 (C. C. D. Del., 1898).

[20] Machen, *A Treatise on the Modern Law of Corporations*, sec. 1928.

[21] Machen, loc. cit.

[22] We refer to "the familiar rule that the stockholder's interest in the property is subordinate to the rights of creditors; first, of secured, and then of unsecured, creditors. And any arrangement of the parties by which the subordinate rights and interests of the stockholders are attempted to be secured at the expense of the prior rights of either class of creditors comes within judicial denunciation." Louisville Trust Co. v. Louisville Ry., 174 U. S. 674, 684 (1898).

[23] That vague but limited class of various sets of rights *in rem*, to which formerly the term property was exclusively applied and which are now frequently lumped together as "ownership," originally possible only with possession, may now include non-possessory interests, but only those which refer to determinate objects,

obligation goes into default, may project his claim upon any individual 'thing' of the debtor, subject, of course, to any real rights of others therein.[24] And also until that time, except for such liens, the freedom of action of the debtor with respect to his individual 'things' is unqualified.[25] But once the aggregate creditors' interests composing this "floating charge" cover, or threaten to cover, the whole of the debtor's fund, the projection assumes a wholly different character. Then the creditors' rights tend to become consolidated,[26] organized, stratified both vertically and horizontally, and thereby determinate, while the debtor's rights with respect to his individual 'things' are more or less destroyed. Thereafter what remains to him, beyond specific exemptions, is an interest, or equity, in indeterminate 'things' and therefore of the character previously attaching to the creditors' rights. Whereas, before, the charge was indeterminate and the equity determinate as to the whole fund, now the charge becomes determinate, *pro tem.*, as to the whole fund, and the equity indeterminate.

The extent of the projection reaches all interests of whatever nature, so long as they are alienable by any means, which went to compose the debtor's fund, except those few which are exempt. But it only reaches to the extent of these interests,[27] except as it may include, as to the general creditors, liens, defeasible or otherwise, which may have been acquired from those general creditors, and which have priority over

So Williston, *Sales,* sec. 258, says, "It is a rule rather of logic than of law that transfer of ownership [and therefore "ownership" itself] cannot be predicated of unspecified goods."

[24] "The creditor . . . has . . . a general right of realization upon his debtor's estate." Glenn, op. cit., sec. 118.

[25] It is well established doctrine that "a solvent debtor owes no duty of trust or otherwise to his creditors with respect to his property." Glenn, op. cit., sec. 281. And, "as between a corporation and its creditors, the former does not hold its property in trust or subject to a lien in favor of the creditors in any other sense than does an individual debtor." Clapp v. Allen, 20 Ind. App. 263, 271 (1898).

[26] Whereas the doctrine of the "race of diligence" in the common law formerly continued the individual status of the creditors even beyond the point of insolvency, the growing doctrine and practice of "equal distribution," which sets a stage of consolidation such as we have described, seems to be superseding it. See Glenn, op. cit., secs. 15 and 280.

[27] This limitation is in general exemplified by Williston's analysis of creditors' rights when property is sold conditionally. See *Sales,* sec. 326. "Creditors of the seller after the property [object] has been delivered to the buyer can have no right to take the property [object] from the possession of the buyer, at least while he is in no default upon his contract. . . The buyer's right is a property right and the seller's creditors, no more than the seller can disturb it, though the seller also has an interest in the property [object] which should be subject to sale on execution." In turn, "As the buyer's right is in its nature analogous to that of a mortgagor, the rights of his creditors should be defined in the same way as the rights of a mortgagor's creditors; that is, the creditors should be given the right to discharge the mortgage; namely, pay the portion of the price remaining due upon the conditional sale, and by so doing acquire the right to treat the full ownership as belonging to the mortgagor or buyer." This, on the general theory that the "buyer's creditors, apart from estoppel or statute, can take no greater right than the buyer himself had."

certain liens of special creditors,[28] and except as it may include special rights running to the trustee under the Bankruptcy Act.

2. *Projection via Administration*

In general it may be stated that whenever—under any circumstances and regardless of the extent of the shadow cast upon the debtor's fund by the "floating charge"—a court imposes upon a fund any administrative officer, other than a receiver, as a substitute for the usual administration, direct or indirect, by those beneficially interested in the fund,[29] this officer is then construed to be a representative of the creditors of the fund and not an agent of the dominant interests. This is true with personal funds in case of death—executor or administrator of a deceased debtor—or of incompetence—committee in lunacy. And it is true with both personal and impersonal funds in the case of insolvency—trustee in bankruptcy, or temporary or ancillary receiver (federal) and assignee for creditors (in most states; in New York and elsewhere to an extent even beyond the property he receives). In all such cases the duty and power of the officer, as a representative of the creditors, is to realize upon the property, so far as is necessary and possible, and to discharge the debts (extinguish the interests of creditors by repurchase) so far as may be, by a proportional dividend. Thereupon the fund, if consumed, is dissolved, or, if not, its equity or remainder is either administered for the beneficiary or distributed to the beneficiaries, the fund disappearing as an entity. Thus the projection of the administrative rights of creditors upon the funds of debtors extends to cases where the shadow of debt does not cover the fund, if the administrative capacity of a person is terminated by death or insanity.

3. *Projection in Insolvency*

In all of these cases the projection becomes also beneficial so far as the shadow reaches—at first indeterminately and eventually determinately. The occasion for such assertion of administrative control is in all cases a situation where it is required for the protection of the interests of creditors, or of the fund, or of both. When the occasion is the threatening extent of the shadow it is described as insolvency. Insolvency is defined in two ways. In common law a man is insolvent who is "unable to pay his debts."[30] This may be described as the dynamic viewpoint. It is the viewpoint taken in the earlier Bankruptcy Acts and in the statutes of many states.[31] But the more modern definition is that of the Bankruptcy Act of 1898: "A person shall be deemed insolvent

[28] See Black, op. cit., sec. 238.

[29] The owner in the case of an 'own,' or personal, fund; the partners, directors and officers, or trustees, in the case of an intermediate, or impersonal, fund, such as a partnership, corporation or foundation.

[30] Glenn, op. cit., sec. 370.

[31] The definition of the law of 1867 and of the New Jersey Corporation Law is "inability to pay debts as they accrue in the course of business." See Glenn, op. cit., sec. 370. In a Massachusetts case in 1849 insolvency was defined as the state

. . . whenever the aggregate of his property, exclusive of any property which he may have conveyed, transferred, concealed, or removed, or permitted to be concealed or removed, with intent to defraud, hinder or delay his creditors, shall not, at a fair valuation, be sufficient to pay his debts."[32] This may be described as the static viewpoint, conforming to our metaphor of the shadow.

Obviously mere illiquidity—the inability to pay debts when due—while it may precipitate insolvency if a forced liquidation must result, does not necessarily connote a lack of sufficient assets, at a fair valuation, to meet liabilities. Therefore the remedy in cases of insolvency due to illiquidity, both for the protection of the creditors and of the equity alike, has come to be an equitable receivership. The state courts have warrant, in their definition of insolvency, for receiverships on this ground. The common law definition is also applied in the smaller cases—those of farmers, wage-earners, etc.—which are exempt from involuntary bankruptcy. But for all cases where the rights of creditors as a whole are projected upon the fund of the debtor involuntarily, so far as he is concerned, the warrant must be that the fair value of the assets (interests composing) does not equal the face value of the liabilities to others (pre-dominant interests incident upon).

a. *Via Trustee in Bankruptcy*

Upon commission of an act of bankruptcy,[33] the filing of a petition and adjudication thereof, title to all property interests of the bankrupt, except those which are exempt, passes to the trustee in bankruptcy,[34] and the beneficial interests therein advert to the general creditors whose interests have thus become consolidated and are now organized and stratified according to priority.[35] Eventually the realized proceeds, subject to

of a person who from any cause is unable "to pay his debts in the ordinary course, as persons carrying on trade usually do." Thompson v. Thompson, 58 Mass. 127, 134 (1849). And insolvency of a trader or merchant was defined by a Federal court in 1871 as "inability of a party to pay his debts, as they become due in the ordinary course of business." See Toof v. Martin, 13 Wall 40, 47 (U. S. 1871). Or, as Glenn puts it, op. cit., sec. 371, "In its ultimate analysis, insolvency is such a condition of the debtor's property that he is unable to meet all his obligations according to their terms."

[32] Section I (15).

[33] Acts of bankruptcy are, (1) fraudulent conveyance, (2) concealment of assets, (3) preferential transfers, (4) permitting judgment, (5) general assignment for the benefit of creditors, (6) appointment of a receiver on the ground of the debtor's insolvency, (7) written admission of inability to pay debts and willingness to be adjudged a bankrupt on that ground (voluntary bankruptcy).

[34] Dated back from the time of his appointment.

[35] Priorities are largely based on various accessory "real" rights which attach automatically, or have attached, to particular creditor's interests. Such are debts due governments including taxes, landlord's liens (distraint), labour claims (analogous to mechanic's liens) supply claims (public service companies, strictly "nolens volens"), secured and collateraled claims. In addition certain claims, not provable or not dischargeable, are also incident upon the debtor's new fund, composed of his exempt property and property acquired subsequent to adjudication of bankruptcy.

costs, are divided, so that the interests may then be said to have become determinate. The title which rests in the trustee is a composite of that of the bankrupt, of that of the general creditors in specific cases, and of that derived from certain special statutory powers conferred upon him by the Bankruptcy Act. The title that is conveyed to a purchaser is that conveyed by "judicial sale," including, unless special warranty by the trustee is ordered, no more than the interest the trustee possessed.

Apropos of our thesis, Remington's comments upon the legal philosophy back of the Bankruptcy Act are worthy of note. He points out that in common law there could hardly be ground for regarding preferences as fraudulent or for nullifying legal liens taken within the previous four months. The common law view is that "whatever the debtor owns he has a perfect right to use in paying his debts and the creditor, on his part, to take payment of his claim." The "race of diligence" is the program. And levies are the order of the day. And he continues: "In law the insolvent debtor does own the property belonging in his insolvent estate; but in equity, as developed in the bankruptcy law . . . he does not absolutely own it. The insolvent estate is, in theory, a trust fund in which all his creditors are equal beneficiaries, in proportion to their respective claims. . . It is only upon some such theory as this . . . that the requirement of the surrender of preferences and the return of property seized by legal process can be justified in cases of insolvent estates. Only so can the debtor's right to use what at common law is his own property, in the payment of any just debt he may prefer to pay, be restricted, and the creditor's right to seize his debtor's property in satisfaction of his just claim be thwarted. The insolvent estate is, in the philosophy of the law, if not in the announced decisions, not his own—that is the answer. He is *not* using his *own* property with which to pay his debts. He has used up all his own property, as equity looks at it, and this is precisely why he has become insolvent; he is now making use of the common fund contributed by all his creditors."[36] Thus the individual interests composing his fund are treated as his property, both in law and in equity, while he continues solvent. But if he becomes insolvent then, four months prior to the act of bankruptcy, the charge constituted by the creditors' interest in the aggregate, which has hitherto floated, becomes a beneficial interest in his fund, which, as a whole, is then converted into a trust fund; the creditors' interests come to be regarded as their capital, and his interest or capital is confined to his equity and his exemptions, less non-provable and non-dischargeable debts. Perhaps this has been the truer picture of the situation even prior to bankruptcy.

b. *Via Assignee for the Benefit of Creditors*

Assignment for the benefit of creditors is a common law procedure available in all cases which do not come under the Bankruptcy Act. But in many states it is controlled by statute in such a way as partially

[36] *Students' Remington,* sec. 64.

to supersede the common law, and in fact, in some cases, to model itself upon Bankruptcy practice even to the inclusion of discharge from debts. Such an assignment is a voluntary transfer by a debtor of all (general) or a part of his property to an assignee, in trust for the payment of his debts and for the return of the surplus, if any, to the assignor. In a general assignment the assignor is completely divested and everything is passed which is by its nature assignable. Being voluntary there is no question of new title, nor can the assignee's right be broader in any respect than the assignor's. Nor is the trust quite parallel to that of a trustee in bankruptcy; for such an assignment always leaves a resulting trust in the assignor. Thus such a trust, being voluntary, does not constitute a projection of the rights of creditors by force of law. On the other hand the dual nature of the trust represents most clearly the actual incidence of the two classes of interest which has existed all along — the floating charge and the equity, the former of which has, until insolvency, been treated as if suspended.

c. *Via Receiver in Equity*

The third class of administrative officer is of a different order altogether, although the practical effect of his appointment may be much the same. This form of administration is the instrumentality which equity uses in many other instances. In cases of common law insolvency it is only used when the insolvency of the party is likely to result in loss to the fund, or property. For this reason it is particularly applicable when such insolvency arises from illiquidity or temporary embarrassments, and it is used to provide breathing space for rehabilitation or reorganization as a going concern. Moreover, from our angle of approach, it is worthy of note that, in addition to insolvency, disputes among, or misconduct of, officers or directors of corporations may also be the occasion for a receivership, in order to prevent waste or deterioration pending litigation. And this, on the instance of a creditor, is clearly an assertion of the creditors' interest, despite the reluctance of courts to interfere in the administration of a fund by its dominant interests.

Receiverships, as a rule, effect no change of title. It is possession only which changes. The property in the receiver's custody is *in custodia legis;* that is, in possession of the court. But the receiver may give a deed at a receiver's sale, not as holder of title, but by confirmation of the court which has power, much as in the case of bankruptcy, to pass title and to require assignment by the debtor. Thus, either during or at the conclusion of receivership, possession may be restored, in whole or in part, where title has remained all along (i. e. in the debtor), or the interests of the creditors may, in whole or in part, be projected upon the proceeds of the property or even, indirectly by way of sale, upon the property itself. The result in practice is most often to reapportion the respective interests, pre-dominant and dominant alike, as if they were all of much the same order and varied only in degree of priority. So that the scaling down of interests is usually general and only varies in degree, according to priority, from the holdings of first mortgage bonds, secured on fixed assets, to the holdings of the final equity.

4. *Marshalling of Assets*

The equitable doctrine of the marshalling of assets,[87] in its application to the rights of general creditors in the fund of insolvent debtors, concerns itself for the most part with the real rights of secured creditors, and therefore does not bear upon our thesis except in that it demonstrates the rule that a creditor's secured interest is first of all a real interest in the security and only secondarily and for the unrealized balance a part merely of the floating charge. In respect of its application to the incidence of debt upon the fund of a partnership and upon the funds of the individual partners the doctrine is of more interest. Under the rule the creditors of the partnership, who are thereby also creditors of the partners, must exhaust the partnership fund before they can proceed against other assets in the funds of the individual partners; and the creditors of individual partners, on the other hand, must proceed first against the other assets in the funds of such partners and not attack the interests of such partners in the partnership fund until these other assets are exhausted. This is a very practical rule of common sense where two sets of assets are each liable for two sets of liabilities. It arranges the respective liabilities of each as primary and secondary. But it has definitely modified the "promise to pay" interpretation of the Roman Law—an interpretation which made, and still makes, the surety equally bound with his principal as an original promisor—in the direction of the more modern principle—as exemplified, for instance, by indorsement and guaranty which are future, contingent and therefore secondary liabilities—which orders the incidence of the creditors' interests.

Another application of the same doctrine is creeping into insolvency practice in certain cases which, while it is obviously not doctrinaire but, rather, wholly a facing of the practical necessities of the situation, nevertheless signifies a radical change in the principle of projection of creditors' interests upon debtor's funds. In effect, one may say, it is setting up a distinction between credit extended on a long term, secured basis

[87] Jenks, op. cit., pp. 234, 235, states that the marshalling of assets derived from the Roman principle of subrogation. Rules as to "order of resort" in early English equity apportioned or assigned various classes of assets as between various classes of creditors or beneficiaries. The doctrine was (a) that personalty is the primary fund for the payment of debts—in fact until the nineteenth century not realty but only its yield could be proceeded against by creditors if it was freehold—(b) that the devisee or legatee of a specific thing takes preference (as to that thing) over a general legatee, (c) that an express beneficiary is preferred over the heir or next-of-kin. Curiously enough, he says that the principle is virtually extinct as to creditors, though still common as to beneficiaries.

almost as if it were capital, and credit extended on a current basis, a mere book account or delay of payment in exchange. In the case of insolvency of producers whose business is affected with a public interest—namely public utilities—where, in the judgment of the court, continued operation is a public necessity or essential convenience the following rule holds: "The supply and material-men and the employees, who furnish the needed materials and service to a railroad from day to day, must necessarily extend credit to the corporation, and as the supplies and labor thus furnished contribute directly to the current earnings of the property, it is held to be equitable and necessary in order to insure continuous operation, that 'current expense' accounts should be paid out of current income before any appropriation of that income is made to discharge mortgage debt."[38] The rule is, in effect, that if the current income for a limited period of the receivership, plus unmortgaged corpus, is not sufficient to care for the claims of these preferred creditors, they may resort to any part of the operating income of the six months prior to receivership which has been diverted to the service of mortgage debt or to enhancing the value of mortgage security. And such diversion of current income, for purposes other than the payment of current debt, can be recovered from the corpus of the fund as against the mortgagees.

This case is interesting to us from two standpoints. We have already mentioned the distinction herein between the secured and the general creditor and the preference which this gives to the latter. In the second place the dynamic theory of contract, as a promise to an act or event without present incidence, seems at first sight to be matched here by a preferred claim which has a prior lien against receipts but no lien against the corpus. In other words income is distinguished from assets. Income, being wholly dynamic, is pledged to one set of creditors, while principal or corpus, is pledged to another. Yet, if we look deeper, we see that here, as in the doctrine of promise, the dynamic character of such property is wholly illusory and the legal doctrine tends to misrepresent the facts. The promise in one case and the income diverted in the other may be a ground of right and a measure of the face value of the property interest. But, they do not constitute either the substance or the incidence of the interest. The right which is grounded on a promise is not a right to performance. It is an interest, equivalent to damages, in the debtor's fund. The right here is not a right to the income grounded upon a prior lien. Rather it works itself out in the form of a prior equitable lien to extant assets. An "implied agreement" is "imputed to the mortgage creditors,"[39] under which fiction property pledged to the mortgage creditors is subjected to this prior lien by reason of the source from which this extant increment of property has come into existence. It is not asserted that the income diverted to the service of mortgage debt can and must be recovered,

[38] Appellant's Brief, Guaranty Trust Co. v. Albia Coal Co. 36 F. (2d) 34 (1929).
[39] Loc. cit.

but rather that an equitable lien lies against property in possession *equivalent* to the amount of such diversion.[40]

5. *Subrogation*

"Subrogation is generally understood to mean putting one to whom a right does not legally belong in the position of the legal owner of the right." It "may involve the creation of a new right in favor of the party entitled to be subrogated," but "the original right measures the extent of the new right." "Subrogation does not depend upon contract, but on the equities of the situation." [41] In spite of the legal fictions and circumlocutions subrogation recognizes that contracts of suretyship, of indemnity (indorsement) or of guaranty are in reality contracts to purchase the interest of the creditor in the principal debtor's fund. And it is this interest which passes if the original or contingent liability in these forms is enforced. Not only is such an interest construed to be an existing 'thing' but, even in early times before it had become alienable, it was already susceptible of so passing by force of law. If it were merely a promise it would cease when it was performed by a co-promisor (the surety) and in no case are the rights of the surety, indorser or guarantor based on any express contract with his principal. His right is not truly on the ground of a promise at all, since this is either extinguished or made to another. It rests on the ground of an interest which he acquires by purchase, that is by exchange.

In effect, then, the right of a creditor – in such a so-called unilateral contract – upon the fund of the surety, indorser or guarantor is of the nature of, but goes further than, his right under a contract of sale. For here he can compel the exchange of asset for asset, whereas in a sale he can usually only collect damages for non-performance. Finally the contingent interest of the surety, indorser or guarantor in the principal debtor's fund is, by the process of subrogation, rendered into a contingent asset to offset his contingent liability.

6. *Reputed Ownership*

One of the clearest cases of projection is the assertion of the interest of a creditor in property in the possession of his debtor which appeared to be his unpledged property and upon the basis of which the creditor may have, or might have, extended credit. Thus a sale may be voided or an unrecorded or unevidenced lien be impeached. The Uniform Sales Act (sec. 26), under "Creditors' Rights against Sold Goods in Seller's Possession," provides that, "When a person having sold goods continues in possession of the goods, or of negotiable documents of title

[40] "The equity of making the bondholders restore to those having the prior equitable right to resort to such income for payment of their claims, the amount so diverted, is held to justify the court in permitting the preferred creditors to resort in such circumstances to the corpus of the mortgaged property," loc. cit.

[41] Williston, *The Law of Contracts*, sec. 1265.

to the goods, and such retention of possession is fraudulent in fact or is deemed fraudulent under any rule of law, a creditor or creditors of the seller may treat the sale as void."[42] And liens may be invalid as against creditors "for failure to record the instrument creating the alleged lien or for any other reason, provided it can be shown that general creditors were misled to their injury, or induced to give credit to the bankrupt, by reason of the concealment or other irregularity which they urge as a ground for rejecting the alleged lien."[43] To make such a pledge valid "there must . . . be visible indications of the pledgee's possession,"[44] the pledgor cannot be custodian and the pledge must be segregated.[45] In other words a possessory pledge is not valid if possession is not taken and shown, nor a non-possessory pledge valid if not recorded.[46] This demonstrates clearly the practical view that the creditor's right is an interest in the ostensible assets. Much the same points of law are involved in determining the rights of a subsequent purchaser, but there, of course, the rights are of the order of property in its strict sense – namely *in rem* – and the issue rests on the distinction between a sale and other forms of transfer ("voluntary" conveyance or conveyance with power of revocation) and between a sale (contract of sale) which is executed (i. e. incorporates within itself a conveyance) and one which is merely executory.

7. *Resolutions of the Debtor's Fund*

As we have seen, the change of status of a personal fund by reason of death or incompetence immediately projects the floating charge as a whole by means of the administrative agency which is appointed primarily as a representative of the creditors. A similar contingency in the case of corporate funds arises in cases of reorganization, consolidation, merger, etc. The practice in protecting general creditors' rights under such circumstances is too complex to be covered here. Suffice it to say that the principle of recognition of an existent interest is well established and reasonably well carried out. For instance, in reorgan-

[42] Glenn, op. cit., secs. 202, 203, states that in America now, "All that is needed is a case where a debtor, now insolvent, is in possession of property belonging to another, who has allowed the debtor to remain in possession under such circumstances as make him the apparent owner of the property. The creditor, in such a case, may use that property in the satisfaction of his debt, without proving that he extended credit in reliance upon the ostensible ownership thus appearing," but "subject to those exceptions that the exigencies of trade customs may demand," such as possession by factors, under conditional sales, or sales with option of return, or sales on the installment plan; under chattel mortgages, where the mortgagee has title and the mortgagor has bailment until default; under consignment; and possession of choses in action.

[43] Black, op. cit., pp. 537-8.

[44] Glenn, op. cit., sec. 230.

[45] Glenn, op. cit., sec. 233.

[46] But the practice is not consistent with the purpose of recording. For the rule does not apply, in this case, merely if a general creditor granted credit prior to the recording of such a lien but only if he attached the property prior to such recording. This in effect protects only secured and not unsecured claims.

ization, the corporation cannot buy in mortgaged property nor even consent to a foreclosure sale, by way of securing new benefit to the stockholders, without providing for the general creditors. Nor can it transfer its assets to any other or new corporation without doing so.[47]

C. *Projection Prior to Default*

If the right of a creditor were in reality the right to the performance of a promise or of a duty, neglect of which, by reason of a breach or tort, gave rise to damages to be executed against the debtor's fund, then the liquidated liability for such damages could hardly arise, in the case of contract, until such breach had occurred; and, in the case of tort, such liability would seem to come into being at the moment of commission, subject of course to adjudication before it became fixed and liquidated. The fact that the law does not proceed on this basis in either case is an indication that it does not follow the doctrine which regards contract as purely a promise and tort as occasioning an obligation of the same order, but that it follows instead the tacit principle that credit-debt is the essential fact and that, as such, it constitutes an interest in the debtor's fund from the moment, and only from the moment, when it arises.

1. *Anticipatory Breach*

Section 63 of the Bankruptcy Act provides that "debts of the bankrupt may be proved and allowed against his estate which are (1) a fixed liability, as evidenced by a judgment or an instrument in writing, absolutely owing at the time of the filing of the petition against him, *whether then payable or not;*" and those "(4) founded upon an open account or upon a contract express or implied." It is the rule to apply the qualifications of "fixed liability," "absolutely owing" and "whether then payable or not" to the classification (4) as well, and to either class the provision (under b, sec. 63) permitting the liquidation of unliquidated claims.

Under the statute, then, a debt is defined as a fixed liability (i.e. one certain as to amount and incidence) which is absolutely owing, regardless of whether it is due or not. It is also provided that certain other liabilities may be converted or construed into debts by a process of fixation and liquidation. Such eventual debts are "founded upon" the liabilities, though the liabilities themselves were not debts at the time of the petition. Thus two separate processes are involved, the acceleration of maturity of debts not due and the construing of liabilities into debts. In theory, the same implication or fiction is used for both purposes. The device is called "anticipatory breach." "The obligor's bankruptcy may itself operate as an anticipatory breach making a claim both owing and due."[48] "The same principle that entitles the promisee to continued willingness [i. e. against repudiation or renunciation] entitles

[47] See Glenn, op. cit., sec. 108.

[48] *Student's Remington,* sec. 41.

him to continued ability on the part of the promisor [i. e. against insolvency]. In short, it must be deemed an implied term of every contract that the promisor will not permit himself, through insolvency or act of bankruptcy, to be disabled from making performance." [49] This fiction may be a necessary basis for construing into debts certain liabilities not absolutely owing. Such contracts as those of sale or purchase, of employment, or of continuing construction,[50] which are still executory, can only be precipitated into present property by some such expedient. But it is clear, I think, that the statute itself is not based on the doctrine of contract as promise and that no such fiction of anticipatory breach is necessary under this statute in order to mature a debt not due. The statute itself accelerates the maturity. Thus it treats all debts, fixed and absolutely owing, as present interests in the debtor's fund regardless of their maturity, and the only issue as to maturity is adjusted by adding accrued or subtracting unearned interest as of the date of filing the petition. The projection of the interest of the creditor in the debtor's fund, once it is fixed and absolutely owing, is here treated as a static or continuing fact and not as a dynamic event. The right is grounded, in the first instance, not in the default upon a promise not due, but in the existence of a form of tentative payment consisting of an interest which has been rendered as one side of a semi-final exchange. Thus it seems that, under the general guise of anticipatory breach, the courts are really maintaining the principle that the interests of the creditors in the debtor's fund exist continuously *pro tanto*, but that they remain in suspense so long as the debtor maintains a margin of safety between his assets and his liabilities. The threat of breach is measured by only one criterion—namely the disappearance of the debtor's equity in his present property. No other potentially available sources, from which to make future payment, are recognized.

2. *Protection of Credits, not Due or Callable, upon the Dissolution of a Corporation*

"In England, the law is established that the winding-up and dissolution of a company causes all outstanding obligations, including bonds and debentures, to mature forthwith notwithstanding that by their terms they may have a longer time to run. The same rule has been applied in a recent Maryland case [1907] where the mortgage expressly provided that except in certain contingencies, none of which had happened, the principal of the bonds should not become due before the time fixed for their payment." It is based on the right of bondholders "after exhausting their security to share in respect to the deficiency in any assets not covered by the mortgage," and also on the fact that dissolution dissi-

[49] Central Trust Co. v. Chicago Auditorium Assn., 240 U. S. 581, 591 (1915).

[50] "The claim of a party to an executory bilateral contract is provable against his bankrupt co-contractor, although at the time of filing the petition the latter's obligation was conditional on future performance by the solvent contractor." Williston, *Contracts*, sec. 1993, citing Central Trust Co. v. Chicago Auditorium Assn., 240 U. S. 581.

pates the business, undertaking, or franchise which is a large part of the security.[51]

Cook holds that such a rule is generally applied in America, though he does not consider the case of mergers, etc. "Of course dissolution does not cancel obligations not yet due even though extending beyond the duration of the company's charter. In distribution, debts not yet due participate with a rebate of interest for the unexpired time," and "upon a sale of the assets and the winding-up of the company, bonds not yet due may be paid at par and accrued interest." In the case of insolvency the rule is certain. "Adjudicated insolvency of the mortgagor operates to mature mortgage bonds in order that they may participate in the distribution of the general assets not covered by the mortgage, in case the mortgage security is insufficient." They "become due on its dissolution, and accordingly the stockholders' statutory liability thereon commences at that date."[52]

In certain cases and in certain states (as well as in England) an employee, who has a contract for his services which is broken by dissolution or not adopted by the receiver, may sue for the unexpired period even before the contract is all due.[53]

3. *Stoppage in Transitu*

Another rule, both of the common law and of statute, has the effect of maturing a liability at the time of insolvency, though the right in this case is a right to security, and therefore *in rem*, rather than a part of the floating charge. An unpaid seller who has parted with possession of goods to a carrier for transportation to a buyer may, if the buyer becomes, or the seller discovers that he is, insolvent, stop the goods in transit[54] and, unless the buyer has cut off the right by transfer of the bill of lading, may resume possession *even if the period of credit has not expired*. He may retain them until payment or tender of price or, after waiting a reasonable time, resell them.[55] This right is analogous to and is usually considered, both in statute or in common law, an extension, or resumption, of the seller's lien rather than a rescission of the contract.[56] It does not restore title to the seller but only possession and, therefore, the usual seller's lien. It originated in and is grounded on the equitable doctrine that one man's goods should not be applied to the payment of another man's debts, a doctrine which very obviously maintains the creditor's right of property until the very latest moment, after

[51] Machen, op. cit., sec. 1813. This rule, if generally applied, would make much trouble in the many cases of outstanding bond issues, where the corporations issuing them have been merged or taken over and dissolved years ago.

[52] Cook, *A Treatise on the Law of Corporations Having a Capital Stock*, sec. 642.

[53] See Cook, loc. cit.

[54] That is until the goods are in the actual or constructive possession of the buyer or one lawfully claiming under him.

[55] Thus the debt is matured at once, even if the period of credit, upon which the sale was made, was prolonged.

[56] But it differs in that a seller's lien ordinarily requires possession.

which it must regretfully see the specific incidence of the right lost in an indistinguishable mass and the nature of the right transmuted into that of the indeterminate rights composing the floating charge. This case is not a projection but rather a *re-jection.*

D. *Projection Prior to Judgment*

The rules of the Bankruptcy Act as to provable claims serve best to exemplify the very nice distinction which the law makes in practice as to what is and what is not present property in all the large class of creditors' rights (choses in action). The presentation which we have heretofore made in the text exactly conforms. The determination, with a few exceptions which we shall explain, is made as of the date of filing the petition in bankruptcy. Present property at that date is provable. Other property is not.

1. Antecedent Property in Contract

   Antecedent property in contract is fully recognized as such. Not only is it not necessary that such claims should be reduced to judgments, but judgments in pending actions on provable claims can only fix the amount of such claims and, usually, all actions against the bankrupt are stayed by the bankruptcy court if they concern a dischargeable claim. The proof of claim is an affidavit and it is automatically allowed unless objected to by an interested party. In other words bankruptcy practice does not recognize the theory that property in contract is of the nature merely of a right of action, but follows the more realistic theory that it is antecedent thereto and only needs to become a remedial right if it is disputed.[57]

   A. Credit-debt. All "debts . . . evidenced by an instrument in writing" or "founded upon an open account or upon a contract express or implied," if "fixed" and "absolutely owing" at the time of petition, are provable as constituting present property "whether then payable or not."

   B. Other Property in Contract

      a. Present Interests—Unliquidated. If such interests would, if liquidated, belong in class 1A (above), and if they are "capable of ascertainment as to amount . . . on [their] face, or by a

[57] Glenn, op. cit., sec. 24, says that if "a judgment [i.e. a remedial right] is not required of the creditor in order to enable him to participate in the distribution of the property" it is because "as the property is already in court for distribution among the creditors, their claim upon it is thereby postulated." This seems to the writer a very lame attempt at reconciliation of the "chose in action" viewpoint with the practice.

It may be noted also that in the case of dissolution of a corporation "the court has discretion to allow a claim to participate even though not reduced to judgment within the time fixed by the court." Cook, op. cit., sec. 642.

simple process of liquidation,"[58] they are provable present property.

b. Future Interests. Property in contract which has not yet ripened into present property, but which is held to become debt upon the ground of anticipatory breach by reason of repudiation, renunciation or insolvency, is by that method of "forcing" ripened into present property and thus becomes provable. This, curiously enough, applies to contracts of employment for the full period contracted, but not to rent not due which, if the lease is not adopted by the trustee, is treated as a continuing contract not dischargeable and therefore as a future interest not capable of being ripened.

2. Remedial Property in Obligations Legally Imposed

A. Credit-debt

a. Judgment Debt. All judgments rendered prior to petition, whether resulting from breach of contract or from tort are provable as present property. All judgments rendered subsequent to the petition but before consideration of the bankrupt's application for discharge, if upon a debt coming under class 1 above, are also provable, less costs. This provision is to permit judgment where needed in the proceedings for ulterior reasons, and to prevent the operation of the rule of "merger." But it is clear that the provisions as to costs, as to impeaching subsequent judgments, and as to staying other proceedings, are based on the theory that the rights represented by such judgments are in reality to be restored to the *status quo ante* and thus to the condition of antecedent present property.

3. Potential Remedial Property

A. Rights of Action for Breach of Contract. In effect, as stated above, such remedial rights are only provable if they have been reduced to a judgment debt prior to petition. If reduced to judgment afterwards, they are in reality reversely merged into the antecedent right and the only effect of subsequent judgment is to fix the amount of liability.

B. Rights of Action for Tort. A claim for damages for tort, not yet reduced to judgment, is not provable as present property. But this is subject to an exception if tort can be waived and recovery had as upon a quasi contract.

4. Contingent Property in Contract

A. Accessory to Other Obligations. The surety of a bankrupt, or his guarantor or indorser, is of course subrogated to the creditor's

[58] Glenn, op. cit., sec. 490.

antecedent property in the debtor's fund if he has discharged, before the petition, the obligation for which the bankrupt, as principal, was liable. If the principal creditor fails to prove, or is unknown, or cannot be reached then the surety, etc., may prove in the creditor's name and, if he discharges the obligation in whole or in part, becomes subrogated to the creditor's rights. Thus in neither case is it the contingent property which is proved upon.

The liability of the bankrupt as indorser, etc., is held to be present property at the time of petition either if such liability was fixed at that time or if it became fixed within the time limit for proving claims. This latter provision is either a curious measure of value of the contingent property at the time of petition or an inconsistent exception to the rule as to the date of cleavage.[59]

B. Principal. Other contingent claims as such are not provable and are therefore regarded as not being present property. But there are two views regarding the definition of contingent claims which may best be demonstrated in the case of insurance policies discussed below.

a. Insurance Policies. Insurance companies are not entitled to the benefits of the Bankruptcy Act. Nevertheless the rules for remedies for wrongful cancellation by the insurer supply the clearest analysis available of the subject of contingent property.

In one view a claim is only contingent if all the facts necessary to fasten liability have not already occurred. On this view damages for cancellation are measured by consideration already rendered by the insured. He is entitled to the present value of past premiums paid, without reference to the insurance already afforded.

In the other view a claim is only contingent if (a) it remains uncertain whether or not the promisor will ever become liable to pay it, or if (b) there is no means of removing by calculation the uncertain or fortuitous elements which might enter into it. Under this second view (b) damages for cancellation of life insurance are measurable by actuarial tables and become the present value of the cost of replacing the policy or, if it cannot be replaced, its face value less the present value of the net premiums to be paid in future. Presumably, if this measure of damages were also applied to fire insurance policies it would merge the two definitions of this

[59] Nevertheless see In re James Dunlap Carpet Co., 163 Fed. 541, 542 (D. C. Pa. 1908), "A contract liability [in general] of the bankrupt, contingent at the time the petition was filed, but liquidated within the year allowed for making proof, is a provable debt." Black, op. cit., sec. 135.

second view, the former of which is obviously not applicable to life policies.

Upon this second view we may distinguish rights under contract as contingent property if they comply with (a) or (b) above. If they do not then the claim is not contingent but rather unliquidated. If, therefore, it can be liquidated, through removing the uncertainty by calculation, it becomes present, not contigent, property and belongs in class 1 above.

In view of the considerations brought forward in the foregoing pages, the antique doctrine which regards the debtor's rights in his property as absolute, and which views these interferences with his control, upon the part of the law, as a mere assertion of the validity of promises and an assurance that they will be performed or that damages will be awarded, must seem to a layman to be a most unrealistic doctrine, and one which is belied by the facts of legal practice itself.

LIST OF REFERENCES

NOTE: — The abbreviated titles in parentheses, which in certain cases precede the full titles of the books, are those which are used in the notes of the text to indicate to which of an author's several works reference is made.

Abdy, J. T. and Walker, Bryan
The Commentaries of Gaius and Rules of Ulpian, 1870, 3rd ed. Cambridge, 1885.

American Law Institute
Restatement of the Law of Contracts, St. Paul, 1932.
Restatement of the Law of Property, Tentative Draft No. 1, Phila., 1929-1931.
Restatement of the Law of Trusts, Tentative Draft No. 1, Phila., 1930.

Ames, J. B.
"The Disseisin of Chattels," 3 *Harvard Law Review* (1889-90) pp. 23, 313, 337.
"Parol Contracts prior to Assumpsit," 8 *Harvard Law Review* (1894) p. 252.
"Purchase for Value without Notice," 1 *Harvard Law Review* (1887) p. 1.

Anson, Sir William R.
Principles of the Law of Contract, 1880, 5th Amer. ed. by A. L. Corbin, N. Y., 1930.

Appleton, Charles
Le testament romain, Paris, 1903.

D'Arbois de Jubainville, Henri
(*Droit Celtique*) *Études sur le droit celtique* (Cours de littérature celtique, vols. 7-8), Paris, 1895.
Les premiers habitants de l'Europe, 2d ed., Paris, 1889-1894.

Atkinson, J. J.
"Primal Law" (in Andrew Lang, *Social Origins*, pp. 209-294), N. Y. & Bombay, 1903.

Audibert, Adrien
"Nouvelle étude sur la formule des actions *familiae erciscundae* et *communi dividundo*," 28 *Nouvelle revue historique de droit français et étranger* (1904) pp. 273, 401, 649.

Austin, John
Lectures on Jurisprudence, 1832, 3rd ed. by Robt. Campbell, London, 1869.

Beames, John
A Translation of Glanville, Introduction by John Henry Beale, Washington, 1900.

Bennett, Charles E.
Syntax of Early Latin, Boston, 1910-1914.

Bentham, Jeremy
Works, Edinburgh, 1843.

Black, Henry Campbell
(*On Bankruptcy*) *Handbook of the Law and Practice of Bankruptcy*, St. Paul, 1924.

Blackstone, Sir William
Commentaries on the Laws of England, 1765-69, 4th Amer. ed. by Geo. Chase, N. Y., 1914.

Blöndal, Sigfús
Islandsk-Dansk Ordbog, Reykjavík, 1920-1924.

Boisacq, Émile
Dictionnaire étymologique de la langue grecque, Heidelberg, 1916.

Bonfante, Pietro
Histoire du droit romain, 1919, French translation from 3rd ed. by J. Carrere and F. Fournier, Paris, 1928.

Bracton, Henry de
De legibus et consuetudinibus Angliae, ed. by G. R. Woodbine, New Haven, 1922; after fol. 159b, ed, by Sir Travers Twiss, London, 1878.

Bréal, Michel
Semantics, 1897, English translation by Mrs. Henry Cust, London, 1900.

Bréal, Michel, and Bailly, Anatole
Dictionnaire étymologique Latin, 2d ed., Paris, 1886.

Briffault, Robert
The Mothers, in 3 volumes, N. Y. 1927.

Brinz, A von
"Der Begriff *obligatio*," 1 *Zeitschrift für das privat- und öffentliche Recht* (1874) p. 11.

Brugmann, Karl
(*Grundriss*, Eng. trans.) *Elements of the Comparative Grammar of the Indo-Germanic Languages*, 1886-1900, English translation from 1st German ed., N. Y. 1888-1895.

Brugmann, Karl and Delbrück, Berthold
(*Grundriss*, 2d. Germ. ed.) *Grundriss der vergleichenden Grammatik der indogermanischen Sprachen*, 2d ed., Strassburg, 1897-1916.

Bruns, K. G.
(*Fontes, Scriptores*) *Fontes Juris Romani Antiqui*, 7th ed. by Gradenwitz, Part II, Scriptores, Tubingen, 1909.

Buck, Carl D.
(*Grammar*) *A Grammar of Oscan and Umbrian*, Boston, 1904.
(*Vocalismus*) *Der Vocalismus der oskischen Sprache*, Leipzig, 1892.

Buckland, W. W.
(*Text-Book*) *A Text-Book of Roman Law from Augustus to Justinian*, 1921, 2nd ed., Cambridge, 1932.
(*Principles*) *Elementary Principles of the Roman Private Law*, Cambridge 1912.

Clark, E. C.
(*Jurisprudence*) *History of Roman Private Law*, Part II, *Jurisprudence*, Cambridge, 1914.
(*Regal*) *History of Roman Private Law*, Part III, *Regal Period*, Cambridge, 1919.

Clark, J. Maurice
The Economics of Overhead Costs, Chicago, 1923.

Cleasby, Richard, and Vigfusson, Gudbrand
Icelandic-English Dictionary, Oxford, 1874.

Coke, Sir Edward
Commentary upon Littleton, 1628, 17th ed., London, 1817.

Commons, John R.
"Institutional Economics," 21 *American Economic Review* (1931) p. 648.
Legal Foundations of Capitalism, N. Y., 1924.

Conway, Robert S.
The Italic Dialects, Cambridge, 1897.

Cook, Walter Wheeler
"The Powers of Courts of Equity," 15 *Columbia Law Review* (1915) pp. 37, 106, 228.

Cook, William W.
A Treatise on the Law of Corporations having a Capital Stock, 1887, 8th ed., N. Y., 1923.

Corbin, A. L.
"Contracts for the Benefit of Third Persons," 46 *Law Quarterly Review* (1930) p. 12.
"Legal Analysis and Terminology," 29 *Yale Law Review* (1919) p. 161.

Corbin (*cont.*)
Preface to Sir William R. Anson, *Principles of the Law of Contract*, 5th Amer. ed., N. Y., 1930.

Cornil, Georges
Ancien droit romain, Brussels and Paris, 1930.

Corssen, Wilhelm
Über Aussprache, Vokalismus und Betonung der lateinischen Sprache, 2d ed., Leipzig, 1868-1870.

Cuq, Édouard
Les institutions juridiques des romains, 1891, vol. 1, 2nd ed. Paris, 1904.

Curtius, Georg
Grundzüge der griechischen Etymologie, 1858-62, English translation by A. S. Wilkins and E. B. England from 4th Germ. ed., London, 1875.

Dalloz,
Répertoire de legislation, de doctrine et de jurisprudence, Paris, 1846.

Dargun, Lothar
Mutterrecht und Raubehe (Untersuchungen zur deutschen Staats- und Rechtsgeschichte, No. 16), Breslau, 1883.

Delbrück, Berthold
(*Grundriss*) See Brugmann and Delbrück.

Dicey, A. V.
A Treatise on the Rules for the Selection of the Parties to an Action, 1870, 2nd Amer. ed., by W. Aldrich, Jersey City, 1886.

Diez, Friedrich
Etymologisches Wörterbuch der romanischen Sprachen, 1853, 4th ed., Bonn, 1878-1887.

Digby, Kenelm Edward
An Introduction to the History of the Law of Real Property, 1875, 5th ed., Oxford, 1897.

Digest
(See Justinian)

Du Cange, Charles du Fresne, Sieur
Glossarium Mediae et Infimae Latinitatis, Paris, 1840.

Dwight, Theodore W.
Commentaries on the Law of Persons and Personal Property, ed. by E. F. Dwight, Boston, 1894.

Elphinstone, H. W.
"What is a Chose in Action?" 9 *Law Quarterly Review* (1893), p. 311.

Ely, Richard T.
Property and Contract in their Relations to the Distribution of Wealth, N. Y., 1914.

Ernout, A., and Meillet, A.
Dictionnaire étymologique de la langue latine, Paris, 1932.

Falk, H. S., and Torp, A.
Norwegisch-dänisches etymologisches Wörterbuch, Heidelberg, 1910-1911.

Festus, Sextus Pompeius
De Verborum significatu quae supersunt cum Pauli epitome, ed. by Emil Thewrewk, Budapest, 1889.

Fick, August
Vergleichendes Wörterbuch der indogermanischen Sprachen, 4th ed., Gottingen, 1890-1894.

Flach, Jacques
Les origines de l'ancienne France, Paris, 1886-1917.

Frank, Tenney
An Economic History of Rome, 1920, 2nd ed. revised, Baltimore, 1927.

Fustel de Coulanges, N. D.
The Ancient City, 1864, English translation by W. C. Small, 7th ed., Boston and N. Y., 1889.
(*Origines*) *Histoire des institutions politiques de l'ancienne France*, V, *Les origines du système féodal*, ed. C. Jullian, Paris, 1890.
(*Alleu*) *Histoire des institutions politiques de l'ancienne France*, IV, *L'Alleu et le domaine rural*, ed. C. Jullian, Paris, 1889.
Les institutions politiques de l'ancienne France, Paris, 1875.

Gaius
Institutes.

Gellius, Aulus
Noctes Atticae.

Gierke, Otto
Political Theories of the Middle Age, 1881, translation by F. W. Maitland, Cambridge, 1927.

Girard, Paul Frédéric
Manuel élémentaire de droit romain, 1896, 8th ed. by F. Senn, Paris, 1929.

Glanville, Ranulf de
De Legibus et Consuetudine Regni Angliae, ed. by G. E. Woodbine, New Haven, 1932.

Glenn, Garrard
The Rights and Remedies of Creditors Respecting their Debtor's Property, Boston, 1915.

Godefroy, Frédéric
Dictionnaire de l'ancienne langue française, Paris, 1880.

Graff, Eberhard G.
Althochdeutscher Sprachschatz, Berlin, 1834-1842.

Grandgent, Charles H.
An Introduction to Vulgar Latin, Boston, 1907.

Gray, John C.
The Rule against Perpetuities, 1886, 3d ed., Boston, 1915.

Green, John Richard
The Conquest of England, N. Y., 1883.

Grimm, Jacob
Deutsche Rechtsalterthümer, Göttingen, 1828.

Hadley, James
Introduction to Roman Law, New Haven, 1873 (1931 reprint).

Haskins, Charles Homer
Norman Institutions, Cambridge, U.S.A., 1918.

Hearn, William Edward
(*Aryan*) *The Aryan Household*, London, 1879.
(*Legal Duties*) *The Theory of Legal Duties and Rights*, Melbourne and London, 1883.

Hempl, George
"Etymologies," 22 *American Journal of Philology* (1901), p. 426.

Hohfeld, Wesley Newcomb
Fundamental Legal Conceptions, ed. by W. W. Cook, New Haven, 1923.

Holder, Alfred
Alt-celtischer Sprachschatz, Leipzig, 1896-1913.

Holdsworth, W. S.
A History of English Law, 1903-09, 3rd ed., London, 1922-32.

Holland, Thomas Erskine
The Elements of Jurisprudence, 1880, 12th ed., Oxford, 1916.

Holmes, Oliver Wendell
(*Papers*) *Collected Legal Papers*, N. Y., 1921.
(*Common Law*) *The Common Law*, Boston, 1881.
"Early English Equity," 1 *Law Quarterly Review* (1885), p. 162.

Homo, Léon
Primitive Italy and the Beginnings of Roman Imperialism, 1925, English translation by V. Gordon Childe, N. Y., 1926.

Hopkins, Grace S.
"*Indo-Europeon *deiwos and Related Words*," (Language Dissertation, No. 12, Linguistic Society of America), Philadelphia, 1932.

Hubert, Henri
Les Celtes et l'expansion celtique, Paris, 1932.

Hunter, W. A.
Roman Law, 1876, 4th ed., London, 1903.

Ihering, Rudolph von
(*Entw.-Gesch.*) *Entwicklungsgeschichte des römischen Rechts*, Leipzig, 1894.
(*Aryan*) *The Evolution of the Aryan*, 1894, English translation by A. Drucker, N. Y., 1897.
(*Geist*) *Geist des römischen Rechts*, 1852, 5th-6th ed., Leipzig, 1906-1921.
(*Zweck*) *Der Zweck im Recht*, 1877, 6th ed., Leipzig, 1923.

Jenks, Edward
A Short History of English Law, 1912, 4th ed., London, 1928.

Justinian
(*Dig.*) *Digest*
(*Inst.*) *Institutes*

Kant, Immanuel
Metaphysik der Sitten, Pt. I, *Metaphysische Anfangsgründe der Rechtslehre*, 1797, ed. by J. H. von Kirchmann, Berlin, 1870.

Karlowa, Otto
Römische Rechtsgeschichte, Leipzig, 1885-1901.

Kent, James
Commentaries on American Law, 1826-30, 14th ed. by J. M. Gould, Boston, 1896.

Kluge, Friedrich
Etymologisches Wörterbuch der deutschen Sprache, 10th ed., Berlin, 1924.

Kocourek, Albert
Jural Relations, Indianapolis, 1927.

Körting, Gustav
Lateinisch-romanisches Wörterbuch, 3d. ed., Paderborn, 1907.

Langdell, C. C.
"A Brief Survey of Equity Jurisdiction," 1 *Harvard Law Review* (1887), p. 55.
A Summary of the Law of Contracts, 1879, 2nd ed., Boston, 1880.

Laveleye, Émile de
Primitive Property, 1874, English translation by G. R. L. Marriott, London, 1878.

Leist, B. W.
Graeco-italische Rechtsgeschichte, Jena, 1884.

Lévy-Bruhl, H.
"La function du très ancien testament romain," 45 *Nouvelle revue historique de droit français et étranger* (1921), p. 634.

Lex Salica

Littleton, Sir Thomas
Tenures, c. 1500, ed. by Eugene Wambaugh, Washington, 1903.

Littré, É.
Dictionnaire de la langue française, Paris, 1873.

Livy (Titus Livius)
Ab Urbe Condita.

Lubbock, Sir John (Lord Avebury)
The Origin of Civilization and the Primitive Condition of Man, 1870, 7th ed., London, 1912.

Machen, Arthur W. Jr.
A Treatise on the Modern Law of Corporations, Boston, 1908.

Maine, Sir Henry Sumner
(*Ancient Law*) *Ancient Law*, 1861, 10th ed. by Sir Frederick Pollock, N. Y., 1906.
(*E. L. and C.*) *Dissertations on Early Law and Custom*, N. Y., 1883.
(*Early History*) *Lectures on the Early History of Institutions*, 1875, 7th ed., London, 1914.

Maitland, Frederic William
The Collected Papers, Cambridge, 1911.
(*Domesday*) *Domesday Book and Beyond*, Cambridge, 1897.
History of English Law (see Pollock and Maitland).
(*Equity*) *Equity*, ed. by A. H. Chaytor and W. J. Whittaker, Cambridge, 1926.
Introduction to Gierke (see Gierke).

Markby, Sir William
Elements of Law, 1871, 6th ed., Oxford, 1905.

Marshall, Alfred
Principles of Economics, 1890, 8th ed., London, 1920.

Meyer-Lübke, Wilhelm
Romanisches etymologisches Wörterbuch, Heidelberg, 1911-1920.

Mitchell, Wesley C.
Business Cycles, N. Y., 1930.

Mommsen, Theodor
Römisches Staatsrecht, 1871, 3rd ed., Leipzig, 1887-1888.

Morgan, Lewis H.
Systems of Consanguinity and Affinity of the Human Family (Smithsonian Contributions to Knowledge, Vol. 17), Washington, 1871.

Moyle, J. B.
Imperatoris Iustiniani Institutionum Libri Quattuor, Oxford, 1883.

Muirhead, James
Historical Introduction to the Private Law of Rome, 1886, 3d ed. by Alexander Grant, London, 1916.

Muller, Frederik
Altitalisches Wörterbuch, Göttingen, 1926.

Oliver, D. T.
"Interests for Life and Quasi-remainders in Chattels Personal," 24 *Law Quarterly Review* (1908), p. 431.

Ortolan, J. L. E.
The History of Roman Law, 1828, English translation by I. T. Prichard and D. Nasmith, London, 1871.

Page, Thomas W.
The End of Villainage in England, N. Y., 1900.

Palmer, F. B.
Company Law, 1898, 14th ed. by A. F. and A. M. R. Topham, London, 1930.

Paulsen, Friedrich
A System of Ethics, 1889, ed. and English translation from the 4th ed. by Frank Thilly, N. Y., 1899.

Planta, Robert von
Grammatik der oskisch-umbrischen Dialecte, Strassburg, 1892-1897.

Pollock, Sir Frederick
"English Law before the Norman Conquest," 14 *Law Quarterly Review* (1898), p. 291.

Pollock, Sir Frederick, and Maitland, Frederic William
The History of English Law before the time of Edward I, 1895, 2nd ed., Cambridge, 1899.

Pollock, Sir Frederick, and Wright, R. S.
An Essay on Possession in the Common Law, Oxford, 1888.

Poste, Edward (ed.)
Gaius, 1871, 4th ed. by E. A. Whittuck, London, 1904.

Pound, Roscoe
(*Philosophy*) *An Introduction to the Philosophy of Law*, New Haven, 1922.
(*Readings*) *Readings on the History and System of the Common Law*, 2nd ed., Boston, 1913.

Powell, Ellis J.
The Evolution of the Money Market (1385-1915), London, 1915.

Regiam Majestatem
In *Acts of the Parliaments of Scotland*, App. I, London, 1844.

Remington, Harold
(*On Bankruptcy*) *A Treatise on the Bankruptcy Law of the United States*, 1908, 3d ed., Rochester, 1923.
(*Student's Remington*) *A Treatise on the Elements of Bankruptcy Law*, Charlottesville, Va., 1911.

Roby, John Henry
An Introduction to the Study of Justinian's Digest, Cambridge, 1886.

Sainte-Palaye, Jean Baptiste de la Curne de
Dictionnaire historique de l'ancien langage françois, Niort, 1875-1882.

Saleilles, Raymond
De la personnalité juridique, Paris, 1910.

Salkowski, Carl
Institutes and History of Roman Private Law, 1868, English translation by E. E. Whitfield, London, 1886.

Salmond, Sir John W.
Essays in Jurisprudence and Legal History, London, 1891.
First Principles of Jurisprudence, London, 1893.
(*Jurisprudence*) *Jurisprudence*, 1902, 8th ed. by C. A. W. Manning, London, 1930.

Schade, Oskar
Altdeutsches Wörterbuch, 2d ed., Halle a. S., 1872-1882.

Schouler, James
A Treatise on the Law of Personal Property, 1873, 5th ed., Albany, 1918.

Schrader, O.
Prehistoric Antiquities of the Aryan Peoples, 1883, English translation from 2d German ed. by F. B. Jevons, London, 1890.

Schröder, Richard
Lehrbuch der deutschen Rechtsgeschichte, 1889, 6th ed. by E. von Kunssberg, Berlin and Leipzig, 1922.

Schulze, Wilhelm
Zur Geschichte lateinischer Eigennamen, Berlin, 1904.

Seebohm, M. E.
The Evolution of the English Farm, London, 1927.

Sherman, Charles Phineas
Roman Law in the Modern World, 1917, 2nd ed., New Haven, 1922.

Sohm, Rudolph
The Institutes, 1884, English translation by J. C. Ledlie, 3rd ed. Oxford, 1907.

Stolz, Friedrich
Historische Grammatik der lateinischen Sprache, Leipzig, 1894.

Story, Joseph
Commentaries on the Law of Bailments, 1832, 9th ed. by James Schouler, Boston, 1878.

Tacitus
Germania.

Tarde, Gabriel
(*Imitation*) *The Laws of Imitation*, 1890, English translation by Elsie Clews Parsons, N. Y., 1903.
(*Transformations*) *Les transformations du droit*, 1893, 7th ed., Paris, 1912.

Terry, Henry T.
Some Leading Principles of Anglo-American Law, Philadelphia, 1884.

Thorpe, Benjamin (ed.)
Ancient Laws and Institutes of England, London, 1840.

Ulpian
(*Ulpian*) *Ulpiani Liber Singularis Regularum.*

Varro, N. Terentius
(*De l.l.*) *De Lingua Latina.*

Vinogradoff, Sir Paul
(*English Society*) *English Society in the Eleventh Century*, Oxford, 1908.
(*Manor*) *The Growth of the Manor*, London, 1905.
(*Jurisprudence*) *Outlines of Historical Jurisprudence*, Oxford, 1920.
(*Villainage*) *Villainage in England*, 1st ed. 1892, impression of 1927, Oxford.

Walde Alois
(*Latin*) *Lateinisches etymologisches Wörterbuch* 2d ed., Heidelberg, 1910; 3d ed. by J. B. Hoffmann, Heidelberg, 1930-1935 (*A-Herctum*).
(*Idg.*) *Vergleichendes Wörterbuch der indogermanischen Sprachen*, ed. by J. Pokorny, Berlin, 1926-1932.

Westermarck, Edward
The History of Human Marriage, 1891, 5th ed., N. Y., 1925.

Wigmore, John H.
"The Pledge Idea: A Study in Comparative Legal Ideas," 10 *Harvard Law Review* (1897), pp. 321, 389; 11 ditto, p. 18.

Williams, Joshua
Principles of the Law of Personal Property, 1848, 18th ed., by T. C. Williams and W. J. Byrne, London, 1926.

Williston, Samuel
(*Sales*) *The Law concerning the Sale of Goods at Common Law*, 1909, 2nd ed., N. Y., 1924.
(*Contracts*) *The Law of Contracts*, N. Y., 1920.

Wood, Francis A.
Post-consonantal w in Indo-European (Language Monograph, No. 3, Linguistic Society of America), Philadelphia, 1926.
Indo-European $a^x : a^xi : a^xu$, Chicago, 1905.

Yntema, Hessel E.
"The Rational Basis of Legal Science," 31 *Columbia Law Review* (1931), p. 925.

Zulueta, F. de
"The Recent Controversy about *Nexum*," 29 *Law Quarterly Review* (1913), p. 137.

Zvetaieff, Ivan
Inscriptiones Italiae mediae dialecticae ad archetyporum et librorum fidem, 1878, Leipzig, 1884.

INDEX

G

J

K

L

Q

R

S

T

U

CORRECTIONS

PAGE		LINE	
116	fn 312	1	_for_ Neibuhr _read_ Niebuhr
194		23	_for_ B.C. _read_ B.C.
540		16	_for_ (Latin) read (_Latin_)
	fn 3	5	for _Diälecte_ read _Dialekte_
	fn 5	2	for _*dhə-mo_ read _*dhə-mo-_
541		2	for _þămelŏ-s_ read _þămĕlo-s_
		31	for _*ueiḱos_ read _*u̯eiḱos_
	fn 6	4	for _*fa-mo-s_ read _*fă-mo-s_
542		1	for _Hausegenosse_ read _Hausgenosse_
		5	for _u̯oiḱi-_ read _*u̯oiḱo-_
543		10	for _dəng_ read _də̄ng_
		25	for _erselbst_ read _er selbst_
544	fn 14	3	for _paternitè_ read _paternité_
	fn 15	2	for _pitā_ read _pitā́_
	fn 16	1	for Ζεὺς read Ζεύς
		2	for πατὴρ read πατήρ
545		9	for _Rom._ read _Röm._
	fn 18	4	for ἂσπαλον read ἄσπαλον
547		14	_for_ Sabinian _read_ Sabine
548	fn 25	2	for _*ĝenti-s_ read _*ĝentí-s_
549	fn 30	5	for _dāyādá-h_ read _dāyādá-ḥ_
550	fn 31	2	for *ῶ-δ-τά read *ώ-δ-τά
		3	for _dévá-tta-h_ read _dēvá-tta-ḥ_
	fn 33	5	for _Idg._ read _Lat._
556		3	As to Oscan this statement is an error. Buck (Grammar, p. 194) does give the verb as _*manfō_, from _*mandhō_, but treats it as a compound like Latin _condo_.
557	fn 50	8	_for_ presente _read_ présente
		4	_for_ indivisé _read_ indivisée
561	fn 56	14	_for_ verfugen _read_ verfügen
566	fn 65	1	for _deiu̯i_ read _deiu̯ī_
574	fn 79	1	for _fuhre_ read _führe_
		2	for _skia_ read _søkia_
575		28	for _*rĕ-i̯o-s_ read _*rē-i̯o-s_
		35	for _*rĕi̯ōr_ read _*rēi̯ōr_
577	fn 85	1	for _r̥jú-s_ read _r̥jú-ṣ_
		18	for _r̥jyati_ read _ŕ̥jyati_
		26	for _reccam_ read _reccan_
615		8	_for_ contigent _read_ contingent

www.ingramcontent.com/pod-product-compliance
Lightning Source LLC
LaVergne TN
LVHW101450200926
848483LV00001B/104
* 9 7 8 1 5 8 4 7 7 7 3 7 3 *